Shelanu

An Israel Journal

Books by Maggie Rennert:

A Moment in Camelot
Circle of Death
Operation Alcestis
Operation Calpurnia
Shelanu

Shelanu
An Israel Journal

Maggie Rennert

Prentice-Hall, Inc., Englewood Cliffs, New Jersey

◤

This book is for B. B. and for E. F., both of whom would rather just be their particular and beloved selves but understand the necessity to serve as symbols too. That is the Israeli burden—and when borne with such grace and humor, it may also be Israel's greatest wealth.

Shelanu: An Israel Journal by Maggie Rennert
Copyright © 1979 by Maggie Rennert

Prentice-Hall International, Inc., London
Prentice-Hall of Australia, Pty. Ltd., Sydney
Prentice-Hall of Canada, Ltd., Toronto
Prentice-Hall of India Private Ltd., New Delhi
Prentice-Hall of Japan, Inc., Tokyo
Prentice-Hall of Southeast Asia Pte. Ltd., Singapore
Whitehall Books Limited, Wellington, New Zealand
10 9 8 7 6 5 4 3 2 1

Library of Congress Cataloging in Publication Data
Rennert, Maggie.
     Shelanu: an Israel Journal.
     1. Israel—Description and travel.
2. Rennert, Maggie—Homes and haunts—Israel—
Beersheba.   3. Authors, American—20th century—
Biography.   I. Title.
DS107.4.R43   956.94'05   78-9561
ISBN 0-13-808808-X

Foreword

What the title means, some ground rules, and a couple of caveats.

Right from the start, I wanted to call this book *Shelanu*. I felt quite uncharacteristically insistent about that, though I can understand the commercial disadvantages of a title people won't know how to pronounce and I'm usually prepared to be reasonable. But this time I just wasn't. And this is to tell you why—though I guess the whole book is really to tell you why.

Let's dispose of that reasonable objection first. The title is pronounced shell-AH-nooh, and it means "our" or "ours." It's an inflected form of *shel*, "of": an ending appropriate in gender and number is added to make a possessive pronoun. Thus, your-my-his-her-their are all forms of *shel* (of-you, of-him, etc.), and *anu* is the ending for the first person plural. Okay? It's simple enough, I think.

But *shelanu* as a concept is not so simple. Among the people of Israel, it's a fierce mutual knowing—and a hang-up, if you will. You can hear it in a soldier captured during the Yom Kippur war saying calmly on his return home, "I knew they'd get me back"—while you know what nobody told him in his prison, that Israel traded an entire encircled Egyptian army plus eight THOUSAND Egyptian POWs to reclaim two-hundred-odd *shelanu*. The trade had to be uneven because Egypt, under no pressure, was in no hurry: its people hadn't even been told about its encircled army, much less all the

v

captives. But in Israel, fifty thousand people out of a population of only two and a half million (most of them, it sometimes seems, dissenters: if two Israelis ever do agree on anything, they promptly form a new political party) managed to sign a petition. It demanded that their government quit talking politely to "world opinion" about Israel's rights under the Geneva convention, international law, etc.: just give the crooks whatever they're holding us up for, and do it pronto. When the returned Israeli soldiers got off the Red Cross plane that had flown them from Cairo, half the population was at the airport to greet them; the other half was back home preparing the "Welcome Home, Shlomo" festivities. And only after a clear majority of the citizens was satisfied that the roses would soon be back in the soldiers' cheeks did the poor guys get a little peace and quiet. That's *shelanu* in operation, and it's what Israel is all about.

Is this maybe just a way, then, of saying the people are patriotic? Or that Israel is a small enough country so everybody feels like one big family? No, because I can't possibly know whether all Israelis are really patriotic; their willingness to serve in the armed forces could well be only a matter-of-fact recognition of the need to fight somebody who's trying to kill you. And anyway, the country isn't so family-size as it used to be: Israeli TV has begun (quite recently, judging from the audience comment) to write in the name of the politician holding forth on your screen—which was never necessary before, when everybody knew good ol' Chaim.

But whatever *shelanu* isn't, what it is is the very essence of Israel's life and people, embodying in exact balance all the idiocy and all the glory that came of the original absurd, marvelous, wholly romantic notion. (I do too need all those adjectives. Because, look at it: who in the early years of this century went around starting up new countries in deserts and against multiple odds—and then also insisted on living in them like everybody middle-class else?) Sure, I guess patriotism is part of it—if you understand patriotism to include quarreling, bickering, name-calling, and varieties of alienation the "alienated" of America couldn't even begin to imagine. And sure it's a kind of family-feeling, because it's in a family that you see people loving the way Israelis love their

vi

country—ruefully, impatiently, and in despite. Wondering why they don't take off for somewhere greener or safer or softer. Asking themselves why they put up with these bastards. And all the time, knowing why: it's because they may be bastards but they're *shelanu*.

Well, that's the best I can do with explaining it. Now for the technical problems that crop up when I try to show you instead. First, Hebrew: I didn't want to sprinkle the pages with phonetic symbols (especially since I'm unable to remember them myself most of the time), but on the other hand I think it's maddening not to know how something sounds—especially names. So I've worked out a scheme that isn't a system because it won't cover every eventuality; but, custom-tailored for this book, it ought to get us by. All you have to remember is a few ground rules: *i* sounds like "ee," the *o* sound is as in the word "forth," and *oo* means as in "book"; if I mean *oo* as in "loop," I'll make it *ooh*. Anything with—*im* on the end is probably a plural (masculine: the feminine plural is —*ot*) and will sometimes give you a shock of recognition, not to say a jolt: e.g., *Phantomim, tankim*. What else? Oh yes, all the *r*'s are rolled, but up front, not the French back-in-the-throat way. That's about all I can think of. If you get stuck, look in the Glossary.

However, so you won't have to go flipping pages all the time, I've pronounced Hebrew words for you in parentheses the first time I used them. The catch there is, though, when is the first time? For you may not be reading straight through like a proofreader . . . I have a working solution (if not exactly a tidy one): I've repeated the parenthetical explanation whenever I felt I should. Which means when I figure you haven't heard it for a while, or that it's a particularly hard one that always gave me trouble, or . . . Oh well, whenever it seemed helpful, that's all. If my intuition misses, fall back on the Glossary.

Spelling out Hebrew, which has a different alphabet, in English presents some sticky problems. I think I've found English approximations for most of the sounds, but they've got one that stops me: I've used *ch* to represent it, which will do if you'll please remember that it *never* sounds like the *ch* in "chair." Okay? I'm still stuck for a description of how it does sound, and the dictionary is no help; like the *ch* in "loch," it says blandly. Which is just dandy, except how many people outside Scotland know how to pronounce "loch"? All I can tell you is, it's kind of a gargled *h*. The farther back in your throat you gargle it, the better; the classiest Hebrew speakers come close to a cat's purr.

Finally, there's the matter of names. Most of the people mentioned in this book aren't famous and probably wouldn't care if I named them. But the way I feel is, they were only going about their lives when I dropped in among them, and they never asked me to say anything, whether kind or not, about them. So if I have unkind things to say—which may happen—I have a right to tell the truth, but that doesn't include a right to make others gratuitously miserable. Thus I decided to shuffle the Israelis' names (except for public figures, of course) and so give myself a freedom that in most cases is not actually needed. Which, when you come down to it, is rather like passing a law that applies only during eclipses of the sun. But, well, ridiculous is better than cruel, that's all.

However, law-making is a tricky business, I found. For it proved impossible to draw geographical lines, even though logic said that my American friends—aware of the hazards of befriending writers and having crossed my path by choice, so to speak—were less entitled to such tender regard. So I ended by changing their names too, and where the line (by that time, right wiggly) finally got drawn was only at members of my own family. The reasoning there is that no adult's entitled to protection from his parents, and besides, my kids had all those advantages, right? ("Name one," and similar challenges, will be ignored.)

Well, being fair-while-truthful isn't the least of the headaches, because writing about real people is hard. But I've done my best. And when I've come to anything I couldn't honestly arrive at a conclusion about, I've at least set down everything I know so you can decide for yourself. Okay?

Contents

I

1 ☞ "You're Going Where?"

My editor thinks I have to begin with some autobiography, and I see his point: you're entitled to know who's talking, and just telling you that I'm nobody's paid propagandist really isn't enough. But I'm daunted, for I have no experience at that kind of writing—though my only previous attempt, a school assignment when I was in third grade, went over big with my father, who carried it around for years. It was titled "My Life in a Nutshell," which I still think isn't bad for seven-year-old wit; and even allowing for the fact that I didn't actually have a lot of autobiography to impart then, the piece is marvelously concise. For in a page and a half (and you know how much room that big, beginner handwriting takes up, too), I managed not only to mention my parents, our maid, and the canary, but also to transmit a clear dislike of my little sister. *That's* talent, baby. But it may have been my finest hour, and I'm scared to try again.

Besides, since this is a personal journal and not a sociological treatise, you ought to be able to spot whatever prejudices, stupidities, etc., anyone looking out of my eyes should allow for—and maybe even more easily than if I tried writing Nutshell II. So I'll just throw at you, fast, the odd bits I think you'll need for determining what kind of mental baggage I took along to the last place anybody I knew expected me to go.

"Maggie Rennert is a poet, critic, and editor" is what it used to say under my column of book reviews. Not graceful, but succinct— and maybe I can do it with my life, too. Like, I've been both a divorcée and a widow (in that order) and I have both children and stepchildren. In the late 1960s, I migrated from Washington, D.C., where

3

I'd spent most of my adult life, to Cambridge, Mass. And now that I think of it, if I hadn't had that experience of setting up a household in a new place, I might very well have quailed more at the idea of trying it in a strange country. (But I didn't think of that then: I'm a noticer by nature but an analyzer only by training, you see.) At the time, I was a widow with one child left at home, a son of about fourteen; he had a father living in Washington and went regularly to visit, but he was in every sense a part of my household. And my son made a considerable difference to it, I discovered when, in 1971, he went off to college—and for literally the first time in my life, I was living alone.

It meant I had to learn lots of small but important techniques for doing things that either a husband or a son had always taken care of. That presented some problems, but they weren't insoluble. And being alone didn't bother me: by then I was a novelist and thus used to working alone anyway, so the "empty nest" meant that now I wouldn't be interrupted because dinnertime could be whenever *I* got hungry. Of course, it also meant that if I wanted some conversation—and, after a day of immersion in the affairs of make-believe people, I often did—I'd either have to invite company or go out. But that too was manageable, for after five years in the area, I'd made friends; and besides, there was usually something going on in town that would be interesting to look in on.

That's where the catch showed up first. Because, though a great deal was going on in and around Cambridge in those years of campus turmoil and political ferment (some of the latter even genuine), looking on couldn't help but give you a dreary *déjà vu* feeling. Especially if, like me, you'd been a college student in the 1940s and seen the first run of the very rhetoric that was now being recycled, with no deference to history and even less charm. (One of my friends described the New Left pronouncements as "quaint," which is the perfect word and I wish I'd either said it or had the nerve to steal it.) Thus, although I was perhaps more comfortable than most in the spectator role that comes with middle age—being an observer was, after all, what I did for a living—I rebelled at the prospect of having nothing to spectate except a road-show version of old musicals starring second-rate ex-radicals (now relabeled "activists") who usually sang flat. True, what had been "the Cause" in the 1940s was now "the Movement," but that seemed hardly enough change. It was no fun to be a spectator when the only show in town was one where I knew how the plot came out.

So I began to consider going abroad to live. And since, with me, to think about something is almost always to talk about it, a largish number of folk in Boston and its suburbs heard of my ruminations; in addition, my temperament and profession incline me to friendships with people who also write long, articulate letters, so arguments for and against, recommendations and objections, etc., were getting airmailed to most of the U.S. and some foreign spots. My idea raised no eyebrows among the literary types I knew—peripatetic authors are not news in the publishing world— who mostly reacted by touting up southern provinces of France, Greek islands, or obscure Edens.

Meanwhile back in Cambridge, I was getting a reputation as either a Deep Thinker or a Rotten Fascist (depending on the specific activism) for such coups as asking why, if the Vietnam war was supposed to be a creature of Wall Street (oh, "quaint" was the word, all right), the stock market showed elation at every one of the practically-weekly "new hopes for peace." In that media-soaked scene of million-words-a-minute public discourse, the merest murmur of common sense or intellectual honesty could get you appointed a guru; but a guru wasn't what I wanted to be. So by the winter of 1972, I was about ready to quit talking and start packing.

But then the whole thing crashed, because I caught a double whammy from Fate: first, a chronic ailment blew up and required surgery, and right after I got on my feet I fell over again, this time clobbered by a new and possibly mortal illness. My friends and loved ones prayed, or tossed reassuring statistics around, or just crossed their fingers; and my relations with everybody became almost exclusively some form of emotional, and sometimes also physical, dependency. I saw the Boston winter from the windows of hospital rooms, and my conversation consisted largely of newly acquired medical knowledge and sulky visiting-hour reproofs ("I wanted my *blue* pajamas. And I've already *read* those thrillers. . .").

I came out in the spring, wafted out, you might say, on my friends' collective sigh of relief both for their own escape from bondage and my rescued future. That future, it seemed, would involve pills, special diet, regular checkups, the whole dreary bit— but an 85 percent chance of living to die of something else, which is pretty good odds. So by summer—convalesced, rehabilitated, checked-up and certified ready to join the world—I had begun Round 2 (involving, of course, several thousand more words) of the process I think of as "making plans." But a few things were different, and that's why I've put all that in here.

For by then, the nature of the discussion had changed on both sides. Anyone who felt at all fond of me was inclined to yell *Go-girl-go* at what was considered evidence of courage; but now

5

nobody was suggesting Ceylon or other exotic outposts. And on my side, the brush with death had first caused long thoughts and then a kind of New Look. I don't mean the world seemed prettified but simply new—the way it looks to a child, who wants to know everything, and in a hurry, and is busy drawing conclusions about what he sees but isn't primarily interested in making a case for or against anything. Part of my sense of hurry was self-dramatization (*Ah me, will I be here to see the roses bloom next year?*) and vanished when the answer turned out to be *Yup*; but something, an up-front feeling of mortality perhaps, stayed with me even when waking up in the morning had once again become a habit rather than a stroke of luck. . . . But I'm worried that you may confuse what I'm talking about with the "born again" feeling, which is mission-oriented. Mine was simply a willingness to inhabit whatever was going on, while finding out about it and without making any smart-talk about it. I had acquired one innocent eye, you might say, while also retaining my former bloodshot one—and the knowledges, wearinesses, and sophistications that came with my age and station. I think the combination is uniquely valuable (though I wouldn't recommend the route by which I arrived at it) for looking at a strange world and its ways, and I've tried to preserve it by limiting the period of time covered in this book. But of course, some of that newness was slowly corrupted, so to speak. (And some of it had to be: I've put in excerpts from my diary, but I've had to annotate them occasionally in the interests of accuracy. Innocence, it seems, doesn't always come up with the truth.)

Back to Round 2 of my "decision-making"—which was getting to be pretty nearly recognizable as that, for I did things as specific as buying a copy of the *Jerusalem Post* at the out-of-town newsstand. And when I started asking people what 20°C was in American weather, they started taking me just a jot seriously. Enough, anyway, to produce the incredulous question at the head of this chapter. Okay, they conceded, maybe I was really going *somewhere.* But, Israel? "You're too old," they said. (A lot of my loved ones lack tact.) I promptly pointed to Golda Meir, who must be at least twenty-five years older than I. And in case Prime Ministers didn't count, I'd also armed myself with a news clipping about a watchman who'd been abducted by Arab terrorists* come to raid his northern kibbutz: he'd succeeded in raising the alarm and thus saving the inhabitants, but he was carried off, presumably to be held as hostage. The story noted, not as news but the way you might give a

*Yes, terrorists were happening in 1972 too. Only, back then, they didn't yet have rocket launchers or invitations to address the UN.

6

victim's address, that he was 54 years old. . . . Faced with this evidence that people even older than I were living along and doing their thing in Israel, the skeptics switched to "You're too sick." That one was easy: "They have more doctors in proportion to the population than we have," I announced, making up a handy statistic. (Actually, it's true. Sometimes, if you get in there and swing, the gods are good to you.)

Some of the other objections were rather easily dispatched: e.g., it wasn't true that I knew nobody in Israel, for I'd met and liked a couple from Jerusalem who'd been at Harvard for a year—and that was twice as many people as I knew when I came to Cambridge. But it was my son's reply to that one that intrigued me, and resounded later: "Mom won't be lonely," he said with assurance, "because she's too curious." (Interesting diagnosis of loneliness, isn't it?) On the whole, though, nobody was really saying me nay anymore. My children—grown, and scattered about the country—not only inclined to look upon the idea as a symptom of recovered perkiness but also, since they'd observed that fifty-year-old widows tend to go traveling, were relieved to find me behaving like other people's mothers. (If, as usual, not quite properly: *She couldn't just go on a cruise, could she* . . .) My editor seemed to find Israel preferable to a Greek island, and urged that I keep a diary (which is one way of weaseling you into doing a book); but he expressed mild amazement that I could have been a Zionist without his ever knowing it.

I wasn't, I told him—actually wondering whether I should speak quite so flatly because I wasn't that sure what Zionism was. The last time I'd had any contact with any Zionists had been in my college days, when I went prospecting among the campus isms. The stated reason at the time was intellectual obligation, but I suspect it had more to do with meeting men—I attended an all-girls' college— than with investigating political philosophies. (It was lucky for me, in the Joe McCarthy-haunted Washington years afterward, that neither the Young Socialists nor the Young Communists had had any really good-looking boys.) The Young Zionists got scratched right at the start, because they so clearly weren't my type: their girls went in for dirndl skirts—a peasant style gathered at the waist but wide and shapeless, and dandy for hiding fat fannies or minimizing thick ankles—and what they all seemed to like best was dancing in a circle. Whereas I, at seventeen, had nothing to hide and fancied the kind of slinky satin dresses Myrna Loy used to wear in the *Thin Man* movies*; and dancing cheek-to-cheek was an important part of my

*My mother, however, fancied demure shirtwaist styles in *good* cloth, with *classic* lines. So guess what I wore.

sex life. Finally, and perhaps most fatal, the Zionists (like all the other socialists, as a matter of fact) were incredibly earnest types—and I held nothing dearer than a good pun, preferably barbed.

Well, more than thirty years later, lots of things had changed (e.g., I no longer thought Oscar Wilde quite such a great writer). But some hadn't, so one of my friends pointed out that Israel might very well be full of Zionists, almost certainly still earnest and probably still not my type. She could see, she said, that my cumbersome medical dossier now effectively eliminated unspoiled island Edens where nobody spoke English and the nearest hospital was half a day away—but there *were* other places with medical sophistication enough to take care of my pills and shots and stuff, and with lots of people who spoke English. Like, even England. The humorist S. J. Perelman had recently announced that he was fed up and was going to England to live.* And he was certainly my type, right? So why did I have to pick Israel?

It was the way she put it that gave me the handle: I "had to" pick Israel because, though I wasn't a Zionist, I *was* an erstwhile liberal. For I am of the generation—sons and daughters of rugged individualists—for whom the dancing stopped, earlier if you got involved in the Spanish civil war but certainly no later than the Nazi-Soviet pact in 1940 (which abruptly shut off that left-wing rhetoric, the first time around). For us, the founding of the United Nations represented a prize won from the hard years of World War II; they cost most of us a lot, and some of us everything, so we felt we'd earned a cosmic-size reward. And for a while it seemed we'd really got it: after the Suez war of 1956 in the Middle East, when the victorious Israelis—who'd chased the Egyptians nearly all the way back to Cairo and who could easily have gone on—turned around instead and went home, it looked to me and my ilk as if Israel, the new nation we'd seen born in 1948, was indeed a harbinger of the new world. Where nations would not claim the fruits of conquest but rely instead on the good faith of the world's men of good will. The Israelis were so gallant about it, too: when they pulled back out of the Sinai, they also picked up and doctored the Egyptian soldiers who'd been left by their officers to die in the desert. (And, until recently—when Saudi Arabia started tending to its international image—young and small and poor Israel paid a larger share of the international bill for refugee care than did the Saudis, who could well afford the cash.) Finally, Israel offered to sit down with its conquered enemies and talk over questions like reparations and

*He later decided it wasn't for him after all.

8

resettlement. Thus, with all that on the record, no wonder it seemed to us liberals that something new and wonderful was happening in the world. And we weren't the only ones who thought so: the guarantee by President Eisenhower (who was no liberal) to the Israelis that they wouldn't suffer by their 1956 withdrawal was approved by virtually all shades of American public opinion.

Well, you know how *that* plot came out. In 1967, the Egyptians took advantage of the returned Sinai land to cut off Israel's access to the Red Sea. There was a lot of vicious radio talk (including calls for slaughter of the unbelievers—which would unquestionably include women and children), Nasser of Egypt kicked out the UN's little peacekeeping force, and Egyptian troops were packed like sardines into Gaza.* But in case all that leaves anyone in doubt about who was the aggressor, the blockade alone is enough: it's a *casus belli* in international law.

Israel was thus entitled to declare war. But it apparently thought there was something better to do, so Abba Eban, the skilled and eloquent diplomat who was Israel's Foreign Minister in 1967, was sent tootling around to foreign capitals to remind them of the 1956 guarantee. And that's when we men of good will started learning the facts of life. For the only thing Eban seemed able to stir up in England was some talk about sending planes to rescue the surviving Israeli children when Nasser had carried out his promise to push the Israelis into the sea.† France didn't come up with even that much of an offer. And in the U.S., President Lyndon Johnson started maneuvering to get a few countries (e.g., France and England!) to send some ships—in maybe a couple of weeks?—to test the Egyptian blockade. It was unclear whether this putative test fleet would insist if the Egyptians said it couldn't pass. Or exactly what good it was supposed to do Israel if a U.S. ship *was* allowed to pass . . .

I don't know how you say "Well, so much for men of good will" in Hebrew. But Israel figured it out, obviously: Eban was told to quit begging with his homburg in his hand and come on home for the war. After which little Israel got us all off the hook by clobbering its outsize enemies so quickly that the U.S. could say *Well, we were*

*Now mentioned, usually with a throb in the voice, as the "homeland" stolen from "the Palestinians," who had not then been invented. Perhaps that's why Egypt didn't set up a homeland for them there—but chose instead to "maintain" (a term used most loosely indeed) refugee camps paid for by the UN. Which meant, mostly, by you and me.

†To be quite fair to the British, their government's shoddiness once again called forth the national gift for sharp satire: individuals writing in newspapers and other periodicals exhibited what was clearly the spirit of Jonathan Swift.

just coming, you guys. Millions of Americans went from writhing in shame to overwhelming relief and gratitude. But we were aware that it wasn't our own government, or even the international enlightened opinion of which we had believed ourselves a mystic part, that did the trick: it was a bunch of faraway people with queer names, alone in the world and fighting for their lives. The way people fight when they know the odds and don't think they can win but mean to die trying wasn't the kind of thing the world had seen much of lately. So the Israeli assault on the Golan Heights—straight up the cliffs, against elaborate defenses dug into rock and manned by professional soldiers who knew the Israelis were coming—is now justifiably recorded among history's legendary displays of valor. And, inasmuch as the Syrians had been for some years shooting down from those heights onto the kibbutz farms in Israel, military historians weren't the only onlookers who were moved to stand up and cheer.

Nevertheless, when the tumult and the shouting died, what was left to see, for me and other liberals, was the simple fact that the Israelis had listened to us in 1956. And if they'd gone on counting on us in 1967, they'd all be dead. . . . Ho hum, back to the drawing board, we need a new political philosophy. By the 1970s, I still hadn't been able to put my hand on a good one. But I'd got as far as figuring out that it seems to be impossible simultaneously to help your fellow men and guarantee your own personal purity, since any ideal you advocate is likely to get some people killed somewhere. On the day in 1972 when I was sitting up in my hospital bed reading a magazine somebody had brought me, I still wasn't minded to go out and join any ism. But neither was I prepared to put up with sly attempts to redefine virtue in the interests of ideological coziness.

That was what the magazine piece was up to. It was aimed at thoughty folk, "intellectual" enough to be able to cope with syntax and fond of feeling *avant-garde* so long as they weren't expected to get *avant* whatever was trendy. But the staff writer had a problem: winning independence from colonial masters, living in communes, wearing work clothes, and speaking bluntly were all In, and Israel had been wearing all those marks of purity for so long that it might be described as prematurely trendy—yet Israel had to be declared Out because being willing to defend one's country was Out-Out-Out. What made the problem particularly sticky was that the Israelis did their defending with such flair. For, only a short time before, a little band of them had popped across the Suez Canal to help themselves to a brand-new radar installation (a gift from the Soviets that the Egyptians had hardly had time to unwrap, so you can imagine how much the U.S. military subsequently appreciated a chance to look it over) and cart it home by helicopter. That exploit—seen from the ground, that slow swaying journey, must've been something: *No, it's not a bird, it's Superman in his sauna bath*—had an engaging student-prank air that tickled the American public; definitely, it was the sort of thing that made life hard for those ideologically obliged to find all Israeli deeds unkosher.

Well, this magazine communicator was doing his best to cope anyhow. Israel, he said, must cease being intransigent and aggressive and hold out the hand of peace forthwith. Tucked into that hand should be the Golan Heights, which should be turned back to the Syrians (who hadn't even *said* they wouldn't shoot down from there at civilians anymore!) presumably to show Israel's faith in everybody else's good intentions. There was more like that, of course. . . . Even a little was enough, though: coming in as it did when I'd just been considering how my life was spent, etc., the article "polarized" me. I put that word in quotes because that's what the magazine would've called it; I call it getting my dander up. Because I guess I felt, like so many Americans who'd been adults in 1967—not to mention people anywhere whose belief in brotherhood was not limited by their own national borders—that we owed Israel,* not only for saving our face in 1967, but for as long as the long train of consequences would last. That didn't mean always giving the Israelis whatever they asked, or automatically consider-ing them in the right. And it certainly didn't mean I thought everybody ought to go pay off the social debt in person, for I hadn't even thought *I* should until I felt like going somewhere anyway. But once pushed, I got mad: since I was about to improve some country's trade balance with my American dollars, let it be Israel's, by golly—if only because they were being shoved around for doing what they had a perfect right to do, try to stay alive.

My, that has a nice round ring to it. But of course what I came up with at the time was a motley collection of reasons, most of them sprung from books I read once I started exploring the prospect of living in Israel. For instance, the fact that Israeli politics, which apparently involved a Thoreau society governed by a Victorian-England parliament, would surely be an interesting show for an *aficionado* of politics like me: that's true enough, but I don't usually

*It's this kind of grass-roots sympathy that's usually "explained" as the "Jewish lobby." Which is nonsense: no matter how you pressure a member of Congress, the bottom line for him or her is votes in the district back home. And there simply aren't enough Jews in enough Congressional districts—the support has to be coming from lots and lots of non-Jews too.

think so fancy, if you know what I mean—it's an explanation rather than a reason. And after a while, my "reasons" were actually a kind of feedback from other people's doubts and arguments. (Which is intellectually untidy, but I'll bet I'm not the only one who arrives at convictions that way.) Not to mention their professions of admiration. For I'm ashamed of this, but it would be dishonest to underestimate the influence of a remark by one of my student friends— about how "gutsy" I was to go "on the road" that way. Like a middle-aged Kerouac, sort of. And especially when you consider Maggie's travel hang-up. . .

Ah yes, my hang-up. It used to be a Shameful Secret, back when I called it a neurosis; but the new let-it-all-hang-out life-style started people talking about *their* hang-ups, and once I discovered I wasn't a solitary freak, I crept out of my closet. My travel hang-up is so full-blown that even though two little granddaughters waited at the other end of the journey, it was all I could do to climb onto a plane. No, it's not that I'm afraid of flying: actually, I have a fine time in flight—until we get to another airport. For, as far as I can tell without investing in a few thousand dollars' worth of psycho-analytic inquiry into the matter, it's airports I'm afraid of. In those great echoing spaces full of people who'll never be anything but strangers, and with mechanical voices booming at me out of the walls, a literally dread-full feeling assaults me and I could easily burst into tears. (Large department stores have much the same effect, though I can dash out of *them* at will. And lately I've come across some covered shopping malls that seem to rate as honorary airports.) Since I can't always avoid airports, lots of people now know that when—for love or money—I simply have to travel somewhere, the details must be all written out and practically pinned to my coat. Then, white-faced and wringing my hands, I am carted to the plane like an express package, and similarly collected at the other end. Nobody has ever been foolhardy enough to try to find out what would happen otherwise.

So you can see why Cathy, a student who'd been to Israel for several summers as a kibbutz volunteer, warned me very particularly that Lod Airport was even more airporty than most. And why there were worried murmurs from all sides. And especially why my son Phil's pronouncement that it made him proud to have such a gutsy mother virtually closed out any possibility of second thoughts.

Getting Phil's *imprimatur* had been practically the first requirement for ever thinking seriously of going forth from Massachusetts to anywhere. He'd been the only child still a schoolboy

12

when a publisher's advance enabled me to quit my job as an editor at a Defense Department-associated "think tank" and try my hand at a novel. Since I'd thus become financially viable without being tied to a salary, shopping for a new school for Phil—who was then ready for ninth grade—didn't have to be limited to Washington, D.C. So when his father and I (we'd been divorced for some time but retained pragmatic-amiable relations dictated by our mutual desire to do the right thing by our mutual child) determined that the day school Phil had liked when he visited Boston was the best fit for him, I rented a house in Cambridge and moved my household up there. It was definitely an uprooting and setting out for unknown territory, but our little household of two survived not only that but even the not inconsiderable struggles and hullabaloos of those awful early-teen years. Perhaps because I'd had previous experience with adolescents (and sons are easier than daughters, I think), I did better than before. But Phil was an extra-difficult kid because, as seems to be rather usual with "gifted" children, he was somewhat uneven: most of the time, he'd be way ahead of you, clearing developmental hazards in easy leaps—and then suddenly he'd reveal a bit of startling immaturity.

But he didn't get fashionably "alienated," and (like most of the math- or science-oriented youngsters, so I think it must have *something* to do with their salvation as teen-agers) he'd picked his way successfully past the drug-culture quicksands that lay all about us. By the autumn of 1972, he had just begun his sophomore year at Yale, where he was not only getting all the math and physics he could gobble but, with gratifying broad-mindedness, was even signing up for the odd anthropology or music course. (I prefer to think that was because of my long-playing sermon on the dangers of unleavened mathematicking, for which I used to use *Star Trek*'s Mr. Spock as a text. But I have to acknowledge that the leavening didn't happen until I was out of the way.) I don't suppose you can say that anybody eighteen years old has really found himself, but Phil at least knew where to look. He seemed to have located his place in his student world; and at home, he'd managed to figure a way to be dutiful without falling into the You're-the-man-of-the-family trap that can await widows' sons. My illness, badly timed in terms of his development, threatened that adjustment for a while; but then he found the handle. (Samuel Johnson's observation about the imminence of death wonderfully concentrating the mind goes for the bystanders too, I guess.)

Thus, when I started my Round 2 ruminations, Phil was pretty well convinced that he wouldn't turn out to be one of those forty-year-old men who still live at home to look after Mama, so he could afford even to be fond of me. I had become, comfortably, his home address—listed as such on Yale forms and repaired to during the sections of his jaunts to Massachusetts when he wasn't busy with his girlfriend or his old school chums. True, I was something of a nuisance because there were chores to do for me, like figuring my income tax and lifting heavy objects. But on the whole I was pretty much what a college sophomore's mother is required to be, a likable woman who's around when she's needed and stays out of the way the rest of the time. Which isn't much of a requirement, but it was still more physical presence than anyone else needed of me. So whereas I could just say "I'm going" to my other loved ones, I thought Phil was entitled to a vote.

I stated the proposition—that I was thinking of not being around anymore, at least not for anything short of a flying-home emergency—during a weekend visit. Which is to say, I sort of slid it onto the table along with the hamburgers done just the way Phil liked them. "How would you feel about it," I asked, very tentatively indeed, "if I took off for Israel? For, well, let's say a year."

He glanced at me sharply and then bent his head, studying the surface of the round wooden table we'd bought when we came to Cambridge—and faithfully oiled and polished for five years. "You'd have to give this place up, I guess." Behind him stood the ranks of ceramic chessmen he'd made in eleventh grade, the nego- tiated settlement of the war to turn Phil into a Well-Rounded Man: he'd been forced into an art class so he could express himself, and— rejecting flowerpots, ashtrays, and even abstract lumps—what he'd expressed himself with, firmly, was chessmen. They were aston- ishingly handsome, but the school and I both got his point.

"Well, I couldn't very well afford to keep paying the rent," I said. Unnecessarily—my son the math genius could figure that better than I could. "Besides, what would be the point? In vacations, you'd be going to your father's." We both knew that where he would probably be going, most of the time, was to his girlfriend's. But I needed the hypocrisy, to make the necessary distinction between leaving him homeless and turning him over to his other parent.

He said "Oh, sure" in a bright voice that didn't match his somber look. Which had nothing to do with the prospect of spend- ing time with his father: there was no reason to believe an additional week together a couple of times a year would strain their pleasant, easygoing relations. The problem lay, instead, in what he was looking at—home. *This* was where Phil had shoveled snow and mowed grass, put up and taken down the Christmas tree, battened

14

down hatches for winter and opened them up again for summer. It wasn't his boyhood home, but it was home.

And I was proposing to move it out from under him, just like that . . . Guilt-struck, I fought back by reminding him that the sentimental picture had contained some real nagging about chores, which now he wouldn't have to do. "And at your father's," I added, "the air conditioner won't stay in the window until you come to lift it down." That was what he'd finally done this weekend, and it was October. *Pow! Take that, you slothful son . . .*

He let it go past, though he could've pointed out that the air conditioning in his father's house wasn't a single dinky little box in the window—which would've reminded me that his father was richer than I was as well as stronger. What Phil said instead was gentle and thoughtful: "It can't be much fun for you, living here alone."

"Oh, it's all right. Just sort of dull, that's all."

He was busy picking at the label on the ketchup bottle. "You've got a right to live your own life, I guess."

The slow, conscientious words wrung my heart. "You've got a right, too," I said, feeling wretched. Because a boy ought to be able to dump his mother when he's ready to, not when it's convenient for her to declare him a finished job. He has a right not to be asked if it's time, too: what eighteen-year-old male could *say* he still needed his mother around—especially if he happened to? "You've got a right to have your mother handy," I told him. "And to feel deprived if you don't."

He lifted his head then and our two looks suddenly crossed like searchlights in the night, meeting in an X of long-stemmed guilts. The kind grown in a mixed soil, half the child-logic of the unconscious, half the greeting-card cultural heritage: a good boy comes home oftener (or writes every week, or makes with the muscles without having to be nagged—check one), and then his Mama won't go away and leave him; a good mother puts her child's need, even a marginal and unverifiable one, before her own hurry-up feeling of mortality, if she wants her children to remember her with love when she does die . . . We hung there, both of us knowing the "right" way to go and not wanting to go that way. And then Phil got us off the hook: "I guess what I want," he said wryly, "is a mother to not come home to." A couple of dogs in the manger, trying to eat our cake and have it too, we laughed amid the clang of clichés in the cleared air of the room . . .

It didn't strike me until I wrote all this down that *where* I was going had had absolutely no part in that—most important, because it

15

was closest to permission-granting—conversation with Phil. I've told you all this so you could see that who was going was (a) a seeker of more interesting spectating for the middle-aged, (b) an ex-liberal debtor of a nation to whom I'd given a bum steer in the past, (c) an *aficionado* of politics curious about what looked like a very oddly shaped body politic, and (d) an aging Kerouac hitting the road (and, similarly, "showing" the society). I can't guarantee all of those *personae,* and there may be more I didn't wot of. But what stands out in the list, I think, is how little those items had to do with Israel, even technically—and when it came down to reality, even less.

Oh, I forgot Item (e)—a coward. Because once everybody went away and all the talking stopped, I discovered that's what I was. There can be few conditions more upsetting than realizing you're scared when you've just been acclaimed as a gutsy heroine. I couldn't possibly go back, but going forward called for just about every skill I was conspicuously without. Except one: if the story of my life reveals any consistent ability, it's at jumping off into space. So okay, all was not lost, what I'd do was arrange some way to make this venture one fast, blind jump—set it up so signing a paper and/or paying out a lot of money would start some kind of conveyor belt in motion. After that, I could close my eyes and (remembering to smile bravely) be carried off to Israel.

2 ⚏ People-Moving

Well, there *was* a conveyor belt—if there hadn't been, I'd have been out of the heroine business before I even got started—but you had to get on it, and I was too busy to. First I had to dispose of the more than a thousand books not going with me. That involved such elaborate classifying and decisionmaking, featuring semifinals and finals and a special "Oh the hell with it" category, that the only way to sooth my battered psyche was to dive into my writing and pull it over my head. Thus it was December before I woke from my typewriter trance—which had been no rest cure either: I was trying my hand at a suspense novel, and I kept falling over my own plot— and ran up against the fact of the date. It was like waking up in the morning to discover you've turned off the alarm and gone back to sleep, a heart-thumping panic (*My God, I've really blown it this time*) followed by frantic effort to save whatever can still be saved.

Nobody can ever have dumped anything more unceremoniously than I did my life in Massachusetts. I began by renting my place for just the rent itself, everything in it thrown in for free, to a couple whose only recommendation was that they agreed to send on after me the five trunks and the cartons of books that represented rock-bottom necessity. My really precious lares and penates got parked in various suburban homeowners' basements to await later determination on whether Israel was worthy of containing my grandmother's tea wagon, etc. The rest of my furniture, I said airily, wasn't worth bothering to ship (oh wow) because beds and tables and chests and chairs could be bought anywhere (uh huh). Considering that I'd paid a small fortune, about five years before, to

17

have that same stuff carted to Cambridge from Washington, you can see that this time I was really going off with just a pack on my back (well, so to speak). The grand sweep gave me a sense of competence—Look Ma, I'm *coping*!—that accumulated like the effects of drinking a lot of beer in the afternoon, the exhilaration climbing in slow boosts so that when I got up to the conviction that I could lick any man in the house it seemed neither sudden nor drunken. From time to time, there were intimations of a future hangover—e.g., it occurred to me that "gutsy" meant there must be something to be scared of—but whenever they happened, I just made another list.

By mid-December, then, I had so many lists that I even had a list of lists. And anyone with my newfound competence could plainly see that, since the tenants would be moving into my place a few days before January 1, it was time to start arranging for that fast, blind jump. So, brisk and confident as Rosalind Russell playing a career girl in an old movie, I phoned the Israel Consulate in Boston to ask how one goes about setting off to live in Israel, please. No, I didn't mean as a tourist; and no, I wasn't going there to take a job or study . . . You'd have thought weeding out those irrelevances would make the Consulate girl's life easier, but apparently it didn't: she still sounded confused when she gave me the number of something called the "Aliyah" office.

There, another girl was clearly knocked for a loop when she heard I expected to leave in two weeks—there was an audible gulp, and then she murmured that I'd better come in and see her boss. I agreed, but the conversation left me feeling as if my brisk-lady costume had sprung a seam somewhere. For both girls had seemed to be thinking up hastily what to do about me: I'd assumed there was a script, but their performances were unmistakably impromptu . . . My frail confidence wobbled, the clickety-click missing a click. But it would be all right, I told myself, as soon as I found out where they kept that conveyor belt. Which must be running smoothly somewhere behind these rather easily unnerved employees of Israel's diplomatic corps.

Well, Revelation No. 1—they weren't that. What they were employees of, I found when I got to the office, was the Jewish Agency, an outfit I dimly remembered hearing of when it was rescuing displaced persons in Europe after World War II. Nothing I'd read in my library book had prepared me for its role in relation to the government of Israel, perhaps because describing that might have taken over the book. The easiest way out—and I don't blame anybody for taking it—is to reach for the handy rubric "quasi-official": back in my Washington-reporter days, that was what we

18

used for outfits like the science-adviser types who flew into Washington regularly to tell the President whether something he wanted might be radioactive. You just typed in "The quasi-official National (Blah Blah) Council"—or Board, or Agency—and then went on to quote the leak . . .

I mention that out of wistfulness, I think: it's so much easier to fly over a thicket than to slog through it on the ground. And the tangled-vine relations of the Jewish Agency (which was, in effect, "the government" in the pre-state days) with the State of Israel makes for quite a thicket. But for now, what matters most is that the Jewish Agency, though quasi, is virtually the whole show when it comes to immigration.* Because, for one thing, it runs the conveyor belt. Which, I learned at the Aliyah office, included a stay at minimal cost (because it's subsidized by you-know-quasi-who) for up to six months at an "absorption center," a kind of hostel with an attached *ulpan* (ool-PON, any kind of adult-education setup) that provided intensive Hebrew instruction. All sorts of other goodies come along with the deal too, like people who help you find a place to live, a job, etc. I mean that "etc." to cover confronting bureaucracy, which is something a type like me sorely needs—if you just hand me a form to fill out, I start to grow airport-pale—even when I'm not turned loose alone in a strange new world.

Of course, though, Israel is a free country, enterable by anybody with legitimate purpose subject to only the usual restrictions (which seem to be fewer almost anywhere than in the U.S.). Thus if I'd wanted to hop a plane and go, I could have; Yaakov and Sara, the Israeli academic couple I'd met in Cambridge, would have helped me find an apartment—and the necessary *ulpan*—in Jerusalem. But to be a rugged individualist instead of a conveyor-belt-borne immigrant would be expensive and nerve-wracking and, most of all, professionally silly: if I was considering writing a book about Israel, why skip an experience that was both typical and, so far as I know, unique with Israel? So the choice was easy—I became an immigrant (thus adding that role to my list) to Israel without actually intending to emigrate from the U.S.

Not that it was easy when we got down to the nitty-gritty, however. I could see it wasn't going to be, even while I was still waiting to see the *shaliach* (shah-LEE-ach: it comes from the verb "to send" and is usually translated as "messenger," but the Jewish

*Even the dummiest new student of Hebrew soon knows the word *Sochnut* (soch-NOOHT, agency; for beginners, virtually synonymous with "Jewish Agency"). I was in the slow-learners class, but I didn't have to learn it in the classroom—I picked it up in the schoolyard.

Agency's is more like an emissary. A quasi-official one, of course—another word means a regular diplomatic emissary). In the anteroom, I picked up an attractive booklet. The cover featured a bottle of milk and a jar of honey—land of milk and honey, supermarket version—photographed in handsome color against a desert landscape. Inside, it looked good too, a nice printing job and the writing polite but not stiff, with just the right amount of humor. But then I started reading—and amazingly, what all that clever work seemed to be designed to tell me was that life in Israel was very likely to prove just too tough for American me. In case I was slow to pick up hints, there were charts and tables to help me out with the cost of housing, the cost of food, etc., for a family of four. In a kind of low murmur in the corners, "privileges" were offered to ease the plight of the (obviously materialistic, soft-as-mush) American immigrant: prominent among them was the right to bring in a car duty-free—the clear implication being that no American would even begin to stir unless he could bring his car along.

All this advice to *olim* (oh-LEEM, immigrants; the singular is *oleh*, masculine, or *olah*, feminine) was presented in a uniquely swing-and-sway style, with every enticing statement instantly followed by a discouraging one; quite often, the ratio was one-to-two. For example, you read that the Jewish Agency would give you a loan (virtually a gift) to pay for transporting your household goods. But before you could even begin to think *Hey, that's great,* you were told that (a) storage facilities are practically nonexistent anywhere in the country and (b) you'd have to get your stuff from the port on your own, too. And even if you succeeded in arranging transport, you might very well find yourself—the cheerful explanatory voice went on, nailing it down with nice clear specific images—with your washing machine on the sidewalk and no way to get it up to your third-floor flat . . . Thus were you invited to come and live in lovely Israel. And if any Public Relations Council gives an annual prize for best-written, best-illustrated Self-Defeat, this one-wow, two-whammies job should be a cinch to win it.

Well, of course I had a swift professional sympathy for the booklet's author, who had clearly had to satisfy some kind of committee with all factions represented (and the Say-Something-Nice party obviously a minority); but my personal reaction was a very American "Oh yeah? Who sez I can't?" If I was irritated, I was also challenged . . . And that word will do nicely too, I suspect, to describe the feelings of the shaliach: reading the form I'd filled out, the poor man must've wished he'd called in sick that day. Because he's supposed to carry out the Jewish Agency's double people-moving mission—to move people to want to live in Israel, and then get them moved over there—but he's expected to use some judgment in the matter. For anyone who decides to go to Israel there are numerous programs, some the Sochnut's and others sponsored by a variety of other organizations. Ready-made niches are available to accommodate practically anyone from pious Jews, who've been waiting all their Orthodox lives to pray daily in Jerusalem, all the way across the spectrum to restless kids seeking new life-styles. (The latter can be sent to a kibbutz where they'll meet other identity-seeking young from all over the world, make themselves useful doing chores, and eventually either find themselves or leave to look elsewhere.) And besides, on the premise that the way to sell a product is to give the customer a sample—very sensible in the case of Israel, which is in fact more than the sum of its parts and so resists all slogans and catch phrases—there's a slew of special arrangements like the one that allows academics to try out the life during a sabbatical year.

And even one for writers' groups to take look-see tours, though of course I'd never gone on one of those (me, travel for no particular reason?!). But in fact my application didn't say I was a writer. I had no real reason for leaving it out, just a habit of double identity I'd fallen into some years before.* I don't stamp my *nom de plume* "Secret" or lie if I'm asked, but I never vouchsafe the information to casual acquaintances—and I consider any acquaintance that involves filling out application blanks very casual indeed. But that accidental fact just about completed the gloomy picture for the shaliach staring hopelessly at my application, with its sparse answers stranded like atolls in a sea of blank lines: if you look out of his eyes, you can see why he spoke to me slowly and hesitantly, while his hand rubbed his forehead. Which must have ached, because he was faced with recommending to the Jewish Agency's embrace a middle-aged widow who had no job or profession, no relatives in Israel, no membership in any Jewish organization, didn't even speak Yiddish, and had never been on so much as a two-week see-the-Holy-Land excursion. Oy. And the information that I'd been hospitalized a year before can hardly have added joy to a

*Ever since a critic called me the "authentic voice of American poetry" (a quote I somehow never have to look up) and urged everybody to keep an eye on me because I was so "rich in promise." But at the time I'd just made that rather difficult by exchanging the surname you see on the title page for another, via remarriage . . . My ex-husband and my new husband, both men of the world, agreed that it'd be a shame if I had to start promising all over again, so neither of them minded too much if I kept on using my former married name in print. I use my proper (i.e. bank and passport) name in all other encounters, of course.

portrait of—well, let's say not exactly an immigrant any poor little country would regard as a real catch.

What in the bureaucratic world (the poor man must have wondered) do you do with a middle-classnik who behaves as impulsively as a youth, and thus crisscrosses categories and flip-flops out of classifications? This one was in no physical shape for kibbutz life—alas, because the kibbutz serves nicely as kin for waifs—but *some* machinery must be activated. Because it was impossible to turn loose on her own a woman who used English words so fancy they made your head ache but had so little sense that she hadn't brought along a single document—and yet expected everything to be accomplished in two weeks (if you could believe it!), which was barely enough to begin the paperwork. She also didn't have anywhere near enough money, even assuming she had more than she said (for middle-class matrons, it was known, always had at least a couple of diamond rings hidden away); and, even more depressing, she seemed unaware of that. So what it probably added up to was this: *if* you could get her settled down somewhere, and *if* this monthly income she said she had (but no proof, of course!) didn't turn out to be a handout from a son or something precarious like that, she just might be able to get along (but wait till she found out how much it cost to run a car!) and it was just barely possible that Israel could gain the only possible asset she represented, a small monthly contribution to the supply of dollars. But to bring all that off would require a whole corps of experts to shepherd, guard, and educate. So okay, here comes a gift for some unlucky absorption center, and God help us all . . .

On the other side of the desk, I'd been examining my surroundings, a not very office-like office, semi-tidy and used-looking. It reminded me so much of the "study" suburban families used to whip up in a corner of the basement that I half expected to hear the washing machine thumping away on the other side of the wall. The girl in the outer room, apparently the only employee, also rather helped the illusion along: she was perhaps just a jot too old to be the shaliach's daughter, but her clothing suggested that she might leave any minute for her 10 o'clock history class; and the way she wandered in and out during our discussion, plus a general informality of manner, definitely bespoke the daughter helping out in Pop's store. Neither she nor the shaliach had any trace of a meeting-the-public manner, nor did their homey-shabby surroundings suggest any such consciousness. They were simply talking to people. Pleasantly, casually—as if visitors dropped in on impulse and whether they went and/or came again was no business of the Aliyah office.

Well, I really hadn't expected brass bands and "Welcome, Maggie" posters. But here I was proposing to pay my liberal debt by helping them out instead of loafing self-indulgently on a Greek island, so you'd think I'd encounter something better than a puzzled frown—plus an increasing feeling that I was applying for membership in some kind of very exclusive club.* It was a bit of an ego-shock. (However, novelists are sometimes lucky with personal dismays, because they turn into phrasemaking: *He had to take the recruiting sergeant to lunch before he could get into the army,* I was writing in my head, for some character to say about another someday.) Mostly because I couldn't see what the shaliach's problem might be. It couldn't be money, for I figured my grubstake—the last of the proceeds from my first novel—was enough to pay my fare, set aside the emergency-return fare, and get a few necessities when I found an apartment. How much could a bed and an unpainted chest and maybe some planks and bricks for a bookcase cost?† And my annuity, which was set at a monthly level designed to keep State Department widows in shabby gentility, translated into—according to Yaakov, who should know about pay scales at Hebrew University—just about the salary of a senior lecturer. Since it didn't seem likely that that bunch was on welfare, it was safe to conclude that my "widow money" alone would keep me from starving.

However, I assumed I would work; I always had, after all. And even if my art didn't sell, I had a trade: Yaakov had assured me that the appearance on the scene of a top-grade English editor (experienced in scientific papers, yet!) would set Israel academic circles dancing for joy. Maybe the prospect of correcting the grammar in some symposium's Proceedings didn't set *me* dancing for joy, but I knew how to do it if I had to. So I couldn't see myself as a potential burden on Israeli society—though I could of course understand that they'd probably rather have somebody who could till the fields—and thus I couldn't see what all the hemming and hawing could be about. I said so at last: "I thought you *wanted* people to come," I told the shaliach. "So what's the hang-up?"

He raised his head and said wearily that they did want people, certainly they did. But this application presented some problems. He turned it toward me, as if inviting me to see it from his point of view, and what I saw instantly was the name at the top— my late husband's name, unmistakably English or Irish. Oh, so that was it: reverse anti-Semitism. Well, we'd see about that. "Look," I

*If I'd remembered that impression, I wouldn't have been so surprised later, when I heard of the hair-raising obstacle course confronting would-be converts to Judaism.
†Plenty. But the real problem isn't that, it's the definition of "necessities" (see 'Dear Folks").

23

said in a tone that all but turned the word into *Look here, my good man,* "under the Nuremberg Laws in Nazi Germany, if you had a Jewish grandmother, that made you Jewish, right?"

"That's right." He answered soberly: in Israel, the days of the Nazi reign of terror are not spoken of casually. Or thought of as debating points either, to be thrown around by innocent, and thus callow, Americans. Now, I am ashamed . . .

But then, I was only triumphant. "Okay, I had a Jewish grandmother. So if I'd have qualified for a concentration camp, how can the Jewish Agency say I won't do?"

The dark eyes were alert, and faintly alarmed. "Oh, they wouldn't say any such thing," he said quickly. Then he added—gravely, but his eyes now looked amused—that it was certainly a persuasive point, and went on to ask me about my grandmother.

I answered his questions—yes, my mother's mother was Jewish*—absently, because I was suddenly remembering Grandma, the reluctant immigrant to America that I'd been told about and the bossy old lady I'd known and loved. She'd been dead for what was now half my lifetime, but I was suddenly behaving very like her. Certainly it was with Grandma's lordliness (sexist, since it stemmed from an apparent belief that men existed to remove annoying details from the paths of ladies) that I asked what other details were bothering the poor wretch before me. When one of them turned out to be only a matter of money—the inflation in Israel, he murmured hesitantly—my response was all Grandma's everything-is-simple airiness (*Just go down there and explain it to them,* I once heard her order my unfortunate uncle, who was supposed to "explain" at the county courthouse that his mother took a light view of anything written in English and thus had thrown the paper out instead of signing it before a notary). "Well, if it turns out that I need money, I'll go to work," I told the man. And when that didn't unwrinkle his brow—it might not be so easy, he seemed to think, especially in "times of emergency"—my patience with all this inefficiency quite wore out. People always needed help, I said decisively. And especially in times of emergency I could be useful: I knew how to take care of children, type, drive a car . . .

*Under Jewish religious law, a Jew is anyone born of a Jewish mother. That matrilineal system makes sense when you remember the desert tribe it was set up for: what with wandering off and raids by hostiles, there would've been quite a few grounds for doubting paternity—which in any case comes down to the testimony of the mother, who may be a young girl with reason to lie. But maternity is, usually, a firsthand visible fact. And if you're trying to keep your tribe from vanishing, it's the only fact that matters . . . Those old sages were very practical societymakers, it seems.

24

What I was doing was of course only Grandma-ly waving the problem away, putting things in simple terms for simple folk. But I realize now it came across like a Zionist dream: he must have seen, peeping out from behind this maniac middle-classnik, the back-to-the-soil ideal of the early pioneers in Palestine, who not only wore dirndls and danced in a circle but also ardently believed that humble tasks glorified the individual* . . . The shaliach awoke from his gloomy torpor and asked me, his manner now quite different, why I'd decided to go to Israel. It wasn't an easy country to live in, he said softly, even in the best of circumstances; and in its short history it had seldom enjoyed the best of circumstances.

Well, I surely wasn't about to deliver my I-owe-them lecture, not at that point: for one thing, I was so irritated I wasn't really sure I still owed these dratted people. And for another, it was entirely possible that by now I didn't so much want to go as simply have to. I was familiar with another situation, though, in which you went on with something just because you'd started. So "I don't have a rational answer," I told him. "It's like getting married. Does anybody really know why they get married?" He was looking at me strangely, of course. Which added to my dissatisfaction with myself (it's a hell of a note, isn't it, when the authentic voice of American poetry can't come up with anything better than *Well, uh . . .*) and suddenly tipped over into outright exasperation. "Look, maybe I don't know why, but I know I'm going," I announced. "If you-all can't figure a way through your rules and regulations, then I'll just have to slip over the border or something. But I'm going to Israel."

Having thus laid down the law (*Just go down there and explain it to them*), I reached for my gloves. Then I caught sight of the girl in the doorway. "You—you don't speak any Hebrew at all?" she asked, her eyes very big.

I told her I didn't, at the same moment the shaliach threw her a glance over my head and said, "Not a word." And they both began to grin, and all of a sudden everything got relaxed and very different, and it was clear that a way would be found through the rules and regulations. I put my gloves down again and started writing a list of what I'd need: birth certificate, doctor's certificate . . .

Nobody told me what had happened, though even then I perceived it was whatever is the opposite of a culture clash. But now I, too, know the missing word the girl couldn't believe I didn't know because I was acting so like it. It's *dahfke*, one of the two

*If this sounds to you as though it came out of the same litter as Maoism, you're right. But do keep in mind the vital difference: in China, you get *sent* back to the land; whereas in Israel the kibbutzim have waiting lists of applicants.

Hebrew words* I agree are truly untranslatable (usually, I consider that claim a cop-out), so naturally I can't define it. But I can locate its neighborhood for you: *dahfke* lives in the same territory as "in spite of" or "in despite" (or, in that sense, "anyhow"), alongside "against all the odds" and "of all unlikely things." Like, imagine on the one hand a hunk of swampland that'd make a great site for a Public Health Service experiment on malaria control but not for anything else. The guy who owns it got title because his family had clout when some war shuffled the other side out and his side in; he lives in swinging Beirut and doesn't give a damn if a few of the more desperate of the local nomads are pasturing their goats there—when somebody comes along who's willing to pay, he sells it anyway. Okay, now imagine on the other hand a little band of revolutionaries, humorless and stuffed to the ears with turgid volumes of clumsy political dogma. Those ears are swathed in mufflers because they're in wintry, decrepit little towns in nineteenth-century eastern Europe—the kind of country where you can't take your mittens off for more than a couple of months in the year and nothing much grows but dark legends. These characters could explain you the dialectics of practically anything, and they're very big on long words in heavy books; but they probably don't have any more agricultural experience than maybe growing a geranium in a pot. Yet it's this crowd that *dahfke* buys that steaming swamp on the other side of the world to go start tilling the soil in . . . Get it? I could give you other examples a lot closer to home, but I have the feeling that's the one that sprang to mind (theirs, not mine: I hadn't heard about those pioneers yet) in the Aliyah office.

So okay. The Aliyah people *dahfke* arranged to get me to Israel, by cutting off enough limbs—on paper—so I'd fit onto the Procrustean conveyor belt. (Editor: Please leave that mishmash of metaphors alone. It's Art, designed to show the joyful turbulence of the time, see?) But it couldn't be done in two weeks. The best they could manage was February 11 (which as it happens is my birthday: once the magic starts working, everything gets tidy), when I could be consigned to leave for an absorption center in Beer-Sheva that had an ulpan for "professionals." Actually, that seemed to mean mostly engineers; but the folks at the office had had enough of my making extra holes in all the punch cards and declared firmly that among that bunch was where I belonged, see. And I couldn't be sent to Jerusalem (where *I* wanted to go because that's where Yaakov and Sara live, but everybody else wanted to go there too, it seemed)

*You'll find the other word in "O Brave New World . . ."

26

because the absorption center there didn't have an opening for a "single." I was so startled by this description of myself, a thrice-married grandmother, that I quit arguing.

In the meantime, an attempt was made to show me, hastily, something of the more normal ways of this new world. But all I learned from being sent to a meeting of people who were thinking of settling in Israel was that they all seemed to think for at least two years. And that I sure as hell didn't belong with that crowd—they were so earnest they didn't even dance in circles. Depressing. But the friend with whom I was staying at the moment comforted me by pointing out that *they* were in the U.S. going to meetings, so I probably wouldn't run into their ilk in Israel.

I was being thus solaced—as well as advised, getting my clothes repacked, etc.—by a whole series of friends around then: the six-week difference between giving up my home and actually setting forth made me a sort of professional houseguest. So I also got to air, in households from Philadelphia to Utah, the Hebrew from the Jewish Agency booklet (*olim, ulpan,* etc.). But I didn't actually spend much time studying it, for advice on how to ship my washing machine could hardly have any relevance for me: the hell with it, I'd take my stuff to the laundromat. I took due note, as a datum about the economy, of the six-figure price (in Israel pounds) of an apartment; but the news that the Jewish Agency would give me a five-digit loan had nothing to do with me (especially since I've never in my life taken a bank loan). That the electric current in Israel was different did register, as, whatever a transformer was, I didn't propose to be bothered acquiring one. A young poet was the only person I knew who didn't have a TV set, so I corrupted her with mine; but nobody had needed my electric blanket, mixer, phonograph, etc., so I'd just dumped all that stuff.* I carried my hair dryer around for a while—it had been needed for New Year's Eve elegance—but after I realized it was electric too, by golly, I abandoned it where I was houseguesting at the moment.

A booklet from Israel's Ministry of Absorption, setting forth the rules for residents of the *mercaz klita* (mair-KAHZ klee-TAH, absorption center) in Beer-Sheva, caught up with me at one point in my travels, so I got to see the dramatic difference between quasi-official and the real thing. For the Ministry effort had no pictures at

---

*By now, this causes me the same wince I noticed when people in Israel heard what I'd done. I soon dropped the subject, in the interests of making friends, and after a while everybody forgot. (Or else they thought I'd just been boasting, which would be a more comfortable explanation for them: it's easier to forgive a lie than such whopping folly.)

all, not even on its cover (cheap gray paper), and it seemed written by a computer inadequately programmed with English grammar and vocabulary. It was also clearly untouched by any makeup or production hand: the pages looked more like copy for a printer than his product. I've seen Marine Corps technical manuals, all about the modular repair of a gun carriage, that were more inviting to read—and my children's Valentine productions in kindergarten were more securely stapled together.

Nevertheless, the booklet did focus my attention on Beer-Sheva, which I'd ignored except for noticing how the Aliyah girl pronounced it: B'air-SHEV-uh, the apostrophe meaning not an omission but a kind of muffled "buh," a hesitation rather than a syllable. (She was being conscientious in front of a foreigner, probably: in daily use, it tends to be a flat "bear.") And, thus awakened to the fact that Beer-Sheva was in the Negev, I took steps to prepare for life in a desert by ditching my workaday winter jacket in Cambridge and my fur coat (which I needed until the last minute) in Philadelphia. That helped to make room in my suitcases—five of them in Cambridge, but I had two airline bags and a straw basket, too, by the time I got to the last of the repackers—for some summery dresses hastily whipped up in Denver.* Nothing more could be added, since all I was allowed on the plane was forty-four pounds of luggage (to live on for two months, while my trunks were coming by sea!) and my Valpak probably weighed that much already. Nobody could squeeze in the afghan an ex-student had knitted for me, before I broke the Israel news, against the chill of a Massachusetts winter. It obviously didn't belong in a desert, but I loved its great squares of brilliant colors, so I rolled it up and carried it by hand, enduring cracks about security blankets all the way across the U.S. and back again, and getting stared at a lot in airports. (And when you remember that I still hadn't heard the word *dahfke* . . . !) But as it happens, it was probably the most useful thing I brought along to Beer-Sheva, so there.

Also weighing down the luggage was a mass of manuscript. For, when the shaliach insisted on applying for an Agency loan for my fare—which, at their special rate, was only $300—so I could hang onto my whole grubstake, I finally got the message that my financial ice might be a bit thin. So I started working energetically, laying up acorns in the form of outlines and rough drafts and at least one half-finished book. (When I got back the manuscript of *Operation*

*Somewhere in the background there, a voice kept murmuring that Denver too was technically a desert, yet it was plenty cold in January . . . But nothing can stand in the way of a wrong idea whose time has come: the Dacron sewing fest went right on.

Alcestis, after it was published two years later, I noticed that it had been typed on seven typewriters besides my own. I wasn't the kind of houseguest who needed to be entertained, you see.) Thus I was not only airport-dazed but also understandably exhausted when, on the night of February 11, 1973, I was handed over to El Al by my son Phil, Cathy and her brother (both Yale students who'd come down for the occasion), and my editor. He was lugging some coming-apart cardboard boxes containing chunks of two mystery novels, and the kids were coping with the luggage—which was more than seventy dollars' worth overweight even not counting what I could carry (two coats, an airline bag, the afghan, the straw basket, and a huge leather over-the-shoulder thing cleverly designed to pass as a mere pocketbook when boarding airliners). Phil had blown a large chunk of his cash on a birthday dinner as well as a gift, so I couldn't have been feeling more lavishly fed and watered, loved and petted. And we were all feeling (a) glad it was almost all over, (b) curious about what I might really be getting into, and (c) a little scared and sentimental.

My final moment had a total and triumphant wrongness: we were moving toward the barrier when it struck me that the battered fur-lined boots I'd been pretty tired of even before I began dragging them across the wintry face of America would certainly be irrelevant in a desert. So I stopped the procession, tugged the boots off, and handed them over. While I stepped into something more chic, Cathy—significantly, she was the one who'd actually been to Israel—made some objecting noises; but I cut her off with an imperious "Just get rid of them." Then I waved good-bye to the little band seeing off, respectively, a runaway mother, a gutsy old lady, and a headache author. And, light and agile in my high-heeled pumps, I marched toward the brave new world.

Before the end of that year of discovery about the weather and the economy of Beer-Sheva, I was writing a frantic aerogram demanding a pair of fur-lined boots, quick. In the interests of saving face, I directed my plea to a friend in Massachusetts: maybe nobody had told her about that airport scene.

From the diary: 1

Feb. 11? 12? How do you tell?

It seems a mite odd to start a diary without knowing what date it is—since that would appear to be a most minimal requirement, I have a feeling of lowering my standards. But all I know is, we crossed (cross?) the International Date Line somewhere en route, so the new day just happened (will happen?) to us: it's there, waiting; February 12 is a function of distance rather than time. (Which means, I guess, that I'm literally flying to meet a date, ho ho.)

Well, I bought this notebook to keep a diary in, so I will. Even if I can't see the Internatl. Date L. (wouldn't it be funny if it really was a line across the sky?) because we have to keep our shades down so people can sleep. I tried to sleep but gave up: there's a small reading light and I have tolerant neighbors, so I read a thriller instead. And also inscribed the free picture postcard of an El Al plane—which will hardly be a real thrill for my grandchildren, as they always see me off on some airplane anyway. (It's a sobering thought that if I die tomorrow, they'll forever remember me against a backdrop of Stapleton Airport.)

But when I went aft to the john (what time? what day? Oh dear), I found an unshrouded window in a lounge space and saw pearly light outside. Several men were standing around the window, all wearing fringed shawls of white silk and swaying together though they seemed to be muttering separately. The morning prayer, my seatmate told me when she woke up for breakfast. It's only for men, and only the very religious, she added—her husband never did it, but when she was a little girl her father used to . . . Well, that explains why there'd been so few; but the implication that they're limited to the old seems wrong, for I saw among those men the husband of the young couple (American) sitting behind me. He came back to his seat carrying his praying equipment in a blue velvet bag with a Jewish star embroidered in gold, very altar-clothy: super-piety manifests itself similarly in arts and crafts everywhere, it would seem.

Unscheduled shock: in London we all had to leave the plane, taking all our gear with us—a disaster for me, as I couldn't possibly carry all my stuff over airport stretches (it had been toted for me virtually all the way in New York, and I was supposed to be met in Israel, so nobody thought I'd have to). No El Al employees in sight, and all other passengers as overloaded as I: what do I do now? The young couple appeared just as panic got a good start, and they not only carried most of my load but when I discovered I'd lost my scarf somewhere on the forced march, he went all the way back to find it for me. So now I rather regret my sneering at super-piety in entry above (this diary is off to a great start, isn't it?). Because maybe religion is the opiate of the people, but what matters when you're physically feeble is that it's the opium addicts who come to your rescue.

All I saw of London was the glittering duty-free emporium. Airportland, with its eternal message: Spend money! I couldn't carry another thing, so it was easy to snub them. I used the Ladies, too, thus costing them overhead without bringing in a cent, and I hope they notice . . .

The young couple are Jewish Agency charges, like me (they're headed for Ramat Gan, which is near Tel Aviv). But not everybody on the plane is—my seatmate since London is a British lady going to visit her Israeli grandchildren (four counting the new one she's on her way to help with), who live on a farm. The very-British accent sounds weird wrapped around the exotic place names in Israel, but otherwise she's a stout and housewifely Grandma with plastic shopping bags full of the bumpy shapes of toys and long-handled things sticking out of the top—just like me when I go to visit.

A dark foreboding: coffee is served only for breakfast, it seems, because kosher means no mixing of meat and milk. Well, I knew that; but I drink my coffee black anyway, so I foresaw no problem. Only, they don't make coffee for the other meals, all you get is a choice of tea or orange juice! That's an adjustment I hadn't counted on making, and I'm not at all sure I can. (Oh come on, you can't go home because of a thing like that. It wouldn't be even borderline-gutsy . . .) Why can't they imagine the existence of a black-coffee drinker, though? I'd have asked them, except that the English lady—happily sipping her tea—was wearing one of those dear-me-these-childish-Americans looks, so I shut up. But grrr.

The loudspeaker announcements are in Hebrew, English, and French. The pilot always ends the Hebrew with "toe-DAH," so that has to be "Thank you." I keep trying, but I can't catch what must be "Ladies and gentlemen."* Saw the pilot, by the way, on one of my strolls forward. He was just emerging from the cockpit, to stewardess flutters. And, for me, plain gawking: he's easily the handsomest man (and I do mean man, with curly hair graying at the temples—not one of those mere-boy types) I've ever seen, not

---

*It's rah-boh-TIE, I know now. But only because I asked: I don't remember ever actually hearing it again in Israel.

31

excluding actors and other pros. They should put his picture on an "Israel Needs You!" poster...

Everybody began grinning hugely at the start of the landing run, and as soon as the plane touched down the passengers applauded! Some were singing, a few practically dancing in the aisles—utterly engaging scene. But I kept wondering why: didn't they expect to get to Israel? (The British lady said they always applaud the pilot on El Al planes. She seemed faintly surprised that I even wondered at it.)

3 ﬣ "'Hell!'" Said the Duchess"

I'll never know when I actually saw Beer-Sheva for the first time, because I can't be sure whether we passed through the town at some point while my pair of befuddled guides was driving round and round, looking for it.

I'd been handed over to these two plumpish, leather-faced men as soon as the Jewish Agency people at the airport finished writing my name and a newly assigned number, and affixing the photo I'd brought with me, into a little blue book about the size of a bank passbook. Meanwhile, the Customs men were breaking the latches on one of my suitcases. It wasn't locked, just tricky to open: I'd assumed I'd be there to do the trick for them. But they went ahead without me, while I was still upstairs being told—by a lady who'd apparently had experience with American fecklessness about identification papers—that I must carry this blue book with me at all times. What she didn't tell me, though, was that she'd read my given names, which are duly recorded on my passport, from right to left, like Hebrew. Thus I didn't discover that I was now "Gloria." My novice parents inserted that name on my birth certificate in the innocent hope that they would thus satisfy both their families, and ever since, it's seen the light only as a "G." on middle-initial occasions. But in document-happy Israel, my "new identity" was a matter that would keep coming up, spelled out in full . . .

Clutching my identity booklet (familiar big-eyed face, hair blown about by the December winds of Massachusetts, looking out somberly above unfamiliar handwritten-Hebrew squiggles), I was deposited—along with my suitcases, one of them closed only by a

33

rope the impatient gents at Customs had kindly provided—in what looked like a pickup truck with a partial roof and a couple of station-wagon seats. This is called a "tender," the British having got their wheels in first, and it's probably the most frequently used all-around utility vehicle. A young man from Canada was already seated inside. A volunteer on his way to work at a kibbutz, he was an old Israel hand and spoke Hebrew: it was he who told me what had happened to my suitcase. He apparently also told the driver and his helper—Tweedledum and Tweedledee to the life—that I didn't speak Hebrew, for, after one abortive attempt at Yiddish, they just grinned and said "Shalom." I said it back, and then we were off into the flattish landscape and the oncoming night.

I kept my gaze glued to the window, but what was out there didn't look exciting. Except maybe for trucks and police cars with Hebrew writing on them: since you otherwise see those blocky, hieroglyphic-looking letters only on the windows of kosher butchers, that did seem an exotic touch. Otherwise, though, all I saw was a road like from New York to Long Island, with palm trees that belong in Los Angeles. The whole view seemed unreal, for me and even for itself—as if this was only what was on the TV screen before the program began.

It was dark, but still early-evening dark with lighted windows, when we dropped the Canadian off at his kibbutz—a place of rustic cabins and tall trees, like any summer camp. After that, what happened was just silence and floating dark. And, once, "Beer-Sheva" on a road sign with English under the Hebrew letters for each place named. We didn't turn the way the arrow pointed, but I figured the driver knew a shorter road. Which seemed good news, because that was an astoundingly large number of "km" alongside "Beer-Sheva." For a while I tried to remember how much a kilometer is,* but all I could come up with was the dead-end fact that it's a thousand meters. So I stopped struggling, and just let the silence grow denser.

That silence was all my own, for the two men in the front seat were engaged in conversation most of the time; the nondriver looked back occasionally as if to see whether I was still there, and then we'd exchange smiles. This cutting-off of speech, which is my

*A kilometer is 62 percent of a mile (I find out every time I look it up) and the usual short way to convert to miles is to multiply by 5 and divide by 8. But since I always seem to lose track of those magic numbers—and especially which one goes where—what I do is divide the kms in half and then just put a little bit back. This works out better on long distances than short, but then a long trip is where I'm most likely to want to know whether I'm almost there or still far away. So I'm happy with my system, and what my son the mathematician doesn't know can't make him shudder.

chief means of relating to anyone anytime, caused me no anxiety, though I can't imagine why not. For surely fleeing through an unknown landscape in the black night with two strangers you can't talk to should be at least a little scary? But it just wasn't. Maybe fatigue had something to do with it—more than twenty-four hours had passed since I'd last been horizontal, and even if you keep your feet up the whole time, your circulatory system probably feels the difference between a bed and a tilted-back airplane seat.

After a while, having no language in common did begin to present a problem—like how to communicate, in some way more seemly than the gestures that occurred to me, my need for a toilet. But just then, the man in the front seat turned around and either asked me whether I'd like to eat or told me we were going to (sign language can be clear, but it isn't useful for distinctions); though he added some words to the gestures, the only one I understood was "kibbutz." Soon after, the problem got solved: we pulled into another setting of dark rusticity, and the inhabitants who gathered round the tender included an American girl who told me where the facilities were.

I didn't get much chance for conversation with the three young Americans whose table I joined (uninvited) when I got back from my side excursion. The dining hall turned out to look rather like a set for a film scene following the big special-effects one (the rains, maybe. But not the elephant stampede—it wasn't *that* battered). A sort of smorgasbord of tomatoes and cucumbers and radishes had been laid out—or perhaps just dropped, since they were as nature had left them—on a central table, along with other nature-girl goodies likewise too much for my bland diet. I found some bread and cheese and poured some tea (I *hate* tea) from a communal pitcher into a small squat plastic cup like the top of the wide thermos in a child's lunchbox. With this repast, I quieted my growling stomach—if not my sharp longing for coffee. Even White Tower coffee, in a thick china cup with a handle and a saucer . . .

Still, at least I could speak again. I began by asking my tablemates a few wayfarer-type questions. But they seemed disinclined to talk about themselves and quite incurious about me—or even about Tweedledum and Tweedledee, who were sitting at the next table and bolting great quantities of farm produce cut up into bowls of sour cream. (They were given to eating and talking simultaneously, so I didn't need to rely on the litter of peels in front of them to know what it was they were consuming.) My own companions ate almost nothing, just sipped tea and smoked American filter-tips and looked lackluster. Since they were all also sallow and stringy-haired, it struck me that they were really no advertisement for the healthful rural life: if this was what going back to nature reduced kids to, I was glad *I* hadn't been pushing communes. (For the benefit of Zionist and other believers in the therapeutic value of the outdoor life, I'd better put in here what I discovered only sometime later: these youths were part of a group of squatters, mostly American and ex-doperidden—though when you've seen them, you wonder how "ex"—who'd moved in on an abandoned settlement. The government was trying to evict them, and eventually did. And whatever had exhausted my tablemates, it was not working in the fields.) I was trying to figure out whether I was supposed to pay for the meal—and if so, where?—when my escorts, still chewing, came to herd me back to the tender. I decided it must be okay: this was probably part of the Jewish Agency conveyor belt, and one of the Tweedles had signed a chit. So I went quietly.

But with an increasing sense of conturbation. Something was not just strange, but wrong—though I kept trying to argue myself into believing it was only strangeness that was bothering me as we slipped silently along empty roads through landscape too black and featureless to be strange. I kept losing the argument, though, to the fact that being driven around at night is something I've always enjoyed. So, that night, what with freedom from both guilt (I wasn't idle, I was *going* somewhere) and responsibilities of either driver or navigator, I should've been having a perfectly lovely time . . . Well, what was stopping me, I finally decided, was only that the lack of comfort kept reminding me of the physical distance I'd come. For, though I had made some small changes on the plane, these were basically the same clothes I'd put on in the Macauleys' guest bedroom early in the morning of February 11—and, since that household happened to be the most decorous and thoroughly polished of all those I'd been staying in, it constituted the worst possible starting point for the no-end dark and no-answers of the night of February 12. Ergo, it was no wonder I was feeling strange, not to mention entertaining infantile whimwhams about being lost in the dark. To psych oneself out is to understand all, right?

Sure. But you know what happens to rationalization. So at some turn in the road, alongside still another black fold of land on that long hurtle toward a mirage of tomorrow, I knew we were lost and doubtless had been ever since we'd left the droop-kibbutz. To go driving on, and on and on, perhaps until we accidentally crossed the border into Iraq.* Or even into something less strictly

*There is no border with Iraq. If you're lousy at geography in good times, it makes hard times just that much harder.

geographical: in *No Exit,* Sartre's hell was a lighted room and endless talk, so why couldn't there be another kind, *all* exit and darkness and no-talk?

Luckily, before I could locate among my sins one that would match this punishment, our being lost moved out of fantasy—because something was being done about it, which proved it was real. We'd emerged onto what looked like a main-type road and the driver's buddy had begun rolling down his window to holler *"Adoni!"* at some bundled passerby. The first time, I thought he'd sighted a friend named Ah-doe-NEE; but after that I figured it had to mean either "Hey, Mac" or "Excuse me."* It didn't sound any more foreign than what I'd been overhearing all along, so I had no way then of guessing the truth: that word represented more Hebrew than I'd yet heard the Tweedles use—for what they'd been speaking, I know now, was Georgian. (The Jewish Agency apparently finds employment for new immigrants even though they aren't getting A's in Hebrew. And almost certainly this pair couldn't read the Hebrew on the road signs. So, since I could at least read the English, we'd have been better off if I was driving. Some conveyor belt.)

But despite those encounters, our journey—into the fourth dimension, I'd concluded, having shifted by then to science fiction: we were caught in a time warp, that's what—didn't take a down-to-earth turn until well past the local bedtime. That's when the boys, having run out of passersby to accost, pulled into what looked like a military vehicle depot and tried their Hebrew on the soldier at the gate. He apparently found either them or their question more than he could handle, and summoned help.

As soon as I saw the young officer come into the headlight-spill, something happened to me. I didn't really know his rank, of course; and I still don't know anything about him. But he looked so *human,* so somebody's-son, with crisp curly reddish hair and an alert, intelligent face . . . Trembling with a desperation I had no idea I'd been containing, I rolled down my window, so he wouldn't go away while I was struggling with the door. "Please," I called. "Wait. Do—do you speak English?"

He peered up, his eyes startled: until that quaver from the darkness, he'd probably assumed there was nothing in the tender but cartons of stuff. "Yes, meddem." He opened the door for me and helped me climb down (which nobody else had done, at our previous stops) and then eyed me gravely as I stood on my wobbly

*Neither, actually—it's much more formal than even "Mister," which is the usual translation. "Oh, sir" is probably closest. (Literally, *adoni* means "my lord." You can see how much good literal translation does you.)

legs. "If you will speak slowly, I believe I shall understand," he encouraged.

I *tried* to speak slowly, I really did. But I had to give priority to being a lady—which was Rule One in my childhood. (Fortunately for my private life, I have managed to override that instruction; but that night, it was probably all that kept me from flying into a million teeny-tiny unladylike pieces.) So I don't think the young officer got to understand all the details of my account—which I had to deliver at speed to keep ahead of the tears forbidden by Rule One—of my surrealistic adventures in Israel thus far. Clearly, though, he understood my fear that he'd vanish: he put his hand on my arm (I, of course, had managed not to dig my fingers into *his* sleeve: such are the advantages of the Right Upbringing) while he worked at gathering the English he needed. He began, "I desire to apologize for my—" Seeing the implications of that, he backed off to try it the other way round: "For my country, I apologize for . . ." The two "fors" got him, and he stopped and just stood there looking miserable. Then suddenly, he made it over the top: with enormous—and enormously moving—formality, he said, "Meddem, I am emberressed for Israel."

Oh my. From what you've read about me by now, you know he couldn't possibly have come out with anything more likely to restore reality for me: here was just exactly what I was used to, back in my own home world—people representing their country, bright young sons solving problems. He rolled up familiar aspects of my life, the Washington years and the more recent Cambridge era, into one neat, gentle, English-speaking reality . . . Even with that, I wasn't quite up to a convincing it-doesn't-matter-really murmur. But at least I was able to take in his assurances: if I would be so good as to wait only a moment—"I must say them that I go out from here, you understand?"—he would himself see to it that I was delivered to the mercaz klita. Yes, certainly he knew where it was, it was in truth a very little distance from here . . . He gentled me back into the tender, helping me up the big step as if he remembered Mama, and then said something to the sentry (maybe he didn't trust the Tweedles not to drive off?) before he vanished into the lighted building ahead.

It really was only a minute—perhaps even less—before he came out again and got into the front seat. "We go now, meddem," he told me briskly, and then turned his attention to directing the driver. It couldn't indeed have been very far to the absorption center, because within minutes we had stopped on a dusty road. Two dark buildings, long and low, loomed at our right, with a pale

38

concrete walk between them that didn't come all the way out to the road. The young officer helped me scramble up to the walk and then left me there while he went back and began wrestling my luggage out, with the help (though that seemed to take some conversation first) of the Tweedles.

Everybody else seemed to be able to see all right, but I have poorish night vision: I couldn't make out much in the darkness around me but a couple of round shrub-shapes at either side of the walk. So I didn't see Ruth until she suddenly appeared before me, a white face in the blackness, and introduced herself as "the house mother"—a term I accepted immediately, though she was probably twenty years my junior. She had been so worried, she said in almost accentless English. (That "almost" indicates not an accent but only an underlying heaviness in some of the consonants, the apparently irremovable mark of the native Dutch speaker. Even for those who manage, with what must be great effort, booby trap words like "mother," it still usually comes out closer to "mudther.")

I tried to apologize for my delayed arrival—*A lady always,* etc.—but when I got to the part about how we'd been driving around "for hours and hours," my voice began to crack. Ruth patted my hand and said it was all right now, and the young officer came up and began to talk rapidly in Hebrew; so when she told me, "I know, I know," I knew she really did (and, even in my state, I couldn't miss the significance of the look of furious disgust she threw at the two Georgians). After that I remember being led across darkness and up more darknesses—lots and lots of spiraling stairs occasionally illuminated by a weak bulb—and that it was the soldier and Ruth who carried up my suitcases. Then he was gone—he kept making trips up the stairs, and I just didn't recognize the one that proved to be the last—before I could even find out his name. And Ruth was showing me a bed and handing me a towel.

I do remember that while I was hunting for my nightgown I found the tax-free bottle of Courvoisier I'd bought on the plane. Suddenly I was in a party mood: have a swig of this marvelous stuff, I invited Ruth, because we're surely entitled tonight. She smiled and told me to save it—there might be other occasions when I'd need it even more, she suggested with an edge of irony that was wasted on me at the moment (but the unconscious never sleeps, aha!). I don't know whether I decided to believe her or just passed out before I could insist, but the bottle's seal was still unbroken when I woke up in the strange room in the morning.

One of the things I woke to was a certainty that I was going to write that book about Israel. Because I sure had a socko opening for it, didn't I: when characters like that army officer just happen and all you have to do is write them down, why struggle with novels? Maybe "Meddem, I am emberressed for Israel" isn't quite as big a reader-grabber as the classic opening, " 'Hell!' said the duchess." (Though, what with the changes in both language and duchesses, that classroom model has surely lost some shock value.) But most readers should be duly grabbed, if only because of the contrast between this Israeli draftee and his American contemporaries—who, though safe on campuses purged of every shred of militarism and bombarded daily with adjurations to LOVE, seem to lack even a smidgeon of that boy's outspoken tenderness for his country. Granted, he probably doesn't go around talking that way every day, either. But in Massachusetts in 1973, kids weren't emberressed when the U.S. stubbed its toe, they were delighted: another satisfying proof of "Amerika," they told the media . . .

So okay, if I had the luck to stumble on an honest-to-God tearjerker opening that even trailed food for social thought, how come you're hearing about it only after a couple of chapters have gone by? Well, life is hard for the honest writer: the answer is, because socko-Israel isn't true even when it's true. For everything happens in context, and to say "I just tell what happens" is a cop-out. You can't: if all you give the reader is your innocence, you're a crook. (That *is* what I mean, but I admit it sounds right peculiar.)

Thus, herewith some contexts that go with the story, though I didn't have them at the time. First, the army officer—who was looking at not just a foul-up but a real need for rescue. He'd have known, too, that he was likely to be the best bet as rescuer, for small-town Israelis aren't out on the streets late at night (it's safe enough, but where would they go? And work days start very early) and Georgians are never likely to inquire at a police station. So he did what he decided was necessary, because the need was there and so was he; whether it was supposed to be his job was irrelevant. And what I was seeing, in that brisk assumption of personal responsibility on the basis of an independent determination, was the paradoxical Israeli pattern—"individualistic," "anarchic" behavior going on all the time in a society so redolent of their opposites that you can't use those adjectives without quotation marks. Because I don't know of a more genuinely collective-minded country than Israel, and it's also as unlikely an example of anarchy as England (which is likewise crisscrossed with the triple regulations of a parliament, labor unions constituting a pseudogovernmental force, and a state church). Thus the young man who elected himself Israel's ambassador that night was—quite apart from the fact of being in the army—surely society's baby, a citizen-man, a member-man. Yet his quaint little speech was just as surely a personal expression; and whatever he was supposed to be doing for Israel's army that night, it didn't include humping suitcases up the stairs of the absorption center. So I can't avoid saying "individualistic" and "anarchic," but I can't get rid of the quote marks.

Another context I was (blissfully) ignorant of was the Georgians. Most of these recent immigrants from the Soviet Union (which lets *them* out with relative ease, for reasons one can quite understand) are believed to be stupid—which may or may not be true, as no one can know until enough of them are at home in Hebrew*—and their predilection to lawlessness and violence seems verifiable. That last sometimes gets exaggerated in the telling, but even among those who take a very dim view of the Georgians, it's recognized that unattractive social habits enabled them to survive as a culture within the USSR. For Israelis are realistic: they don't fall into the automatic American polarization between total all-God's-children-are-lovable tolerance and xenophobic isolationism. Thus virtue is not a prerequisite for acceptance, and dark assumptions about Georgians are not a mark of the bigot. (What does mark the bigots in Israel is their rejection, in favor of a belief in permanent no-goodnik-ness, of the consensus that education will make the Georgians, or at least their children, Georgian *Israelis*.) So it was natural for the soldier and Ruth to assume that Tweedledum and Tweedledee (only a foreigner would have called those two anything so innocent) were probable brigands who'd had robbery or extortion in mind—and therefore to be horrified to discover I'd been tootling through the night in such dubious hands.

(Since I know brigand types are not much for fearing consequences or enduring frustrations, I have a few dark assumptions of my own. Because the Tweedles must've wanted to get back to the bright lights of Tel Aviv, and I was right smack in the way of their whim-gratification . . . But I had one thing going for me, I think: if our stop at the illicit settlement—which the driver who couldn't find Beer-Sheva located unerringly, on back roads and in darkness—was for a delivery, and thus a payoff, they'd be quite unenticed by my roped-up suitcase and other battered luggage. When you're feeling rich, you don't bother with a small and withered orange not worth

*Even for the immigration-experienced Israelis, the Georgians represent a special problem, because very few people (including other Russian immigrants) speak their language. And they rarely speak any other: their province is not one of the USSR's more advanced, and the Jews there got an even smaller share of everything than the other benighted.

41

squeezing. And my silence probably helped, too. A hectoring voice from the back seat might well have ruffled their benign mood . . . Ah well, maybe I'm just dramatizing. But if they hadn't tried the army base—?)

Now for Ruth's own context, which, at least up until the time she heard what had happened, was a workaday one. Thus it provides glimpses of, among other things, the elaborate organization of immigrant machinery and the catch-as-catch-can actuality it comes down to. For Ruth's experience with the conveyor belt left room, when I didn't show up, for lots of nothing's-really-wrong assumptions—e.g., I could have stayed over in Tel Aviv, and somebody forgot to tell her or just couldn't get through on the phone. Uncertainties, whether caused by people or the telephone service, were commonplace in her job. And even if something *had* gone wrong with the delivery of this American who'd been seen at the airport six hours before (according to somebody in the office there who'd long since gone home) and a ruckus later developed, Ruth was in the clear. She'd been there, waiting to do her job, right?

Right, but it wasn't as easy as that. For, though when I first heard Ruth say she was the "house mother," I assumed she lived there—if the light had revealed her dressed in pajamas and bathrobe, it wouldn't have surprised me—she didn't, and she'd gone home at the end of her workday. Which means she picked up her toddler at the kindergarten and her baby at the babysitter's, cooked dinner, cleared up, and put the children to bed; and then, because her husband was there with the children, she went back to the mercaz klita to wait. Maybe she was only trying to get out of the dinner dishes (if she did), but if so, it proved a lousy trade. Her own flat is much better heated than the one-room office with its kerosene stove; and at home, she'd have been in bed by then because she had to get up at 6.

Well, so she was conscientious. But what made it possible to be was the casual mingling of working and personal lives, so remarkably different from the careful compartmentalizing when I was a working mother.* In Beer-Sheva, it was typical for fathers, too, I discovered later: the bus I used to ride downtown from my first apartment made a special stop every morning for the driver to drop his small son off at kindergarten. I was the only one who ever

---

*Especially when I first began. A man could hurry an editorial meeting because he had a golf date, but a woman who had to pick up her child at nursery school knew better than to say so: it would only be "proof" of the folly of hiring women. In Israel, though, all workers' children come first. Even if Ruth had been required to come back that night, if she'd had no one to leave her kids with, that would've been an acceptable excuse.

seemed surprised, and everybody waited patiently while Daddy walked the little boy across the street.

Something larger and more important about the shape of the society shows up, though, if you look at the slight difference in the young officer's and Ruth's reactions to me-as-victim. They were both angry, but the boy showed his by riding to the rescue, wielding his sword against injustice, etc.—not out of character for a twenty-year-old male practically anywhere—whereas thirty-year-old Ruth exhibited what I've come to recognize as the grown-up Israeli's characteristic consciousness of what I guess is the limitations of citizenship. What I mean by that clumsy term is that the Ruths, "emberressed for Israel," are also inhabited by a wry knowledge that they will be again; there's a sad citizen-awareness that official "They" will goof and goof again, and you can't personally repair all the damages. But so far as it's practically possible, you try. (Throughout my stay at the mercaz klita, I always got whatever advantages Ruth's powers enabled her to arrange for me. Nobody ever *said* how I came to be teacher's pet, but . . .)

Whatever the form it took, however, what was on display in both cases that night—the individual sense of personal participation in making the society work—is absolutely typical in Israel. Since it co-exists with the sort of cynical awarenesses that go with being a citizen in America or England, an odd light is cast on ordinary discourse involving politics. That's almost always slurring: Israelis criticize their government more often than Americans (perhaps because Israelis are more often molested by theirs) and with similar gusto. But, though the free-swinging, no-holds-barred "knocking the feds" spirit *seems* to be the same, when the usual consensus emerges (the government is a shambles, the economy a mess, etc.), the resemblance suddenly runs out. Because even the sophisticated Israeli can't quite shift his gum and ask what else is new. They want to, you can see them trying; but it just hurts too much. "*Ma la'assot?*" (ma la-ah-SOAT, literally "What to do?"), they say, and shrug—and it comes off like a would-be sophisticate mispronouncing *C'est la vie*. The struggle for casual chic at political dismays is almost always a form of social climbing, for a passionate Zionist or gung-ho adherent of a social or religious orthodoxy is likely to be containing a wrath hardened into Samson-like despair; and even a moderate is apt to be writhing in deep, unexpectedly personal shame. It's true that jokes abound, jibes travel swiftly, and the humorist is admired. But all the wit is edged and rage-full, rarely zany and never really lighthearted—though, if there's been influence from American or British humor, it may seem so at first. And

43

then the American, jabbing away joyously with the irreverence characteristic of his own culture, suddenly discovers with horror that he's drawn blood . . .

Well, all that was all there, right from the first, in the details of the people-moving machinery and barely glimpsed Israel. I couldn't see the world in the grain of sand, but that didn't keep what I'd seen—the vast and lonely desert night, the disorganization under it, and the individual improvisations trying to close gaps between the plans and the uppity actuality—from becoming my own context, part of the package I was going on with from that first night.

From the diary: 2

Beautiful downtown Beer-Sheva

First morning is for business—Ruth took me downtown to buy a pair of socks and go to the bank. That's my order of priority, not hers, and as a matter of fact it seemed to amuse her that I rated socks so highly. But I couldn't find any clean ones, not without unpacking five suitcases before breakfast. And I don't like the feel of shoes on my bare feet.

You walk into town from the absorption center, though it really seems long enough to warrant a bus. There are some buses visible when you turn onto the big street, but those are headed for Tel Aviv: the three Hebrew letters in their up-front signs spell EGG-ed, which is the name of the driver-owned co-op and virtually means "intercity bus."

Ruth had to get back, so we went to the bank first. But she promised to point me at the department store (A department store! I didn't feel ready . . .), where socks would be visible at a ground-floor counter so I wouldn't have to remember the word. (Well, if I stay in sight of the door, maybe . . .)

At the bank, I deposited my grubstake check and changed the money in my wallet. (Foreign exchange is upstairs, presided over by a very pretty—in fact, beautiful—girl named Simona whose native language is obviously French, but she speaks everything.) I knew the rate was 4.20 Israel pounds to a dollar,* but I didn't realize what a lot it would look like: I came out holding a wad of bills like a movie gambler's. The only face I recognized on them was Einstein, who's on the five. ("You got two Einsteins for a——?" would make weird dialogue. Must find out who that is on the ten.+) There isn't any one-pound note, it's a coin.

The "IL" like "$" before a number stands for "Israel lira," which is the same as a pound. Obvious question—why both words (they're used equally and indiscriminately, says Simona)—brought odd answer: it's "easier." Why should it be easier to create confusion with the Italian word lira, *especially when you've already got confusion with the British pound (which is worth around two dollars and thus a lot of Israel pounds)? Well, it turns out they need a second word because money gets talked about in the plural a lot and*

---

*Since those good-old-days, the rate has climbed to almost 20-to-1.

+Bialik, the Hebrew poet. It took a lot of tries before somebody recognized him, but then everybody turned out to know about him. (Which, come to think of it, is the way it should be with poets.)

"pound" is awkward to pluralize in Hebrew but lira can be given the regular feminine plural, lirot *(lee-ROAT). Ruth, looking a mite defensive, pointed out that there's more than one word for "dollar" in English too. (Yes, but "buck," etc., are slang. Which I suspect she knows, and what's involved here is neither language nor strict logic. So I shut up.)*

In Beer-Sheva being in a hurry doesn't mean you don't have time for mid-morning coffee, so Ruth took me to a coffeehouse near the bank. The place was abuzz, but the waiter never hurried and nobody seemed to want him to: there's a distinct three-hour-lunch ambience (a little hard to recognize at first, because in the U.S. it doesn't go with cheap-joint décor featuring formica-topped, iron-legged tables), and it's clear Beer-Sheva wots not of rat races. The customers tended to look more like the midnight-haired willow-maiden Simona than like Ruth (who has yellow hair and a square Dutch face), the waiter called out "Deux cafés" to the counterman, and the buzz of presumably-Hebrew sometimes turned out to be French when I listened closely. So I wondered aloud whether one could maybe get along in Beer-Sheva with French? Oops, faux pas: *Ruth said severely that it was absolutely necessary to learn Hebrew. I backpedaled hastily—I only meant in the interim, see, that's all I meant, honest . . .*

Useful Note No. 1. To order coffee, say "Nescafé blee chah-LAHV": "Nescafé" (sometimes shortened to "ness") seems to mean any kind of non-Turkish coffee, and the rest means "without milk." What you get then is half a cup of coffee; for normal people, the rest is milk, with the whole thing whipped to a light-tan froth. Since they're very small cups to begin with, this turns out to be right expensive—one can be a nonconformist in Israel, but it costs.

Ruth taught me the coins so I could go buy socks on my own. The one-lira looks like a silver dollar (though a little smaller and lighter, I think, than those passed around Washington by Senators from western states). But alas, so does the half-pound, which is almost the same size, so you have to look for the ½ written on it. These are worth, respectively, 100 and 50 agorot *(plural of* agora, *which looks sort of Greek, doesn't it?); but one should learn promptly not to equate agorot with cents . . . The 25-agorot coin is the size of a quarter (well, it is, by golly) but it's gold-color; so are the 10, which is smaller than a nickel but bigger than a dime, and the 5, which is smaller than a dime. Neither of these has the kind of edge that makes a dime handy as a screwdriver: Israelis must just have to use screwdrivers. There's a 1-agora piece that looks like the zinc pennies of World War II, only with a ripply piecrust rim that makes it even less likely to get taken seriously.*

The coin lesson reminded me that I'd seen one of them before, so I dug out the 10-agorot piece I'd been carrying since I left the U.S. and told Ruth about my son Phil's parting joke. He'd apparently come by this single Israeli coin, from one of the much-traveled young who abound on college campuses, and tucked it away until my farewell-cum-birthday dinner, at which he produced it grandly. "Here you are, old girl," he announced with a dreadful red-hot-sport smirk. "Have yourself a ball in Israel."

Well, Ruth smiled—broadly, and almost convincingly. But, across that little table, I was just too close to be fooled: she didn't think anything at all was funny, she was just trying to be polite to a fond mama, and it wasn't easy . . . Okay, I know humor's supposed to be almost untranslatable. But Ruth's English surely embraced "to have a ball" and she certainly must know my son's gift was worth exactly .042 cents. So it wasn't because of language that the joke had fallen flat . . .

The answer didn't emerge until sometime later, when we'd started talking about our children—and "Oh," said Ruth in that unmistakable things-falling-into-place voice, "your son is a university student?" She'd thought he must be older, she explained. But he was the son who'd given me the coin, was he? This fact verified, Ruth smiled. A great big, relieved, for-real smile.

It was a kind of culture clash, I see now. For Phil's wit had not only laid an egg, it had shocked Ruth. Because in her culture (maybe all Israelis?*), what an American son is supposed to give his mother is a big fat check. So for Phil to make a joke of not doing that was really Too Much, and my approval of him was—well, it was as if I'd boasted of how cleverly my son wiped his nose on his sleeve. Ruth recovered quickly: after all, her job involves dealing with foreigners and their strange ways, without showing shocked disapproval. But things didn't get made all-right again until she found out Phil was a student. That's a group to whom antic naughtinesses are permitted; and American students especially, since they're so young, can be quite outrageous . . . So then, only then, Ruth—who likes me and doesn't want to have to be sorry for me—was able to relax and smile upon my comic son.

Useful Note No. 2. Don't try to share jokes. At least, not for a while.

---

*It's pretty general, all right. But see Chapter 17, "Phil's Israel," in which my son and I come face to face with Israeli notions of what's fitting and proper for mothers and sons.

4 ☑ "O Brave New World . . ."

The real "first day" in a place isn't the first, or even the second or third. It happens on whichever one of the early days the surrounding landscape stops being always in the fringes of your vision and your chief preoccupation ceases to be the task of wrapping the environment around yourself, which is a form of problem-solving rather than looking. So I choose for my "first" day one somewhere in the first week, when I already knew how to get black coffee and which street the department store was on. I had acquired a few more contexts, too: e.g., one reason Ruth had had time to escort me to town personally was that the boatload of immigrants from Argentina who were to be my fellow students at the ulpan had not arrived. (I still hadn't discovered, though, how often that sort of thing was likely to happen.) Thus the school bell I'd hurried to come in time for had failed to ring and I myself was at leisure. No one seemed to know exactly when school would begin—all I could find out was, when I went down for breakfast each morning, it wasn't Today—but I was hardly suffering from a yearning to travel some more, and it seemed pointless to go look up Yaakov and Sara in Jerusalem for a single day's stay. So I spent my precarious day-at-a-time holiday just looking around.

On that real-first day in Beer-Sheva, then, I was still new enough to be trailing comparisons with home, but I had nevertheless acquired some subliminal awarenesses. Of, for instance, the sweet-blue sky with little puffs of fleecy cloud—a wide-open sky like Colorado, but prettier, more like a picture for the baby's room; I was

48

still noticing it, but I'd already thought up that comparison, if you see what I mean.

What I was most actively still noticing, though, was the warmth: in a body prepared for Massachusetts in February, my very bones felt positively stroked by the sun in Beer-Sheva. Sure I'd expected it—sort of. Back in December, I'd been reading the temperatures listed in the *Jerusalem Post*, and Phil had taught me how to translate the C figure ("You go nine-over-five times whatever the temperature is, and then add thirty-two . . . what do you mean you can't do it in your head?"). So I knew that 15° Centigrade was 59° Fahrenheit, and 20° was "really" 68°—when nine-over-five goes in evenly, I *can* do it in my head—but I didn't understand what that would mean to flesh and bones. And thus to the spirit: a temperature of 50°F (9/5 × 10°C, + 32) not only feels deliciously warm, it feels *benign.* So that along with the physical fact comes a sense of dazzling luck, of having somehow been awarded an extra spring, that becomes a watershed event in the mind. But it's almost as hard to recall—even with notes in a diary—as labor pains: you can talk about it later, but you can't really remember the feeling . . .

Well, thanks to a casual occurrence, I can come close, though. Writing this chapter in another February, I knocked off work at noon to go out for cigarettes (in Beer-Sheva, you fit your work around the stores' schedule, not the other way round). And there at the *macaulet* (ma-CAUL-et, a Mom-and-Pop grocery store), I ran into an Israeli acquaintance who was shepherding some visiting scholars' wives around Beer-Sheva. He hailed me with the special joy of one who's been making conversation all morning and is wearing down: these ladies were from Massachusetts, too, he announced, his voice practically trilling in rapture at the unimaginable coincidence. Well, fair enough—in a lifetime that's included both diplomatic and literary soirées, I've been rescued often enough myself to acknowledge an obligation to pay back. So (after only the teeniest reproachful look at him, I swear) I began to exchange the names of Massachusetts towns with the ladies, and to ask those inane questions no visitor can answer except inanely. And then all of I sudden I was rewarded for my churlish virtue: "It's so *warm* here!" said the strange lady, on a note of marvel that I recognized at once . . . I stood there in my heavy slacks and boots and two sweaters and fleece-lined jacket, all standard garb for winter in rooms with stone floors and stone walls that even above-freezing temperatures can't warm up—in fact, the way you get warm is to go out and stand in the sun in front of the macaulet at noon—and I stared at the visiting lady with her coat thrown open and her face turned gratefully toward the lucky, benign sun. And I *knew*, I really remembered.*

Well, I too had my coat thrown open when, on a morning in February 1973, I strolled out to explore Beer-Sheva. But first, to get a newspaper. That mission meant going "to town": Hebrew newspapers could be bought at a nearby kiosk, but foreign-language newspapers like the *Jerusalem Post* (which is the only one in English) were in a more exotic class, I'd learned.

I'd also learned by that time that the handsome buildings on the corner—after you followed the dusty, unpaved street of the mercaz klita to the big street with the buses—was a youth hostel. As I turned the corner, a pair of tall, springy-striding, sunbrowned young emerged from it. Unconscious chauvinism led me to assume they were American (who else has such vitamined children, walking the earth with such confidence and so much equipment packed on their backs?) but the voices drifting back to me seemed to be speaking Swedish. That was a guess based on little but Bergmann films, though; I think now it was probably Danish. All the northland folk (including many Germans, but I can recognize German) flock to southern Israel to soak up the marvelous sun during the winter months, but the Danes had charter flights directly from Copenhagen to Eilat, the Red Sea resort about 250 kilometers south of Beer-Sheva. And their tall young, who have no guilt—*their* fathers defied the Nazis to save the lives of Jews—wander the land cheerfully, smiled upon by the society (which has a very long memory in these matters).

The young pair, who were interested in going somewhere, pulled ahead of me rapidly. I lingered, trying to believe in this amazing, wholly undeserved spring—and I'm not just talking about the odd crocus or violet: in gorgeous (literally!) colors, fringed flowers with thick spiky leaves covered the youth hostel's courtyard and spilled over onto the street. They weren't in beds but growing as ground cover, like the pachysandra we used to plant in Bethesda, Md. to cover the spots where grass couldn't be coaxed to grow.† But back then in my suburban past, and even more so in the climate from which I'd just come, it's a longish time between planting

*This isn't recalling labor pains either, but it should help to show you how it was: that first February, I got a laugh when I announced to some fellow inmates of the mercaz klita that I wasn't going to shave my legs because I really needed the warmth. But by the next February, nobody would've even giggled—it wasn't wit, it was wisdom.

†What the flowering ground cover was covering in this case, though, was an intricate pattern of flexible piping for irrigation. But how could I have known? Where I came from, things just grew: if you wanted to have a garden, you exchanged one kind of growing for another. But you never really had to start at zero.

things and seeing flowers. So this lavish bloom implied for me something long ongoing, not just a difference in when spring begins (which I'd seen by moving from Washington to New England) but an air of always-spring. Or maybe even, if I could get my mind around the strangeness of this happening when it wasn't even hot out, of always-summer. Because when I saw, on the street across from the absorption center, brilliant clumps of red and orange and purple bougainvillea climbing over high stone garden walls and spilling down the other side, what came to mind was the *summer* chore: what went with lavish bloom was garden furniture, lemonade for the kids and Tom Collinses for us, and domestic promises to get around to the trimming and clipping this weekend for sure . . . But that memory took me too far—I thought suddenly of my young slogging to class through the cold dismal rain in New Haven or shoveling out the car in Denver to drive the children to school, and I just got too guilty. I had to get out of there.

In the next block, the display didn't arouse personal guilt, for its message was simply an impersonal one about Time. Far, far in from the street I could just glimpse a great crumbling stone mansion that looked as if it had been closed up practically forever. And with a special brutality, for under the stone arches where you would expect windows, concrete had been slapped on roughly, all the way to the top on each side of the front door. (It's only the Negev version of boarding things up: in a desert, wood is too precious to be used for that. But the effect is so much more hardhearted, somehow.)

In New England, such a grand house with such lavish grounds would probably have been turned into a private school— but in New England, all the titles would be filed in some county office and the private school would have no doubt about whom to buy it from. Here, there was too much history for clarity. One intelligent guess is that the house was the residence of some biggie—maybe the commandant?—when Beer-Sheva belonged to the Turks. Back then, it was less a town than a trading post, and hardly anybody lived there but customs officials and the troops that protected them (from desert brigands, mostly). When the British wrested Palestine from the Turks in 1917, Beer-Sheva was just part of the booty. It profited a little, maybe: under the British, there was a new town plan. Nobody seems sure how much of it ever got carried out, but there *are* streets that meet at right angles—which is not your usual urban vista in Middle East desert towns.

But mostly it remained a corner of Empire without a Kipling, a hot and dusty place where nothing much happens. Except big overarching things that go on over everyone's head—like becoming part of the Palestine Mandate awarded to Great Britain by the League of Nations (an outfit given to leaving the status as much quo as possible, especially when a great power was *in statu*). In daily fact, Beer-Sheva went on being the place where the desert Beduin, ever indifferent to who owns what, brought whatever it was they had to trade, paid tribute to whoever could catch them, and then went away again. In any case, the British, whether as outright colonial masters or solemn Mandaters, constituted a very minor item in the history of the Jews. In which the whole caboodle of Johnny-come-latelies, Britons and Turks alike, were regarded as pretenders anyway: Abraham (always called, in Hebrew, "Abraham-our-father," which ought to make his place in Jewish history right clear) planted a tamarisk tree and swore an oath at the well at Beer-Sheva. (The name means "well of the oath.") It says so, unmistakably, in the first book of the Bible. So if anyone is to feel conscience-stricken about land taken by conquest . . .

Well, in 1947, when the United Nations undertook to relieve the British of the Palestine Mandate, which had become more trouble than it was worth, the intent was less ambitious than clearing historic titles: it would be enough, it was felt, just to divide the land—though not equally—into a state for each of the two kinds of Palestinians, Arabs and Jews. (Oh, didn't you know? At the time, the Jews in Palestine *were* what was meant by "Palestinians." The Palestinian Brigade that fought with the British Army during World War II—when Egypt, incidentally, was on the other side—was composed of Jews.*) The UN mapmakers charged with deciding what went where apparently didn't think much of the Biblical account of Abraham's tamarisk tree as a claim to Beer-Sheva,† so it went into Arab Palestine—as opposed to Jewish Palestine, which promptly became Israel. Arab Palestine remained nobody's-baby-land, as its inhabitants were mostly just not interested: it wasn't the Arabs but the Jews in Palestine whose national liberation movement had made the Mandate unattractive for the British. The Emirate of Transjordan, established (under the kindly eye of the British) in 1921, became the country of any Palestinian Arabs who wanted one. They were Jordanians; the rest remained simply "Arabs."‡

*Including Moshe Dayan, who's probably the best-known of the lot. Born on a farm not far from Haifa in 1915, he is as certainly a Palestinian as he is an Israeli.
†Israel thinks differently, of course. I myself incline to believe in "statutes of limitations"—so to speak—that run out in, say, a generation. But the way I see it, Israel has valid claims to Beer-Sheva in anybody's book, and doesn't have to fall back on the Bible.
‡Some had passports of the Arab countries from which they'd come to Palestine, drawn by the jobs created by the Jewish pioneers' activities. But a passport was an insignificant technicality, as nobody was going anywhere much.

The Palestinian Jews, willing to pay almost any price for an end to colonialism, accepted the UN decision. The Arab nations—as distinct from the relatively few Arabs who were actually native to Palestine—did not, and I guess everybody knows what happened then: five Arab armies, mostly trained by the British and equipped by just about anybody who wanted some of that yummy oil money, jumped the new State of Israel the day after it was officially launched in May 1948. Among this sporting crowd was Egypt, which apparently was moved to try to pick up what was lying around, so long as it was close by and pretty much undefended. So that's how come, when those Arab armies ended up running for home (pursued by Paul Newman, Frank Sinatra, and the cast of *Exodus*), it was actually the Egyptians who dropped Beer-Sheva in flight, so to speak. Easy come, easy go: if the commandant of *their* garrison had had time to move into the Turkish commandant's mansion at all, he certainly didn't get to feel it was home before he moved out again.

The Israelis who settled in Beer-Sheva after most of its 3000 (the highest estimate) Arabs had fled didn't come to collect customs for the government but just to live and work there, and they didn't have a commandant. They were socialist-idealist pioneer types who not only would have recoiled, for ideological reasons, at the notion of residing in a mansion, but who also aspired to things like indoor plumbing and maybe someday even electricity—both of which were mightly difficult to introduce into an old house with stone walls umpty meters thick. A woman I know who was one of the small company of Jews in Beer-Sheva then doesn't remember that there was any discussion about the use of the Turkish-leftover buildings in town; what was practicable was used, and presumably nobody gave much of a damn. (She does remember, though, a hassle about the first public building erected, the local cinema. It seated 1045—she remembered the precise number, without hesitation—and was noisily denounced, not because anybody was against having a hall, but because of its absurdly grandiose size . . . It's still in use, as you'll see in "The Dark and the Cold.")

Well, in the Beer-Sheva my friend's children now take for granted—any place you were born in has obviously been there forever—that stone mansion on the main road into town has gone on yielding, speck by silicone speck, to Time's erosion. But its erstwhile elegant landscaping has gone in the other direction, has been added to rather than subtracted from: maybe at first there was coexistence, before the struggle for survival started and the delicate and deliberate plants succumbed to what takes over when you start having a garden in a desert and then stop. The winner—harsh stuff, capable of living on next to no water, and of quick and effective self-defense—

has now taken all. The great, cactus-y shrubs crowd into and over each other in matted impenetrability, looking like a dehydrated, dusty jungle. Here and there, though, they suddenly line up in a row; and the spiky branches of those, fed on the nutrition once supplied for a flower bed (by a Briton homesick for his suburban garden?), are noticeably longer than the other shrubs' branches. Down front, where the estate borders the street, a chain-link fence long lost to the perpendicular has been thoroughly conquered by an especially fierce-looking bush: one of its thick tentacles, bristling with gigantic thorns all along its edges, has thrust through and now goes on growing out over the sidewalk to menace the passing pedestrian. By the look of it, it could easily do as much damage as the teeth of a crocodile. And I wouldn't care to bet that even an expertly wielded machete would make a dent in its tough fibers.

Israelis are not much for confrontations, though: the thorns may be capable of tearing the flesh of the unwary, but even that much hostility can be rendered futile if you're simply wary. So the citizens of Beer-Sheva—who have institutions to care for them collectively but who also know that just about any job may go undone while several Ministries quarrel—accept the need for individual meantime wariness, walk around the menace, and get on with their peaceful pursuits. I've watched them doing that, absentmindedly and casually, from that first day. The only thing that's changed, between then and now, is that I've learned how typical it is—a very metaphor, neatly applicable to a thousand aspects of the life of the country.

That street intersects with the one marking the border (so to speak) of the Old City. Rechov (ruh-CHOVE, street) Herzl—named after Theodor Herzl,* the founder of Zionism—is urban enough to sport a traffic light. Which doesn't say "Walk" and "Don't Walk," even in Hebrew, but gives you instead alternating language-proof figures of a green walking man and a red standing-still man. Crossing to the opposite corner, I took the little green man's word for it more readily than I ever would now: Israeli drivers characteristically turn corners by roaring up to the intersection and then braking suddenly, so that they come around with a scream of rubber and virtually out of control, in a wide wobbling loop that can get you no matter which side of the road you're walking on.† (Traveled exquisites tell me that

*He's on the 100-lira note, and everybody identified him at once. But it's not a fair test, as he has a unique Smith Brothers black beard (enough of it for both brothers).

†Naturally, I assumed this skill was passed down from father to son, via homemade instruction. You can imagine how staggering it was, to learn that all Israeli drivers must take formal (and expensive) courses in order to be licensed. So the incredible truth must be, somebody's *teaching* them like that!

kind of there's-no-tomorrow driving can be seen in Italy, and some say also in Paris. I don't think I want to go see.)

Across the street, a public park surrounds the Negev Museum, which is topped by the mosque that came with the town. A museum seems a clever way to cope with a mosque in a newly Jewish town: you don't tear it down, which would be cruel to any Muslims still around; but neither are you forced to leave it to the tender mercies of the populace, many of whom are refugees from Arab lands and tend to have strong feelings. At least, that is, until their Arab culture—which likes confrontations, particularly with symbols—has been tempered by the wait-and-be-wary Israeli *Weltanschauung*. Thus it looks to me like definite civil smarts to arrange things so the mosque, its status changed but not demeaned, gets both official protection and unofficial inattention (the fiercest among the local inhabitants being the least likely museum-goers).

The woman at the newsstand, a shack small enough so that she could reach any wall from her chair, looked very old and withered and huddled. Some of that was doubtless because of her layers of sweaters and scarves (did I look like that to the visitors from Massachusetts the other day, I wonder?), and some was also a result of contrast with the nearby park—all sunshine and flowers, gaily colored benches, and even the most luxurious of summery triumphs, real grass. But it was her close-up surroundings that were most responsible, I guess. For the array of magazines pinned up along the walls of her little booth framed her with pornography: against a total background of plump breasts and parted thighs being peddled in half a dozen languages, the small, muffled figure would simply have to look old and dried-up and sexless.

Her eyes, the color of Worcestershire sauce, were set deep in a face as wrinkled as a walnut shell and nearly as brown. I'd already discovered she had no English, but she did know some French and German—which I'd studied in high school and college, respectively. Her French was unlike either the kind in *Le Peau de Chagrin* or the diplomatic-reception kind I'd been getting by with since I read that. And though I'm not very qualified to judge, I think her German wasn't very: I suspect it was more Yiddish. But I understood perhaps one word in four, so we talked.

And she acquired the information she wanted—that I'd come from "Boston"* in America, and I lived at the mercaz klita. She got her question answered, too: yes, I had been in New Jersey, where her

*You learn quickly to forget about suburbs and townships unless the Israeli you're talking to is an academic, in which case Cambridge, Mass. is likely to have an identity for him; otherwise, it's better to stick with "Boston," which everybody recognizes.

cousin's son lived. She didn't seem to expect me to know him, à la the caricatures, but even that much connection brightened her eyes and seemed to stir her to some kind of expansion. At least, she agreed to keep a *Jerusalem Post* for me every day (which I had discovered was necessary, or they'd all be gone when I got there). Then, moved to something approaching friendliness, she volunteered the information that there would be no paper tomorrow because today was Friday. I looked uncomprehending, so she tried visual aid—first pointing to the masthead and then, when that didn't seem to do it, opening the paper to show me the magazine section inside. I got it: oh, this was a *Sunday* paper . . . *"Je comprends."* I nodded to show her I understood that a Sunday paper cost more, and opened my purse to get the extra money.

She sighed, and tried German. When I finally got the point that there would be *kein* newspaper *morgen*—because tomorrow was *Shabbat* (Shah-BOTT) and newspapers were among the never-on-Shabbat items—she sat back, tired but triumphant, and regarded me with the closest she could have come, I think, to a smile. I thanked her as best I could. To do that properly, I'd have had to say "I would have walked all this way for nothing tomorrow" or some variation of that, and I couldn't: I didn't seem to have any subjunctive, French or German, lying around in my memory. So I just said it was a long walk from the mercaz klita.

The newsstand lady couldn't see the connection and took it for a change of subject. Her sauce-colored eyes narrowed and so did her lips as she remarked—with half-concealed amusement and certainly some scorn—that it probably wouldn't be long before I got my car. I said I wasn't going to get a car, and saw immediately that I couldn't possibly have told her anything more interesting: she seemed to come alive all at once, even lifting her head so that more of her scrawny neck emerged from its wrapping the way a turtle's head comes out of its shell. I guessed at rather than understood what followed in a kind of spastic torrent—first a rapid spate of words and then, as she remembered, a recapitulation conscientiously paced for the slow student. *"Je comprends,"* I kept saying; but she still went on explaining, in detail and at length, the amazing rights and privileges that were mine as an immigrant. And still, every time she thought I'd finally understood, I shook my head again and announced, *"Je ne veux pas,"* or, even more emphatically, *"Kein auto."*

Eventually, some certainty got transmitted. It must have, because she stopped trying to think up new ways to educate the retarded and began to believe me—my French, my German, or maybe the set of my mouth and the fanatic light in my eyes?—despite common sense and all the givens. Her opaque gaze swept over me efficiently, adding up the probable cost of my wardrobe—tweed topcoat, smoothly tailored slacks, a handbag that didn't stint on leather or try to get by with trimming.* Logic said I could afford a car, so her attention turned inward to consider a wild surmise. I recognized her look because I've seen its like before. For example, in a reporter who puts together a telephoned tip, an apparently routine handout from a government bureau, and the arrival in Washington of a certain lobbyist—and suddenly spies the outline of a major scandal with Pulitzer-prize possibilities for himself . . .

Well, the newsstand woman was at least as experienced as any Washington reporter with the sudden deaths of presumptions, not to say the revealed nakedness of emperors. So if the world had changed again, and it was no longer incontrovertible that Americans couldn't live without cars, well, she could absorb that. But—said the dark eyes in the weathered face suddenly burning with newsman-lust—she was sure as hell going to be the first to start telling it around. As soon as she'd checked the story out . . . She went about doing that patiently, in her semi-German with a dash of French when necessary, and I stood there in the sunshine patiently answering questions from the nudie-lined cave. Yes, I'd had a car in Boston. I told her what kind—smiling, because I was remembering then the note I'd had from the student who now owned my Dart, a minimal car boasting no adornment and nothing not absolutely needed to make it go. Doug had painted a racing stripe down its side, he reported in a letter that caught up with me in Utah, and he was now vroom-vrooming down the streets of New Haven. (Ha. That was one used car that really had belonged to an old lady, one who didn't even drive it to church on Sunday, so it simply wouldn't know how to vroom. And a racing stripe would probably peel right off its demure black flank . . . But one of the reasons I gave Doug the car was that he wrote like that.)

I'm almost certain it was my fond smile that misled the news-stand woman: she read it accurately as reminiscence, but then she made her own guess as to what it was reminiscence about. And,

*She would almost certainly get the sum wrong, as no ordinary Israeli is familiar with the kind of eclecticism the American consumer can exercise. There, the owner of such an expensive coat would not have bought bargain-basement slacks from a clearance table (where mine had landed because the advent of bell-bottomed pants caused the unloading of all other styles. But that in itself is a phenomenon too capitalistic for Israelis to grasp easily). And in Israel, where income is usually a function of education, taste usually goes with money and the un-garish can be assumed to be expensive. But in fact my handbag was manufactured in Hong Kong and bought at the five-and-dime in Harvard Square; I would rather doubt that it was really leather.

apparently, began pursuing her researches—because it was right after that, I remember, that I got into a language problem again. This time it was because I lacked the word "widow": when she asked what kind of work my husband would be looking for in Israel, *"Mein Mann ist gestorben"* was the best I could do. I probably looked pained, but that was only because the German sounded so immediate—as if he'd just died and I was breaking the news—and anyway didn't seem to fit: my husband was lanky and too boyish for *mein Mann*, which clearly is portly and wears a watch chain. I didn't care for *mon mari* either (too short, and maybe dapper), but in French I could at least make it clear it wasn't yesterday; so I started out bravely, *"Depuis—"* And then I saw that it didn't matter how many *ans* I'd been a widow, because the whole dialogue was off on another track.

For, while I'd been wrestling with the question of how to manage nuance without vocabulary, she'd been arranging her research data logically. And now she got the picture—I had had a car in America, but only while there was a husband to drive it. And what she had here was not a news story but a tragedy, a familiar one: her face changed, and she made a small sympathetic sound . . . Looking through her look—it was like a view through two windows, one behind the other—it suddenly broke over me what she saw: there I was in my Sunday silk and maybe a hat with cherries, sitting sedately behind my husband while we motored down the golden roads of America. For that was the way it was among the luxuriating citizens of the unimaginably soft life her cousin's son's letters kept reporting. And yet, when you came down to the things that count, what was so different there from what she herself remembered? One day you're at home, fixing the goulash the way your Otto likes it and thinking that the Spanish shawl on the piano really should be cleaned again—and the next day, it's all gone. All of it, the good provider and the dining-room sideboard, the predictable future years and the easy present, all vanished in an *Augenblick*. And all you really know is, you're somehow alone in a faraway land where they speak a barbarous language and do things boldly and sort of gracelessly, and where you yourself have become a very different woman—so different that it's even hard to remember sometimes the way it was. But of course you do remember. Like the American woman, standing there with that remembering fond smile you recognized right away . . .

Oy vey, she knew how it was, she said, her face soft with sympathy. And I stared at her in fear and horror because she didn't, but all of a sudden *I* knew how it was. I don't know how it happened, but it happened: the prepared ground of social science split abruptly, revealing the individual dark underneath—the separate, personal, permanent wound the Nazis left on the people who were chased out of where they thought they were at home. Something a lot less than the death-drama, but maybe worse because it couldn't be buried.

Like most Americans—and certainly nearly all writers—I'd tried to come to terms with the fact of an Auschwitz, and of the organized and deliberate and coldhearted murder of millions. And how could any poet (which is a form of nationality) have failed to be struck by the fact that the citizens of Goethe's hometown had been proud of the efficiency on display in neighboring Dachau? Eventually, like most other writers, I'd put it pretty much to rest in a poem. After that, the itch gone from the subject, it became a political-science fact, something for a citizen to guard against. But history, definitely history.

As it was, too, for the newsstand woman. Only, for her it had left an echo altering the sound of things, a waver in the glass that would have to ripple her recognitions. She saw me as one of the chased-out because that was, for her, the shape of goneness and of a past different from a present: "ago" would instantly mean More and "now" Less, and all changes assumed to be not by choice, because of the way the real world had once ended for her in a moment. Whether that moment came by being locked in a freight car and having her flesh stamped with a number or by beginning a rat-scurry (cringing with the shame she couldn't identify a guilt for) to safety through the sewers of Europe, what it meant was the sudden loss of her onetime citizenship in the world of cause-and-effect.

So that, by now, the stopped-time reaction even overrode the news from the observable world in which she functioned. For in Israel, and even in provincial Beer-Sheva, women do drive cars; and a middle-aged woman, especially if she got reparations payment* from West Germany, maybe was even more likely than a young one to manage the 20,000 to 25,000 lirot a car cost Israelis in 1973. But in the view from stopped-time, facts don't matter: good providers' middle-aged relicts—*like us,* I saw her thinking, and was briefly shocked (but it was true, she was probably only a few years older than I)—could only hope that getting up early and working late would bring us enough to make a living. With any luck, there might be a successful son and daughter-in-law to come around and take us for a ride on special occasions. But we ourselves would never buy cars or go off for a holiday at a spa, or do whatever it was she thought of as the prerogatives of solid status. Those were lost—permanently, because

*Perhaps the "sale price" of Otto's business. Which Otto never got to sell, but somebody had been profiting from it for twenty-five years.

all losses are permanent—to catastrophe, whether it struck two or twenty years ago and whether via a heart attack or a Nazi edict. Thus she "recognized" in me (all her observed data and previous conclusions about my wealth become at once irrelevant as soon as she knew I was a widow) a comrade, a foreign member of the universal order of the pushed-out . . .

Well, sure it's a culture gap, one that's just harder to bridge because of the stopped-time obstacle: how could I put it in any language she'd understand? But eventually her daughter or daughter-in-law would (assuming that Israel, like any small country that can manage to, keeps moving along the same technological-development path the U.S. trod) come to see a car the way I did, as a symbol not of opulence but of servitude. I still burned with resentment of those years and years of driving on demand, to and from schools and shopping centers and horseback-riding lessons and dancing and music lessons, picking up and delivering at Scout meetings, doctors' and dentists' offices, arriving and departing airplanes, and the annual Patrol Boy parade and Science Fair and God knows what annual else. So that I couldn't possibly be reasonable by that time: the very first item on my left-behind list had been my car, and the last thing I was likely to do in Israel would be to replace it, at great additional cost and trouble. In short, the correct translation of *"Je ne veux pas"* and *"Kein auto"* was "Free at last."

Whew. But at least that outburst must make it clear that I wasn't exactly a dandy example of the species American Widow for that woman to run into . . . Okay, though, telling is my trade. So somehow, sooner or later, I could think of a way to get across the news about a society in which middle-aged widows owned any damn thing they could afford (which was often a lot more than most Israelis could) and were free to do anything anybody else could do—including, by the way, picking up and going to live half a world away because the notion took them. It might not be an easy communications job, but that wasn't what gave me the feeling of frightening chasms opening under my feet. It was the fact that I, whose trade is seeing as well as telling, had utterly failed to see. How else could it have come as such a surprise to me that to be chased out *hurts*, and goes on hurting? I thought of myself as a thoughtful and compassionate woman, capable of imagining others' dismays; I know my faults (I should, for I've been told about them frequently, and colorfully) but nobody ever said they included callousness. And yet . . . All right, it was shame that clobbered me as I stood there in the sunlight, warmed by my extra spring, and looked into—and out of—the prune-dark eyes of the newsstand woman, who belonged to here only because she got chased out of where she once thought she belonged.

I kept seeing traces of that, along with all the welcome and curiosity, all over Beer-Sheva as I walked around that morning, without an interpreter and with no real mission except, you might say, to leave my calling card. Doubtless the universal welcome I met with was at least partly a reflection of myself: if you walk down a street anywhere in the middle of a sunny morning, with a delighted sense of having lucked into sunshine and a childlike curiosity about the brave new world and all the wonders in it—if you're personable, prosperous-looking, obviously interested in what's going on but representing no authority or any other threat—you're very likely to stir up benignity on all sides. Especially when most of the people encountered are erstwhile immigrants, because there's an inherent flattery involved. What now-experienced bicycle rider fails to smile upon the learner wobbling along, with training wheels bravely raised a couple of inches off the ground?

Besides, now that I have myself seen the weather that precedes a bright day in February, I know that anyone who's got through it is a citizen of a hard-up land, and thus very much in the market for heartening. For a Beer-Sheva winter really batters the soul and spirits. The rain that marks December and January isn't just weather, it's something you have to hold out against, like brainwashing—and everyone has a breaking point. It's a "tropical" rain in the sense that it pours in sheets (there's no such thing as a raindrop, it seems) and all at once; but it's quite untropically cold. And there's no tropics-like sense of relief or welcome about *this* rainy-season rain: it crashes down like a swift blow from some capital-p Power ("Throw the book at the crummy little bastards!"). In Beer-Sheva, yesterday's dustiness abruptly becomes a strangely slippery, sucking, primeval-ish mud reminiscent of quicksand; it doesn't take much imagination to feel that evil forces lie in wait for your first misstep.

People get up in the morning in cold bedrooms, go to work in cold offices, and come home on buses—where all the windows are closed, to keep the outside cold from mingling with the wet-wool-smelling inside cold—to apartments in which the cold and the damp, closed up all day, have been free to do their worst: the walls and everything they contain are graveyard-clammy, and in a one-story house or top-floor flat (or anywhere, if you cringed from opening the bathroom window after your shower), mold is removing the ceiling paint in curls like somebody peeling an apple. You can, with effort and at cost, manage to provide yourself with a brief, planned snugness by closing off a single room or a corner of one and huddling over a heater; but that has to end at bedtime . . . *I can't remember,* wrote a G.I. I knew, then creeping into Italy via foxhole jumps, *what it's like to be warm or dry or clean* . . . I hadn't thought of him since World War II, but his words came back to me during my first winter as a householder in Beer-Sheva.

So, sure, when I turned up—brand-new and apparently happy to be there—I was a welcome sight to the "cadre" who kept shops or worked in the Post Office, or to any of the people who just happened to be crossing a street on some errand of morning business when I stopped them to ask directions. None of them was ever too busy to talk to me—to ask if I was an *olah chadasha* (oh-LAH chah-dah-SHAH, new immigrant, feminine) or to advise me that I would soon learn Hebrew: *liat-liat,* they'd add with a smile. It's pronounced lee-OTT, and I assumed it meant "Be patient" or "Everything'll be just fine." (Actually, it means "slowly," but I'd got the idea, all right. For sahv-luh-NOOHT, "patience," and Ye-HEE-yeh tohv—literally, "It will be good"—are both such common advice to olim that they've become automatic joke material, like the tag lines of TV commercials in the U.S.)

At each encounter, anybody within earshot who spoke English would come over to contribute information and/or amplification. This is standard practice in Israel, I've learned since*—and I've also learned that it may well include, right along with the courteous impulse, efforts to enlist or educate or lobby you. All of which is, I guess, a function of that deep-down caring that makes politics so emotion-laden in Israel. For, though the society is faultlessly tolerant in its political forms (even avowed enemies of the state can be elected to political office), the populace tends to no such cool rationalism: a political party you're opposed to isn't just wrong, it's benighted, accursed, doomed to drag the country to imminent disaster—and any other charge suitable for screaming at the top of the voice.

Well, maybe what I'm really describing is the way people always are in a young society that has had no practice in feeling safe. Because, wildly incongruous as the notion seems, a good deal about that morning in Beer-Sheva reminded me of an account I read once

---

*And I've also become "absorbed," it seems. For yesterday in a Tel Aviv restaurant, I heard an American tourist wondering to her husband whether they needed to go back to the hotel and change, or was it okay for her to go to an art-gallery opening in pants. I leaned right over from my table and told her it wasn't necessary to dress up . . . I'm a veteran eavesdropper, anyone who's ever dined out with me can attest; but only in Israel would it occur to me to *participate* in what I'm dropping eaves on.

of the early days of Cherry Creek, Colorado. I've forgotten the year it happened (it'd be over a hundred years ago now, though) but I remember the anecdote, which was about the people of Cherry Creek rushing out to greet arriving wagon trains from the East. *We've got a school!* they called out—in simple civic pride, in the hope that the newcomers would be persuaded to stay, perhaps in an attempt to temper the vista of shambling extemporaneous buildings and dusty/muddy streets . . . No language problem troubled communication between the Cherry Creek cadre and the new arrivals; but on the other hand, I was in better shape to receive Beer-Sheva's vibrations than anyone just jumping down from a prairie schooner could possibly be after a journey to Colorado. Perhaps most important, though, there's this in common: the inhabitants of both places were people who took off for an unknown land and then *didn't* strike gold there. For the Colorado settlers, most of the gold turned out to be on the other side of the Rockies, in California. And for the Moroccan and Iraqi and other so-called "Oriental" Jews who made up most of the population of Beer-Sheva in 1973, the gold was on the other side of an educational and cultural Great Divide—in the established cities up north where *Frau Doktor* presided at coffee and *curricula vitae* were sprinkled with the prestigious names of ancient European universities.

In both instances, too, people had managed to survive in a new land but not to get what they'd come for. Having made a home in a hard place, they'd maybe grown to love it; but they knew it wasn't San Francisco/Tel Aviv, where all the excitement was—and which itself was no match for "back east," where all the civilization still was. So the mere arrival of anyone who'd left Boston to come among them was surely heartening. And more than that if it could be seen as a harbinger. For the tired people who'd made a dusty/muddy town could dream of a fine city under their wide skies, but it needed you, the newcomer: *Stay with us, join us* must have been the silent plea informing the settlers reaching up to help a lady down from the wagon. And also the welcome in bits of three languages that surrounded the olah chadasha.

Well, who knows? But doubtless one of the reasons the comparison stirred in my mind was the similarities in physical environment. In Israel, the speed of modern life has collapsed Time even while the repetition of ancient wars has also stretched it out again, so there is and there isn't (I know, but that's the way Israel *is:* always, infuriatingly, a special case while also typical) a real resemblance between Denver—which is what became of Cherry Creek—and Beer-Sheva. Oh, not in the Old City, the "downtown."

63

But elsewhere in town, sparkling modern buildings rear suddenly out of the desert quite as Denver does out of the plain, both of them abrupt innovations in a wide landscape under a wide sky. So that the visible sense is of uppitiness, a kind of cockiness if you will: Man has marched into all that nature and started piling up his blocks . . .

Ah, but in Beer-Sheva there's that wound, a peculiarly twentieth-century phenomenon and much more corrosive to the mind and soul than any of the causes (e.g., worn-out farmland, brushes with the law, just plain bad luck) that made some migrants to the American West feel pushed out of where they'd come from. Thus, though I can believe a Cherry Creek settler may also have secretly thought the new arrival a bit crazy to have left the East, I don't think he'd have needed the amount of reassurance it took before the Beer-Sheva cadre could quite accept the phenomenon. The wound-haunted question appeared there over and over, testing to see whether I would hold up as what I purported to be. Yes, I was actually born in America; no, I hadn't gone there from any other country first. Those answers couldn't do the trick entirely, of course: some of my questioners had also been native-born Germans and Austrians and Czechs and Hungarians, and they'd learned how little that meant.* But America was said to be different, the speculations behind the eyes conceded. And from the evidence of my clothes, my coming couldn't have been inspired by either destitution or extreme piety (my uncovered head, not to say also pants and lipstick, flouted any notion of strict Orthodox beliefs). So maybe it was true, maybe I really hadn't been chased out of anywhere . . .

I'm sure other possibilities were being checked out, too—I'm sorry I can't supply examples, but remember, I was trying to understand the French of a woman with a lisp, or—on the basis of a college course in Goethe twenty-five years before—the Yiddish being spoken by an old man who hasn't used it much lately. Lucid these encounters weren't, but the process of silent verification going on was clear enough. And I could certainly see, when the evidence proved too much for disbelief even among the wounded, the original smile of welcome broaden and brighten. It was true, was the verdict: I had *stamm* come to Israel.

The word *stamm* (pronounced like "stomp" without the "p") is, like *dahfke*, genuinely untranslatable. But *stamm* is a little easier to get at because it resembles the "just because" of childhood: things

---

*Those who'd come from Arab countries (they were the ones with whom French—of sorts—was the communicating language) had no such problem to reckon with. In Arab lands Jews, whether native-born or not, have seldom or never had full rights as citizens.

stamm happen, or people *stamm* do things, like the grown-ups' affairs as seen by children. Thus "unexplainably" doesn't define it, because the implication is that an explanation (if perhaps an unreasonable one) does exist. *C'est la vie* or *That's how the cookie crumbles* convey a proper sense of helplessness, of a cause beyond ability to predict; but they won't do either, because they're talking about randomness, which can be understood. Whereas *stamm* doesn't try to understand, it simply surrenders.

Maybe I did have a "because," though, for staying to live in Beer-Sheva: it had something to do with that morning's discovery of wound and appeal, of Dachau past and Cherry Creek present, of people at once too hurt to believe easily in luck and yet full of frontiersman confidence. Originally, I'd only been passing through; after I'd done my duty toward the typical experience of the mercaz klita, I'd go to Jerusalem and be introduced around by Yaakov and Sara and settle down. But when Beer-Sheva came out to greet my covered wagon, calling out their brash frontier boasts and with their eyes haunted by what I—in my American-frontier brashness?—had carelessly assumed was all finished, something happened to me. Love? Guilt? Or, after weeks of moving about as a guest in other people's households, followed by that night of being carried about in a dark *terra incognita*, I was just ripe for joining a common effort that so obviously wanted me?

Or else, that morning, I *stamm* decided to belong to Beer-Sheva. And then set about making up reasons—some of them even valid—to fit.

From the diary: 3

Le steak blanc (February)

Dining hall wasn't open yet, except for breakfast (coffee, plus the bread and hard-boiled eggs that seem to be part of the décor here), so, the first night, I went scouting in town for a place to eat dinner. And thus met Yoshua-né-Jacques, born in Morocco, I'd say about twenty-six years ago. His corner café is off the main streets but should be easy to find again, and it can serve as an extra translation-base. For Yoshua (yo-SHOE-uh) speaks French and he's open when my English bases in town—the lovely Simona at the bank, and the lady in the candy store (she speaks impeccable British and was clearly written by Dorothy Sayers)—are both closed for the day.

Yoshua does most of the cooking, right up front on a blackened grill like a householder's backyard barbecue (if you know some non-fussy householders, that is). Chopped-up salad vegetables and other side items are in plastic bins under the counter, but anything really complicated comes from inside a metal structure behind Yoshua: a little door at waist level slides open sideways—as if for putting wood into a Franklin stove, which is what that structure most resembles—and you get to glimpse the brown, sweaty face of a very old woman as a dish is quickly handed out.

Small, paper-thin slabs of meat were sputtering on the grill when I climbed onto a counter stool. At a backyard barbecue, those steaks would have been for the smallest children, but at least steak seemed a safe idea. So I said "Biftêk, s'il vous plaît"—congratulating myself on finding a food to fit within the doubly narrow confines of my diet and my French.

Yoshua grinned. "Nous avons steak blanc, Madame." He seemed proud, either of his English word or of his waiter-suggesting-haute-cuisine manner.

It did seem a shame to lower the tone of the dialogue, but I had to say I didn't know what "white steak" was. He brought out the raw materials from another plastic bin and held them up, wet and glistening, to demonstrate—in one hand biftêk, a scrawny cube steak, scored to tenderize it (which I always regard as ominous), and in the other, "steak blanc," a pork cutlet.

It was unmistakably disappointing to Yoshua that I didn't want white steak, for he'd clearly expected something more swinging of American me. Because, I gathered from our hit-or-miss conversation, cocking a snook at the religious authorities and cashrut (cosh-ROOT, kosherness; "kosher" itself is actually cah-SHARE) is the swinging thing to do in Beer-Sheva . . . Well, I had to insist on non-white steak, but, by pointing at my middle and miming pain, I did the best I could to indicate I wasn't just an Establishmentarian. I think I succeeded, for he nodded amiably and began to grill me a cube steak—alongside a pork cutlet for a real swinger down at the end of the bar. (He cooked both steaks the same length of time, I noticed: trichinosis may be the punishment for those who ignore cashrut.) My steak turned out to be juiceless and very nearly taste-less: I know now how "leathery" got to be a cliché.

Yoshua leaned over the counter and talked to me while I ate. Beer-Sheva's night life, he said in answer to my question, consisted mostly of a single discothèque, which was not only expensive but had a ridiculous rule (I lost part of this, but maybe "No table-hopping"?) the effect of which was—I got this part all right—that you had to leave with the same girl you came in with. If you were young and breathing, you died on the vine in Beer-Sheva, man: that was the gist of the message, but the language is not really mine—because when I translated Yoshua, it came out to almost exactly what I'd been told a few years earlier by a depressed young soda jerk in White River Junction, Vermont.

Then we got around to my answering his questions, and Yoshua perked right up. Especially at the news that I was a widow, because what goes with that plus "American" is "rich." For a rich American widow, he had a special manner, even more your-wish-is-my-command-Madame. He's a good-looking boy, very big and strong, with coal-black hair—a lock of which falls forward (quite naturally, I think) over his forehead—and dark sleepy eyes that lend themselves to gazing romantically into a rich American widow's. Actually, though, he rather resembles a poet I knew once, a hand-some man who looked more like a truckdriver than a poet and generally managed to make sure literary ladies noticed that fact. So I saw Yoshua's attempt to come on like a gigolo as a case of closing the circle—the Populist Poet's Comeuppance, you might say—and it rather destroyed the impact.

Oh, that's his mother, inside the Franklin stove: he answered quite readily when I asked. He didn't seem to suspect telling me that would diminish his charm for me.

5 ב "... That Hath Such Wonders in It"

Well, for wonders there's nothing like the instant view, so this chapter will be mostly diary notes. But first I'd better explain why it will all sound so different, though it's about the same town on the same morning.

A Friday morning, which is what alters everything: if I'd gone out for my newspaper and then straight home, I wouldn't have seen *this* Beer-Sheva. (Which makes you think, doesn't it, about fresh and wide-eyed views. Like, what if an observer comes into downtown New York on Yom Kippur, when department stores, hotels, etc., are open and there's nothing to tip him that he's looking at the untypical? If he wrote, "My taxi slipped quickly through the wide, quiet streets"—well, he'd be telling what he saw. But could you recognize New York?) For, as noon on Friday approaches, Beer-Sheva undergoes a sea change: the pace of the action quickens sharply—when I noted in my diary that the town "wots not of rat races," I hadn't seen a Friday there—and the average age of the characters drops about twenty years. A heavy percentage of passers-by are clearly young, and uniforms become numerous in the impromptu encounter groups that hail each other, stopping in their tracks to exchange a pattern of Hebrew like rain on a roof. (Though I should report that very few of these rumpled, open-collared soldiers are "in uniform" as the term is used in the American army.) But even these gregarious types wear a definite air of going somewhere, and in a hurry: once in motion again, they twist in and out dexterously, getting around whatever's in their path without breaking stride. Somehow, these uniformed, passing-through young make everybody else look moseying-along.

68

Where most of them were going that morning was to the Egged bus station. For Beer-Sheva may be a trifle pushy in calling itself the "Capital of the Negev," but the Negev desert *is* a dandy place to put army camps (not to mention also an airbase or two, but the government always calls those "Somewhere in Israel") and Beer-Sheva is both their (relatively speaking) metropolis and their gateway to the north. It doesn't surprise me anymore when, the minute an Israeli I meet hears that I live in Beer-Sheva, he's apt to join the 80 percent or so who have told me—often in almost exactly the same words—*Oh, I know Beer-Sheva. When I was doing my army service* . . . These are usually professional associates, so that turns out to be ten to twenty years ago, and they don't know Beer-Sheva. Still, their comments do provide a handy informal view of the town's growth; it's a little specialized but probably more reliable than the civic boosters'.

Thus it would be fair to say that a nice sampling of the country's eighteen- to twenty-one-year-olds can be seen tearing through town on any given Friday, usually heading home for the Israeli version of Mom's blueberry pie. And no wonder they look purposeful. For, to get this far, they've already negotiated a ride up from the desert, which may take some doing; now, they can be in Tel Aviv or Jerusalem in another couple of hours, but only if they catch the right bus—which also may take some doing. In such a tiny country, no Israeli can ever really be very far away from his home; but it's not like the U.S., where the distance is the only important factor and where, especially in the western states, the 113 kilometers between Beer-Sheva and Tel Aviv would amount to only about an hour's drive and no significant expedition. Here, it can be that. And to get from a Negev army base to the third and most northern of the big cities, Haifa—that's about 200 kilometers—may mean waiting for an extra bus and takes a minimum of four to five hours, including waiting time. (Warning: I got that estimate from an Israeli friend, so assume it's optimistic: an Israeli's "It's only a ten-minute walk" can mean anything up to about five miles.) Besides, if you don't live *in* Tel Aviv or Haifa and will then have to catch a local bus from there— well, the one thing certain is that you won't have much of Friday left when you get there. And Israel's weekend is only one day long: if you want to be sure of getting back to camp in time, you'd have to start back early enough Saturday evening to reach Beer-Sheva before the last bus down into the desert leaves at 11 or 11:30 P.M. In short, your travel time may be just about equal to your time at home, which is itself only long enough for your mother to wash your uniform while you're seeing your girl. That's assuming your girl (because she may be in the army, too) also got leave and got home.

69

Life isn't easy for the Israeli young, is it? But hitchhiking, which is called *tremping* (TREMP-ing, presumably from the British "tramping"*) can improve matters, and it's a safer and more respectable way of traveling than in the U.S.; here, giving a ride to a soldier—in a country with a citizen army, he or she would be somebody else's young son or daughter—is considered a social duty, so tremping can be speedy and efficient. The only risk in it is for the "observant" soldier, who may be still en route when the sun goes down and Shabbat begins.

I'd better deal right now with that word "observant," which for me, as a novelist and thus an observer-by-trade, is a source of irritation. What it means in Israel is a Jew who obeys the strictures of Orthodox Judaism (the only kind officially recognized by the religious authorities). There are literally hundreds of those rules, all of which "observant" should presumably cover. But it's actually more a social than a religious term and thus gets commonly applied only in interface matters like *cashrut* and the sabbath—e.g., an apartment-to-rent ad calls for an observant tenant who'll keep the kitchen *casher*; or, if you're planning a Saturday outing in the car, you don't invite your observant friends along.

A certain amount of (strictly official) "observance" is forced on the society in general by the political fact that the religious parties can deliver swing votes in the Knesset's majority coalition. But, since the society is dogmatically egalitarian and socialist-oriented, what happens then is either hilarious or appalling, depending on whether absurdities move you to satire or rage. For the closing-down of the town by early afternoon on Fridays—so everyone can get home before sundown, when the buses stop running for Shabbat—sends the citizenry scurrying around in a compressed version of the American family's Saturday shopping; but the system can't match capitalism's response to such commercial-urgency situations because no group of workers can have fewer rights than any other.† Thus do the ideologues of church and state combine to produce a spectacle that, like Christmas eve in a department store, starts from piety but doesn't do much for its image. Unless, unlike me, you can see why God should presumably be served by sup-

---

*However, a roadside spot set aside for soldiers seeking rides is a *trempiada*. The pseudo-Spanish sound of that makes me wince (and all these borrowed words doubtless give Hebrew purists real fits). But it does offer a glimpse of the layer-on-layer melting-pot influences on the language.
†The military, firemen, and the usual other public-service personnel are excepted. This doesn't cause any hassle, because the religious tenets permit Shabbat-breaking necessary to protect life (a primary and absolute value in Judaism).

planting the gentle, considerate pace of daily life with a me-for-me scramble that turns Beer-Sheva into a miniature Times Square.

This Friday double whammy from church and state puts considerable strain on individual virtue too. For, even normally conscientious types are more or less compelled to cheat on their working hours—a practice so general that you soon learn not to try to get any business done on a Friday. Which is to say, if you can arrive at an office at 8:30 A.M., you may be able to get a start; but by the time you find out who's the next person you must see (there always is one—even in the unlikely case that you're in the right office, nothing is ever completed by one signature or stamp), he's gone off to join the beat-the-crowd crowd. Like, for example, at his bank, which closes at noon. In Beer-Sheva, that's not lunch hour, so nearly everybody shoving in the crush at the bank counters is supposed to be at his desk somewhere for another hour or so. (After which he goes home for midday dinner: the lunch-counter sandwich and the business lunch are still relatively uncommon in Beer-Sheva.)

I've been saying "his" because it's usually the fathers of families fighting the battle of the bank, since the mothers—who usually work, too—had to get home by noon because that's when their pre-schoolers are let out of the *gan*. That's short for gahn yell-eh-DEEM, which means "garden of children" (like the German word *kindergarten*, but a gan takes nursery-school-age children), and is the day-care facility you'd expect to find in a society that's all in favor of working mothers. Only, there's that doctrinaire catch: the *ganenet* is also a worker, and thus entitled to time for her own frantic pre-Shabbat shopping, right?* It's already unfair that she has to wait until noon, by which time things get very frantic downtown. That's why the old and/or infirm, who know that, are no longer much in evidence by noon—when determined teenagers, just released from school, beat it into town to buy the new records they absolutely have to have for a Friday-night party. True, that's not what the religious intended the kids to be doing on Shabbat. But when your power comes not out of popular conviction but out of party politics, your writ can run only so far in a free society . . .

Well, *I* didn't get out of the way of the teenagers, or of anyone else trying to get into the downtown stores before they closed at

---

*Also true of the grade-school teacher, though her charges are more self-sufficient. But that brings about an interesting situation, for "latchkey children" was a term used in the U.S. years ago, to dramatize the heartlessness of capitalism, which forced mothers to go to work. Yet latchkey children are an everyday sight in Beer-Sheva, the housekey on a string around the neck bouncing as they play—just as if Israel weren't a progressive society.

about 1:30, because of a sort-of culture clash. Israelis who say they want to go somewhere don't mean to fiddle-faddle around town for a couple of hours on the way, so to the girl in the mercaz klita office, sending me via the main street (she knew I knew it, because that's where the department store is) seemed the easiest way to direct me to the *shuk* (an Arabic word pronounced like "shook," but it's been taken over into Hebrew, where it rhymes with "kook"). The shuk is an open-air, farmers'-market-type place, but its stalls sell just about everything from apples to zippers and prices are determined by haggling—via finger signs if necessary, but the stallkeepers can count in quite a few languages. It's also strictly caveat-emptor turf: if the pitcher you bring home from the shuk leaks, that'll teach you to look smarter next time. (And you're lucky you didn't get your pocket picked as well.) The really big day at Beer-Sheva's shuk is Thursday, when the desert Beduin come in to market their produce and arts-and-crafts work; but what I wanted was souvenirs to send the folks back home, and brummagem can be bought there anytime.

So that's where I was supposed to be, and well before noon, too—instead of right in the middle of the main-street scene at its dizziest hour, which is no place for the frail and bewildered. For Beer-Sheva's main street isn't exactly your grand avenue to begin with, so when all the cars and tenders and buses turn out it doesn't take long to work up a regular big-city traffic mess, complete with mindless honking and squealing near-misses. And on the sidewalk, things were no less cluttered, for though the soldiers had mostly made it out of town by that time, the local population was still augmented by just about everybody from the surrounding Negev area who could get there. Including, conspicuously, pairs and trios of very large, very sunburned folk, toting enormous quantities of various commodities, who plunged along as if carrying the life-saving serum to some verge-of-death case. These are the delegations from *kibbutzim* and *moshavim* (a moe-SHAHV is a cooperative farming community, which means in practice anything from subur-banites who chip in to pay for crabgrass-control to something like a collective farm). They come up of a Friday with major banking and purchasing missions, both communal and personal, plus long lists of errands ranging from changing the children's library books to matching some green wool for a half-finished sweater; besides which, they probably have to get the truck back by a certain time. So their highly organized manner is understandable, but it makes them distinctive. As does, also their dress—like, shorts when every-body else is still winter-wrapped—and a general air of deepbreath-ing nature-boying . . .

But the problem isn't just additional people, it's extra commerce also: two flowersellers, for example, had spread their wares on opposite sides of the street (but quite in sight of each other) and were offering carnations, iris, and snapdragons in exactly the same colors and at exactly the same prices. They seemed to be doing equally brisk business, for each was surrounded by a ring of people buying flowers or waiting to, or asking how much each kind cost— and meanwhile reducing the traffic flow on both sidewalks to one slithering or wriggling pedestrian at a time. But at least those customer-clumps could be got past, and their effect was confined to the sidewalks, unlike the pushcart selling strawberries in the street at the corner. (Perfectly safe: I've told you how the drivers take corners, so there was no danger from cars turning into the side street. And those trying to come out couldn't move anyhow.) The real all-out traffic strangler, though, was on the opposite corner. There, a more elaborate cart, with a glassed-in heating cupboard amidships, peddled hot corn on the cob. Virtually irresistible, especially considering that most people would still have had no lunch, so it stopped practically everybody. And its customers, spilling over sidewalk and two hunks of street—as they waited first for the corn, then for the communal salt, and then for their change—weren't any mere traffic block, they were more like an army of squatters.

Beyond them stretched the way I was supposed to go: *Keep walking straight down the main street until it just ends.* Where it ended, the helpful girl had explained, was where the desert began, and there I'd see the shuk . . . Well, that made sense in terms of cities I had known: Beer-Sheva must begin at the desert just as Boston did at the waterfront, and for the same reason—that's where trading goods had been brought in originally, in olden times. Also, having the desert at one end of town sounded like Denver, which has the Rocky Mountains instead. Since they're highly visible (which was more than I could expect of the desert), they do wonders for me: only in Denver, where even I can tell which way is west, can I feel geographically competent and talk like a regular grownup.

Which is a rare treat, because I was born with virtually no sense of direction. (One of my poems opens with the line "Imagine the man who first made a map!"—which I think transmits the special awe of the inept for the ept.) Thus I get about by unwinding mental spools of thread in a perpetual labyrinth, never quite certain of my way even to familiar places and certainly never taking any liberties with any instructions I've been given. So when somebody tells me that's the way to the desert, that's how I go, see. With the blind devotion of the fanatic.

Only, this time, no way. For, peering down the main street, I could see that the vista of knotted pedestrian and hooting vehicle traffic apparently went on as long as the street did. Once I spotted a shopper wiggling past a standstill clump—holding a shopping basket aloft, as there wasn't passage room for both a body and a basket—but even that much motion, itself as unpromising as the last trickle in a dried-up stream bed, was on the other side of the corn-cart barrier . . . Well, things had to be that bad before I could do it, but I did it, I dared to try common sense: surely, I reasoned, the next street parallel to the main street would also go down to the desert? Once before, I'd got that bold: on a long-ago afternoon in Washington, I decided it was quicker to drive around a block—and ended up hours later somewhere in Baltimore. With a vision like that dancing in your head, it's hard to be brave . . . But bravely, I turned and, negotiating the narrow strip between the strawberry customers and the corn customers, set off at right angles to the main street. Maybe I couldn't have done it except for the comfort I derived from the warm, throbbing flank of a taxi I sidled past. It meant hope—not of transport, for it had been waiting for some time for an unlikely chance to turn into the main street. But it was a sign, because the taxi had come from *somewhere*, no? So if I could keep my head, I'd find a street to turn left onto. And if I could only remember that, I'd get back on the way to the desert.

What happened after that can be seen in the following diary extracts.

74

From the diary: 4

Gunslingers and gals

I was told that English courses became compulsory in the secondary schools rather recently, so I figured that made recent adults—most likely to have studied it, and most likely to remember high school— my best bet. Very scientific, what? It worked, too. After a false start: several of the young people I accosted said "A leetle only" when asked whether they spoke English, and I took their word for it and let them go. But then came a lean and stringy fellow, and it occurred to me (maybe because he resembled my stepson) that he might be just modest. So I hung in there, and sure enough . . . The trouble was my question, which seemed to them to mean a school exam in which maybe they didn't get an A: for all they know, I'm about to ask them for the past participle of something. Once I took to announcing firmly that a little English was enough, everybody managed.

More than 50 percent of the young I stopped this morning were chyellim (soldiers—pronounced chigh-el-EEM, singular chigh-AL) on their way home. Generally slouching along, notably lacking in spit-and-polish, and each one also carrying a plastic shopping bag—sometimes emblazoned with advertising—or else the kind of pseudo-basket made of woven plastic strips. In either case, most unmilitary; but in the latter it was possible to glimpse the contents. A particularly friendly and fluent fellow (his girlfriend majors in English, he said, and enforces lots of practice) had a jumble of clothing in his: a certain familiarity with the way a nineteen-year-old male will pack a perfectly clean shirt makes me hesitate to say it was laundry, but it certainly looked like that. And if it was, there was a lot of it. (Hi Mom, I'm home—and then he's off to parse sentences with his girl, leaving a puddle of dirty socks and underpants in the kitchen? I guess: how different can things be, even in faraway lands?) This lad had lots of black curly hair, very white teeth, and bounding energy—not to mention, also, leave for longer than just the weekend, which may explain his big grin and bright eyes as he told me all about Irit (ear-EET), who makes him go to all the American films and doesn't let him read the Hebrew subtitles. I wonder whether there's a Hebrew equivalent of "She's the greatest thing since sliced bread . . ."

After that it was something of a shock when, as we parted company ("Ciao," he called cheekily, though he'd started out with a respectful "meddem") and he turned away, I very nearly got poked by the black snout of the gun sticking out from under the sweat socks in his shopping basket. I "recognized" it as an Uzzi—by which I mean, mostly, that American newsmen have told me over and over about Israeli soldiers patrolling the streets with Uzzis. Of course nothing I've seen so far matches that story, but doubtless it's a good thing anyhow that TV brings the world to my door so I can spot an Uzzi from the merest glimpse?

A little later, it looked for a minute as though the media were finally coming through, because across the street there was a boy with his Uzzi slung over his shoulder. Besides, he appeared to be carrying an automatic in his other hand, and you can't get much more armed-to-the-teeth than that. Only, once I got closer, I saw it wasn't a handgun: it was black and L-shaped, but it lacked both sights and trigger. The rumpled chyal hurried toward the Egged station, swinging this object insouciantly—a very model of the Israel-as-Sparta all the liberals back home were always warning about . . . Except, the picture didn't quite fit somehow—maybe because he, too, had a shopping bag (a little one this time, but enough to spoil the image)—so I checked it out. And about fifteen minutes later I not only knew that the gun-shaped thing is the Uzzi's firing module (my term for it, as nobody seemed certain of the English name; but whatever you call it, you can't fire an Uzzi without it), I'd also learned that it's forbidden to carry the weapon without disarming it. So in militaristic, gunslinging Israel, if your gun won't fit in your shopping bag, you have to tote that module conspicuously unless you want to risk being stopped by the MPs . . .

By that time it had become pretty obvious that no member of this shopping-bag army was patrolling the streets with his Uzzi. So why were they carrying it at all, I asked. Well, not—it turned out—because they just feel undressed without it, but because infantrymen are responsible for their own weapons. So unless you've got a buddy who can babysit with yours over the weekend, it's safer to take it home with you: left in the barracks, it may be picked up by some son of a bitch too lazy to clean his own. (That last is a free translation.) So much, then, for the gunslingers who get mentioned so consistently in dispatches—to headshaking and lip-pursing peacelovers back in Cambridge. I suppose it wouldn't do for some reporter to reveal the sober reality of a society that handles weapons, sure, but doesn't glorify or even trust them. All I can say is, now that I've been able to compare these chyellim with the love-beaded young men on Ivy League campuses who talk so chillingly of the "aesthetics of revolution"—well, it isn't the shopping-bag bunch I find scary, baby.

If the Israeli officials had any propaganda savvy, they'd have a soldier call an American hotshot reporter with an offer to Tell All about the repressive army ruling. ("For us chyellim, life is a hell of *dodging the MPs . . .") That way, you'd get investigative reporting, see. And the slavering-for-war Israeli would be exposed to the world as only Irit's feller, chomping popcorn at the flicks.*

When it comes to the girl soldiers, however, I've probably benefited by the American media sloppiness, which photographs the pretty girls and lets it go at that. Because it never bothered me back home when the TV news showed me a chyellet (pronounced chigh-ELL-et) helping Golda Meir settle a wreath on a tomb; but now that I've encountered the chyellot around town, I find I've got mixed feelings. They look cute, they really do, in their miniskirts—which are so mini that pantyhose become an important part of the uniform. (Not a single run have I seen, but it does make you wonder: how does a pantyhose army march?*) And instead of those awful clumpy butch oxfords, they have skinny little black sandals that look both comfortable and flattering. The whole things amounts to that welcome phenomenon, a sexy outfit that actually gets worn only by women young enough to look right in it. (For a while I thought it might be hard on the fat girls, but today I saw one and it isn't: she had a jaunty air of I may be tubby but I'm sexy, too.).

But I dunno, the chyellot make me feel querulous anyway. Surely I don't want to see the girls actually fighting again, as they did in the 1948 war; yet their present role, which makes them something like the airline stewardesses of Israeli society, is much too adorn-and-serve for my taste. I mean, I'm no devout feminist, but when I learn that the chyellot help out in the elementary schools (teaching, taking kids on outings, etc.) and type letters in the captain's office—and all the time looking pretty, too—I begin to break out in a rash . . . But I'm also no ideologue: I believe in asking people what they think, not telling them. And the answers I've got so far are all plus. For, not only do all the women say they enjoyed being in the army, but those who work at the mercaz klita (and thus could be questioned at length, and in English) are still young enough so they haven't had time to develop any distorting good-old-days feeling about it. And finally, the current girl soldiers I've been talking to all seem to take their responsibilities very seriously: maybe they're cast as society's little helpmates, but they fill the role with a pride that's genuinely touching.

Possible light on the puzzle today, from a thoroughly English-speaking chyellet (she was tall, slim, grave, and beautiful, with a dignity that quite overrode her Busby Berkley uniform) who told me that going to the army is usually the first break with home. All of a

---

*It doesn't, dummy—do the U.S. Marines take beachheads in their dress blues? Back at the base, the *chyellot* wear slacks.

sudden you get to stop being the So-and-Sos' daughter and become a chyellet, anonymous and—in your free time, at least—on your own. The army has rules, but she says they're certainly not the in-loco-parentis kind, and the officers have no orders to serve as duennas. So it figures, I guess, that girls would indeed go for a combination offering both new freedoms and the comfort of tradition. It may not look much like it, but maybe it's really liberation.*

And with it comes total public esteem, for everybody seems to have some fond memory of a school-days chyellet, or of having been handed a mug of hot coffee after a hard day's war or training. (I know, I know—tending and nurturing again. But if it's so gracefully given and gratefully received, what makes it bad?) And I saw it myself this morning, when I accosted that lovely, serene chyellet at the bottom of the Post Office steps—and we stood there talking in the sunshine, all the time under the benign gaze of a guard up on the top step. (I guess he was guarding something, though he spent the whole time sitting in a tipped-back folding chair.) His satisfaction was writ clear on his sleepy face: there was a chyellet taking proper care of a foreign visitor, col b'seder (cole b'SEH-dare, literally "All in order"; b'seder is used like, and as extensively as, "okay"). True, that gent didn't seem likely to stir very much even if everything wasn't in its proper place. But clearly our tableau relaxed him even further . . .

This chyellet, by the way, was enchanted to learn of my connection with Cambridge, Mass. (She'd used the word "suburb" for her hometown, so I was able to abandon my standard "Boston.") And the news that I'd actually lived near Harvard Square really made her day—which was a little embarrassing, as what I mostly did at the Square was go to my bank. But she didn't ask why I went there: maybe it didn't occur to her that anyone needed a reason . . . What she did want to know, it turned out after a while, was whether I'd ever run into Simon and Garfunkel, whose songs she heard on the radio.

Oh my. There was—how shall I put it?—an inescapable impression from the way she spoke that she thought S. and G. were students at Harvard, perhaps given to minstreling away on campus between classes. And how do you go about delicately dispersing an impression? Particularly since there could be language problems: her English was dandy, and she had a little French, too; but I've already learned how difficult it can be to summon up a subjunctive . . . I weaseled: well, I said, I had never seen Simon and Garfunkel. (She nodded, recognizing common sense—I was pretty old, and even

*In a later discussion, I heard that most women have met their husbands either in the army or at university—and attendance at the latter is by no means general in Israel. So if the army doesn't offer liberation, it does at least widen the choices . . .

in America the old probably stayed home a lot.) But yes, I told her, I did know some of their songs. (I should: Phil gave me a whole album one Christmas.) And yes, I knew the words of the one about the bridge . . .

So that's how come I stood there in the bright blue-and-white weather of flowering Beer-Sheva and warbled "Lak a bri-idge o-vah trou-bled wa-ter." As they say in those old show-biz movies, I sang my heart out—doing my best to sound exactly like the jukebox wail that used to fill the student snack bar while all those earnest arguments went round and round and nervous fingers fiddled with crumpled cellophane packages. The cardboard hamburgers, my favorite Yankee Doodle cupcakes, the coffee that comes in a plastic cup with a wooden stirring-stick . . . Oh when shall I see their like again?

The chyellet didn't have to choke back any tears—she was happy, so all-lit-up happy, just to have the latest news of the international-youth country (the wine of it must be that fruited yoghurt) she could hear of only dimly and as long as the transistor's batteries held out. What luck to have encountered a traveler from there: "Ah, did you once see Shelley plain?" Well no, dear, I didn't . . . I feel so bloody guilty: she was so sweet, and surely somebody owed her something better than a precarious future in a tiny land kept islanded by surrounding enemies?*

Over at our left, a small dirty man paused in the act of weighing pears at his corner fruit stand; his customer turned her shawl-wrapped head and smiled uncertainly. But up at the top of the steps, the guard only looked proud and confident. No matter how strangely foreigners behave—even if they suddenly break into loud, quavering song in front of the Post Office—you can trust a chyellet to handle the situation.

---

*Well, maternal feelings were all I had to respond with, back then. But now, I'm not at all sure that girl wasn't getting something more valuable, despite her hard life, than her contemporaries smoking pot on Cambridge Common.

From the diary: 5

A grain of sand

More about what happened after I turned off the main street this morning.

It was really quite reassuring at first, for there were people, and business going on—but decorously, inside stores. It all looked so normal (I mean, there was even a bookstore!) that I went on for an additional block in the wrong direction: it was nice and peaceful, and up ahead, I could see there was a cross-street I'd be able to turn left on.

Well, I shouldn't have been looking up ahead, for just then I stumbled. When I looked down to find the cause, what had tripped me turned out to be an edge of the next large square of concrete. It was just like the sidewalk behind me except that this square was tilted up at about a forty-five-degree angle, with its opposite edge disappearing into sand—which was what lay ahead, sprinkled with more slabs of sidewalk. Some of those were even lying almost flat, but no two were still lined up squarely or remained linked together: they looked rather like grave markers in a ruined cemetery.

The way I felt, standing there looking out over that, was rather like when I first heard of the uncertainty principle (imagine the man who first realized there was no map!). It's the way you respond, I guess, whenever and however the news first reaches you that, viewed cosmically, you're a virtually invisible jot whose fate is forever up for grabs ... But that message had reached me some time ago (what is writing poems if not an attempt to defy it?), so it made no sense for me to react as if somebody had just stolen away all order or stability. Could I be so frail that a mere display of municipal messiness socks me so hard? After all, sidewalks crumble in Massachusetts, too.

Well, but that's it, I finally saw. For in Cambridge, and in Washington, when old sidewalks crumble or crack, what's made that happen is likely to be a tree root: looking down as you step around it, you see the brown, gnarled root and the revealed earth. Which was always there, under everything—and suddenly wasn't, in Beer-Sheva. I mean, dammit, who ever even thought it necessary to define "earth"? It's just the dark, dampish stuff that was "dirt" when I dug a hole in it to bury a caterpillar who died in spite of love and a lavish shoebox home. (I remember I wasn't sure what services were appropriate, so I made my little sister sing our school song. She never did grasp why she had to render "Crim-zun and gold, crimzun and gold" in the birch grove, but at least she learned that might makes rite.) Later on, when I was the mother, dirt was "soil" and I added things to it to make my garden grow. So that's what earth is—dirt, soil, the diggable actuality of the abstract "land" you buy with your house.

And that's precisely what wasn't there this morning. Because it seems that in Beer-Sheva, when two paving stones move apart what's revealed isn't earth but sand. Not the pale, fine sand of beaches but desert sand, which is kind of caramel-colored. You don't sink down in it as much as you would on a beach, but it doesn't seem to pack down like earth either.* And—here's where the wallop comes in—in Beer-Sheva it's not the sidewalk that's usual and belongs there, it's the sand. For sidewalks are temporary and transient, but the desert is a permanent fact of life.

What's shaking me (and maybe has been, one way or another, since I arrived) is how long facts of life are in this place. "Old" was always, of course, a relative term: as a native of a region where the American Revolution was the local history, I snickered at talk of "historic" Denver. But here, where anything less than four thousand years ago is practically recent, I know better than to mention a town only two hundred years old. And yet, its sidewalks may well be a lot older than the one this morning: that was concrete, not cobble-stones, and you'd have to assume the Israeli settlers twenty-five years ago had higher priorities for their concrete. So the sidewalk may even be rather recent . . .

What I have to get used to is a new kind of personal vista, nothing like the small and limited ones I know—Washington, a city-slice contributed by Maryland and Virginia and still tucked in be-tween them; the tidily defined towns and farms of New England; and Denver visibly stopped by the great mountains. Forget all those, along with notions of old and older, of starting and growing and stopping: they're all irrelevant here. Where the desert isn't just down-near-the-shuk, it's at the end of a street facing in any direc-tion; it's everywhere, in short, that isn't town. For the desert isn't just older, it's forever—and everything else is temporary. Not just sidewalks: everything in Beer-Sheva, with no distinction possible between Abraham's tamarisk tree and the strawberry pushcart on the main street, is equally flimsy and upstart.

What happened this morning was that, with an almost audible click, the Old City and the mercaz klita and the shuk and

*It sure doesn't. So you walk not on it but through it, while it slides into your sandals and, eventually, out again. Which is probably why Ruth found it so amusing that the first thing I should think I needed in Beer-Sheva was socks.

81

the soldiers and the flowers—all of it, and all the people in the streets—turned into a film set with actors (no, extras hired by the day) parading before it. The truth about the crumbling mansion and the worn stones, no matter who left them here, is that they're all just planted hastily, plunked down on top of the desert for a while. The only really old thing around is the desert, sand on top of sand on top of sand, forever and ever. You can set down a street and run a bus along it, nail up a house and raise generations in it, and you're still temporary: whether tomorrow or a thousand years from now— which, is not up to you—everything will disappear into the only-and-always reality of tawny sand.

Later.

    When I read that over, the startling, embarrassing truth leapt right out: what I was trying to tell about was—incredibly— falling in love. It sounds awful, writ bold like that. But it's there: I'm a critic, by golly, and I couldn't miss a thing like that in a piece of prose. Besides, now that I've got enough distance to be at least a little clinical, I can recognize the symptoms, which were there this morning: the swift this-is-what-I-want certainty, the conviction that you don't want to go away from it ever. It's true, isn't it? Admit it.

    I can see one possible how-come (literary-psychoanalytic stuff, but that doesn't make it automatically untrue) right off the bat: viz., the obvious difference between earth and sand is that sand is empty (okay, so it's really teeming with microscopic somethings. But when you look at it you don't see science) and always shifting— and those two things add up to the very opposite of "home," right? So suppose what shook me was less cosmic revelation or existential awareness than the not-yet-absorbed realization, I stand not upon the earth of home but in an alien place without roots? *From that point on, it figures to be much like the phenomenon of kidnap victims joining their kidnappers' cause or released hostages telling the press how kind were the hijackers who refrained from blowing their captives to smithereens: people who find themselves suddenly powerless tend to join the powerful (even when they must know the power is temporary and lacking in long-term substance. But when you're looking at it, you don't see political science). So maybe that's what I was doing, too. Finding myself in alien corn, I avoided tears by joining it—because whatever you fall in love with is ipso facto not alien, right?*

    Or else the above is just Maggie-the-writer, entering to clutter up a simple fact with smart-talk, and what happened was that I stamm fell in love. And even if I could figure out which is the right answer—jolted by awareness of being a passing pimple on the indifferent desert, I ran for emotional cover? Or an inexplicable but authentic emotion overcame me, and the only thing odd about it is its object—I wonder whether I should really try. Because if you play chess against yourself, who wins?

All right, leave it alone: you don't have to understand everything, and certainly not in the first week.

But I wouldn't go around talking about it, you know?* People might not want to make friends . . .

---

*I've left this sage advice in, lest I come off sounding more emotionally daring than I've a right to claim credit for. But in fact I did make friends, and thus learned I wasn't the only one to experience what may be something like the "rapture of the deep" phenomenon: quite a few people in Beer-Sheva chose to settle there because of what sounds like my experience. (None of them can explain it either.)

6 ↙ Boats of the Negev, or Something Like That

The Altschul Absorption Centre was so named—one could learn from a not very prominent sign—to acknowledge the generosity of Jeannette and Louis Altschul of St. Louis, who I assume would have spelled it "Center." I never passed that sign without thinking of T.S. Eliot, whose spelling also began in St. Louis and switched to British (though he would seem unlikely to have felt comradely about the Altschuls and *their* fondness for a foreign culture). This odd mental linking went utterly unmolested, neither added to nor altered by more information, because during all the months I lived at the mercaz klita, nobody ever mentioned the Altschuls.

Many Israelis flinch from these reminders, sprinkled all over the landscape, of the benevolence of Jews abroad. It's not clear whether this reaction is to the vulgarity of the whole business or to the fact of dependence, but it does seem to come down more heavily on the Americans; perhaps that's because a lot of Israeli movers and shakers, even when they are intellectuals, seem to be patsies for a title, and many of the British Jewish contributors are Sirs and Ladys. But in any case, my antennae pick up a certain implication that the British do these things high-classly, whereas American generosity is uppity and naïve. That remains mostly a matter of my own judgment—because when I asked Israelis, they usually denied what I'd observed*—but, though my perceptions

---

*One who didn't, and knew the behavior I meant, condemned it as an attempt to imitate the *goyim*—who presumably are believed to refrain from such self-advertisement. I can't see how that follows. But he's never seen the pews with memorial plaques in Cambridge, Mass. churches, so I guess he's free to sociologize unhampered.

84

continued, my attitude changed after a while. At first I found this Americans-slurring damned irritating, but then I began to recognize the element of injured pride—the human phenomenon of resentment of the benefactor (which Americans learned about from postwar France, among others). And finally I came to recognize it in its context, which is the psychic damage done by erstwhile colonial masters. The departing British always seem to leave a kind of second-degree-snobbery syndrome behind, like an infestation of fleas; I choose that simile because I read somewhere that fleas can live on, even in an empty house, for twenty-one years . . .

I think Israel has been less affected by the syndrome than many other British (and French) ex-colonies, and even what there is is on the way out: the younger sabras' deliberate brashness and scorn for "manners" is at least in part a way of killing those Mandate fleas. It takes a while to see all that. But most people soon recognize that what's on view isn't really anti-Americanism, and if they've been bridling, they stop.

Oh my, I've wandered a far piece, haven't I. And you still don't even know what the mercaz klita looked like. Well, there are two long buildings, about twice as wide as they are tall, made of huge concrete blocks with shadow "stripes": i.e., the striations look indented, but when you touch them the surface is actually smooth. The blocks are stacked with the stripes alternately vertical and horizontal, like a parquet floor; the arrangement may be dictated by some structural necessity, but it looks ornamental, like a good way to get pretty without getting expensive. Each building contains three stories of "flats" (there's the legacy of British nomenclature again) above one-story pillars, which widen as they rise. So maybe they can't properly be called pillars? Well, whatever they are, they do support the buildings that line up in parallel on opposite sides of a campus-like stretch of grass (big enough for boys' pickup soccer games) and shrubs and bisecting concrete walks. At one end of this landscaping is the dirt road where the Georgians' tender deposited me on the night of my arrival; opposite, at what amounts to the fourth side of a rectangle, a small sign directs you to the "Dining Room" and its equivalent in Hebrew, French, Yiddish, and Spanish. Shallow stone steps lead down to a small plaza and the communal dining hall, which has a sliding-door window wall that can make it virtually one with the plaza for festivities. At night, that is—in the daytime, the windows are closed and drapes drawn over them to keep out the sun.

Since there's a bank of shored-up sand and rubble rising at the opposite end of the plaza, it doesn't seem to be sunken by accident and I wondered why anyone would go to the trouble of digging it out. But once I learned how the merciless sun beats down on the campus strip above—so that, fresh out of a shower in one building, you're drenched with sweat by the time you cross to the other—I stopped thinking in terms of aesthetics. For putting the whole little complex (it includes also a small building housing the washing machines, like an apartment house's basement laundry) below ground level at least creates shadow on the one-story stone dining hall and the tiled plaza, and that's the only way to get shadow without the enormous trouble and expense represented by the greenery in the campus strip above. I'm making such a thing of this realization because it was an introduction to a primary daily consideration in Beer-Sheva, the business of arranging to get light without admitting too much heat. It doesn't take long to learn you'd better hide from the sun, but if you're fond of house plants, you can't keep the sun out of the house entirely—that's just one example of what I mean, the recurring need to think of ways and practical means.*

The fact that the mercaz klita was designed—it didn't just grow, in the haphazard, plenty-of-time American way—emerges most clearly after you first see it late at night, when the random lighted windows of individual flats have gone dark and all that remains are the institutional lights, one beside each flat door. Then, the long low buildings, lifted on their pillars and strung with rows of evenly spaced lights, look very like a pair of ocean liners riding the night. Each building also has two staircases enclosed in curved sheathings of stone whose rounded rising bulks (the lights on the stairs within them hidden from sight outside) look like smokestacks and quite complete the silhouettes. A well-known Israeli architect won a competition with this design, Ruth said—and added, her tone denying personal association with the whole notion, "It was supposed to be 'Boats of the Negev,' or something like that." That came out only after I'd remarked on the effect, and if I hadn't already appeared to have got the message she would probably never have admitted to anything so la-de-da: her look said she herself disdained such stuff but maybe it was all right for me, a writer and thus permitted to get fanciful . . .

The flat I'd been assigned to was one of the 42 two-bedroom units—each with a back balcony overlooking the green "common" between the two buildings—in Binyan Aleph (Building A). In Binyan

---

*Of which artificial lighting for plants is not one: electricity costs a fortune per kilowatt hour in Israel.

Bet, which faces the common, the first floor is given over to class-rooms, offices, a lounge, and other administration facilities. The flats there begin on the second floor, and their balconies look out over the desert.

The front door of Binyan Aleph is on the non-campus side of the building: the sign telling about the Altschuls is just outside the main staircase (it has a small glassed-in lobby space, whereas the stairs in the other "smokestack" just begin). You come off the staircase onto a windswept gallery—the first, second, or third, depending on your destination and your empirical discoveries, since there's no sign telling what numbers are on which floor—with the red-painted flat doors on one side and on the other a stone wall that's breast-high for me and waist-high for most men, but certainly high enough to keep a toddler from falling over. It takes a puffing fifty-four steps to climb to the topmost gallery, where I lived in No. 40, but the view from there—particularly during the orange- and purple-streaked desert sunset—is worth it. That is, if you're not fussy about your coiffure: the winds of both winter and summer whip along there in force, sometimes strongly enough to actually threaten your footing if, like me, you're neither small enough to be sheltered by the gallery wall nor heavy enough to withstand much buffeting. I weigh about 110 pounds and sometimes, going along the gallery to visit in No. 32, I'd have to tack like a small boat in white water.

When you came into my flat from the gallery, you'd be in a kind of vestibule. On your left it becomes a kitchen, because of the sink and two-burner gas "platter" (it's just a stove top, with no oven or broiler, sitting on the counter beside the sink) along the far left wall; the rest of the kitchen fixtures are a small refrigerator and a table the size that nightclubs consider big enough for two. The door to the bathroom is at the right and just ahead are the two bedrooms, mine the lefthand one. If a family is occupying the flat, this kitchen-cum-entrance-hall becomes the dining room—because something always has to be cooked for children even though three meals a day are served in the communal dining hall—and the general center of the household.

In No. 40, though, it was a sort of no-man's-land, at least at first. For I had, briefly, a flatmate, a spinster from Argentina who'd already "graduated" and had a job and and was almost ready to move into an apartment in town. She didn't seem to be my type (she wore a hairnet at night, went to bed early and without reading, and was prissily tidy), so the lack of a language in common didn't really matter; she managed to communicate (a) disapproval of my gregariousness (it must've been that, since when I invited fellow students up we'd just sit in my room and talk) and (b) instructions on how to light the kerosene heater, which sat in the exact middle of the kitchen area—where it did both of us minimal good but was fair. She soon moved out and I never saw her again, but while she was there the kitchen-lobby was mostly only what you crossed to get to the bathroom or answer the doorbell. And the two men who shared No. 41 next door didn't even regard their kitchen as living-space: it was filled with luggage and cartons, piled with only passage-room left. But in No. 39, inhabited by an Italian widow and an American divorcée and the little son of each, the table was in the center of the area and whenever I went in there, somebody was sitting at it or playing under it, and something was simmering on the stove.

The flat's balcony, which can be entered only through the bedrooms, is also shared space, but in No. 40 the sharing was pretty well limited to use of the clothesline. Some people used the balcony to store possessions or the boxes the stuff had arrived in (it's wise to save the wood from crates, for use when you move to your own apartment*), but ours was bare: my flatmate either had few possessions or had moved them out before I came, and I'd arrived in February, which is still rainy-season enough so I hadn't yet learned to think of anyplace roofless as suitable for storage. (In Beer-Sheva, it is: you just take the stuff in during the few rain months.)

The balcony's low outer wall is like the gallery's out front, except that down near the bottom it's pierced by an inset hunk of pipe. Every morning, after the floors have been washed, the rinse water—dirty, but it's still water, see—is poured out there, arcing beautifully through the sunlight to fall into the rows of circular depressions containing shrubs three stories below. (Each shrub lives in its own dimple of soil, which holds onto water and whatever enriching stuff has been added to make a garden in that desert soil.) Nobody could possibly be walking down there—rebellious types disinclined to stick to the concrete walk might cross the grass, but they couldn't wiggle in between those great thorny bushes, not without a suit of armor. Still, though I was on the top floor and didn't have to worry, I did wonder at first whether people in the flats below might be deluged if they happened to be on their balconies at the wrong time. I checked, and it's all right: the parabola dictated by the angle makes the falling water from above just a passing rainbow to

---

*And not for just the obvious bookshelves, etc.: foam rubber is cheap and readily available, so the handy and ingenious, given a little wood, devise all sorts of furniture. A two-year-old of my acquaintance sleeps in a darling little bright-red youth bed; you'd never know that under the paint on its wooden side is a stenciled "General Electric."

anyone on a balcony below. Nice, huh? I like a mind that can dream up both "boats of the Negev" and ingenious ways to recycle the wash water: as an introduction to Israel, it was impressive.

Maybe my flatmate had been around long enough to learn to recognize the sun as enemy, but for me the high, roofless balcony was very heaven. I'd take a blanket and lie out there after I washed my hair (which made it not loafing, you see, and thus guilt-free), listening to the 2 P.M. English news and reveling in such un-February warmth. It wasn't much past February, either, that I discovered another lovely fact: by the time I finished hanging my single line of wash out on the balcony, the pajamas I'd started with would be dry. The desert air has obvious drawbacks, but it's really great for anything you *want* to get dry . . .

I've been talking about No. 40 as my flat (though briefly shared), but it was only the bedroom that was actually considered mine: the word *cheder* (CHAY-dare) means "room," and it was the one used in the Hebrew sentence I learned when, quite early, we were taught to give our addresses (*Cheder Arba-im, Binyan Aleph, Mercaz Klita Altschul, Rechov Yitzchak Sadeh 11, Beer-Sheva*).* But "flat" was what they said when speaking English—a confusion that may stem from the early kibbutz (the country's good-old-days and still vaguely its social ideal), where your sole individual holding would be one room . . . Well, there in my individual room, my bed was along the wall I shared with the kitchen and opposite the door leading to the balcony. The bed was the "inconspicuous" Hollywood kind meant to look couch-like without your having to strip it every morning and make it up every night. But under the washed-out-aqua bedspread, also meant to be inconspicuous (you could get a tan one that just about faded into the wall), the hump of pillow at the head undid the effect. I fixed that by hauling the pillow out, folding my "security blanket" afghan around it, and leaning it against the wall: it not only acted like a bolster when you sat on the bed in the daytime, but the bright wool squares also sparked up the pallid décor.

The cheder needed all the individuating it could get, for the bed and the desk—and the desk chair, which I used for a night table (it was the only way to get a lamp within reach of the bed)—were all

*We all wrote our names and addresses on our *machberrot* (notebooks), some people adding a bold "Israel." It reminded me of my children, who used to go on from "Washington, D.C." and "U.S.A." to "The World" (except Phil, who wrote "Planet Earth" and "The Universe"—and I think some galaxy was also in there somewhere). Maybe Israeli children do the same? But "Israel" was as far as the Hebrew vocabulary of the ulpan students would go.

straight out of a motel, the middle-quality kind that doesn't belong to a big chain or ultra-violet the toilet seat but is clean and respectable and approved by your motorists' guide. (This impression was enhanced by the long drapery at the glass door leading to the balcony: it was an American-motel print—mine was brown and orange, but I bet it came in blue and red, too—that a traveling salesman would feel right at home with.) The exception was the wardrobe, which wasn't the light motel-neutral wood of the desk but some thinner stuff to which a walnut stain had been applied. It was the largest object in the room, though puny in terms of use: down one side, four shelves provided about the same "drawer" space as a nursery chest of drawers, and the remaining hanging space—one bar, one hanger-width deep—was just about long enough if everything was doubled and tripled on the hangers. I didn't really have that much hanging stuff, either, for books and manuscripts and a ream of typing paper, all of which went into the desk drawers, and some bric-a-brac had pretty much filled my suitcases; clothing, especially the hanging-up kind, had been well down on my priority list. When you think of a husband and wife sharing that same space—*two* winter coats, Sunday (no, *Saturday*, in Israel) good blue suit *and* best dress . . . Well, maybe it was the kibbutz mentality at work again: a couple who labored daily in the fields and tossed their overalls into the communal laundry wouldn't need much room to hang up the peasant skirt and homespun trousers they dressed up in for the Saturday evening History of Zionism lecture.

There'll be a short pause here while I examine my soul, or something. Because I just reread the last couple of pages, and I can see they sound somewhat condescending—even, not to mince words, snotty—and it bothers me because I don't think that's the way I felt. Like most of the Americans at the mercaz klita, I'd come with a sense of at least semi-pioneering, an unspoken but nevertheless real expectation of having to rough it: we wouldn't have been surprised (and in fact might even have felt a certain satisfaction) if we'd been given army cots to sleep on. So why should I now be giving the impression that I sneered at the mercaz klita accommodations for falling short of the Waldorf?

Well, partly it's the old tricky business of reporting innocence while burdened with later sophistications: whether I intend it or not, my description of the cheder and its furnishings is imbued with a certain amusement. For, you can't help a small giggle once you understand that the fantastic luxuries provided for immigrants are a "known fact" to the Israeli public: the faction that grumbled about it was overruled by the progressive realists who insisted on putting the country's best foot forward, but neither side doubted that all this was indeed lavishness. Which of course is true, if you remember the tents and/or huts in which most of them began their life in Israel. To reproduce those conditions would hardly attract the immigration the country needs, though, so it's an argument in which both sides were right. But I suspect that being in a position to see both sides sympathetically now produces that note of over-view superiority you may be hearing here. It may be impossible to avoid (Query: Are all historians *ipso facto* snotty?). But at least don't imagine me standing around with a smirk . . .

However, you can trust any impression I've given you of my surroundings as sort of unfinished, half-baked. Because it may be a surprise to be confronted with something resembling an American motel, but once you are, the resemblance starts dictating comparisons and what you would have accepted as just exotic (*here I am in a faraway foreign land where everything is different*) suddenly seems just incomplete. Thus to an Israeli, for whom a cube of stone with window and door is a finished living space, supplying a wardrobe is lavishness—so why shouldn't it stand out in the room, on display like that? Whereas for an American, used to built-in and unnoticed closets, the effect is of a piece of machinery with its lid off and the works exposed, a job somebody forgot to finish.

The works-on-view effect was most noticeable in the bathroom of Cheder 40—maybe it wouldn't have been to a European, but to me it was nearly all news. Because sure I'd seen a water heater before, when I was a homeowner: it was a tall white cylinder down in the basement, something for husbands to worry about. (And when I lived in apartments, I never saw it at all.) But I'd certainly never seen one prominently on display in the bathroom, a squat round white-enamel thing, sixty-eight centimeters tall and forty-nine in diameter, bolted into position high on the wall by a pair of braces that looked meant to hold up a bridge. (They'd better be substantial, come to think of it: water itself is very heavy, and its cylindrical container can't be tucked into the right-angled meeting of two concrete walls but must be held at arms' length, so to speak.)

This object is called a *dood* (rhymes with "food") and is not only visually conspicuous, it doesn't do its work in the undercover American way either. Somewhere on the wall outside the bathroom there'll be a switch and a night-light sort of bulb that glows redly, like the exit light in a theater, when the dood is on. When that is can be the result of a communal agreement designed to take advantage of lower electricity rates in off-hours—or, as in the mercaz klita, an institutional arrangement* with the same purpose—or else left to individual shrewd "systems" that depend on your remembering to turn the dood on an hour before you want to take a bath, etc. Since electricity rates always rise, usually by fantastic increments, dood-handling is a frequent subject for informal seminars once new-comers get out of the mercaz klita and into paying their own electric bills. Everybody's got a system, based on firm convictions about what saves most kilowatts, and advice gets trotted out with the inevitable frequency of suggested remedies for a head cold. And besides, doods seem to have a sort of prescribed half-life, like a radioactive isotope: unless you have a brand-new one, your luck may run out at any moment. Thus, at any given time, somebody you know is going through the three weeks or so of cold-water living that it takes to replace a dood, or else knows somebody who is and is offering the use of his shower and other solaces. (Broken doods have now happened to me enough times, and I've heated water on the stove to wash in during enough cold days, that I no longer harbor even the smallest pioneering impulse.)

But if the dood was the most conspicuous it wasn't the only exotic touch—and most of the others are also in the bathroom, which may have been the most foreign-landish experience of my early days in Israel. For example, I got quite excited about the toilet, which I described in my notebook as a marvelous instance of straightforward simplicity brushing nuisance complications out of the way. That may have been partly because fixing toilets that wouldn't stop running was my chief item of handyman expertise as a homeowner—God knows how many Saturday mornings I spent driving to Sears for a replacement for the little bar that hooks into the ball that rises with the water level in the tank. So it was almost as a technician, you might say, that I celebrated the ingenuity of the Israelis, who'd dispensed with all those moving parts and even with the tank itself: there was nothing behind the toilet but a rising pipe with a valve about midway up the wall. You flushed the toilet by turning the valve to let in water, then turning it back again when you'd had enough—thus custom-tailoring your use of water to the visible need. Like shifting gears yourself instead of turning the whole problem over to automatic drive, by taking not-much trouble

*There, the dood comes on automatically, deep in the night—scaring me into fits on my second night (during the first, I was too exhausted to notice anything) when I woke to see that red glow reflected in the transom above my door. After a minute, I managed to realize it wasn't wavering so probably wasn't a fire. I got up and went to look, which is how I discovered that thing right next to the refrigerator was the switch for the dood.

you effected economies and also eliminated the nuisances resulting from complexity. Simple is better, I wrote enthusiastically, and hooray for the intelligent, simple Israelis.

Yeah. Right there you have a bright, shining example of the dangers of writing about a society on insufficient evidence. How in the world do people spend a few weeks in a place and come up with a book telling you about it? I know I'm a slow generalizer—other writers jump from the observed artifact to the Large Truth while I'm still turning the thing in my hands and figuring how to describe it— but even if you get to the generalization slowly, what confronts you is apt to be the same booby traps. And the primary one is usually a product of people messing up logic, which is what happens here. For nice simple toilets like that still do exist, in kibbutzim and in the homes of practical types like Sara and Yaakov (whose Jerusalem house is full of luxuries but who are not likely to change a perfectly good working toilet just to be chic). But the Beer-Sheva apartments I would come to live and visit in were mostly built in the last half-dozen years or so, by which time everybody had up-to-date American-type toilet tanks with little handles or buttons to push that would give you pre-set amounts of water you could use only in multiples of itself—just as if you were living in careless, water-rich America* . . . Without American distribution of goods, however, so that the snazzy latest-wrinkle toilet in my present apartment has a plastic tank (made in Israel—a home industry developed to compete with imports?) that seems to work on the old rising-ball principle; but if it breaks, finding a replacement gidget could be quite a project. Bah. I look upon the damn thing the way a member of the French Academy looks upon *Franglais*, although my Israeli friends are all pleased about how *moderni* (moe-DARE-knee) my place is.

Nevertheless, when it comes to books in running brooks (but not sermons in stones: after living for a while in archaeology-happy, sermon-prone Israel, I'm for sticking to running brooks), the shower in the mercaz klita still holds up pretty well. I think it was probably the original kibbutz model, its only lavishness the fact that it was, after all, indoors. Though just barely, as the bathroom was a good-sized room but the shower wasn't cut off from the rest of it by so much as a curtain, even. There was no bathtub, which I can still say "of course" about: everybody I know has one, but it's a thing you supply for yourself, like kitchen cabinets. My current brand-new apartment had space left for a bathtub (an official recognition of the

---

*Well, that's the way America has always thought of itself. But as I write, Denver is facing a water shortage—and it's not likely to be the only city in that plight.

facts of real life), but the owner had to get one put in. It cost him 2500 lirot, which was at the time the official monthly salary of a Cabinet minister.* The government Thinks Kibbutz; if you want to get middle-class, you have to be prepared to pay plenty.

Back in the mercaz klita, though, a bathtub is still sternly unimagined. Even the shower involves no more construction complexity than using a different kind of stone square (but just as slippery as the rest!) for one corner of the bathroom floor. And maybe, just maybe, the floor there slopes, ever so slightly, toward the small drain—actually, a circle of iron with a few slits in it—set in the middle of the space. Above, a hot and a cold pipe, each with its blatant valve, rise to a rudimentary shower head: once again, all the works in plain view. And any American newcomer whose pioneerish aspirations are frustrated by the motel decor of his cheder can stop suffering as soon as he takes a shower. For you have to establish your own mix of hot and cold, and in the process you have to get pretty well soaked—and either scalded or frozen, for a length of time depending on the speed of your reflexes—because the only way to reach the valves is *through* the water. Which is falling straight down from a height of nearly two and a half meters, so if you use anything more than the merest trickle, it bounces and spatters off the slick floor tiles and the virtually solid drain all during these preparations and wets down the entire bathroom while you're still trying to get a temperature you dare enter.

With enough experience, it's possible to keep the spray from quite reaching the hook on the back of the bathroom door where you hang your bathrobe (with your slippers prudently tucked into its pockets); leaving it outside is the safest way, though, and once I occupied the flat alone, I took to leaving my towel outside, too. Towels—one, once a week—are supplied but bathmats aren't. So I bought one, but that proved of doubtful worth: it may be just a jot less chilling to step out onto a soaked bathmat than a wet stone floor, but you really have quite enough chores after your shower without adding more things to wring out.

What needs wringing out may vary slightly with the season, for you get dandy condensation drips in winter if you succumb to the temptation to heat the bathroom by running the hot water for a while before you enter,† but you can avoid that in summer by

*Without, however, the privileges and allowances that add up to as much again per month.
†Either because of a pioneer complex or plain stupidity, I didn't think of this. But when I remarked that it took a towering faith in hygiene to get myself into the shower in February, Avi (the first Israeli I got to know well in Beer-Sheva: you'll hear lots more about him) told me nobody with any sense even went into the bathroom until the hot

opening the window. Which opens onto the gallery outside your front door, thus presenting another kind of problem: presumably people *can* look in, or the window glass wouldn't be frosted, right? (I mostly choose modesty. But there's a point in the summer, like about when the temperature starts getting close to 40°,* where I tend to abandon my standards—if it will catch me any passing breeze, I'm for letting 'em look.) Thus, one way or another you're apt to end with all the contents of the bathroom—the sink, the toilet, and the looming dood on the wall—all rinsed and dripping. Like the window, whether it's opened or closed. And like any clothes you were dumb enough to take in there.

So there you are, standing naked† in the upper lefthand corner of a two-meter-square sea on which it keeps raining. But don't despair, there's a way out—via energetic wielding of the Israeli artifact of artifacts, the *sponja*. The word, pronounced like "sponge" with an "uh" on the end, is both noun and verb; but don't make the mistake of believing it describes anything, for a sponja isn't made of sponge and doesn't absorb water. What it does is *push* water—it belongs, I guess, to the genus Windshield Wiper. The working end is closest in size to the window washer's squeegee, except that the rubber edge is wider. (And if you're speculating that somebody confused the English words "sponge" and "rubber," I doubt it: the word for that strip is *goomi*—GOOH-me—which means any kind of rubber, including sponge-rubber erasers.) And of course the handle is much longer, because you use a sponja standing up, as if using a mop.

Only, when you ply a mop, you're picking up water. A sponja just moves it, and the only available place to move it to is into the slits in the drain—people with pinball experience may hit a slit right off, but for the rest of us, it takes practice—and the floor you're moving it over is slippery, flat, and non-absorbent. Thus the water, if poked even a little too hard, immediately sends out amoeba-like extensions in unexpected directions. The odds are, with any given swing you'll drive some water back over your own feet—and the fact

---

water had been running full force for five minutes. Maybe ten, he added, eyeing me with the mixture of concern and scorn ("This one shouldn't be out without a keeper, so I suppose I've got to be the keeper") that came to inform our relationship ever after.
* 40°C is 104°F, and 34=95. For numbers between, use Phil's Phormula (see Chap. 4, "O Brave New World . . .").
†And, in my case at least, looking like an illustration for a medical textbook. For, the first time I took my clothes off in that icy bathroom in February, my body went on red alert even before it was wet: a complete map of my circulatory system, each and every capillary distinct, appeared instantly on my skin . . . It wasn't exactly attractive, but it certainly was instructive.

that old hands sponja barefoot would indicate that experience does no more than alter the odds somewhat.

This is the after-shower drill I worked out. Start by shoveling the water in the shower square itself, guiding small amounts into the drain. (This gives you a chance to study the best angles, as well as to practice wrist control, body English, etc.) After that, you move outward, sticking to open areas: it's silly to sponja under the sink, for example, while water is still dripping down its sides. I prefer to sweep an aisle, about three floor tiles (sixty cm.) wide, to the bathroom door, and thus to my slippers. By then, I'd be no longer actively dripping; so, by leaning against the door while I dried one foot at a time, I could end up shod on my relatively dry island. Of course I developed this method in winter, when it's urgent to get to the towel and bathrobe; in warm weather, standing on a cold floor is desirable and it's cooler to work naked, so you can start off in any direction and sponja your way over to the sink. The idea there is to get to the rag under it, which is protected and thus probably dryish.

However, those rags are like the pencils kept besides telephones: they vanish randomly, according to some not-yet-understood natural law. (I put it scientifically like that so I won't sound paranoid. But we know, don't we, that They come in the night and snatch trophies . . .) So when you get to the sink, the rag may be gone. But don't panic: toilet paper, unrolled past the soaked outside layers to the merely damp part, will do to wipe the sink. Then you can wipe down the toilet seat, too, though that's never a really permanent job: the dood is right overhead and condensation will come sliding down its sleek sides for quite a while afterward anyway . . . I can't make this operation totally economical, for you have to re-sponja your way, wiping out your footprints, back to your original aisle. (But, given a universe consisting exclusively of flooded floor and sponja'd floor I don't think even Phil could figure a perfectly efficient system.) There, you lean the sponja against the wall, put your robe on, and beat it to your room for a rest.

It's just as well, really, that you have to develop a sponja technique right from the first, because it's the most prevalent and universal factor in Israel's daily life. (Which is doubtless why the Ministry of Absorption is, like all Israelis, unaware of any necessity to prepare the newcomer: it's so *there* that they just don't see it.) What mostly explains that is stone floors, which are absolutely everywhere, without regard to sociological or economic distinctions or previous conditions of nationality. If you get homesick enough for American-way touches to go to some trouble and/or expense, you can find real hamburgers and even bourbon (those aren't accidental for-instances, they're what you get to dreaming about in frontier-town Beer-Sheva): "everything's up to date in" Tel Aviv, not to mention tourist-conscious Jerusalem. To find a wood floor, though, I think you just have to get on an airplane. Because I never saw one anywhere in Israel, not even in the super-elegant places where some money-is-no-object Foundation or Fund has paid for a dazzling building and dazzlingly overpriced paintings and sculpture to go in it (and, by the rules of the gift, for nothing else. Alas.). And not even when Israel itself is putting on the dog for distinguished foreign visitors,* who are housed in yummy little chalets complete with hot and cold canapés, in Jerusalem. Elegance and endowment funds may determine the number and size and gorgeousness of the carpets in the showplace buildings, but underneath them are those tile floors again; after the dignitaries have been whisked off for cocktails and mutual-tribute speeches, the carpets are picked up and out comes a battered-looking prole in high-button work shoes—and the bucket and sponja.

I don't like using the word "tiles" for these floors made of stony squares, because I'm afraid you'll think of the asphalt- or vinyl-tile floors of American kitchens and public buildings (oh my, remember the man in overalls who comes around after hours with a rotary-brush machine and produces a wax sheen that results in a mirage at the end of every corridor?). The Israeli tiles, which could never be waxed like those in my nostalgic parenthesis, are square, but that's about the only similarity: they're very hard—if you wore diamond-soled shoes and scraped your feet a lot, you just *might* scratch them—and they're neutral rather than decorative, with the floors the same all over the house. (Importing super-elegant tiles from Italy for the bathroom is the thing in the conspicuous-consumption set, I hear—usually in the course of sad tales about orders getting lost or strikes at ports—but I don't know anybody who has them.) Variations occur because of age, which may mean a change in design policy at the factory; but the usual floor is beige or light tan, with or without dapples or flecks, and the standard size is twenty centimeters square.

That last explains, by the way, why Israelis know how many meters your apartment is; they tend to use that rather than the number of rooms as a description. When I reported back to the

---

*It says something significant about the Israelis that these are likely to be musicians or scientists or artists. Even writers: here, the scrivening trade has a built-in prestige (which can, alas, quite turn an American writer's head).

mercaz klita that I'd found an apartment in Beer-Sheva, Ruth asked how large it was*—and Avi, who'd taken me to look at the place, said "Forty-eight meters" while I was saying "Two bedrooms." (I was awed: what an eye he must have!) Their system has a clear advantage in terms of accurate description—e.g., I have another two-bedroom apartment now, but it's sixty-four meters. And it's handy, too: if you want to know the size of anything, you can lay it on the floor and count squares.

However, the reason I've taken off from the sponja at such length is that I think it involves a great deal more than just the stone-floor fact of Israeli life. Not consciously, though: "*That's* what you pick to write about?" asked my friend Thereza, throwing me an incredulous not-marble-nor-the-gilded-monuments look. She knows about my choice because I had to check out the word "sponja," for one of the things you learn in Israel is that a word in constant use, even if it's clearly not confined to the slangy, may not be "real" or "proper" and in fact may not even be Hebrew in the Academy sense. (Sometimes the daily-use word has a "correct" synonym—which may be known to nobody but a couple of professors at Hebrew University—but quite often it's a Yiddish or Arabic word that came to fill a need and just stayed.†)

Well, it turned out there is a "Shabbat word" (i.e., elegant, dress-up) for "sponja." It's *shtifat-rizpah* (floor-cleaner—only it's *rizpah* that's "floor": we're in a right-to-left world here, remember) and unused but not obscure; everybody I asked looked surprised but produced it promptly. (Each of them also told me that nobody ever says it.) Including a fifteen-year-old boy who's learning English in school, and if a sponja was what I wanted to talk about, why, okay: what did they call a sponja in America, he asked politely. Um. Well, I said, we don't really have any . . . He stopped in his tracks and just stared: "In America the peoples they don't cleaning their house?" Ha. I know this kid well—he's the son of friends, and I've been in his house when he came home from school, entering with a noticeable disdain for household cleanliness—so his horror at American dirty slobs who don't even sponja could easily have been answered with a you're-another sneer. But my country deserves something of me, so I rallied round the flag and explained that

---

*"How much are you paying?" is a more likely first question, but Ruth is used to dealing with Americans. Who, quite unaccountably, flinch at perfectly natural questions about money.
†Or sometimes it supplies a special humorous or ironic color, like the Arabic *habibi*, "my friend" (buddy, pal): if you use it in direct address, it's like calling someone "baby" in English.

though we hadn't evolved the sponja, we did have primitive methods. And yes, a word for something *like* a sponja . . . He went away saying "squeegee" over and over, so he wouldn't forget it before he had a chance to show off in class.

Maybe I should've said "mop," though. Because in the first part of the regular household sponja-ing operation, it gets turned into a mop, sort of, with the addition of a heavy homespun-looking cloth: even pristine in the store, it's almost always a dirty-gray, with maybe a red or blue stripe at each end. This is frankly called a *shmatta* (SHMAH-tuh, rag) but currently costs the equivalent of a dollar. Which is a lot to pay for a rag, but not, I guess, if it has some kind of non-objective inherent value. As does indeed seem to be the case, for Thereza, who is neither conventional nor at all reluctant to adopt new or strange ways, refused even to consider the merits of the old skirt I'd torn up and was using for a sponja rag. But why should I pay a dollar for a rag when I already had a rag, I argued. Thereza had no idea which old skirt I meant and thus no way to know how closely my rag duplicated the qualities of the shmatta, but she "knew" it wouldn't get the floor clean. And she's normally a logical woman.

But sponja-ing is not logical, it's prescribed; everything about it is. You dip your shmatta into a bucket of cleaning compound (after some mistakes with stuff that turned out to be water softeners, I found a brand helpfully named Rizpah), bring it out dripping, slap it down on the floor, and wrap it around the sponja by folding up alternate corners of the oblong cloth. I've never quite mastered this craft or sullen art, but among the talented, the rag stays on until it's unwrapped—after you've slopped the cleaning water around the floor as if it were the deck of a ship. For sponja-ing, though it requires skill, isn't much for finesse: small objects are picked up and set on tabletops, etc. before you begin, but anything left on the floor after that has to be able to survive regular lapping by water-cum-Rizpah. And the deck-swabbing analogy is even more apt for the second half of the process, when you take the wraps off and get even more carefree: clean water is simply poured onto the floor and then raked with the (now naked) sponja from room to room and finally out the door.

In hot, dry Beer-Sheva, that has a very pleasant social effect. For example, where I live now my way to the grocery store takes me through a kind of mews lined with little houses, each with its walled front courtyard. At noon on a Friday, the gates and the front doors within stand open on a vista of glistening floors; the sponja cloths are wrung out and pegged to the clotheslines, and in front of some houses, the damp traces of finished jobs are cooling the air that's drying them. In front of others, little children on tricycles, dogs, and I zigzag around barefoot housewives raking the last of the rinse water into the middle of the narrow street. Nothing can keep the heartless midday sun from finding us, but in that space between the whitewashed walls of the little houses, something cool and clean and sparkling is fighting back against heat and dust and desert drab.

That's what it's all about, I think—and it's why even progressive Thereza won't have the sponja custom treated like an ordinary domestic routine, amendable and open to individual option. It's a genuine ritual, culture-woven and emotionally weighted: that dimple-kneed tricycle jockey, grown up and far from home, will think of it wistfully; when he's old, it'll be his remembrance of things past. If he's religious, it'll also be part of the preparation for the Sabbath, which is thought of as a queen *(Shabbat HaMalka)*: in addition to cleaning your house, you're supposed to bathe, don fine raiment, etc. to welcome her . . . But that pretty story isn't a likely one, for a very large proportion of the Israeli population (in the street I was just talking about, I'd say it reaches 85 percent) is non-religious, and a smaller and noisier percentage is actually anti-religious. So it's quite likely that although the sponja-ing gets done on Friday because of Orthodox religious feelings—that's what arranges the work week—most of the time what the house is being cleaned for is not Shabbat HaMalka, but weekend visitors.

That the sponja ritual is a community one but the community is more national than religious shows up in the *way* of it: there's a distinct flavor of the kibbutz (and that's probably where Thereza's involvement stems from), an air of institutions associated with bareness and simplicity.* Certainly it doesn't go with, say, the tea wagon inherited from Grandma—or with anything else too old and/or frail to withstand the sponja rigors. Which fact, of course, people being the way people are, rarely stops anyone from hanging onto precious possessions: young Golda Meir may have come pioneering with nothing but a pack on her back, but there are other old ladies who've been patiently wiping sand out of the carved legs of middle-European sideboards for forty years. (And in case you think I'm sneering at them, guess who insisted on growing morning glories in Beer-Sheva—though it meant virtually custom-tailoring an appropriate climate out on my balcony?) Thus in Tel-Aviv and such established places, the sponja philosophy and the bourgeois

*I think it's significant that the only American newcomer I know who had no trouble learning to sponja is a former nun.

appurtenances have been rubbing up against each other long enough so that both have altered somewhat.

But Beer-Sheva is in more than one sense a frontier place, with middle-classness really only just beginning to confront the sponja, so to speak. Which raises some interesting questions—e.g., a very expensive kind of imported sofa and chairs, squat and legless and upholstered in velvety corduroy (an ugly design, and it's hard to imagine any material more inappropriate for the climate!) is on view in the shops frequented by the chic young-marrieds. Right now, the young couples seem to sponja as ritually as their elders.* But for how long, if they're going to buy furniture that's so obviously neither waterproof nor liftable?

Well, anywhere except here, you could recognize that kind of pattern—the descendants of wooden-bench pioneers saving up to buy velvet sofas—and safely predict the changes it foreshadows. But when it comes to Israel, that's not so easy: for one thing, traditional beliefs and practices have a way of going on living side by side with their own refutations. But also, the ritual here is supported by what you might call a coalition. For the means, the sponja routine, preserves the *chalutz* (chah-LOOTS, pioneer) tradition of those dance-in-a-circle early Zionists; and the act itself preserves the Shabbat tradition, which is perhaps dearest of all to those for whom Israel represents a chance to live a true Jewish life.

I hope my personal skepticism doesn't give the impression that I just brush off the latter, because I don't mean to do that. What I do mean to say, though, is that the same thing is being seen through different lenses. For it can be argued that it's the *society-making* aspect of the Jewish religion which is operative in many of the daily-life prescriptions for the devout—and thus the "observant" and the heirs of the atheist kibbutzniks are obeying traditions handed down by people who were playing the same game. The name of it is establishing civilization, or linking arms against the primitive; and you're winning it so long as the tribe holds off the desert. In short, it's Man vs. The Great Shrug, whether your weapon is the concept of one God and an immutable Law or faith in human perfectibility and the true communal grit that triumphs over tyrannies.

The way people in Beer-Sheva, whether religious or not, think of being clean is, I think, similarly a case of that "coalition."

---

*Young women who want to rebel against Mama don't do it in the kind of terms American parents see. A defiant daughter may refuse to get married (if she holds out until she's, say, twenty-five, she'll really be hurting Mama); but once she does, the options—unless she goes to live on a kibbutz—are pretty much limited by the need to buy an apartment, furnish it, etc.

Because they don't define the word but feel about it, and in a way different from my own experience: clean is something I like to be (actively when I'm dirty or hot, absentmindedly the rest of the time), but it seems to be, for them, something they *have* to be. And it would be foolish to insist that that has nothing to do with all the emphasis on distinctions between "clean" and "unclean" in Jewish religious writings. But ritual baths and other cleansing rites run through hundreds of cultures and sects—there's nothing unique about such notions, though Orthodox Judaism has perhaps had time to accrete more dizzying complexity than some. (Nor is there anything especially Jewish about the sort of simpleminded reductionism that equates the odor of Clorox with the odor of sanctity: all religions seem to be troubled by examples of that kind of thing.) So I find it more persuasive to explain the deep and passionate feelings about cleanliness on view here to people's need to preserve the distinction between themselves and the surrounding Arab culture (which also includes ritual handwashing, etc., but doesn't visibly go in much for hygiene). That social explanation doesn't by any means preclude the religious one, especially since the latter could have been similarly inspired a few thousand years ago . . .

But whatever you want to call it, that emphasis is, in Beer-Sheva, reactive and defensive. For a very large proportion of the city's population came out of the Arab world, and it shows:* what the winds from the desert are carrying around this dirty town is the detritus of a society that's strong on group identification but hasn't yet had time to produce a really customary, taken-for-granted civic consciousness. So home—and still quite often, *only* home—is Civilization, to be guarded with an ardor verging on fanaticism. Against what? Well, call it Middle-Eastness—a bundle of attitudes and ways including lassitude, resignation, irresponsibility, easy violence . . . In the better neighborhoods (which here tends to imply resources like education or youth or political viability, not just cash), the apartment-house hallway or the immediate street is part of what's to be defended: committees see that the stairs are sponja'd, energetic delegations brave the municipal bureaucracy to get the road repaired, and disputes end in nothing more dangerous than a shouting match. But in general, the defense line is still drawn at the family's own front door.

---

*To the point where you can even make a handy rule-of-thumb: if you see someone carry a crumpled cigarette package to a container instead of dropping it where he stands, he's almost certainly an American (or some other variety of "Anglo-Saxon") and you can go ahead and speak English.

Well, I didn't note all that by peering down from my balcony at the mercaz klita. But for expertise at cultural anthropology, you probably can't beat the ad man (I think that's probably internationally true, too)—so I did pick up the first hint while I was still only listening to the English news. Which was followed by a washing machine commercial* in which the announcer assured us that this machine would get our clothes *as clean as you can wash them yourself.* Not, please note, cleaner: that's the key difference.

American manufacturers tell you why their machine is better, the generic argument for washing machines having been long established, so I can't make a direct comparison. But I can compare the Israeli ad with American spiels for dishwashers, because they were not yet that common when I was a young housewife; a dishwasher didn't cost so much as to be only for the very rich anymore, but it was still a major investment. Thus you got a generic sales talk: it was explained to me that I needed a dishwasher because I couldn't put my hands in water as hot as it provided to get my dishes "scientifically" clean. So I owed it to the health of my family to . . .

Ha. An Israeli housewife, who isn't nearly so humble, wouldn't be persuaded by that, she'd be insulted. *She* doesn't bow before words like "scientific" or "germproof"—mirror, mirror, on the wall, she is the cleanest of them all and you better believe it, habibi. (Or she believes she should be. So if she suspects she isn't, she's not going to admit it by buying a machine.) Still, she'd like to get out of doing the work. Thus she will buy a washing machine (most people do, though the cost is proportionately much greater than the dishwasher investment was for me), but only as a mere substitute for her own expertise. Not quite as good, of course; however, in an imperfect world, an acceptable compromise—and if you pitched your ad any other way, you'd lose.

The washing powder used in her machine isn't "germproof" (unless it's imported), because that's an irrelevant promise in an Israeli household—where the lady of the house could well be a biochemist and thus no patsy for the simplistic "germ" talk that bullies American housewives. Or else she recognizes no bacteria because a kitchen presided over by a pious Orthodox woman can't harbor anything harmful. (Once you get a look at the amount of constant cleaning required for *cashrut,* you're tempted to agree.) Only "assimilated" households, of Jews corrupted by living in the

*Only one of the English news broadcasts has commercials at all, and they *never* keep you waiting for the news while we hear a word from our sponsor. All the news and weather are given first; unless you want to hang around for a reprise of the headlines, you can leave before the commercials even begin.

103

Diaspora, can have germs, see? And of course Arabs* have them, but they can't help it, they don't know any better.

Some notes on the Jerusalem connection:
Well, it's taken me three weeks, but I've finally overcome the telephone hang-ups—Israel's, and my own—enough to get in touch with Yaakov and Sara in Jerusalem. There wasn't any real hurry, as I hadn't written them the exact date of my arrival and, since I'd insisted on riding the conveyor belt straight to Beer-Sheva, they weren't expected to do anything special about me. So, as the only inhabitant of the mercaz klita who didn't have a nervous cousin waiting anxiously in Tel Aviv, I stood aside during the first mad scramble for the phones. And for a while after that, lacking any such noble excuses, I just put it off—as I would any phone call anywhere.

Thus, by the time I got around to it, I already knew where the coin phone at the mercaz klita was—out on the first gallery of Binyan Bet, near the office—but I'd never actually seen it used. So I didn't know it took not coins but special tokens called ah-see-moan-EEM (I *think* that's right†) until I walked right up bravely and read the English version of the "Instructions for Use" on the wall. Then, feeling relieved (it was rather like having the dentist break your appointment, an escape with honor), I surrendered my turn to the queue that had already formed behind me and went back along the gallery to ask how you get telephone tokens. In the Post Office, they said; but they had some in the office and sold me a few.

Back outside, I had plenty of time to read and ponder the Instructions. And to be fascinated by their curiously hectoring tone, which I suspect has something to do with too-literal translation; maybe it's the Hebrew language that's responsible for the maddening-the-people-are-children attitude that seems to inform all Israeli officialdom. ‡ "Pay attention" (to your tokens) has such a chiding, parental sound—you expect it to go on wearily, *I've told you a hundred times. . .* The man who was talking on the phone did go on and on (in Spanish), so I had plenty of time to decide that "Pay

*That is, enemy Arabs—Israeli Arabs don't have germs. (Most of the time, that is. But when the liberals want welfare allowances increased, the Arabs—like any others among the poor—are discovered to be living in insupportably unhygienic conditions.)
†This is a permanently sad story based on the fatal fact that what I first seemed to hear was "Simenon," probably because of the psychological gimmick that makes you substitute a known sound for an unknown one. I did soon realize it wasn't Simenon as in Georges, but it left some kind of scar: I still tend to use the English word, and if I am pushed to the Hebrew word, it comes out with an audible quaver of doubt. (But I'm less neurotic about the singular: a token is an ah-see-MOAN.)
‡I doubt that, since the same tone turns up in England. Maybe it's the language of socialist governments?

104

attention to the quantity of tokens in the aperture" probably meant you were supposed to watch the small glass-covered oblong on the face of the telephone box; true, it wasn't exactly an aperture, but I could see the man's token in there, resting. So I paid attention. But nothing happened until the man finished, at which point the token vanished abruptly from the little window. The man lifted a small door below (a real aperture, but not watchable, since anything in it was invisible) and stuck his finger inside—it seemed to work like a miniature version of getting a piece of pie at the Automat—thus demonstrating the final, brusque instruction, "Regain tokens." He didn't regain his token, and I wondered why he should expect to: clearly, somebody had answered his call.*

Then it was my turn. With a respectful eye on the Instructions, I lifted the receiver and listened for "the dialling tone," inserted a token, and watched it appear in the little window. Whereupon the tone promptly stopped, and tentative dialing of a couple of digits only confirmed lifelessness. So I hung up, worked the Automat-window gimmick, and regained my token. Rereading the Instructions yet again was no help—they no more considered the possibility of their own error than the impatient parent telling you for the hundredth time. But logic insisted that a demonstrably in-order phone was not going to go on the blink just when I stepped up to bat. Unless . . . Abjuring paranoia, I grasped my token firmly and stepped up to the plate again—thus discovering, via a kind of act of faith in probabilities, the important fact that Israeli telephones have to be allowed to "cool." Nowhere is this written down— certainly not in the Instructions—but a word-of-mouth campaign should be started immediately. (Americans particularly must also try to remember that the phone needs to rest after each digit, too. Do not dial rapidly but always with a certain stateliness, giving it time to relax from getting you an 8 before you ask it for a 3, etc.)

This time, the system worked: I listened to the dialing tone, paid attention to my token, and finally got to dial the number I'd been carrying around. It was Hebrew University's, and had been given me by someone else; but I thought it useful for reaching Yaakov too, because where else would I find him in mid-morning? Even if he was in class, I could leave a message, for as a department chairman he must have a secretary (or at least half a secretary?) who, the odds were, would be able to speak English.

Luckily—because I hadn't yet grasped the Rest Principle of Israeli phones—after I dialed 02, the area code, I had to stop to look at the next digit. This allowed the machinery to recover from

*You should always expect to regain tokens—if not your own, then several predecessors'.

105

summoning Jerusalem. So when I finished, the thing actually began to ring, giving me a heady sensation of success. So heady that I forgot the Instructions, I'm afraid. A voice said something with "University" in it, I gave the name of Yaakov's department in English and then, as insurance, added "Professor Manor." There'd been, briefly, a puzzled sort of silence, but now came an "Ah, so" sound—I was on my way, clearly. And then, quite suddenly, I wasn't. It wasn't so much a click as an abrupt cessation of the breathing hum of contact, but it was unmistakable: one minute I'd been tuned in to the stream of life and the next minute I was dead. I stared numbly, still holding the receiver, and that's when (so to speak) the penny dropped: I hadn't hung up, but my token was gone from the little window. I'd failed to pay attention to my token, and this was what happened to you—no little warnings, either spoken or beeped. Just doom, utter and instant . . .

Well, I know the trick now—you put in four or five tokens, enough to fill the window, and keep more ready in your hand, all before you begin. Then you PAY ATTENTION, for the tokens will slide off to the right and out of sight, soundlessly, from the moment the connection is made. (That doesn't go for local calls, though. Which was why the man who used the phone before me hadn't had to watch *his* token.) Thus, if you're calling an institution, like a university or a hospital (heaven forfend, says my informant: *never* try to phone a hospital!), it can cost you four or five tokens just to get through the switchboard, especially if you don't know what extension you want. And we won't even *mention* the emotional tension: that silent slipping-away is awfully nerve-wracking.

But that's all wisdom I didn't acquire right away, of course. What happened immediately was that I put in *two* tokens and tried again. And what I got was a lady in Jerusalem who answered in Hebrew but quickly discovered the need for English. She rose to the occasion nobly: no, she wasn't Hebrew University, she reported, and in fact her number was—she gave it, stopping to think how to say each of the six digits in English, and a token slid away while she was working at it. I knew better than to leave a lone token in the "aperture," so I added another while she was asking me how long I'd been in The Land, and where I was speaking from. Beer-Sheva? Ah, then I must remember to dial 02 first, because that was the code for Jerusalem. I thanked her hastily, lest she tell me to pay attention: either I just happened to get for my wrong number the very author of the Instructions or else the Ministry of Communications really reflects the spirit of the people, because her handling-a-retarded-child manner exactly matched the tone of the official prose. (And

106

she was even better at giving me information that didn't quite fit—like, if I'd got her in Jerusalem from Beer-Sheva, you might think I already knew about the 02, right?) She was kind to me two tokens' worth—I regained the third one afterward—but at no time did we take up the curious question of how I'd managed to get connected with a number bearing so little relation to the one I'd dialed.

Still pondering the chances of my dialing four numerals wrongly out of six, and in such unlikely ways—e.g., you could read 8 for 3, or put your finger in the 5-hole rather than the 4; but how could you mix up, either digitally or visually, a 4 and a 9, a 1 and a 6?—I hung up and tried again. That time, I got two people speaking to each other in Hebrew (presumably in Jerusalem), neither of whom could hear me, apparently. After that was over, I found I was too low on ammunition to risk another sortie, so I had to retreat until I could bring up reinforcements. Which meant a trip to the Post Office, since I'd already had my quota from the mercaz klita's stock of tokens. And what *that* meant was another valuable orientation lesson, because I waited till after lunch—and thus, since it was a Wednesday, learned the importance to a well-organized life in Beer-Sheva of remembering that stores close on Tuesday afternoons and banks and the Post Office on Wednesday afternoons.* (That's in addition to Friday afternoons, when everything is closed.)

But every setback has its advantages: Yoshua's coffee bar is near the Post Office and he has a pay phone (not at all usual) and it was in working order (even less usual). So the next time, I didn't have to fight alone. He came out from behind the counter to help me, after tossing a remark to his ever-present coffee-sipping buddy—it was clearly a *Whaddya know about that?* comment on the fact that he, Yoshua, was actually about to traffic with Hebrew University. (Question: if I asked a man at a Nedick's in New York to help me phone Columbia University, would he also be thus half puffed-up, half amused?) He did it, though: it took him three tries, each time with the little window stuffed with tokens, but he finally got through the switchboard and to a department. Where, with an unmistakable air of *Hey look at me, I'm calling a perfessor!*, he asked for Professor Manor. And then, abruptly, Yoshua was all out of joy. *"Rock rega,"*† he said into the phone, and told me sadly, *"En*

---

*Not bad for a beginner, but actually it's only the Post Office *bank* that's closed on Wednesdays. So you couldn't pay your electric bill, but you could buy asimonim.
†"Rega" (pronounced REH-guh) is a second, so this is literally "only a second." But what it, and half a dozen common variations ("Rega, rega," everybody on the bus hollers when the door starts to close), all come down to is "wait a minute."

Anglais." He handed over the telephone as if it were a ceremonial mace: for a little while, he'd been the big hero man-in-charge but now his dark eyes were dull-black with defeat.

It wasn't fair, it really wasn't: so what if he couldn't speak English? Look at how he'd just flipped from one language to another without even stopping to think. Which was more than I could do, so it would have taken me awhile to find French to console the suddenly crumpled Yoshua in—and what if the English-speaker got tired of waiting and went away? I grabbed the phone.

I might as well have paused to be gracious. Because it was an *English* English-speaker, we were connected with the Sociology Department, and the British voice was a stranger there itself. He turned out to be a visiting scholar who'd answered because nobody else did and he was expecting a call; but he knew Yaakov, so when he heard the name he hung on. (It was the wrong department for a call *to* Yaakov, but maybe it was *from* him)? Now, though, there was nothing useful he could do, the visiting social scientist said regretfully, for he didn't know Yaakov's extension and he couldn't read the phone book on the secretary's desk, and there was nobody around to ask. . . Well, I was in Beer-Sheva, I explained while my hopes and another token dropped, and I'd had a terrible time getting the University at all ("Oh, I can imagine," said the sympathetic Briton in Jerusalem), so if he could just get the switchboard for me—? Sensing non-cooperation, I added quickly, "You simply jiggle the button a few times" and silently cursed my luck: I *would* run into one of those academics who make a point of coming on all unworldly.

I sure had the wrong number there. For he'd love to oblige, the genial voice told me warmly, but it just wasn't on, dear lady. One couldn't possibly get the operator, and even if one could, the odds were overwhelming that she'd give one the wrong department again. I hadn't been long in Israel, had I? His tone suggested that that was the kindlier assumption, and he didn't wait for an answer before he undertook briskly to give me a bit of advice, if I'd forgive him. Viz., that it was a waste of time to go bumbling about in the fastnesses of the University, the drill was to call Yaakov at home instead. He was in the book, and some helpful bod would surely look up the number for me . . . It was like one of those reception-line handshakes from the First Lady, moving you on while being gracious. I remembered then that he'd been waiting for a call when I got in his way, so I thanked him and moved on.

Yoshua didn't have a phone directory, and besides, the ability to *read* Hebrew—I've already discovered—doesn't necessarily accompany an ability to speak it, and this didn't seem the right moment to risk another defeat for Yoshua. So I thanked him too and moved on back to the mercaz klita (after ten minutes in line at the Post Office, to stock up on tokens again). I got back there in time to catch the office girls before they left, and one of them got out a very tattered phone book of small-town thickness and turned to the section for Jerusalem. Only, then came the next catch: how did you spell "Manor," she wanted to know. I had no idea how to spell it in Hebrew, of course, but I said confidently, "With a *mem*." (Like the first letter of "Maggie," which is how I could get confident.) Yes, the girl said patiently, but *mem* what? *Aleph? Ayin?* Neither, one of her colleagues suggested: maybe just *mem nuhn*, with nothing in between. . .

I waited humbly, wondering why, with only three possibilities to cover, they didn't just try one at a time.* But I was hardly in a position to get bossy about it, so I held my tongue. Except for trying to answer questions pursuant to the discussion, most of which I could neither fathom nor answer. Like, what country did my friends come from? (Now I think that maybe had something to do with how you Hebraicize your name.) And then, when that drew a blank, when had they come to The Land? (I suppose, since there were successive waves of immigration, that might provide a clue to their origins.) I didn't know that either, except that I was sure it wasn't any time recently. All I really knew, I said finally, was that he taught at Hebrew University and she was a scientist somewhere else. I'd met them in America, I added, meaning it by way of apology for my lack of helpful Israeli context for them. But it was perceived as more of an anthropological explanation, and a satisfying one—oh, in America, everybody said, nodding, understanding that in that strange cold land people didn't know anything important about each other.

Eventually, the conference adjourned with a concurrent resolution favoring trial-and-error in the phone book. And then at last they showed me the listing: Manor, Yaakov and Sara, I spelled out slowly. ("Manor" begins with just plain *mem nuhn*.) I asked whether listings of married couples always gave both names like that, and the girls looked astonished. Of course, what else? They were two people, weren't they? . . . Blushing for my male-chauvinist native land, I hastily copied down the phone number (not forgetting to precede it with 02, as three voices duly reminded me). I didn't want to have to go through all this again.

*The short answer is, because they're Israelis: if it's possible to discuss a thing, they will.

But I didn't use my hard-won information right then either, for I couldn't see myself trying to leave a message with a baby-sitter. So I held off the next venture till about 7 o'clock last night, when I figured they'd be home from work but probably not yet gone out for the evening. Then it was that, clutching my hoard of fifteen (!) tokens, I listened for the dialing tone, paid attention, remembered to begin with 02, and turned the dial *very* slowly. . . When Sara's voice sounded in my ear, as clear as if she were in the next room—ah, the wonders of modern technology!—I couldn't think of a thing to say after I'd managed a quavering "Sara? Is that you, Sara?" (because one should always check out a miracle). I mean, *What hath God wrought* has been done. But it was the only thing that occurred to me.

Sara must know lots of other women who pronounce her name Americanly, but I imagine none of them quaver. So she said "Maggie?" And *she* knew what to say next: "Where are you speaking from? Quickly, give me the number." That, it seems, is a routine Israeli precaution, since it's known that what God hath wrought can be precarious even if you obey all the Instructions. . .

I'm going to Jerusalem next Friday (which means it has to be an overnight visit, as there's no bus on Shabbat). I have crisp, efficient bus instructions—elaborate enough even for me—and when I arrive, I'm to call them from the bus station. The telephones are in sight of where you get off the bus, Sara said—and added helpfully (in view of my apparently somewhat distraught state) that it would be this number but *without* the 02, remember. . .

Ah well, at least it was a switch.

From the diary: 6
Two climates of the Middle East (March)

I woke this morning with a headache—but neither the up-front sinus kind nor the wallop of migraine—and a feeling that if I wasn't exactly sick, I was sure as hell ailing. Though in some new kind of way. The first explanation that occurred to me was the kerosene heater; but no, I hadn't forgotten and left it on all night. Besides, judging by what I've learned from reading newspaper stories ("Four Found Dead," the address always in a slum: in the U.S., kerosene stoves are definitely not part of any lavishness), the fact that I'd waked up at all disposed of that hunch.

High blood pressure, then? It was supposed to give you headaches. But high anything didn't fit, for when I first tried getting out of bed I discovered that someone had sneaked in in the night and untied all my muscle-strings. However, I decided as I stumbled around my cheder, my head didn't really pound and as headaches go, this one ranked well below a good-sized hangover. So finally I declared myself formally not-sick. What I felt was just "funny," and that vague description was as close as I could get. Defeated on all fronts, I dragged my oddly heavy body off to school.

Ruth was on her way from the parking lot to the office when I crossed over to Binyan Bet. "Boker tov," I said, too listless this morning to watch my accent. (Perhaps because for Americans "Good morning" has to sound crisp, boker tov always tends to come out very middle-western, with a sharp "r"—"BOH-kur." What the Israelis say is closer to "baw-care," and the whole intonation is softer and just not so brisk somehow.)

Ruth stopped and shifted her armful of envelopes out of the way so she could peer at me. "You look pale. Didn't you sleep well?"

"Like a top. Whatever that means." I couldn't remember anything unusual showing up in the mirror when I brushed my teeth; but it's quite a while since I last looked good in the mornings, so I don't really study the view. Now that I'd been reminded, though, my headache returned, sneaking across the top of my skull and down behind my eyes, which felt parboiled. "I woke up with a headache, that's all," I muttered through my stiff upper lip.

Ruth took another look and then said if I was sick, we could go over to the Kupat Cholim* clinic, which was right near by, and—

---

*The largest of the health-insurance plans. I didn't have to be a member because olim get free medical care for the first six months.

I wasn't sick, I interrupted: I didn't have a sore throat or any other coming-down-with-something symptoms. All I felt was just, well, funny... She eyed me with concern (and I thought rather oddly, too, but I wasn't paying that much attention to how she looked) and told me there was aspirin in the office and if I didn't feel better soon to let her know. Then she hurried on her way and I went to see whether coffee and a roll would help. Though the dining hall suddenly seemed very far away, almost too much trouble to be worth it... I feel as though I'm walking through water, I told myself—and promptly felt much better, since that at least was an improvement over "funny."

But having named the name didn't help much in class, where I seemed to be an even duller Hebrew scholar than usual. I wasn't walking through water, I was immobilized in thick air while new words, however conscientiously chanted, dropped soundlessly out of my mind the next second, and even words I'd thought I knew failed to come when I rang for them. That apparently made the teacher a bit cross, for she scowled a lot and sounded snippy. She'd seemed to me a rather attractive woman—thirty or a few years over, very well groomed and with a nice flair for colorful combinations of sweaters and scarves to ring changes on her tailored skirts—but now I thought uncharitably that I'd underestimated her age. And her face had a pinched, thin-lipped look and her hair seemed not only dyed but tired of it, and I didn't give a damn if she didn't like me...

At hafsaka (hoff-sah-KAH, an interval or intermission, in this case a mid-morning coffee break), I went to ask whether the mail had come yet—the thought having struck me that maybe nobody at home liked me anymore either, as it seemed a long time since I'd had a letter. When I set foot in the office, it was instantly clear that I was some kind of celebrity: heads turned, typewriters stopped, and This is the one was in the air. Fortunately, before I could respond with irritation (not to say paranoia), Ruth came out of the inner office. And all began to grow clear...

What it was all about was the chamsin (cham-SEEN),* which seems rather like the south-of-France mistral, at least in its effect on health and spirits. That is, it's a wind—something I find hard to credit, because winds are supposed to be cold, like the biting

---

*The Arabic word, and the one in constant use. The Hebrew word is shah-RAHV (which I didn't discover until I heard it on the radio) and the powers that be, ardent about Hebrew, would rather have you use it. Nobody does, perhaps because during chamsin nobody feels very obliging; perhaps, also, there's an unstated feeling that it's sort of pushy to re-name what's so obviously an institution.

"Montreal express" that torments Boston winters—coming more or less predictably at certain seasons (except that it can really come when it damn pleases: if it's not the "right" time, whom do you sue?) and doing something to the ions in the air. I can't remember whether it makes more or fewer of them happen, but I hear there's a machine that, for lots of lirot, will either add ions or take them away . . . Anyway, the chamsin gives you a headache, tightens your nerves, sours your temper, and makes everybody seem at least a little hateful. It also gives a lot of people that pinch-faced, drawn look I'd suddenly seen in my teacher. It was visible on the people in the office, too (though there's individual variation: that business of the hair lying down and looking like a nylon wig doesn't happen to everybody).

What made me news was that Ruth had seen The Look on me, but it's an accepted *"fact"* that newcomers are immune to the effects of chamsin. For at least the first go-round, you're supposed to be able to walk virginal and merry through the wretched few days (it usually blows itself out then, though of course there's no guarantee) while the Israelis are nursing their headaches and reminding themselves grimly that it's only in Arab countries, see, that people murder each other because of chamsin. Among the mercaz klita's employees, this given had really been tested: they'd all had experience with not-yelling at pain-free, nerveless olim who expected reasonable behavior. Thus when Ruth reported that, precedents notwithstanding, the American Maggie showed clear signs of being chamsin-struck, it was a real news flash. And naturally, one of those Israeli instant discussion groups started work on considering all the possibilities. Like, maybe Ruth had misread my symptoms, maybe I'd heard about chamsin and was reacting "psychologically," maybe I'd been in Israel before and had lost that initial immunity. (If I hadn't come into the office when I did, I'll bet new political parties would've begun forming.) Thus, when I showed up, drawn-faced and tense—yet still, it turned out under questioning, ignorant of the meteorological facts—and answered irritably that no, I'd never been in Israel before (and asked even more irritably whether somebody wasn't losing my mail), well, I can see why I caused quite a buzz. Even my ill-temper brought confirmation, and was received with the joy of finding a wonder in their midst.

And with that pathetic hunger to be joined that seems to crop up all the time. "You see, you're really an Israeli," a typist said, happily welcoming me into the common misery—and with not a smidgeon of regard for the fact that it doesn't really represent great pro-Israel propaganda. Even without the chamsin, that sort of *thing would set my teeth on edge, for it's like the Israelis' characteristic attempts to make everybody admirable "really" Jewish. And it always irritates me: can't they be satisfied with Einstein and half the world's best musicians, for God's sake?*

(Later, a post-chamsin day).

P.S. Well, it's true, what I wrote; but I don't feel right about it because it's excessively ill-natured, too. I mean, here you have a few besieged and beset people, just a leftover handful and their children, who are barely managing to hold on to a lousy little hunk of desert and strip of seacoast in the face of hordes of enemies—and of what's worse, the sneaky-snide behavior of plummy Christians who're themselves much too well-bred to launch a pogrom but don't mind when some slob does. The world has a way of making these people feel pretty rotten most of the time, and they certainly must be always aware of being few and insecure. So no wonder they grab at every "proof" that they're more numerous than they seem, that somebody else is somehow deep-down and mystically one of them.

What stirred up those second thoughts is, this morning we had songs in school. A young man from some kibbutz goes around, rather like the visiting music teacher when I was in third grade; accompanying himself on a guitar, he teaches ulpan students the songs they would have learned as children in Israel. These are not exactly folk songs in the pure sense, I guess, but more like the equivalent of "I've Been Working on the Railroad"—I don't think that's really a folk song, yet I never met an American who didn't know it.

There was a distinct sense of occasion, with the other "baby" class coming to our classroom for the event and a great preparatory bustle and scraping of added chairs and a formal exchange of "Boker tov"s for mo-RAH (teacher, fem.; masc., mo-REH) and tal-mi-DEEM (pupils). The minstrel in the plaid flannel shirt is not only engaging but experienced: he knows just how to pace himself for people struggling with the strange words of the songs. Our teacher would write the title and sometimes the first verse on the blackboard while the visitor sang it through once, then we'd follow as best we could from mimeographed little booklets. (The verses have to be written on the stencils by hand, because most of us can still read only script.* I can recognize a few of the printed letters,

---

*I don't know why they don't teach script and printing at once, like capital and lower-case letters in English—"aA, bB," etc. But even in Israeli first-grade classes, the two alphabets are taught separately, script first.

deduced from signs around town; but that's unreliable for learning purposes, as merchants like to get imaginative, with slanting or shaded lettering to confuse you.) Then we'd all repeat a line at a time, with a "review" every couple of lines. The songs are simple, for the most part, with a rhythmic repeated chorus. So even if you get lost, you can catch up when the next chorus comes around.

Most evident about all the songs, though, is that they're all about peace, and full of gentlenesses—though not "antiwar" because they're not anti anything, just wistful and hopeful. "Jerusalem of Gold," which I'd heard of as, in effect, the anthem of the Six-Day War (written by Naomi Shemer, it was a popular song in 1967 and thus was sung by the soldiers who retook Jerusalem), turned out to be not an anthem at all: I learned the word for "violin" in it, and that's not a word you're likely to acquire from a war song, right? (What it is, really, is a love song to Jerusalem, poetic and sensual—with very hard words—celebrating the coppery light and the special odors. "I am your violin," the instrument of your music, says the singer, addressing Jerusalem like a Cavalier poet to his mistress.) But then, the actual national anthem, "Hatikvah" (which we did not learn, by the way), is a gentle pastoral melody chosen for a new nation that wasn't planning on summoning anyone to combat. True, in twenty-five years it's been played over a lot of war dead. But the title means "the hope."

The song that got to me most was called "Ma-CHAR," which means "tomorrow." It's a pretty tune, swingy and melodic, and the words are less "poetic" and more truly poetic, if you see what I mean, than "Jerusalem of Gold."* Tomorrow, the song says, the soldiers can stay home and do all the things they'd rather have been doing today. (Exactly the way we young felt about being caught up in World War II—not particularly scared and certainly not exalted, just interrupted.) Tomorrow the air will be full of the sound of joyous bells, and the people will come out on their balconies to welcome peace. Tomorrow whatever has been broken or destroyed will be rebuilt, by our own hands, in our land . . . A very touching version of "There'll be pie in the sky, by and by," I said to myself, clinging to toughness. Until we got to the saving realism of the last line, and then I succumbed absolutely to what may be a uniquely Israeli blending of sentiment and clearsightedness. "Va eem lo machar, az machrotym" (And if not tomorrow, then the day after), it

---

*I'm told "Machar" is also by Naomi Shemer, who seems to be the Hoagy Carmichael of Israel. (I meant that in the sense that her songs become "classics." But now that I think of it, she also sings them with a similar engaging amateurishness.)

115

promises, cheerfully acknowledging an imperfect world with a shrug built into the line: you can hear it even if you don't understand Hebrew.

It's a campfire song, I'll bet. The two teachers, their faces soft with reminiscence, forgot to be morot *and just sang out, standing in front of the blackboard with their arms linked and swaying together like schoolgirls or bunkmates at summer camp. For a moment, we were forgotten by all "our adults"—the two women, one in her thirties and the other in her twenties, who have known wars and rumors of wars all their lives, and the young kibbutznik who must surely have been a soldier in at least one war. A stubborn crew who put not their trust in princes, or even tuneful promises, but* dahfke *trust . . .*

I've been remembering now the appalling array I once found in a newspaper library, where I was researching for an article, of sample pages from Arab elementary-school textbooks.* These were used in the refugee camps run by the UN—on my money!—and treated children six and seven years old to repeated cruel caricatures of the Jew (actually, most of the drawings markedly resembled the king of Saudi Arabia, which may be why they had to label the figures) who, they were being taught, lives only to kill, ravish, loot. With incredible thoroughness, these children's thinking is thus carefully poisoned at the source: they can't even learn to read without absorbing this stuff. And most of them—especially the girls, since educating women is still considered a bizarre notion in most Arab countries—will never get to learn more than these literacy-of-hate primers provide . . . When I can read enough Hebrew, I'll look at some Israeli primers;† but they can't possibly be anything like that, for both religious and political orthodoxies would oppose such hatemongering on principle. Besides, you can see the refutation on any street—where Arabs (and their language) are all over the place, casually going about their business.

*The Anti-Defamation League collects specimens and so, at one time, did the UN (certainly not a pro-Israel source!). In addition, some wives of American diplomats who served in Arab lands confirmed this for me. And it was a member of a church committee visiting the camps who first told me about it.

†I did, starting with borrowing a first-grade reader from a neighbor's child. The stories are all Dick-and-Janeish—Sara gets a present from Grandpa, Tamar and Nir sing a song that seems to be a Hebrew version of "Rain, rain, go away," and Rami and Dana sail a paper boat. The only "propaganda" in the book is a picture of Chaim Nachman Bialik (tsk, tsk, those people who couldn't recognize him on the 10-lira bill must have been daydreaming in first grade) who, the caption says, "loved little children and wrote beautiful poems for them." Which may or may not be true but apparently doesn't inspire great awe, for the owner of the book had undertaken to color Bialik orange—and did a sloppy job, too.

Well, shalom alenu (peace to us; the more frequently heard shalom alechem, which is also in the song, means peace to you-plural), I sang today, in a song with repeated lines and no hard words like "violin." Like Israeli kindergarteners, we clapped our hands to the rhythm and sang of peace—30 miles from the border with Jordan, 120 miles from the nearest Egyptian school teaching six-year-olds whom to hate. And I couldn't help it, all of a sudden my eyes were stinging with tears (I don't give a damn if it is a cliché, that's exactly what it feels like) for these pathetic, marvelous people. Maybe foolish people, too, it occurs to me now that the tears have stopped pricking: it could be called quixotic to teach your kids to value peace while, no farther away than from, say, Washington to Richmond, Va., their contemporaries are learning to value killing them. There's a legitimate argument there, and certainly an old one—the temptation to fight by outdoing the enemy at his own game is always lying around. But the Israelis don't buy it. And neither do I, I guess; though I'm not at all sure I wouldn't change my mind if I were they.

I'm not, though—my chamsin vulnerability notwithstanding—and the difference showed up at the song lesson this morning. Because I wept, but they didn't: they really believe, you see, in that lovely specific peace to come . . .

Oh, wouldn't it be something if, machar or machrotym, it turned out they know what they're singing about?

117

7 ⌐ The Huddle

I'm embarrassed about this now, but it's the truth, so you can go ahead and giggle: the first notion I had for a book about Israel was a kind of imitation of *Canterbury Tales*. For, the mercaz klita, at least while it was still not much of a reality, seemed a setup for choosing a dozen or so representative characters. Who, like Chaucer's, were wayfarers spending time together, weren't they? So . . .

Fortunately, though I may get some dumb ideas, I'm not really stupid. Thus it didn't take me long to discover that not even by the most determined metaphor-juggling could the Tabard Inn and the mercaz klita in Beer-Sheva be shoved into the same topological ball park. Not because of the scene: to the perverse—and who's more perverse than a writer with a pet notion?—opposites are no problem because they can be used to suggest each other. What made the idea a no-go was the characters: no matter how long I sifted batches of mercaz klita inhabitants, I'd never find a Wife of Bath. Because these people were traveling a road together on a common journey, all right; but what I'd failed to take into account was the separate inward, and very perilous, journeys going on at the same time.

For, like Chaucer's characters, the people I met had brought along their past lives and used them in interacting. But not one of them could have announced himself with anything like the assurance of, say, the Clerk of Oxenford, because whatever any of the immigrants had been, they had no way of knowing whether they could continue being it in the new land. Some, like the idealistic American couple Yehuda and Yael Artzi, didn't propose to continue the way they'd been going at all: born Bob and Sally in affluent Suburbia, those two had rejected their actual pasts in favor of what they considered their real heritage.* Others were more like Anita and Rafaelo, who'd come from Argentina out of a kind of practical idealism only lightly tied to ideology. They were not really Zionists, since they didn't believe all Jews should live in Israel—they had only decided that *they* should. (An attitude perhaps reflected in the fact that Rafaelo became Rafael, a respectable Hebrew name, after a while; but Anita, whose name would have needed rather more changing, remained Anita.) And among the Russian immigrants, there was a whole spectrum of expectations. The central one seemed to depend largely on whether they saw themselves as immigrants or refugees—a view that might vary with the mood of the moment.

But it's fair to say that nobody had any substantial supply of certainties. Unlike the pilgrims clip-clopping along the road to Canterbury, the people in the mercaz klita were navigating inexpertly in an element strange to them (which Yehuda acknowledged was true of him, too: he was quite aware that you don't make a thing happen simply by issuing a manifesto). Worried and confused, the only thing they could be sure of was who was along on the journey, the face or voice just behind or beside them as they were carried toward a destination that, when you came to think of it, was only said to be there. They huddled, trying not to think of it. Hoping that the winds and the currents would take them in the general direction of the shore—and that when they got close enough, somebody would have set out the promised buoy to keep them off the rocks. In short, as you may have deduced from my shift of metaphor, if there was a model for what I was seeing it was not *Canterbury Tales*. It was something much smaller and more ephemeral: *Lifeboat*. I recognized it as soon as I saw the huddle.

Of course, *Lifeboat* doesn't hold up perfectly either. But it fits in the sense that we were, like passengers on an ocean liner, random within the framework of a single initial selection—the loose "professional" category† that made us a group. But it didn't really:

---

*Their choice of a name makes their position clear: Yehuda Artzi means "Jew of my land" (i.e., The Land). I don't know why his wife picked Yael (which is a kind of gazelle), but such "nature names" are very frequent among Israelis in her age group.

†Admittedly, the majority would also have been classified as "professionals" by the U.S. Civil Service Commission. But it wasn't what you might call rigidly applied anyhow: we had a prospective farmer from Chile and a couple of tradesmen from Argentina; and some of the Russians' "professions" weren't the kind you go to college to learn.

an Argentine mining engineer and a Russian medico are not necessarily going to have much to talk about together even if you give them a common language. (I'm tempted to say that only in Israel would that need to be explained, but I don't want to be unfair: artificial people-lumping is a characteristic of Social-Think, an international phenomenon. But probably only in Israel would anybody *act* on such a notion and expect it to work without cops to enforce it. And then engage in an orgy of blame-assigning when it didn't.)*

If the planned "professional" tie didn't bind at the mercaz klita, neither, for the Americans, did national origin. Partly that was because people sensed that it shouldn't, that "absorption" meant *not* being guided by one's past. But the Americans were probably not numerous enough to constitute much of an ethnic group anyhow, and they'd also come at different times and were thus not usually in the same ulpan class or at the same stage of the absorption process. (Yehuda and Yael, for example, had already finished their Hebrew instruction; and so had Annabel, the divorcée in Cheder 39.) The local branch of the Association for Americans and Canadians in Israel had a committee that visited newcomers in the mercaz klita (my "welcome lady" brought me delicious brownies), and an AACI counselor tried to guide the bewildered through the bureaucratic maze that awaited them after "graduation." But once beyond the problem-solving point, the American connection tended to become pretty much limited to the usual manifestations of the expatriate condition, like borrowing books (you'd be amazed at what you'll read, so long as it's in English, when you're laid up with the flu). Few Americans in Beer-Sheva got chummy on the basis of nationality alone, though the acquaintance might begin that way: e.g., Martha was not the only fellow American in my ulpan class, but she's the only one I became friends with. And many Americans made a particular point of *not* hanging out with compatriots.

The group from Argentina, a much larger percentage of the mercaz klita population at the time, also had an expatriate organization (which took in many South American countries and thus, with a whole slew of national rules to hamper it, wasn't as effective as the AACI); it held occasional parties and organized bus trips with a Spanish-speaking guide. But the Argentines also tended to locate

*These hullabaloos eventually change things, though: e.g., later batches of Americans at the mercaz klita had known each other back home or were headed for a common destination. And the Social-Think policy of assigning housing according to a "mix" of national origins was also at least eroded. (No policy was actually *supplanted* by the Labour government. It just got nudged, in greater or lesser degree but not completely out.)

120

themselves less by nationality than by empathy. At the mercaz klita, they chattered in Spanish, of course, and some of them did some coffee-and-cake visiting in each other's cheders*; but if you looked closely, you could see that those were the ones who would probably have visited each other in Argentina too. And even though they all tended to be at the same stage of Hebrew-learning, what formed the friendships was still the huddle: people might have a language in common and a Hebrew-homework headache in common, but what brought them together was the particular fears and longings they had in common. And that had most to do with the kinds of people, not nationals, they were.

But the premise there is of course an ability to manage some kind of communication. That problem kept the Russians in a strictly-Russian huddle, usually—and not only because of language. For it was really remarkable how little language in common you needed if you had empathy to begin with—plus, I guess, intelligence and/or perception (what I mean is a kind of quickness, a mental agility and resourcefulness: I know it when I see it and so would you, but I don't know the word for it). A natural talent for languages is more like an ear for music than anything to do with learning ability—I always got high grades in school language courses, but I don't have the gift—and of course is a great advantage. But probably most important is whatever it takes to be unafraid of making a fool of yourself. Character, personality, maturity, past luck,+ and a whole mess of other factors all have a part in getting you over that hump of fear, so I didn't even try to figure out which lack explained the Russians' on-the-whole smaller ability to surmount it.

But at least one reason, I came to see after a while, was societal: in the Soviet Union, intellectual status is such a life-and-death matter that one simply can't take risks. (Actually, you can see a similar fearfulness in the West, in the loftier reaches of the oldest and stuffiest Academes. But there, it's by choice.) Their closed, narrow-focus society also meant a pretty complete lack of reference points in the non-Soviet world. Imagine, for example, how it would be if you tried to make friends with someone who'd never been out

---

*The plural of cheder is chadarim. But I typed it the way I talk, and then decided to leave it alone because it gives you a better view of the tolerance (and sometimes ingenuity) required of my Israeli friends.

+E.g., my own liberating experience of having dared in the past and suffered no traumas. For when I tried out my skills in Washington it was usually in party situations—people felt benign, perhaps flattered that I'd try to speak their language when I didn't have to, and generally inclined to think my goofs cute. Thus, though I'm still untalented, I'm also still un-timid.

of the Tennessee hills, didn't know anyone else who ever had, and had no access to radio or TV. You might interview him and learn local history and weather wisdom (and maybe some folk songs), but even with the advantage of a common language, what you'd get wouldn't be dialogue but instruction. Which was really what most talk with Russians, even when it could be managed, amounted to.

When I try to think what there was between me and the Argentine couple Anita and Rafaelo that made friendship possible without either English or Spanish, I arrive at some of what I was talking about above. Like, some sort of minimal language bridge (Anita's Yiddish to my German, or my high-school Latin hastily "converted" to what I'd hope was a Spanish word: both very rickety bridges indeed!), plus the social self-confidence that permits daring. But what may be the real key was simply that the same sort of thing seemed to strike us funny—maybe that *is* a common language?— which just leads back to the combination of personality and a comprehensible society.

I met Anita and Rafaelo via my ulpan class, though at the beginning I sat between Martha and another young American woman in a first-row huddle of our very own. During the first week, we had all learned to say things like where we lived and what our profession was. The method was practical: the teacher spoke Hebrew to you from the very first day, so you not only acquired minimal vocabulary but also began deducing some principles. Like, if she used *"At"* (that's a broad "a," remember: aht) to talk to me and *"At-TAH"* to the man behind me, by the time she'd spoken to each of the dozen members of the class everybody knew the masculine and feminine for "you." The same process extended to whatever verb went with it—e.g., if she asked me *"At gara b'mercaz klita?"* and him *"At-ta gar b'mercaz klita?"* it was obvious which was the feminine form of the verb. (The meaning of the verb was established by pointing out differences leading to easy deductions. *"Ani,"* the teacher would say—pointing to herself so you knew that was "I"—*"lo gara b'mercaz klita. Ani lo lomedet. At lomedet. At-ta lomed. Ani melamedet . . ."* Thus, though limited to the present tense and to unsubtleties, we could deduce "live," "learn," and "teach.")

So far, so good. But when we reached sophistications like "Where are you from?" I got into trouble. By the time she'd been around the class at least once, I could recognize *"Mi-EYN at?"* (or at-ta) all right; and if I'd been allowed to answer *"Ani mi America,"* all would have been dandy. But no, she had to get fancy: you weren't allowed to say "America" (which in fact all the Israelis use), you had to say *Artzoat Habrit,* which is "United States." Now normally, I'm quite a fusspot—both by nature and as a result of my years in Washington—but becoming an illiterate changes you. So, as a new convert to simplicity, I may have been engaged in an unconscious rebellion that set up a mental block; but whatever the reason, I simply couldn't retain *"Artzoat Habrit."*

Lacking any natural gift, I needed lots of repetition to learn. So I'd managed fine with the announcement *"Ani gar(a) b'mercaz klita,"* heard over and over. But there just weren't many Americans in the class and most of them couldn't manage you-know-what either (Martha could, but she had an Israeli husband),* so my ear was deprived. And finally, there was the fatal fact that though everybody says "Roosiah," the Russians were having to learn *"Brit Hamoazoat."* (Soviet Union, United States—you can see why the similarity; but when you're going by ear alone, it makes your head swim.) And the majority of the class was irrelevantly Argentine, with a few extra oddments like a woman from Tunisia. Thus, if I did catch one correct *Artzoat Habrit*, a slew of *"Ani mi Argentina"*s would get in the way while I was trying to hang on to it; and the odds were, a few Russians would also crop up before the finger pointed to me. Sitting next to Martha, so I could hear the magic words at the penultimate moment, might have solved my problem. But the teacher foxed me by skipping around the class instead of taking us in order.

Thus, even when we'd progressed to giving whole little "autobiographies" and I was able to inform the class that I was a widow (al-man-AH) and a novelist (so-FERR-et) and how many children I had and even what city I came from, I still couldn't say which nation had supplied this boon to Israel. Until one day I realized that I didn't have to, by golly: the teacher, who was determined to speak nothing but Hebrew (though she could speak English just fine, I'd discovered after class), could be hoist on that petard. And she deserved to be—skipping around that way and ruining my chances! So one morning, when the smile and the dread question *"Mi-eyn at?"* arrived at me, I answered smoothly, *"Ani mi Argentina."* There. Let her argue, if she dared.

She didn't try: she just broke up, as did the class, which by that time had had experience with my *Artzoat Habrit* struggles. And during the coffee break soon after, the dumpy little Argentine woman with the tall red-haired husband—I'd seen them sitting in

---

*That's Avi, and I wouldn't put it past him to have rehearsed her every morning at breakfast—she probably repeated it all the way over to school on the bus. Martha was one of the very few day students in the class and thus got to say *Ani lo gara b'mercaz klita*. But the teacher made her say where she did *gara*, so she had an extra sentence to learn.

the back row, but we'd never tried to talk—came up to me and said, grinning, *"Ani mi Artzoat Habrit"*—pronouncing the bugaboo words carefully. I recognized it as communication in addition to an attempt to be helpful, and I'm usually pretty good as a mimic, so I responded with a nice sample of the autobiographical information I'd heard Rafaelo give in class. (It's amazing how much Hebrew I can remember, so long as it's not *useful* . . .) Thus, with a mutual giggle and by wielding our limited mutual language, did the slow business of friendship begin. What it went on with was that slim Yiddish-German connection I mentioned, and an ability on both sides to recognize some bit of "modified" or pseudo-language. And doubtless experience at playing charades helped: Anita's transmissions were particularly ingenious, and she'd have been great to play with in a parlor game. Rafaelo's specialty was literature—he'd read a lot of English literature in translation (a hell of a lot more than I'd read in Spanish lit, I'm ashamed to say, though it's my trade and not his)—and you have no idea how useful fictional characters are as an international language. It works like algebra, I guess, through the use of symbols: whatever language you've read Shakespeare in, Iago is the deepest-dyed of villains and "Falstaff the fool confronts forever the prig Prince Hal."* And what literature is most likely to help with is gossip, which is also likely to be something people who find the same things funny and live in a mercaz klita will want to communicate.

I think the best illustration of our grab-a-word-from-anywhere form of speech is what happened some time later, one evening when a mouse ran across the floor of my cheder. I did what came naturally: I screeched like hell and ran for help. Rafaelo answered their door and, though he probably couldn't be sure whether it was a mouse or a rat I was gibbering† about, he grasped the problem, turned me over to Mama to be restrung, and went off to give the whatever-it-was its quietus. Anita, product of a culture in which no woman had to feel ashamed of being afraid of a mouse, was a great comfort. So I did get persuaded that the menfolk would handle things while I huddled in Anita's kitchen being plied with coffee and *There, there*—but as soon as I felt better, logic emerged and took away all the comfiness. Because it occurred to me that

*Wonderful line, isn't it? It's W. H. Auden, but I'm sorry I don't remember where.
†If I'd had the sense to gibber in English, the Yiddish-speaking Anita, would have understood because it's *Maus* in German—which I could've figured out by way of *Fledermaus*. The Hebrew word, by the way, is ach-BAR. Rolled out properly, it sounds more like a lion, doesn't it? (Happily, I've never had to use it again, except metaphorically.)

where there'd been one mouse, there were likely to be others, right? (Alas, with me logic lasts only long enough to grease the skids to imagination—immediately, hordes of mice were scampering over my face while I slept. Et cetera.)

So I surely needed more consolation, but how say what was bothering me now? Inspiration came: *"Oolye yesh mishpacha"* ("Perhaps there is a family"—mish-pa-CHAH turns up regularly in class), I suggested piteously. Well, Anita the comforter also had a handy supply of words heard during those oral autobiographies in class. *"Lo, lo,"* she soothed, her heart full of compassion. *"Hoo lo nissooi"* ("He's not married").

I have to admit we didn't do much for women's lib, because we were still laughing when Rafaelo came back to escort me to my mouse-free home. And from the look on his face, it was clear we'd reinforced his conviction that even when you remove the mouse, the women will still work themselves into hysteria. Ah well, you can't win 'em all . . . But you see what I mean by ingenuity? This kind of communication depends on snatching up anything lying around on your mental shelves that may apply, and of course its efficiency is bound to increase, for the better you know the other person the easier it is to know what applies. (Maybe the reason it tickles me so is that it's really a form of poetry—making metaphors, talking of something as if it were something else, stirring up multiple resonances from a single word?) Like *"Andiamo!"*—which I decided one day was probably close enough to Spanish to transmit "Let's go!"; but even if it wasn't, Anita and Rafaelo had also seen how when somebody in an opera sings that out, the chorus wheels and makes for the wings—or a bit of dialogue from one of those old foreign movies ("English subtitles by Herman Weinstein," it said for years and years—what ever happened to Herman, does anybody know?).

Well, I hope I've made it credible because it's true: in this mishmash of pidgin Hebrew and odd tags from one or another language we didn't quite have in common, Anita and Rafaelo and I covered such subjects as child-raising techniques in Argentina and the U.S.; American politics (easier than you might think, because *Time*'s Spanish edition at least provides mutual familiarity with names); interior decoration; diets (Anita was always trying to lose weight); and whether that Russian couple in Binyan Bet had really phfft. Once, I remember, we even got into the classic philosophic wrangle over free will vs. predestination. And I ask you, leaving aside things like a local bond issue (we had our equivalent of that, though, in rumors about the administration of the mercaz klita), how different is that from your Saturday night with a friendly neighbor couple?

But the real news I bring you is not about how widely we ranged but how deeply. Because something lovely and exhilarating and altogether marvelous happens to people when they reach-reach-reach with all their might, standing on their tippest tiptoes and straining across the chasm of no-speech, *willing* each other to understand. Most of the time it's such fun, too: finding something that even looked as though it might work, I'd toss it out and hope Anita could field it; similarly, she'd drag out some half-remembered *Time*-ologism, give it a little twist to render it relevant, and send it bumping along (*Time*, you see, would have to be a grounder) in the hope that I'd manage to scoop it up. And when she did, or I did, we'd look at each other with the purest delight and love, like victorious comrades in arms.

We didn't win them all, of course. Sometimes we had to wait for reinforcements: Anita and Rafaelo's daughter Susanna,* who was about nineteen, had been given private English lessons (this is apparently typical for the upper bourgeoisie—or maybe just the Jewish sector of it?—in the society they came from). She was a bright girl and probably talented besides, so she spoke English thoroughly and seemed able to translate in and out of Spanish effortlessly. Thus whatever seemed important and unyielding would get saved for the weekend, when Susanna came from the *nachal* where she was doing her army duty. (A NAH-chal is a frontier settlement staffed by chyellim and chyellot who guard the border while learning agricultural skills. It's a form of military service many young Israelis choose, as quite a few of them dislike the necessity of learning the arts of war and prefer to feel they're doing something affirmative too. But a nachal isn't for the soft or faint of heart—it's very, very tough duty.) Susanna was beautiful, really beautiful, with delicate features and a wealth of wavy hair of the auburn color dyes try for and miss, and she was a very nice girl too, sweet and kind and merry. So she would sit there over the coffee and cakes and alternately *"Dile a Maggie"* in English and "Tell Mama" (or Papa) in Spanish whatever it was us old folks simply hadn't been able to manage. Then, after the little table had been cleared and the Hebrew books set out, she'd help everybody with the homework, too.†

---

*Both "s"s are sibilant, so the Spanish Susanna is much softer than our buzzing Susan.

†And, it should be acknowledged, provide the necessary vocabulary for some of the more interesting adventures of my epic, *Swingin' Yehuda* (see "Diary 7: The busted dood").

Scenes like that are pretty typical in Israel, where the children, who pick up Hebrew quickly in school and at play, do interpreter duty for their immigrant parents. But the case of Anita and Rafaelo was even more-so, for they'd sent their two older children to Israel more than a year before, to stay on a kibbutz. If Susanna and Ricardo were happy there, then Mama and Papa and thirteen-year-old Miri would come for good, was the idea. An intelligent one, for the children were the key consideration: Rafaelo told me he and Anita were not dissatisfied with their lives in a pleasant and civilized small city; but the wild inflation threatened any concept of a future, and the increasing political turbulence made even sending your children off to college insupportably risky. So they decided to get the kids out of there before it was too late. (Which, even in 1973, it almost was: while they were en route to Israel, the money they were bringing—from the sale of their house, car, etc.—was abruptly devalued, so they arrived with their resources cut just about in half. And then, back in Argentina, political assassination became so commonplace and so capricious that it was quite accurate to say Ricardo was physically safer as an Israeli soldier than he would've been as a university student in Buenos Aires.)

Thus Susanna and her brother, who attended a boys' boarding school up north and also came home for most weekends, were actually less children of immigrants than Israelis welcoming immigrants. (Though Ricardo, who hadn't profited that much from those English lessons back in Argentina, didn't do much interpreter duty.) Susanna lived a Hebrew-speaking, Zionist-pioneer life; i.e., a little group of brave and energetic young, tilling their fields and guarding them.* So, except for her looks—the fair skin tanned but not yet dejuiced by the harsh desert life—and her manners, which were still Spanish-Jewish-bourgeoisie (than which there may be no combination more mannerly), she had become entirely an Israeli. Which meant, to us inhabitants of the mercaz klita, a person full of special knowledges and arcane information we couldn't hope to learn in detail yet, but maybe the general idea could be explained to us . . .?

Now that I've had time to look back, I know what the scene in the kitchen—the young girl patiently explaining, the elders throbbing with questions—reminded me of: it was the day in August 1945 when the newspapers abruptly burst into headlines about a place called Hiroshima. And all over America, people dragged in their high-school-physics-student sons and daughters—if you didn't have one, you went to a neighbor who did—sat the kid down, and

*About a year later, Susanna married a fellow soldier. And, last I heard, they had become one of the founding families of a new kibbutz in the desert.

127

demanded to know *What's all this about this here nuclear fission?*
The resemblance has something to do with a dawning new age,
maybe. (Not the most warming notion, that, considering the gap
between our visions of the Atomic Age—with wars ended by the
instinct for self-preservation, and all that cheap energy we'd have,
we could feed the whole world—and what's happened in it so far.)
But our new age was full of old roles. I kept recognizing that,
sometimes with a start. Like when, describing my daily life in a
letter, I said I still had no hair dryer but could usually borrow one
from— And there I halted, shaken by the knowledge that I'd been
about to write "from a girl down the hall" though the lender was in
fact a married woman with teen-aged children. There were other
clues (e.g., my total lack of interest in cooking, though other women
made all sorts of ingenious snacks, etc.), but that one was unmistakable—I was playing dorm, enjoying a kind of grad-student existence as an adult but with few adult responsibilities.

Well, I don't suppose it hurt, for a while: I'd been somebody's
mother for more than half my life then, and maybe I was entitled to
a little rest. But it's also perhaps just as well that I got shoved out of
the role, and more or less back where I belonged, by the later arrival
among us of Rob—who'd been a grad student quite recently and was
far more entitled to the role. What happened was, he was in need of
what I happened to be able to supply. And the first "rule" of the
huddle was, when you're needed you go.

Strictly speaking, Rob shouldn't have been in the lifeboat
with us, for he came equipped with everything the mercaz klita was
supposed to arrange. He had a job—complete with rank, salary,
subsidies, fringe benefits, and assorted courtesies and emoluments
—at the University in town; it was new and still expanding, and an
American Ph.D. who could be acquired without all the additional
costs represented by a wife and children was a real prestige
bargain. So it wasn't the Jewish Agency conveyor belt but a university functionary who brought Rob to the mercaz klita. And he
didn't even need the cicerone to talk Hebrew for him, because he'd
supplied himself with four years' study—the scholarly way, via
grammars, as well as with cassettes—and his Hebrew was thus
already beyond the level of our most advanced ulpan class. That
wasn't the only way Rob had taken thought and made preparation,
either: he'd bought a stove, a refrigerator, and all the other household amenities the acquisition of which provides us less fore-
handed types, who have to buy them in Israel, with marvelous
lessons in empirical Hebrew (spoken through gnashed teeth). In
short, Rob was just about as far as you could get on the other end of

the immigrant spectrum from my own muddled, impromptu jump-off into space.

So Rob's stay at the mercaz klita was really a form of "storage"—of a valuable commodity belonging to the university—until his shipment of household goods came (by sea, which takes two to three months); after that, the university would find him (and subsidize) a place to live. But in the meantime he had a lot of preparatory work to do—except for a department chairman who'd come down once a week from Hebrew University, Rob was the sole local representative of his rather abstruse academic specialty—and living at the mercaz klita would not only leave him free to do it, it would also oil up, by daily use, his perhaps too-correct Hebrew. Or so went the tortuous logic of people-planning. And you know what always happens to *that*: Rob was assigned to a cheder near mine, and almost from the first moment I encountered him on the gallery and offered to show him the way to the dining hall, the language he got daily-use practice in was English. Because Rob, for all his princeling status, was in the lifeboat, too. And what he appeared to need (as Ruth may have perceived, hence his room assignment) was a mother.

Not literally, of course, but he did come on that way—he was actually twenty-nine, but he seemed of indeterminate university-student age.* And most of all, he was a very experienced, almost professional, baby. Everyone enters a strange situation wearing some kind of armor, and his (clearly not new, and polished to a high sheen) was obvious weakness, a kind of ducked-head, terribly vulnerable look that said *Maybe I'm not supposed to be here?* What it called for in response was *Sure you are, sonny. Come right in*—and in any group of his elders (and his contemporaries, too, so long as he stuck to college campuses in the era of passionate emphasis on gentleness and sensitivity), it probably always worked . . . It worked here, too, for when I first led him into the dining hall, everybody immediately assumed he was my son. That figured, since I was known to have a student son and here was an American youth who'd turned up in the middle of an ulpan term, like a visitor from outside. That impression got corrected, of course. But it also partly prevailed because, given Rob's and my ages and personalities, into a sort of filial-ness was the only way a relationship between us could go.†

*Not really a con—he just thought of himself as A Student, and so everything about him *stamm* went with it.
†Odd couples happen, but not this kind to me: my hang-ups and character flaws all go the other, you-big-Tarzan, me-little-Jane way. Not only do I have no history of angel-of-mercy love affairs, but I used to feel betrayed and defrauded by a husband who had a cold in the head and thus rocked his hero image . . .

Given the imbalance of need—Rob had come looking for mothering, whereas, whatever I might be looking for, an extra son wasn't part of it—*my* concept of a son dominated. Which, since it was clearly much tougher than he was accustomed to, probably did him good.

For me, though, having Rob in the picture made two major practical differences. The first was that from then on if I wanted to match observations or discuss my reaction to an experience, I could do it not only in English but in my own language. For Rob had *both* come out of a world I knew *and* would be living like me (i.e., a "single" in a milieu of families) in the new one: Americans I'd met fit one or the other category but not both . . . And the second was that, with Rob around, my communications facilities took what you might call a quantum leap. Because he'd done, at some point, his characteristic intensive thing with the Russian language. (For no real reason, only that he simply wasn't your smattering type: people like Rob can't pick up a dictionary without reading the whole thing and a grammar too.) He'd developed a great fondness for it—and he persuaded me too, it *is* a pretty-sounding language—and thus he loved to speak Russian whenever he could. Which gave me, for the first time, a hope of learning what the Russian olim around me were really like.

It seems so odd, though—not to say coldhearted—to describe the relations between people so bluntly in terms of needs to be filled; I don't feel happy about letting it stand that way. And yet, that's what I was talking about, the shoal on which my *Canterbury Tales* idea foundered: nobody would do as a pilgrim because everybody was needy but the needs were met by other humans, not supernatural interventions. These relations could *contain* ordinary friendships: if Anita and I had inhabited the same town, in either her geography or mine, I think we probably would have become friends anyway. But still, there was a difference. If I look at it as if reviewing a novel, I guess I'd say the difference came of the situation having as much weight as the characters, whereas in ordinary friendships situation is an originating but minor factor. And certainly the heightened intimacy produced by that language-stretching exhilaration was a special function of the situation. But it was more than a matter of speeding up a relation based on liking; there was always something else, sort of alongside.

I think it must have come from the fact that nobody could feel certain or safe, but I don't know the name of it. I saw it most clearly, though, one day when I was feeling ill and decided to skip the midday dinner. I was standing at my bathroom sink when I saw Anita reflected in the tilted-open window: she was hurrying along the gallery, carrying a covered plate—and she was a virtual echo of a day in Massachusetts when, just out of hospital, I was looking from an upstairs window and saw my friend Janice arriving bringing me a casserole. Physical detail was different, but you would've painted the figure much the same—the hurrying woman, carrying the covered dish, come to tempt the invalid. Only, Janice had been wearing the abstracted, sort of somber look characteristic of people glimpsed alone and unaware of observation; but as Anita drew closer I saw that she looked, unmistakably, scared.

I think that's the difference, though there are all sorts of possible side explanations, of course. Like, Janice knew what was the matter with me and what would make me better, whereas Anita not only didn't have information, she probably had misinformation—"news" was disseminated in the anxious mercaz klita society at a speed that would dazzle CBS, and it was always imaginative besides, so who knows what the grapevine had decided was ailing me? And then there's the temperamental variation, too: Janice is an American, Anita a Latin, and to be unflappable is a quality encouraged by only one of those cultures.

But even when I've allowed for those and other variations, I'm still left with an extra dimension on one side. For Janice brought the casserole because she was kind, whereas Anita was not only kind but *threatened*. In a way I've seen in myself too, since then, for it's strongest in the mercaz klita but it seems to inhabit life in Beer-Sheva generally—somehow, alongside the concern for friends' adversities and the normal social nag at the back of your mind about So-and-so who's sick or moving or in some other crisis and you really should go, there's an extra obligation like a volunteer fireman's. If a member of the huddle is in trouble, you drop what you're doing and go: even if you can't do anything, you belong there, joining in the worrying. Thus, if Janice's husband were out of a job, I'd be concerned and try to help if I could. But when, at one point, the job-finders were having difficulty getting something set up for Rafaelo, I was frantic—in almost the same way he and Anita were. Which is not to say that friendships elsewhere were not precious and also sometimes intense, but there is a difference between being one of a group of boats bobbing in the same anchorage and being *in* the same boat: a threat to the viability of Janice's household couldn't have the same fear-force for me as a threat to Anita's. Because we immigrants in Beer-Sheva had individually varying abilities to survive if the wind rose and the seas grew heavy, but the best way, really the only likely way, was for all of us to make it together.

And for that, every hand was needed and had to be kept in

good shape—even if its chief contribution at the moment seemed to be doing comic turns for low-morale moments. (But let's not knock it: my imitation of Avraham, the mercaz klita's administrator of nuts and bolts, was good enough for the regular Bar Mitzvah and wedding circuit, if I do say so myself.) So it wasn't a matter of too-bad-about-Maggie but of too-bad-about-Us. See?

From the diary: 7
The busted dood

My dood is broken. I could call it a crisis of the first water (if, that is, I allowed that kind of low joke into this high-class notebook), but I also have to admit this episode has produced a great picture of Israel that any observer should consider a piece of real luck. And I do, I do. But, well—I'm not only a writer, I'm a bather too. And to give up hot water for my art . . .

Frankly, though, it wouldn't have been a crisis if I hadn't been a procrastinator. Because a little voice has been telling me something must be wrong—like, a persistent drip long after the last effects of a shower should have dried up—but I refused to call a little extra dripping in that bathroom an emergency. So I waffled, finding reasons for inaction. (N.B.—Could this be beginning of absorption into the anything-to-avoid-trouble local culture?) Then came the morning when it was all of a sudden crunch-time: water was spilling over the rim of the white enamel soup-plate-like thing attached to the bottom of the dood—and that couldn't possibly be condensation because in fact the shower the night before had been noticeably tepid. So, as I dressed and got ready for school, I knew I'd have to Do Something. And finally, peering in from the bathroom doorway on my way out, it struck me that all those gallons (no, litres) of water are suspended upside down there—and if the drip turned into something less restrained while I was out . . . Convinced of emergency at last, I grabbed my Hebrew reader and fled.

Luckily, I didn't get a chance to waver. For, lounging at the foot of Binyan Aleph's main staircase, apparently doing nothing but taking the sun (which, at 7:30 A.M., you can still take), was Moshe (Moe-SHEH). He's a burly overalled fellow seen around—usually accompanied by a skinny lad who carries the toolbox—fixing this and that in one of the flats. And running into Moshe was a great stroke of luck because, if I had to tell my tale at the office instead, I'd probably be referred to Avraham, an uptight meanie who doesn't like Americans or women (and for all I know he has a real mad on at writers, too). But in the general psyching-out of the mercaz klita staff, Moshe is rated as a nice guy—not too energetic, and lacking English, but an engaging figure, big and clumsy-looking, like Yogi Bear. Since he's never trammeled by any Puritan work ethic, he always has time to give you a big grin and a cheerful Shalom as you go by in your odd American hurry.

This time, I didn't stop with a "Shalom, Moshe" in return but begged him to wait a minute, bevakasha *(beh-vock-a-SHAH, "please").** *Perhaps because he was charmed by the notion of anybody thinking he might be going anywhere, Moshe inclined his head politely. Then he waited, his ripe-olive eyes speculating— mildly, of course—on some abstract question like* Would you say this was a handsome woman or wouldn't you? *(Don't sneer, Maggie: it beats* I wonder how much her shoes cost, *which is the question you usually stir up in Beer-Sheva.) I proceeded to identify myself as Maggie—except for formal occasions (which I've experienced so far only while visiting in Jerusalem), nobody ever seems to have a last name—from Cheder Arba-ihm. Moshe nodded and pronounced, "Amerreekah," looking happy to know both me and the word.*

The situation, I considered, simply couldn't be more en-couraging. So I began, "Ha dood sheli" (my dood—fortunately that ha *is the same for all genders, as who knows what gender the damn dood is?). But then I stuck there, because my vocabulary depends largely on the activities of Yo-SEF, the hero of our reader. Yosef gets up in the morning and washes and shaves and drinks coffee and eats breakfast—each at a specified time, so we can learn quarter-hours. But, rather oddly considering how many things in Israel get broken, Yosef lives in a world of perfect repair. (Hmm. This is a case for the next episode of "Swingin' Yehuda"!†)*

"Ken?" Moshe gave his "Yes" a you-don't-say inflection. He tried a bit of Hebrew but drew a blank, so he went back to ken, *this time as yes-yes-go-on.*

Well, who needs "broken" anyway—it's the symptoms that count, right? "Ma-im," I began. Confidently, because Yosef uses lots of water. (The word is pronounced more like "mime," but I'm going to insist on spelling it so as to show it's plural: ma-im *and* shameyim, *sky, have no singular, though nobody knows why. I could hazard a guess—can they be hangovers from a pre-One-God-era?—but it wouldn't be tactful to suggest that in Israel.)*

*Well, yes, but you'd only pronounce it all-out that way, usually, if you intended irony. It's generally compressed to 'Vak'sha.
†The underground saga "Swingin' Yehuda" (in Hebrew, it becomes Svingin, which is pretty swinging) is designed to counter the dull adventures of Yosef; it appears in serial form, and is awaited by my classmates with an avidity that makes me feel like Dickens. Svingin Yehuda gets up not at 6 but at 10, and doesn't take the OH-toe-boos to work; what's more, he specifically doesn't wash or shave before he strolls into town to the coffeehouse. He also doesn't have a wife: Yosef's Chana, who lives only to supply us all with the feminine form of wash, dress, drink, etc., is just a bit too much like one of those Dickens heroines . . . The adventures of Svingin Yehuda are about to terminate, since I'm doing so much homework that I might as well just do my homework. But he may represent the high point of my literary career, for I'll never again have such devoted fans.

134

"Ken," said Moshe. Meaning, I think, don't go on. Perhaps sensing that this could lead to labor, he didn't sound interested in hearing more.

And maybe I couldn't give him any more, for the exemplary Yosef drinks water and washes in it but it never falls on him. However, Moshe looked Moroccan, and the French word is easy . . . "Ma-im descend," I announced. And in case he didn't know how water descended, I raised my arm and brought it down slowly, wiggling my fingers all the way. ("Rain!" any charades player—except maybe in the Negev—would have shouted at once.)

Moshe just stood there, viewing the performance and comprehending (I think) but definitely fighting it. I needed a punchline that, if it perhaps couldn't be expected to stir him to action, would at least raise my news to bulletin level. I prospected for a word, couldn't find either Hebrew or French, and then that grab-any-language mechanism clicked on. "Ma-im descend," I said, and finished dramatically, "Kaput!" It was unlikely that Moshe spoke German, but maybe kaput had reached international status?

Apparently it had: my dood was "lo kaput," he assured me promptly. And with ill-concealed scorn: (Women! All her dood needs is a good smack. Or at most, a turn of a screwdriver). But our tête-à-tête had moved him, huzzah: he levered his bulk away from the wall he was leaning against. And he even grinned at me with affection, which was the last thing I'd expected. But I understand it—I had made him a polyglot. Hebrew and French (and probably Arabic) were a habitual mixture and so didn't count; but a man who could say "kaput"—he rolled it on his tongue with delight and pride—as well as "Amerreekah" was a sophisticate indeed. He beamed upon me gratefully.

A week later. The dood got certified kaput promptly—Moshe went up to my cheder (the very same day!) and turned off the electricity for the dood. Apparently it's on its own fuse, for all the lights still go on except that little red one. I've been taking sponge baths with potsful of water heated on the stove, supplemented now by a deal to allow me occasional showers next door at Cheder 41. This may cause some official eyebrows to lift, since two men live there.* But it isn't fair to bother Cheder 39, where the two women and two children keep the shower pretty busy and there's always a bucket of

*It caused considerably less than it would have in Massachusetts. To the gung-ho Zionist types on the staff (Ruth is only a mild example, possibly because you have to come from eastern Europe to be the real thing), liberated (hetero-) sexual behavior is ideologically fitting; and to the "Orientals," it's naughty but not noteworthy.

something soaking in there too, waiting to be washed. So the hell with it—any gossip that starts up can't hurt me (and it may do something for the morale of the beat-up middle-aged American next door).

Every time I've seen Moshe since D-Day, he's smiled tenderly and said "Kaput," with an air of fond reminiscence. I can hardly wait till the anniversary—I bet he'll send me flowers. I've seen him sort of often, too, because he's kept tracking in with one or two other men and peering up at the wounded dood. That is, until today, when they Acted: I came home from school to find a great gray blotch of raw cement on the wall and everything in the bathroom, and from there to the front door, under a thick fall of gritty stone-powder. They didn't even cover up my toothbrush, damn them.

The fallen dood is sitting, fat and huge, on the gallery beside my front door. I can squeeze by it, but one of the inhabitants of Cheder 42 is decidedly plump, which may present a problem when other people come home. Presumably somebody will take the dood away pretty soon, though.*

Meanwhile I can't say I'm suffering too much: carrying my soap and towel next door isn't much of a price for the uplifting experience of having produced a three-word sentence using three languages. I can probably dine out on that for years. Not to mention crowing triumphantly at all those who were so sure I couldn't cope with life in Israel—and will now have to eat their sneers!†

*Naïve, naïve—why would they do that? It stayed right there until they had to move it to get the new one in, a little over two weeks later.
†Pretty cocky. However, there's always hope for someone who notices really useful things—like that the dood is on a separate fuse.

136

From the diary: 8

The committee bird, and Prometheus in the P.O.

Two essence-of-Israel glimpses, both in the same March week!

I

It was during hafsaka at school. I was leaning on the first-floor gallery wall of Binyan Bet, just outside the classroom. Talking, but only theater-intermission chitchat, and watching, in the same idle spirit, Nature burbling around in the campus strip between the two "boats of the Negev." Nature-watching isn't normally a passion with me: I mean, I'm respectful enough to spell it with a capital and I don't start fires in it, and I'm even capable of occasionally noticing its larger attributes with either admiration or fear; but most of the time, I'd have to deny any rumor of a Thing between us—we're just friends.

That morning, it was really looking good enough to attract whistles, though: a benign and indiscriminate sun was beaming on the whole visible world, and the payoff for all those rainy days was showing up in spring signs like a general greening look all over the place, with twitting and humming and comings and goings by little birds and even the odd butterfly. Pretty, and heartening, but still not what I'd write in my diary about—until into the scene strolled a rara-avis-in-spades, the damndest-looking bird I ever saw. And I do mean it strolled: it didn't fly or do anything sudden or quick, and in fact it didn't even go in for that twitchy dipping of the head that makes birds bird-like. On spring-tasting days when the grass is just getting a start, the worm and grub supply must be especially good, and a creature that doesn't store food can't afford to pass up a special; so every bird visible out there was bug-to-mouthing it busily, working top speed at the birdlike job of feeding its face.

But not that baby: it just stood around, rather the way penguins do. (That's the only kind of bird I ever watched seriously. Some were on exhibit in Washington once and I kept going back because they all looked to me like T. S. Eliot, formal and chilly and clearly only dimly related to other birds.) This fellow wasn't nearly penguin-size, of course; it was noticeably bigger than the sparrow-ish types hopping about, but only blue-jay-size or, at most, dove-size. It was obviously not a stranger or a menace, for its arrival on the scene created no to-do among the little fellows. So, though it wasn't acting like a bird, they seemed to know it was one anyway.

137

In fact, so far as looks went, you might even say this one was a kind of Ur-bird: strolling onto center stage, it stood there as if charged with exhibiting attributes of birdness—in a minute, you felt, lines pointing to it might appear, leading to tiny type in the margins explaining what each feature was an example of. For, quite as if it had been constructed from odd parts (samples, or maybe leftovers?), it had some of everything. Like, it was mud-brown but it had conspicuous black-and-white slanted stripes too; it had a robin's chubby body but somebody else's (maybe a kingfisher's?) kind of tail; it had skinny sandpiper legs but it didn't scurry—in fact, its walk was something like a duck's, only with more amble and not quite so much waddle. Not that it ambled much, though: it took a few slow steps, looking Eliotishy lost in thought, and then raised its pointed-cap head (black-and-white stripes, with a fuzzy black fringe over the forehead) and peered around. At one point it fluttered its tail a little—thus revealing another touch of black and white, this time in polka dots— but no flying came of that maneuver. In short, it didn't do anything birdlike, not flying or hopping or perching or hunting for worms or making any identifiable sound (I wouldn't have been foolish enough to expect it to sing, but I never caught even a squawk) or even poking for parasites among its breast feathers. And now that I think of it, I'm not sure it could do that last: the way its head was set on its neck, maybe it couldn't twist its head around that far if it tried. It didn't try.

Well, if it was standing out there waiting for somebody to say "Hey, look at that weird-looking bird," I came though, all right. Martha looked, did a double take, and said she'd never seen the like. Neither, I proceeded to discover, had anyone else whose language I could make a stab at. It had apparently never been seen in Russia, Argentina, or Brooklyn, and I myself can swear to Washington and the Boston area. I may not be a big bird-noticer, but I couldn't forget a hodgepodge like that if I'd ever laid eyes on it before.

Naturally, then, nobody knew its name. So, lacking any knowledgeable birdwatchers to ask and in a hurry because class was reassembling, I decided it was a committee bird. And I'm afraid I spent quite a while in class dreaming up the proceedings of the committee meeting, e.g., a factional dispute betweeh the Plain Browns and the Pro-Stripe splinter groups, with the Polka Dots as an up-for-grabs swing vote. The deadlock is finally broken by a pipe-smoking, let-us-reason-together chairman: "Now look," he says with weary patience, "there's room for every point of view if we're all willing to compromise a little . . .")*

*That sort of activity during class may explain why I never learned the future tense of Hebrew verbs.

For a couple of days, it seemed that a "committee bird" it was going to stay, too, for my inquiries ranged farther afield but with no better luck. Martha reported that Avi had not recognized the description and was puzzled about why I cared what the expletive bird's expletive name was anyway (since I'd found it, I could name it, was his typically free-soul reasoning). Ruth didn't think she knew its name either but promised to come and look next time the bird showed up; predictably, when one appeared the next day and I tore into the office hunting for Ruth, she was out somewhere settling somebody's problems or something dreary like that. Every other Israeli I applied to—my teacher, the girls in the office, etc.—said kindly, "Tsipor" (bird) when I pointed, even though what I was asking was not my usual "Ma zeh?" but "Ma ha shem?" ("What's the name?")

Eventually I ran into the mercaz klita's director, a slim dude of such battered good looks that you felt he must have spent decades touring the provinces as the second male lead in a Noel Coward comedy, his negligent younger-son air changing not a whit though the gray crept into his hair. (This impression was underscored by his English, which was so super-British that everything he said tended to sound like Tennis, anyone?) *When he too disappointed me, I was vexed: the mercaz klita ought to import somebody, perhaps from the local university, I told him, to give us inhabitants a lecture on the flora and fauna hereabouts. He threw me the most incredulous look I've ever seen—offstage, anyway—and muttered vaguely. I let it go, aware that I was becoming an anecdote (and no doubt justly: in what language is this lecture to be given? And among all these people with housing and employment problems, not to mention some really social-worker-meat items like maladjusted kiddies and aged parents, who the hell has time to worry about the flora and fauna? The Americans grow more incredible every day, m'dear. Care for a spot of tennis?)*

Finally, yesterday Yehuda Artzi, who's been here only a few months longer than I have but has read everything about Israel, said he remembered once seeing mention of a hoopoe bird, but he didn't recall what it was supposed to look like. He believed, though, that it was indigenous to The Land, which in the time of Jacob included such areas as . . . and off we went into the History of the Jews. While I was extricating myself, the bird went away again. (I never see it go, it always just disappears when I'm not looking. And it always simply appears when my back is turned, too: all of a sudden, it will be just standing there on the ground.) But now at least I had a clue to run down. I scrambled up the stairs to my cheder and tried the 1960 Webster's I'd dragged along instead of sending it by sea with my books—it's only the "Collegiate" edition but it did its share, all right, toward my overweight charges. So if it didn't have "hoopoe" listed . . . It did, hurrah: "Any of a family . . . of Old World non-passerine birds having a slender curved bill." But that didn't sound too promising, for, though Israel is the oldest world I've ever set foot in, I think what "Old World" means is Europe. And I don't know about that bill—the committee bird didn't have a fat bill, so I suppose it was slender; but I'm not at all sure it was curved. Hmmm. I turned to "nonpasserine" and got "Zool. Not passerine" first. But then somebody relented enough to add "often designated esp. birds of the order Coraciiformes (see CORACIIFORM)."

If you tell me to "see," I'll nearly always go look, and this time I was extra-curious: had the proofreaders been consistently on the ball with that double "i"? Yup, it turned out. But that was all the satisfaction to be found in "Of or relating to an order (Coracii-formes) of arboreal nonpasserine birds comprising the rollers, kingfishers, hornbills, hoopoes, motmots, and allies." Do tell. My grandmother had a serving platter hand-painted with a series of fish, all beautiful Della Robbia blue and with every tail in the next fish's mouth, all the way around the rim. I not only remembered the platter yesterday, I also felt suddenly willing to bet that painting plates was what people who wrote Webster's entries did for a hobby . . . But I didn't lose my head, and I did look up the one word left unexplored: passerine birds belong to an order or equivalent group "comprising chiefly songbirds of perching habits that range from the titmice to the ravens and birds of paradise, and including more than half of all birds."

So okay, the committee bird doesn't sing or perch and thus is probably nonpasserine, all right. Which means it's an oddball, or at least a minority, bird—which also figures. Because I see now that, whether or not it's a hoopoe, it ought to be Israel's national bird. You couldn't ask for an apter totem than this creature made up of bits from all over bird-dom, arboreal, Old World, peculiarly spelled, and refusing to be passerine like everybody else . . .

II

This one doesn't involve wandering in the backwaters of biology or any other departures from my characteristic behavior. What I was doing when it happened, in fact, was tedious and daily—standing in line at the Post Office. And, like a prisoner in solitary, I had coped with my unhappy surroundings by removing my attention; I wouldn't

140

call that kind of reverie really thinking, but I wasn't intaking data, that's for sure.

Thus, so far as I was concerned, the voice from behind my right shoulder came out of nowhere. And it was almost disembodied: I suppose I did recognize it as a woman's voice, but it was a very low contralto and not especially feminine. It just sounded like a pronouncement—except that it was clearly asking a question: "Efshar lekabel esh?"

Even before I started turning around, I'd begun to translate the words, perhaps because they were slow and distinct, like the way the ulpan teacher talked to us. And within my means, too—ef-SHAR is "it is possible,"* and I knew it was followed by the infinitive; lekabel, "to receive," is a commonly used verb and one of the earliest you learn; and esh is a word you're bound to have run into in a mercaz klita or any other public institution—where the red-painted fire-fighting boxes are all labeled with the two letters that stand for "Fire." So, with a completeness and speed far above my average for Hebrew comprehension, I got the message: "It is possible to receive fire?"

I got it so fast that I was in fact unaware of translating it. Thus what was striking me dumb, this time, was the answer floundering in a mind just jolted back from wandering abstractly. Well yes, it's possible, I was thinking. But isn't it a bit dangerous? I mean, Prometheus— Fortunately, by that time I'd turned around enough to see the well-dressed lady behind me in the line. She was holding an unlighted cigarette and looking up at me patiently. And, clickety-click went my perception machinery, slogging back onto the job and registering that I had a lighted cigarette in my own hand . . .

I gave the lady a light and said " 'vakesha"† politely when she said "Toda raba," and I don't think she thought I was anything more than just a bit slow-witted. Besides, she probably didn't expect much: her slow, clear pronunciation may have been the product of a guess based on my American clothes and the fact that I was carrying the Jerusalem Post. That could explain the very formal request, too: there are less elegant ways to ask someone for a light. (Still, she was an elegant-looking lady, so maybe she always talked that way anyhow.)

But in fact I was thoroughly shaken. For I'm not very fond of Hebrew, so far anyway, as it seems to me a half-baked, imprecise language—rather like speedwriting, in which the context provides

---

*It's perhaps more often met (alas, alas) as ee-efshar, "it is not possible."
†In Hebrew you say "please" for "you're welcome," like the German Bitte.

you with the odds, so to speak, for guessing the meaning. For example, the same three-letter word, spelled daled-vav-daled, could be either "uncle" or "David" (I know what you're thinking, but you can't, because there aren't any capital letters in Hebrew)—and, for all I know, maybe a couple of other things too.* So I've been entertaining a certain contempt for the language, a feeling that Hebrew may be all right if you like guessing games but if you really want to say anything . . . Until all of a sudden in the Post Office I got the message of antiquity, of monumentality and the echoing thunder of prophecy and declamation.

It's one of the righter languages, Hebrew is, for talking about receiving fire—and the ends of worlds, and the wrath of God, and justice and judgment. So what if it's not so great for saying "uncle" in?

*E.g., dood—spelled *daled-vav-daled* too!

142

8 ⬩ The Russians

I should make it clear right here that my previous knowledge about Russians—as distinct from the Soviet Union, which I studied in Poli. Sci.—was virtually zilch when I arrived at the mercaz klita. Back in the Washington days, I'd been to the Polish embassy (slivovitz, delicious ham, people dull) and, when the U.S. was particularly wooing the Yugoslavs, I went to their soirées (more slivovitz, beautiful embroidery, people charming); but if the Soviet embassy gave any parties, we didn't have to go. So my acquaintance with real-life Russians, as opposed to Dostoevski's and Chekhov's, was pretty much limited to a few How-do's at Soviet-bloc wingdings.

My husband saw more Russians than that, as negotiations do go on even when there's no summit meeting and the TV cameras are out to lunch. I have a vivid memory of him one workday evening at home, looking up from doing the domestic accounts to say that if I had to write a check tomorrow, it'd better be for less than—um—twenty-eight bucks, because that's all there was in the checking account. He turned back to eye the discouraging balance, and then suddenly grinned. "Funny thing, you know? Twenty-eight was the number of times the Russian delegate said 'capitalist imperialist America' in this morning's meeting. I was counting, to keep awake . . ." So I guess you could say my connection with the twenty-eight-dollar capitalist wearing out the seat of his good gray negotiating-sessions suit on behalf of the US of A gave me some derivative knowledge of the Russians. (Not that I needed tips on Communist rhetoric, though: I've belonged to three unions, two of which the

Communists tried to take over in the late forties, and I'd seen that dialectic-'em-to-death technique for myself.)

We should throw into the pot too, I suppose, the fact that I'd read Crankshaw* and—'way back in European Dictatorships (3 credits)—I'd learned something about the machinery of totalitarian government. I never made any attempt to put together what I knew, or thought I knew, about the Russians. (Why should I, when I lived in a Washington milieu of experts? I could always ask a government Sovietologist, or even my own newspaper's specialist.) But in general what I came equipped with, by 1973, was an impression that the Russians had once been like the characters in Russian Lit; then, after the October Revolution (the beautiful, tragic girl in Vincent Sheehan's *Personal History*, plus the later-admitted delusions of Edmund Wilson), they had become Orwell's characters and you had to feel sorry for them. Also somewhere in there was, of course, the ineradicable impact of Garbo's adorable Ninotchka. But I always knew that wasn't really-real.

I think I'm making myself sound dumber than I was. But if that summary is a little cruel, it's accurate in its linearness: I did actually imagine a sort of progression, from people who talked to each other in clumsy translation to people who believed *Pravda*. It was because the Russians at the mercaz klita turned out to be all those characters at once, not just the end product of the chain, that taking their measure amounted, for me, to a prolonged series of little shocks and discoveries.

The first surprise, and the simplest, was the Russians' size. There were exceptions, of course, but in general both men and women ranged from merely hefty to hugely fat. Tamara, a physicist with whom I could talk a little on my own (she had some English and learned Hebrew so quickly that, quite soon after her arrival, she could say anything I could understand) was about thirty-six, I think. And, though I'm aware of the incongruity of the Scottish-lass word applied to a Russian Jew, "bonny" is what fits Tamara—a big, bonny woman with a fair, fresh complexion and very rosy cheeks. (High color seemed common among the Russians, particularly the blond.) In America, she would surely have been directed to the Stylish Stout shop, but she didn't seem to know that or act like it: she moved with that awareness of herself as a woman that sometimes gets described as sexy. (It's actually nothing so blatant or tinny, and "womanly" would probably be better if it hadn't been so messed up by

*Edward Crankshaw, *Cracks in the Kremlin Wall* and other works.

144

phony images of women. But let it go—I can't right all the world's wrongs in a parenthesis.)

Tamara was a divorcée with an eighteen-year-old son who somewhat resembled Phil—black curly hair, dark eyes, the same way of hunching tense and oblivious over a chessboard—but looked as though he'd make one and a half Phils. Since my son is neither short nor skinny and Tamara's son was probably not exceptionally tall and not fat, the impression may have been a result of differing self-images or culture-attached values (American boys slouching diffidently because size doesn't matter that much, Russian boys hulking because it does?). But it was so clear and prominent that it crossed my mind at one point that if the two boys ever confronted each other in a war—which God forbid!—we'd better make sure Phil had superior weapons . . .

The Russian men at the mercaz klita were, though often hulking, hardly yummy-looking; there were of course exceptions, but even the exceptions didn't seem likely to provoke much female fluttering. (Though I may be being unfair, because they were in part victims of their culture, which seems to go in for very blatant dentistry—maybe for the same reason as among the Beduin, where it's a sign of wealth?—that leaves gold- or steel-capped teeth flashing in the sunlight.) Only one of the exceptions, a psychiatrist from Leningrad, was actually good-looking. And—I don't think I mean the connection I may be implying here—he was, I learned, the son of an American Communist who a generation ago rejected his native land in favor of the higher ideals of the Soviet Union. The father had married a Russian woman but apparently (his son was not sure about this) made an attempt to register his child's birth at the American embassy; he was (understandably) turned down . . . Had his father ever expressed any regret for his emigration, I asked Eugene. He didn't know—he'd been too young for such chats when his father died. And his mother, he said, was not likely to tell him if she knew of any second thoughts.*

The second surprise wasn't really quite that, it having been borne in upon me previously that the Soviet society wasn't actually classless. But I wasn't prepared for the extent of the class-consciousness dividing, more firmly than even the British Mayfair-vs.-Cockney, the Moscow and Leningrad types from those hailing

*Eugene spoke some English (anything not absolutely minimal needed Rob to interpret, though), but he had learned it at school. He was so interested in learning more English that I had a feeling he intended, whenever he could, to reverse his father's route all the way. Thus I wasn't surprised to hear recently that he'd re-emigrated to Canada.

145

from places that tended to end in "stan" (and whose women wore "native" costumes and would have looked like Dolls of All Nations except that they were too fat—arms like tree trunks—and steel-toothed). This geographic class labeling was so prevalent that you couldn't possibly miss it. It was also quite obviously of desperate importance to the immigrants, which caused settlement problems for the Israelis: a Russian from Leningrad would regard a job offer from anywhere but, say, Tel Aviv as a put-down—and fight it with the fierceness aroused by a threat to the very self. And certainly now that I've seen, close up, the whole-life-determining weight of that geographic class distinction, I understand why dissidents in the Soviet Union are punished by having their permission to live in Moscow withdrawn. That's a severe penalty indeed. For whatever it also means in terms of torn family life, it surely means a de-classing, with all the implications of that for one's own future and one's children's.

I got a good look at this mechanism when Tamara apparently tried to project it onto Americans. (That may make her sound dumb. But how else should she try to grasp the incomprehensible, if not by applying what she knew?) The incident began with an insignificant confusion when she asked Martha and me where we were from and we interpreted it differently: "Boston," I said, answering *Where have you come here from?* And "St. Louis, Missouri," said Martha, who was still young enough so that where you're from is where your parents still live. Well, Tamara, who had taught physics at the university level, had of course heard of Boston (and certainly of Cambridge, Mass.); but "Missouri" was obviously the provinces, or maybe even the Wild West . . . Immediately, her manner changed, differentiating sharply between Martha and me: Tamara was job-hunting and ambitious, and clearly she had decided that, career-wise, I was the valuable one to know; from that moment on, she more or less ignored Martha and turned her energies to buttering me up. Which, in the actual circumstances, was pretty humorous. Because, except for the couple in Jerusalem (whom I had never mentioned), everybody I knew in Israel was an immigrant— whereas Martha's Israeli husband, Avi, not only himself would have constituted a valuable professional contact for Tamara but also seems to have old buddies in every science enclave in the country.

Among the no-surprise-at-all encounters were what I came to think of as "by the book" Russian behavior. Sometimes the book was written by Dostoevski, as in the case of the smoky parties in Binyan Bet, with too many people piled into a room (but sitting, not moving around, American cocktail-party-style) and vodka, and, after a while, the dark sad-sounding singing. It was easy then to remember the books that take place "in the town of K——" or some other capital letter followed by a blank, with people who address each other by those long, impossible patronymics while they describe their tearing sweeps of emotion and finally reach Myshkin's conclusions, or Alyosha's knowledge . . . And in fact though I don't really know whether the Russian immigrants at the mercaz klita were actually moodier than anyone else, it was clear that there was among them a greater societal acceptance of it: a Russian's friend, turned away by a short answer and a brush-off gesture, would merely shrug and wait till the mood had passed. No offense was taken, and if any attempt was made to explain to foreigners—which was rare, and required persistence—it was less an explanation than, even from analytical and articulate types, a kind of verbal shrug: that's how we are, others can't really understand us. I saw some commiseration but nothing that looked like telling a cast-down fellow Russian to buck up, and certainly nothing like trying Americanly to kid him into cheerfulness.

But there was one by-the-book case that, if you've read *Oblomov*, you'll think I'm making up—a roommate of Rob's who for the first few days seemed much like the other Russians (he was a writer of sorts, which gave him Moscow-and-Leningrad status) and, though apparently not anybody's special buddy, still socially acceptable. Even though he didn't go to the ulpan and seemed to stay in his room most of the time between meals. And then he took to staying there all the time, mealtimes included, except for occasional ventures into the kitchen he and Rob shared, where he made himself some tea. Other Russians came to visit him (including the doctors, several of whom came repeatedly) and maybe brought the old bun, and somebody must have provided him with cigarettes. But before long, he'd gone all the way into the protagonist of Goncharov's novel, spending all his time lying on his bed, speaking only occasionally to visitors, and mostly just looking up at the ceiling.

The Israeli staff at the mercaz klita may not have read *Oblomov*, but they weren't having any anyway: in due course, a relative—remote and apparently reluctant, but nevertheless a relative, and in Israel that's what counts—was located living on a kibbutz, and I gather some pressures were applied. So one day Oblomov was whisked off, presumably to the kibbutz. And presumably "Sent to Kibbutz——" appeared in his dossier as evidence of the assimilation of one more Russian immigrant, and bureaucracy was thus tidily satisfied . . . I can't say I blame the Israelis: no institution could have tolerated that for long. And particularly not an absorption center, which fears epidemic depression the way a summer camp fears conjunctivitis.

But "by the book" left Masterpieces of Russian Lit. and moved on into distinct Orwell touches when I got to talk more to more Russians. Like when Fanya, a biologist, "explained" to me the banning from Moscow of a well-known dissident—an event duly reported in all the languages in which news is dispensed in Israel. My question to Fanya (translated for her) was framed in terms of attempting to understand Soviet policy: since a world-famous physicist must surely be an asset to a government hungry for technological expertise, why, I asked, would they want to cut off this man's ability to work? But Fanya answered the query in less Machiavellian, more tourist-information terms. It was simply that there was a limit, she said (uneasily, I thought), to the number of apartments available in Moscow. So of course so eminent a person would have a permit to live there, but then the man had become "political . . ." (The word, in her voice, clearly described a public-health menace, like a known typhoid carrier.) However, ordinary people, people who avoided excesses and just went about their business, could live wherever they liked. Not Moscow, of course. But anywhere else where there were enough apartments and people had a proper reason to be, they had no more trouble getting a permit than they would in any other country . . . Told that in America one didn't need a permit to live in any city, Fanya looked surprised, and politely incredulous.

What was involved was a confusion of concepts of authority, according to the trained-eye slant I got from Vered, a social worker at the mercaz klita. She was a chic, handsome woman with the kind of built-in-the-bone good looks I've seen before in Polish women, and nothing about her (unless you happened to glimpse the number on her arm) would have given you a clue that she'd come to Israel direct from Auschwitz. She'd then been living in Beer-Sheva for more than twenty years, and there was no immigrant problem she hadn't seen—and, apparently, no language in which she couldn't at least cope. Her English, less accented than Thereza's, was just about as fluent; there was no need for an intermediary in communicating with Vered, so we would get to talking. About Beer-Sheva, her job, the setup at the mercaz klita, etc. And one day she mentioned that she was sometimes accused by her colleagues of favoring the American immigrants. (I couldn't have helped her disprove it: she certainly was very helpful to me.) She was trying very hard not to show favoritism, but the trouble was, Vered confessed, it was really the way she felt.

Why, I wondered. Could it be that English was the foreign

language she found most comfortable? Vered smiled and said it was something best explained by example. Like, did I remember what I had said when I came into her office this morning? No? Well, I'd knocked lightly, waited to be told to come in, and then asked politely, "Are you busy right now?" and offered to come back later if she was. That was typical of the Americans, who would themselves make the distinction between what was pressing and what could wait, and who even when seeking help with something immediate would often apologize for having to interrupt her and/or thank her afterward. Whereas no Russian, she told me flatly, would ever knock. And some, even most, would barge in, charge across the room, and issue demands—often while thumping a fist on her desk. So, though she tried to be fair, to exercise an equal amount of ingenuity in extricating what the client wanted from the intricate coils of Israeli regulations, it was nevertheless true that she *felt* more like problem-solving for the Americans . . .

A matter of different cultures, I suggested. Perhaps something to do with the way the two societies looked on displays of emotion? No, Vered thought, it had more to do with concepts of government. The Americans tended to seek information—Could this or that be arranged? How did one go about getting the necessary piece of paper?—and to understand that there was machinery to be worked. They *consulted* her, and maybe identified with her to some extent: they might not be social workers, but they had some other special competence that they had exercised, sometimes sitting behind a desk, on behalf of others. (Listening, I realized suddenly that what she was describing was in fact egalitarianism: it was the Americans who could have addressed her as "Comrade.") Whereas the Russians, she went on, frowning, made no attempt to understand and certainly not to identify. She was Authority, which one bullied unless one had to be afraid—and the distinction there had to be clear, so they came on strong: *I am masterful, not timorous. So you see I am a person who'd better be treated right.* Even those Americans who wanted special treatment tried to get it by enlisting her; but the Russians tried to wrest it from her, seeing their problem not as a matter of maneuvering a spaghetti-tangle of programs to yield something specifically useful but as a question of compelling this presumably reluctant functionary to give them what they needed. Their bullying was sometimes followed by threats, Vered said wearily. But in any case their assumption seemed to be that the best motivation for a social worker would be a need to end an unpleasant scene. Which notion of course completely ignored the human factor . . .

It all sounded, I commented, a little like the fable about the

149

sun and the wind competing to get a man to remove his cloak. (The wind tries to blow it off, thus causing the man to wrap it around him even more tightly. Then the sun does his thing, and of course the man takes it off voluntarily.) Vered agreed but said sadly that she was afraid it went deeper than a mere dispute about efficacy of means.

And I guess it does, at that: the key may be that the Americans expect justice (I think they still do, despite the now-fashionable lack of faith in government; and in 1973, and especially in a sample embodying a large percentage of idealists, it was certainly true) but the Russians, apparently, understand only power. In whatever terms they can command: accustomed to having no voice, they use their bodies; they don't vote but demonstrate. And not like American demonstrations, which often strike observers as inauthentic because of their blatant contradictions in terms—i.e., Harvard students on Boston Common shouted through bullhorns that they were "the people," though youths at least as entitled to that label would have slung them out of there promptly but for the protective ring of cops (who wouldn't volunteer for the job) around the speakers. Just to be able to *charge* "police brutality" is more power than the Russians are used to. So how should they imagine a milieu that expects to have rights—including the right to ask, without banging on a table?

But if the Russians had trouble imagining something outside their own frame of reference, so did I—and my blind spot needed several shoves before it really got dislodged. My first awareness came after I noticed, one day, that the ulpan class was skimming very lightly over a certain lesson. This one, about our previous homes, seemed very like the earlier ones that had required us to tell about ourselves and our environment and thus—sensibly, I thought —provided a vocabulary that would be of practical value. So why did the teacher seem unwilling to dwell on this one, which used handy words like kitchen, bathroom, etc.?

When I ran into her after class, I asked her. She'd never liked that lesson, she said, looking distressed—if she had her way, it wouldn't be in the book. Why? Well, because it always became a "propaganda contest" between the Russians and the Americans. What invariably happened in that lesson, she went on angrily, was that the Russians started lying—which she didn't think did anybody any good, and she didn't want it happening in her class. Like *what* lying? Well, for example, the Russian woman who had described her five-room apartment in Moscow this morning . . . The teacher eyed my surprise and said disgustedly, "Didn't you know? She'd have to be a member of the Presidium to have an apartment like that. And in Moscow yet!" The Russian woman and her husband (both of them engineers) and their school-age child *and* the maternal grandparents—who had gone unmentioned in this morning's description, but who'd come to Israel, too, and were living in the mercaz klita—probably had had a three-room apartment. Just maybe with their own kitchen, but that was stretching it, my mentor indicated, because it would be a rather privileged standard of living.

Why had the Russian woman lied? Clearly, out of a kind of patriotism, the teacher supposed. Stirred up by envy of the American, Jeffrey, whose turn had come just before—and who had, if I remembered, described a house of nearly unimaginable luxury. I remembered Jeffrey's presentation, all right: I'd been listening closely, trying to pick up the necessary Hebrew for when my own turn came. But the California house he'd described was no mansion, so where was this unimaginable luxury? "Even for the baby, there was a room," the teacher pointed out. Not to mention Jeffrey's bragging about all those bathrooms . . .

Well, I could see how it happened. Jeffrey had mentally roved the upstairs, improvising words if he needed to, intent on getting the right Hebrew word for everything relevant. (What had preoccupied him about his son's room, in fact, was that it was under the eaves—and how do you say "eaves"?*) In the process, he'd listed the bathroom absently, because that was a word he already knew, and obviously without any special awareness that he'd already mentioned a bathroom downstairs. *He* wasn't counting bathrooms, but others clearly were—including the Israeli teacher, a mother of two (who had doubtless noticed for her own reasons that the baby had a separate room) . . . I got the message at last, and, feeling contrite, "apologized" for Jeffrey: I could see now that it had been unfortunate, but certainly his intent hadn't been—

The teacher shrugged—that wasn't the point. (Or maybe it was, because that made the whole thing even worse? I kept that notion to myself, though.) All right, I understood, I told her. But was it really necessary to skip the lesson just to avoid this problem? The Americans, if only they were told, would readily see the need for sensitivity . . . That wouldn't work, my teacher said flatly. The Americans took so much luxury so much for granted that sooner or later they'd slip; and the Russians couldn't be expected to perceive it as anything but chauvinistic boasting, which would inevitably

---

*Who knows? Talk about "relevant": in all the time I've lived in Israel, I don't think I've seen a single eave.

151

arouse the more spirited among them to compete. It was best just to avoid the confrontation.

Well, I don't know whether any of the Russians were giving any thought to the Americans' sensitivities, but one I heard surely wasn't. It happened the first time there was a concert in Beer-Sheva: tickets were available to immigrants—said a notice in Russian, English, and Hebrew—at a reduced price. Apply at the office, etc. As a group of us stood reading it, a Russian woman said something obviously shocked and maybe incredulous. "She's astonished that people have to pay," Rob told me. The woman realized he was translating and, turning to him, delivered a polemic. In the Soviet Union, she announced (with flashing eyes and dramatic gestures), concerts and ballet performances, plus of course vacations at the Black Sea in summer, were everybody's due, provided naturally to the people as their right. Only among barbarous grubby materialists would The People be expected to shell out for "culture" . . . "But somebody has to pay the orchestra their wages, no?" I heard a man wonder in Yiddish, from somewhere behind me. (He sounded old, and not American.) The Russian woman, who didn't understand Yiddish,* thus didn't have the answer and went on declaiming.

Well, it figures, of course: a totalitarian government must supply bread and circuses; and, from what one hears, the bread supply isn't that good, so the circuses had better be. (Besides, if a three-room apartment for a three-generation family is such a luxury, it would make sense to get people out of the house often.) So that the Russian immigrants were bound to discover with dismay the disadvantages of freedom—a government that Takes Care of You is sure to be missed. Anyway, *It was better where I came from*, though perhaps illogical for an emigrant, is humanly predictable: you're likely to hear it from a newcomer to your office staff, a new arrival in town, etc. But the everything-is-bigger-and-better-in-Russia bit was, as a matter of fact, usually several layers thicker than just that: e.g., the airplane was invented in Russia, Rob and I learned, without even asking. (Our informant was so like a comedy-skit Russian that we had to avoid looking at each other to keep from

*Quite usual, especially among the big-city types, who had little exposure to either the Jewish religion or its culture and traditions. And in fact—though this was rarely mentioned out loud—some of the Russian immigrants weren't even Jewish (I knew myself of one, who admitted it): if they could fake it (i.e., with false papers, or by marrying a Jew), their chances for getting out of Russia improved. So nobody really blamed them, though the religious got a bit unhappy—and argued (with justice) that the non-Jew might have kept a truly devout Jew from his place in the Soviet let-'em-out quota.

laughing.) Another time, Martha, who'd been to Russia as a tourist, agreed with a proud lady from Leningrad about the art triumphs on view in The Hermitage—but then got clobbered because she hadn't said it was the *greatest* in the *world*. National pride, it was clear, was thoroughly internalized. And of course it was in dramatic contrast to the Americans, who were a singularly unboastful bunch, perhaps because chauvinism has always been out of fashion except among right-wingers and nobody seemed to be that. (That's why I found the teacher's charge about that classroom incident personally irritating, since it so definitely wasn't the Americans who were politicking the lesson up. But of course it wasn't a matter of who was to blame.)

However, even the most caricature American Rotarian noisily proclaiming that God's country is the biggest and the best wouldn't have been likely to boast about how much information was available to him—which was, in fact, the most important difference that emerged. But having the whole world brought to your TV screen, laid on your doorstep every morning in an eighty-page newspaper, available in the public library of every town, is—well, it's like having two bathrooms in your house, I guess. So if I had difficulty seeing what the Russians' life must have been like in specific detail, their problem was more severe: if you're not accustomed to a flow of information, it may be well-nigh impossible to imagine that somebody else is.

Thus, even later, when I'd got to know a few Russians well enough so we should have been able to see each other as more than national figures, I still kept running into their assumption of ignorance of everything Russian (and most things of importance were, of course, Russian) by everybody in the West. Again and again, I'd turn out to know some hardly esoteric fact, available to any ordinary American newspaper reader—and certainly to anyone who could even recall grammar-school "units" on People of Other Lands, etc.— and my Russian acquaintance would first boggle and then, often with considerable emotion, struggle with the conflicting needs to avoid calling me a liar and yet not believe in the image of America I was thus implying. Fanya the biologist, for example, knew I was a writer; so who would possibly guess she'd be surprised that I knew who Dostoevski was? She was, though. (I'm not going on mere perception: she said so, in Russian, to our host on that occasion. He comes from the Balkans and can read Russian and so is expected to know about Dostoevski.) It blew Fanya's mind, even when our host confirmed that Dostoevski really-truly could be read in English translation. And even might be, by Americans (though he himself had a little trouble with the fact that I'd got *The Brothers Karamazov* out of the public library. He just couldn't believe that of the capitalists).

Still, Fanya is intelligent, so once she'd absorbed the idea that the never-imagined was nevertheless probably true, she seemed less surprised when it emerged that I had heard of Lysenko. I didn't have the straight of him, though, she indicated. Well, I could believe that, as my knowledge was at little more than Sunday-supplement level. But what I wasn't prepared for was Fanya's adding that it was of course understandable, since my information came from the West.

As soon as I recovered, I did try explaining that it wasn't the State Department, honest, that had told me about Lysenko. But she and the man from the Balkans were already exchanging amused smiles. "We are all victims of propaganda," he announced even-handedly—thus presenting me with a debater's coup. Because I could hardly argue that everything American authority had taught me was solid-gold, capital-T Truth without any error, confusion, or (most frequent of truth-twisters) faddishness. I knew in my heart— you might say—that if a "discovery" that acquired characteristics can be inherited had been proclaimed by a Western source, it would've earned exactly the same thumbs-down reception American scientists in the 1930s gave to the announcement of Lysenko's theory. But how do you go about proving a negative like that? (Especially if all you're operating with is some high-school biology and a few editorial brushes with history-of-science papers.)

I should explain, though, that the man from the Balkans was not merely scoring a cynical debating point—he believes firmly that everything put about by the American media is dictated by the U.S. government.* As a doctrine, it's unshakable: any example of the press sassing the government (and those are certainly easy to come up with) is simply declared part of a devious propaganda campaign the end of which has not yet emerged, but you can be sure "Wall Street" (which means, to him, the government) is behind it. It's simply not possible to move him any more than Fanya toward real comprehension of a milieu in which people may not be pursuing a Platonic Ideal of Truth but are free to push their individual versions

---

*He's not the only Israeli with that notion. I once listened to a man from South America psyching out the U.S. government by means of an article in a news magazine: he was too sophisticated to believe the article, of course, but he was using the fact that the statement had passed "the censors" to guess at official intentions. Even when an American known to him to be distinctly leftist backed me up that there were no censors, he couldn't quite believe he'd lost his premise.

154

of truth—and where even if what you hear may be propaganda, it's not necessarily the *government's* propaganda.

That inability to grasp even the idea of multiple sources, of many voices equally powerful (or powerless), proved general among the Russians, however intelligent and perceptive they were. (And even however trendy—one university lecturer in American Lit. clearly saw Norman Mailer as some kind of chief of an American "academy." He was bringing that news to Israeli college students, but, so far as I could discern, they didn't believe him.) What's odder, I guess, is that it should also be true of Israelis, for God knows there are plenty of voices to be heard in Israel, usually all talking at once. But to my friend from the Balkans, and his ilk, they're all only puppets anyhow.

Well, in order to be fair in describing the chauvinisms of others, it's necessary to core out one's own—a difficult, maybe impossible, task. For Americans, too, are provincial, in the sense that they believe their own to be the only useful, or maybe even viable, way. You hear that, in Israel, most clearly in their complaints: many Americans seem virtually unable to remember that Israeli Theys don't have to woo them, either commercially or politically. They can surely see that, although Israel's is an industrialized and democratic society, being a voter or consumer there doesn't provide even minimal power. But somehow the knowledge keeps slipping out of the consciousness of people accustomed all their lives to being able to write their Congressman, take their trade to another supermarket chain, etc.

Still, there's a difference between that provincialism and the Russians', and I think it lies in the fact that the Americans tend to feel they *ought* to see out of the other guy's eyes. It's the difference between "commitment"—which held sway (well, verbal anyway) in the U.S. for a few years in the 1960s and among a limited number of citizens—and "tolerance," which has reigned longer and wider and deeper (perhaps because it leaves room for thinking up better ways, a favorite American trait). Thus, if we're all shaped by our conditioning, the American shaping contains the traditional consensual tolerance that says with a shrug, *It takes all kinds* and disposes of disagreement with *That's what makes horse races.* So that an American charged with failing to respect somebody else's way of life is apt to feel guilty—or, at the very least, to argue that he hasn't really, so there.

Whereas for the Russians nothing seems to exist side by side, and virtue, like government, is central and single. It's a smallish difference but a vital one, I think. And less a matter of dictatorship vs. democracy than of a central One vs. a scattered Many. (In fact, central government may explain why Israelis sometimes fall into Russian rather than American responses.)

Or the whole and only answer may really be that, as a British friend once told me, America is not only unique but intrinsically unbelievable. Unless, of course, you were born to it.

From the diary: 9
Linens day (April)

This is a weekly event presided over by Avraham, who seems to be the mercaz klita's Assistant Sec'y for Administration; he's apparently outranked by Ruth (if I stick to these State Dept. terms, I guess she's an Undersecretary), but he's the handyman Moshe's boss.

Linens day goes like this: one day a week, right after lunch, Avraham appears and unlocks a door on Binyan Aleph's first-floor gallery, just to your left as you come up the main staircase, and thus reveals a secret supply room in what looks like just another cheder. At exactly the hour specified for Binyan Aleph to receive clean linens (Binyan Bet has its own weekly D-Day and H-Hour), Avraham sets a table across the doorway and seats himself behind it— sunburned, muscular, beetle-browed, and ready to hold off anyone driven wild by the sight of the stockpiled sheets, towels (and wastebaskets! bedspreads! saucepans!) visible in the room behind him. Where hover, also, two handmaidens—the Moroccan chambermaids who wear their hair in a long thick braid down the back and giggle a lot, thus always seeming somehow schoolgirlish. Standing in the gloom behind Avraham, who controls the room's only exit, they look like captives, brunette Rapunzels whose hair just wasn't long enough to get the liberating prince up there.

During the specified hour and a half—and not one minute longer, habibi, you can count on that—you must collect your sheets and pillow slips and towels and join the queue that eventually stretches a good way along the gallery. When you reach the altar and pass the ritual test, you're issued replacements—equally tough white muslin sheets (the weave is almost dense enough to use for sails), equally threadbare towels, etc. And, if your bedspread has worn out (or you're mad enough to just want another color!) or you need a wastebasket, this is your moment. First, though, you give your family name and the number of your cheder, which are checked off on a long sheet of the cheapest possible mimeograph paper. Next, Avraham actually looks at you! He has to, to make sure you're not some ringer; but he keeps it to a minimum—one slanting upward glance through the overhang of his eyebrow. Just so might a man under siege peer, fast and sidelong, from a chink in the shutters to check on the enemy out there . . . That ordeal over, he unwraps your returned linens enough to see whether you actually do have the number you purport to have. And then, his face closed like a fist on the pain the act of giving apparently costs him, he calls out the number of replacements you're entitled to. The old linens are handed back to one of the women, and the new are handed up by the other—who gives you, from behind Avraham's back, a nervous conspiratorial smile that wants you to know she's not a daughter of this Avraham. He examines your portion (maybe she slipped you an extra towel en route?) and after that, you're free to carry off your loot.

Unless you've got a problem or special request. In which case you'd better state it in Hebrew, since Avraham will brook no discourse in any other tongue:officially anyhow, he lacks the smallest understanding of English, Russian, Spanish, or even (most incredible of all, considering the years he's confronted immigrants at the mercaz klita) Yiddish. Since Hebrew is what the people on the linens line are just learning—mostly, though once in a while you get a well-prepared type or a rabbi—the special-request supplicant will usually try to find some common language or, if desperate, simply point. A venture of that sort is always doomed, for Avraham will see no gestures. And at the first sound of an alien tongue, he ducks his head even further, hunches his shoulders, and, with every appearance of being about to paw the ground and snort, waits for the wretch to either come up with Hebrew or fade away. For the queue, all this adds a nice touch of drama. And for Avraham, it serves to discourage inroads on his 756 wastebaskets, 349 mattresses, etc.

I've been curious about the always-fierce Avraham, but all I've been able to dig up about him, from one of the girls in the office, is that he comes from Russia or Poland and is a graduate of one of the nastier concentration camps—which doubtless explains his manners but makes his purported lack of Yiddish even more unlikely. (And nearly everybody from Poland can speak some Russian, I've noticed.) Oh, and also that "He's a big Zionist," with the office girl delivering the line like a Massachusetts liberal explaining Ronald Reagan or a Unitarian acknowledging a Holy Roller. That was clearly that, so the next resource was Ruth. How did it happen, I asked her, that Avraham, who couldn't speak the immigrants' languages and seemed notably—er—unsympathetic to them, should be employed in an absorption center? Ruth looked uncomfortable and said well, he wasn't really such a bad fellow. But when I persisted—Okay, but why not set him to work in, say, the Post Office?—all I got was a brush-off: "He's a big Zionist," she remarked, and that was that again.*

I knew I'd be at the end of the linens line today because I

---

*That wasn't a brush-off, it was as much explanation as she could provide without discoursing for hours on the Israeli political scene. When I read these diary entries, I feel sorry for Ruth. What was she supposed to do with an interviewer who had apparently never even heard of ideology as a job requirement?

stayed in my cheder to listen to the news in English; in fact, the only people who came after me were the Belgian couple, who must have loitered for the French news. I didn't need to worry about missing my turn and I could see familiar faces along the queue, so I went off to circulate and chat. For the Americans particularly, because they don't see each other that much otherwise, linens day is that kind of occasion—like country folk meeting in the general store, there's a lot of "Hi" and "How you been?" The young couples tend to divide the linens-day chore, and whoever's turn it is usually brings the baby along so the other parent can have a nap. Thus I also get to hold a baby, which is something I like to do from time to time.

The Argentines look on the linens line as a social occasion too, though they're less efficiency-minded and more formal about it. For example, Rafaelo would never let Anita tote the load of laundry, but she generally comes along to keep him company. And so do the other wives, so it becomes for them a church-social sort of event, women chatting with women and the men going in for mild backslapping and guffawing. This segregation seems virtually compulsory, even for those who don't enjoy it. (Rafaelo brightens when I hail him, because I constitute rescue: a foreign woman may not know her place but she's entitled to courtesy anyway; so if I start talking to him, he's temporarily excused from men-in-groups bonhomie.)

The American socializing quickly becomes the cocktail-party variety, with the quip—rather than the Spanish inquiry about family members' health—the dominant tone. The Russians on line hardly socialize at all, partly because they're few and are always together anyway. Most Russian immigrants are housed in Binyan Bet; Binyan Aleph's consist of, aside from a scattered "single" or two, large families with numerous outriders, who inhabit a row of contiguous flats along one of the lower galleries. (Probably they were sent to our building because of their space needs. Though it may also have been to keep the Moscow-and-Leningrad types over there from feeling déclassé, for our Russians are distinctly "lower class.") But in addition, I think they're pretty much immobilized by their own ground rules: they take queuing very seriously and consider that if you step out of your place you lose it—as some careless Americans have now learned, the hard way—so they're pretty much limited to talk with whoever's ahead or behind in the line. But even there, the conversation seems absentminded, both speakers always watching for an opportunity to move up. They never quite forget, it seems, that what they're there for, principally, is to get things from Avraham.

Linens procurement is a woman's job among the Russians, I see. Sometimes she brings the little ones along, though not for the same reason as the Americans: The Russian families all have old grandmothers who watch the children too small for the gan yele-dim. *The Russian toddlers you see on line are always remarkably quiet, eyeing you impassively out of very round faces and staying very close to their mothers; in their funny shoes and their nearly always too much clothing for a Beer-Sheva afternoon, they tend to look more like dolls than real children. The Spanish-speaking tots usually don't rove far from parental pants legs either, and they also seem to me rather demure; but they do play, usually with some small toy they've brought along, and if they stare it's briefly and with active curiosity. Occasionally you even hear an Alberto being scolded. But it's always more likely to be a Stevie who's plucked down from an attempt to climb the gallery wall. So far, it's never been an Ilya.*

(Later)

The Russian families, now that I think of it, are Avraham's real clientele. Not that he treats them any more kindly—in fact they usually fare worst, as they're not only the most recent arrivals and so shortest of Hebrew vocabulary, but they always seem to want more things. That's the key, of course: it's they who really test Avraham's stockpile defenses, and I wouldn't be surprised if encounters with them are the only ones he enjoys. Because they know what's valuable, see . . .

Anita disagrees, thinks Avraham is just an all-around misanthrope: "Hoo lo ohev col ahneshim."* Well, maybe it's true that he not-loves all people, but I think he not-loves the Russians least. His reaction to the Argentines seems to vary with class, with the few working-class types rating about like the Russians but the gentlemanly ones like Rafaelo inspiring extra-dirty looks—it's their disdain, I guess, that gets to Avraham. All he wants, really, is respect for his values. And what he gets from most of the Argentines is ladies and gentlemen enduring an irritation (almost Britishly, except that their language obscures the comparison: Spanish flows, and there are no clipped cadences like "Oh quite."). Making the occasion as gracious as they can but, in effect, snubbing Avraham. It must sting.

But the Americans actively infuriate him because they're not even snubbing him. Whether or not he can understand English, he surely comprehends the Americans' light-mindedness: visibly and audibly, they are simply not taking the whole linens-day shtick seriously. They don't even stand in line properly—they lean against

---

*Tsk tsk—*ohev* has to be followed by *et*, and how about that *ha* in front of nouns? *Who lo ohev et col ha-ahneshim.*

the parapet, dart in and out, shift from foot to foot, jiggle the coins in their pockets. And they call out to each other sallies of what must be obvious as public wit, meant to bring general laughter . . . People speaking a language you don't understand are always likely to make you twinge a paranoid twinge; especially if they laugh a lot, you'd have to feel they were laughing at you. And I guess there really is, by now, something faintly provocative, a sort of In-group anti-Avraham black humor among the Americans on the linens line. "Ech omrim [how do you say] 'Please sir, there's a six-inch hole in the middle of the sheet you gave me'?" somebody asks plaintively. And from somewhere down the line, a gagster sings out in pseudo-worried tones, "But how much is a six-inch hole in meters?"

Thinking it over, I can't remember anything said today that wouldn't have been said if Avraham was known to understand English. But when I write that, I see it isn't a defense, it just makes things worse. Because to perceive the repartee as good-humored, Avraham would have to understand much more than the language; he'd have to know about a people who will mock authority and yet— most difficult to grasp—quite mean to obey it. To the Americans, the linens bit is no burning hardship; standing in line is real pioneersy and the churlish Avraham a quaint native, part of being in foreign parts. But to Avraham the Americans must seem not just foreign but incredibly alien: I don't think he can imagine that they really don't want more than their share of sheets, any more than he can imagine an employee—no, no, a worker—being praised or rewarded for handling the public tactfully. For to comprehend the balance of powers that informs such a relation between functionary and citizen would take a vocabulary of social contract that comes not with the English language but with rights not merely ordained but long ago won and passed on, taken for granted now and with built-in recourse mechanisms in case anybody tries to deny them. If the U.S. Government owes you a Social Security check, it's yours: you don't have to know anybody important to get it, and you don't even have to be first in line. Look how petted you are—manufacturers try to find out what you want so they can make it, and then even woo you to buy it. "Sorry to keep you waiting," says the functionary you can telephone instead of having to go and see (and if you do go to his office, he'll be there—or a substitute will—for all the hours of every working day).

What all that produces is maybe the most precious civil right of all, the right to levity: there's a lightheartedness in the Americans on the linens line that's visibly unique. Anita and Rafaelo are just as ungrabby, but they're not so irreverent, perhaps because they can't be so unworried. They respond with dignity, but the Americans (the

North *Americans, I should've been saying all along, of course)*
respond with mockery—of the process, the scene, themselves—in a
common understanding that nothing is sacrosanct. The mockery
isn't primarily hostile, for it falls on the deserving and virtuous as
well as baddies. It makes use of common terms of reference
brought from the U.S. (e.g., "beautiful downtown Beer-Sheva"), and
fractures Hebrew ("Anybody holech-ing *to town this afternoon?")*
merrily and without intending disrespect. And, although maybe
what Rafaelo and another Argentine man were quietly discussing
today was a better way to do the linens exchange, the speculations
in English about how many man-hours would be saved if etc. etc.
had a very different air: for one thing, nobody was especially
quiet or saw any need for tact. (Another marked difference, by the
way, was that the English discussion could include a woman—most
unlikely among the Spanish contingent.) The U.S. discussants
wouldn't talk any differently if Avraham understood, and they'd be
surprised if he bridled—as he may have today: I'm not convinced of
his total incomprehension—because the right to improve on what-
ever's going on just comes with being American. Everybody's as-
sumed to have it, and if they don't use it that's only because it isn't
their thing.*

Well, what it comes down to is, I guess, that I love my lucky
people—their cheerful acceptance of each other and the casual self-
respect that grants it unthinkingly to others. (Including children:
"You said five minutes, Daddy," pipes a Stevie, in the bright toddler's
precise diction and expectation of never being pushed around. And
Daddy doesn't tell him not to be impertinent, he leans down and
answers the complaint.) But I can also see how that very self-esteem
strikes Avraham as arrogant, the ebullience merely childish and the
frivolity feckless. What must infuriate him most, though, is that
there is no comeuppance: the Americans don't get humbled, or
grow up, or live to regret—they prevail. Because Avraham can deny
them a wastebasket or an extra sheet, but he can't make them think
it's anything but funny, all this fuss over a pile of five-and-dime-
store junk.

By now, we've all evolved anti-Avraham techniques. What I do
is give my name and number and then put my stuff down and say

---

*As the vexations mount, efficiency becomes every American's thing. But their
revisions of Israeli systems run into culture clashes. Like, if it doesn't occur to you
that anybody will rip off those battered sheets to sell in the shuk, you don't build in
safeguards against that. And the premise that saving time is Good is actually all
wrong for Israel, where the public's time is nothing to worry about (what could an
Israeli kept waiting do, write his Congressman?) and the employee will be paid
whether he finishes today or next week.

162

nothing, in Hebrew or anything else. This gets me my linens (and a scowl), and if I need anything more I apply to Ruth. Which not only gets me what I want but, since I carefully explain that I'm only going over Avraham's head because I didn't know enough Hebrew, lets me get in the needle . . . Recently, though, we had a newcomer, an American salesman type accustomed to plying "personality." The wastebasket had been omitted from his cheder, so he had a legitimate beef; and what with that and his great track record, he was sure he could charm Avraham. He tried, in Yiddish, and got the treatment, of course. And as he stood before the altar, ignored but not yet willing to be crushed, a mocking voice from the queue called, "Say, you got him eating right out of your hand, Marty." Marty called back, "I sure do"; then, grinning, held up his hand with a couple of fingers "missing" (bent backward out of sight), and the gallery resounded with American laughter. By the time Marty had clasped his hands over his head in the winning-prizefighter gesture, whatever had to be translated had been rendered into Yiddish and then Spanish, and the polite Argentines were visibly hiding smiles. (The Russians just looked dumbfounded, either not quite understanding or else shocked.) And "Way to go, man, way to go," somebody was shouting jubilantly.

Avraham must have been mystified at the way victory had been snatched from him; that day anyhow, I couldn't help being sorry for him. But eventually, I suppose, he'll have a brighter day: sooner or later, the Americans will come to value even his sheets and towels—when enough years have gone by so the consumer goodies now traveling Israel-ward in their trunks have been worn out. When they're forced to buy sheets of inferior quality at double the price, maybe they'll take sheets more seriously (or else go home).

But for now, Avraham suffers—from, I think, a painful wrenching away of his own history. For how can he respond with anything but anguish when these newcomers make light of what came of those earnest comrades, only a generation ago marching and singing and building a land out of nothing but a dream and a will? He must know that Israel needs immigrants to ensure it as a continuing reality. Yet he must also suspect that these alien feckless spirits will "absorb" as much as they are "absorbed": the habit of mockery is just something people don't give up—and it's infectious. Avraham himself may be immune, but the Israeli young probably aren't. So the dark vision that torments him, I think, is filled with light, ironic future voices, calling (maybe not even in Hebrew anymore) Way to go, Yehuda, way to go . . .

From the diary: 10
Pink lizards and orange air (April)

Maybe, every once in a while, I need a reminder—Negev Notes!—that the environment around here doesn't mean just the folks or the mercaz klita. The real environment jabbed me twice this week. And the second one, last night, was quite a poke.

But the first, a few days ago, was just a mild nudge that began with Rob, looking shaken, popping into my cheder to seek succor for his shattered nerves. It seems some some kind of lizard got into his bathroom, doubtless through the window. It had probably been there for some time, plastered against the wall near the dood (enjoying the heat?) until for some reason, it moved—and thus Rob, who was shaving, caught sight of it in the mirror. But only from the corner of his eye: "If I'd really seen what it was," he kept explaining mournfully, "I could never have. . ." The fact is, though, he did see something skitter high on the wall, and he reacted instinctively to what he perceived as a threat: he grabbed the sponja and clobbered the invader.

Rob's remorse indicated it didn't need much clobbering, though. "Such a harmless little thing," he wailed. "Nobody could possibly be afraid of it."

Well, I'll bet I could. It may be small and apparently doesn't breathe fire (It didn't even have any way to defend itself. One swipe and it was dead. Stupidly, uselessly dead) but, from the description, it looks a little like a dragon—and even a little is enough. "Nonsense," I said. "Of course you were frightened. Why wouldn't you be?"

"Of something no bigger than this?" His thumb and forefinger measured off maybe a couple of inches. "And pink, besides?" He shuddered. "When I looked at it—afterward—I felt sick. It was like a baby, all pink and innocent. They just eat flies and bugs, and they can't possibly hurt you." Then off he went again, into his I-am-a murderer routine.

While I sat there thinking that a pink lizard would sure as hell scare a lot of people I know. I myself have done next to no drinking since my arrival (not on purpose, but naturally arising alcoholic occasions seem to be few in Beer-Sheva life. The way it's looked so far is, you can get booze if you want it, but you nearly always have to make the move yourself), so I didn't really think the DTs were looming on my horizon. But even I, if I should run into a pink lizard . . . "There, there," I told Rob, and "Now, now." Plus a lot of chitchat designed to ease the pain, for a graduate of campus peace movements and Zen flirtation and love-love-love, of discovering that he was human nevertheless.

After a while, I plied him with coffee and cookies and a line of fancy-mixed "science" (mostly derived from an editorial rewrite I got stuck with once, and thus had to become an instant expert) about peripheral vision, the rods of the eye, messages flashing to the retina, etc. Then I segued into a kind of anthropo-philosophy, eclectic and custom-made for the moment's crisis: There is no innocence in nature. The possibility of wandering into the territory of a larger animal is a natural hazard—in Rob's set, "natural" is a key word and has to be used a lot if you aim to soothe—in the life of a lizard . . . Eventually, he calmed down; when I sent him off, I could be reasonably sure he would stop washing his hands pretty soon.

Susanna came home for the weekend the next day. So, over coffee in Anita and Rafaelo's cheder, I asked her about the pink lizard. Oh, them, she said (using a word for them that I promptly forgot).* They're cute little creatures. They live between the stones or something, and they like to come out in the spring and bask in the sun. But they never come up as high as the fourth floor of a building, she told me positively.† So I must have got the facts wrong.

Yeah, well . . . I didn't argue. But I've been inspecting my bathroom walls closely, from the doorway, before I enter. And I tell myself that I, too, can wield a sponja. Even if life in this foreign land holds a few hazards, I can cope.

Okay. By last night, though, I wasn't actively thinking about staying on guard against a hostile environment, especially since what I was doing was something civilized and familiar—going to the movies. In Beer-Sheva, that's not exactly a simple venture, as there are several kinds of tickets and so you have to be able to say more than just "One, please" in Hebrew. But Rob hadn't seen the (American) film and was willing to go with me, which would take care of the box-office Hebrew. And he even knew approximately where the theater was.

We set off in good time for the second show, which was said to begin at 9:20. It was possible to get there on two buses, but by the

---

*The word is "gecko," dummy.
†Of course they do, why wouldn't they? A stone wall is a stone wall, and what lizard can count stories? Israelis are always telling you flatly that something you've seen doesn't exist or something that can't, does; it's like their assurances that practically anywhere you ask about is "a ten-minute walk." Either charming or maddening, depending on how you're feeling that day about life in Israel.

time we came out of the movie all the buses would have stopped running; so it made sense to walk across town instead, and thus be more sure of the way home. It was still only dusk-dark at most and very warm—in fact, it had been so warm all day that there was a chance the theater might be air-conditioned. Just in case, I took along my old, stretched-out lavender cardigan. But that was only for use against the icy bite of artificial air: my thin blouse, short cotton skirt, and socks and sneakers were more than adequate protection from the weather (as were Rob's short-sleeved summer shirt, chino pants, and sandals). So I carried my sweater and—since I had to tote my distance glasses and my cigarettes as well as money—a smallish tan summer purse slung over my shoulder. Rob doesn't smoke and he had his glasses on and his wallet in his pocket, so he went empty-handed.

We found the theater all right, after wandering off our course only once, and got there in enough time for Rob to negotiate the tickets and even for me to buy some candy at a nearby kiosk before the first-show crowd started coming out. Not many people went in with us for the second show, but that seemed to figure: a town whose buses stop running by 11 P.M. is a town that goes to bed early. Soon after we sat down, I began to wish I'd gone to bed early, too; I was pretty tired, I discovered, and the film wasn't really rousing me. (Nor was the experience, which wasn't a first: I'd been to a movie in Beer-Sheva before, with Martha and Avi.) So I just relaxed and let the English-speaking voices fill the air; from time to time, I'd check the French subtitles against what the characters said. Rob was amusing himself by reading the Hebrew subtitles, which appear in a line below the French (sometimes, in a longish speech, the printing has to begin at about the actors' knees), and once, when there was a funny difference, he leaned over to whisper it to me; but, like me, Rob isn't much given to talking in the movies. So I ate my chocolate—which he didn't want any of—and just watched and listened in a semi-drowse. At intermission (all movies in Beer-Sheva have a hafsaka, whether the action on the screen allows for it or not*), he went out and got a Coke, but my delicate innards don't take well to fizz and I was too lazy to go look for a water fountain. Which

*Yes. A perfect example of high-handed Israeli individualism. The projectionist just stops the film wherever he feels like it (or maybe when his coffee break comes), and he almost invariably loses a bit of what follows when he starts it up again. That's how come I once saw, in Beer-Sheva, what must be the only showing of Olivier as Henry V without the once-more-unto-the-breach speech. It probably came along just after hafsaka, and the (probably not English-speaking) guy in the booth wasn't really deft . . .

isn't likely to be found in Beer-Sheva anyway, I've learned by now: in this dry climate everybody has to drink a lot, but what they mostly drink is sodas. So, though the chocolate had made me thirsty, I decided it wasn't worth it and stayed in my seat.

Thus, when the movie ended, I'd been sitting still all the while and was not only sleepy and thirsty but also a little stiff. Israeli audiences never bother with the cast names and other stuff that rolls up after the last scene (indeed, if the scene ends with a slow fade or a lingering glance, half the audience is gone before it's over), and I was being slow and fumbling about the business of putting my glasses away, collecting my sweater, etc., so we were the last to leave the theater. The single remaining attendant, looking decidedly impatient, was waiting to shut the door behind us as we emerged into the lobby. With me still tucking things away in my purse and saying to Rob, "I'm not really mad about the idea of walking home. And I've got money, so if you see a cab—"

"Well, I don't think—" He broke off to steer me past the glowering employee. The doors clanged shut behind us instantly. "I'm afraid there's a problem," Rob said, uncomfortably enough to attract my attention. So I was looking up at him, in mild surprise, when all the lights behind and above us went out abruptly.

And then I didn't need to be told what the problem was. For a strange, frightening dark that wasn't really dark but sort of orange moved in and swallowed us. Rob's face was almost invisible, and for a moment I half-thought he had been carried away. Or that I had— the feeling was rather like having been tossed into a sea. Only, a very dry and oddly warm one.

Rob's voice, queerly muffled, was explaining that he'd had a feeling, when he went out at intermission. But he wasn't sure, so he didn't say anything. "I should've told you. We should've started home then," he said angrily.

We had moved forward tentatively from under the brief shelter of the movie theater's mini-arcade. And it was clear, right then, that I had no time for Rob's breast-beating routine, not now. For there was nothing out there but the orangey whirl, entirely blotting out the bowl of stars I'd got used to in the night sky of Beer-Sheva. And indeed blotting out nearly everything: down at the end of the flagstoned walk leading to the street, I could see the silver-painted base of a street lamp glimmering darkly. But all I could see of the light at its top was a faint yellowing of the dark-orange up there, and it looked very, very far away. "What's happening?" I whispered.

"A sandstorm, I guess."

I glanced over my shoulder. Dark, black dark: the last man in the theater had doubtless gone out the back way and was halfway home by now. And out front there was nobody visible: in the deserted street, nothing moved—everything had been carried away by the dark and turbulent sea of air.

Rob at least was sure which way to go, so we set off. After a few steps into the terrifying thickness, we held hands: it was the safe and sane thing to do, but I think we would've wanted to anyway. For, by the time we reached the corner, it seemed we were the only things alive in the whole whirling world.

I really don't see how I'm going to explain this in a book, because it sounds so utterly contradictory, that coexistence of everything in motion and at the same time a stifling stillness. But that's the way it felt, because there was no real sense of being in a wind: we stumbled, but only because of the difficulty of seeing the ground, not because of any problem in keeping on our feet. In fact, as we struggled slowly*—a pair of scared babes in a horribly enchanted wood, running from the wicked witch who'd cast this spell—I kept wanting to push the air out of my way. It seemed solid, thick and heavy, like something you could move aside with your hands. And then maybe you'd be able to see.

Even the fact that millions and billions of tiny prickles were stinging my face didn't seem to have anything to do with a wind; it was just one more awful thing happening. But it was the thing, I think, that finally stirred my fuddled mind to attempt some defense by rounding up the stored information that went with the word "sandstorm." That didn't turn out to be much—the word "burnoose" (probably filed for potential use in word games) and a few travel-ogue photos of Arabs in flowing robes—but it was enough to make me get smart: I tied my sweater over my head, bringing the sleeves up to cover my mouth and chin, like the Arabs in the pictures. That left nothing showing except my eyes, and, after a moment's thought, I dug out my glasses and put them on. They were meant for distance and distance was precisely what I couldn't hope to see, but at least they kept the sand out.

Rob had no extra equipment (in his case, glasses weren't extra), so about all he could do was keep his head down. He admired my ingenious headdress, though, and considered doing the same thing with his shirt. But he had no undershirt, and this way, he decided wryly, it was a smaller area that was getting sandblasted.

---

*You see what I mean? You had to sort of *deduce* the wind. For that was why progress meant struggle, of course. But I didn't remember it that way until I wrote the word.

168

I don't know whether I've ever been so grateful for an attempt at humor. Because he was tense as all hell—I could feel it in his hand, and he practically gave off rays besides—so it represented real gallantry. I recognized that because I'd had half a lifetime's experience of being the mother, observant and responsible and guiding, and I knew how hard it could be when you were scared yourself. But mostly I was grateful for the relief: I own little sense of direction anyhow, and on our walk to the movies I'd simply followed Rob absentmindedly, talking about something else all the way. So I had no practical way to be responsible, and I certainly couldn't guide—even if I could see, or breathe, and even if I hadn't been feeling that the top of my head might come off...

Thus the burden of getting us home—or of at least getting us somewhere out of this hostile whirl—was all Rob's. I clung to his hand like a child, and if I made any effort at all to play a part in our survival, it amounted to little more than gasping, from time to time, that he was doing fine. (You big-strong-man, me little-helpless... Ugh.) I don't like saying that, of course. But I see a couple of things now about it. Like, that what we were both doing—Rob effectively, but even I weakly—was concentrating on what was expected of us, clinging to a frame of reference even while the physical evidence was busy wiping it out. Awash in a world where nothing was visibly in its place, and almost nothing was audible at all, Rob was still being a member of a civilization that says a man must take care of women, and most especially Mama; so, nightmare or no, he did.

But my presence must have reassured him, too, I suspect. Because what causes a good part of the panic of being out in a sandstorm is the sensory deprivation. I remember hearing once of experiments in out-of-touchness, involving floating somebody in body-temperature fluid that he can't feel because he's wearing some kind of allover suit; he can't touch the sides of the tank and it's always dark and always the same temperature and utterly silent. If I recall correctly, what was mostly proved was that that was the short way to psychosis. I can understand why, I think: old nightmares of being lost in the night, of homelessness, or of smothering or drowning, lie frozen in the mind and are instantly warmed to life by fear (which of course then sets up physiological panic-manifestations that make the feeling of smothering very real). And then perhaps, unless you're very strong and/or lucky, infancy takes over: maybe in an Antarctic blizzard, it's not the cold but the wipeout of the world—also by a blinding whirl, only theirs would be white instead of orange—that makes people want to stop trying, just curl up in the snow and go to sleep and die. I've been trying to think what might have happened if I'd been out alone that night, and I suspect it would've been something very like that, stumbling in blind circles until I gave up in that special, cut-off despair. Whether I died would depend on where I'd curled up in my infantile huddle, I suppose, and on how long the storm lasted and whether anybody just happened to find me. But all those factors would be beyond my control (especially the first: in my ignorance, I'd probably pick the worst place) or even my interest . . .

Well, I don't know. For, even without Rob to hold on to, there was one definite, and perhaps saving, stimulus to the sense of touch. It didn't happen all the time, but at some point I could feel my bare arms and legs being sort of silkily stroked. Despite Rob's assumption that if he took his shirt off his torso would get "sand-blasted," it wasn't like that at all—it was delicious. Soft, and languorous. (Oh wow, did I say "saving"? Come to think of it, that feeling may have been the fatal invitation instead—to come lie down and get stroked to death!) I asked Rob about it this morning, and he thinks it was probably electricity in the charged air coming and going rhythmically and making the hairs stand on end. He apparently wasn't troubled by it. But his legs were covered, and his arms are of course much hairier than mine: maybe you only get that sleek, sort of furtive stroking effect if the hair is sparse and downy. (Or maybe Rob, busy leading the troops, simply wasn't as vulnerable as I was?)

Get back to what happened . . . Okay, but I can't be very specific, because all I know is that at some point before it was actually over, it began to be. We were still wandering, stumbling over invisible curbstones, stifling in the loaded air; all the water seemed to have been blotted out of my body—and I'd been thirsty to start with. Still, somehow the whole thing had become a problem instead of a nightmare. Perhaps that happened when the search-lights came on, one at our right and another at our left; they looked very far away, but then, everything did. "It must be the air base," Rob said, relieved—maybe because it showed we were going the right way. But the really heartening effect was just the news that there was somebody else out there, even though they weren't aware of us. Like in one of those science-fiction stories where the few people who've believed themselves the only survivors of a nuclear holocaust suddenly hear a radio signal . . . Later, when we also heard the strained, thick sound of a siren—probably the police, we agreed, and began looking for something instead of just peering as we fumbled down dark-orange streets—it either set off or rein-forced a changed feeling, that we were going to make it. The searchlight beams crossing in the thick sky, the image of a police car slipping through the streets, reminded not only of professional protectors and defenders, who presumably knew what to do and how to do it, but of me, Maggie, a citizen, a friend of friends, a member of an ordered world.

I must have let go Rob's hand, because I remember being surprised, and stumbling in a nervous effort to keep up, when we turned the last corner and I saw the dark blotch of the mercaz klita. Binyan Aleph looked like not anything so clearly defined as a boat, just a black splotch in the all-pervading burnt-orange, with hazy yellowish shimmers that must be the lights along the galleries. There were no lights in any of the cheders, though. Or on the staircases either, but Rob, charged with the energy of triumph, forged ahead and found the entrance to our staircase—and then, for the first time, we were indoors.

"Be careful, it's slippery," he warned. Once in the enclosed staircase, I'd taken the sweater off my head and we were using it like a mountain climber's line, Rob holding one end while he felt his way slowly upward in the blackness and I hanging on to the other end. A few steps up, my purse, swinging from my shoulder, hit the banister. So then I had that to hold on to, too. And I needed every hold I could get, for under my sneakers the sand, carpeting each step and piled in the corners, wasn't gritty, as you might expect, but like walking on glass.

When I went fishing in my purse for my key, though, the sand on it was gritty. I didn't wonder then how the sand had got at my keys, inside a zippered compartment inside the zipped purse (which also has a flap closing over the outer zipper!), but I suppose it prepared me subliminally for when we turned on the lights in my cheder. I'd left everything closed up except the kitchen window, high in the wall and opening onto the gallery. The refrigerator stood underneath. Its top, and the objects on it, looked like a beach with half-buried abandoned toys—and more sand had cascaded down its side and was lying in drifts on the kitchen floor. I wasn't about to cope with that problem right then, though, so we tacked between drifts. "Come on, I'll buy you a drink," I said, and Rob said he could sure use one and followed me into my bedroom. (I kept my bottle in the wardrobe, out of deference to the official shape of things. For, although I occupied Cheder 40 alone, the kitchen was theoretically communal and only my room was my own.)

The situation looked better in there. There is no window, only the door leading to the balcony, and I'd left that closed and locked, with the curtain drawn across it—which I've learned you're supposed to do when it's hot, and it had still been quite warm when I

171

left. The balcony door was still closed, but a visible pile of sand, with veritable dunes at the corners, outlined its bottom edge; more sand had drifted over to the side of the wardrobe and was piled up there. The room was stifling, for there seemed to be a shortage of air everywhere, and certainly in this closed-up box.

And the last thing we needed, probably, in a temperature that must have been close to 100 degrees, was a slug of brandy. But my hoarded Courvoisier was for special occasions, and this sure as hell was one. So I got the bottle out and, from the top shelf of the bookcase, the little handleless Arab teacups somebody had bought for me at the shuk. Fortunately, I kept them turned down—because when I lifted one, it left its circular mark (no, more than a mark, actually an indentation) in an invisible film that must have been half an inch thick. "How did it get in here?" *I wondered, eyeing the stone wall above the bookcase.*

Rob offered no answers, just sat there on the end of the bed, sweating. He gulped his brandy and held out his cup for another. I obliged, then put the bottle down and felt my soaked hair, which had not benefited greatly by being wrapped in a sweater: it was as wet as if I'd just climbed out of a swimming pool. "It's unbearable in here," I said impatiently. "We've got to open that door." I heard Rob make some kind of objection, but I was already at the balcony door, pulling the curtain aside—this was my house, and I had survived and was back in charge, see . . .

I unlocked the door and just turned the handle, but I never really got to open it. Instead, I got hit with a solid wall of boiling air, a good ten degrees hotter and fiercely, unmistakably inimical. It was like a leak in a submarine—I staggered, holding frantically to the door to keep from being swept off my feet. But losing ground: by the time Rob leaped up and crossed the room, I'd already fetched up, still hanging grimly to the door handle, with my back against the wardrobe. He pried my fingers off the handle and began struggling to get the door closed. When I went to add my weight, he yelled, "Stay back—the glass may go!" and turned, trying to hold the door with his shoulder while he yanked at the curtain, pulling it over between his body and the glass panes.

In the end, though, it did take both of us to get the door closed against the raging out there. I wanted to put the desk chair against it, but Rob said no, that might only concentrate the force on the glass in the upper part. (Right? Who knows? I do know now, though, that quick "sciencing" applied to distress of mind is a gimmick that works both ways, doesn't it?) That was the last of Maggie the manager, in any case: from there on, we just sat on the bed, with me leaning against one wall and Rob the other, and sipped brandy. He opened his shirt and used the tail to wipe his face and his glasses and I just sat there, being neither Mama nor even hostessy enough to offer a towel. Whatever it was that had started beating madly in my chest during the struggle with the door was now in my throat, threatening to choke me. When I felt up to it, I took my shoes and socks off—sand I hadn't even felt pattered onto the stone floor—but then I had to rest: the air was thick and hot, all but unbreathable. Some more electrical goings-on, I guess. Because it reminded me of a time when a hurricane came through Washington. When the eye passed over, I was sitting in the kitchen of my battened-down house; the electricity had failed, but my husband and children were home safe and with me, my daughter's eyes sparkling with the adventure of the thing, and it was even cozy there in the candlelight. Until suddenly something altered, invisibly but unmistakably, and in a moment it was all I could do not to scream. Phil, who was then about five months old, had no such inhibitions: he let out a piercing wail—though, a second before, he had been smiling and gurgling, showing off his repertoire to his gathered family and apparently charmed by the flickering yellow light. I can't remember now what his father said while I was trying to quiet the frantic baby, but I think it had something to do with electricity and air pressure and stuff like that. It would pass in a few minutes, I remember he assured the big-eyed, suddenly silent ten-year-old...

But in that stifling room in Beer-Sheva, the same sort of scream-feeling didn't pass in a few minutes, it went on and on—while Rob and I tried to tell each other we had really-truly been out in that and while the sand drifted silently, unstoppably, into the locked stone-walled shelter that shouldn't, by any logic, have been so frail. We marveled that the lights were still on and wondered whether the water was, but neither of us got up to see. And after a while it became obvious that we really had nothing more to say, it was just that neither of us wanted to be alone. Well, I did, in a way: my clothes were sticking to my sticky body and I wanted terribly—as I imagine Rob did, too—to stand under a nice cool shower; but I didn't want it more than I wanted human society. And he seemed to feel the same way, for he kept saying it was late and he ought to go along and let me get to bed, but he didn't make any attempt to do it. And when he did manage to stagger into the bathroom and wet some towels, I felt instantly frightened though he stayed in sight. I draped the damp towel around my neck, and it did help—for a few seconds, anyhow—but what I was really grateful for was that he'd returned.

It was about 3 A.M. when, finally, something seemed better or else we just felt better. Rob went to his own cheder, but before he left, he resoaked both towels and warned me not to open the balcony door. (He also stood looking down at me for a moment, wearing a look I didn't quite fathom. Asked him about it this morning: I was wondering how you call for an ambulance in Beer-Sheva, *he tells me. I must have looked even worse than I felt.)*

When I heard the front door click shut, I moved just enough to yank the bedspread down; I could hear the sand (our clothes must have been absolutely loaded with it) as I kicked it off the end of the bed. Then I lay down and put one wet towel over my head and forehead—but not over my eyes—and the other over my front, and apparently passed out in the next second. With the light on. Nothing on earth could have made me turn it out.

P.S. I was told, this morning, that last night's was the worst sandstorm in local memory. (The people who told me had heard that on the Hebrew news: they were all asleep in their little trundle beds when it was happening.) Ain't I lucky? It's apparently also rather late for sandstorms. Ruth says they nearly always have a lulu in early April, just before Passover*—but after all the housewives have finished getting ready for the holiday, which involves a spring cleaning in spades, as the rules require not only washing out cupboards but also changing to special Pesach dishes, etc. So then they have to do it all over again . . .

What a peculiar people the religious Jews are! Because if year after year God keeps undoing all their devout labors, wouldn't you think they'd conclude He's maybe ordering a change in the rules? In any other group that ascribes all events to God (or even gods), they'd surely take it as a sign. But no, God is good and is God—and also sends sandstorms just before Pesach . . .

---

*And maybe did in the time of Christ, too? I don't see why not. But it never seems to turn up in any of the dramatizations or "biographies"—perhaps because of the same European and Middle Ages slant that gave a Jew born in Bethlehem most unlikely fair hair and blue eyes—though everyone's emotions and reactions are affected by the charged air of even the mildest sandstorm. And if you're imagining a re-creation, surely a factor so relevant and dramatic (particularly in a film, no?) must be worth including.

From the diary: 11

Going to Jerusalem (May)

The first time I went to Jerusalem, I remember I told Yoshua the day before (yes, I had finally reached the professor on the telephone, thanks) and he thought it only right and proper—clearly, if I'd been so unfortunate (or so slovenly) as to have failed to lay my eyes upon Jerusalem, I must of course rectify that forthwith. There was a distinct proprietary quality in his gracious advices, part of which was simply the general Israeli attitude: they're all absolutely nuts on the subject of Jerusalem, I've seen by now.

But the big point Yoshua wanted to make was that I could now go there directly, right through the West Bank instead of having to head first west toward the Mediterranean and then make a nearly right-angled turn inland again. Which ridiculous journey (it's quite insane, if you look at a map) was required before the 1967 war, when that chunk of land was Jordan's and they wouldn't let any Jews pass through it. Technically, it's still Jordan's—pending peace talks, Israel has elaborately refrained from annexing the West Bank and Gaza, despite pressure from the opposition parties who insist that all the Biblical lands still belong to the Jews (and that Ben-Gurion shouldn't have given them away in the first place)—so the West Bank, which lies between Israel and Jordan, remains an "administered area"* run by the Ministry of Defence. Yoshua, whether or not he understood these legalities, was aware that it wasn't part of Israel (though, after six years, I guess he'd forgotten all about the still-awaited peace negotiations). But he felt that he and his fellows who'd fought in the Six-Day War had given me this gift, the name of which he perceived as rationality: now that there was once again de facto peace, the Arabs having got foolish in 1967 and again been taught a lesson, it had become possible to do things sensibly. Among those things was traveling from Beer-Sheva to

---

*The complexity and absurdity of this is obvious, and it keeps creating all sorts of daily-life problems, which end in the Knesset catching hell from both Jews and Arabs. But the ultimate example (maybe!) of the mess created for people by international gavottes is the recent brouhaha when the Minister of Defence decreed that women in the West Bank should be allowed to vote. Which is law in Israel but is counter to Jordanian law, and administered areas must be run under their prevailing law (otherwise it might be considered annexation, see?). So a huge—even for Israel—hooha erupted: the Arabs would now be entitled to charge imperialism (imposition of the conqueror's customs, e.g.), chances of peace would be impaired, and besides it was Interfering with Others' Cultures, a cardinal sin for Israelis . . . Studying the lifelong-Progressive names now raging against votes for women, I couldn't decide whether to laugh or cry.

175

Jerusalem—which Yoshua had certainly not gone to war for, but he felt gracious about his part in arranging this convenient by-product.

I suppose because all the other Israelis had done as much, a similar proprietary pride was evident during the bus trip. A man sitting beside me turned out to speak some English and kindly offered explanations of puzzling sights (no, there had not been a forest fire, those rows of black and withered stumps out there are what grape vines look like when they're cut back for winter). And, in the fashion I now know to be usual here, everybody else got into the act, too: this was Chev-ROAN—marvelous dazzle of bottles and jars and vases, blue and gold and green, all winking in the sunlight—of whose glass I must have heard, even chutz-l'AHretz (outside The Land)? I had, I assured them, once I recognized Hebron glass. And over there, a burnt-out, rusted-out hulk of a defunct truck serving as monument, was the site of the terrible bloody battle to open a road to besieged Jerusalem in 1948,* twenty-five years ago this very spring. (Yes, I knew about that battle. It was in the movie.) A dozen voices told me, in at least three languages, why the houses out there all had blue doorways. They belong to Arabs—to VIP Arabs, in fact, which is why they're so large and handsome—and Arabs believe that blue keeps the devil out. (Or more precisely, I suspect, enough of them still believe it so that biggies among them had better do it.)

What I should have asked about on the bus—but I didn't, alas—was the impressive display of against-the-odds agriculture in Arab villages near Jerusalem. For the steep hillsides near the road must have been stonier than practically anywhere, if the terracing stone walls, in curving rows all the way down every hill, are an indication of what was lying around in the ground. The sight of all that effort is truly awesome, maybe because it's individual-sized—one person at a time, one day at a time—and therefore emotionally comprehensible. During years and years of days of sun and rain and seasons, people in that landscape of flowing robes and an occasional donkey had worked their lifetimes away, digging out and piling up literally millions of stones so they could grow a day's food on those tiny terraces. That's old, you know it when you look at it; that's about as old as you can imagine . . .

That look of permanence, of the Arab farms having been there all the way back to the era of one-stone-at-a-time, impressed

---

*It was taken by the Jordanians, who didn't have Israeli-type scruples about molesting other peoples' cultures. And who so thoroughly molested the city that they acquired the mantle of legitimacy: it's quite commonplace to talk now of "returning" Jerusalem to them!

me enough so I brought it up on Saturday morning. We were all sitting around the table in Yaakov and Sara's house, having coffee (real, perked coffee, my first in Israel!) and several varieties of cakes, some of them brought by Sara's mother and by two old neighbor ladies for whom this visit was, obviously, a Shabbat tradition. The talk had been proceeding mostly in English, for my benefit, with everything going along sunnily until one lady asked me about my trip up from Beer-Sheva—and I don't know what madness possessed me, but what I chose to talk about (at length and in detail, yet!) was that careful, stone-wall terraced landscape I'd seen. And then I added the fatal remark: "I hadn't realized the Arab agriculture was so sophisticated." Oops. You can't miss the news of a gaffe—heads go up, backs stiffen, and the air is suddenly full of withheld gasps. So I knew I'd said something dumb. But I thought it was about agriculture (which figured, as a consequence of deciding to talk about something I knew virtually nothing about). "Or perhaps contour farming isn't really a new development?" I ventured apologetically, by way of a save.

It didn't save a thing: the silence, already utter, became loaded. Finally competent Sara took a hand—no, it wasn't, she said. Then, with the question about contour farming thus disposed of, she added, gently but pointedly, "Those stone walls were built by the Jews, Maggie. Long before there were Arabs living there." Everybody proceeded to look politely elsewhere, while I sat there recalling that a heavy Zionist argument for the establishment of the State of Israel relies on the fact of the Jews' return . . . Then one of the ladies began to talk brightly about the problems of teaching Jewish history (she was a retired teacher, I gathered) and ,having thus established me as a victim of lousy education, passed the coffee cake. And Sara's mother, a brisk chic tweedy lady, launched into a funny story about her own geographical confusion when she first went to the States. (The story sounded true, but not for Sara's mother, who would've studied up beforehand. I'll bet it was some other Israeli it happened to.)

My dropped brick may have reinforced Sara's intention to take me on a tour of the city that Saturday (in the car. And Yaakov had gone off to take care of his correspondence, which ought to indicate how "observant" was the milieu); this trip had at least been proved necessary, though it meant organizing all four kids—it was early March, and cold as hell—and using up her only day off from work. In my Washington days, I'd had experience of doing involuntary guide duty for visitors to my nation's capital; I hadn't thought it fun, so I was guilt-struck and kept demurring. But "You don't understand how it is with us," Sara said finally, raising her head from the business of getting her two-year-old's boots on. "For an Israeli, since 1967 it is the greatest pleasure, to show people Jerusalem." Her blue eyes, large and intelligent, surveyed me with a kind of scientific curiosity mixed with mildly scornful amusement. Once again, Oh. For, if they really wanted to see Washington's sights, I used to tell houseguests, it was much better to go on one of those conducted tours. It's true I did get a charge out of looking at the Declaration of Independence behind glass in the Archives building, and I especially liked Lincoln and the words hewn into the wall of the Memorial (". . . we must think anew, we must act anew, we must disenthrall ourselves . . ."). But those amount to pretty small potatoes beside the visible glow of Sara's "greatest pleasure."

Well, the difference is, I guess, that I never had to fight to get Washington back after somebody'd taken it away from me* and kept me locked out of it for nineteen years. Sara didn't hammer the point, and in fact she tried conscientiously to be only flatly instructive: Here was the barbed wire . . . No Jew could go beyond this point until after the Six-Day War. (She didn't even make the useful propaganda point that the edict had applied to all Jews, not just Israelis or even just Zionists—thus "correcting" freer countries' notions of citizenship. The Israelis, even brainy and sophisticated ones like Sara, seem to be inept propagandists.) But her painstaking understatements in fact had the effect of highlighting the emotion they were restraining.

All I remember about that first tour was all those hills—the city lies in a bowl of them—with history all over every one. But I'm afraid the only history that gave me a real feeling of cozy partisanship was the story about the Hill of Evil Counsel—a name the naughty Jewish colonials didn't make the Mandate authorities privy to, and so that's where the British built a fine mansion for their High Commissioner. From which he could look down and wonder what the natives were sniggering about in secret glee . . . But neither the Western Wall's great hewn stones bearded with accidental interstitial grasses (old, very old, is all I felt) nor the dig nearby (very-very old) that promised great leaps of knowledge about antiquity

---

*Nobody mentions this, but I hear it whenever I listen to the old-hand Israelis who were around before statehood: there's a special bitterness for them stemming from the fact that they were ex-colonials who'd finally got rid of the British—but the Jordan Legion that proved too much for the embattled Jewish farmers and thus conquered Jerusalem were British-trained, -fostered, and maybe even -funded. So what was involved was more than Jews vs. Arabs—and indeed, some of the old Arab families felt little empathy with the attackers.

stirred me to any real emotion—though the latter, it was clear, did at least that for Sara. But for me, a single look out over the desert at dusk seems to do more than all of history-dripping Jerusalem.

Which leads me to why I started this entry, after another Friday when I toddled back from J'lem with my evening dress (Janice made me pack one in my suitcases, on the grounds that I'd need it before my trunks arrived, and she was right) and the jewelry and stockings and shoes that go with it all tucked in a plastic shopping bag along with my toothbrush and pj's. For this one was a big-deal weekend, since Yaakov and Sara were entertaining a foreign Nobel laureate, plus a whole slew of other Prominent Persons from abroad. Chinese lanterns dangled in the garden and well-dressed, well-educated folk moved about beneath them, conversing in a handful of languages and with impeccable grammar, I'm sure, in all of them. (The Israeli intellectuals are really funny: they talk a mile a minute and are chock-full of ideas, which they discuss in any terms that seem relevant. Thus American sociological terminology will pop up suddenly in the midst of a rapid discourse in the kind of Hebrew I'll probably never be able to understand.* And of course all quotations, place names, etc., are in the original languages, so that Descartes appears abruptly in an incomprehensible dialogue—as though he'd stuck his head in to make an announcement to a class of Hungarians . . .)

That sort of thing is undeniably interesting, and often fun besides. For Teddy Kollek, the mayor of Jerusalem, is a real charmer—one of those genuine political talents who get you even though you know being charming is their trade—and Isaiah Berlin looks and sounds satisfyingly like everybody's idea of a Great Man of the Age; and I guess I've got enough fan-club impulse so that when the Arthur people are talking about getting together with next week turns out to be Rubinstein, I feel that I'm really Up There. In a sense then, these weekends among the movers and shakers are less foreign and more like home (with an occasional upward-mobile touch, even) than anything else about my life in Israel. So why is it that on the way back to Beer-Sheva this morning is when I started to feel at home? To be precise, it was when the bus had passed the last of the roadside kibbutz fields and the easy green (including trees

---

*In one hilarious instance, Hebrew wasn't all I couldn't understand, viz., when a British visitor told me his field was Arab "sonse," which is how Oxbridge pronounces "science." I took it for "sonnets" and professed amazement that the Arabs had any; he assured me that in 600 A.D. they'd etc., etc. (while I went on wondering whether Arabic lent itself to iambic pentameter). Eventually, we deduced cross-premises. But it took a lot of—peculiar—dialogue before the thing got unscrambled. . .

that "just growed"!), and the brown hills speckled with clumps of pasture grass began to appear. This is the time when anything that's going to grow in the Negev had better hurry, so it's "flowering" now. But it's still a landscape in which a tree is apt to be a sudden and heartlifting sight, a land where a cloak-wrapped woman on a plodding donkey—a picture so Christmas-like that your mind automatically fills in the figure of Joseph walking alongside—turns up right there beyond the bus window.

And then come the black tents of the Beduin encampment, with a few goats trailed by girls (so skinny, with such pipe-cleaner legs) waving their not very business-like little sticks over the herd. And a feeling of this-is-where-I-belong takes over: I remember how country-cousin my slacks, designed to keep my legs warm, looked the first time I got off the bus in Jerusalem, where fashion comes first and women were wearing nylons and boots like those I discarded before I left America. (Or, if they did wear trousers, it was as part of sleek and beautifully tailored suits made of imported tweeds.) They were wearing fur coats then too, not fuzz-lined bulky utilitarian jackets, and hats instead of scarves tied around their heads... But in my bus, what was chic then was whatever kept you warm—and now it's whatever keeps you cool—and my plastic-bag "luggage" was only a lighter version of the great rug-wrapped bundle that belonged to the Arabic-speaking women sitting behind me. It jolted along in the middle of the aisle and everyone stamm had to climb over it; when we arrived in Beer-Sheva, one of the women set off down the street from the bus station, carrying the bundle on her head.

That's because here where I live, it's Asia, see. And back where I came from this morning, where there were delicacies to eat and thousands of books and Verdi's Requiem recorded at the highest level of technology—that's Europe. The survivors of the early settlers, and their children, having secured their land—by lots and lots of blood, sweat, and tears, over and over again—have managed to return (those of them who were lucky, or talented, or both) to what my grandmother left in old Vienna, maybe. I guess that's what the scene reminds me of, with the music and the lantern-spangled garden, and ladies and gentlemen of slow and elegant dignity—like something out of Arthur Schnitzler (only it's philosophy, not flirtation, that sparks the repartee). But it's all so different, down here in Asia. And I'm not at all sure how well Yaakov and Sara know that—though Yaakov (who came to Israel as one of the children rescued from post-Hitler Europe; Sara, though, is a sabra) gets all dewy-eyed at the idea of a group of immigrants and once asked me nostalgically whether the Sochnut still gives you a cot with a straw mattress when you settle in an apartment. (It does, I hear: the Artzis got them, along with a primitive primus-like thing to cook over, and a couple of rolls of toilet paper. They didn't really need the last two items, but tradition is tradition . . .)

Well, I don't suppose it makes any in-the-last-analysis difference, this Europe/Asia thing: they're all Israelis. But it isn't the "last analysis" I take up residence in, so it makes a difference to me. Thus, scratch any notion that I could do the immigrant bit in Beer-Sheva and then move on to J'lem. For, maybe it's because my huddle is here, but this—Asian Israel—is the Israel I'm at home in.

From the diary: 12

"Occupant," Beer-Sheva (June)

By the end of May, I knew I just had to move on from the mercaz klita. "But why? Think it over," Ruth argued, sounding hurt. She looked around the now rather cheerful little kitchen that was my very own, in a whole two-room flat all to myself. (Well, I couldn't actually use the other bedroom, since it was officially supposed to be available and Avraham regularly came around on inspection trips. He would've just loved finding that I'd spilled over into it, but he never did—I stowed some books in the closet there for a while, but that's all. And I always kept the door of that room closed.)* My trunks had arrived, and even the incredible ordeal-by-Customs had been eased for me because Vered, who happened to be visiting in Haifa at the time, volunteered to go with me through the port hassle.

That act of generosity gave her a real education, by the way: there's of course nothing lacking in Vered's Hebrew and, as a social worker, she's certainly used to coping with bureaucracy; but she nevertheless ended up livid and shaking with rage after we'd trotted back and forth between functionaries, describing endless repetitious zigzags, in the broiling sun for most of a day. "Unbelievable!" Vered would burst out every hour or so, and "A scandal!" Then she'd launch into a tirade in Hebrew addressed to the nearest Israeli (if he was an official, he usually ignored her, and if an ordinary citizen, whatever he replied seemed to end with a shrug and "Ma la'assot?") It was a wonder, she would fume when it was English's turn again, that the immigrants didn't all turn around and go home. Something must be done about this . . . I just listened, dulled by heat and exhaustion and up to noting only that an enraged citizenry is apparently an international phenomenon.

My shipment from home hadn't included furniture, my foot-lockers were easily disposed around the cheder as tables or seats,

---

*I couldn't ignore the rules, or be overtly defiant to Avraham, because that would give him a weapon against Ruth (who outranked him but could hardly forbid him to inspect). However, once when he'd irritated me particularly, banging on my front door like a storm trooper, etc., I did pull a psychological jujitsu stunt. Breathing hard and generally putting on a show of guilty nervousness, I let him in. (In terms of art, twisting my hands and the other bits of business may have been overdone; but never mind, they worked.) As he approached the empty room, I mimed outright panic. He fell for it, throwing me a look of pure venomous triumph as he flung open the door—on a vista of stripped bed and bare desk and shelves, all demurely awaiting a theoretical roommate . . . His face was a treat, it really was.

and an extra bookcase for my crate of books was scrounged for me the moment it could be managed. (The empty crate, out on my balcony, would be perfectly safe from rain until next winter. And it did nicely as "garden furniture.") Thus Ruth had a right to be a little hurt, not to say puzzled: everybody had done everything to make me happy, so why should I want to leave the mercaz klita?

I told her it was because I'd signed a contract to do a suspense novel and I had to get to work on it. Which was true: I'd already started, in fact—first versions, outlines, carbons, and several kinds of typing paper littered my room, and the "Rosetta stone" I needed for my intricate plot (it had columns listing where characters were, where they said they were, and where other characters believed they were, at crucial times during a mythical week) was tacked to the door of the wardrobe. A letter from my editor, setting forth an objection I'd have to get around somehow, was Scotch-taped to the wall above the desk—from where it loomed whitely at me as I lay in bed, a last-thing-at-night and first-thing-in-the-morning Grim Warning. And worst of all, I couldn't do anything about it first thing in the morning, which is the best time for me to work (not necessarily morning, but whatever time is right after breakfast time). Only, at the mercaz klita that natural rhythm was defied every day: first thing in the morning was really that—7 A.M.—and I was off to my ulpan class instead of to my novel. Which meant that I sat in class with half my mind elsewhere, and only got around to my book during a couple of squeezed-in hours later, after my Hebrew homework. By which time it was a near-schizophrenic effort to recall what Guy Silvestri was supposed to be detecting in "Buxford," Mass., on a certain Tuesday.

Well, thanks to my literary littering, Ruth could see for herself I had logistic problems that no amount of staff good will could overcome. But people usually stayed in the mercaz klita for at least six months, and indeed one of Ruth's recurring headaches was easing them out—which could take several months more. So my yen to flee the nest early wasn't something she ran into routinely, and she was worried about sending such a ragged-feathered fledgling out into the great world of Beer-Sheva (population at the time probably about 80,000, including a very large percentage who were babes in arms). Without any more Hebrew than I had at present, she put it delicately—what she meant was, the only thing that gave me the title of second-worst student in my class was that the worst-worst guy had a tin ear and I could at least mimic—how could I possibly manage? I'd manage, I argued; I'd already made some Israeli friends in town, all of whom were minded to be helpful.

183

Umm, she said, and Yes, but. In the end, what most comforted her, I think, was that these Israeli friends included Martha's husband, Avi. He really rated: he had fresh experience, since his American wife was hardly less of a greenhorn than I, and besides, he himself had lived in the U.S. and thus knew the peculiar ways Americans react.

That was about how things stood this week, with me determined and Ruth's doubts at least somewhat quelled, when the university came up with an apartment possibility for Rob. It's over in an older, less elegant shikun (neighborhood, quarter) than the one around here and is inhabited preponderantly by Moroccans and other "Orientals"; it isn't a slum, though, as these are apparently the people who settled in and bought flats and have had jobs for, some of them, nigh onto twenty years. But the jobs tend to be blue-collar and, except for a few renters who've landed there via ads on the student-lounge bulletin board, college educations are not the neighborhood norm. Rob went over to look at the place, and from his description it seemed rather like a lower-middle-class neighborhood where I lived once in Somerville, Mass.—and where, I assured him, I got along quite well with the neighbors and nobody raped me or ripped off my TV.

But he nevertheless decided to turn the apartment down. His chief reason, that it's on the ground floor and right next to a school yard, both of which will mean noise, constituted no drawback for me: I'm pretty tired of running up and down four flights of stairs, so the first floor sounds good; and, unless somebody is talking directly to me, no amount of buzzing life (and particularly not the shrieks of playing children: where would I be if that had bothered me!) dents my concentration.

I can see from the way I've been writing, above, that I probably would have wanted that apartment unless a cockroach opened the door for us when Rob took me over there to see it. For, though admittedly very small—forty-eight square meters: I don't know how much that is in feet, but it's minimal even in Beer-Sheva—it has two bedrooms, which means a workroom that the door can be closed on, oh joy! The back balcony (on the ground floor, a back porch is what it would really be) has been closed in to make a dining alcove, and what was originally the back door now opens into a kind of pantry off the kitchen instead. Which is handy, as it has shelves—except for the side taken up by the dood—and the kitchen doesn't: the only place to stow things there is the couple of shelves that come with the sink-and-drainboard unit. But who cares? I left my good china and my first-wedding silver packed away in a basement in

Massachusetts so I could travel light and unburdened by "bourgeoiserie." So my few dishes and pots can fit easily on those underneath shelves—the bottom ones are actually just part of the floor, but think how good for me all that stooping will be. And for canned goods, liquor, and all the rest of the stuff that inhabits kitchen cupboards, there's that roomy pantry.

Besides, the place does have the one amenity that really counts, a bathtub! And it not only has an up-there shower—the kind you stand in the tub for, and I must remember to buy a shower curtain (I suppose they do have them here?)—but also one of those "telephone" showers that you can hold. The bathroom is very tiny, which must have been a source of fun-and-games and/or irritation (probably, given the nature of people, both) for the young couple who were the previous tenants. But it's big enough for me anyway, and it's just been repainted. The rest of the flat is a trifle grimy-looking but it'll be repainted this week, and the broken trissim* will be replaced.

The lopsidedness of the apartment's appointments—e.g., luxuries of the bath but minimal kitchen—was explained when I consulted the mercaz klita shepherds about my taking the place. For it seems the flat was bought for the daughter of the landlords (who live just across the courtyard). She doubtless ate often at Mummy and Daddy's and did little cooking on her own; but the toilette of la jeune fille is no place to stint on technology. She also had a telephone, of course—its jack is still there in the living room (no, I mean "salon"). However, despite all this coddling, she moved on, as les jeunes filles will: she's now working in the U.S. (near Boston, actually) and is engaged to be married to an American. When it became apparent that she wouldn't be back, at least not to live in that apartment, it was rented to my predecessors, the young couple who lived there for a year or a little less, while they were waiting to buy a brand-new flat. They had a baby (my work room was the nursery) and lots of expenses—what with down payments, plus kitchen cabinets and closets to buy—so the telephone, a heavy expense in Israel, was taken out. Which is too bad, because it would cost nearly a thousand lirot installation fee again. But I don't have to

---

*Slatted wooden or plastic blinds that don't tilt like Venetian blinds but just roll up and down via a cord. There are many varieties (representing not competition but different times of manufacture), but nearly all of them vanish into an oblong box above the window when rolled up. When they're down, they admit only tiny pinpoints of light and almost no air—which is often desirable, in this climate—and if you let them collapse entirely, they'll keep out both altogether.

worry about that because there's a miles-long waiting list for phones anyway.

(Look how much I know about everybody! A small town is really a remarkable experience—abridged novels all over the place.)

Ruth, Vered, and Devora—she's the other social worker: there's one from the Jewish Agency and one from the Israel Ministry of Absorption, both of which outfits settle immigrants (and yessir, I would say that indicates a certain bureaucratic unstreamlining)—all think this flat is a good deal for me. Because though the lease runs for only a year—any longer would be crazy, in a leaping inflation—it can be renewed. And presumably again at a reasonable rate, for the owners are sensible people able to appreciate the advantages of a quiet, solvent tenant like me; and the current rent, IL325 a month (about $78 at the present rate of exchange) demonstrates that they aren't interested in a capitalist fling, just in paying the taxes on the place. Anyway, we know they're not rent-gougers because—and this seems to be a typical factor in doing business in Beer-Sheva (because it's in Israel, or because it's in a small town? Try to find out which)—the wife is a social worker and Vered knows her. It seems that Mrs. Ben-Ari, a woman of honor and a real patriot, is precisely the right person to conduct Maggie into the dark wood of life in unsheltered Beer-Sheva. She speaks English and, since she's aware of my fledgling status and flimsy Hebrew, will even cope with ordering the gas connected, etc. Which, even without the etc., I happen to know is no small thing: those who have gone from the mercaz klita before me—for example, Yehuda and Yael Artzi—chill the blood with their tales of what this sort of thing involves. (In fact, it was almost enough to make me chicken out. But Martha staunchly pledged that Avi would never leave me alone with All That.)

The consensus is that I'm better off "going on the private market" (which is more expensive than the officially assigned housing, but at IL325 that's hardly a problem) because the flats provided for immigrants—like the Artzis', which is brand-new and cost virtually nothing per month and even that is applied to the purchase price—involve regulations that would strangle me. For, under the rules, I'm a "single" and am thus supposed to get only a room in an apartment shared with other singles (a setup actually inferior to mine at the mercaz klita right now). That prospect was so clearly ill-fitting that, almost immediately after Vered first talked to me, she wrote to Jerusalem explaining that she had this-here important American writer who was, what's more, no chicken and couldn't be treated like a college kid. Back came an answer in practically record time, like two to three months: okay, the author-ities were so impressed that Vered had permission to go ahead and apply for a whole one-room apartment for me, all to myself!

So, clearly, it's got to be the private market. But a furnished flat (which can only be had on the private market) usually belongs to somebody going abroad for the school year or something like that, which means they probably wouldn't be renting it until August or September (which was when I'd normally be leaving the mercaz klita, and I'll bet the staff had me on the back burner till then). And they'd probably want it back in a year: an annual need to move house is often the price of "going private" and is virtually certain with a furnished apartment. So, what with the advantages of having an English-speaking landlord right near by—and somebody we know, see—Devora advises that it pays to buy a few sticks of furniture. Which is just a one-time expense, and then you're through. And if the expense is too much, Vered says, she can get me various forms of special no-interest long-term loans, outright grants awarded for "settlement" costs, etc. (The shape of a division of labor between the two social workers begins to show up vaguely at this point. Or at least, it seems that Devora gets people apart-ments and Vered helps them move in.)

I don't know why she would think I'd need any such help. For, at $78 a month rent, I should have plenty left over just from my widow money.* I've saved some by living here so cheaply, I still have my grubstake money, and of course there's the advance I got when I signed the book contract—all of which adds up, so long as the dollar is worth at least IL4.20, to more money per person than most people in Beer-Sheva have to spend. So why would I want to tap the Jews of the world who've contributed to the UJA or whatever? Or the Israel government—if that's who pays for the subsidy on my apartment rent I'm told is my "right." (Rob's IL325 would have been subsidized by the University, too. Fantastic.) Well, if it's my right, I can presumably abjure it. For I don't see that I'm likely to founder, though my Israeli friends warn that everything's expensive (but they also volunteer stuff they can let me have). I don't have to pay the Customs that just about doubles most prices. And anyway, nothing's expensive if you don't want it—and I sure as hell don't want to acquire a mess of consumer goods.

But the whole business seems a little curious. Because if you

---

*Well, but Vered is an Israeli. The widow money comes in a government check, and to her that means it may never come, as everybody knows governments are notoriously irresponsible.

read the arrangements backward to what they're designed to care for, the image you get is a refugee who's (a) shocked and bankrupt and (b) lusting for middle-class living. Either it's an overlay, the new immigrant acknowledged but not replacing that shawled and fleeing figure of Jewish Agency tradition, or else somebody's done some acute observing and consumer goods is what the immigrant wants most even if he's shocked and bankrupt.

Last day at the old homestead.

Well, it's all done: Avi took me over to the apartment, checked to see what the most immediate fixing-up needs are, showed me the fusebox in the hall and where the grocery store is, and read me the lease. (Which he says is standard, but it sounds oddly landlord-favoring for such a worker-oriented society. Must find out why.*) I can borrow an electric hotplate from the mercaz klita—deep in Avraham's secret stores and he'll scream, but Ruth can make him produce it—until the gas is hooked up. Which it visibly is: I can see the nice shiny copper piping leading to where the stove was, and it's where mine will be, too, because it's the only possible place to put a stove; but the job will still take a fee of IL50 and some days anyway. (Avi's explanation: Because they're a bunch of fuckin crooks. *Colorful, but must find other answers.)+ The place needs a little scrubbing, but Martha will come and help me with that.*

Yesterday I signed the lease and went with Mrs. Ben-Ari to the municipal center to register it. We also had to buy government stamps: every transaction, however small, has to be decorated with these special stamps in an amount linked to the size of the deal. They're bought at the Post Office—most people keep some 25-agorot ones on hand, to stick on receipts, etc.; but a rent contract requires a special trip. We zigged and zagged on buses between her home, the court building, and the P.O. in the Old City; by the time I got back here, I figure I'd used nearly half of my twenty-ride bus ticket. And I was exhausted: Mrs. Ben-Ari tears around at the pace of one who has never had more than minimum time.

But we did get to sit down, briefly, at a coffeehouse when we finished—she's such an energetic type that even her leisure seems to

---

*Roughly, because the society started out so *very* worker-oriented that the laws gave tenants just about everything—once in, they were set for life, with the landlord virtually their indentured servant. So leases now tend to be landlord-protecting, in an attempt to even things up. (It's all very similar to the situation in socialist England.)

+Do. But they're not going to be all that different, habibi.

hum, but apparently one must be ceremonious because otherwise it'd all be too materialistic, like America. She can't be much younger than I am and looks older, as she outweighs me considerably and has pouches under her eyes. Her hair is coal black, so very black that I wonder whether it's dyed. She's a sabra, the oldest one I've met so far (here in Beer-Sheva, anyway). Mrs. Ben-Ari speaks Arabic—fluently, it would seem, since where she does her social work is Gaza, one of the "administered areas"—and maybe French too, but I didn't check that because her English needs no supplementing. She has a brisk, very executive manner and is impatient-patriotic, like Vered and others, but rather more bossy about it: not so much Something must be done as They'd better hop to it. Like so many of the locals I've met, she speaks of the government in a way that calls to mind the word "dratted." (It's not actually in their vocabulary, but that's the tone.) It surprised me that her given name turned out to be Caroline, but she seemed surprised in turn when I asked whether her parents had come from England. No, it was just that, when she was born, girls were being given names like that (the pervasive British culture again, seeping into everything!) . . . I find Mrs. Ben-Ari a bit daunting, but I like her. And nobody could doubt that she'll steer me right.

This morning Martha and I drove over to the flat with some cleaning equipment, but the painter was not finished. In fact, he was about to start on the salon. Mrs. Ben-Ari had said I could choose the color, but right now she was at work and the painter spoke no English, so we had a problem. His buckets, much-used and slopped over, implied a mix of lightish colors and I didn't see any green—which I wanted but don't know how to say anyway. However, the situation appeared to resolve itself when the painter indicated that he wanted money or he wouldn't continue. Which might mean postponing the moving but was otherwise dandy, Martha and I agreed: now we could wait and Mrs. Ben-Ari would explain to him what color I wanted. (Especially desirable since my initial attempts—like asking "What colors do you have?" in what Martha and I considered impeccable Hebrew—had drawn only a startled look.) So when he repeated the thumb-and-fingers "gimme money" gesture, I shook my head and said "Geveret Ben-Ari" and pointed over toward her apartment. He said she was "b'avoda" (at work) and I nodded and told him "Ca-ashare he choseret" thus concluding an on-the whole satisfying demonstration that my Hebrew was up to the demands of ordinary life. (Well, he choseret is the present tense and "When she returns" clearly calls for the future, which I don't have. But Martha—who didn't have it either—thought the present *tense had been adequate, considering the man's rather unsophisticated Hebrew.)*

However, this afternoon Martha turned up again to report, with not too well suppressed giggles, that she'd telephoned Avi at work and, in the process of describing our encounter with the painter, she'd repeated proudly my very conversation. Avi, it appears, could hardly restrain his laughter. Because it turns out I'd confused (lovingly, he seems to have ignored the fact that Martha did, too) TSEV-ah, "color," with tsiv-AH, which means "army." We'd better get on over there and make sure the guy wasn't doing my salon in olive drab, said Avi. And then he hung up and presumably went to tell the fellows in the office the latest immigrant joke.

Oh well. We drove back across town, telling each other it didn't matter because the painter hadn't started anyway. And besides, it was a perfectly natural mistake, Martha assured me again as we hurried down the walk between the dusty little trees. (But still, they're trees. And there's even grass, along the strip between the Ben-Aris' house and mine.) When we got there, the painter had gone—and his job was finished: Mrs. Ben-Ari was not yet home from work, but my salon walls were the much-whitened pale orange (so that it comes out sort of peach) that you see all over town; the paint, the cheapest possible whitewashy kind, was already dry. The painter had not done what you could exactly call cleaning up, but his equipment, which had been standing around in the flat on all my previous visits, had been collected and taken away. Ah, the mysterious Middle East . . .*

Well, there was no way to solve the mystery at the moment, and anyway, the flat was now ready to be cleaned. Martha turned out to have got the sponja technique down cold, so, except for the bathtub—which was not only grundgy but also spattered with the enamel paint used on the walls in there—I didn't really have to overdo for my advanced age and frail health. And it's clean and can be minimally lived in. Especially since, as a final surprise, Martha dug out of her reticule a genuwine shower curtain, brought from her Chicago apartment—and not needed in the Beer-Sheva one where handy Avi, awaiting his bride's arrival, had built a stall around the shower . . . Love is truly an ennobling emotion, spreading joy all around it.

---

*Ah, innocents abroad . . . No mystery: Mrs. Ben-Ari had either already paid or the painter knew damn well she would, so he always intended to do the work that day. But when the two Americans turned up, why not take advantage of a chance to pick up a little extra? They're so rich, and so ignorant, that Geveret Ben-Ari will probably never hear about it . . .

So, that's It. Tomorrow's the day—Maggie, an ulpan dropout, takes up life in the heart of Beer-Sheva. I've been making New Year's-type resolutions, which indicates at least qualms. Ruth's square, troubled face and earnest doubts getting to me, despite the reasons I summoned up to persuade her that it was time?

Well, maybe, but it is time: the kick has long been gone from the dormitory fantasy, and I want to be a grown-up because the grown-ups can make their own rules and go to bed whatever time they want. And I don't care if that means I'll now have to do my own sponjaing and shopping and cooking . . .

I have a feeling the sandstorm has something to do with my sense that this is enough of the sheltering institution. Which was necessary, God knows—how would I ever have coped if dumped alone into this mystifying society?—but institutional life isn't Life in Beer-Sheva. Where people know when a sandstorm is coming (I'll bet most of the moviegoers that night lived around the corner, or they wouldn't have come out) and what you meet is not other confused new arrivals—who are interesting and thought-provoking, there's no doubt—but Mrs. Ben-Ari. I could've lived in the mercaz klita for a year without running into anyone like her.

So I want to be a member of the regular, going-to-work life of Beer-Sheva. I'm still also a member of the huddle, but I've just jumped a square, that's all—catching up to the Artzis, for example, whose current problems are not about the mercaz klita and the shipping regulations but about schools and health services and repairmen. That's the mainstream now, and I'm impatient to be in it. If I'm going to live in Beer-Sheva, let's start.

And reasons are only reasons: I stamm want to leave here, that's all. I just went out on my balcony for a last look over the desert night (one thing I won't have anymore, alas, in my ground-floor flat is that high, wide view). Out there, in the black with the close, curved array of stars overhead, things are nothing-in-between and uncompromising: there's the big old sand down here and the big old bowl of sky up there, both of them always imperceptibly in their own long-term motion and not responsive to what anybody does or says or legislates or feels. No wonder the long-ago people who were born to such a landscape got busy at once with theologies . . . I thought of that once before, but differently because it was a different landscape: standing among great trees in a starlit grove in Vermont, I suddenly saw why all that abundant wheeling order would stir you to inventing, or recognizing, God. But here, I feel, it would happen for another reason—to deny the vast indifference, to blur the bare harsh visible facts. The result not of a moment's grateful awe but of every day's knowledge of fear. And thus the belief more passionately held, more likely to mean bloodshed (and tyranny?) . . .

Out there that single radar mast, or whatever it is, is the only thing reaching up, the only attempt at connection. I treasure it more than all those leafy verticals connecting earth and heaven in Vermont: this single, frail, man-made try, with its absurd little ruby dot of light on top, is so utterly brave. Not to say uppity. And heartening in a way abundant Nature can't be, as the searchlights in the sandstorm were more precious, more there, than the million-zillion candlepower of the every-night moon.

See, I knew all this had something to do with that sandstorm . . . All right. One last look at the hived slumber up close and the blackness beyond. Tomorrow I'm off to join the little bumptious band that dares to set up a town and conduct loves and wrangles and business in it, just as if anything could be counted on besides entropy.

II

9 ⬿ "Dear Folks"

I'm lucky to have some of my letters home, written soon after I moved to my first apartment, because they tell more about my discoveries and encounters than either my notebook or my memory could. The following extracts were addressed to several friends and relatives and therefore emphasize their own special interests. Some of the recipients are self-evident, but anything "miscellaneous" was either for my son Phil or my editor (and friend); anything about money was almost always addressed to the latter, but so were just-wandering thoughts because I had to write to him very often.

1.   "I don't know what I would've done without Thereza—she's an Israeli I 'picked up' while riding the *sherut* (sheh-ROOT, an intercity group taxi) to Jerusalem. Soon after that trip, which we spent talking (in English, mostly: it gives Thereza no trouble), she biked over to the mercaz klita one Saturday to invite me to go swimming with her family—they have a season membership at the Desert Inn pool. (As in the U.S., the middle class tends to do that. There is a city pool—in a desert town it's not a luxury—but that's frequented more by the poor.) It was awkward at first, especially as I was just about to go out; but apparently something I'd said gave the impression that almost the only Israelis the immigrants meet are professionals employed at the mercaz klita (which is true), and she thought that was un-good and decided it should be repaired, by golly . . .

"She rather reminds me of Janice, for she, too, has two jobs as well as a husband and a pair of kids to care for (and parents to make flying visits to in J'lem: they're old and she's their only child) and yet

195

somehow manages time for individual, inner-directed kindness. Only you'd have to imagine Janice doing it without a car or a dishwasher, and not only no microwave oven but all meals to be got 'from scratch.' This Thereza has reddish hair, but lighter than Janice's and springy-curly. No other physical resemblances, but a similar air of impatient energy, of *Let's do it. Now.* I think she's older than J., but her kids are younger, maybe eighth and sixth grade. And oh yes, there is one more resemblance—her husband is good-looking, too.

"Anyway, Thereza didn't know what her picking up the Israeli's burden was going to get her into, I'll bet. Because she ended up taking me shopping—you know what an ordeal that is in the best circumstances and these weren't, for we had to buy a lot of stuff in a hurry. Like a bed, for starters . . . I'll probably never be in more danger in Israel than I was while trailing Thereza in and out and up and down the side streets of Beer-Sheva, me in the numbed state shopping produces and her with her fine indifference to moving vehicles (it seems to be habitual with her, God help us). Hair-raising. She acts as though it's against her religion to cross with lights, or even at corners. And there's plenty of opportunity for perilous zigzagging, because first you buy the bed and then you go somewhere else to buy the foam-rubber mattress. In this case, to a Hungarian upholsterer Thereza has patronized before and from whom, talking a mile a minute in several languages (the only Hebrew I recognized was *"zot omeret,"* which means "which is to say" and seems a bit fancy for dialogue with an upholsterer; but maybe he was a Ph.D. in the old country?), she wrested fantastic concessions like having the slab cut and covered in a single day! Anyway, then you go to a certain street where freelance tender-drivers foregather, and you hire a guy to take your bed home for you—along with the desk and chair you bought in two other places, and mountains of portable stuff like a pillow, sponja, bucket, etc. Plus you: you ride in the truck too, of course. I don't really remember what-all we bought—I just kept shelling out lirot and writing checks (the English signature squinted at dubiously but accepted because vouched for by Thereza). The rest of the time it was a matter of choosing between death and losing sight of Thereza as she darted obliquely across the street from between parked cars. Death seemed less of a risk: I could never find that Hungarian again by myself.

"Her final coup was persuading the man with the tender to stop off at her house (which is *not* on the way) to pick up one of those pole-and-shelf bookcases she and Jan had left over after they did something or other to their house. It's got four shelves, but one of them needs new brackets—which we didn't have time to shop for, as she had to get to work. I'm supposed to get them myself—'butterflies' brackets—and I've got the words written down so I won't forget. So, as a by-product, I now know the word for 'butterflies'—it's *parparim*. Pretty, no? If a little exotic in my vocabulary . . ."

2.   ". . . and everything, but everything, turns out to require the services of somebody with an electric drill. (Except things electrical, and those clearly require a son or husband, for you couldn't expect to be able to hire somebody just to cover up the naked bulb dangling from the ceiling; but only the knowledgeable dare attempt it, as you have to unhook and rehook connections and at 220 volts, experiment is perilous, baby.) Those yard goods I once whipped into drapes and tacked up by myself are now reduced to covering footlockers: they ain't gonna be drapes because you can't just buy a curtain rod (even if you had an electric drill to put it up with), you have to have curtains made at a draper shop and then *they* come and put them up. Since apartments are generally owned and this is thought of as a once-in-a-lifetime expenditure, the whole thing is pretty damn expensive. So, for now, I've pasted some bright orange paper onto the panes in the living room's French window. Otherwise, the only way to avoid being on fishbowl view—and I'm practically at eye level, too, from the courtyard—would be to lower the trissim and live in darkness . . . I got the orange paper from Gladys, a woman from the AACI who took me under her wing. She works at the hospital and this paper comes between new X-ray plates. (Naturally, she saved it. You don't throw out valuable paper, not here.)"

3.   "I know now that what happened is, Peggy—who's been sending me my widow-money checks because I didn't want to change my address too often—put air-mail postage on the envelope but forgot to *write* 'Air Mail'; so, since it wasn't a special air-mail envelope, the letter came by sea. With the result that I was buying and buying and my check hadn't arrived—and that check amounts to substantial lirot. I wasn't stony broke, mind, for I still have money in my dollar account. But I didn't want to 'go into my capital' (I'm still troubled by occasional visions of Phil falling dangerously ill and my suddenly having to fly home) so I started turning on the old ingenuity. Fun in a way, but nerve-wracking. And bad for work: I'd wake in the morning with my head full of a brilliant new improvisation that would save IL100, instead of a brilliant new character or plot wrinkle . . . Still, it's been an education, for now I know how it feels to be poor. Not let's-be-Bohemian poor but nickel-nursing poor,

like if I go to the dentist that means I can't order drapes, and like postage Counts. What happens, mostly, is that there's a hesitation between you and every move, grimming everything. I'm not much given to impulse buying (that's just not the kind of impulses I get) and if I have to be a consumer I like to get it over fast; but, last month, I got my nose rubbed in consumering because I had to take thought, weigh, and worry. Not a nice way to live.

"Not least grim about it was that Vered, the social worker at the mercaz klita who had always 'known' my check wouldn't come when it was supposed to, kept offering to get me declared needy or something so I could get financial aid. Whereas I, aware of the realities of vote power in the U.S., knew damn well the govt. pays, and on time (dunno about welfare and Social Security crumbs, but this is a bought-and-paid-for deal, no poverty program: you could borrow from a bank on the basis of it). So I wrote Washington and said Hey, my check didn't come—and, just about the time Vered started explaining that Israel would never let me go hungry, I began drowning in forms in triplicate from departments and bureaus in D.C.: Dear Madam (Voter/Taxpayer), the U.S. Treasury and 57 other varieties of civil servants are all hunting down your missing check this minute. To receive replacement check, please return Form 4893 A, notarized . . . Ah me. Thus were the disadvantages of both cultures winding around my legs as I struggled to thrash on through Chapter 4."

4. "My refrigerator still hasn't been delivered (it's promised for next week) but Avi came up with a sort of one to use in the meantime. Somebody else was using it, it seems, but it got sprung— for which I'm right grateful, what with the tropical temp. But I'm also puzzled: I can't figure out how this thing works, for it has no motor; you do plug it in, but how can that make anything cold? I swear it, though, there *can't* be a motor: there's never any noise, for one thing, and for another, there simply isn't room for a motor—it's just a rectangular box, more squared-off but not much bigger than the portable TV I had in Mass., and it sits on a table. The outside is white, the inside insulation-silver, like radiators. There are no shelves—you just pile things ingeniously, balancing them on each other—and of course no freezing compartment, but I bought a plastic ice-cube tray and it *does* make some ice cubes. I didn't notice any periodicity about that (still the phenomenologist, you see!) but Yehuda Artzi apparently did: he says he stops in on Thursdays because that's when he can have an ice cube in his drink. I giggled at his wit, but after he left, I started wondering. Now another Thursday has passed, and you know what? He wasn't being witty.

198

"Can the thing have argon or something running around inside its walls? (If not the right element, forgive: it's ages since I took chemistry. But you know what I mean.) But if so, why heat the stuff—which must be, mustn't it, what the electricity does? Oh, if you've an inkling, explain, explain . . . P.S. it has no controls either, needless to say. Just plugged-in or not plugged-in."

5. "I'd met a woman (Hilda, a Dutch-born Israeli) who teaches English at one of the high schools, so when I knew I was going to stay in Beer-Sheva I asked her how to volunteer English-conversation help to high-school students coming up on the *bagrut* (that's the dread college-entrance-exam-in-spades, much tougher than our kids' S.A.T.s). Because it seemed to be something I could contribute, as Hilda'd said the kids who do all right on the written exam tend to flounder on the oral even when the questions are quite as predicted and there's nothing to make them especially nervous. Lack of practice in actually speaking the language does it, apparently . . . Hilda was delighted and so was her department chairman (who came over to the mercaz klita to see for herself, I suppose, that I really do talk grammar—and who can blame her?). But what it finally came down to was, one venture into the high school itself was enough for me: the kids are noisy to begin with, and the sound echoes and re-echoes among the stone walls until it becomes the very Essence of Airports and I die, I faint, I fail. So I invited them to come to my house instead, one afternoon a week—which may weed out the too-timid, or those who have to go home to take care of the baby, but it was the best I could do.

"The size of my group varies, but the hard core consists of two boys and a girl, all seventeen and all absolutely top-grade students (Hilda is said to be a really inspired teacher, and it sure looks that way: these three are her students and they not only know their stuff but also obviously adore her). With those three—all charming—I've progressed past the kind of 'rehearsal' talk I was told would be like the bagrut oral and now, except for the fact that it's I who set the opening topic, we just talk. Like a seminar, but with me listening to the English as well as the content and sometimes halting the proceedings to correct a pronunciation or construction. Yesterday's subject was the army service that lies ahead for all of them next year—Esther (called 'Estie') for a year and a half and three years for the boys, Amir (Ahm-EER) and Elie. (Hmmm, I don't know, that spelling looks too feminine. But if I spell it 'Eli,' you'll read it with Yale in mind. Well, it's short for 'Eliezer' and just remember it's pronounced like 'Ellie' but there's nothing effeminate about it in Israel.)

"The first answer came from Estie, who said with an air of

faint surprise that going to the army was simply something you have to do if you're an Israeli. She didn't sound as if she was merely repeating some kind of early-conditioning stuff, but just in case, I set it up so she could be only instructing foreign me in Israeli customs. Was it true, I asked, that one could choose to go into the police instead? Yes, it was. Well then, were any of them planning to do that? No? Why not?

"That caused them a little trouble. But finally Estie said it was because you don't meet very nice people in the police. Whereas the army, I should understand, was usually a very pleasant experience in terms of making friends: you met people like yourself only coming from another part of the country. The implication, I think, was that the police are somehow déclassé (and perhaps that the unlovely types one would associate with there would not be only the crooks). I decided not to press that, but I did try the argument I'd made with kids in Cambridge: I had read that the police were shorthanded, I said. If that was true, then shouldn't they, since they were willing to serve, be willing to go where service was obviously needed? And perhaps, if enough kids like them made the same decision, the quality of the *mishtara* would thus change for the better.

"Elie, who's the best English-speaker (probably natural talent—he also speaks French and some Arabic, as his people came from Egypt) and seems also to be something like their leader, burst in to say somewhat irritably that it was enough of a service to give up three years of your life to what was basically irrelevant and useless. Perhaps encouraged by that frankness, Amir then pointed out that there was a difference: if the government needed him in the *mishtara*—yes, excuse it, the police—badly enough, they could send for him and then he must go. But it was not a thing to volunteer for.

"Estie was nodding and Elie was looking approval, so I gathered that was the definitive statement. (And a gutsy one, what? Because Israeli kids do not talk back to teachers. And when I was seventeen, I'm not sure I'd have had enough self-confidence to argue in a foreign language—and with somebody who was also correcting me, which is hard on even less fragile psyches than a teenager's.) So I abandoned my researches in favor of doing my style-coaching duty and we talked about why I *must go*, used socially, implies that you'd stay if you could and is thus politer than the *I go now* that may seem to say the same thing . . .

"But what I've reported to you is probably a not-untypical portrait of the attitude to army service, for these three (judging by their extracurricular activities at school and the way other kids talk of them) are popular though, as they're so bright, they're also pacesetters. Estie is very pretty in a dark Biblical-looking way—melting dark eyes, black wavy hair in braids or ponytail—and Elie is distinctly handsome, a golden boy who's going to win all the prizes, you can see it. They're both 'Oriental Jews' (Estie's family is Moroccan, has a huge number of children, and the mother is very religious and virtually illiterate; the older sister is the first, and Estie the second, to even aspire to go to university) and as such are at once typical of the region and of lower social status. Amir, who has carrot-red hair, is an only child and is also the only one of the three students to have been outside Israel (perversely, though, his English is the worst—because most heavily accented); he may be something of an aristocrat by contrast with the others. They all treat each other in very comradely fashion, but my antennae tell me Estie prefers Amir. He's got pimples, but that doesn't seem to matter . . ."

6.   ". . . a *'platta'* that sits on the drainboard—it's a two-burner gas stove top like the one I had at the mercaz klita. (Actually it has a third teeny-tiny burner in the middle for keeping sauces or water hot. You buy a teeny-tiny saucepan with a pouring lip to go on it.) It's Avi's and has been supplanted by the fine new stove he and Martha got from the U.S., so I can keep it. I've begun proceedings to buy an oven—very involved business because if I want to use my tax-free privilege I have to first get a paper from the man in the store and take it to Customs and then go back to the store and order one and then arrange for its transportation (and if that doesn't sound like enough, remember that the man who speaks English isn't always in the store and the Customs office isn't always open and even when it is, it's jammed and you'd better count on a whole morning of bench-sitting). The oven-cum-broiler I'm buying is electric and slightly larger than your electric broiler but not much—if I had in mind to cook a Thanksgiving turkey, I could just forget it. It will cost IL400, which is about 100 dollars (and that's *without* Customs!), plus another something-like-20-bucks for a table to put it on.

"This combination of gas on top and electricity underneath seems pretty standard even for 'modern' one-piece stoves in Israel . . ."

7.   "The way I got 'discovered' was, something appeared in the *Jerusalem Post* that I took great exception to—enough anyhow so, though I know I shouldn't be spending the time (not to mention giving away my prose for free), I wrote them a letter. It was a good one, I admit. In that death-dealing satiric-urbane tone I haven't used much since I stopped book-reviewing (maybe I should make one of

201

my characters a book reviewer so I can show off again?). Well, my letter appeared last Friday—I'll send a copy as soon as I find it—but before that, in fact by the next mail, came a note from an editor asking if I'd ever written for publication (naturally, I'd used my real surname) and would I be interested in doing the odd piece for them, etc. Elating, what? Okay, okay, I know, I *am* sticking to the new book, I am *not* frittering away my time on journalism. But you see what a huge talent I am, right? So tell 'em, down at the office . . ."

8.   ". . . perfect capsule illustration of the differences in political systems. It happened when Ze'ev (the apostrophe means make it two syllables, like 'Zeh-ehv,' but I mostly just say 'Zev') took me to Ashdod to pick up the TV set I'd ordered from Holland. (Dealing in internatl. currency turned my head: I watch the rate of exchange of the Dutch florin with a sort of proprietary interest now.) Ashdod is a smaller port than Haifa and closer to home, but the Customs ordeal, trotting with papers from station to station, was almost as incredible. (No more, I vow it: I've got an electric radiator coming from England, but after that I won't, no matter what. The hell with a washing machine: washing my clothes in the bathtub is infinitely better than having to go to a port again.)

    "Well anyway, Ze'ev—the husband of another 'mixed' couple I've met, only this wife is Canadian—had got us up to the next-to-last step and we were waiting for the clerk behind the counter to acknowledge our presence. Just then a man walked in and marched right up to the counter, ignoring us. And the clerk, who'd up to then seemed to be mentally calculating his income tax and unprepared to be interrupted at it, immediately rushed over with an eager Can-I-help-you-sir air *I've* never seen in Israel. But the sir wasn't next, we were—so, my American ire aroused, I said 'Hey!' loudly. Everybody ignored me except Ze'ev, who said 'Ssh' and wouldn't tell the clerk we were next (as I strongly suggested) or do anything at all except shake his head and mutter to me to wait, I didn't understand the situation. So I stood there simmering until the man finished his business and what seemed to be a few How's-the-wife jocularities too, and then at last we got to have our paper rubber-stamped thrice. The explanation came as soon as we were safely out in the corridor: 'That man was Yigal Allon's brother,' Ze'ev told me, his tone conveying *You see, there was a good reason*—not to say also *Aren't you glad you behaved yourself?* Clearly, I was supposed to be not only satisfied but probably also honored to have thus rubbed shoulders with the great.

    "You can imagine what *that* did to my American ire. Partic-ularly because it brought back something that happened one night a few years ago when I was catching a late flight from New York back to Boston. There were about twenty of us, all weary-looking, standing on line for boarding passes when along came a small, dark man being obsequiously ushered by two uniformed airline types and accompanied by two of those briefcase-toting politician's-aide types. 'No need to wait, Governor,' said one of the uniforms. 'If you'll step this way—'

"Well, I think it may have been Volpe—a Republican who wasn't Gov. of Mass. then but had been and was at that point maybe some kind of Nixon appointee, like White House staff or something. And I also think, because it was real late and he looked tired, he would have stepped this way all right. Except that the remark was heard on the waiting line, and people looked around and a few smiled, apparently recognizing him. One of the aides behind presumably-Volpe made a small minatory noise in his throat. But I suspect his boss didn't need any help, for the weary look was already being replaced by a frank-and-open political-rally grin. And 'Are you kidding?' he asked the airline equerry. He waved loosely at the waiting people. 'These folks are Massachusetts *voters*, son. You think I'd be dumb enough to just—' The rest was lost in the laughter from the audience. Including me, because it was funny all right. And engaging, and people so responded—*Oh, go ahead, Governor*, and somebody else promised, *We won't hold it against you* (and of course the inevitable comic called out, *I'm from New Hampshire myself*). But in the blinding sunlight of the port at Ashdod, it was more than engaging, it was positively endearing. Enough to give you a lump in the throat, even if, like me, you've never been a fan of Volpe. (If that's who the guy was.)

"I told Ze'ev the story, right then and probably wearing a fond, reminiscent smile. So he could see I thought it significant and enjoyable, and thus he tried to be polite; but it was clear that he didn't get the point. And why should he? Yigal Allon is a biggie in the ruling Labour Party coalition and has been in and out of various Cabinet posts; he's doubtless a Minister of something right now and if he isn't, he may be tomorrow. But that's up to Golda Meir, and all she needs (if that—she's a right powerful lady and prime-ministers away firmly) is the consent of a small group of top party pols. So it's clear that the Customs clerk, whose advancement doubtless depends on being well-thought-of in Labour circles, had reason to butter up Yigal Allon's brother; and it's equally clear that neither Allon nor his brother had any practical reason to need to butter up the waiting citizenry. Which meant Ze'ev (as I was visibly an immigrant), an Israeli of voting age—who, depressingly, took his non-status utterly for granted . . ."

9. "I'm definitely a local Sight, especially with the folk from across the courtyard who've all heard about Caroline Ben-Ari's American tenant. (Some of the neighbors in my own entry are perhaps just as curious but more dignified about it, as they're a social cut above the out-and-out 'Orientals,' it seems.) Kids sometimes shinny up to steal a peek into my salon through the French door that opens onto an abbreviated balcony just big enough to step out on. The grown-ups are more restrained, but they do peer if the door is open; and if there's the odd excuse to come calling (like, collecting the monthly house dues, IL20 per apartment), the neighbor with the real business is always accompanied by two or even three others who'd like a look at the presumed American goodies, too.

"I don't blame them—how could I, when I'm so nosy myself?—but I'm afraid I disappoint them. For there's nothing enviable in sight except maybe the TV set. I not only don't have a newer, more elegant living-room suite than theirs, I don't have any: what you sit on in my salon is the standard iron cot from the Jewish Agency. (I've replaced the straw mattress, which produced hives on the backs of my legs every time I sat on it, with a foam mattress. But it's covered with a spread, so they don't know that.) And it'll be months before the chair and rug I've ordered are produced by Danish Interiors. (They don't take single-item orders, but I attached myself to Martha and Avi's order for the chair and to Miriam and Ze'ev's for the rug. Both couples have cars and will bring me my stuff after theirs is delivered.) The only small consolation for the neighbors is a huge table lamp I bought, in a burst of luxury-hunger, after my check finally arrived. It has a base of white stone and a cylindrical shade of tweedy orange-and-white silky stuff, and I found it in a shop that specializes in luxury notions and is distinctly tourist-oriented.

"The lamp is a real discovery for the neighbors now because Martha and I brought it home in her car one morning; most people were at work, so its arrival went unnoticed. Though it stands on one of my footlockers, it's still a conspicuously lavish note in the utilitarian decor. (Any kind of lamp is anyway in Beer-Sheva, where putting a light fixture over the ceiling bulb is la-de-da enough.) Faces brighten at sight of it—here, at last, is a touch of the foreign—and I'm asked, hopefully, how much it cost. Because the exotic must also be expensive to be fully satisfying: when I tell them IL180 (about $25) it's clearly pleasing. I have a feeling it would help neighborhood pride if I'd put it in the front window. But that's not where I want to read.

"And that would also interfere with traffic to the little front balcony, which is where my clothesline is. That means it's also right beside the entry on the courtyard, which now seems to have become a major gathering place for women wheeling baby carriages, etc. At first, I smiled and nodded a lot while hanging my wash, figuring I was making everyone's acquaintance. But the gatherings kept coming, and one day, what was clearly a spokeswoman stepped forward and asked me shyly in Hebrew-English whether that was indeed a single wash. I was puzzled, because it really wasn't much quantity—I can only do a bucketful at a time, and anyway I can't lift much weight—but then I looked at my deep-purple towel and washcloth hanging next to a pale-blue nightgown and some red socks, and I got the idea. Yes, I assured them, I had washed all those colors together, honest—all these things had come from America, yes. I know it got translated, because I heard either *echod* or *yachad* (which mean, respectively, 'one' and 'together' and either way add up to the same news), but I'm not sure it got believed. For I'm still collecting murmuring groups alongside my clothesline. If you ask me, the American textile industry owes me . . ."

10. "Thank you for your nice letter—I think it's great that you're old enough now to write letters to me!—and I'm so glad you and Maggie liked *I Love You*. Yes, I wrote it in Israel. But I didn't draw the pictures. Somebody else had already done that. All I did was make up the words.

"Most children here can't read it because people in Israel have their own language, Hebrew. The children learn English in school, but not until they're older.

"Yes indeed, I've seen camels—they're all over the place here, even though where I live is a city. I don't think a camel even in a zoo is really very pretty, but up close, they're just plain ugly. The long neck looks like a big snake, and the small head at the end of it has mean little eyes. Camels are said to be bad-tempered, too (and *very* smelly), so when I see a few grazing in an empty lot I usually decide to walk on the other side of the street.

"We also have sheep around, and some small black goats. They belong to the desert Arabs and are not brought into Beer-Sheva as often as the camels, which are sometimes necessary for transportation. But there's one flock of sheep, belonging to an Arab who lives in town, that I used to pass every day on my way to . . . ."

From the diary: 13

The dinner party (Aug.)

I've been so busy reminding myself that those who live alone and work alone can become recluses if they don't take steps to ensure a social life—So put your shoes on and go out, you hear?—that I failed to intake a vital, non-psychological datum: my apartment lies athwart lots of people's paths home from the university and the hospital, and it's also right near one of the town's few supermarkets. That's in Mercaz HaNegev, a sort of merchandise-mart-looking structure that also houses regional offices of several government agencies, etc. So there are numerous reasons why people may have business nearby—and why not stop in and see Maggie, who's all alone and doubtless longing for company?

For a while all I did was make instant coffee. Unless it was afternoon, in which case I opened soft-drink bottles and occasionally —Rob and Yehuda Artzi have remained rather American in this respect—constructed highballs. Paper cups are expensive (you buy them for so much per cup, like valuables!) and have to be bought downtown, so after a while I was spending a lot of time washing cups and glasses. And of course lugging bottles home from the super-market and then back again,* and in the interim juggling them around in my odd little fridge's shelfless innards. Busy, busy social life—and fortunately, not as busy as it could've been, either: every time I got back from buying more soda and snacks, I'd find a couple of notes stuck in my door by callers who hadn't found me at home.

So my recluse worries would seem to have been just a jot unrealistic—Take off your shoes and go wash your hair quick, before somebody else drops in, you hear?—and it isn't scarcity of company that's the problem. Umm. Well, part of the error was my Tuesday "At Home" idea, which not only bombed but had fallout, too. For everybody who wasn't coming the next Tuesday felt duty bound to come tell me so; thus I represented an extra chore for them, and they represented more impromptu entertaining for me—and what I ended up with was not an at-ease salon but a series of enforced tête-à-têtes. Lovely. And what's more, sometimes people who were coming next Tuesday would drop by to tell me that, too . . .

In short, hardly anybody seemed to dig the idea of gathering regularly for an afternoon's leisurely talk. I know why now, I think: purposefulness is the keynote of Israeli daily life ("What's it for?" the

*Nearly all bottles—including some you wouldn't expect, like ketchup and bleach— are returnable, and you pay sizable deposits.

unstated but always-present question), probably because every-body is so very busy. After all, they have only a one-day weekend and most breadwinners have two jobs (e.g., Avi teaches at the university after work in his regular job. And even has some kind of third part-time deal too, as a consultant). Then there's the constant need to fit in with complicated schedules: the stores are closed Tuesday afternoons, the banks Wednesdays; the supermarket closes for the morning by 1:30 but the macaulet may stay open till 3; the Kupat Cholim clinic closes at noon and if you didn't get there by 8 A.M. and take a number, you may not get to see the doctor by noon. (But if you're there for a shot, it has to be before 10 A.M.) These outfits reopen in the afternoon, usually at 4 but it could be 5. But govern-ment offices—which you have to visit a lot, since almost nothing is done by mail (Americans who at home hadn't set foot in the realm of officialdom since they went to get a marriage license now spend hours sitting outside some misrad or other)—don't reopen in the afternoon at all.* So, even though I'm prepared to believe that all these schedules do fall into the back of your mind eventually and you just know without thinking, I don't see that that would make you any less harassed by Time.

And yet, watch it there, Maggie. Because if an American is asked what he or she likes about Beer-Sheva, the answer (mine, too) will inevitably include something grateful about the slowed-down pace of the life. And it's true: next week will always do as well as tomorrow, and if you have an inquiry that somebody has to tele-phone to Tel Aviv about, you're told to come back for the answer in three or four days (and for all I know, that may be hurrying things up for the benefit of the impatient Americans). The combination of a hot-country mañana frame of mind and a culture that puts human relations decidedly before business—so that if two clerks are conversing or a working mother is instructing her children at home via the office telephone, you not only wait but you're sup-posed to wait—adds up to a pace that will drive you mad unless you can disenthrall yourself and come to believe that things don't necessarily have to happen, and certainly not on time. So, the busy people rushing around and the general non-concept of deadlines are both true, and oh Lord, I've got another paradox. What if my book about Israel turns out to consist entirely of statements fol-lowed by "On the other hand"? Oy. (No, oy va voy is what they say: at least get the local color right, will you?)

*This has been changed since, so now *some* offices reopen in the afternoon on *some* days. I predict with confidence that this won't last. Because, since nobody can remember a particular Ministry's house rules, the safest thing is to go in the morning—which will eventually mean P.M. hours will be "proved" not to pay . . .

Well, you can buck the indolent culture if you're rich enough and determined enough, but it would still take a lot of luck, too. Like—Social Notes from All Over—my first dinner party, which came off this week. The problem of not enough dishes was solved when it turned out an American poet was here last year or the year before, being a visiting scholar at the university, and when he packed up the wife and kiddies and departed, he left behind not only dishes but also a dandy Teflon-or-something-lined Dutch oven—just what I needed.* The stuff has been circulating around the English Dept. ever since, with people (except the religious, who wouldn't let non-casher crockery into the house) using these dishes until their own arrived, etc. The last on the string were the Artzis, who are now pretty well settled in. So Yehuda appeared lugging this huge box—not only dishes but things like a bread knife and cutting board, too—and I accepted the gift, seemly because of both my immigrant and poet statuses. (Though as to the latter, I'd say that poet owes me Spode, at least. She said modestly.)

So I was virtually equipped to throw a dinner party. But, since things would still be a little rough and I wasn't sure the Israelis would perceive the fun of camping-out, I limited my guest list to Americans and mixed couples. And if I was going to do it, I might as well do it right—it would be a proper dinner party, I told the Artzis, and Martha and Avi, and Miriam and Ze'ev. With me, that made seven, which was pushing the facilities a little. But any fewer wouldn't be a proper dinner party . . .

Somehow this enterprise began to assume a dressing-for-dinner-in-the-jungle aspect. I think it was when I began to make lists as I had in my Washington-wife days—and then realized that, this time, I was the only one around to carry out the chores on the lists. And, this time, every single one of the raw materials had to be bought separately and lugged home from all over Beer-Sheva. By Friday afternoon, too: there would be no running out for something forgotten when I realized it two hours before dinner Sat. evening.

Well, as I said, with enough time, money, and musclepower, you can do it: who would have believed, e.g., that it was possible to find curaçao in Beer-Sheva? I did, though—a single, dusty bottle for IL75 (!) in the super-luxury clip-joint shop that even had imported cheeses. And was accustomed to sell them only an occasional sliver at a time, so the man couldn't believe his ears—or the size of my check—and I found out what it's like to be a millionaire on a spree:

---

*Ha. You couldn't ask for a more typical example of how a problem in Israel can get solved—by an out-of-left-field present from a bountiful American, of course. And of course the connection via the arts . . .

Yes, Modom, Sairtainly, Modom, *with forelocks respectfully tugged . . . But alas, once I'd left behind the bowing shopkeeper (and his wife, who was summoned to help with this windfall: there's two, alas, whose rich-American-widow assumptions will never get dislodged), what we had was not Mrs. Vanderbilt sweeping to her limousine but Maggie hiking to the bus in the heat, loaded down with baskets and plastic bags and holding her bus ticket in her teeth.*

It got wilder and wilder, too: I found myself hunting through fruit-and-vegetable stores (whose wilted stock an Iowa farmer wouldn't have rated good enough to feed to the pigs) for this kind and not that kind of onion, if you can believe it. And then I decided we'd have to begin with martinis (which I haven't had since I came here: another American and I once tried to teach a Beer-Sheva restaurateur to make one, but something went so wrong that we paid for the "martinis" and then gratefully drank beer instead). Gin turned out to be no problem—for a fabulous sum, it was easy to find (oh, that British legacy again?) a good brand of real gin—but the vermouth was something else. Perhaps, just perhaps, if its influence could be kept slight enough, like about 1-to-8 proportions, the resultant cocktail might be wounded but not fatally.

That brings us to on-your-own time on Friday, when tomorrow's party would stand or fall on what was assembled in the kitchen now. I stowed my shopping lists and began on a logistics chart. For I've always been a great fan of the do it in advance and then pop it in the oven when the doorbell rings approach, but you have to have someplace to put what you've done in advance. And what I had was my little Scotch-cooler-size mystery refrigerator, in which the soda and the wines (in order to get the latter to "room temperature") would also have to be stored. Clearly the only feasible plan was an in-again out-again one, with everything taking carefully timed turns in touch with the coolth. (I tried an intermediate station, the bathroom sink filled with cold water, for the bottles. But the temperature was in the high thirties* on Saturday, so the cold water didn't stay cold.)

Still, by Saturday afternoon I was in good shape, the salad stuff washed (a serious business in Israel, where it had better not be just holding a tomato under some water for a minute) and scraped and chopped and whatever else had to be done to its component parts; and the canapés were ready to be popped into the oven and meanwhile were taking their turn popping in and out of the refrigerator at a rate calculated on the basis of the cream cheese in

*35°C is 95°F, so figure it from there.

them—which I thought was probably more vulnerable than the anchovy paste. Since the meat course was one I'd done often in grander circumstances, the only problem with it was that the Dutch oven couldn't possibly get a turn on the ice; so the entrée was stowed in a bowl, a pot, and a plastic refrigerator dish—two of which had other duties and would have to be switched en route.

But the table, which had taken a lot of thought, was working out nicely: the large wooden lid of my book crate, laid over the tiny two-person Jewish Agency formica and iron table, would stay in place once I hammered some brads into the crate-top's underside so I could tie it to the legs of the table. If you put your elbows on it, especially at either end, it tended to tilt into your lap, true. But why worry? Guests at a proper dinner party wouldn't put their elbows on the table. If they did, though, they'd get splinters—I discovered that at the last, or I might have sandpapered the cracked and knotholed plywood. But, inspired, I dragged out some of my supply of Gladys's orange X-ray paper and covered the wood with several thicknesses, thus also practically making an even surface too. Then I was ready to lay over all that the linen cloth my mother once embroidered (as a way of whiling away summer afternoons on the tall-tree-shaded patio of her summer home. Mind-blowing, if you let yourself dwell on it). Luckily the tablecloth, intended for much larger—not to say also more orthodox—tables, hung down lavishly on all sides, thus concealing the construction that had made this one possible.

So far, so good. But it was at around that point in my preparations that things began to happen. First, the water went off. Hafsakat—ma-im (literally, "water intermission"), explained the lady next door when—barefoot and minimally clad, hair and eyes wild—I knocked on her door. Timidly, I asked could she (because she was an old inhabitant and had a phone) perhaps phone somebody and see at least how long it would be before the water was restored? She raised her fine eyebrows: Goodness no, phone whom? Or had I forgotten it was Shabbat? Behind her I could see her Shabbat-afternoon visitors seated among polished tables and starched doilies, drinking tea and eating the little cakes she baked every single week. (Proper European cakes, too—of German origin, she worked at preserving her burgherin status among the Moroccan hordes: in her way, she'd been dressing for dinner in the jungle for years.) No thank you, I mumbled, I wouldn't come in. She said graciously that the water might return before long, and I mumbled some more and fled.

Back in my own jungle, I gambled that the water would return in time and used up all my ice water for the absolutely necessary rinsing of the George Spelvin pots and bowls that would have to

210

reappear on stage later in another capacity. For my hands, I used some of the gin (which does not lather well. Try to remember that). And when it looked as if I'd better get dressed and the hafsaka was still on, I used the lukewarm bottle-chilling water in the bathroom sink to wash my face and then dumped cologne liberally on the rest of me—which had been working hard, and sweating heavily, all day. Then I donned my party frock: talk about whited sepulchers . . .

But the water turned out to be the least of my troubles. For at the next scheduled refrigerator-reshuffling, I discovered it wasn't even as cold in there as that poor little thing could get. Panic. It wasn't a hafsakat-chashmal, though, because when I absent-mindedly flicked the bathroom switch, the light went on. So recovery set in and I was able to determine that only the dining alcove and the kitchen were affected. Only! But even if I could get the refrigerator into the salon—a doubtful feat—I'd still be in trouble, for the kitchen is windowless and needs artificial light all day anyway. And, while dining by candlelight would be glamorous (and certainly possible, as I was using my ancestral candlesticks, placed in interesting asymmetry, to cover a couple of spots in the tabletop where the longshoremen's hooks had penetrated), cooking by candlelight would be impractical in a too-small space and with a need to wash and re-use things, in a clickety-click hurry. So, what to do?

Well, I didn't need light in my workroom, did I? Or even the salon, if it came to that . . . I carried out one of the two little Jewish Agency stools (using the other to prop my door open for light, as the hall light only stays on for thirty seconds or so after you push the button) and, tucking my elegant gown out of the way, climbed onto the four-inch-square stool to reach the fusebox. I made plenty of noise doing all that, but part of the lady next door's class awareness was that she didn't stick her head out to find out what was happening—which any of the Moroccan neighbors would have done . . . After enough climbing down to find out what I'd turned off, and then up again to pull out another of the six fuses, I got quite good at the operation. Which had to be conducted in a delicate, not to say gingerly, manner, because these aren't the little round covered-up fuses of an American home but permanent ceramic holders that you wrench out: all the connections are visible (you can actually watch the electricity snap at you while you tug!) and, especially if your hands are sweaty, the ceramic is slippery. So unless you're deft, you're likely to fry.

And you'd also better have a head for mapmaking, I discovered, because the jurisdiction—so to speak—of any given fuse is not necessarily related to the floor plan of the flat. (Like, you can't take out just the workroom, because the bedroom goes with it.) I failed to size up these allegiances fast enough, and thus blew the salon (cum bathroom) fuse too, which was just a jot disheartening. But in the end, I triumphed—thanks to my stint in the mercaz klita, where I learned that the dood has its own fuse. I tested, and it was true here, too. So if I remembered to put it back half an hour before time to do the dishes, I could get by: I hadn't used any hot water for a bath, and what was stored in the dood would do for now, right? Oh-kayyyy. With a flick of the wrist I borrowed the dood's fuse for the kitchen and dining alcove, and the bedrooms' fuse for the salon. Nothing to it when you know how . . .

Now that I think of it, the fuse-switching and the refrigerator gavotte would make a fine farce, played fast and light. It was even funny while it was happening, in a way: the more ridiculously the odds against me piled up, the more determinedly flossy I got—so that I not only mixed my martinis and stowed the pitcher to chill (by jamming it in at an angle between two bowls and letting it lean on a Pepsi bottle), I also suddenly decided to chill the glasses, too . . . I wasn't drunk, honest. And I wasn't hysterical, though I was laughing. It's just that—well, I was engaged in a comic battle to the death, on behalf of something I didn't really care that much about but when They decided to do their worst I had to show 'em . . .

The water came back on before the guests arrived, but not enough before for a bath—especially as I was then mixing the salad with one hand while switching things around in the fridge like a speeded-up silent movie. There was a small incident or two, like when a bowl of noodles that probably should not have been balanced on a soda-bottle top fell off; but by that time I had more than enough composure to simply scoop the whole mess back into the bowl and get on. Certainly nothing that small could have kept me from arriving at the triumphant moment when, with everything ready, I lighted the now purely decorative candles on the table and then carried one into the dark bedroom to find my earrings. Then came the knock on the door. I thrust my dirty feet into my high-heeled shoes, stopped off to put the candle back on the table, and answered—the smiling perfect hostess.

It was a lovely party. Martha arrived early, without Avi—who'd been called to miluim (reserve duty) yesterday, too late to come tell me—but toting a homemade cake and a bundle of forks and spoons that were extra so I could even keep them. (Avi's mother's? Heavy silver plate with curly engraving culminating in an unreadable initial, definitely middle-European and long ago.) Ye-huda and Yael came next, lugging folding chairs; Miriam and Ze'ev, assigned the lightest chore because they're the most recent acquaintances (ah, delicacy), brought a plastic bag of ice cubes. But all the guests, having apparently caught the spirit of the thing, were dressed to the teeth.

Well, the martini glasses were not really frosted, I'm afraid: some might even say the rims were only just coolish. But the contents of the pitcher had had a longer turn and were tingly cold. And I fear that's where my exact impressions stopped coming, for I had two of my vermouth-hiding martinis and they knocked me for a loop. I remember assigning Martha and me to the two ends of the table (Avi's absence left it better balanced) on the grounds that Martha had nice manners and I had inside knowledge, so we were the least likely to put our elbows on the table. And I know I got courses on and off, accompanied by the appropriate wines; but it seems to me that by coffee time Martha had to take over.

Perhaps, though, that was also because my fuse problem was then under general discussion and Yehuda was trying to do something about it. (He has no professional expertise and no previous knowledge, but right after he became a Beer-Sheva householder he took up home electrician-ing—guess why—and is now quite skilled). That took my attention from my kitchen duties, but it also produced my warmest glow of the evening. For, since I had never even heard of fuse wire (five voices promptly informed me that some should always be kept on hand), it looked as though not even Yehuda could help—until a great light bloomed and I said I'd bet the wire inside those twisters that close plastic bags would be as thin as what Yehuda was describing to me. A hunt ensued and one, just one, of the paper twisters was found: it was holding up a drooping plant stalk, from which it promptly got snatched (while all the voices said you must save things like that, Maggie). We all held our breath during the peeling. And then, by golly, I'd been right! "Good thinking, Maggie," said Yehuda as he wound the new wire onto a fuse, and I knew everybody would remember this useful discovery and maybe even tell everybody else. I felt wonderful. I had been tried and found brilliant, a great resource for myself and the friends beaming proudly upon me, a true asset to our little society. In short, I felt almost adequate. And it's lovely.

Happily, it was Ze'ev rather than his plastered hostess who, before the guests departed this soignée dinner party, climbed on the stool and restored the dood. But since only one fuse had been mended, the best he could do for me was to give me back my bedroom light by blacking out the salon. Which was good enough, really. Only, somehow after they all left I didn't feel up to taking advantage of the great opportunity to wash the dishes right then. Or even to bathe, though that was probably perfectly safe because with the bathroom door open, there was a nice shaft of light from the bedroom. But how can you clean up after a dinner party without a 3 A.M. old movie on the TV? After a full twenty seconds' consideration, I decided you couldn't and went to bed.

Something is clearly wrong with the wiring in the dining alcove—probably it's those wall lamps Yehuda had doubts about when I made him put them up for me originally—because I've blown that same fuse twice since the party. Mrs. Ben-Ari says her husband knows a man who may be able to come fix the wiring if he's back from miluim and they can go see about it maybe Saturday. Okay. Meanwhile, every time the lights go out I simply yank out the fuse and rewire it—I haven't had time to go buy fuse wire yet, but Yehuda came by with a supply on Sunday and showed me how to twist it, too (he apparently wasn't convinced of my learning ability when I'd watched the night before). Martha took the tablecloth home to wash and iron; it's too large for my washbucket and anyway, I don't have an iron. The orange paper that was under it on the table has an interesting swirly design in spots, where something got spilled and color ran, but it's a trifle tatty, so one of these days I guess I'd better take the extended table apart again. But no sweat: I've seldom felt so able to cope, so thoroughly on top of things—even though, now that I examine the matter, that doesn't seem too justified. But it feels delicious, so to hell with logic. That's from another culture anyway.

10 ע Geveret Maggie's Frigidaire

The affair of my refrigerator—my real one, that I bought and paid for, not the phenomenon Avi lent me—is, as multum-in-parvo events go, a dilly. For it went on for months and months, happening, like the weather, under and around everything else. And visible through it (if you knew how to look, and sometimes I didn't) was the essential fabric of the people and life in Beer-Sheva in the spring, summer, and early fall of 1973.

The first revelation came when, shortly before I was to leave the mercaz klita, I finally ordered a refrigerator for my new home. For me, that was practically long-term planning; but the Russians who were then doing the same thing had arrived perhaps only a week before. And even those Americans who had not shipped one from the U.S. took care of the refrigerator chore as soon as they'd settled into the absorption center. Only I, it seemed, required the immediate and specific apartment on my horizon before I would do something about putting a fridge in it.

Though it was an unquestionable necessity, no matter how pioneery you wanted to be, in a climate where more than half the year is summer and summer is hotter than most Americans ever experience even for a few days.* What was a surprise, though, was the *way* people provided for this necessity—and what happened

---

*Readers of my Silvestri novels, which are set in Massachusetts, may have noticed a certain emphasis on descriptions of piled snows, crisp air, and other raptures I got carried away about as I sat typing, with a wet towel around my neck, on a 40-degree (that's 104-degrees F, baby!) day in Beer-Sheva.

when, seeing it as only a necessity, I saw it differently from the rest of the huddle.

But first, the Russians, whose behavior was not entirely a surprise because, for them, this was part of the reward for having made it out of the Soviet Union to the West, where all goodies dwell. The chief reward in Israel is an apartment—a whole, brand-new one with its very own, unshared, kitchen and bathroom. But the way that comes to them is via a government, just like back home, so it occasions no change in behavior: what you do is fill out forms, berate the social workers, and generally try to bully or bribe your way into a better deal than the next Russian. Old stuff. But to actually go out and buy something (with money supplied by the Jewish Agency*), and to get to be a consumer who chooses, that's a first. The same thrill applies also to buying cars, but that comes harder even for Russians who arrive with substantial (smuggled) money: the immigration people in Israel know that a car wasn't a taken-for-granted part of even the Leningrad-Moscow life-style.

Anyone can get money for a refrigerator, though. Promptly, too, for the absorption people's aim is to get the immigrants into their own flats as soon as possible. And a special need existed right then, for, under a new rule shortly to take effect, immigrants' right to import Customs-free would be limited to goods from their country of origin. For the Russians, that would mean getting along with the Israeli product (which may well have been the legislators' intent). It presented no particular problem for Americans, from whose country of origin most of the available consumer goodies came anyway. And it didn't even hurry people much: Martha and Avi (using Martha's immigrant privilege) and the Artzis would have bought their Fiats† promptly anyway, and the same went for my Dutch TV set. And it was the memory of kerosene-heated winter, not the edict, that stirred me to order my British electric radiator with uncharacteristic promptness. (It came in midsummer, so I actually had something on hand before I needed it: there's no doubt about it, Israel changes you.)

Well, but a refrigerator was something else. You only had to see the Russians translating for each other from a General Electric

---

*These can only be described as sort-of-loans, and please don't think I'm just a sloppy reporter. For the way it works is, if you stay in Israel, the loan is forgotten about; but people who decide to leave the country are hit with bills for the whole staggering amount. So you owe it but maybe you don't, it all depends. (And the rules vary for different kinds of loans, too.) Not exactly your typical banking practice, in any case. But that's the way it is.

†A typical choice. Nobody with either a conscience or a need to pay for his own gas was interested in an American fuel-guzzler.

brochure—featuring lots of colored ink and photos of actressy-looking ladies revolving revolving trays—to recognize the thrill of a lifetime. Which it was: when else had they had a chance to ponder and discuss, to debate whether the two-door kind was better than another freezer arrangement (for several U.S. brands were represented: I just remember GE's literature best because they'd apparently gone all-out) or whether self-defrosters were worth the extra cost? Listen, rapture is rapture. That's what I saw, and to call it something less because it was only about a refrigerator would be like the self-blinding elitism of the U.S. heavy-"culture" types who put Shakespeare on TV—preceded by an explainer in a living-room set to wise up us proles. Nuts to that: let the people see, and let them alone. So I'm telling you, their eyes shone and they smiled at each other and couples held hands lovingly above the brochures. These people were enraptured by becoming consumers, with all that that implies of ad-man wooing (you, YOU, are so important to a rich slick-paper green-ink corporation!) and the surrender of practical knowledge to false comparatives.* Not to mention the identification-dreams—of oneself as slim and lithe and girlish like the pictured housewife or as the provider of the kind of smooth luxury-filled household a wife like that would live in. (Okay, nobody told me their dreams. But that's what it looked like, all right.)

It's worth noting here, too, that the chauvinistic boasting theretofore endemic suddenly vanished then. *Nobody* said they'd had bigger and better fridges in the Soviet Union, neither the woman engineer who'd lied so bravely in class about her Moscow apartment nor her poorer compatriots who had probably never had *anything* new, much less something so big and gleaming and surrounded by superlatives. The fact is, once presented with a ticket to membership in the consumer society, the old everything-is-better-if-Russian belief simply melted away. Freedom of speech hadn't made that change, maybe because they couldn't imagine it. But this didn't have to be imagined—you could see it in the picture, and all you had to do was decide on which corp. to bestow your favor . . .

Tamara, ever intelligent, recognized that she was a novice and consulted me for consumering tips. Which proved awkward: I'd been living in apartments in Massachusetts, and the last time I

---

*Frozen foods were rare in Beer-Sheva and much too expensive for regular family use, and most people lived so close to the paycheck that large-quantity buying was unlikely; so *all* the freezers meant for American TV dinners and easy noshing were probably too big and what difference did it make whether they were on top or on the side?

remember buying a refrigerator, in a Washington suburb, I was also buying a house. I think my then-husband, a professional economist and quite capable of comparison-shopping refrigerators, dishwashers, etc., did the actual purchasing. But the chief parameter was the layout of the kitchen, and most discussion was with a lady sent out by the electric company to help people plan kitchens—and who didn't care what brand we bought so long as they all used electricity.

Well, but by the time Tamara approached me, I knew better than to try to describe a milieu so alien. So I explained about *Consumer Reports*, but, except as a guide to how her colleagues in America probably did things, that wasn't much help—how recent and/or applicable would it be even if she got hold of a copy in the U.S. Library in Tel Aviv?—and it sounded off-putting besides, with overtones of *Don't bother me, go look in a book*. The problem got solved when I realized that the characteristically thorough Rob had quite recently bought a refrigerator in the U.S. to bring to Israel. Since he spoke Russian, Tamara couldn't feel that I was fobbing her off; it was just that he could explain better. (He did, including considerations of repair service and spare parts, which I hadn't even thought of.) I wondered briefly why Tamara hadn't asked Rob in the first place, but then I realized she wouldn't think a bachelor would know about such things: refrigerators are for families.

But if the Russians' consumer ecstasy was engaging—as all wholehearted emotion tends to be—the American immigrants' less conspicuous absorption by what I came to think of as the "unreal-money madness" was depressing. There'd been signs before, like when I refused to buy a car: my distressed compatriots besieged me with facts—look, unless I moved quickly I would lose this many thousand lirot, which translated to that many dollars. That time, I pointed out that I couldn't be "losing" money by not-spending it for something I didn't want (and of course, the more I said it, the stronger became my resistance to a car). And yes, thank you, I did understand that after the cutoff date my decision would become irrevocable ... After a while, they eased off—which is to say, "Maggie has an anti-car hang-up" so what was the use—or they fell back on the age gap, which usually got obscured by the automatic-Bohemian status that goes with my trade* but could be revived to prove I was just too old to change. Some may also have concluded

*And is reinforced by my habitual, obviously preferred, way of dress. I got used to that assumption in Cambridge, when the college students seemed unable even to consider the possibility that I might have been wearing sneakers and jeans for my own reasons (i.e., most shoes hurt my too-narrow feet, and I hate shopping) long before such a costume became a Statement.

that I was poorer than I seemed (perhaps all that confabbing with Vered meant I was living on handouts from the Israeli government?) and was ashamed to say so; in those cases, tact forbade pushing the matter anymore.

But when it came to the refrigerator, the assumption was that I was just cringing from the prospect of facing bureaucracy again, so *Maggie, you can't put it off forever* nagging became the duty of the huddle. (*I know, I know. I'll do it tomorrow, or anyway next week,* I promised, over and over again.) Money, for the reasons I've explained, couldn't be the problem. So nobody felt any need for tact when I declared—much too shortly before I was to leave the mercaz klita—that tomorrow, really-tomorrow, I was going to order a refrigerator. What kind? Well, why not the same as I had in my cheder now?

What every cheder had was an Israeli-made refrigerator, a "Model 10" size (which apparently does not mean the cubic capacity, though you might think so) that stood about five feet high, had a freezer compartment along the top and shelves on the door, and in fact was much like any other refrigerator except that everything in it was smaller. (Well, not quite like—American designers have discreetly fenced off the coils and other "works" that frankly hang out the back of the Israeli number. And they also seem to have found somewhere else to put the motor so the hump of its casing doesn't take up half the bottom shelf. Minor considerations.) And if the inside of the door has indentations for only eight eggs instead of eighteen, why should that prove a problem when I had to go shopping often anyway because I couldn't carry many groceries at a time? Nor was merchandising logistics likely to trouble me, for eggs are sold here in flat cardboard trays of thirty each, or else individually—the dozen/half-dozen concept seems unknown—so why couldn't I buy eight at a time?

In short, I proposed to buy a refrigerator that appeared to do everything they're supposed to do, that was big enough for one person's uses, and that I could afford—and you wouldn't believe the stir, concerned or hostile or both, this logical decision caused. Now I can see that it may have also looked like a statement asserting superiority (in the sense that every thumbs-down judgment of the popular implies that you're made of classier clay), but at the time I was simply puzzled by what seemed some kind of failure to communicate. So when Americans accosted me on our daily rounds or came to my cheder in the evening to "educate" me, I countered all arguments politely. Yes, I realized that if this fridge proved too small I'd have lost my duty-free "rights" and the cost of a bigger one would then be wild. But why should it prove too small? I wasn't planning on having babies: were they all so oriented toward future growing families that they couldn't see I was going the other way? (Well, but what if I got married again, Jeffrey's wife argued: okay, no babies, but that wasn't big enough for two, even. I said that even if I managed to contemplate such an unlikely happening, I couldn't imagine myself marrying a man who didn't own a refrigerator too—and she giggled and gave up.)

As to doubts about the trustworthiness of Israeli technology, well, there was a difference between a dood, which GE, Westinghouse, et al. weren't peddling in Israel, and a refrigerator, which had to compete. And Israel was not after all a primitive society—the Israelis had presumably managed to work jet fighters and other machinery just fine in the Six-Day War, right? All those mechanics and maintenance men must be distributed around in peacetime jobs now, so if my refrigerator broke down, the repair man could come right over and spare parts would be no farther away than Tel Aviv. (As I mentioned, I hadn't thought of this on my own. But I learn quickly: it came out sounding as though that had been a real datum in my decision-making.)

Still, all this reasoning-together got nowhere, really. Because, it finally dawned on me, what was bothering everybody was actually my refusal to borrow money—or, more precisely, my insistence on a distinction between my own money and the Jewish Agency chit or its equivalents from half a dozen other sources that had become almost universal currency. Which wasn't even always necessary: some Americans had come with large sums from the sale of houses and cars back home, but many of these took the usual loans anyway in order to preserve their own money for items not underwritten by officialdom. (That sounds mean and dreadful, I know. But, though I wouldn't do it myself, I can't wholly condemn because I remember how I felt when I went from reliance on a paycheck to living on publishers' advances. Watching your bank account decline steadily is panic-making, at first anyway—and these young people, in a situation full of uncertainties, were probably panic-prone.) Some were spending their own funds, but with a kind of Whee! vacation-drunkenness perhaps occasioned because, for the moment, they had more money than they'd ever had at one time. And certainly, if they stayed in Israel, more than they were likely to accumulate again.

Well, the Whee! feeling could be counted on to vanish. But my sense of being the only sober guy at the party might well not, because there was a strong possibility that I was looking at a bunch of incipient alcoholics, you might say. For the society itself, I was

220

slowly realizing, went in for an economic drunkenness that might make "absorption" *mean* a loss of reality about money. The problem got worse, much worse, after those early days when I was fumbling to identify it (would you believe 43 percent inflation? And that was only the last time I looked: it changes almost daily) but even then, there was such a gap between what people could earn or save and what they needed that, in most cases, it was impossible to function on "real money" alone.

I've read about the inflation in Germany after the first World War, but that's something different: if you need a wheelbarrow-full of money to buy a newspaper, you don't even try to cope. In Israel, though, the inflation was both controlled and uncontrolled—which meant that if you were an honest wage-earner and didn't invent something that made a million or win a lottery, your income and your major needs would be permanently on two different scales. Thus you could take your IL3000 or 4000 a month (then a very good salary) and go buy bread and other basic foodstuffs at prices kept low* by government subsidies and everything would more or less fit together—at least well enough, anyway, so you wouldn't be confronted with the wheelbarrow situation. But the same IL3000-a-month breadwinner was likely to owe IL100,000 or so on his apartment and half as much again that he'd borrowed to buy a car, refrigerator, stove, closet, washing machine, TV, and heater—just for starters: if he had a taste for even mild luxury, it'd be more than that—or anything else with a price the government can't control. (Israeli industry was hugely helped out by the government to compete in export markets, but that didn't do much for the at-home price. Production costs were so high and productivity so low that a foreign producer could sometimes get his goods all the way over here for little more, even with import duties, than an Israeli firm charged.)

What made the unreal-money purchaser in Israel different from the overextended family in the U.S. paying for a mess of stuff bought on the installment plan is that in the States the car or color TV *could* get paid for, because its cost was usually in the same ballpark as the buyer's salary in the first place. But here, the thing got paid for right away: installment buying requires an assumption of an at least reasonably stable currency, which Israel definitely

---

*So low that an incredible amount went to waste, for the bread was delicious when fresh and why eat stale bread when you could have a new loaf for practically nothing? The sight of bread in the dustbins bothered much of the citizenry, but *ma la'assot?* The original dogma had been set by nineteenth-century immigrants from Russia and Poland, who knew damn well that revolutions started with bread riots; and dogmas just don't get altered easily—even though, for a sizable portion of the current population, bread was not their basic food when they came. Rice was, or beans.

didn't have. So the consumer took a loan (at interest rates reflecting the likelihood of currency changes) to make the purchase and then started paying that back. Forever, because it was more than he could reasonably pay to begin with, since he'd taken out five other loans to pay for other things. Like, eventually, his *children's* apartments, refrigerators, etc. Because a young couple in Israel was apt to be very young: marrying at twenty-one—with the man still in service or just out, and thus unlikely to have even a fair start on a university degree and the salary levels it brings—was not at all unusual even among sophisticated families. And what young couple could buy an IL120,000 apartment without help?

What it all came down to, ironically enough, was that in Israel, where ownership was the way of life and all arrangements were intended to be permanent, nothing was really owned. I guess that comes of clashes between the vision cherished by the early immigrants, driven from their original homes and hungry for stability, and the realities of wages now earned not via Zionist hoes tilling The Land but through things like being clever with computers—and earned by a population in touch with and longing to be part of the rest of the world. If that sounds too vague, I have lots of specific examples of the way the society crossed itself up. Like, that young couple's apartment I mentioned above would have two bedrooms. But the government (via free maternity care, child allowances, etc.) and the demographic needs of the country and the whole spirit of a war-threatened society all urged young couples to have as many children as possible. If they did, though, in five years their two-bedroom apartment—with all its built-in closets and huge expenditures justified because they were once in a lifetime—would be too small (or they would have changed jobs or done some other modern and non-visionary thing); nevertheless, since they "own" the apartment, they then sell it, along with a lot of the contents—all representing only a ridiculously small percentage of real money. So what was actually owned, and what could possibly be permanent, in such a setup?

An even better example is the automobile, which was clearly a luxury and the government did everything it could via towering taxes, onerous regulations, etc., to keep it that way. Which made sense: the last thing a country so small and poor and oil-less needed was a lot of roads (beyond those necessary for defense), traffic problems, the whole shtick. But the same Israel government—which couldn't help it, no government could, because of the clout of the religious—turned off public transportation on Shabbat, the only non-working day of the week. So a car of course became *the* most wanted possession, auto ownership mounted despite all the obstacles, and the whole spectrum of automobile-society problems socked the already feeble economy. (There's even an extra, almost-too-tidy absurdity involved in these two examples, come to think of it. For young couples, like immigrants, are encouraged to settle in underpopulated areas like the Negev. Where of course they're most likely to need a car. And the young couples' Mamas and Papas, who live in Tel Aviv and work every day but Shabbat, are certainly going to have to have a car, because it's the only way to get to see their children and grandchildren.)

Well, maybe we seem to have come pretty far from my refrigerator. Not so, though, because this was the society the Americans in the mercaz klita were about to join—a society severed from economic realities (and from a few others too, it sometimes seemed) in which unrealities extended outward from the "real" unreality like buying a 120,000-lirot apartment to a nothing-matters way of thinking about money altogether.* But many of the Americans I knew were, like me, from a culture where financial prudence was chic—where you bought things on sale, investigated advertising claims carefully, and bragged if you pulled off a thrifty coup. And yet from here on in, none of that would make any sense. For, first of all, the very terms had changed: it would now be thriftier, in fact, for me to borrow lirot to buy a great big refrigerator because one thing you could be sure of was that when I paid it back in three or five or whenever years, my dollars would be worth more lirot than they were now.

I'd already been advised of that particular verity by Rob, whose filial duty it was to instruct me in economic sophistications. But when I heard it from Yehuda Artzi—one of the most idealistic of the immigrants and certainly the most gung-ho Zionist—what we were discussing was the intra-huddle situation created by my insistence on buying a refrigerator solely in terms of what I needed and could afford, exactly as I had done back home. Which constituted a defiance of the generally accepted value of "absorption," plus a kind of reproach. Rob, who was not great on human relations, may have been blind to it (or preferred to be); but Yehuda, drinking beer in the kitchen of Cheder 40, had come to make peace and sense. So when I disposed of that currency-logic by saying that

*This is a bit unfair to some of the intellectuals and others—including Knesset members, and some of those even within the Labour coalition itself—who were extremely aware, and worried. But they were all either out of power or lacking in sufficient clout to make a difference—and the "grass roots" surge that might have empowered them was just not there, in 1973.

playing money games was not what I had come to Israel for, he nodded gloomily. No debate, for that wasn't what he'd come for either and we both knew it. Yet here he was, forced to take the practical rather than my honest-and-pure approach—because, we agreed, of the differences in our situations, his lirot vs. my dollar income, his wife-and-kiddies obligations vs. my no-dependents freedom. And what that came down to was, something was wrong, very wrong.

Well, just the fact that we were always *talking* about the damn refrigerator was wrong, I burst out, glaring at the squat white bulk of the fridge in the gloom. Never in my life, I said passionately, had I spent so much time talking and thinking about Things—where to get them, how much they cost, which was the best kind—and I was sick and tired of it. Of struggling for my identity, which was what it amounted to: the Artzis and I might have known each other back in the States, I pointed out (perhaps not quite accurately: he was an academic and he wrote poetry, but we moved in very different circles and I was a lot older). But was it possible to even imagine that we would've sat around there chatting about consumer goods, in detail and endlessly? So, though he and Yael had convinced themselves they were "coming home" to Israel, it didn't look much like that to me. In fact, what it looked like to me was that this was a society in which I definitely didn't *want* to feel at home.

Because for one thing, it was just too damned stupid around here. I'd never believe another anti-Semite, I said—aware of some need to lighten the mood by a little wit (but too angry to make a good job of it)—because where was all this purported money-shrewdness the Jews were supposed to be so good at? For, as even an economics fool could plainly see, my chief practical value to Israel was the dollars I brought in; and yet, here was Israel virtually coaxing me to spend them in the interests of personal profitmaking rather than country-supporting. Well, nuts to that—so far as I could see, the right thing to do was spend my dollars on an Israeli-made refrigerator. And no, it was not *dahfke*-idealism, I snapped (doubtless furious because Yehuda's jibe had been better than my own wit), it was a simple refusal to be pushed into altering my personal self. Governmental stupidity couldn't make me become a Thing-worshipping full-time heart-and-soul consumer, and neither could local social pressure for conformity . . .

Well, enter here another revelation. For, that night I didn't yet understand why, but I did not add *And especially such a wretched hypocritical conformity.* Because one of the things you learn in the huddle (as in any expatriate group, I guess) is that

224

there's only one game in town: who else recognizes jokes with tag lines that depend on old TV commercials, will remind you when Mother's Day is coming, and does the same things for a cold you do? So I reined in: maybe young people with growing families had no choice but to alter their outlook—I said, donning a more-in-sorrow-than-in-anger look—but if so, that was their business. If I didn't have the problem (back in Cambridge, I probably would've said *If I prefer not to sell my soul*), that was my business. Maybe, as people kept telling me, you had to learn to live with a lot in Israel (careful non-mention of the obvious question *Why the hell should you?*). But I refused to learn to live with imperialism, and particularly the pressure-y social kind that can't let you alone unless you conform . . .

Well, what that diatribe is, in the huddle's terms, is a mild form of the I'm-leaving threat—and the response to it is always dominated by that fact even when it comes from one of the people who use it a lot, enjoying the flutter of attention it provokes. But I hadn't been given to that, so it was especially alerting coming from me. Thus, nearly all talk was suspended in favor of *Now, now* variations. In this case, custom-tailored: was I so sure, Yehuda asked, that life in the mercaz klita—which was after all only one big, months-long Moving Day, wasn't it—was so like the real life of Beer-Sheva? And wasn't it possible that a lot of attention to purchasing appliances had gone on in the U.S. too, only with a husband doing it, considerately out of my sight and hearing? Mightn't it make sense that having to do everything myself for the first time—because, though I'd set up household as a widow before, there'd been a son around, right?—would make me feel irked even without the special difficulties of Israel? . . . Yehuda is a clever young man. And, as in a family, members of the huddle know all about each other, and thus what handles to use.

And he either spread the word or else some of the others were more perceptive than I'd thought. For, after that night, things shifted: since I'd waited so long to order a refrigerator at all, people opined, I should probably take advantage of the prompt-delivery aspect of buying an Israeli one. And of course for a person alone, a small fridge was quite practical. And so it went, all my arguments re-pronounced with a judicious air (sometimes in the very same words!). Other talk (not to me, but the boats of the Negev are full of leaks) was about the individualism of the artist—we must remember that dear Maggie is after all a creative writer—naturally running into problems in Israel's group-oriented society. That one was followed by a marked rise in non-consumer-oriented conversations with me—and it may have been a coincidence, but the next time I saw Yehuda, what we talked about was a visiting poet scheduled to lecture at the university. Some big social thinker also pointed out—doubtless while puffing on a pipe; it sounds like that anyway—that Maggie's societal attitudes stemmed from an era when activism on social problems was seen in terms of individual, personal gestures. (Well, that's true enough: the liberals of the 1940s would boycott a corporation, refusing to buy its product because of its employment policies, whereas the students of the 1960s would mob the firm's representative when he came on campus or sit-in in the admin building because the university owned stock. You could argue about the comparative effectiveness of the measures, but I have no doubt our way was better for the participants: *we* didn't feel anonymous and alienated but virtuous and individually responsible for the way things run.)

What links all this rationalization—the true and relevant as well as the foolish and inapplicable, the spurts of honest thought as well as the précis of Sociology 101—was the phenomenon, here seen in bud form, of *Save the group*, which closes ranks over just about any rift the moment it looks too threatening. It's what, I realize now, keeps the impossible compromise (all right, that's a contradiction in terms. But that's what it is anyhow) between the Orthodox and the non-pious rest of Israeli society operating somehow, and that makes the most argumentative people on earth suddenly stop arguing. It's easy to see it as merely a function of the political system—like the swing vote of the religious parties—or of the need to suspend quarrels when threatened from outside. Both of those are true, and, since people like explanations (and writers of books about Israel are in the business of serving them up), everybody seems willing to stop there. But if you stop with logic you don't get even to the halfway point in figuring out the sudden way Israelis—apparently by common but unspoken recognition—abruptly shut down opinions, arguments, philosophies, beliefs, and even (hardest of all to turn off) irritations, on behalf of a wholly non-rational and almost reflexive We.

Well, so I not only got what you might call forgiven, but as time went on I even became a very symbol of simple idealism. And the beauty part of the story is, time did go on. And on and on: I moved to my apartment and set up housekeeping "temporarily"—a term believed, originally, to mean about a week or ten days—with the ice-cube-a-week wonder Avi had provided. And the nice man in the appliances store, the one who spoke English and had been so patient about telling me just which piece of paper I had to take where and then bring back (because there was a substantial discount for immigrants even on Israel-made goods. So I ended up sitting on benches outside the very same offices as the GE purchasers were waiting at. Heigh ho)—this very nice man even assured me he knew somebody who would bring the refrigerator to my house for me. As soon as it arrived, next Wednesday . . . When I turned up at his shop on Thursday to say nobody had come, he couldn't have been more surprised. Well, he was going to Tel Aviv himself on Sunday (a business day in Israel) and he'd personally see what happened.

Several weeks later—it seems there'd been a strike at the plant—the nice man told me he'd bring the refrigerator out himself on Tuesday after he closed his store. That Tuesday afternoon, my "At Home" was still on, so several people were at my place when the refrigerator didn't arrive. With the happy result that after that I no longer had to keep going downtown to ask what had happened—thus, each time, running the risk that the refrigerator would appear in my absence and be taken away again—because friends who had business or shopping there would stop in and do it for me. In Hebrew yet, so there would be no language problem. (Which was not sizable anyhow. What was really meant, I think, was that a tacit message would be delivered—like, if this guy thought it was safe to shove a lone ignorant foreigner around, it wasn't; she had savvy, Hebrew-speaking friends.)

A less happy result, though, was that after a while practically everybody was participating. For friends told other friends, my conversational-English students told other youngsters, and the neighbors were all alerted anyway in case the refrigerator came while I was at the supermarket. (I hardly ever went out during the day otherwise, for either it was scheduled to come or somebody was coming to tell me the latest results of a trip to scream at the shop man; and in the crevice moments, I was trying to write a novel, too.) The strike at the plant was over, but it had naturally caused a pileup of orders. Then there was a strike of truck drivers, including the ones who drove the refrigerators down to the Negev. And of course there were holidays—lots, because there are lots of holidays in Israel anyway, what with the religious plus the national ones, and a large percentage of them went by while "Geveret Maggie's Frigidaire" went on being unfinished business.

I should explain the quote, I guess. That "Frigidaire" was only the usual turning a trade name—presumably the first one encountered—into a generic term that then becomes the everyday-Hebrew word for it (e.g., *ness*, which is probably short for "Nescafé" but means any instant coffee). "Geveret Maggie," though, is a little more complicated. For sometimes it was simple confusion caused by the fact that both the first and last names on my door were equally alien and without connotation. Which led some of the neighbors, reading from right to left, to believe they were calling me, quite formally, "Mrs. Maggie"—which, the knowledgeable among them informed the rest, was the custom among Americans (a cold and formal folk, obviously). Then too, there was a special problem because my married name does look, in Hebrew, a little like a girl's name; as in the case of "David Brinkley," who becomes sort of cute as *Brinkli*, my last name sounds like a diminutive. In other cases, though, it was a way of first-naming but with due respect for my age and station. As with my high-school students, for example: they knew in which direction my names were read, and Estie even called me Maggie sometimes (the boys, more hesitant, preferred to avoid the problem). But a teacher is a personage in the culture of Beer-Sheva and you don't go around talking about even an irregular and part-time one as just plain Maggie—certainly not when you're on your dignity with the man in the refrigerator store . . .

Thus it was Geveret Maggie's Frigidaire that got inquired for, usually at least twice a week, through June, July, and August, while I nursed my foodstuffs through the steaming summer in Avi's magic box. And while everybody's tone got stiffer and stiffer, the store-keeper more and more apologetic, and all the Israelis increasingly unhappy. It was wholly, hugely embarrassing—simply as an act that couldn't get off the stage, aside from the little matter of actually needing the refrigerator—because to cancel the order would only mean starting another wait, this time at the bottom of a list. And the embarrassment doubled when trucks began to be seen almost daily, delivering brand-new crated GE refrigerators (the hugest size, of course) to the Russian immigrants who had finished at the mercaz klita and were moving into the Jewish Agency apartments on Metzada; it's the main avenue, with the supermarket lying on the other side, so everybody had to cross it often.

If that sight left me feeling a little grim, that was nothing compared to what it did to the patriotic Israelis—for not only was I victimized, I was the only *idealist* and I was being victimized. *Eempawssible.** *Incroyable. Lo na-im* ("not nice"—a heavier con-demnation in Hebrew than it seems in translation). My Israeli friends ground their teeth and went tearing down to the appliance store. And Thereza at least—plus I don't know how many others—explained to the man how bad it all made Israel look. (Whereupon *he* ground *his* teeth and wrung his hands too, swearing on his

*This is the way Thereza pronounces "impossible" (emphasis correctly placed), and I've grown very fond of it: it sounds extra-exasperated, somehow.

children's life that he was aware, terribly aware every waking minute, of the plight of that very nice American lady, such an idealist—and oh God, an artist, too!—and he'd told them and told them in Tel Aviv that it was a scandal, a disgrace to The Land.)

The patriotic suffering was not always shared in my neighborhood, though, where some people were less high-minded. "Why didn't you buy an American frigidaire?" asked Shoshana, a student at a vocational school. What could I say? Well, at least she was proceeding intelligently, checking facts out for herself, so she was owed education . . . I said, more haltingly than just my Hebrew required, that I'd wanted to do a good thing for Israel; when she simply stared, I told her as firmly as I could manage that it was good for Israel to buy things made here instead of abroad. She blinked, then began to check out that I was really American and thus could really-truly have bought an American refrigerator, etc. In the end, she regarded me in silence, chewing her gum. Finally she shook her head. And, making an effort to remember the English (from school, presumably), she leaned forward to poke a grimy finger into my shoulder. "You coocoo," she pronounced cheerfully, gave me a great friendly gap-toothed grin, and sailed off.

By that time, of course, I wasn't sure Shoshana lacked wisdom. But she didn't represent the only neighborhood response, for the *yekke** lady next door wasn't able to dismiss me with such cheerful realism. But in her own way, she also implied that I was stupid: it seems there are *two* Israeli refrigerator manufacturers, and the other one—which as a matter of fact made the fine refrigerator she owned—was much superior; so if I had only taken thought and been thorough . . .

Meanwhile, somebody—I suspect it was Hilda, who believed in forthright displays of power†—threatened to bust up the man's shop unless he came up with Geveret Maggie's Frigidaire by next Wednesday. He didn't, but he came out to my house to explain why he couldn't; he also explained to Thereza, Yehuda, Selma and Isaac (another American couple, very religious and more Hebrew-speaking

---

*An almost untranslatable name for, basically, German Jews. But embracing also their (sometimes actual, sometimes caricatured) qualities—fussiness, insistence on "order," documents, detail, a million little things that in the Middle East tend to be considered silly. *Yekkes* have dinner at dinnertime, no matter what, in a society that favors felafel, a dinner you not only carry out but walk around eating.

†Perhaps that's because, according to the story I heard, she managed to stay alive—all alone, at the age of six—in a concentration camp through the silent kindness of a guard officer who habitually dropped a hardly-smoked cigarette on the ground near her and then stood there to make sure she didn't get lost in the scramble for it. With it, she could buy a piece of the occasional rat the prisoners caught.

than practically anybody), Miriam and Ze'ev, Gladys, Rob and of course Avi—some of whom weren't currently inquiring but they had,* and he recognized them and stopped them on the street. The sufferings of this entrepreneur were really tragic, because Yehuda and Rob, who could use telephones at the university (not everybody's privilege, but they had Ph.D.s) and who both spoke Hebrew more than adequately, each had a try at calling the plant itself—and got the same runaround the poor shopkeeper had. So his helplessness was authentic, if infuriating.

Oddly enough, he's really what I remember best about the whole refrigerator hassle. Which memory tended to suppress (for if I'd thought I was getting my nose rubbed in consumering when I complained about it to Yehuda that night in the mercaz klita, well . . .), so the affair slipped almost entirely out of my notebook and I'm unable to say just exactly when the refrigerator did finally arrive. But I know it was past early September because I got a New Year's card then, at *Rosh HaShana,* from the storekeeper! (I couldn't possibly forget *that*: Rob had just come by, bringing in my mail as he came. So, as I didn't recognize the Hebrew return address, I was saying he'd better have a look at this for me, please, while I opened the envelope. And then I pulled the card out and it was obvious what it was, and we simply went into hysterics. I'm not sure—though I made Rob read it to me when he finished rolling on the floor laughing—whether the card was meant as a personal gesture, a way of apologizing, or a "progressive" attempt to do business Americanly and nobody thought to take this particular customer's name off the list.) I know I had the card around, propped up on a shelf of my bookcase, for weeks before I had the refrigerator.

But it did come (maybe the last week in September?) one day, without any kind of warning. I was ill with the flu and Hilda had come over, accompanied by one of her sons: she had to get back to work, but she'd figured she could do my shopping for me and then her son could bring it to me. So I was sitting in my salon of a brilliantly sunny mid-morning, wrapped in my bathrobe and writing a shopping list while sniveling into a much-used Kleenex, when somebody knocked and Hilda went to answer the door. The next thing I knew, they were wheeling in my refrigerator and the place was full of people: two men, one holding the dolly and the other doing nothing in particular; Hilda slanging both of them in flashing-eyes, rapid-scornful Hebrew; and a trail of neighbors who'd been

---

*Among the inquirers was, also, Mrs. Ben-Ari. I wasn't surprised when I heard. But I wonder who else I didn't hear about, because they didn't tell me either.

outside with the baby carriage or hanging out a wash when they thought they saw the unbelievable happening. (Among them was Shoshana, who apparently decided to help Hilda out and fell to with a will: the Hebrew they were flinging at the two refrigerator men was not in my vocabulary, but I could tell from the winces of other neighbors that it wasn't supposed to be.)

And then of course, the minute there's a visible gathering, another one, of the curious but not yet sure about what, immediately begins to form. In the end, not everybody could get in: some people stood outside, peering through the French window and passing the word to those who couldn't get that close; around back, small boys scrambled up to look in the windows of the dining alcove and see at least the scene, if not Geveret Maggie's Frigidaire. What the scene mostly consisted of at that end of the flat was the two men, shrugging and proclaiming—obviously—that they didn't know nothing, while they tried to edge past the two shrieking women and then through the throng to the only way out, the front door. So the kids didn't get to lay their eyes on the Frigidaire, but the scene was surely worth shinnying up for.

I never tipped the hapless delivery men: I couldn't get close enough, and besides, when they escaped a lady from upstairs was congratulating me in precarious but formal English that made me feel as though I'd won a prize. I suppose I had—people kept coming all day to see it. When they did get to see the refrigerator, it was briefly clear that they were disappointed (this, *this* cheap little thing, was what all the fuss was about?). But after a moment, what was important about it would get recalled and they would turn to me with grins of pride and relief: it was Israeli-made and it had got here. And it even worked—you could hear it humming. Rejoice, rejoice. The whole thing was a goddam festival, that's what it was. I'd broken out my pretzels and some candy for the children, and somebody ran up to her own flat and brought down some little cakes and then somebody else brought nuts.

Sometime toward the end of the fête, Hilda's son did go to the supermarket and bring back my groceries; half the neighborhood watched me put the refrigerator items away. But it had been too late for Hilda to go with him and, though he could read English, my shopping list had been meant for her interpretation. So, when the show was over and everyone was gone, I discovered the terrible truth: he hadn't bought any Kleenex.

Well, it was a good day and a bad day. But certainly a Beer-Sheva one.

From the diary: 14
Local color (August)

I have a lizard!

I discovered him last night, when Fran (did I mention her here? She's about twenty-eight, single, has been teaching at the university for a couple of years) and I decided the blessed cool evening air from the desert rendered practical the luxurious Scotch tipple we just felt like anyway. So, still talking, I toddled into the kitchen and opened the pantry door onto my liquor supply. And there, on the wall as if stuffed and mounted, was a dragon-lizard, regarding me with his beady little eye . . . I slammed the door and jumped back, shaking even while I was also thinking coolly that it really wasn't that little and not pink but light brown with spots and you just can't trust Rob. "There's a lizard in there," I called over my shoulder. "Not the pink kind I've heard about but—"

There was only one kind, Fran interrupted—they just weren't pink anymore at this time of year. And they were harmless and, what's more, very stupid: I could get the bottle and be gone without the critter's even noticing. But if I was afraid, she'd—

No, stay there, I told her. Though if she'd been a man, or even a boy, I know I would've shrunk back prettily and said Yes, please. Why the difference? Women's Lib getting to me? Or just that here, where I've never been a pretty young girl, the relevant models of women are intrepid independent types like Fran and Hilda—so it's their club I try to get into? Well, I don't know, but social-climbing isn't strong enough to cancel fear, or instinct, or whatever it was that had twitched my muscles before I could even make a lizard policy. So that I ran—for the same non-reason (vive-la-différence variation excepted) Rob had clouted his own first-glimpsed lizard.

Okay, but I wasn't the only creature of instinct around, I told myself as I began reviving enough for a little policy-making. Thus I started beating—at first tentatively, then emphatically—on the pantry door with the flat of my hand, making some noise and even more (I hoped) vibrations. To the resultant what-the-hell? from the salon, I said I didn't mind coexisting with the lizard but I didn't want the sight of him setting off my instincts; so the idea was, he'd get out of the way while I got the Scotch . . . Fran, sounding struck with the ingenuity of the scheme, said okay but surely that was enough noise? So I opened the door. And it wasn't enough noise: there he was, still spread out. I could see why Rob kept wailing about being a murderer, because the thing's hands and feet may or may not have

232

*exactly five fingers each (I wasn't really cool enough to count them),
but there is something babyish about the way they hold on . . .*

*"Nu? Is he gone?" Well, by the time Fran finished saying it, he
was—in a movement so quick as to be really invisible. I think I saw
the start of it, but that may be only because he was facing upward
and made a looping turn (fortunately, not toward me); and I know
what join of the wall he disappeared into, but I didn't see him
disappear. Though there's an unshaded 100-watt bulb in that very
small room, and I was looking right at him.*

*"Yes, he's gone," I called, cool as you please. I took the
bottle—just a jot hurriedly, but only the mean-spirited would call it
snatching—and closed the door. Very, very firmly.*

*In the reassuring light of this morning, I put the bottle away.
Nobody was home in the pantry—he's probably out in the sun somewhere. Now that I've had some time to think, I can see that we'll be
able to manage. For it wasn't that it wasn't enough noise: a creature
so low in the evolutionary scale must have a very small brain, so it
takes him quite a while to dig that he's threatened and he'd better
head for home. But that can be worked out, all right—knock on the
pantry door before you get the glasses and soda out . . .*

ADD VOCABULARY
*Protektsia: Originally Russian, I think (but that doesn't mean it's
new—probably Golda-Meir-generation Russian). At first, I took it for
"protection," like a gangster with a bought-off cop. But clearly that's
too illegal and illegitimate. So then I figured it was only "clout,"
which also involves knowing somebody influential but not necessarily non-legit. That's closer, but protektsia is broader because you
don't even have to exercise it to have it—like, if you have a relative in
the housing office he doesn't have to say "That's my brother-in-law"
when your application comes up—and of course it's not so in-and-
out as clout even when purely political, because here the same
party's been in office for twenty-six years . . .*

*One of my problems is, everybody uses the word for practi-
cally everything, and with or without specific knowledge: the usual
answer to any how-come-they-do-like-that question is "Protektsia"—
generally accompanied by a wise look. Indeed, Jerry Kirschen, who
does the "Dry Bones" cartoon in the J'lem Post (he's a newish American immigrant, which may explain why his Schuldig character, constantly bumping into absurdities, is so popular with the Americans)
has a running gag about it: you send in for a protektsia card, see . . .*

*Ruth was my protektsia at the mercaz klita, which ought to
show it doesn't have to be a relative and can be quite legitimate; what*

that amounted to was, if the rules gave her a choice, she chose what was better for me. It also shows the second-degree effect, because I doubt that she'd ever actually have warned off the enemy Avraham; but he just knew that if he harassed me, he'd irritate Ruth.

I've got a different kind of protektsia now (though it's regarded as more routine than that, really: if everybody didn't work the bureaucracy as best they could, everything would come to a dead halt), procured for me by Selma and Isaac after a round of sicknesses caused by stupidities at the Kupat Cholim. Once again trying to play it straight, I'd gone to my neighborhood clinic when I caught a virus—and without taking any history or making an examination, the doctor just handed me a prescription. I got very much sicker, as I was allergic to one of its ingredients. (Which I found out because I knew my own history and I got somebody to look the stuff up in the pharmacopaeia for me, thus providing myself with data the health service wasn't interested in. Oh well, now I know.)

Selma is an energetic, community-action type anyway, so when they heard of my plight (Isaac, who loves to play anagrams, dropped in for a fast game with me and discovered me languishing), she got hold of Aharon (Ah-ha-ROAN), who's a doctor at the hospital; he and his wife are members of the same very Orthodox congregation as Selma and Isaac. Aharon's medical specialty is irrelevant to my needs, but he told them to bring me over to his house, which is nearby. There, in his tiny little study, I got my first real medical care in Israel, though I've been to Kupat Cholim several times for this and that. Which is to say, he took my medical history and probed (carefully: clumsy examination can set off a week of symptoms, so I may be lucky Aharon was the first) my surgeried abdomen.

A couple of days later (which is record time for Israel), Selma appeared and took me over to Aharon's office at the hospital. There must have been two dozen people waiting outside, but we went right in. True, our mission was only administrative (we had to get a referral chit), but I'm sure everybody out there was saying, "Protektsia." In a sense they were right, and I don't like the feeling: it makes me angry, because what Aharon had done was tell the doctor at the gastroenterology clinic about me (he's not American but speaks English, I'm told) and he put me on his project. That amounts to simply working the machinery by hand, so to speak, because the automatic way isn't doing the job. And it was in fact the only sane, practical, and medically responsible thing to do with a chronic case that needs maintaining drugs and, from time to time,

234

such resources of the hospital as X ray and blood chemistry.* So why should it have taken protektsia to arrange it?

Yet without Aharon's intervention, I'd probably never have got there—or if I ever did (after how many more bouts of illness caused by blind bumbling?) it would be after things had got acute and there were no choices left but more surgery. Or else I would've gone home first, compelled by self-preservation . . . That was the obvious possibility that brought the huddle-response from Selma and Isaac. They hadn't been in the mercaz klita—no need, as they didn't need instruction in Hebrew and they'd both been in Israel before—but the huddle now, while less huddled, includes just about all the Americans who are still in any stage of settling in. (And, perhaps because the hassles come thick and fast then, the save-the-group spirit is even more marked.)

Aharon and his wife, Phyllis, are Old Inhabitants who've been all settled in for quite a while. They're both wonderful people, but something of a shock to me because they're also such Beautiful People types: he must be more than six feet tall and she nearly that, and they're both always beautifully dressed (with the money-cum-taste eclecticism that likes fashion but regards it as only fun), slender, athletic, and terribly handsome. Indeed, Phyllis is, by any standards, professional-beauty beautiful: if she wasn't Miss America of, say, 1969, it's because she didn't bother. (They have one child, of about kindergarten age, which provides a clue to their ages. But Phyllis doesn't look like anybody's mother.) They're California types, sun-kissed and lucky and always rushing around to ski somewhere or skin-dive somewhere else, while they talk gaily and intelligently in that best-schools English that almost entirely looses Americans from their regional origins. But, amazingly, all this also goes with being 100 percent cashrut and Shabbat purists, and strict observers of each and every holiday and ritual. (He answers the phone on Shabbat when he's on call from the hospital, but that's all. And that exception is permitted, and in fact prescribed: Orthodox Judaism, I've been discovering, is more "pro-life," passionately and in detail, than the Cambridge hippies are capable of imagining.) I've always thought of Orthodox Jews—the term calls to mind black-clad figures seen at prayer by the Western Wall, etc.—as, at the very least, old and stodgy. Are Aharon and Phyllis typical, I wonder?†

---

*Not to mention a watchful eye for weight loss, pallor, etc., since my wounded gut doesn't absorb food reliably.

†In a way, they are. That is, nobody else is so good-looking, and doctors earn more than most other people. But many Orthodox here are chic and well-educated children of the rich, quite unlike the old-and-seedy image.

Everybody takes problems to Aharon, I gather: he functions for the Americans here rather as the old-time wardheelers used to in big-city precincts, where if your children got into trouble or you needed a job, you went around to the Democratic Club to see Boss So-and-so, whose door was always open. (Be careful with that analogy, Maggie: lots of readers consider "politician" a dirty word and have no idea of the virtues of wardheelers, so they're apt to think of Aharon as some kind of chiseler.) Except that the payoff for Aharon isn't your vote for the party but, I guess, just the satisfaction of lighting a candle in a dark world. What it is is a personality type, a form of mental health, and very hard to describe—for the same reason that niceness is the most difficult attribute to give a character in a novel. But I've run into these high-hearted, genuinely loving people before (my maternal grandfather was one, and once I worked at a publisher's with a young woman like that): when you see one, you always know it. And so does everybody else, for they're actively cherished by any community they turn up in.

But wait a minute, I can't just leave out Aharon's obviously deep religious feeling as a factor. His enormous willingness to put himself out for others (there are almost unbelievable stories about the trouble Aharon has gone to to help people, and I can believe every one of them) may be an enthusiastic performing of the mitzva—and there are 613 mitzvot!—required of the pious Jew. So, though Aharon never proselytizes, presumably he does get some kind of religious glow from his good deeds. (And hope of heaven? Find out.*)

Not to mention from just living in Israel: the other day, he told me, they lacked a minyan (ten men, a kind of quorum required to constitute a congregation) for the daily prayers at the synagogue, so he went out to recruit a couple more. A construction crew was working down the block, and when he accosted them and stated his problem, two of the men (sighing, Aharon says) went back with him and muttered their way resignedly through the prayers. "Now where, where in the whole world except Israel?" asked this sweet man with pure delight shining out of his eyes, "could you just go out and pick up a couple of bricklayers to make a minyan?" Well, he made his point. But he also made another for me, because nowhere

---

*It turns out to depend on whom you consult. The frantic individualism of Jews extends to matters that are flat-out dogma in other theologies—causing this questioner, at least, to think wistfully of the easy old days of just calling the Information office at the Archdiocese. Wouldn't work with the nearest Jewish equivalent, though: the Israeli Chief Rabbinate has *two* Chief Rabbis, who disagree and are co-equal! But there's enough controversy about heaven and after-life in general so it's hard to see how any true believer can really count on it.

in his story was there the smallest condemnation of the backslid Israeli bricklayers who had presumably once been Bar Mitzvah boys and so knew the words but now had to be hauled into the synagogue. I looked hard, but I didn't see in his voice or diction or face any trace of the self-congratulating righteousness of the "unco guid"—if anything, Aharon seemed to think it had been nice of the guys to come along. So religion, I see, can be (at least when it's Aharon's kind) something truly lovely.

(Which reminds me, add another refutation of the notion of Jews' shrewdness with money. Because Aharon, if he'd stayed in the U.S. and even if he stuck to his Hippocratic ideals and didn't become a society doctor—at which he would undoubtedly make a fortune!—would certainly earn a great deal more money than he ever will in Israel. They live well here, but they could do that in America without Phyllis working too. And, since they're very religious and very generous—they'd doubtless regard mere tithing as niggardly—over the course of Aharon's working life Israel would get a lot of much-needed money, and in dollars yet. Except, Orthodox Jews are supposed to come live in Israel: it's a holy duty or something. Thus do the Orthodox cut their own financial throats, it would seem . . . Strange people, and certainly not very practical.)

Street scene.
Walking to the hospital today, I saw a Beduin woman on her own. Which is news, because they seem to go about always at least in pairs, and even then young women will be shepherded by an older, duenna type. I'm told, too, that the husband and wife I saw alone together downtown were probably "progressives."

But this woman wasn't quite unaccompanied, for she had a little boy with her (age uncertain: these Beduin kids are often so undersized that, though he was no bigger than a four-year-old, he could've been as much as eight). To put it more precisely, she was with him—he led the way up the street, checking back over his shoulder, his look as wearily authoritative as a safari guide with a tourist group in tow. He was dressed in shirt and shorts and sandals, like any other little boy, but his exotically clad mother—veiled and gorgeously embroidered—was a real greenhorn up from the desert; there was no doubt about who it was who was solemnly and importantly in charge of getting them through the labyrinth of entries to the right clinic. (Of course I don't know she was his mother. But she was slender, which for Beduin women usually means young. And anyway, I saw her eyes, proud of him and laughing at him too, and I think so.)

Well, one look and I knew: here before me was none other than James James Morrison Morrison Wetherby George Dupree, of the marvelously rhythmic Milne poem, who "took good care of his mother/though he was only three." Whenever, reading aloud to little Phil, I'd get to the last of James James's injunctions (the line repeated but always slightly varied) to his mother, "If you want to go down to the end of the town/ you'd better go down with—" I'd stop before the last word and Phil, bouncing ecstatically in his crib, would screech "Me!"

A Beduin James James seems stretching things, though: this kid wouldn't even understand the poem.* But, well, art is universal . . .

---

11 ⬚ The Shesh-Aleph Bus

The street I live on is named for a Russian poet, and the bus stop is near the intersection with Einstein Street. Bialik Street is up at the next corner, where the macaulet is. And an unpaved little semi-street leading to the schoolyard beside my house is named for the Arab poet Ibn Gvirol.

Bialik is probably the only one whose works may actually have been read by the inhabitants of the neighborhood, thanks to a definite educational effort. But even there, it probably amounts to only a few holiday-related lines quoted in a newspaper: Bialik's Hebrew, I'm told, is much too difficult for most people. Ibn Gvirol seems to do a little better, for Estie told me about him with an admiration obviously shared by the other students. But they're Youth, modern and privileged: not many of my neighbors went to secondary school in Israel, and probably none of them to the kind of track therein that's meant for the university-destined. Still, though, streets are named for Bialik and Ibn Gvirol in Tel Aviv, and there's one for my own street's Russian poet in Jerusalem, too. (And that's only from my own limited experience. Who knows how many other places also?)

And I haven't heard anyone mutter discontentedly or even say "Ma la'assot" about our neighborhood street names. When I've asked about these namesakes, I've usually been told they were "men of intelligence" (a finger points to the forehead in a gesture you might take for "nutty" except that the finger doesn't wiggle and the look is admiring). Usually, that's also that: it's simply understood that people of imagination ought to be celebrated. I think "imagination"

239

is what they mean, for, though *ish chacham* means an intelligent man and there are other words for "imaginative," etc., it's clear that the everyday meaning is a knowledgeable fellow, a brainy guy—the possessor of a quality clearly distinguished from both mere shrewdness and university degrees. A brainy guy, it becomes apparent, is one who's always likely to come up with a good idea . . . Thus the people who now live on these streets have a certain cultural assumption, you might say, in common with the original street-namers in Tel Aviv and Jerusalem. But they haven't really acquired the early settlers' culture: when *they* build a town, they'll name a street for their own ish chacham. (And here in Beer-Sheva, they may have begun to do so, for Ibn Gvirol obviously was added after Einstein and Bialik.)

This kind of not-quite inheritance, one culture rapidly overlaying another, is on view all over Beer-Sheva. Which is a city of, now, 100,000—a figure I'm told so often, and so pointedly by people who know I'm a writer, that I'm suspicious: my guess is, they're hoping it'll go that high pretty soon. (Maybe I'm wrong, though. Chamber of Commerce-type local puffery is crude and naïve here; but the crude and naïve may also be telling the truth.) My bus line is the Number 6—"*shesh*"—which, a few months ago, went only a little farther on; where the Artzis live, less than a mile from me, was the end of the *shesh* line when they moved in. But now we have the *shesh-aleph* (equivalent of 6A) too, and I have a choice of two buses home from downtown.

Actually, I have more choices than that (e.g., both the 7 and the 8 go to the hospital, which is within walking distance of my house), but I didn't know it for a while because the bus lines are part of that Big-Town Think people go in for. So I spent a lot of time standing around at bus stops before I discovered that if I wanted something in town, almost any bus would go there; people giving me directions always specified the bus that would take me nearest to my destination and never mentioned that if I walked around a corner, I'd be on another bus line that would do, too. The truth is, Beer-Sheva is a small enough town that even I, a middle-aged lady of sedentary habits, can probably walk from almost anywhere to the *mashbir* (the department store) on the main street of the Old City. But, ssh. Whether you call it Couéism or alpha waves, the Israelis have long been practitioners of the hopeful self-fulfilling prophecy: if you talk Big Town often enough and believe in it hard enough, it'll be true.

In fact, puffery does come true in Beer-Sheva: you can ride out on any bus and see it happening. So I don't mock it much anymore—partly because I *live* in Beer-Sheva now. And one of the things that means is that I, too, have a passionate interest in the progress of the new Conservatory of Music, which is shaping up as something very handsome indeed and will doubtless be a much better place to go to concerts in than that great old stone barn the first settlers built. Besides, Beer-Sheva's bus pretensions are part of something I can't mock anyway. Because, just when I'm about to get unkindly witty about civic delusions of grandeur, I think of Los Angeles, where people just flung down a city without bothering about how anybody would get in and out of town. And then I hold my tongue, or at least start pulling my punches: city planning is easy mockery-meat, but if *somebody* isn't willing to be earnest-lugubrious, look where you-all end up.

Well, where I end up is in a queue waiting alongside the mashbir, where the shesh and shesh-aleph buses both start. At this spot, Israel's rampant individualism is controlled: reminiscent of the mazes used for rats in psychology experiments, a waist-high arrangement of horizontal piping with lanes one person wide winds around and ends at where the bus door will be. (I should think the ugly metal apparatus—but what do you expect, wood?—would also be uncomfortably reminiscent for concentration camp survivors. Can't be helped, I suppose.) This structure really amounts only to what you might call a strong suggestion, though, for you could easily duck under the piping and usurp an earlier place in line. But I've never seen anyone try that except children, who are promptly scolded and returned to their proper places.

Occasionally, some smart aleck will try sidling in from the outside at the point where the maze delivers the customer to the bus door. (Late arrivals who've come when the queue has already started to move also stand there, but they wait; their aim is to avoid the bother of winding through the maze but not to evade its purpose). When a lawbreaker tries a short-cut maneuver, what you do is call out *"Yesh tor!"* ("There is a line!") and the cry, taken up all along the line, causes the intruder to back off, holding up his hands apologetically and saying he was only something-or-othering. However, if that social pressure doesn't work, then most of the time nothing happens except a protesting murmur, a grumble of people telling each other *"Lo na-im, lo yafeh"* ("Not nice, not pretty"*) and a general shaking of heads in the international what-is-this-country-

Yafeh (or *yafa*, the feminine), means "pretty" or "beautiful," both literally and figuratively, and sometimes just "fine." The slang word "*yofi!*" is used all by itself and may be only an emphatic form of "okay," but it's often meant ironically. Very like the American slang use of "Beautiful!"

241

coming-to fashion. Meanwhile, the outlaw may be climbing the bus steps . . . Americans, I'm pretty sure, would raise a lot more fuss. But then, the concept of fairness is much more a part of the American psyche. (And Israelis, I've seen again and again, are simply not very warlike.) Soldiers seem to be the only legitimate exception to the bus *tor*, but this nice gesture works both ways: I've never seen a soldier enter a bus ahead of anyone except another soldier. And both chyellim and chyellot are among the first to offer a seat to elders, pregnant women, etc. (Soldiers are often waited on first in stores, but that seems to be something decided by the storekeepers—who are all, unless they're past fifty-five, in the reserve and doubtless remember how short a leave can be.)

This day I want to tell you about, the shesh-aleph bus came before the shesh, which meant that everybody on line could take it. But the line was short, because anybody might be inclined to walk if they could on such a fair and pleasant day of sunshine—the warm and pleasant kind, not the killing sun of summer—and sweet white clouds scudding across a baby-blue sky. I'd been shopping and was going home: I was toting the plastic shopping bag without which one doesn't usually leave the house in Beer-Sheva, and it was filled and heavy. So I took a seat near the front of the bus. And, after maneuvering my plastic bag to keep the chocolates I'd bought out of the way of the sun, I settled back to watch the passing scene.

Which at the moment was in the bus itself, as people were still getting on. A young woman with a baby and a shopping bag caught my attention at once, for I could empathize with her logistic problems: my first baby got past twenty pounds before she consented to start walking, and I myself weighed only ninety pounds at the time. This young mother was having even more trouble, though, because she was also vastly pregnant and thus had a great frontal bulk to maneuver, along with the shopping bag and the wriggling eight-month-old (around there, anyway—still in plastic pants over a diaper, and the bare feet had not been walked on but the dimpled knees looked as though they'd done some crawling). Besides, her shoulder purse had slipped down and was dangling near her calf. She was twisting, trying to haul it up and extract her bus fare, but she couldn't see very well around her bulge. So she sat down on the front seat across from the driver to continue her struggles. The two front seats are informally reserved for the old and the lame and anyone in difficulty, and she certainly qualified on one score. (The window half of her seat was occupied by another qualified candidate, an ancient wisp of a man who had already fallen into a drowse.)

Once she sat down, more people entering obscured my view of her. But when the door closed and the bus began to move, I saw she had things under control. She'd hoisted up her pocketbook and unzipped it—thus delighting the baby, now sitting on her knee and strategically located for poking fat little hands into the inviting bag. His mother managed to fend him off and find her change purse while also bracing herself and him against the wild swerves and lurches by which traffic moves through the Old City.

Private cars offer a somewhat less dramatic motoring experience, at least if their drivers know better than to try to hurry (Gladys, who's lived here about five years, gives you a nice, smooth ride); but they, too, must contend with a populace inclined to take automobile traffic lightly, like Thereza, or to stroll Mediterraneanly, pausing to greet friends in the middle of the street. Bus drivers, who are supposed to maintain a schedule, thus have a problem. Most of them solve it by speeding up whenever they spy a few yards of empty street and then jerking to a stop a microsecond before the bumper dirties the pedestrian's sleeve. So he usually escapes injury. But the bus riders don't: the seats are made of metal and of course have no upholstering, springs, or other folderol. Possibly it would be easier on the spine to let go and just fall off, but nobody seems to have the courage to try that.

Eventually, the young woman managed to pay her fare, leaning out over the baby to hand the driver the coins as he drew up to a stop at the edge of downtown. The baby, cheerfully open to all adventures, liked this one too: he crowed, waving his arms as if inviting the newcomers into the bus, where such interesting things happened. In the narrow space, he represented a mild obstacle. But people managed to wriggle past him and his gestures. And they usually smiled: he was a very pleasant baby, and if you noticed him you would certainly smile.

By that time, we had progressed from the mashbir to its ancient and still thriving ancestor, the shuk. All the bus lines stop there, for nearly everybody has some business sometime at the shuk. Tourists are not the only ones who buy rugs and embroidered blouses on sale there; Israelis, who can stand closer acquaintance with the chicken or fish they plan to eat than I can, buy them sickeningly fresh and cheaper there; and even the fainthearted favor the shuk for fruits and vegetables. Most people go at least once a week, usually very early in the morning and lugging all the bags and baskets they own. An American I know (one of the Old Inhabitants who does good works at the AACI) has observed that Americans can be considered "absorbed" into the life of Beer-Sheva when they can (a) do *all* their shopping at the shuk and (b) carry the results home on the bus. He has a point. For Beer-Sheva has some European aspects, I'm learning—like the Israel Philharmonic visits and the local chamber-music concerts, a coffeehouse that bakes delicious Viennese pastries, and other such (probably yekke-inspired) touches. But the shuk is dirty, noisy, crowded, given to haggling and thieving and always distressingly frank about entrails: the shuk is Asian all the way. There are Americans in town who are used to living in places where English is not spoken, and some have had comfortable experiences of residence in France or Italy; but even they feel startlingly far from home in the sweaty, haggle-babble air of the shuk.

The stop at the shuk thus always converts the atmosphere of any outward-bound bus, whatever it was like up to that point, to the distinctively Asian. Immediately, every vacant space is filled and overflowing, and that includes the aisles: all the new arrivals are laden with baskets and plastic bags and more exotic containers, often precariously roped together and with the odd squash or eggplant poking out, and obviously nobody could store all that on a lap even if a seat were still available. So the aisles are full of things to stumble over, which inevitably gives rise to conversation ranging from a polite *slicha* (slee-CHAH, "pardon," "excuse me") to angry Arabic and Hebrew and Yiddish and Russian and Georgian and who knows how many dialects in which people ask what's clearly "Why can't you look where you're going?" In addition, there's the encounter factor, which is apt to be pretty high in a small town (*slicha*, I mean even in a city of 100,000 population). The resulting greeting of old school chums, co-workers, neighbors, and buddies people (or their husbands or sons) did army service with fills the air with a few additional languages, because someone who addresses strangers in Hebrew to say something irritable will use Serbo-Croatian or French or Spanish or English to shout "Hi, how've you been, how's the family?"

And finally, while the sound level is rising, so are the smells. Some of them come from pungent stuffs in the baskets underfoot, but many of them quite certainly emanate from the salami consumed in the recent past rather than the one going home now. The new arrivals are many, are crowded into a too-small space, and have been standing in the sun and/or dragging heavy packages and perspiring freely; in addition, the more Asian-oriented members of the Beer-Sheva population tend not to have the same regard for daily baths or such easily washable clothing as the European-culture types.

So the bus is crowded (and noisy, and it stinks) even before it stops next—as, again, they all do—at the *tachana hamerkazit*, the Egged bus station for intercity travel. This stop almost invariably means a net gain in the number of passengers and the new arrivals are very likely to have luggage. Rarely suitcases but plastic bags, backpacks, etc.: foreign students (particularly the towering Danes and Swedes) helplessly batter everybody around with their huge backpacks and the impedimenta hanging from them. But even more mind-blowing is the first time you get poked by an Uzzi slung over the shoulder of somebody-in-Beer-Sheva's son or husband coming home on leave. It doesn't hurt (except psychologically: I'm usually reminded guiltily of the letters I owe to friends in Massachusetts), and the contrite soldier always swings around—thus bopping somebody on his other side—to say *"Slicha, Geveret."* But it takes a while before you quite get used to it . . .

After that the bus lurches on around the corner to what is intended to be the replacement of the Old City. The would-be new city is a scattering of new government buildings—City Hall, the court, etc. (so people will have to go there, and sooner or later it *will* become the new city, see?)—around some beautiful, carefully tended garden areas with brilliant flowers and lush ground cover (humph, it ought to be: the sprinklers are going half the day, and you can hardly walk by without getting sprayed). There's also an arcade, with shops lining it and a café at each end; characteristically for Beer-Sheva, one is "Anglo-Saxon" (the proprietor is actually from South Africa) and features delicious and very rich cakes, and the other is "Oriental," given to spicy and nutty tidbits and with a TV set mounted on the wall. It's interesting that Mrs. Ben-Ari took me to the latter for our ceremonial coffee, whereas Thereza and her friends are habitués of the former. (Which goes to show, I guess, that even when Israelis lack religious and political schisms they'll at least insist on two coffeehouses.) But just behind this sudden clump of innovative architecture and intercultural bustle is a patch of dusty plain whose own new and ultra-modern building is still on the drawing board at some Ministry—and there, a couple of camels are mooching along, waiting for their Beduin owners to come back from a day's trading at the shuk . . . It's all so absurd, and at the same time so endearing, that I don't know whether to indulge my taste for satire or my local pride. (So I've settled, you see, for simply reporting it.)

Well, it was at that stop—when I was sitting in the bus with the round eye of a fish regarding me from a nearby basket and the edge of a cardboard tray of eggs bumping the back of my neck—that the fat man got on, adding himself to the already unimaginably crowded passenger load. That he should even try was incredible, and seemed to indicate a light view of the laws of physics; that he should try it when he'd obviously been to the shuk before he hiked over here to pay his electric bill—well, it was just too much. If he hadn't been so *fat*, if he hadn't had not two but *three* great bundles in his hands (and a ceramic towel rack tucked under his arm!) . . . Clearly I wasn't the only one who felt instantly that this simply was not possible. The driver said so, angrily, and hissed the door-closing mechanism to make his point. But the fat man came on anyway, ignoring both fact and advice and counting, apparently, on the beachhead he'd established when he thrust one of his baskets through the door and up onto the top step. The driver could still shut the door and hurtle off with the fat man's groceries, but he wouldn't: nobody in Beer-Sheva would do that.

So the bus driver—a slim, lithe young North African with a marked (and certainly intentional) resemblance to almost any rock and roll singer—rolled his eyes and muttered, but he waited. And the fat man, wheezing and sweating from his walk in the sun, toed the first basket ahead of him along the top step, put down another, and paid his fare. Then he picked up his stuff and stood aside so the door could close.

He couldn't go anywhere, though. It would have been a tight squeeze anyway, what with his bulk and his bundles; but now the lively baby in the front seat, his waist encircled by his mother's arm, was leaning out into the only air left. He was waving his arms in swimming motions. He was talking happily to himself. And, quite effectively, he was blocking the last remaining inch of aisle.

The fat man glanced from the baby to his own full hands and then looked around for somewhere to put something down. There was nowhere: he'd only managed before because the bus door was still open then. Now, even though my own abilities to arrange objects in space have been much sharpened by my experience with the shelfless Mystery Refrigerator, I could see that there was no way. The fat man was totally immobilized—he'd have to keep on holding his possessions, and thus couldn't possibly hold anything for support, while the bus pitched and veered along—and the only possible variable in the picture was the baby. Who wasn't about to move unless his mother moved him, and one look made it apparent that there would be no help from that quarter: aware only that she had the baby safely pinned down, she was busy at the other side of her bulging belly, rearranging pocketbook and shopping bag in the limited, sloping space. She hadn't noticed the fat man's predicament, and she wasn't likely to.

246

His sweating, three-chinned face sober, the fat man considered his plight in silence for a moment. Then he bent his head— the only thing he could move—and said to the baby, *"Slicha, kätzele."* He had a loud voice, you could hear that, but he spoke gently; if he'd had any free hands, he'd have patted the baby.

The baby's mother heard. She looked around, uttered a small sound of apology and dismay, and hauled the baby in. The fat man smiled broadly, his face becoming a veritable caricature—the circle with the upturned curve inside that children draw for a nice/kind/ cheerful face. Then he set about trying to put his stuff down, now that he could at least bend over. Voices rose immediately, warning about imperiled eggs and threatening vengeance for the least tomato damaged, and possessions were either moved or defenses were erected. My nearby fish must have been relocated by a millimeter or two, for it waved gently as if somehow restored to its natural element; but it never quit glaring at me. The fat man shouted back either polite reassurances or the Hebrew equivalent of *Ah, your mother wears army shoes,* whichever the dialogue seemed to call for. And the bus hurtled on past the half-finished Conservatory, turned sharply into Bialik Street, and veered into the bus stop—once again demonstrating, for our little class in applied physics,* just what happens when bodies in motion abruptly cease being in motion. Now that we were in the smaller, residential streets, turns were frequent. So words and vegetables flew and rolled, elbows and feet and knees suddenly bumped and trod and poked each other, and the only thing unswerving was the eye of that fish.

It was still on me when we got to my stop at Einstein, by which time enough other people were debarking so I could elbow my way out, too; I'm not really good at that yet, but I'm learning. Through the bus window, I could see the baby, who'd apparently grown fond of his close-quarters chum during the ride: he was trying to stand up on the slopes of his mother's front, to watch the fat man moving himself and his gear into a clearing now available farther up the aisle. By that time, the driver had turned on his radio—it was almost time for the hourly Hebrew news—so if there was a chorus of protest again, I couldn't hear it for the strains of

---

*Somebody remarked on this—claiming, I think, that Israeli city buses defied the laws of motion—in a letter to the *Jerusalem Post*, which launched an epistolary debate that continued until the definitive word was finally uttered by the most prestigious professor of all who'd entered the controversy. I can't remember the arguments and I haven't the clips because I sent them to my son Phil for an opinion. He wrote back, eventually, that nobody had really laid a glove on Newton, so forget it. (But get a good grip on something when you ride the bus, Mom.)

pseudo-American pop music trailing out of the bus as it turned onto Avenue Metzada for the last leg of its trip.

But I knew, and I still know, that the fat man's *"Slicha, kätzele"* had put everything in place and maybe said it all. For "kätzele" is Yiddish, meaning "little cat," "kitten"—but why translate it literally? It means "sweetie-pie," "dumpling," and in the American South, "sugar." It's whatever, depending on where you grew up, you call babies and other soft, dear little things . . . So *"Slicha, kätzele"* is a two-word sentence in two languages: one revived after centuries, successfully urged into daily use by determination and even fanaticism, until after a mere fraction of a single century, it's a working fact.* And the other is the language despised by the early Zionists because they thought it the mark of the chased and cringing Jew running from a pogrom-shattered "Fiddler on the Roof" *shtetl* in an unwanted corner of eastern Europe, then from the Warsaw ghetto, and eventually from organized death among the busy burghers of Greater Germany . . .

Few people in Beer-Sheva speak Yiddish, and those are rarely young; the only ones I've ever heard voluntarily speaking it, apart from a few drifted words, were employed to work with immigrants and sometimes needed it to do their jobs. You can hear Yiddish in Tel Aviv, where people in tourist-oriented shops have a similar need for it and where many old people who came from Europe very long ago congregated and have remained. (Oldsters like that in Beer-Sheva don't speak Yiddish and never did: they speak Ladino or Maghrebi, two lesser-known dialects stemming from Jews' sojourns in Latin and Arab countries, respectively.) Only very, very recently has there been a glimmer of Israeli interest in Yiddish: finally, it would seem, some people feel safely enough established so that the odd Yiddish-theater venture can occasionally claim a place in the arts spectrum. And there is a Yiddish newspaper—Gladys buys it for her old mother, but that takes some doing in Beer-Sheva. In short, the movers and shakers, the leaders of Israel, didn't like Yiddish on principle; now, the population doesn't like it because it's just too foreign. Yet it survives, as if to show that a people accustomed to surviving-anyhow will keep on doing that even when it's no longer outsiders who're running things.

And what the Yiddish *"kätzele"* showed, that day on the

---

*How, is beyond everybody—including me, though I should be in a superior position for figuring it out: I went to college with an Irish-born girl who felt just as determined, and even fanatic, about restoring Gaelic (and their movement even had Yeats, surely as silver a tongue as you could ask!). So I got to watch a similar effort close-up. But I still don't know why theirs never got off the ground and the Zionists' did.

shesh-aleph bus, was that it was not really foreign at all: it's Israel as the fat man himself was Israel, this stern imagining brought to reality by larger-than-life brave dreamers with heads full of socialist theories—and now inhabited by very different people, who are mostly neither socialist nor very interested in theories. They came from everywhere, just as David Ben-Gurion, the "father" of the new state of Israel, and his little band of never-give-up pioneers had hoped and urged and dreamed and planned. But what happened was, the odds and ends of people shaped by everywhere else overflowed the planners' slots for them in Israel; their baggage of language and custom spilled over into the new land, reshaping it.

For planners always have trouble with human facts, and the one that confronted these is particularly hard (for non-planners too, sometimes) to absorb—the sad, strange truth that people go on loving what didn't want them. So the luggage that, it was believed, would be kicked aside before arrival at the promised land—where one would walk tall as a Jew at home in the Jews' ancient home— was in fact brought along to the little flat where Mama and Papa settled in and began struggling to learn Hebrew so they could understand their children. Thus it's been there all the time: along with the ancient gnarly tongue that had for so long been used only for prayers, there was also the softer tongue—theoretically the mark of disgrace but actually the sound of home and thus beloved. (I wasn't surprised to learn that the Yiddish noun for "Yiddish" is *mamaloschen*, "mother tongue.") The stern and powerful might deplore it, but what could they do? They weren't running a tyranny. And come to think of it, what could a tyrant do either, against the kind of gentle pressure that, like the effect of water on stone, you can't see happening or ever really put a stop to? So Hebrew has words for "baby" and "darling," all right. And the fat man could speak Hebrew, all right. But when he wanted to speak tenderly, to a baby, he softened it . . .

It isn't only words that the fat man has softened, though: he's typical of the whole process of accommodation between the dream and the daily life. The founders of the state never entertained an image of the fat man on the shesh-aleph bus, and some of them and their later followers, I suspect, didn't have any images of people at all. (Some did, surely: who would be nutty enough to accuse the down-to-earth Golda Meir—who came to Palestine as a flaming young Zionist kibbutznik in 1921—of being able to think only in abstractions, even though she's still a passionate socialist?) But even those among them who did imagine the future inhabitants of a Jewish state as particular Yitzchaks and Sarahs with individual faces still saw them as marching in from the fields—shoulder to shoulder, singing, something like those thick-limbed mammoth capital-W Workers who used to stride all over "proletarian art" and the 1930s murals in U.S. public buildings. These new citizens of the new nation* would be big, weight-bearing people, sunburned and outdoorsy, nourished on home-grown vegetables that nobody would think of cooking with a sauce . . .

Okay, maybe I'm exaggerating the early Zionists' naïveté. But, give or take a cliché here and there, it's pretty certain that they— those incredibly brave pioneers who made fields happen where there'd been only malarial swamps—weren't ever really thinking in terms of a fat man squeezing onto a bus in Beer-Sheva (population 100,000!) with a load of vegetables he didn't grow for himself.

The thing about Israel is, it got away from the original planners† because, in a sense, they were too given to over-swift *lumpen*-concepts. (A marked, and noticeable, example was their attitude toward the few poor Arabs they found squatting on the land: nobody doubted that, once these fellows saw what a proud and independent collective effort could do, they'd realize how they'd been exploited for centuries by fat-cat sheikhs and caliphs and they'd stand up and join the workers' struggle.) But the Jew was not a concept and was an individual, and he'd not just been waiting to return to Palestine, he'd been living, for generations—in this or that land, changing it if it was a free country (has anyone yet written a dissertation on the Jewish comedian as a cultural influence in American life? If not, it ought to turn up any minute) and in any case being changed by it. If he said prayers at all, he certainly repeated the references to Jewish-history places and events in Palestine; and every year at the Passover *seder*, he repeated the traditional promise, "Next year in Jerusalem." But the same service also says the Messiah is coming, and nobody thinks it means on the next bus.

So, once a land started being restored out there, Jews all over the world gave money to buy more acres and occasionally bought a certificate announcing that a tree had been planted in their name,

---

*I find it typical that they were still debating what to name the new country while the UN was getting ready to vote it into existence in 1948—and, in Washington, there was panic because the scroll to present to President Truman when the U.S. recognized the Jewish state had to be made up with the name left blank pending word from Tel Aviv. It was Ben-Gurion, just as argumentative as the rest but with a gift for keeping his eye on the ball, who got behind the "Israel" faction and pushed it through in the nick of time.

†Not all, of course. An oft-told story—maybe apocryphal, though it does sound like old on-the-ball Ben-Gurion—has him saying that Israel would really come into nation-hood when a Jewish cop arrested a Jewish prostitute in Tel Aviv. But perhaps it's significant that he had to *say* something like that to his troops.

and thanks. But none of that added up to any intention to pack up the wife and children and a couple of sets of old parents, sell the business, and go live in some weird place . . .

Jews did just that, of course—they came, with families abruptly diminished and no chance to sell the business, from Europe to Palestine because practically nobody except a little group of wild Palestinian Jews who'd slipped into Europe (and some of whose exploits would make today's TV daredevils look namby-pamby) was even trying to beat the Nazis' "final solution"; later, they came from places like Yemen and Iraq because in Israel a Jew could be safe at least. But even those refugees carried possessions with them—it's a trademark of refugees, that—and not everything in those bundles was as tangible as books and samovars. And the non-refugees, coming from Argentina and Chile and South Africa and England and the U.S. for an assortment of reasons and sometimes no really important one, brought along even more openly and consciously a whole complex of demands and expectations, plus habits of freedom and self-esteem that the Zionist pioneers camping in a wilderness wouldn't have had time to develop in their native lands even if they'd had the opportunity. In short, these arrivals from Latin and Arab and Anglo-Saxon cultures resemble Ben-Gurion just about as much as the average American resembles George Washington. And much the same goes for the recent arrivals from Russia: though they speak the language a lot of the heroes of the State of Israel were born to, they are nothing like that bunch (which fact I suspect Golda has trouble remembering, for it seems to me she tends to think of the new Russians as too like the old), and the way they got here was by slugging it out with bureaucracies and outwitting government agents. Which was hardly the experience of the eastern-Europe-born founders of Israel: neither the Tsar of all the Russias nor the hard-riding, Jew-hating Polish aristocrats could have cared when a young David Green, e.g., took off to become Ben-Gurion in Palestine.

So this land was born of imagination and is now inhabited by the unimagined: the fat man, wheezing as he climbs three steps onto a bus, and his tender Yiddish are ludicrously out of synch with the vision of the muscular, determinedly Hebrew-speaking fathers of his country. And he is still imperfectly visible to the movers and shakers—I suspect that many of the people I met in Jerusalem, most of them brilliant and all of them deeply patriotic, have little concept of the fat man in Beer-Sheva and perhaps only a dim notion of the bus driver who dreams of knocking 'em dead in Las Vegas. (I make that distinction because I know they do volunteer work with "disadvantaged youth" in Jerusalem. But I suspect the assumption is that if they can only get the lads into steady jobs as, say, bus drivers, that'll do it.) If I tell them, they're politely unbelieving—Maggie's *so* colorful—or else patient with my ignorance: they've seen before how immigrant cultures got absorbed and people became Israelis. (Yes, but an Israeli, now and in Beer-Sheva, is something different: showbiz success is the Desert Sands in Vegas, not enthusiastic applause from desert kibbutzniks. Television has brought about one world—if a distinctly shoddier one than was dreamed of.)

This gap between the power center and the grass roots is not unheard of in the U.S., of course. I know that from firsthand experience, because the Washington news service I worked for worried a lot about the gap (and so did my late husband, who was always urging his colleagues to put down their copies of *Foreign Affairs* and start reading the *Reader's Digest*). But, partly because it *was* worried about, the gap was not so great: people in Washington might have a skewed idea of how much detail about a bill coming up in the House anybody in the heartlands really wanted to read, and the vision of "Peoria"—a generic term for the heartland—was colored with scorn for the yokels; but still, Washington had a clearer idea of what things were like in Iowa than Jerusalem has of Beer-Sheva. Maybe that was because the knowledge was both easier and harder to acquire: easier because there were lots of newspapers, all in the same language (at the news service, we all took turns with different "local" newspapers: mine was St. Louis, and I read the *Post-Dispatch* every day, with particular attention to the readers' letters), and harder because it was expensive to send a reporter out to the Midwest or the West and keep him there while he scouted around.

But they *did* send a man to look and listen, because it mattered what people out there were thinking—if you were going to write an advance piece on a state primary, for example, you had to know before you stuck your neck out. That's the key difference: nobody in Jerusalem sends a scout to Beer-Sheva, though it would cost only bus fare and he needn't even stay overnight, because nobody needs to know—either for purposes of beating the competition with a pre-election "think piece" or of getting re-elected—how the grass roots in Israel are growing. If you're an Israeli politician, you sit in your office in Jerusalem or Tel Aviv and the mayor of grass-rootsville comes to you; what he tells you is going on back home is whatever is likely to get him the biggest appropriation. If you're a real all-out populist, you may, from time to time, glance at one of the Hebrew University polls—relatively new, and admittedly skimpy.*

*The profs were integrity-full enough to warn that there *was* this teeny-tiny consideration to be kept in mind—the sample was obtained by telephone. Which in

252

Well, what it adds up to, from my own point of view, is that the fat man on the shesh-aleph bus was mine, all mine: that day, my last need for making a home in Beer-Sheva got filled. Because I'd acquired sufficient household goods to get on with, a circle of friends with whom I had various kinds and degrees of relations but always a place that was mine and uniquely mine, and enough money to live on—and now I also had the most necessary living condition of all for people like me, news to tell. It all cost something, like the great distance from my family and other loved ones in the States and like the facts of a rather hard life in which I did things slowly and by using my own muscles; but then, everything costs something.* Lugging my purchases across sleepy Einstein Street in the bright, gay, clear sunshine under the wide and tranquil sky, it suddenly came to me that I was—despite a lifetime of half-believing that Morose is More and anguish an essential if you're not a clod—happy. *Happy*, believe it or not. And they could laugh if they wanted, back in Cambridge, but there were objective evidences of it: I never cried, because I had nothing to cry about, but I had something to laugh about almost every day; my weight was holding and my color good; I was working well and liking myself; and I had emotional time and space now to turn my attention and compassion outward . . . It was very, very hard to realize, but that's what I was. Happy.

Among people who let things slide, and then come through in the clinch. (No wonder I felt that I fit: my specialty, when I worked as an editor, was the "crunch job" that had an impossible deadline and/or had been botched.) Among people who, like the fat man, first insist on doing what looks impossible and then somehow make the operation viable. And preferably with a tender "Slicha, Kätzele" rather than a "Lady, will you please get your damn-fool baby out of my way?"

An American, I'm pretty sure, would have waited for the next bus; but then, Americans (in the past, at least) could entertain reasonable expectations that a next bus would come and it might even be less crowded. The fat man doesn't count on any such thing, though; he solves the instant problem, any way he can. That he's thus typical is obvious: Israeli ingenuity is noticeable all over the

---

Israel isn't only the socio-economic limitation it might be in the U.S., for phones are not only expensive but also unavailable (waiting lists can run to about three years!) in development towns, etc. Thus the survey has to skew geographic and probably age groups, and who knows what else? Integrity is not enough.

*The hard life may be cheaper than it seemed: just back from the mile walk needed to buy my daily paper, I found a letter from the U.S. mentioning that So-and-So, who's about my age, had been warned about the sedentary life of a writer and was buying an exercise machine. I laughed and laughed . . .

way of life, and instances strike you the minute you look about you at a household, a town, a factory, a kibbutz. What's also true—though it takes more time to notice—is that half the time the resourcefulness shouldn't have been necessary. For Israeli ingenuity, like the fat man's determination, is often needed to render viable a situation that common sense would have avoided in the first place.

But sometimes I'm not so sure that last judgment really makes any difference. For common sense, like efficiency, somehow doesn't strike you as so important if you spend enough time in Israel. What you come to respect instead is something not at all common-sense—the dahfke spirit of I'm-gonna-do-it-anyway, an indefatigable uppitiness that would be profoundly irritating if it weren't so profoundly awesome. Maybe the latter reaction wins out because, deep down, we're all scared; and the powerful visual assurances all around in Beer-Sheva of just how indefatigable, and uppity, man can be are consoling, heartening, life-supporting. (Of course you could argue that what I'm talking about is a special sample, Jewish man with his back to the wall. But I don't think much of that argument: we've all got our back to the wall, the whole bloody human race. And James Joyce, a fellow of admirable awarenesses, wasn't kidding when he made his universal voyager à Jew.)

So I can't really make fun of the shesh-aleph bus lurching along Avenue Metzada, which has plenty of room for four lanes of traffic and a center strip wide enough for good-sized (future) trees—but right now, I can cross that street with Thereza-like indifference to safety and be at less risk than I was when I dutifully watched the traffic lights in downtown Boston. How can I laugh at this pretentious avenue, though? For what better way is there than to combine the lessons of the past with buoyant hope for the future? Somebody in some Ministry (well, this is Israel: probably *three* somebodies in three Ministries) researched Highway Board reports from half a dozen countries before the width of the center strip, grades of curves, etc., were determined; then Avenue Metzada became a reality after time was duly taken out for Shabbat, miluim, the workmen's wives having babies, and holiday preparations and celebrations.

When I say holidays, I'm not talking about something like a Washington's Birthday Dollar Sale. Let's see, there are Chanukah and Pesach (Passover) and Succot, all examples of the kind that kill the better part of a week, and Purim* and the one where everybody

---

*My favorite, combining aspects of Halloween and April Fool: the children dress up in costumes and the adult keynote is all-out zaniness. (The Purim "weather report" on

254

goes out and plants trees and the one where everybody goes to a campfire. Also, Independence Day—which may or may not include a big parade, depending on the outcome of the debate between those who think it could make Israel look militaristic and those who don't give a damn if Israel does look militaristic—and the day of mourning for the fall of the Temple a few thousand years ago and another for the victims of the Nazis and another for the dead of Israel's wars. And oh yes, let's not forget Simchat-Torah (the joy of Torah), a day of dancing with the Torah scroll. I've left out some real biggies, like Rosh HaShana (the "head of the year," or New Year) and Yom Kippur, the Day of Atonement. And then there's a slew of other holidays that are sort of optional: any given Israeli may or may not be celebrating one of them, and to a varying degree, too. Also, I haven't bothered to mention interruptions like running out of funds or into strikes, because they're variables (a term meaning, in Israel, that it'll surely happen but you don't know when or how often).

But still, the fact is, Avenue Metzada did get built: it's there, ready for the future with its clumps of four-story stone buildings on stilts lined up along both sides of the street. Most of the flats are occupied, in series like a string of freight cars, by new, newer, and newest immigrants—in that order as the shesh-aleph bus travels outward. Thus, nearest my own street, Arab music wails from radios and TVs get turned on earlier (on Israel's channel, the Arabic broadcasting begins at 6 P.M., the Hebrew not until 8); a little farther along, where the Artzis live, Spanish is what's mostly spoken; and it becomes Russian in the farthest-out section that required the addition of a shesh-aleph bus. Especially out there, the apartment houses have the same Someday look about them as does the broad avenue. But let the future fill it in a bit and *yeheeye tov:* their white stone will become tanned, as our older buildings have, by the invisible drifting of sand. And their stilted forecourts will also be linked to the earth by pepper trees and fast-growing bougainvillea,* so that they look as if they're supposed to be where they are.

---

the English news is like the old-time Bob and Ray radio routines. And oh, the sly takeoffs on literary and art criticism—not to mention dance, easily the best of the lot—in the *Jerusalem Post!*) There's dancing in the streets, and people hit each other with little plastic hammers that squeak. You're supposed to get good and drunk, and the most abstemious Israelis arrive at the whoopee! stage very quickly. This is all to celebrate how the wily Esther outwitted wicked Haman, who ordered death to the Jews. I'm told the Rabbinate takes a dim view of Esther (who, one gathers, did not behave like a good-Jewish-woman) and would rather skip this one. But the populace just likes it too much.

*That much landscaping "comes with" the new flats. Any more is the product of the inhabitants' cooperative efforts: each house has its own *Vad* (committee), which executes the will of the majority and collects the necessary levies, too. (My block's precious couple of trees and strip of grass was costing only IL20 a month apiece, but everybody must've chipped in plenty at the start.)

255

The job could be done better, maybe. And certainly prettier—those concrete hives, abrupt in the wide and empty landscape, don't seem to make sense: when there's no shortage of room to spread out, why go up instead? To nasty suspicious types like me, the first answer that suggests itself is bureaucratic rigidity, a style established early on in Tel Aviv, where there was never much space to spread out, and now absurdly continued here. But inquiry reveals that (though nobody would of course be so foolish as to eliminate the bureaucracy explanation) the tradition involved is probably defense. That's been modernized, too, with underground shelters equipped with business-like air vents and yard-thick concrete walls; but the original principle was the stockade, a familiar feature of the American western. And if whoever's in charge seems reluctant to depart from it, well, these people were defending Beer-Sheva in 1967 while I was watching baseball games. So it's hard to assume I know better . . .

Anyway, in terms of the Utilitarian ethic of the greatest good for the greatest number, this works. And better than housing projects I've seen in the U.S. Here, thrift has been designed into this housing not to please the stockholders of an insurance corporation but to make the money provide a maximum number of families with light and air in every room and a courtyard and play space for the children*—and it's managed without the anonymity that can make public housing in the U.S. a horror. For sixty-four families live at my address but a maximum of eight share an entry. Thus if somebody's kid crayons on the walls in the hall, I know who did it; and if I should suddenly scream in the night, it would be seven families' direct business. (That much is established by the design. But general Israeli nosiness would of course make it the business of a lot more.) All of which is not, I know, enough to stop the winces of Americans who feel obscurely that there's just something immoral about not having your very own acre. For them, eight families will still cause shudders. But, granted its own terms, this seems to me a successful solution to the problem of providing equal self-respect along with equally modern kitchens. And for me, it simply *feels* better than before, when I lived a lot better but also with the knowledge that a hell of a lot of other people never would.

The catch is the usual one here, that it's all so fragile—all the

*Each family also has a balcony, which I like—perhaps because I still feel a need for a "garden" or a "porch." But many people in Beer-Sheva think the balconies a real tradition-hang-up: fine for Tel Aviv, they say, but in the desert it's too cold when it's cold and too hot when it's hot, so who can sit out on them? They have logic on their side, I have to admit. And they're beginning to prevail.

elaboration of planning and construction and technology only make more poignant the fact that this, too, is just plunked down on the desert. A dozen yards from the buildings with all their refrigerators and bathtubs and ingenious uses of every square meter of space, the "lone and level sands stretch far away." Ozymandias lurking right behind the dustbins can be a bit scary.

But what matters most, all the time, is that this is *not* the work of my-name-is-Ozymandias-king-of-kings but of the abused of kings (and presidents and chancellors). Maybe they're sometimes individually arrogant or brave or silly, but they're always also people huddling together against the scary . . . You have to have faith in *something*, I think, and I guess this is where I've come to put mine—on these never-say-die survivors, good at kindness and not so great on common sense. So, wait till you see our new Conservatory . . .

From the diary: 15

Dynasties (Sept.)

Martha and Avi came over this evening. And, while he treated my cracked kitchen faucet with his wonder-working epoxy, she sat primly on my iron-cot "sofa" and said "I'm pregnant," all pleased and pink-faced. She looked solemn and wondering, too—I was the first one they'd told and that's always an occasion that combines a feeling of formality with a lingering incredulity (now it's really real...) Part of the pink may have been embarrassment, too: Martha comes of a culture that's proud of "keeping yourself to yourself"—to use their own odd phrasing—and sometimes it still shows. She's come a long way in learning to inhabit this one, though; and I ought to know, because I've been around practically since the beginning. Which was a little hairy, what with Avi's way of inviting the world and his brother to dinner; buying huge quantities of stuff in the shuk that was usually rawer, so to speak, than his American wife had ever seen before; and bounding up at 5 A.M. for an early-morning swim before work! Eventually they managed a compromise—mostly Avi's way, but that figures: it's his turf they decided to take up residence on (and in a Beer-Sheva summer, an early-morning swim makes marvelous sense)—but Martha lost a lot of weight and went about in a considerable daze for a while.

Not to mention standing in tears amid the Rabbinate's alien corn. That bunch is no joy at any time, but it's far from at its best when an Israeli Jew brings home a not only foreign but non-Jewish-born bride. For the Rabbinate wants to be sure that her conversion is for-really real,* and it knoweth not diplomacy...Always that gap between religions and their bureaucracies, isn't there? Because Ruth, the mother of King David, was a woman of another tribe and the fact gets sweetly celebrated every year at the appropriate holiday: the "sheep," it appears, are way ahead of their "shepherds"... (Incidentally, it's kind of thrilling, reading that "Your people shall be my people" speech in Hebrew. But it had to be with help: the vocabulary is antiquated and very, very hard.)

Well, but they did make it—I remember Avi lighted up like a

---

*Of course if they'd allow civil marriages they *could* be sure. But no, they prefer—and get—hypocrisy. For, though there was nothing to stop Martha and Avi from getting married in the U.S., the religious law's definition of a Jew depends on the mother; and Avi wanted to insure against possible future hassles over the legitimacy of not only his marriage but his children. So Martha not only got converted but in rabbinate-approved style, with every base touched.

Christmas tree with the joy of having finally managed, against all the obstacles, to be all legal-and-proper installed with his own wife in his own flat. Which was littered with wedding-present crockery and cheese boards and electric whatsisses, both American and Israeli versions, for which he'd now have to build cupboards. Hell, he'd have built a jet plane in the salon if that was what was wanted, and you could see it written all over his face.

It's hard to remember that all that "past" was less than a year ago. For everything is so speeded-up in our little society that I didn't even stop to think it odd, this evening, that I should be feeling so—well, dynastic. (The same is true, though to a somewhat lesser extent, of the way I feel about Miriam and Ze'ev's baby, which is due earlier: I know them an even shorter time, and Miriam was already wearing a maternity dress when I met them.) All babies coming to Us, it seems, are part mine—I was not only busily suggesting names tonight and offering (unsolicited) grandmother-type advice, I was also thinking godmotherly, practically elder-of-the-tribe stuff. Which is curious to begin with, but what's curiouser is that in such a short time I should feel equipped to make baby policy, so to speak. Our speedy coming-together includes such knowledge of each other . . .

But arriving at this baby isn't going to be speedy enough for Avi, I predict, for I've never seen a man more ready for fatherhood. Which figures for any normal man past thirty. But in Israel it may always be helped along by those European horrors that most sensible survivors prefer not to talk about, just let it all slide away and get forgotten.* Thus it was Martha who told me Avi had been in a camp at the age of four—and nobody has to tell me that a child torn from his parents at that age and in such circumstances (Avi's were better than my friend Hilda's, though: he at least was with his older sister) will be marked by it in some way (even if only by the starvation diet that went with it). So maybe Avi would have loved children anyway—why not? He's an outgoing and affectionate man—but not, I think, with the all-out, immediate, and wistful joy so evident in the way he regards all children. Who all seem to adore him in return: toddlers tug at his pants legs to pull him down on the floor so they can climb on him just one more time, and six-year-olds hold long, earnest Hebrew conversations with him. And it doesn't

*This sounds too hung-up, and they're not: Avi will answer relevant questions, as will Thereza and others. But none of the friends who've been perfectly willing to give me brisk factual accounts of how it was would willingly go to a public memorial ceremony (Avi went once so I could see what one was like—an effort I've never stopped being grateful for) or read books about those times.

have to be children he knows, either: once, when we were driving through town on a Saturday afternoon, he stopped the car to admire a little girl of about four who was skipping along on the other side of the street. Maybe on her way to a birthday party, because she was all dressed up in spanking-clean white pumps, pink socks, and a ruffly pink party frock, and there was a bow in her neatly combed hair. And, "Isn't that some sight," said Avi, shaking his head in wonder, like a tourist appreciating a sunset.*

So it would be hard to imagine anybody happier than Avi must be right now. He had to participate in this evening's discussions—e.g., the merits of "natural childbirth," the comparative merits of the local hospital and the one in Ashdod—because he's the only one who can arrange for any of them, but of course he doesn't give a damn about the details. He'll fix it, he'll fix everything, he says, and I believe him: I wouldn't like to be a bureaucrat who tries to get in the way of whatever Avi's arranging for Martha's confinement. It's clear that Avi, denied room at the inn, would make room at the inn ... But it's also clear—now that I'm thinking my long thoughts—that stern-disciplinarian-wise, Avi's likely to be somewhat inadequate. So, since Martha will have to be the no-no meanie—with the first one at least, until Avi learns a little self-defense—it may work out somewhat better for the kid's psyche if we get a girl this time.

Note that "we." Ah well, it's infectious, this utter joy—my attempts at long views and prudence are only dues paid to my parents, particularly my mother's constant Is-this-really-wise? pullbacks from happiness. But I don't owe that anymore: I'm the elder of the tribe now, and I have babies coming who'll get born into debt and hazard my mother never imagined—and I feel wonderful about them, happy and excited and eager. (I feel, in fact, like my own Christmas poem about the birth in the manger. It ended, "Every baby born has come to save the world"—and I don't think I really knew until now what I meant by it.) Nuts to looking ahead, and even to making pronouncements: like the Israelis, I figure we'll all learn whatever is necessary to take care of our babies, and if something is needed and we haven't got it, why, we'll make it. Welcome, welcome, babies. We'll do all right by you, somehow. Yeheeye tov.

*Whenever I think of that moment (which I found heartbreaking) I always recall that in 1967, when Nasser was threatening to throw all the Jews into the sea and Egyptian troops were lined up in Gaza all ready to jump off, some kind hearts and gentle people in England offered to help Israel—by sending planes, to take the children away! You can imagine the déjà-vu feeling that "charity" must have given Israelis ...

12 ⚡ Fun and Games

The following reflections are based on calendar or notebook jottings from several months of what turned out, a very little time later, to be the last of the Days of Innocence. Most involve jaunts, though never very far, since the whole of Israel has been said to be about the size of New Jersey. I think that means before the Six-Day War in 1967, but it doesn't make much actual difference because if Israel in 1973 was bigger than New Jersey, the increase was mostly not in inhabited parts. Where people not in a Beduin tribe, a monastery, or a military base live is still largely within the Old Testament's "from Dan even to Beer-Sheba"—and that grand north-south sweep amounts to about 600 kilometers, or somewhere around 360 miles.

It was hard to remember that fact, though, because traveling from Beer-Sheva to Haifa took about the same time as from Boston to Denver. True, one is by bus and the other by air, but you still feel that you're journeying a like long way from home (and in fact the bus trip may actually feel longer, because then the miles and miles of land can be *seen* going by). Besides, the people around me whose concept of a "whole country" is Israel-sized were always subtly influencing me—the neighbors taking their children to visit grandparents in Hadera (not far from Tel Aviv) would be visibly packing the car with provisions and baby equipment for a long trip; or a woman would tell me, "My mother still lives in Givatayim, so naturally I don't see her very often." That kind of conversation is often very trying anyway, as I discovered when I tried to explain why I wouldn't see my grandchildren much even if I'd stayed in Massachusetts. For there simply is no way, short of doing lots of laps, to travel anything like 1800 miles across Israel.

For the sabra who's never been abroad, non-Israeli notions of distance are virtually unimaginable even short of the huge U.S. distances. (That causes one of the parent-children problems that sometimes crop up here, by the way: Thereza and Jan, like most people who came from small European countries, were used to hopping over a border or two for vacations, to go to university, etc., so they're always aware of how tiny Israel is; yet, to their children, it's the world. Thus the parents see the kids as hopelessly insular, and the kids consider their parents weird.) Especially since the illusion of size is supported by the weather report rolling up on the TV after the nightly news; it goes through four or five regions before it arrives at the letters meaning Negev. Which is not just Big-Think, for Israel does truly have a wide variation in weather: from Dan to Beer-Sheva can quite commonly mean from snow to blossoming spring, on the same day; and the Mediterranean country of Tel Aviv is in a wholly different meteorological league from the land beside the Dead Sea. So no wonder you lose track of the fact that it's all happening in so small a space.

My calendar is marked, on an early-spring day, "To Dead Sea"; a notebook entry about it says, "My God, if you thought the *Negev* was a desert . . ." Yes. The Dead Sea is the lowest point on the face of the earth, all the guidebooks tell you. But you know that before you reach it: nothing can be as empty of life, and even the history of life, as the Judean Desert. The end of the world—nothing moves, or can have moved for eons and eons, over those great gray-brown hills of sand baking under the merciless sun. Not even, it seems, the lizards of the Negev, which now looks positively fertile by contrast. In *this* desert, Georgia O'Keeffe's bleached skulls would be too much a reminder of life: even death, if it's recent enough to leave bones still around, is too time-tied to be in place here . . . Until you get right beside the Dead Sea itself, where a few things do remind you of the U.S. desert O'Keeffe painted. Like a couple of spiky-branched shrubs—no leaves, of course, just your basic Chinese-art shrub—all their arms encrusted whitely with salt. They look not only dead but pickled, but at least they're there, they're *something* . . .

I waded in the Dead Sea, which seems no wider than the lake I used to swim across at summer camp. It must have some currents, or freshets, because it moves—though no, in nothing like waves: forget the "sea" part, it's much more like a lake—and the surface sparkles (that's the salt, I guess) under the sun. On the opposite shore, about as far away as the boys' camp used to be, bluish-purple

shapes of something (gun emplacements?) in the Hashemite King-
dom of Jordan shimmer in the heat; if I had my distance glasses
with me, I'm sure I'd be able to see something specific over there. In
Israel, on the height behind me, they're building a luxury hotel. I
made a face when I saw it, but now I think wistfully, what if the
Jordanians built another one on their side and the guests of each
rowed across for lunch, or to buy souvenirs . . . I realize what's happened to me, and I can't believe it. Not only am I thinking of luxury
hotels as something Good(!) but I'm being like an Israeli: today it's
dirty, or half-finished, or swallowed in sand, or warstruck—but
tomorrow, ah tomorrow . . .

I meant to taste the Dead Sea but I chickened out because
when I looked down at my legs they were oily. Ugh. These warm,
heavy (but buoyant—it's said that you can't sink in the Dead Sea
because of all the salt), languidly moving waters are supposed to be
good for you if you have psoriasis, and baths in it are used to treat
arthritis and troubles like that. Okay, if you're suffering, it's doubtless worth it. But, even back in the car, scrubbing at my shins with a
wet cloth, I couldn't get rid of the ugly, sticky feeling. Awful. If you
need to bathe in Dead Sea water, do it from a luxury hotel, where you
can jump right into a hot shower afterward . . .

High on a hill at another point (when I say "high" I may be
talking about sea level, remember, or a couple of feet above: the
Dead Sea itself is 400 meters *below* sea level) I saw what must surely
be the world's most effective anti-war demonstration. It was a
monument to a terrible event, presumably described in the ex-
tensive Hebrew on a sign nearby. One day some years before—an
Israeli woman who teaches English told me—an Israel Air Force
plane got lost and the pilot tried to make it home by coming in over
the Dead Sea, as he had neither radio nor navigation equipment. But
the trouble was, he was coming in from the direction of Jordan, and
there wasn't supposed to be any Israeli plane where he was.
(Perhaps he was also flying very low, which would make sense if his
aircraft was damaged but would look like an attempt to get under
the radar?) And he didn't answer the radio or give any other signal
asked for, and he was heading direct for the Israeli base, coming in
fast. There was little time and no way to know for sure who he was:
thanks to busy arms salesmen in peace-loving countries, both sides
in any Middle East confrontation may have the same kind of aircraft.
So the Israelis did what I guess they had to do—they shot him down.

And then they went out and picked up the pieces, and the
dead pilot turned out to be one of theirs after all. You can see how
anybody would feel about a thing like that—but add to it then the

263

special anguish of a country in which every single life is personally, agonizingly precious. And in which the religious precept, which of course affects the cultural tradition of even the most non-religious, insists that *anything** must be done to preserve life . . . So the angry and bitter and heartsick people got a sculptor to make them a monument that would remind them of what war had led them to.

And this is what he did: he took the blackened and broken fragments of the fallen plane—ugly, jagged, torn, charred lances and hunks of metal—and dumped them helter-skelter into what is clearly, from its shape, meant to remind you of a toilet bowl. And there it stands, stark and nasty, the perfect symbol of what a war is . . . *We* had a monument made, the Israeli woman had said. I wondered whether that meant the Air Force, so I asked her whom she meant by *we*. She eyed me with faint disgust: "The people of Israel," she said. "Who else knows better than we do about wars?" She looked at the black, ugly thing for a moment and then turned away, shaking her head. There were tears in her eyes . . .

It seems to me quite remarkable that I've never seen any mention of this monument in the U.S. media. You'd think television news, which keeps whining that it's limited by what can be shown in a picture, here would have one that might even halt the hand carrying the beer can to the mouth. Is it the toilet bowl that bothers them, do you think? American TV may consider such references not-nice unless they're in commercials. But in that case, where's the counter-culture, which makes such a point of being *both* anti-war and not-nice? I haven't seen this in any "underground" newspapers either. Well, maybe it's just that, what with Israel supposed to be so aggressive and militaristic, it would be too risky to let Americans see how much Israelis, who know better than anybody, hate war.

Notebook entry: "Avdat. And the true Fran revealed." That was when Fran kindly volunteered to drive me down into the Negev, to see the ancient ruins of Avdat (Ahv-DOT). On the way, we stopped at Sde Boker, the kibbutz deep in the desert where Ben-Gurion retired to; he was said to be studying the religious commentaries, now that he had time. (But he hadn't, apparently, developed any meekness:

---

*The sole exception, I believe, is that you must not deny God. But you're supposed to do anything short of that to stay alive. Which may explain why the pious Jews weren't the ones who tried the suicidal actions against the SS. (The non-pious did—and an ex-underground fighter I know is still bitterly anti-religious because of that. Though it now makes no difference, since they're all Israelis and defending Israel *is* trying to stay alive.)

there was a story that he'd asked one of the soldiers who guard the kibbutz, a religious guy, to help him with some complicated inter-pretation he was reading. The soldier said okay, after he got off duty—but the old man would have to put on a *kipah*,* as it was forbidden to handle the sacred writings with your head uncovered. Some time later, but before the guard was off duty, Ben-Gurion came flying out of his hut, white hair furiously rumpled and eyes blazing. Where did it actually *say*, he demanded triumphantly, that you had to wear a kipah? . . . Ah me, if only B-G hadn't had to wait till he was halfway through his eighties to turn his attention to the follies of the rabbinate!)

Well, Fran and I didn't see the old boy, but we saw what he saw: you stand on the edge of a cleared plateau beside the tidy kibbutz, with its neat little white houses and the dazzling modern school and flags flying—and you look down at what is clearly the beginning of the world. The steep cliffs shadowed only by the shadows of themselves look like what might have been left after boiling seas had been sucked away: a million years later, say, when every drop of water or trace of sea life had been burned off to become just part of the caramel-colored land, you'd end up with this leftover seabed of dead mountains and abysses, utterly dry and terrible. And awesome and beautiful, for in the great pitiless light an amazing array of colors is visible, a tiny palette with immense subtlety. They're not even real colors, I guess: the purple and blue and gray and green are the delicate hues of mold, the unwanted life that grows in the cold and the dark of the back of your refrigerator on some bit of cheese or old bowl of leftovers you forgot about. The colors of life-in-despite, though, may be the most beautiful of all— particularly when they're grand in dimension, the heights soaring, the depths frighteningly deep, and the whole site seeming wide as the world . . . *Go to the Negev*, their old leader told them, and came down here himself to set an example. But all it did was make them sore as hell, buzzing angrily in their half-a-million-lirot apartments in Tel Aviv, coaxing the tourists while the air got thicker and thicker with auto exhausts and even the blue Mediterranean might have an oil slick. Oh, why didn't they listen to the old man? The tourists might have come anyway—they'd be crazy not to want to get a look at this grandeur. And the Israelis would be a very different people now, I think, safe here from the squalors and quarrels, pettiness and politics, and all the sad legacy of an advanced society . . .

---

*The skullcap usually called, in the U.S., a *yarmulka* (which is Yiddish).

Oh come on, I know why, don't I? For much the same reason that the Beduin are now saying to the would-be preservers of the primitive, *You go sit in those picturesque black tents: you can rail against the evils of technology just as well there. But we'd rather have our babies survive infancy, and we think it's great news that an ordinary everyday woman, nobody special, can expect to live past forty-five.* And, as the arrogant heir of the Age of Reason, of inventions and discoveries and the gift of Time it took centuries to hand me, I couldn't possibly have the gall to tell other people they shouldn't want it—all of it, even if they later find out that a lot of it isn't worth the price . . .

Avdat was the fastness of the Nabbateans, a gone people who lived well, all right. You can still wander through their shadowed stone rooms—so cool to come into, ducking your head, from the desert heat—laid out upstairs and down, in and out, in what looks like a marvelous example of expert town planning. The key to their good life was the system of underground cisterns, dams, channels, and catchments, storing and irrigating with the flash-flood waters of the desert winter and the odd millimeter of rainfall. With clever engineering and hewn stones, they used the water that *is* there, even now, in the desert.* Nobody can really be sure why Avdat stopped flourishing. That the settlement was wiped out by marauding nomads is one guess—but when you stand way up there on their highest level, where the wind never stops and you could surely see a rider from any direction while he was still days away, it's hard to figure how they could have been successfully attacked by anything short of aircraft. The economic explanation, that it was because the caravans (from rose-red Petra to Gaza, and also to the Red Sea; then, later, religious pilgrims going down to Santa Catarina in the Sinai) stopped coming, seems a bit more likely: changes in the shape and direction of trade, wars, and other human activities do happen, and civilizations that can't fit the new configurations just wither away, I guess . . . (I wonder how it would've felt, though, out there in all that immensity with never a caravan coming by anymore. Can a civilization die of loneliness, just like people?)

Well, back to my note about "the true Fran." It's because we were in this wadi, see, near Sde Boker; we'd scrambled down to take a close look at a big round rock tilted upward at an angle.

---

*Just below Avdat there's a demonstration project where Israeli agronomists, having studied the Nabbateans' "technology," now use it to grow crops year after year on just the desert's 100 mm. of water per year (and that's optimal!). Imagination and respect for the past—plus the good old dahfke spirit—seems to be the winning combination, all right.

Because it didn't look quite real—it was so smooth, and it even had something like a piecrust rim all around—I went thrashing through some scraggy thornbushes to touch it and make sure. I had just started to work my way through the brambles again when I didn't exactly see but sort of perceived the presence of something. I looked up and there above my head, poised delicately on top of the rock, was a beautiful tan creature with slim graceful legs. A gazelle, I concluded—it must be.

Fran didn't know for sure what it was either, but she knew a perfect photo just asking to be taken. So she aimed her camera and started figuring the light, etc. "Better hurry up," I said, not exactly helpful. "He won't be there long—they're supposed to be very timid." I stood still, practically on one foot, so I wouldn't set the underbrush crackling and scare him off. Fran said, just as softly (neither of us, it appears, ever thought of simply shutting up!), that she had it now, she thought. She bent her head over her camera and then added wryly, "He left." She let the camera swing loose from its sling and I came over to join her in mourning the now-lost photo. He'd been so beautiful, we agreed. Almost like Bambi. Probably quite young, whatever species he actually was . . .

It was during this sorrowing session that we glanced once more at the deserted point of rock, and abruptly discovered it wasn't deserted anymore. Standing up there just as Bambi had stood—but looking quite, quite different because I couldn't see his trim ankles now but neither could I miss a set of antlers you could hang a rowing crew's hats on—was what was clearly a veritable Grandpa of gazelles. And he was staring down at us, his head slightly lowered (to give us a real good look at his antlers?), and, well, nothing at all timid about him. "He's mad at us, don't you think so?" I asked, just refraining from clutching at Fran. Who at least had her camera to clutch, but she wasn't trying to take the old boy's picture. "He probably thinks we meant to hurt the kid," she suggested—and there was that in her tone that was reminiscent of ghost-story sessions when I was about eight and always there was one girl who said ghosts weren't real . . .

I don't know what was going through Fran's mind but mine was full of bits of advice from books, like about moving very very slowly and holding your hand open. Only, I wasn't sure that was meant for gazelles—who, anyway, were always supposed to run away. This one sure didn't though: he shifted his stance slightly, and I could swear he snorted . . . "Listen, it's *his* wadi," I said: and Fran said we'd really finished here, hadn't we. And—well, to make a long story short, we beat it out of there. Backwards at first, until we had enough distance. And then we just turned tail and fled . . . Ladies and gentlemen, let's hear it for Fran and Maggie, co-winners of the total-timidity title for 1973. And let's not hear anything, ever again, about timid gazelles.

About that "true Fran" note—well, it did cross my mind that maybe, back that night when I first discovered my lizard in the pantry, I could've been wrong to try so hard to make it as one of these-here intrepid independent women. And that maybe she stayed there in the salon that night, lazily calling suggestions and observations, not because she was tired or lazy . . . Independent, okay. But when I said intrepid, I may have been going a bit too far.

Then there's another note, even briefer, that looks like a mere date for lunch but was, I blush to say, more of a story than that. Though even the recording of the lunch date represents a kind of triumph over the hazards of life in Beer-Sheva, for what happened was, my ex-husband wrote that he was coming to Israel. He wouldn't have much time, as his schedule called for only two days full of meetings in Tel Aviv—doubtless I remembered how those official trips went— but he'd phone me when he arrived (he said in his naïve American way) and we'd get together, okay? . . . Well, I did indeed remember those trips, where he hit four capitals in five days and if you wanted him you'd catch him at the appropriate U.S. Embassy. Yeah. Except that now I'm not a Washington wife but a resident of Beer-Sheva, who gets in touch with people by walking over to their houses and leaving notes if they aren't home. So only *contemplating* trying to phone the Embassy in Paris or Rome or Athens made gaskets blow in my head.

The upshot was, by the time I got around to even calling the Embassy in Tel Aviv—to break the news to my former husband that I didn't have a phone—it was too late to manage anything but a lunch up there, with him due at something afterward and me having to catch a sherut to Jerusalem. (Yaakov and Sara and their kids were about to leave for a year in the States, and I had to go say good-bye.) But that would work out just fine, I realized then, in one of the sudden flashes of pseudo-efficiency that occur whenever I've just about messed something up totally. For if I got an early enough bus, I could also knock off a promised visit to the publishers in Tel Aviv for whom I'd done a children's book; they wanted me for a planned project, and I'd promised to at least come look at it. What with my general reluctance to travel anywhere, it had remained a "some-time" prospect, but now all of a sudden it was part of a zip-zip scheme. He could call me at the publishers' office when he got through with his Embassy morning, I told my ex-husband, and we'd arrange where to meet. Right, he said, sounding relieved: here was a normal-type setup, like in real life . . .

Well, it was hot and I would be doing a lot of traveling. I didn't have to get all dolled up in my lady-author suit (which would never survive the bus trip anyway), but I couldn't go in my usual garb either: Israeli publishers aren't *that* informal. So I chose a dress that rated as sort of dressed-up because it came from India and had been expensive (ten years before, in Washington's Georgetown—but I'm not much for rethinking my wardrobe attitudes) and was also cool. My sneakers had to be forsworn, but Israeli sandals went nicely with the dress. As a special-occasion touch, I added a long string of black beads from Africa and, thus togged out, off I went. (It would never occur to anyone in Beer-Sheva to wear stockings—or makeup either, for that matter—in the summer, so I didn't even think about such frills.)

I seemed to look all right to the folks in the publishing office; one of the editors even commented on my dress, because it was a kind of cloth and print you simply can't get in Israel. And they were helpful, too, in the matter of where to take my visiting former spouse to lunch (or let him take me, which meant it could be somewhere expensive, since he's lots richer than I am). He liked the good life, I explained—since they knew only me, that might need specifying, I figured—like dining at smart places and all . . . You can usually count on editorial types to know that sort of thing: I was directed to an air-conditioned Dizengoff Street establishment that was In and had good food too. So, clickety-click and none of Maggie's mess-ups this time, when he called I told him just where to meet me. And I sailed out of the office, feeling all brisk and efficient.

My ex-husband had grown grayer since the last time I'd seen him, about a year and a half before. I myself still had the same color hair, perhaps a trifle streaked by the sun; and if I'd gained any weight (which is never too likely), it wouldn't have been visible under my smocklike dress anyway. So there was very little for him to say—and that's why, I think, he made the idle observation that probably set the whole rest of the thing off. Because he eyed my peasant dress and bare legs and sandals and the beads made out of beans or something, plus the deep tan you acquire just by walking to the supermarket in Beer-Sheva, and then he said pleasantly, "Well, you look like you've gone native."

I'm pretty sure it was not a hostile remark and I'm certain I didn't perceive it as such. What happened was something quite impersonal, like maybe a devil taking over my tongue. Anyway, that's the best I can do to explain why I answered demurely, "Of course. I've been living in the desert, you know." And why that's the way it went on from there, I'm afraid. Like, entering the air-conditioned restaurant, I shivered delicately—my thin desert blood, y'know—and when he asked politely whether I came here often, I said I got up north to the bright lights only rarely. Which was true enough (for one thing, I was usually at home waiting to see whether my refrigerator would come). I don't lie. But I must admit you *could've* got the impression that to go to Tel Aviv I'd have to sell my camel . . .

Besides, even without the presiding devil, some accidental facts helped out the image-making. Like, it was hot and I was thirsty, so I welcomed the beer with such enthusiasm that it would be hard to imagine I had several bottles of the same brand at home. And I'd eaten breakfast at 6 A.M. and the coffee at the publishers' hadn't been exactly filling, so naturally I ate everything in sight and yes, thanks, I would have dessert. My former husband, who diets, watched me with envy and (since I am, after all, the mother of his son) kindly concern: while I was polishing off a huge wedge of chocolate pie, he was looking at my tanned but skinny arms and the work-worn hands that do in fact wring out the wash in the hard Beer-Sheva water . . . Thus the whole thing was really a mixture of representational and impressionistic art, you might say. I mean, when he asked me about my life in Beer-Sheva, I told him about my primitive fridge because it was news and colorful, right? To go on and mention that it would be perfectly possible to have the latest model GE would have been dull . . .

There's noplace to go in Tel Aviv in the afternoon "siesta" hours, so we walked over to his hotel to enjoy the air conditioning. There, it was surely natural that I should look around the dim bar in wonder: after all, I hadn't been in one in quite some time and you don't get touches of tourist-elegance much in Beer-Sheva anyhow. But—well, what's the use of making excuses, the fact is, I stamm got carried away with building my sunbrowned-Zionist-pioneer role. So when we went up to his room to see his fine view of the Mediterranean, I bestowed a single rapid glance on the ocean and then began exulting over the marvy luxuries on display. Like the toilet in his bathroom, which didn't have a valve to turn but a real sophisticated flush mechanism. And, *soap*, I cried in rapture, and promptly tried it out (perhaps also giving the impression that a towel was something of a luxury too?). He had one of those airline souvenir bags—you know the sort of stuff, books of matches, little cakes of soap, etc.—about which I exclaimed deliriously (stopping just short of clasping them to my bosom, I'm afraid) before I apologized for my raptures by explaining that matches cost ten agorot a box and even then half of them didn't work ... The poor man, looking worried and guilty, promptly pressed on me some very nice matches he'd picked up in Stockholm (they work just fine, though I've used only a few: the box lends class to my salon, I feel) and then all the goodies from the airports of four or five countries plus all the cigarettes he owned. It was the least he could do for such a brave little pioneer, up from the hardships and hazards of the desert for a rare treat ...

Oh, it was a disgraceful performance. I felt so guilty that when I got to Jerusalem I confessed all to Yaakov and Sara. Who were a mite troubled over what my chalutz routine might have done to the potential tourist trade—but they began giggling while they were still trying to reprove me ... I tell myself I didn't really do Israel any harm: my ex-husband is no dope and I may have overdone the act enough so ... Well, anyway, he knows how to look up the production figures on soap in Israel.

But I haven't been so ashamed of myself since one day at the *Washington Post* when I was sitting with my feet in my desk drawer and thinking about what to do next, and then a troop of schoolchildren being conducted on a tour of the *Post* (How Your Newspaper Is Made, a unit in fifth-grade social studies, maybe?) was ushered past the open door of my office. In the blink of an eye I was sitting up straight, typing madly with two fingers on what any fool could plainly see was a Scoop ... But, that time, I blame bad influences for leading me astray. Because I wasn't the only one: people were calling out "Copy! in brisk commanding voices—which so startled the copyboys that they actually came at once, on the run. And an editor who was lucky enough to have a hat in his office promptly stuck it on the back of his head, hot-reporterwise ...

Well, Israel changes you, see. Now, I can pull a stunt like that all by myself, and even without a script.

From the diary: 16

Highlights of the TV Week, Beer-Sheva (first week of October)

A new month, but that's not an upsetting fact this time: I'm in pretty good shape, even sent off the dedication for book #1 today, and I'm well into #2. The secret of working here, I find, is to put in double-time on holidays. For people are careful to invite you over—everyone seems very upset at the notion of anyone spending a holiday alone—but they don't drop in. They can't: they're either knee deep in visiting relatives or they are visiting relatives.

So all that really has to be settled right now is the title of the first book. We're having a slight argument, but a compromise looks easily possible. I was writing a no-sweat letter to New York about that this morning when I became part of a most Israeli scene. For from my workroom window I can see a new house being built, and many of the workmen are Arabs (from Gaza: they commute this way every morning while Mrs. Ben-Ari goes the other way). And as I glanced from my window at about 11 A.M. one of the Arab workers was praying. He'd spread his mat on the ground and was kneeling, occasionally also leaning forward to touch his forehead down too, in the direction of Mecca (which seems to be, more immediately, the direction of the supermarket). I was considering this exotic scene (including what it must mean in terms of job performance, for I've heard prayers are required five times a day and at least some of those times must fall in working hours) when I saw Avi drive into the apartment house's parking lot at the back of my house. He got out of the car, carrying something that glinted in the sun, and I leaned from the window and called him.

No, nothing was wrong at home—Avi wasn't at work in Dimona because there was some kind of nuclear-engineering confab on at the university; he'd taken advantage of being in town during morning shopping hours to stop and buy me the new shower head, and then figured he'd drop it off on his way. No thanks, he didn't want coffee. He didn't have time to come in, and anyway he'd drown in the stuff at the conference, as it was full of foreigners and Israel would be putting on the dog, probably with china cups even . . .

So he handed the shower head in at the window and turned to go back to his car. And there we were, for a moment, all in a line—the Arab now rising and rolling up his prayer mat, the Israeli off to his nuclear shivaree, and I setting the plumbing down on my desk

272

while I finished writing to a publishing office in America. It was a little like a picture I remember seeing in my stepdaughter's first- or second-grade schoolbook, in a unit on Transportation: there was a bridge with a train going over it, under the bridge a boat, and over it an airplane... Only, how can we three line up so easily for a snapshot, the Arab and Avi and me busy in our pursuits worlds and centuries apart? But we did, we do, so I'll have to explain it somehow. Won't be easy, though.

Next morning.

Watching TV last night, I realized I haven't written a thing about it yet and it's surely going to be news to Americans. But I can't figure out whether good or bad news. For it certainly is a nice change to have not-so-beautiful people on view: I don't mean they're ugly, for they aren't (one of the women who comes on regularly is in fact quite lovely, and the Arabic lady announcer, though she doesn't strike me as terribly attractive, is a real looker to her audience); but it's clear that people with teeth parted in the middle are not banned, if you see what I mean. And to see a non-sylph-like singer may be a shock at first, but it's pleasant.

The most conspicuous difference, though, is that TV-watching in Israel is a real activity, not an accompaniment to something else; and the absence of breaks from commercials means that if you get up to go to the bathroom or fetch something to eat or drink, you'll lose a hunk of the plot. That notable absence becomes rather fun, however, when what you're watching is an American series with its built-in plot break for the commercials. "Hawaii Five-O" (which sounds cuter as "Havaii Ha-mesh Ef-fiss"), which has a great wave rolling up to mark the spot, is particularly delicious: when the big wave promptly uncurls again and the action goes on, it's hard to keep a straight face.

I don't watch "Havaii Hamesh-Effiss" much, though, because it's really too awful; most of the other Americans here, who also will sit through damn near anything in English, agree that that one is Just Too Much. But everybody watches "Ironside"*—well, not Jan, who hates TV; but even he lets the kids put on "Ironside." It's on Saturday night, right after the news—late enough for people to have got home from outings, early enough so even the early risers haven't gone to bed. And it comes to a welcoming audience, too, for there's of course been no TV all Shabbat. Which is officially from sundown Friday to sundown Saturday (the times worked out by the

---

*This has since been succeeded by "Kojak"—and, at least in my neighborhood candy store, a lollipop is now called a *kojak.*

book: the emergence of three stars marks the arrival of sundown*),
and the religious don't turn on the radio or TV on Friday night or
Saturday because that would come under the definition of forbidden "work." (That's why they don't turn on lights either.) But the
habit of compromise prevails: English news is on radio at the
regular afternoon time on Saturday, but the evening half-hour
contains a summary of the past twenty-four hours' headlines "for
the benefit of observant listeners." It sounds as if the Hebrew news
on TV does the same, but I can't be sure: Kissinger turns up all the
time whether it's new news or old . . .

   I have grounds for an inference that Beer-Sheva audiences
like the American cops-and-robbers imports because of their
exotica—big American cars squealing around corners, street scenes
of New York, etc. That this is taken literally (as case histories for
cultural anthropology, you might say) was revealed to me by Yoshua
way back one day in February when, seated at his coffee bar, I
became alarmed because there was a loud bang somewhere nearby.
When I looked out, there was nothing to see but a passing Israeli
soldier with an Uzzi and a tall Arab in long black robes; he had a
rifle slung over his shoulder (plus the usual long dagger at his belt),
but he clearly hadn't fired it, and the chyal was carrying the module
that showed his own weapon was disarmed. Besides, nobody in the
place except me had even stirred . . . Embarrassed, I had to admit to
Yoshua that I'd been afraid. And he decided it was the Arab I was
afraid of: "Ah non, Madame," he soothed. "Cet homme, il est
Bédu . . ." Les Bedouins, he went on to explain, were simply primitifs from the desert, and thus carried arms as a matter of course. But
in The Land it is understood that guns are for war—and now we are
in 1973, when it is since six years peacetime, Madame . . .

   In the ensuing discussion (because of course others in the
coffee bar got into the act), I got the message. Which was that it was
natural for the lady from America, where people were all the time
shooting at each other, to misunderstand. For it could be seen on
the television that the people there shoot guns to see who is fastest
(this was illustrated with quick-draw gestures) or for high spirits at
festivals, like les primitifs. It is simply their culture . . . Well, I'd have
understood that comment even without the accompanying shrugs,
because we'd just learned "tarbut" (tar-BOOT) in school—where the
message clearly was that the Israeli idea is to live in peace, not
reform anybody. So we don't interfere with the tarbut of the Beduin,

*You don't have to do this stargazing for yourself, though: the Shabbat moment is
given—for most places, anyhow—on the Friday midday news broadcast. (Courtesy, I
suppose, of some university's Astronomy Dept. Israel is a very odd country!)

or the Druse, *or any other nonconformist group of good citizens.* *

But—to get back to TV—we apparently don't like somebody else's *tarbut* well enough to put it on in prime time, either: imported westerns are in the *"children's hour"* *("Smith and Jones" had a run then)* or late at night, like *"Eesh Veer-JEAN-ee-ah"* *("The Virginian"),* which comes on only, apparently, for the benefit of people like me who can't stand the thought of a mere-midnight bedtime. *Westerns are not prime-time stuff because they're simply not exotic enough: who wants to be told about a bunch of roughly dressed fellows tearing around a dusty landscape, forever shooting at each other in revenge for previous shootings? Except for the amusing revelation that their job is tending grazing animals—which hereabouts is women's work, or even children's—it's all just too like* les primitifs *of the Negev.*

But more dramatic than all the dramas, I find, is the sports program. I started watching it because this is the easiest Hebrew to understand. For the guy says "Shtay neckadot" *as the basketball goes through the hoop, giving you solid grounds for assuming that means "Two points," and then the figures on the scoreboard jump two points—a nice audio-visual lesson. But when we get a broadcast of a big game, well there, habibi, it isn't the words, it's the feeling. I mean, I've heard excited reporting, but the Israeli TV announcer makes everybody look phlegmatic. I guess it figures that in a little, poor country suffering always from a yearning to be recognized among the nations, sports—particularly those that don't take a lot of expensive equipment and can be played in a smallish place—would not only be important but have a noticeable emotional content for the public, too. And whole games on TV (and even, very occasionally, a live game, by satellite!) are still infrequent enough to be big events, for the reporter as well as his public.*

But what that means is, since these big games are nearly always international, the reporter is first of all an Israeli. So when the Israeli team scores in a basketball game with one from, say, West Germany, the announcer is not only enthusiastic but also patriotic—and his high, excited "Shtay neckadot, shelanu!" *might be thought over-emotional for the winning run in a final World Series game. A foul-line shot duly sunk is apt to get a little less drama*

---

*But of course—and this is one of those facts of Israeli life Americans keep losing track of—*everybody's* getting interfered with in a sense, since Israel broadcasting is a government monopoly. It's modeled on the BBC (though *they* recently acquired a competing network, which Israel hasn't got up to yet) but isn't quite such a closed system, perhaps because Israeli newspapers incline to an American-type shrill dissent. (And the public isn't as meek as the British public, either.)

(though from what I've seen of Israeli basketball, that looks like the real news); but every basket earned, whether or not it evens the score or does something else crucial, gets the same joyous celebration of "Two points" followed by not "Israel" but the ecstatic ring-out-wild-bells "shelanu!" The other team's baskets are duly noted—and as "Germania," not "Them"—in a kindly voice and with something that may be "Well played" added occasionally. Our announcer, you see, knows about sportsmanship and all that. But his feelings just get the better of him . . .

Some Israelis (Ze'ev is one) don't like such amateurish display of Israeli unsophistication, but I don't see that that would have much effect in toning the announcer down: he's practically a civil servant, so he probably doesn't have to worry about audience reaction. (What may change him is more contact with non-Israeli broadcasters—every time the local boys go abroad to cover something international, they come back with some borrowed mannerisms, usually from the big-time Americans.) I don't care, though, for I think he's utterly endearing. And he may constitute a better portrait of the people of Israel—including the sophisticates, who share his feeling but just don't think it nice to be so noisy about it—than I can come up with in my book.

Later—An exception to what I said at the start of this, about working on holidays. (You can't make a flat statement about anything in Israel!) Because Miriam came by, and she strongly advises against trying it on Yom Kippur, which is coming up this weekend. Even the nonreligious take this one very seriously, at least to the extent of trying not to disturb the sensitivities of the religious, who are fasting and praying all day—like, nobody drives (partly because some of the religious, particularly in Jerusalem, may get mad enough to stone your car). So clearly, it would be offensive for me to be heard typing that day. I've worried about that on other holidays, but people always told me it was b'seder and none of my neighbors ever seemed offended or angry. However, this one is different, it seems.

Anyway, it would be too depressing to be alone in the dead silence of Yom Kippur, Miriam says—better come out to their house in suburban Omer for dinner on Friday, the eve of Yom Kippur, and then make a weekend of it, coming back with her when she drives in to meet her Sunday-morning class at the university. It sounded nice and convenient, but I really hated to take that much time off from work; on the other hand, though, I was at a good stopping place, and I would like to meet Miriam's sister, who used to do journalism and

is coming for dinner Friday night with her husband and children . . .
Oh come on, said Miriam. Surely you're entitled to a little break?

I have no character: in mid-afternoon on Friday, Miriam will come to get me and my nightie and toothbrush. And my wash—bring it along, she said, and we'll do it in her machine. Then it'll have all day Saturday to dry.

Well, when you look at it that way, I won't really be losing so much time from work. I'd have had to take time out to do the wash anyway, right?

13 ⤝ Maybe We Should've Fasted

I was practically ready when Miriam called for me the afternoon of the day before Yom Kippur, my mystery story and its plot problems stowed away and my "overnight bag," a shopping basket, stuffed with a couple of days' underwear, pajamas, two blouses, and—most fortunately, it turned out—a pair of slacks. Extra packs of cigarettes and a couple of thrillers, both advisable when visiting a non-smoking and too-literate household, were tucked into the corners. Miriam made the rou ds of my flat to close windows and lower trissim while I gathered up my heavy laundry—literally heavy; i.e., sheets and towels—and stuffed it into a pillow slip. The prospect of holiday seemed really pleasurable, perhaps because though not-working was shadowed by guilt, I did feel entitled to a little whirl of washing-machine leisure.

Hurrying, because Miriam wanted to get dinner early, we tossed my stuff into her station wagon among the bulging plastic baskets that showed she'd been to the shuk. The streets were full of traffic, all apparently headed homeward and in a hurry. Everything already had a closed-up look: there were people on duty in the hospital to tend patients who couldn't be sent home on leave, but the patients were having no visitors and nobody was trekking to the Emergency Room. Across the road, the parking lot at the university campus was virtually empty. Even those faculty members who had not left yesterday for hometowns up north had, like Miriam, shut up shop early today to allow time for holiday preparations.

Naturally, everything about that day and evening stands out in memory, perfectly clear and shining—for the same reason, I suppose, that any American can tell you exactly what he was doing just before the news flash from Dallas in November 1963. But I think for me it was especially distinct because that day before Yom Kippur was also the most "American" I'd had since coming to Israel. For Ze'ev came out of the house to unload the car, and he was followed by a small, short-haired, mongrel named Charlie Brown (I don't want you to get the idea from that, though, that Miriam and Ze'ev are one of those whimsical-type couples; the dog had been named by his previous owner, Miriam's young nephew. And they *are* the kind of people who wouldn't try to change it). I'm not your instant dog-lover type, but Charlie Brown was really a most engaging animal: he escorted us load-bearing humans from the curb to the front door with an air of earnest responsibility any industrialist would rejoice to find among the workers. The triangular brown-and-black face was also extraordinarily expressive, and there was a wide variety of noises to go with it: when Miriam strayed from the path to speak to the next-door neighbor, Charlie Brown gave her a tolerant *You're such a flibbertigibbet* look—followed by a mild reproving bark that said, quite clearly, *But do remember you have perishables in that bag.*

Then, too, there was the house—box-shaped, three bedrooms and bath upstairs, powder room downstairs, patio out back—which was the standard model in the developments that sprang up, called into being by the veterans' home-owning yen and their G.I. loan money, just outside many American cities after World War II. Though here there were Israeli touches, of course. Like, no basement (under the floor tiles in any single-family home in Beer-Sheva and vicinity is just plain desert) and the addition of a concrete shelter, which could have been mistaken for a garage except that it was in an enclosed courtyard you couldn't drive a car into and it was probably too small for anything but some Volkswagens. What the shelter becomes, in such Israeli houses, is a sort of substitute for the basement of the U.S. equivalent: laundry equipment (though not, of course, a furnace) is kept there, and bicycles, and a whole mess of stored stuff.

Miriam and Ze'ev were renting this house (from the university, which owns some houses and flats for the same reason it subsidizes rent on others, as an inducement to attract faculty) and were camping out in it until their own new house, now being built in a newer part of Omer, was finished. But it had been worth while to install their American-bought kitchen appliances—the basic ones, anyway—so it was an American kitchen into which I came. And tied on an apron, which was something I hadn't done before in Beer-Sheva, where if you're too dressed up to wipe your hands on your shirt you're probably at the Philharmonic concert, but certainly not

279

in a friend's kitchen. I was wearing a dress for the same reason I was hurrying to help out in the kitchen: if we could get through dinner in time, we were going over to the Orthodox synagogue to hear the *Kol Nidre* sung. This was the Sephardic version, Miriam had said, and she thought I'd probably not heard it and would like to. I'd brought along a scarf to cover my head and even worn (ugh) stockings, reasoning that people who forbade bare arms would undoubtedly veto bare legs too.* So, slipping the already buttered garlic bread into the oven beside the roast chicken (most un-*casher*, of course: butter and meat mustn't cohabit), I was dressed up Orthodoxly.

Miriam's sister and brother-in-law were not—they were dressed appropriately for driving down from a university town in the north with three boys aged around fifteen, eleven, and seven (plus all the food you have to take along with three boys when there are no Howard Johnsons to stop at along the way) and the fluffy, tan dog who was—surprisingly, since she looked definitely spanielish—the mother of Charlie Brown. (He apparently had no Oedipus complex, for he acknowledged her coolly and as a stranger. It was the boys, particularly the youngest, he seemed to remember and welcomed lavishly with leaps and licks.) But this family arrival, with spates of talk and dogs and kids in constant motion, was very American: Sally and Reuben dashed upstairs to Orthodox themselves, but what floated down was the familiar sounds of enforced son-washing. Sometimes the dialogue was peculiarly Israeli: *Mom, where'd you put my kipah?* is not exactly a line I associate with suburban America. However, the culture and the language were definitely American, for Reuben, born in Israel but taken to the U.S. as a youngster, was now—at probably thirty-five or a little less—an American who happened to be bilingual in Hebrew. I've met other Israeli-Americans like him: they're probably traceable to economic depression in Israel in the 1950s, which caused many families (particularly when the father was an academic, or a doctor with some in-demand specialty and thus easily employable in the U.S.) to transplant themselves and their children. Now Reuben, a scientist, had brought his family to Israel via an exchange-professor deal, thus leaving a way back if Sally or the children found the life unbearable. (Something like that happened with another such family I knew—only there, it was the daughter who came back, with an American

*Correct. But, as I've noted on other occasions, obeying rules doesn't always bring about the planned effect. E.g., Phyllis, who turns out for work with her long shapely legs encased in sheer black nylon—a requirement because she's observant, but it produces a lot of the other kind of observing. She certainly looks sexier than even she could in (forbidden) slacks.

280

husband and two children.) Sally was the product of an American university and seemed very like your normal American university wife—slim, clever, and tense. And Reuben appeared to be one of those quiet, humorous, salt-of-the-earth men you often see married to a high-strung woman. The children were doing all right in school and had made friends, but they didn't like living in an apartment instead of a house with a yard. The two older boys had brought sleeping bags, for going to Aunt Miriam's meant a chance to sleep out, which was now a real treat.

Downstairs, Ze'ev was unfolding chairs and opening bottles, and Miriam and I were snatching things out of oven and refrigerator. And we all managed, by eating with unseemly haste and postponing dessert, to scurry through the twilight and get to the hot, overcrowded little synagogue just before the *Kol Nidre* was sung. It turned out to be startlingly Oriental music (which figures, I know; but I simply don't think like that, so it surprised me). That's all I remember about it, though: it was just too hot in there, and I felt too claustrophobic, to really enjoy the music.

I do remember the blue-gray world we came out into. It seemed especially wide just then. And flat, for the only thing tall in Omer is a ziggurat—a nice exotic touch beside the community swimming pool. The sky was too hazy for stars, as if the great inverted bowl had a scum of something coating it and needed washing; the lights of Beer-Sheva (now diminished by piety, since Yom Kippur had begun; but the hospital, the army depot, the automatic traffic lights of the grand avenue in front of the city center, and other impious outposts were lighted anyway) were strung across at lower left, as if the pattern of the bowl were showing at one point.

And nothing moved: just outside the entrance to Omer, the road to Tel Aviv glimmered whitely, but nobody was getting off a bus and no car was turning in. There was almost no wind, so everything was motionless except our own little clump of figures short-cutting across lumpy desert and then winding down the tidy streets between houses. They were spotted with light—an upstairs room in which a small child was being put to bed, somebody cleaning up in a kitchen, and here and there a dim "bug light" from a patio where people presumably were sitting. Almost home, we encountered somebody else out, walking a dog. It was a man we knew who worked at the university, so we stopped and Miriam introduced her sister and brother-in-law while the children went ahead: I could see their outlines, black against the deepening night, as they halted before the house. The dogs heard them and began to bark (Charlie Brown demanding bossily *Well, what are you waiting for?*) and Ze'ev muttered and hurried ahead to quiet them. The front door wasn't locked, but the children, now used to living in an apartment house, didn't know it.

Once inside again and sitting at the big table, I knew Miriam had been right in urging me not to spend Yom Kippur alone. The hushed world out there was peaceful, but only when seen from a lighted group of voices; alone, it would have seemed a day-after-the-bomb quiet . . . So I was aware of, and grateful for, the ordinary-life buzz—the seven-year-old, visibly half asleep, being persuaded into bed upstairs; the dogs who took to quarreling and had to be separated; the men helping the two older boys spread out their sleeping bags outside; and finally all the grownups collecting, to help or talk, in the kitchen. It was all so *normal*. By which I mean, I suppose, American.

With Israeli touches here and there. The first, invisible one may have been the very fact that we were all staying overnight—and that Miriam and Ze'ev, who still had another army cot and the sofa unfilled, didn't think of themselves as having a full house. But a noticeable reminder of the cultural difference arose when we'd finished cleaning up and Miriam took some steaks out of the freezer to defrost for tomorrow. Ze'ev, who had a dandy new grill, said good, we'd have a cookout—and was promptly overruled by his wife, who observed that it would be a bit gross, wouldn't it, to eat outdoors when the people next door would be fasting? Ze'ev glanced around for support and found none: I was clearly with Miriam, and Sally was articulately shocked at such insensitivity. (Reuben, looking amused, said nothing.) Well, we were going to *eat* tomorrow, Ze'ev pointed out. To say nothing of right now, when it was already Yom Kippur and we were nibbling crackers and drinking. So why was it insensitive to do it on the patio in daylight? . . . But he was complaining, not arguing: his gesture (and a Hebrew remark to Reuben, who laughed) made it clear that Ze'ev the born and bred Israeli was resigned to these occasional outcroppings of the mysterious, intricate hypocrisies of the Anglo-Saxons. No cookout, okay, *b'seder* . . .

After talk about the ways of people and the human condition—all normal, terribly normal—and taking my turn with the only shower (you brushed your teeth in the powder room downstairs, to avoid keeping the next bathrobed figure waiting unduly), I fell asleep on a rollaway bed in Miriam's study, surrounded by textbooks and dictionaries but finishing one of my thrillers. I slept well: a typewriter in the room, grinning at me, doesn't bother me so long as it's somebody else's.

The war began the next morning, or at least when it was still morning for our lazy, holidaying household. Breakfast was tidied away, and Miriam and I had done my wash and were spreading out my towels—including the black one, my cherished favorite—on the patio in the sun. Sally and Reuben were out there too, sunning themselves, and Ze'ev was in the salon demonstrating the virtues of the stereo to the oldest boy; the other boys and the dogs ran at leisure in the empty land, unreclaimed from the desert, beyond the yard. I went to the shelter to make sure nothing had been left in the washing machine, and Miriam stopped off in the kitchen to put a light under the coffee, which everybody had thought sounded like a good idea.

When I came back in, through the front door, we had a visitor—a very tall, svelte young woman, wearing hiphugger pants that left a tanned midriff bare; she was accompanied by a remarkably cute baby in a stroller. Ze'ev introduced us and I said *Naim ma-od*, as I'd learned in the ulpan. Then I gave my permission for them to proceed in Hebrew, because the visitor didn't speak English, and I played drop-a-toy-and-pick-it-up-again with the baby while the grownups talked over my head. Until it occurred to me that I could get the coffee and leave Miriam free to come in here, so I went out to the kitchen.

Not a moment too soon, apparently, for Ze'ev called "Miri!" almost at once. Miriam made a face, not about the visitor ("Neighbor from down the street. Nice girl. Teaches second grade in the local school. Her husband's an army officer, so he's away a lot") but about the difficulties of being married to Israeli punctilio. Which was maddening because it seemed so inconsistent: they dressed informally, first-named strangers, and scorned hypocrisy; but once inside their own houses, everything was immediately square and by the book—and you were somehow supposed, Miriam grumbled, to both bring the coffee promptly *and* be there every minute hostessing . . . Ze'ev called her again, noticeably sharply, and Miriam left me to bring the coffee and fled.

The coffee and cake were ready, I had nothing to do but put the last few things on the tray. Then all of a sudden I heard Miriam's voice in the salon saying "Oh my God." Not loudly, yet there was something about it— Well, I wasn't the only one who felt that, for as I left the tray standing on the counter and ran in, I saw Sally and Reuben coming in from the patio, too. Miriam was sitting in the armchair as though she'd fallen into it, and she looked pale and stricken. But Ze'ev, instead of attending her, had his back turned and was fooling with the radio again—which I observed angrily:

culture clash or no, this simply wouldn't do . . . But then I saw Sally stop in her tracks and clutch her husband's arm. So whatever was being said in Hebrew, though clearly something upsetting, wasn't about Miriam . . .

The TV set, which Ze'ev had apparently turned on also, suddenly bloomed into life. The picture was only the standard screen-filler, the Knesset building in Jerusalem; but it should have been the test pattern, because there wasn't supposed to be anything on on Yom Kippur. And music was coming from it—Beethoven, I thought—which also wasn't supposed to happen. "What *is* it?" I asked belligerently of all the knowledgeable grownups, like a vexed child. But I think I knew: I think the music had already told me by the time Ze'ev—looking abashed at this failure of his duties as a host—turned and said, "The Egyptians attacked us. From across the Canal. But don't worry, Maggie. It will be all right."

As though he had raised some kind of standard that recalled everyone to obligations, voices began explaining to me what the girl from down the street had come to the house to tell us. I had many more interpreters (their faces still showing shock, but also concern and perhaps guilt: the visitor couldn't speak English, but all the others, who could, had thus mistreated me) than there was news to interpret, for so far there'd been no announcement. But the neighbor—whose husband was in the Air Force, not the army, and was in fact the equivalent of a brigadier general—had known since last night. Presumably because of his rank, they had a phone (the only one on the whole street), and her husband had called a little while ago to tell her it was definite, we were at war and the official announcement would come soon . . . While all that was being explained to me, the girl said Shalom and left—on her cool, chic way down the street with her adorable baby, to tell everybody to turn on the radio and TV that they'd of course turned off, whether out of piety or resignation, for Yom Kippur. "Beethoven, isn't it?" Miriam said as the *Eroica* swelled into the room. "It's always Beethoven for a war," she added, sounding like Miriam again. Then she got up and brought in the coffee.

It was Miriam who generally assumed responsibility thereafter for the chore of translating for me—it was in Miriam's voice, I remember, that I heard about the Syrians having simultaneously attacked in the north. But everybody took a turn when necessary, including the oldest boy, who had suddenly become one of the adults instead of one of the kids. After a while, though, nobody needed to translate, for Ze'ev, roving the radio frequencies, came up with the BBC, which had a bulletin. Then Reuben collected his wife and son and went out to find the younger boys, and presumably tell them what I was still trying to absorb. And couldn't: the fact that somebody was actually trying to kill me—Me!—kept slipping out of my grasp.

Other people were apparently better able to cope with comprehension. For a great rushing-around soon began, mostly started by Ze'ev, who seemed at once the least afraid* and the most practical. The first thing you do in a war, according to Ze'ev, was what's apparently the first thing you do in Beer-Sheva in *any* crisis: fill everything with water in case the water goes off. So feet raced up the stairs and the bathtub was turned on full force, somebody filled the little sink in the powder room, and all kinds of plastic jars, saved coffee cans, etc., were dug out of the far reaches of top shelves in the kitchen. Thinking of containers became a kind of ingenuity contest— until "But will it hold water?" somebody asked as Miriam came up with yet another potential vessel, and we all began to giggle. We didn't stop until Ze'ev pointed out that the electricity, too, might go off. And then the game changed: Reuben, the tallest, was exploring the top of the kitchen cupboards for the extra candles, Sally dispatched the middle son to their car for the flashlight kept in the glove compartment, and transistor radios were routed out of corners.

But after that it stopped being a game, I think. For—I don't know whether the Hebrew on the radio told us to or it was simply the result of facts sinking in—somehow we became organized, all the ingenuity marshaled in aid of a rational program. The first step of which was to clear out the shelter: the washing machine, the piled trunks and cartons (Miriam's tons of books and bric-à-brac, left packed because life had been going on without them while they were coming by boat from Canada, and they'd only have to be packed up again when the new house was ready), and the still-crated dishwasher and drier would all have to be moved out into the courtyard. The shelter was jammed, with everything an intellectual takes along when she knows she's going forever plus every appliance an Israeli whose new wife has "immigrant rights" can buy in America, once and for all and last chance. The moving job was mostly for Ze'ev and Reuben and the man-boy, but an eleven-year-old can also lift a carton of books and Sally's American-girl tennis muscles gave her, too, a place in the yo-heave-ho chain. Even Miriam, who couldn't tote, had a specialized executive function: she

*The army would take care of it in a few days, he was certain. That assurance, I discovered later, was very common among Israelis on Yom Kippur.

knew what was in all the boxes and trunks, and thus what could be piled on what, which could be left in the sun, and other vital details. So only the littlest boy, frankly frightened, and I were unfit for navvy duty. But I saw a sociological role I could fill: I got a deck of cards (they were exactly in the drawer the efficient Miriam directed me to) and collected the little boy. We sat on the kitchen doorstep—so he could see his parents—and I did my bit. What did you do in the war, Maggie? I played Go Fish with a scared little boy.

All right, but funny-funny comes down to a serious question that I think must turn up in all such caught-off-guard situations. When dailiness suddenly alters, in a moment, there's a sort of general hold-still pause,* while you shift yourself from the familiar Here to the strange There. And then begins a process of locating yourself in the There. Sally and I—both of us, I think, having the writer's habit of looking from inside and outside simultaneously—probably formulated it more directly than the other adults. But the question (here stated more flatly than any of us were capable of then, I'm sure) that emerges for everyone, immediately after the realization *Here I am in a war* is "What do you do in a war?"

The short answer is, "Join an army." Which is to say—again drawing it more crudely than the way it actually happens—you get yourself a spec number and start learning the drill. You become, in other words, a societal unit good for some things, not so good for others, in some respects a total liability. The clearest example of what I mean is probably Miriam, who that morning was an extraordinarily perceptive and competent woman, a scholar to contend with in faculty debates, a demanding person with a tendency to perfectionism and none whatever to clinging-vineness—yet who, that afternoon, was primarily A Pregnant Woman. And, as such, our greatest vulnerability. For what we were doing was setting up a self-sufficient defense unit to ride out the unknown for however long it took. And Miriam was *ipso facto* not self-sufficiency-meat: she could require doctors, hospitals, all sorts of outside services nobody knew whether we could count on.

Because of my age and chronic illness, I was probably the second most vulnerable member of the unit. Not from my own point of view: *I* knew I wasn't going to collapse and wouldn't need

---

*Even for the Israelis, who, as I hope you've seen, don't go around thinking about war. True, everybody's in the army; but everybody isn't a general, and you don't run armies by acquainting every man with the latest strategic estimates. So citizen armies are not made up of men who think of themselves as soldiers and they're not married to army wives. And, though some of them may know what to do *after* the pause, they still need that hold-still moment.

emergency outside help. But looked at administratively (so to speak)—well, let's say you'd think twice before taking somebody with a chronic illness on a small-boat voyage around the world, or on any other venture where you might be out of touch for a long time. And yet that, in a way, was what our small society had to prepare for.

So long as I could be kept functioning, however, I was a distinct asset in the matter of our other automatic vulnerability, the children. For, in a situation where adult experience may have to substitute for pediatricians, child psychologists, and the whole spectrum of expertise intelligent parenthood nowadays scans for advice and counsel, to be about twenty years older than the other adults is an immediate qualification. In short, my spec number in this army stood for The Old Sage—expert on first aid, health care, nutrition, and possibly even midwifing . . . That the general attitudes were somewhat short of logical should be clear from the fact that I myself had borne only two children, the second nineteen years before, whereas Sally had had three babies, all more recently. But even for the usually logical Miriam, logic took second place: it was not the presence of her sister but of an Older Woman that eased fears. And certainly it did so for her Israeli husband, for to Ze'ev—raised in a tribal-haunted culture and not one of those first-time prospective fathers who studies the prenatal-care book—old wives and their implied lore rated at least as high in terms of reassurance as any obstetrician.

Well, if you're the Old Sage, the first thing to do is act sagacious. Which I figured required an air of unflappability, presumably reflecting a belief (one I have never actually held) that there is something practical and effective to do about everything. So I ordered Miriam to sit down and put her feet up for fifteen minutes (which couldn't hurt anyway). She obeyed without question, amid nods and gratified looks from the others. The general relief was unmistakable: Maggie was in charge of the unborn baby, and with that matter visibly in hand everybody could get on with other concerns . . . You see what I mean by illogic? For surely Miriam herself, and Sally and probably Reuben too, knew as well as I did that at Miriam's stage of pregnancy, if the baby was born it almost certainly would not survive, not even if we'd had at hand skilled obstetricians and the resources of the best-equipped hospital. Yet we had not all suddenly become TV sitcom characters blandly carrying out our plot-compelled roles; the element of illusion was recognized but recognition couldn't be afforded, was what it amounted to. "It's possible to save a *seven*-month baby," I whispered to

Sally in a moment alone in the kitchen. "But you know . . ." She leaned her head against the refrigerator and closed her eyes and said "I know." But when she opened her eyes again the dialogue was over—I had had the small relief I was entitled to, and that was enough—and we wouldn't have said any more even if Miriam hadn't come in just then . . . But I swear to you there was also, at the same time, a sort of cooperative myth, a collective and deliberate hallucination maybe: if it happened, I'd boil water or something magical like that, and then everybody would scurry around and it would all end happily.

The second thing you do in a war is follow the leader. In this case, that was principally the Israel government, which almost from the first was on the air with news and instructions (in several languages: even for me, rich in translators, it was a relief to be addressed in English, and I waited for the next scheduled English as though I really needed to depend on it). Leadership also came from the experienced among us, chiefly Ze'ev but also Reuben as house scientist, and anybody else who had experience with whatever we were trying to do at the moment. The channeling effect of organization extended to the information coming in, from which we selected what most directly applied to us. Thus, though of course the whole war mattered, the words "Jordan" or "Hussein" in a broadcast would stop all activity. Had the Jordanians (who are nearest the Negev) entered the war yet? And if so, in what manner? Because their shooting at us was an immediate danger, but if they just sent troops to join the Egyptians or Syrians, that was something for somebody else, down in the Sinai or up in the Golan, to take care of.

However, considerations like that were practical, not fearful. For it surprised me when I thought about it afterward, but the truth is, nobody seemed to be really afraid of dying: nobody made any last wills or even faintly valedictory statements (at least, not in public), and I don't remember thinking of my faraway loved ones at all that day except to wonder once, fleetingly, whether they'd heard yet. Ze'ev thought of the people next door, who had not planned to eat until sundown; he went over to see if they needed some of our fruit, etc. But what we were primarily focused on was carrying out our own assignments and contributing what we could to the next fellow's.

Thus I was collecting medical supplies to be taken into the shelter (internal medications in the Pan Am bag, external stuff in the Gladstone, so they couldn't be confused in the dark), beginning with Miriam's pills and mine, and the youngest boy's allergy pills, and then extending into all other imaginable needs for medication—

288

burns, falls, choking, fainting, vomiting, diarrhea, broken limbs, bleeding, coughing (cough syrup would do double duty as a mild sedative, I figured: I even got pleasure out of the dual-function aspect of that). Sally's specialty was nimbleness and energy—as the only woman in good health, unhampered by pregnancy and in the prime of life, she was the women's muscle-man, so to speak—so she did most of the running up and down stairs to collect items and receptacles to store them in. (Toilet paper, cotton, Kotex, and bandages in the laundry hamper, which could also be sat on in the shelter. Oh, we were really clickety-clicking along. Meanwhile Miriam sat on the kitchen floor pulling out canned and processed foods so we could decide what to take to the shelter. (Sally, go ask Reuben whether, in case of radiation, the cans would be better than the packages, or would it all become useless anyway.) Most of the milk would be for Miriam: the little boy could do with one glass and the others could go without entirely for a day or two without damage, but we didn't know *what* equipment Miriam's baby might be developing just today so we couldn't take a chance. Whiskey and brandy were requisitioned for the Gladstone bag—which meant not only medicinal use but first priority for external use. A supply of lemonade stood on a corner of the dining-room table, covered with newspaper to keep it cool because the refrigerator was not to be opened casually: the cold must be preserved in case the electricity went off . . . Oh, you just wouldn't have recognized Muddled Maggie the mess-up expert. All wars, it seems, produce individual Finest Hours.

As a troop in other people's departments, however, I wasn't really hotly in demand: somebody climbing around nailing a bed-spread up for a blackout curtain could do a lot better for an assistant than six-thumbed Maggie. But there was one job I was useful for, and so was the littlest boy (whose own department was dog-feeding)—we were the chief radio and TV monitors. For, though much of the mobilization of army reserves was being done by individual messengers from the man's own company who simply went to his house and told him to come on* (the religious man next door to us was plucked from the synagogue), the units had code designations so they could be summoned by radio. These were meaningless expressions—chosen by the men themselves, so they were often silly (e.g., "ice cream and cake"†) or reminiscent of rock

---

*Avi, I found out later, spent the first afternoon and half the night driving a commandeered bus around Tel Aviv and environs, picking up the men of his unit—who were all packed and waiting.
†Neither this nor the subsequent one were the actual codes used.

and roll groups' titles—and the magic word was not broadcast formally (perhaps for security reasons?) but sort of slashed across whatever else was being said, like subliminal ad techniques. An announcer would be reading a message from the head of a foreign government, say, all about how he and his people wished the people of Israel to know their hearts were with us—and suddenly there'd be a static-like brrr and a voice would say (in Hebrew, of course) "Dancing artichokes" quickly, twice. And then the news-reading voice, quite unaware, would go on reading while the men who belonged to the unit that had chosen "dancing artichokes" got up and took off for the war . . .

Interesting, isn't it, that in Israel—which I'd have been willing to bet was the worst place in the world to keep a secret*——I'd never heard of the code system. Well, of course any among us who happened to be listening to the radio would also be alerted, but the job was just made for my physical qualifications, once I was taught to recognize the sound of the key word well enough to call Ze'ev if I heard anything like that. (My colleague, the littlest boy, didn't need remedial instruction: he even knew what the words meant. I really was the bottom of the manpower barrel, you see. But I had ears, and we didn't waste *anything*.) Each call would be repeated a couple of hours later, so all I had to do was alert Ze'ev; I didn't need to worry about possibly sending him off to war on the basis of one fast brrr and an approximation of a Hebrew word.

But I was also, like everybody else, required to lend ingenuity to blackout problems (which got heavy priority after an Egyptian airplane was reported shot down on its way to Tel Aviv). We licked most of them, but took one defeat—thanks to an Israeli twist in the typical-American-house powder room. Windowless, it had a sky-light, but two stories up, set in the roof. And the way to get to the roof of a two-story Israeli house is via a two-story ladder, which we didn't have. We sure had to do *something*, though, for that nice round light shining out of the roof would be handier for a ma-rauding airplane than the big glass patio doors we'd just carefully covered up.

Nothing we tried worked: it was our first defeat in the war. And a heavy one, for with eight people in the house and nervous tension high, a second toilet is very damn valuable. But we could still use it during the day, we consoled ourselves—though, after several of us had gone in there and unthinkingly switched on the

*That was well before the Entebbe rescue of the hijack hostages. After that operation—a masterpiece of speedy, absolutely secret planning—I wouldn't make any such bet, ever.

290

light (it was pretty dim in there even in daylight), Ze'ev climbed on the sink and removed the bulb from the light fixture on the wall. Which took care of habit-causing slips. Once it got dark, we'd see whether, if the door was left open, light from the salon would shine in without also shining out the skylight.* The prospect of leaving the door open was dismaying, but nobody said anything—maybe because they were all thinking, as I was, that if we had to live in the shelter, we'd get a lot less privacy than that . . . Three morals to that story, in case observations about what to do in defeat are useful: 1. Pick out any consoling factor you can locate. 2. Accept defeat but not permanently: any kind of plan is better than nothing. And then, 3. Shut up about it.

Triumph, somehow peculiarly personal, in a second blackout problem—the clouded-glass strip alongside the front door, meant to let daylight into the little entry. Nobody thought of it because we didn't see it as a window; but, we discovered at the first blackout survey that evening, any light downstairs shone right out through it. We tacked up a blanket over door and all and then tore around hunting for something dark and thick—and just the right size, for if it overlapped, it would interfere with closing the door. Then somebody came up with my black towel, washed in peacetime and forgotten, out on the patio, when war came. It was folded to fit and promptly nailed in place (blessedly, the door frame was wood, so we didn't have the usual Israeli stone-wall problem), and it stayed there all through the war, a model for the neighbors—who, lacking black towels, were desperately tacking up all sorts of things that got in the way of the door or weren't lightproof or kept falling down . . . I can't remember whether it was I who thought of using my towel, but I know I felt honored by the choice right from the first; and when Miriam returned it, relaundered and neatly folded, after the war, she handed it over as if presenting a medal for my contribution. I still have the towel, a bit frayed at the edges where the nails started trouble, but usable. And every time I see it I remember just how it was, all of it—the small fears that left no room for the big one, the shelter so thoroughly stocked with provisions for every imaginable emergency that there would've been no room for all of us to squeeze in too, the bathtub with dead mosquitos floating on top of the water that was nevertheless too precious to let out, just in

*The experiment worked, and leaving the door open was immensely preferable to being alone at the bottom of a narrow black pit with a cold circle of starlight twenty feet over your head. (A fancier arrangement, worked out later, restored privacy: the small flashlight I carried in my purse would, if placed under the sink and covered with an inverted basket, provide a light invisible from outside.)

case. And most of all, the nail-biting tension of listening for the crackle and mystic Hebrew words (or facsimile thereof) that would summon Ze'ev. That was the greatest nervous strain I suffered in the war, yet I could hardly complain: it was so absurdly little to contribute.* I'll always keep my black towel, always.

And I'll keep, too, the memory of the moment the war finally became real. It wasn't the TV pictures of men in Tel Aviv and Jerusalem doffing a *talis* (prayer shawl) to pick up a gun, or even the radio voice in English confirming the dark news that had been coming in in Hebrew and that I'd seen in Miriam's face even before she began to translate. Or Moshe Dayan trying to tell a people quite unwilling to believe him that we'd win but this time it wouldn't be like the Six-Day War, that Egyptian armies had crossed the Canal and all that stood between them and us were stretches of Sinai. (*What if we had given the Sinai back to them?* In the blacked-out house, we remembered pieces in *Harper's* and the *Atlantic* urging the intransigent Israelis to abandon the delights of war and make peace possible . . . We didn't know it that night, but when some of those articles were being written, the Egyptian army had been practicing Canal crossings for more than a year—and Sadat, having spent a fortune on it when his people were hungry, probably couldn't have got away with calling it off even if he wanted to.) The sad, homely face of Golda Meir, telling us we'd regain the advantage lost by the surprise attack but it would cost— Well, when she said that I knew it must have already cost, and the war almost became real.

But what actually did the trick was when we went for a late-afternoon walk, all of us, dogs included. The move was dictated by two "commands": for health reasons, I thought we all needed to get out of the house, and the ways-and-means command also thought there just might be a two-story ladder over at the construction site where Miriam and Ze'ev's new house was going up. We started to walk over there, and on the way we passed the entrance to Omer with the road to Tel Aviv that, last night, had glimmered so white and empty in the dark.

There were no cars on it now either: the radio, all day, had been urging *Stay off the roads†* in order to keep them clear for

*Now, though, I wonder whether the real contribution wasn't to my own sanity. Because if I hadn't been so busy with my frantic monitoring, who knows what frightening awarenesses—that, as things were, had to seep in slowly—might otherwise have hit me hard and all at once? (Moral: Focus on one tiny job, preferably one that's a strain . . .)

†That's why Sally and Reuben and the children stayed on for several days, despite Sally's almost immediate—and persisting, and later tearful—yearning to go home. It was instinctual and understandable (I myself have had it, in the face of a blizzard

vehicles on official business (which in Israel doesn't mean official vehicles only: buses and trucks and even some private cars get called up, just like people.) But the road was full of people, walking, alone or in twos and threes. When we got closer, I could see they were all in uniform, with packs on their back and a few with weapons—but they weren't marching, they were walking, keeping to the sides of the road as if it were still the everyday road to Tel Aviv and a sherut might come tearing past any minute. And they were all going one way: it was the road to Tel Aviv but they were going in the direction *I* was familiar with, to Beer-Sheva . . . I grabbed Reuben's arm. "Why is everybody going to Beer-Sheva?" Maybe something had been left out of the translations? Maybe there was fighting on Bialik Street?

"They're not going to Beer-Sheva, Maggie," Miriam said quickly. "They're going to the Sinai. To the war."

"*Walking?*"

Ze'ev, his patriotic fervor apparently aroused, broke in to assure me that *Zahal* (TSAH-hal, an acronym for the army reserve, which is of course most of the army) didn't depend on hiking soldiers making it to the battlefield in time. They would be picked up, he said, by buses carrying their units down from the north or by anything going where they were going. But meanwhile, if they knew where their units were headed, why not start south?

Why not indeed? If you know you have to go to war and you know in which direction it's going on, why not just start? We were close enough to the moving, matter-of-fact men so I could see the folds in their uniforms—the shadow squares still showing where that khaki shirt had been folded and stored on the top shelf of a closet until, a few hours ago, it had been taken down and put on because somebody came by and said *Turn on your radio* . . . That's when it became real, when I looked at the men who last night and this morning had been either irreligiously enjoying a holiday or hungry and praying in the synagogue—and now, without ceremony, without bands playing or flags flying or even anyone visibly in charge, were quietly availing themselves of the nearest means at hand* to do what they had to do.

---

warning: you just want to get your own family into your own house and lock the doors . . .). But Reuben, a strong man, sensibly withstood semi-hysterical appeals, and the rest of us helped him as much as we could.

*An interesting fact about means at hand emerged after the war. The Tel Aviv police, it seemed, had been swamped with stolen-car reports on Yom Kippur. But they cleared up most of the cases as soon as the mobilization was finished—the stolen cars had been snatched by resourceful types in need of transport to the war, and the cops just made the rounds afterward and collected the cars where they'd been left, outside army depots, etc. A typical case of Israeli problem-solving, that "crime wave."

This is the way war, when it has to be, ought to be: something embarked on soberly by men carrying clean underwear, just taken from the bureau drawer, tucked in their packs and plastic bags of hastily prepared sandwiches and fruit in their hands. Walking silently, perhaps still listening to the wife's voice or the baby's cry in their heads. And obviously not listening to the voices I'd grown used to in Cambridge, where the only babies mentioned were Vietnamese (and sometimes only *North* Vietnamese) and where voices didn't speak but chanted "Make love, not war," ignorantly or disingenuously overlooking the less lucky who didn't have a choice . . . What I was seeing, I realized, was the common man—something wonderful, and not the political symbol and even more unlike the phony The People of campus rallies. Simply, Man, civilized and responsible and self-respecting, needing not harangues or rallies or dreams of glory or pay incentives, just a good reason to be brave. And then, all by himself and without even a slogan on a button, he *is* brave, incredibly brave . . . Listen, you rhetoric-spouting arty-farty bleeding-hearts-in-restricted-areas-only, take down your posters of Che Guevara (who wrote in his diary that what the peasants need is a little more terrorism to make them see the light!) and if you're still spouting about "the aesthetics of revolution" and suchlike twaddle, wash your mouths with any of your land's twenty dozen brands of cheap, easy-to-get soap. And if you have to have a poster—if all the social love you're capable of is the fan-club kind—I'll get you one of Chaim, an accountant of Beer-Sheva who was saving up to buy an electric heater when he was interrupted by somebody trying to kill him. That is, if they don't succeed. If he's around to photograph when the uniform is washed and ironed and put back on the closet shelf.

Heroes are real, and are us.

There was no ladder left behind at the new house. We trailed back home, the boys listening to the transistor for Ze'ev's code, behind the frisking dogs who didn't know there was no room for them in the shelter. The littlest boy had raised the question, and it occasioned much adult confabbing. And a final, agonized semi-decision: we would give each dog an infant-size dose of antihistamine, which we had plenty of and could spare and which we figured would make them sleepy. So they wouldn't be frantic, but they wouldn't be helpless in case . . . (*In case there was no one to take care of them* was the rest of the sentence. But it didn't get said in meeting.)

It was when we got back home that the title of this chapter was born. In a general rest half-hour, when Sally hunted up writing

294

paper and offered me first use of the typewriter, as befitted my age and station. Only, because of my age and station, I really knew better: I'd been a writer for long enough to know you can't say anything valid about what's happening until it's not happening anymore.

But, tempted, I proved weak. So, while Sally scribbled, I typed—a page and a half before I recognized the predictable idiocy of the attempt. For the way to write journalism was to dash out, commandeering transport and phones (if I could find the old press card that was probably still somewhere in my wallet), and get through to that American editor who'd written me, shortly after I arrived in Israel, that "if things hot up out there," he could use something from me . . . So I didn't try to write journalism, I tried a short story. And discovered what I already knew, that it was not possible, not then and not there.

I don't know what Sally wrote: I didn't ask her and I didn't show her my own abortive effort. But when I handed over the typewriter, I saw that she too had a title. "Maybe We Should Have Fasted," she'd called hers. Whereas mine said "Should've." That's the difference, you see, between the old hand and the tyro.

From the diary: 17

The Home Front (October)

Checked our blackout last night, and it was perfect. And so was Beer-Sheva's: its little string of lights across the bottom of the sky is wiped out. You feel like saying But I just saw them, they were there only last night . . . Miriam and Ze'ev and I went to the home of Geula, the young woman who'd brought the news of the war. Mostly it was to find out if she knows something extra about what's going on, but also, I found, because it was the neighborhood thing to do. Except for dire emergency, nobody can use her telephone because it has to be free for incoming calls, so that isn't why. What it is, I see (and Ze'ev apparently somehow knew: he has a sure sense of his society), is that she's the center of reassurance—not only as the only military wife on a civilian street but also because the Air Force, admired and respected by nearly all Israelis, has always been regarded as a kind of aristocracy, it seemed to me. If so, it's a true one: Geula can't be more than twenty-five and she's alone with two little kids (one has had a slight fever all day and is droopy and cranky), but she was being—and I mean this divested of any pejorative or snobbish sense—the lady of the manor. Sort of responsible for all of us. Telling us that though things did look bad at the moment, it will be all right, we'll see. Giving advice on blackout problems, offering to share her baby aspirin: a real General's lady for all she's so young and so chic (she looks as though she ought to be skiing in Colorado) and, doubtless, worried about her husband, since Israeli officers don't sit in headquarters. Especially in the Air Force, where they're all so young. (God, how old can he be? Thirty, even?) And, unless we're going to get down to fighting on Bialik Street, it's the Air Force that has to be the equalizer . . .

In the morning, a funny story—or maybe someday it will be—that began when, opening my trissim, the first thing I saw, just across the empty street, was an Arab with a gun. Not the desert rifle you see them with around town, but something shorter and automatic-looking, and business-like. He was walking slowly, turning his head from side to side to eye the sleeping houses one by one . . . I was scared—close-up, specifically, personally, mouth-dry scared. Jumping back from the window, I put my shoes on with shaking hands. It couldn't be, I told myself, there hadn't been even a phony report, this time,* about their reaching Beer-Sheva. (But if they had,

*A reference to a *really* funny story about the Six-Day War in 1967, when the Egyptians announced they'd taken Beer-Sheva. The residents, busy piling sandbags in

nevertheless? And if this wary-looking Arab in dusty robes was an advance man . . . ? How close was the airbase? . . .)

The best thing to do was to get downstairs, pronto. And as soon as I did, end of drama: the Arab outside was an over-age Beduin serving in the Home Guard, Miriam said matter-of-factly, and went on to ask how I wanted my egg. (I must stop getting nervous over armed Arabs.) I don't think anybody noticed me trying to recover my cool, for they were all hovering around overflowing baskets of groceries in the middle of the kitchen floor. It seems Ze'ev went to the local macaulet when it opened, at 5 A.M.: the radio had promised milk and bread deliveries to the Negev, and the experienced Ze'ev knew that whatever arrived wouldn't last long— and we sure needed milk. Sally was not experienced, but she couldn't sleep and was downstairs when Ze'ev came down, so she went along. They'd managed to get nearly everything on the list, she boasted, waving it proudly. I took it, and I don't know why I began reading it—except that I always read everything, I guess, and it was mostly in English (probably because it was originally Miriam's regular shopping list, begun in peacetime).

But "cigarettes Mont Blanc"—English, but in Hebrew order— had been added by Ze'ev, and so had "choc. bar," followed by the name of the brand I'm famous for addiction to. So I knew these two items were for me. And Ze'ev, looking up just then to discover me eyeing them with a peculiar look on my face (I'll bet: here I'd been survival-thinking, and look at this frippery!), promptly assured me that it was okay, those things were in one of the baskets some- where. Of course it had been necessary to compromise a little, like, one of the packs of cigarettes was another brand. But they'd found the giant-size chocolate bar . . .

It was so ridiculous: the catch phrase of World War II—Don't you know there's a war on?—rose absurdly to mind, but Ze'ev had not yet been born when that was going the rounds in the U.S. The best I could do was to explain, somewhat prissily, that I hadn't thought they'd be shopping for anything but essentials (particularly when, five minutes before, I'd been contemplating the arrival of the enemy at the door). That only puzzled Ze'ev: but these things were "essentials," no? His bearded face full of astonishment that Maggie,

---

front of the hospital, only grinned. But an Israeli patrol out in the desert believed it, and promptly reorganized itself as a guerrilla force to take the town back. So they were still skulking out there when, the war abruptly over, another patrol went out to look for them . . . The newborn guerrillas weren't about to fall for an old trick like Egyptians in Israeli uniforms, but it was prudent to hold their fire—so when the lieutenant called "Yossi! Danni! Where are you?" they didn't shoot him before Yossi recognized him.

297

usually fairly bright, should fail to understand something so simple, he explained that the things on the list were all needs shelanu. *Couldn't I see that?*

I could. And that, naturally, he'd put the needs shelanu *on the list and trudged out early to try to satisfy them: what else is a man supposed to do? Especially a Jewish man, even one who snorts with impatience at the religious and doesn't believe in coddling them with sensitivity. But he still knows he must be responsible for "the stranger within your gates." It says so, in Torah.*

Well, that one will never be a funny story. But among its resonances, which I'm pretty sure will keep on ringing in my head, are everything from the innocent frontier-days Israeli competitiveness—get there fustest with the mostest—to the equally typical Israeli courage that insists on life-as-usual for as long as and however that can be managed. They really seem to know, somehow, that if a war changes you too much, you'll lose even if you win. (Actually, the word for them is "gallant," but nobody seems to know it, in Hebrew or English.)

Shelanu *isn't a club that's hard to get into: all you have to be, as a matter of fact, is willing. But once you're* shelanu, *you come first—no matter how foolish or unworthy the immediate issue or behavior, we take care of* shelanu.

To be looped into shelanu *is one of the nicest things that can happen to you.*

14 ⚄ Our World at War

I had learned the Hebrew words for "Egyptian" ("Syrian" is practically the same as English, thus no problem), "missile," and "shelter" by the time private auto traffic was general enough so Sally and Reuben and their children could go home. But even while they were still there in Omer, which meant two more who could translate effortlessly—and the boys could manage quite well, too—I was still wrung with anxiety, every time, between the spoken word from the radio or TV and the moment, a split second afterward, when somebody finally told me what was happening. In that interval my mind would race out of control, imagining what could possibly have been said (nobody can tell me anything now about the speed of thought!). And, no matter how brief the hiatus, I was filled with rage of incredible proportion—I wanted to scream and smash, to bring the very house down around our ears if somebody didn't tell me *instantly* . . .

I thought I'd learned, before that, how hard it is to be one of the dim-witted; but I didn't really know the half of it. Not to be able to understand, not to know what's causing the looks that cross people's faces as they listen, is more terrible than you can imagine. The feeble-minded must contain, always, a huge fury. And the deaf, waiting for the interpreting hand's sign language, must be even more formidably at the mercy of this anger: an intelligence equal to comprehension if it only had the key is a torment.

Though, when you lack the key, even your IQ turns off, it would seem. For I knew better—of course I did—than to interrupt with questions ("*What* airplane? Did he say the Egyptians were

firing *missiles* at Tel Aviv? What was that about Washington?")
while the others were listening. But I couldn't stop myself. "In a
minute, Maggie," somebody would say, sacrificing a second of
attention he or she must have wanted just as desperately as I did.
"Ssh" and *"Please,* Maggie!" the voices said. Ever the educator,
Miriam appealed to reason: "I can't tell you if you don't let me listen
first. Now you know that, surely you do." Yup. But it was like telling
a drunk to wait nicely for somebody to open the bottle. Sometimes
I'd be able to remember to be quiet (when I did, when I actually
managed to shut up through an entire news broadcast, the muscles
of my legs and arms ached by the time the effort—apparently quite
physical, too—was over). But then the news would say something
partly comprehensible like *"Sooria"* followed by *"tankim"*—and
trying to be good was hopeless: all vows forgotten, I was ready to
grab the bottle and smash it open . . . I don't know how they
managed to put up with me,* but they did. Their voices would
occasionally grow an edge of irritation, but all tempers were kept
(though I'll bet *their* arms and legs ached with the effort!) and they
went on doing their best with practically-simultaneous interpreting.

It was mainly because of my frantic need for news, more
often than the four-times-a-day English broadcasts, that the consensus was against my going home. Nobody was worried about my
safety there: my apartment house had shelter provisions, and
everybody in Israel always knows that the neighbors will take care
of any lone person, especially an older one and especially a foreigner. But nobody in my house spoke English nearly well enough to
supply my need. Mrs. Ben-Ari, who just might be well enough
equipped,† was across the courtyard; but she was too well equipped
in other respects—e.g., as a fluent speaker of Arabic with considerable personal prestige among the Gaza Arabs—so she was not
likely to be sitting around the house listening to the radio. Thus,
until the situation was less fluid ("until they know we're winning,"
was the way Ze'ev put it), I'd be better off staying where I was. And if
Ze'ev got called up, I'd be needed there, to drive Miriam to the
hospital if anything happened.

So, after the others had left, Miriam and I drove to Beer-Sheva

---

*Yes, I do know, I guess. It was *my* form of nervous breakdown, and it was tacitly
understood that we were each entitled to one.
†Doubtful, actually. The ability to speak English can be far short of an ability to
translate into it, instantly and orally. The level of skill I'd been demanding—which
only Miriam, who had professional talents, could really meet, and then not always—
is pretty much confined to the *crème-de-la-crème* simultaneous interpreters like
those who work at the UN.

to pick up some more clothes for me. We stopped at the university*
on the way, and there got the car blackout-proofed. By teenagers,
who'd been given the job of applying dark-blue paint to all but a narrow vertical strip of each headlight, and who were empowered to
stop all cars on the street or anywhere else. The merry little band we
ran into was working the hospital and university parking lots, and
talk about practical disposition of resources! *Never* have I seen such
a perfect right-man-for-the-job setup: given authority to make a
mess, the kids were having a ball. Everything in sight—including the
teenagers themselves, of course, and the occasional innocent
pedestrian, too—was marked with dark-blue evidences of their
enthusiastic labors and the abundance of paint they'd been supplied. When we got back to Omer that day, it took an hour's work
with a razor blade to secure for us the vertical slits of light we were
entitled to.

At my apartment in Beer-Sheva, silent and stuffy, we found
everything untouched. My mail was mostly irrelevant even when it
wasn't: a letter from my editor, still discussing the title for my first
mystery, was an example. (The discussion having been interrupted
at the crucial time, a bland acceptable-to-all-factions title was
chosen in New York, so the cover could be printed. And that was
that—war, it seems, solves literary problems marvelously.) My local
"mail" consisted of a combination of notes stuck in my door—by
those who could write English—and verbal Hebrew memos left with
the lady next door, and they'd mostly been answered by that time,
one way or another. For practically everybody I knew had come by
at some point, it seemed—and been told, if they could understand
Hebrew or German, that I'd gone off the day before Yom Kippur in a
station wagon driven by a pregnant young woman wearing blue
jeans and a plaid smock. No, not my "daughter." (Martha had been
elected to that role by my neighbors, we'd discovered soon after I
moved in.) This was the other pregnant one, who some said was a
professor at the university—which obviously taxed the credulity of
the yekke lady next door . . .

I know all that because my three English-conversation students, by asking next door in Hebrew *and* writing me a note in
English (with, I was absurdly pleased to see, only one spelling
mistake and that a very natural one) constituted a kind of Rosetta
stone. Rob, too, had tried both languages and both written and oral
conduits. So I did that, too: Miriam left a Hebrew message for him,

*Which was of course closed. Part of the faculty could've gone to work (e.g., Miriam,
and men like Yehuda Artzi—still, for all his passionate Zionism, a foreign national),
but what for? Nobody of student age was likely to be around.

with her address and an invitation to come on out (Rob had no car, but he could always hitch, or even walk), with the lady next door and I Scotch-taped a note, addressed to "Rob et al." on my own door. Then we took off with the clothes and a few perishables rescued from my fridge—plus the rest of my wash, which would now also get comfily machined—to check on the rest of the folks, Miriam's *chevra** and mine.

Two men had come for Avi late in the morning of Yom Kippur, Martha reported: that was how *they'd* found out about the war. She'd fed them all and packed sandwiches, while Avi dashed across the courtyard to the people he knew who had a phone. Here was his mother's phone number in Tel Aviv: if anything went wrong with Martha, they were to (a) take her to the hospital (easy enough, since Martha had the car) and find her an English-speaking doctor, and (b) call his mother and tell her to get hold of her sister, who spoke English and was a doctor. Having thus arranged for the care of his American wife—by a family that spoke Hebrew, German, Czech, and Hungarian but not English—Avi went off to the war. He was now in the south but not at the front—near Eilat, it seemed, where he was keeping the beach safe for future tourists while the rest of the army kept the Egyptians too busy to bother about the Red Sea. (That was clearly a direct quote from Avi himself.)

Martha couldn't come to Omer with us, thanks, because Avi might be able to call again. The way he did that was as follows: he called his mother, who then called the Hungarian-speaking family across the courtyard. (Avi's mother, after thirty-odd years in Israel, spoke almost no Hebrew.) If Avi thought he could call again, they came and took Martha over to their flat to wait; otherwise, they just gave her the message. So of course she had to stay right there. And her only problem at the moment was that she kept getting indigestion from all the goulash etc., she consumed at the neighbors' while waiting for the phone to ring. . . In my role as mother of the race, I pre-scribed Chiclets. And Miriam taught Martha how to say *My doctor says that's a no-no* in Hebrew.

Selma and Isaac were both at home: they had to be, Selma said mercilessly, because Isaac was ashamed to be seen in public in his civilian clothes. He said that wasn't it, but I could see he really was hiding. And so was Yehuda, when we got to the Artzis': I began to realize then how hard it must be on the American men, not to be

---

*Pronounced chev-RAH, this word is almost indefinable, I think (though I tried, in the Glossary). It's your gang, your bunch—not necessarily associates, and maybe not even all fond of each other. But everybody not a hermit has a chevra, I guess.

able to do anything* . . . Fran had driven up to visit a friend in Haifa for the weekend and apparently ended up in a man-who-came-to-dinner situation rather like mine, for she wasn't back yet. We left a note in her mailbox—she had a car and could get to Miriam's on her own if she didn't want to stay alone when she got back . . . I called Thereza, who wasn't worried because she'd phoned my yekke neighbor and recognized the description of Miriam. Jan had been called up but was coming back. I couldn't quite figure out whether that was because Israel needed its experiments in desert agriculture more than it needed a fiftyish clerk at an army post (which makes sense, but no army will often do what makes sense) or because he'd got stationed near Beer-Sheva anyway.

Our next stop was Miriam's, at the apartment of a faculty colleague. Linda was American but she'd been married to an Israeli longer than either Miriam or Martha and was really part of the local rather than expatriate community in Beer-Sheva. In fact she was so thoroughly comfortably set up—including even ready communication with her husband, because he was some kind of information officer and thus could get to a phone virtually at will, and they had one at home—that she was on Miriam's go-see list only because she was very, very pregnant. But the faculty had rallied round: another colleague, a single Israeli woman, was staying with Linda, with the car keys and the Kupat Cholim membership book in her purse, just waiting for the first pain.

Thus Miriam and I were about to take off to go get helpful somewhere else, when the phone rang and we had a mission—to go get Linda's young sister-in-law, who'd arrived at the Egged station. Linda had been expecting the girl, she said. Her husband had called that morning to say his sister had been got out of the army post and put on a bus to Beer-Sheva, where she'd stay to help Linda instead of going on home up north . . . *What* army post? Everybody looked amazed at my amazement. No, of course women didn't serve in fighting units anymore, but had I forgotten that the war began with a surprise attack? So this girl, nineteen years old and doing her regular army service, had been on duty (perhaps because, as a beginner, she was least entitled to home leave for Yom Kippur?) when all of a sudden† the post was under bombardment. The

---

*Not even listen for the code, which was all Ze'ev was doing since he'd gone to the army office in Beer-Sheva and they told him to go home and wait. Miriam's sunny willingness to tootle all over town may well have been aided by the desirability of getting out of Ze'ev's increasingly mopey presence. (And it may explain why they both wanted me around.)

†If you notice a certain discrepancy between this situation in the Sinai outposts at about 2 P.M. and the fact that Israel's mobilization of reserves had begun in the

Israelis felt very strongly about not letting the chyellot get into the hands of the enemy, so there'd been efforts, right from the first, to get to those pinned-down posts and evacuate any women along with the wounded; but the trouble was, half the Egyptian army was in the way. And then, at last, an armored vehicle succeeded in getting in and out again.

Well, I wasn't planning to write any news stories, but a first-person report, this fresh from the Sinai, was irresistible anyhow. I was busy priming Miriam (who'd have to interpret, as the girl didn't speak English) all the way down to the bus station . . . But I'd never make it as a war correspondent. Because the moment I laid eyes on this kid just off the bus from the war, I forgot all about stories, either fiction or journalism. When Miriam went up to her, I was sure we'd got the wrong chyellet, for this one didn't seem to be waiting for anybody but was just standing there, all but asleep on her feet. She was quite tall—maybe five feet seven—but she looked about twelve years old, with long hair tied back in a ponytail and baby fat still plumping her cheeks and the soft little chin. She was dressed in a tan uniform of shirt and slacks and carrying a small carryall bag, and everything about her was all the same color, the color of dirt. I mean everything, right down to the bare toes poking out of her sandals: I've mothered active young sons, all of whom took positive pleasure in getting as dirty as they could and staying that way as long as they could, yet I've never in my life seen anybody as dirty as that girl. But, come to think of it, I've never before seen a girl who'd been lying on her face in the Sinai for several days.

She murmured muzzily* as she climbed into the car. But then, she roused and began to ask questions—where her brother was now, how Linda was feeling, and had the family, especially Mama, heard that she was out? Miriam answered her while also fending me off ("Did she see the Egyptians . . ."), and then asked her how *she* felt. What she said, in her oddly muffled† voice, was not really an answer: "She just keeps saying how dirty she is," Miriam

---

morning, so did Israelis. The question of who dawdled in alerting the front line had a direct effect—and that's putting it mildly—on the subsequent elections.

*What she was saying, Miriam told me later, was "I'm so sorry, I'll make your automobile all dirty."

†It wasn't her natural voice, I discovered when I ran into her once, with Linda, long after the war. The muffled voice may have been a leftover effect of the bombardment, which had disturbed her hearing temporarily; most of that wore off before she got to Beer-Sheva, but perhaps there was still a bit left. Or it could've been just exhaustion and dryness. (I didn't recognize her when I met her again, by the way. And Linda asked her if she remembered me and she said of course she did; but I think she was only being polite.)

told me. And I could see it for myself—the girl loosened her hair and let it fall forward while she felt of it with her filthy hands. A look of disgust crossed the dirty babyish face, and I knew why Miriam was driving so fast: whatever else there might be to do for this kid, the first thing was to get her to some soap and water.

The girl had heard my questions, though, and she got the drift. At least she clearly detected that the American woman was anxious, for she made an enormous effort: leaning forward from the back seat, she spoke to me directly, looking into my face the way people do when they're urgently trying to break through the language barrier somehow. *"Col b'seder,"* she said, the brown lips in the brown face trying to smile . . . It means "Everything's okay," a stock statement and the answer to stock questions. But it's also what you might say to a toddler after he's had a tumble and before you send him back out to play—and that's the way the girl said it to me, with a weary kindness that filled me with instant, terrible shame. (And not only me: Miriam winced, and then sped up some more.)

We got the girl to Linda's and up the stairs, and found the other women already running a bath for her. She wouldn't sit down anywhere, but she did allow herself to be talked into a cup of coffee—I guess she agreed that she might fall asleep in the tub otherwise—while Linda laid out half a dozen great soft towels. Then it was ready, a huge hot bath thick with sweet-smelling bath stuff, and Linda's best imported soap and two kinds of shampoo laid to hand. We made the girl leave the door open a crack, because we were really worried: normally, people will wake before they can drown, but maybe not in the state she was in . . . She was all right, though: after a while we heard the shower, and Linda peeked in and said she was rinsing about ten tons of shampoo froth out of her hair.

We were all, all four of us, so bloody guilty—every one of us was older and richer and better educated than that kid in there, and we could hardly stand it. But Linda and her houseguest at least could do something about it: one of them was finding robes and slippers and the other was busy whipping up a nice light omelet. Miriam and I loitered pathetically, like kids too young or too clumsy to be allowed in the game, just on the off-chance that we could maybe pass a bath towel or something. But there was no recreation leader to say everybody had to be allowed to play. And there were no requests from the bathroom, and all the jobs were taken. So, eventually, we crept out of there.

It was the day after that I woke, out in Omer, with an awful feeling that something terrible had happened to my son Phil. I mean, I was really stricken, as though with actual knowledge. I struggled and lost—the feeling was so strong that in the end I couldn't possibly keep it to myself. I was just telling Miriam and Ze'ev when Carole, another of Miriam's faculty colleagues, drove up; she'd come out to Omer to check on them. Carole lived in the Old City, in Beer-Sheva, and had a phone. Let's try calling Maggie's son, she said—it was still early morning in the eastern U.S., not time yet for a student to be gone to even an early class, so if we could get through we ought to be able to catch him in. While we were discussing it, a neighbor dropped in. She'd heard you could make overseas phone calls, she said. But only collect: there was enough personnel to work the connections, apparently, but not enough for the paperwork, too. Well, that was no problem—I wouldn't have wanted to charge up an expensive call on Carole's phone anyway. (It's always awkward because it's hard to guess how much you owe people, as there's no separate list of long-distance charges like the one that comes with your phone bill in the U.S.)

I don't know how it happened, but the news that we *could* do it made it an immediate necessity. That's the way we behaved: we scooped up Carole's two little kids—who looked bewildered by this extraordinarily short visit, but were unprotesting—and we jumped into the cars (we even, for no known reason, took Charlie Brown along) and all drove like mad to Carole's house, as if we had to make a deadline. Nobody even questioned the validity of my "awful feeling": I was treated like somebody who'd had bad news. People said reassuring things to me, but they were all attempts to cut down the alarm—like, that maybe it would turn out to be only something minor that was the matter with my son—and nobody suggested for a minute that there might not be anything to it at all. I can't understand that: *why* didn't anyone balk at this sudden, frantic journey? Or even say "Oh, be sensible"—which would be in character, normally, for Miriam and certainly for Carole? I have no answers. Only a guess that we were all hysterical, and had been for several days (maybe the whole damn country was, too), and that a sudden belief in magical powers of divination just went down as easily as ice cream down a sore throat. And, for me, it was of course especially easy: if I'd ever had any doubts about my "feeling," the fact that everybody else instantly took it so seriously disposed of them without a trace.

The phone call took quite a while. During which, naturally, the self-perpetuating tension perpetuated itself busily, not hampered at all by the fact that I asked every ten minutes what time it was now in Connecticut. Ze'ev had been doing all the wrangling in Hebrew, so when he called me to the phone I didn't really dig, for a moment, that this was It—we'd done it, we were through, it was somebody in the United States of America who was asking what number we were calling!

That's when I also realized I didn't know Phil's phone number. It was written down somewhere at home, along with his address—which of course I knew by heart, so I hadn't even looked at the entry in ages, and I certainly hadn't picked it up to take along to Omer . . . "Just get Yale University, in New Haven, Connecticut," I told Directory Information, trying to sound ladylike and a shade peremptory, like my mother. The next voice I heard was Yale's own operator. I gave her Phil's name and college and she gave me the number of the phone in his room—and there the wheels stopped again: she couldn't put the call through because it was collect and *she* couldn't accept the charges. She explained that to this caller who didn't seem to dig the simplest facts. And she truly wanted to be helpful, so she pointed out patiently that now that she'd given me the student's own number, all I had to do was hang up and call it, see?

Some gasket must've blown in my brain when I tried to make it take in that I was really supposed to surrender this single, frail, frantically won connection. Or maybe it happened when an operator in New York or New Haven or somewhere broke in to ask Yale if she was still connected—because that's when I began to scream. I, who never-never-never shout at operators and am notorious for my meekness in the face of any regulation anywhere—well, all I can say is, the worm turned, baby, like you wouldn't believe. "Listen, goddammit," I yelled, at both operators indiscriminately—they were both guilty, weren't they, of behaving as though everything was all right and it was just a normal day?—"I *can't* call back. There's a war on, and I was damn lucky to get this connection. I'll *never* get another one."

The Yale operator made a small, doubtful sound; but it was in answer to a telephone company voice, not me. Omigod, they were going to ignore me, just pull a plug on the troublesome public: they are Power, and I've offended them . . . "Put the call through, will you?" I shouted. *"Please."* And then brought up what I guess seemed my only weapon: "Listen, I'm his *mother!*" (I can hardly believe it, but that's what I yelled. And in earnest, yet.)

Amazingly, the New York operator said, presumably to the Yale girl, "This call is coming from Israel." She sounded reproving. I heard her, but I couldn't turn off the passionate pleading: "Listen, he'll *pay* for it. I swear he'll pay for it . . ." And then, utterly without warning, my son's deep voice said "Hello?"

"Phil!" I screamed it. "Are you all right?" Behind me in the

307

room, I felt rather than heard the stir as everybody waited urgently, celebrating and yet fearing.

Sure he was all right, said Phil sleepily, why wouldn't he be? He sounded bemused—I've never been the kind of mother who called up much, even from Massachusetts.

I was still at least half out of my mind, but the other half was suddenly aware that I'd been making a spectacle of myself. Before my friends and, the way I'd been yelling, doubtless half of downtown Beer-Sheva, too. Not to mention God knew how many operators half a world away . . . Well, I wasn't going to do it before Phil, too: I could still save *something*. "I don't know," I said meekly. "I just—got sort of worried, that's all." Which was about as accurate a description of what I'd just got as—well, suppose a dinosaur suddenly appeared on your patio, and you said *Look, Charlie, there's a lizard out there* . . .

Phil was coming fully awake now, there in his room at Stiles with the alarm not even gone off yet to begin a perfectly normal day of gamboling on probabilities and sliding down gradients and doing whatever it is you do with a Lagrange multiplier. But Phil awake is unfailingly logical, so he proceeded to ask the logical question. Why was I worrying about *him*, he wanted to know, when I was the one who was in a war?

Why indeed? Would you believe that it wasn't until I sat down to write about it that I put together my sudden "ESP" fear for my perfectly safe nineteen-year-old son and that terribly tired and dirty nineteen-year-old girl I'd seen the day before, just off the bus from the war?

Well, if you're a parent, I guess you can believe that. But here's something even harder to believe, unless you've lived in Beer-Sheva: when we got home to Omer, Miriam and Ze'ev and Charlie Brown and I, waiting for us on the doorstep was a new immigrant! From Canada, which was why he'd been given Miriam's name and address by the AACI: he was coming to Beer-Sheva and he was an academic too, so it figured. Only it figured for some lost, already long-ago day in Toronto, in a time before the last Soviet missile was all dug into place and the Egyptian soldiers had practiced Canal crossings long enough . . . The new arrival (dressed—in that heat!—in a proper dark blue suit and white shirt *and* tie) had gone over to the university, he told us stiffly. And there he met a girl who said she knew Miriam and was about to drive to Omer herself. So he'd been dropped off here—he concluded, his voice having a hard time believing itself—and told to tell us Fran had to go deliver a message and she'd be back soon . . .

308

We herded him inside and got some lunch—for Fran, too, who'd turned up by that time—and he ended by staying the night and then for several more nights. He was given the rollaway bed in the study, and I moved up a notch to the proper guest bedroom. Where there were two beds, but Fran, who suffers from insomnia, preferred the sofa downstairs so she could not-sleep without disturbing anyone.

So we still had plenty of room in case anybody else was lost or lonely. And I still had enough chocolate and cigarettes, and while we were in the Old City, Ze'ev had gone to the pharmacy and got a supply of my gut pills, too. True, one small problem loomed: I was beginning to run out of thrillers to read in bed, and what was available in that house was all too elevated to be an inviting substitute. But doubtless, if the war went on long enough, somebody would turn up with a Nero Wolfe in his pocket.

From the diary: 18

Between the mosquitos and the BBC (Oct.)

Last night was dreadful. Physically, to begin with: it's hot and still, and the mosquitos are god-awful. Indoors, with all the windows closed and shrouded in blackout stuff, you feel you're smothering; if you want a breath of air, you have to go outside or turn out all lights inside so you can open windows and doors. But then, the minute you do either one, you're mosquito-meat. I've never seen such mosquitos: they're virtually kill-proof—even if you get one occasionally, it's always full of blood, indicating a long and successful career. But mostly you can't get one: they light on the ceiling, and by the time somebody assembles enough stuff to stand on (nobody standing on just a chair can reach) for a swat, the mosquito drifts off lazily. After a tremendous amount of climbing up and getting down, plus precarious teetering on the edges of things and one or two gravity-defying leaps, Ze'ev actually clobbered two (2) mosquitos—both times leaving bloodstains on the ceiling . . . The temptation to get out the spray and let 'er rip is almost unbearable. But so are the effects: we sprayed the first-floor trissim from the outside before dark, and even that mild measure made the air in the living room close to unbreathable. Vengeance-spraying, it's clear, would damage us more than the mosquitos.

(Oh my. The minute I wrote that, it dawned on me that the mosquito conflict may be a goddam parable. More than a little wobbly, since the Arab armies are not natural forces and are not proving—thank God—anything like so unconquerable. But there too, the Israelis keep having to pull their punches: to publish the truth about what Syrians do to prisoners of war might damage the chances of POWs still alive, to smash Damascus would damage the U.S. ambition to become the Arabs' protektsia and thus cause more of those mysterious "administrative" Washington delays in sending us ammo . . . Israel irritates me—and doubtless the rest of the world too—by constantly turning into a paradigm.)

Well, we in this house have one consolation now: Ze'ev got convinced at last that the water wasn't really going to go off (at least, not unless things get so bad that we're living in the shelter anyway), so now we get to take baths. I went upstairs early last night, to do just that in the hope that a little soaking would relieve my poor red-welted body. But I couldn't really soak, for the downstairs toilet is better than nothing but still not what anybody would really prefer to use, so I couldn't keep the upstairs bathroom inaccessible for too long or my conscience would itch worse than the mosquito welts. What luxury it is to live alone! (Did you hear about how poor Maggie suffered in the war? She had to share a bathroom, you know . . .)

Another reason for coming upstairs early is, they're watching Israeli TV down there, a kind of "special" on the war. It's a good job, I can see that even around the language barrier. (The TV people— perhaps because the grim bureaucratic grasp on their necks is loosened now?—seem to be having their Finest Hour.*) But the trouble is, it divides me from the group. What causes the separation, I think, is the inevitable delays between the pictures I see on the screen and my understanding of their meaning. Brief moments, but they make a fatal difference because the others can react emotionally and I'm forced into cerebration: I can't help trying to stretch my small Hebrew to cover what's being said, even though I know help is on the way. As a result, we become two different kinds of audiences, so to speak—as if the others are reading a poem, but I have to proofread it. So they take in through their senses and respond, nice and direct, whereas I'm busy pasting together what I see and the puzzle-and-solution sequence I hear in two stages. That difference didn't matter when all news from the outside world amounted to bulletins on the single question* Are they gonna get us? *Back then, I stayed anxious a split second longer each time, but it was still the same kind of reaction as everybody else's. Now, it isn't. They're getting consoled and heartened;* and I, I guess, am reverting to type.*

For I am, after all, the only one in the group with personal experience of how foreign policies get made, and reported, in the U.S. Miriam and Fran have all sorts of esoteric academic knowledge I'm not privy to, but they've always been only consumers of political reporting and I've been a producer; and Ze'ev was actually in the 1967 war, but I doubt that he thought of himself as a "unit of firepower"—which was what he'd have been in the analyses of it I was editing. So, once winnowed out of the group by the language gap, I run to a different kind of rumination, I suspect. And my poor friends, along with all the rest of Israel, will be getting deluged with "think pieces" in the Hebrew press soon enough—they don't need me psephologizing in the salon tonight. So, "I think I'll take a bath," I murmured (real noble, like Titus Oates strolling out into the

---

*This doesn't mean we were getting cheery lies from the TV. But the view of other Israelis, in other towns, does reassure—as does the simple fact that someone's taking pictures—that things are being coped with, familiar places are still there. Only, for me, it had to be less effective: a picture of a talking soldier is only that, until you know that what he's telling is how the rocket attack missed the kibbutz's dining hall.

311

blizzard so Scott and the others could struggle on unhampered to the South Pole), and took myself upstairs for the general good.

Though of course the starting-point of analysis isn't depressing: everybody, even the least analysis-prone, must've worked out by now that we're relatively safe. For Israel isn't yet in a position you can call comfy, but Egypt hasn't even got as far as the Sinai passes despite such advantages as the two-front war, surprise, an all-but-unbelievable superiority in manpower, and—until mobilization here got under way—super-armed professionals facing over-age Israeli reservists and kid trainees. So if with all that going for them, the Egyptians didn't make it, logic says they're not going to. And in the north, where Israeli tanks were outnumbered 80 to 1,* the Syrians have clearly blown it. They may in fact have been pushed quite a way back; I'm skeptical about govt. claims, so I just don't know. But it's obvious from the nature of the Golan terrain that it's not a front you can stand still on: the winner of the first clash is automatically halfway to either Damascus or Haifa, with air support the only x factor. Which Israel may have, even though the Air Force must also be busy down south.

Well, that's the good news. But I can hear, in govt. pronouncements, etc., the groundwork being laid for the casualty lists to come. It figures they'll be staggering, for the Israeli forces absorbing the initial attacks on both fronts must've been chopped to hell. It's not that there ain't no miracles: that little girl soldier getting out of the Sinai alive may well have been one. But there aren't unlimited miracles ... And it's sure going to be a miracle if how-come questions don't do serious damage to this society. Like, things were definite enough so the mobilization had already reached down as far as Avi by mid-morning on Yom Kippur, so how come the war now turns out to've started in early afternoon? What the hell was the govt. doing with the precious hours of advance info? And why didn't they send planes over to spike the preparations, as they did in 1967?

Possible answers to that last question: 1. They couldn't. Because the Egyptians also remember 1967, were on the watch for a similar strike, and maybe have some nice new Russian weapons waiting for just such a move.†

---

*I accepted this figure because it came from an outside source that couldn't possibly be Israeli propaganda; the same was true of the reported 600-to-1 manpower ratio at the Suez Canal (though the mind reels). But I dismissed accounts of the fantastic new Soviet antitank weapon the Egyptians had, because nobody except the Israelis had yet reported it. And clearly I wotted not of ammunition shortages.

†I try to leave these innocent ruminations untouched, but "maybe"?!? Egypt's array of SAM missiles arrived at the Canal via the American-engineered disengagement in 1970. After *three weeks* of "confirming" Israel's warnings that the Egyptians were

2. *The Israelis suspected a trap. If the Egyptian threat was a phony and Israeli planes drawn off to the Canal area left the field clear for Syrian attack— Well, that's standard military risk. But Israel is so vulnerable once air is knocked out that Intelligence would have to be guaranteed 14-karat.*

3. *Political reasons—e.g., U.S. public's anti-war mood. The left-wing infrastructure's already managed to create Israel-as-aggressor image of 1967, so American public opinion would immediately turn against Israel if it struck first. No explanation would even get heard.*

Well, for Golda's sake, I hope it wasn't No. 3. Because she must know that without public opinion, there'll be no supplies for Israel (everybody except the Americans seems to know what a truly responsive govt. the U.S. has!); but it's still a hell of a reason for a hell of a decision. In Golda's place, I have to admit, I'd probably have made the same (presumed) decision—to hold off and let the enemy be visibly the aggressors. But oh God. Poor Golda.

The Israelis don't seem to see it in those terms, not yet anyway. (How can they, ever? Could the parents of a 19-year-old killed in the Sinai on Yom Kippur bring themselves to identify the cause as some well-intentioned trendy moralism half a world away?) But even writing that down makes me feel sick. About the future, too: are people going to die in poor countries everywhere so American idealists can feel cozily virtuous in their anti-war purity?

All right, I'm sensible and mature. I don't wallow in hysteria, I try to get a wider picture. So alone upstairs, I turned on the transistor radio. And, after ten minutes of tuning into the outside world, I was choking with rage. For what I got was the BBC. Which has always been a little hard to take (e.g., it's "guerrillas" who engage in high jinks like killing unarmed athletes at the Olympics, though in Ireland the terrorists are "terrorists" to the BBC too). But now their smarmy pseudo-reporting that says it's too bad about the poor Israelis but . . . (what follows the "but" is a clear implication that after all they deserve it, don't they) is worse than being shot at. It's Chaucer's "smiler with the knife."

The BBC dirty-pool gimmicks are quite easy to spot. Like, Arab governments' press releases get read out straightforwardly ("Egyptian armies advanced umpty miles since this morning . . .") while the Israelis' are always preceded by a disclaiming "According to" or the even more doubt-stirring "Israel claims that"—thus getting

---

moving missiles up, the U.S. finally protested to the UN. About 30 missiles stayed where they were after the talking finished, and they were still there on Yom Kippur. It may be shame that caused that fact to slide out of my American memory.

313

it across that your wise BBC knows what the Arabs say is valid* but what Israel says is only propaganda. A neat trick, if just a jot slimy, what? I've heard literally dozens of other gimmicks too, all the kind of examples I used to save for my class lectures on How to Read a News Story Warily.

It's not just these nail-downable points, though, it's the whole tone. The disdainful voice that seems to be smelling a bad smell whenever it has to say the word "Israel." The clipped, brisk accent that makes such small work of courage, love, and any other old-fashioned notion that conflicts (and it's remarkable how often honorable notions do) with the oil-money ethic. Because of course that's what it is, up front: anti-Semitism may make the work enjoyable besides, but Arab millionaires must own half of England by now, so naturally British "progressives" and soi-disant radicals dance at the ends of their oily strings. What makes me especially angry, I guess, is that I remember when radicals were against millionaires. It hurts to see the theft of the heritage left by honest, brave people who fought to keep millionaires from walking over everybody else.

I don't mind so much about the Conservatives, who are only greedily busy protecting their sterling. Thus the fact that the son of Britain's Foreign Minister heads a syndicate angling for a billion-dollar development deal with one of the Persian Gulf oil emirates (a setup that sure sounds like a conflict of interest, doesn't it?) is just another big-money scandal, nothing to get emotional about . . . That information comes, oddly enough, from the BBC's own Business News program. Doubtless they assumed business-news listeners wouldn't care if a Conservative Minister wasn't so kosher. (Ha, they forgot about me. I feel like a spy. But it's only that I'll listen to anything in English, even business news.) Or maybe it was plain stupidity, some producer either not getting the word or being too dumb to see that this darkens the would-be white hats? Or—cheerful thought—maybe some bright boy managed to slip the item in, in the hope that somebody would pick it up and bring it to public atten-tion. (On second thought, he couldn't have been a very bright boy. Not if he really expected investigative reporting.)

Well, upstairs alone with the BBC last night, it suddenly occurred to me that I was really hating. I'd turned out the light so I could pull up the trissim and get some air, and I lay there in the dark

---

*Even, it seems, when refuted by the BBC's own correspondents. For their man in Damascus protested openly at one point because, though he reported he was actually *looking* at the results of an Israeli air raid, his home office insisted on broadcasting instead the official Syrian denials that there'd been any.

trying not to let it happen to me; but the unctuous voice of Prime Minister Heath was enough all by itself, it seemed, to start up physical symptoms of rage. Will I never be able to hear a British accent again without immediately seeing a slimy-hypocritical monster who blands real people to death? I finally got my fists unknotted, though only by bribing myself with Hate the sin but not the sinner—*that way, I didn't have to give up all hatred altogether.*

It was hardly what you might call a victory. And it wasn't enough: I had to have help, I decided, and got up to see if anybody was still around downstairs. Somebody was—from the top of the stairs, I could hear the radio muttering down there—so I crept downstairs in my pajamas, hoping that wasn't the new immigrant in the salon.

It was Fran, propped on her sofa-bed but not reading. "Is that news?" I asked, nodding in the direction of the Hebrew-spouting radio.

"It's supposed to be. But it isn't, unless news is another high-minded call for all the combatants to stop fighting—now, but not last week, of course." She made a face, then apparently recollected her duty to me. "You want me to tell you what—?"

"No, thanks." I didn't want to know what it said; in fact I hadn't even been trying to understand the words myself. What I wanted was only to listen to the Hebrew radio voice, gnarly and anonymous and not at all snotty. Or cool: nobody speaking Hebrew last night could be cool, bland, or anything else BBC-ish. So it came to me then that here, with the language I didn't understand, was where I belonged because it was the language I did understand in everything but words. It's the language of people whose children's school bus is ambushed by those called heroes* in Arab capitals— and excused, in BBC and other progressive circles, as having suffered so terribly at the hands of the Israelis (it's seldom stated how) that they just couldn't help doing "this terrible thing." The name of what these people do is killing children deliberately, as a matter of policy. But that cannot of course be actively celebrated, so it becomes a "terrible thing," a vague term implying large forces before which we're all helpless . . . Another example for my class on how to spot gimmicks. Except that it's too elementary: I can't believe anyone doesn't already see through that one (or couldn't if he wanted to).

Nobody in the house could sleep last night, it seemed. Pos-

---

*Some heroes! A school bus, traveling a regular route and making regular stops every school day, should be as easy to hit as a shooting-gallery duck. Easier, if little David drops his geography book as he's getting on, thus giving the heroes even more time to aim.

315

sibly not even the newcomer, though he apparently didn't feel free to come trailing downstairs barefooted, as Miriam did and then, after a while, Ze'ev did too. So, at any given time, there was always a voice in the dark speaking English—but this time hesitantly, in broken sentences that were certain of nothing. And yet hated nothing: oh, down there among the voices that didn't know but did care, the mosquitos were fierce and it was smotheringly hot. But it was the right place to be.

For I'm beginning now to entertain a real dread that Israel will prove a prototype, and after it will come mass-production abandonment of morality to feed moralism. (My guess is that's pretty much the way things will go: Israel will get neatly labeled whatever's considered immoral, so the New Moralists can be selfish and still feel good.) Hating the sin but not the sinner could turn out to be the best I can do. For we may be getting down to an all-out war between the Warms and the Cools, between people who will kill only the enemy who attacks them—and then will cry about it—and people who'll kill anyone anywhere anytime, just to make a propaganda point,* and then feel good about it. And for me, even if it's too hot where the Warms are, it'll always be too cold among the Cools.

---

*Not hyperbole: see numerous "explanations" after random spraying of automatic fire in airports, etc. "We wanted to make the world pay attention to our cause," said one such hero. The world paid attention. What's bothering me is, why didn't it also gag at such an admission?

15 ⌁ In the Dark and the Cold

I finally ended my visit in Omer after it was certain that Ze'ev wasn't going to be called up. He found that out, and why, by hitchhiking to Tel Aviv: what the Beer-Sheva provincials had been unable to tell him was that he'd been assigned to a "cripple unit." I doubt the army called it that, but Ze'ev did—and in his accent it was even clearer that a "creeple unit" wasn't likely to be called unless the Egyptians were ordering coffee at a Dizengoff café. (The error had been caused, apparently, by somebody's listing him as wounded in 1967. Which he had been, but the damage to his hand was invisible and wouldn't have affected his life unless he'd been a concert pianist.) I stayed around just long enough so Ze'ev wouldn't feel he'd driven me away (like most people who feel unjustly dealt with, he was now injustice-hunting); then I discovered a need to return to my typewriter and took off.

When I got home, Rob came over—as arranged during elaborate discussions in Omer, since the general assumption was still that I couldn't possibly cope—to put up my blackout and guide me to the shelter if the sirens went. He stayed over for the first couple of nights, but after that, since he wasn't an Israeli, he was capable of believing that I wasn't really nervous. Perversely (although this sort of thing happens often enough so maybe we should stop calling it that), as soon as he'd left we had our first air-raid alarm. I followed the sign that said *"miklat"*—I'd managed to learn the word for "shelter," but I could've simply followed the neighbors anyway— and then stood against a wall in a large L-shaped underground room that I didn't even have time to investigate before the all-clear sounded. We all trooped out again, one of my neighbors clucking as she brushed at the back of my shirt, which had picked up stone-grit from the wall. So much for my friends' fears about Maggie-all-alone.

There were two other alarms in succeeding days, but by that point—which, with the advantages of hindsight and research, I figure must have been still well before the Israelis actually turned the war around—the public attitude was already one of irritation with whoever had presumably let maybe one plane slip through somewhere or hit the alarm button with his elbow. Slovenly, slovenly. So careless, these boys. No consideration for the public, everybody muttered—standing there in a town that could be reached by a MiG from Egypt, and certainly from Jordan, in less time than it's taken you to read this chapter so far. The Israelis are incredible. (Or maybe it's citizens of free countries I mean? Because there was something awfully "American" about the *chutzpah* of the public.)

Well, that's part of why it really doesn't matter about what was happening on what date, in the progress of the war. For, to the Israeli public, and certainly in provincial places like Beer-Sheva, the good times are when you can afford to grumble. And there's nothing between them and the bad times, for in Israel, it seems, there are no victories. I see by the record that on October 16, Sadat was making a victory speech in Cairo. Which should have set us chuckling, because not only had an Israeli force broken through and set up a beachhead on the Egyptian side of the Canal,* but Soviet Premier Kosygin had already determined, presumably from evidence gathered by a spy satellite umpty miles in the sky, that the Egyptians were getting clobbered; he flew to Cairo abruptly (apparently because the Russians could see themselves getting sucked in, like the U.S. in Vietnam). But in Israel, nobody was celebrating. And they didn't even when Golda Meir announced the first really good-news report from the war. Oh, maybe the Knesset broke into applause. (And, if I know Israel, six professors—representing six budding new political parties—probably sat down to write 6000-word pieces that could all have been titled "Why the Hell Did It Take So Long?" but none of them would be.) But in Beer-Sheva, and other towns like it, everybody's attention was on the casualty lists.

In a way, that was maddening: sometimes I felt like screaming, "Don't you crazy people know you're *winning?*" But it would've

*This was always referred to as "Africa," from the very first beachhead—when it *was* probably newsworthy that Israelis had set foot on what was after all another continent—to long after they controlled the road to Cairo and it was just another place to come home on leave from.

been useless anyhow—there simply is no kick, for Israelis, in any war. Victory parades are for Cairo: in Israel, the only important news about any battle, even a victorious one, is *Who got hurt? How badly? Is Shlomo all right?* Taking the long, or objective view, I can see that this dolefulness, this utter refusal to rejoice, in fact becomes a powerful psywar weapon for the enemy; and certainly it makes domestic political power virtually irretrievable once a war starts— because the public doesn't blame leaders for that ("He kept us out of war" wouldn't have been a persuasive campaign slogan in Israel, whose citizens understand the lack of choice) but neither can it be mollified by anything short of having the war end completely. (The *only* public rejoicing I saw in Israel was when the prisoners of war were returned from Egypt. Boys coming home, that's a victory, you see . . .) Which means no political capital can be made of victories, there are virtually no morale-raising results, and—most important— there's a constant, severe drag on Israeli leaders trying to horse-trade at the negotiations table. Because Sadat, whose people still believed they were winning glorious victories, could tell Kissinger that if the U.S. didn't make the Israelis behave, he simply might not be able to hold back his spoiling-for-blood populace; but in noisy democratic Israel, you didn't have to be as brainy as Kissinger to detect the bring-the-boys-home pressure on Mrs. Meir. And if *she'd* ever threatened to bomb civilian targets, as Sadat did,* she'd have got not cheers but riots . . .

So I'm truly not exaggerating when I say that the only al-together bright moment I remember in the whole dark tunnel of October and November in Beer-Sheva was the day the rains started. It was, after all, my first experience of them (it may be hard for you to remember, as it certainly was for me, but by Yom Kippur I'd been in Israel for just under eight months). Thus I couldn't figure out for a moment what the excitement was about when I heard children calling out, clearly happily, in the courtyard. When I looked out, small forms were capering, school books tossed aside: *"Yored geshem!"* (yo-RED GESH-em), the children cried out, dancing and laughing. Mothers leaned from windows and began yelling them indoors, and some came down and snatched their elated kids and abandoned jackets and lunch bags into the house. Quite frantically—

*Just so you don't get the impression of nerves of steel, etc., Sadat's threat apparently scared me enough so I wrote a just-in-case letter handing on my wisdom to my son Phil. I've forgotten what my wisdom was, but I have his return letter, thanking me for it though expressing surprise that I'd really been scared: Phill didn't recall even hearing about the Sadat threat. (And with his mother sitting in range, he *was* rather paying attention to the news.) Presumably, if it got reported at all, it was only lightly, in a context of just-more-Arab-rhetoric. But that isn't the way it felt in Beer-Sheva.

the mothers in my neighborhood seemed convinced that a child with some raindrops falling on his head was only one step from pneumonia.

It's yored-geshem day, then, that divides, in my mind and memory, the hot blackout days and nights from the cold and dark that the year ended in. Though of course it wasn't really that decisive: the rain doesn't come like the rainy season in stories I've read about Africa, all in one drowning moment; in Israel, it just means that now it *can* rain, and pretty soon it will start to, and it'll be cold indoors. And then will come the endless mud and the kind of days when you go stand outside in the sun to warm up a little . . . So when I first got home from Miriam and Ze'ev's, it was still all bustle-time, with everybody charging around filling in for people who'd gone to the army and individuals' view of the progress of the war pretty much concentrated on prospects of David's or Yitzchak's next leave. The Israeli landing in Egypt, which for the rest of the world seemed to be a signal to start yelling Stop-the-bloodshed,* meant to us that chyellim whose turn for leave came around would now be bringing their laundry home from "Africa" instead of somewhere else. Or a little boy in the courtyard telling me his *Aba* (AH-ba, father) was *b'beit* (at home. And that's the last word of his discourse I understood, I'm afraid: his Aba was going to take him somewhere for some treat, I think). That's what mattered, to everyone—and not from where but only for how many days.

This is where I ought to tell about the not-very-funny thing that happened to me during those days. I hate to, but I *said* I'd tell the truth—and anyway, one comforting bit of news I've picked up over the years is that my unconscious is no more loathsome than other people's. So here it is: looking on at this war, with its intimate mingling of front and home front (even "Africa," after all, was not really very far away), I couldn't help remembering my own youth in World War II and feeling—well, jealous. And maybe scornful, as if this was a phony war (which God knows I knew wasn't true, for this was also the time of the casualty lists) and my own the "real" one of deprivation and loneliness and the bed that at first you continued to sleep only in your own half of becoming, slowly and inevitably, *my* bed instead of *ours*. I resented—I guess—these new young women,

*This shot was neatly called by Golda Meir when the war was only eleven days old: "I am certain that when we have brought our enemies to the verge of collapse, representatives of various states will not be slow in 'volunteering' to try and save our assailants." Which cynicism came as no surprise, of course, to a people who remembered the world's silence when Jordan took over Jerusalem by conquest in 1948—a silence that endured until the Israelis took it back in 1967, and a chorus of demands for "internationalization" (at least) of the city immediately arose from peacelovers abroad.

who could talk to their soldier husbands on the telephone and would see them again not in years but in weeks. Maybe I was simply envious, on behalf of twenty-year-old Maggie, of women who were not suddenly married to an APO number but participants: however hard that made things, it also meant they could do their fearing of death and injury in much smaller clusters of nights... Well, I told you this wasn't nice. And after a while (sigh of relief) the feeling went away.

But the Israelis saw it very differently: to them, the everyday absence of fathers from home was an enormous factor. So enormous, in fact, that even the religious relented—and the TV stayed on on Saturdays, for the benefit of mothers trying to keep the kiddies occupied without Daddy around to help. Which was part of more of a problem than it sounds like, for most women worked anyway and they'd now added other chores both at home in Daddy's absence and at work, where at the very least, the office was shorthanded. (For nurses, it was such a sizable problem that organized aid was supplied: teenage volunteers were assigned to babysit with the children of nurses and other hospital personnel, so Mama could go to work in outside-school-hours and late-night shifts.) And they were often coping with money shortages too, for the army paid the lost salaries of the citizen soldiers, but only up to a certain amount and only for their major jobs: if your husband's salary was higher than the set maximum, you just lost the difference. So, since most Israeli husbands had more than one job, belt-tightening became part of the increasing dark and cold. It wasn't that anyone would actually go hungry, you understand: there was swift machinery for dealing with such a plight. It was more like—well, Martha and Avi, as a childless couple with professional-level earning capacity on both sides, were probably hardly typical, but the kind of financial beating they took shows what I mean. Because her salary, once intended as savings for the horrendous expense of a trip to the States to see her parents, got moved out of that luxury category; and part of Avi's regular salary, the whole of his second salary, and his extra consultant fees were all blotted out. For a young couple trying to get a head start before the children come, that sort of blow can make a permanent difference in their future.

People like me, and the other "unconnected" Americans, weren't suffering financially (except by choice, via voluntary contributions), but we were all job-hunting as though we were about to starve. Our intense concentration, the way we scrambled after every opening—and there was even an active trade in *rumors* of jobs—resembled a 1930s depression picture. (But of course in actuality it was very different, for what we were all after was not money but a way to be of use: the non-Israeli young men felt even worse than the rest of us, I guess.) Once, when my students told me of openings at the Post Office—high-school students were useful there because they could read non-Hebrew addresses, but they could only work after school, as the authorities felt strongly about not interfering with education—the tip didn't do me any good because you had to be able to read Hebrew and heave packages around too, but I rushed up to the Artzis' and passed the word to Yehuda. Who all but kissed my hand, though an American citizen who had a contract with the university (which was closed, of course) was in a vacation-with-pay position, if he cared to see it that way. Yehuda didn't. And when he got to the Post Office at 7 A.M. the next day, only a few other beneficiaries of this precious tip were already on line. He landed the job and worked there until he got even more useful work teaching high-school English in a development town far down in the desert. (Most of these jobs, since they were not "volunteer work" but replacement of regular workers, had pay attached. Americans usually contributed the extra pay to the war effort.)

What with my physical limitations and my frail Hebrew, I was, as you can imagine, in real trouble in the non-citizens' job-hunting contest. Especially since the only thing I had going for me, my English, was also available from every other "Anglo-Saxon" in town—all of whom also had job connections, family, or other forms of protektsia I lacked. I used what I did have shamelessly: when I saw the Beer-Sheva stringer for the *Jerusalem Post* downtown one morning, I backed him up against the wall of the mashbir and bluntly begged for anything, any teeny inside tip about the possibility of a job anywhere that I could do. I've used my journalistic connections to get jobs before, of course. But this had no relation to long lunches, casual inquiries, and the odd comradely drink, baby—this was out-and-out Gimme, and, since it was not a newspaper job I was looking for, a blatant demand for protektsia-type favoritism: Gimme in the name of the guild, so to speak . . . The poor man, wiping his sweating face, said he himself was just coming from the hospital, in pursuit of a tip that they needed somebody to keep medical records in English. But he hadn't had a chance: by the time he got there, the place was already jammed with "Anglo-Saxons," most of them a lot younger and a few with science degrees, even . . . We stared at each other in mutual hopelessness, and then I let him go—both of us thoroughly ashamed.

I finally got a job, by a combination of luck and having learned by then not to ask questions, just grab and run. It happened when I was hanging around at the university, where I did a small writing chore for the man in charge of its public information (he was one of my few contacts, since I'd done a freelance bit for that office once, shortly after I came to Israel). I'd finished that and started on a self-appointed task, cleaning the type and changing ribbons on the typewriters. By that time, some people at the university had noted the futile job-seeking swirl of misfits like us foreigners, exhausting ourselves in hand-tailored efforts to serve a society that needed every pair of hands, and an attempt was being made to set up the necessary machinery.* The "guidance bureau" was still in the drawing-up-rules stage then, but in Beer-Sheva everybody hears everything: while I was in the office, a phone call came in from a local secondary-school principal in need of a replacement for an English teacher gone to the army (she'd had some kind of interim arrangement, but now, with the new "bureau," she hoped . . .).

Well, as I said, I'd been learning. "I'll take that one myself," I told the secretary, snatching the message slip from her hand. She looked a little doubtful—surely this wasn't the way the new job-finding bureau was supposed to work?—but she knew who I was: thanks to my constantly mailing manuscripts at the central Post Office, everyone in town knew that. And a *soferet* (book writer, fem.) is a person of prestige and surely must have such on-the-way skills as a high-school-teaching certificate? I think what decided the question for her was that she worked in a university, a feudal society in any country—where status Counts and is read from small signs. And the way the information guy had spoken to me, I clearly had status . . . So she let the chit rest in my inky grasp (in the Zionist ethos, that wouldn't be a mark of un-elitehood: the notion that dirty hands constitute a virtue in intellectuals, which many U.S. leftists seem to associate exclusively with Maoism, was a basic tenet of the Zionists they now despise noisily). The phones were ringing, and the poor girl had lots of other things to do . . .

In those job-hunting days, I went around dressed better than had been my daily wont; so when I'd washed my hands and combed my hair, the image in the Ladies Room mirror looked reasonably teacherish to me. Experimenting, I arrived at a facial expression suitable for someone who's taken at least a few Ed courses. And then (still busily thinking myself into the role), I found out who was driving somewhere near the school and soon presented myself in the office there. The principal was delighted: how marvelous of the university to have sent someone so quickly. She conducted me

*Israelis are good at learning from experience. The wastefulness of our every-man-for-himself job-hunting led to arrangements being set up, after the war, for channeling local volunteer labor to where it's needed in wartime.

upstairs to the Teachers Room, a buzzing sanctum full of coffee cups and smoke, and turned me over to my "colleagues."

My heart sank: it looked like the employees' lounge of a factory, full of union members who knew not only their jobs but the ropes. They were all very busy shop-talking (of the conversations I could understand, the only people I ever heard discussing students in that room, though, were a couple of Americans: all other talk seemed to be concerned with time off, new rules, and other entirely employee-oriented affairs) or grading papers, and the bell was surely going to ring soon. A sweet-faced Israeli woman who looked like an easy winner of anybody's Teacher of the Year award loomed out of the haze and showed me the schedule of classes (all in Hebrew, my God!) and told me, in an exquisite Mayfair accent, that wherever it said "Benny" it meant me. Then she was called away . . . I'd have been sunk except for a sudden sight of a vaguely familiar red-bearded face. He turned out to be an American from the university faculty (math or some kind of engineering: in the social context in which I'd met him before, it hadn't mattered which) who'd landed himself a spot here early because his wife knew the principal. He'd been teaching math (long enough, too, to have learned to call it "maths," British-Israeli style). It wasn't too bad, he encouraged me. The main thing was to keep control of the class, that was all: don't try to relate to students, and don't worry about their actually learning anything. He told me that with the look of a parent telling an adolescent child that this may be puppy love and it would be wise to proceed with caution. Suppressed amusement quirked at the corners of his smile, and his eyes were resigned: you have to pass on your wisdom, though you can practically bet you'll be dismissed as an insensitive clod and your wisdom ignored.

That was It—the bell rang, the American math teacher and the Israeli English teacher both disappeared, and I took off for the classroom listed on Benny's schedule. It took me a while to find it, of course; so when I arrived the class seemed pretty well out of control already. *"Boker tov,"* I said authoritatively from the doorway, and got to finish my entrance in almost complete silence: it was the only time in my teaching days there that anything I said received near-perfect attention.* I wrote my name on the blackboard, and then wrote it again in Hebrew to make sure they'd pronounce it right. Then I announced that, since this was an English class, *anachnu*

*Except if you count the day I finally lost my temper with a persistent smart aleck and, one inch (make that a centimeter) from knocking his teeth down his throat, yelled "Out, junior. Scram. You split. NOW." I think I can say in all modesty that there wasn't a single student who failed to learn *some* English that period.

324

medabrim rock b'anglit. I didn't have to think of a way to top that display of mastery of Hebrew (which perhaps would have been more convincing if I'd been able to say "We *will* speak only in English") because a very pretty little girl had risen from the first row and was approaching my desk. "Yes?" I said icily, keeping control of the class.

Trembling, she asked that I pardon her please, Geveret Maggie (natch. Oh well, it wasn't worth making an issue of), but here was the roll-call book . . . I thanked the monitor—who turned out to be a good English student, and the handiest thing in that class—and called the roll with, I'm pretty sure, an effective air of having been just about to do that anyhow. And from there on . . . Well, let me put it this way: I made a real sacrifice for the war effort, I did. If you doubt me, let's hear *you* give the rule for doubling the final consonant to make the simple past of verbs like cancel, travel, refer . . . Without looking it up first, friend. Because I sure didn't get to: the only way I knew what any of Benny's classes was up to (he had a dazzling variety, some of which talked about gerunds and others struggled with "I am, You are, He-She-It is") was to go there, write my name on the board, and hope for an English-speaking monitor. If Benny had a lesson plan, I never knew it, and it would've been in Hebrew anyway. But even without a word on paper, without my ever having seen his face or heard his voice, the absent Benny became a constant and major influence on my life—his every reported word, thought, and mannerism (imitated when I thought I could get away with it) pondered for clues to how he'd managed to control the class and also, it was clear, both be liked and teach at least some of them something. One thing sure, none of Benny's loved ones could have hoped any more passionately than I did for his safe and prompt return from the war.

Which kept going on, I'd better remind you. Because I think I'm making this sound too much like a lot of fun, and it wasn't: any time things lightened for a minute, you'd find that your next step— the one required just to do your job and your shopping and live, there among your neighbors—brought you right smack into the dark again. For a while there, I'd half entertained a notion that the persistent Israeli darkness of outlook, the refusal to celebrate victories, etc., was a kind of cultural neurosis, some sort of sick compulsion to be morose. But, no: if there really are voices talking to you out of the wall, it's not paranoid to hear them. So that the battle at the "Chinese Farm" (an Israeli agricultural-research station right near the Canal, easily overrun by the Egyptians in their surprise crossing and then bloodily retaken by the Israelis about two weeks

325

later) was doubtless a major factor in convincing the Russians that the Egyptians couldn't win and thus was probably the turnaround point of the war; but *I* remember when the Chinese Farm battle was because the son of a woman I knew lost a leg there. He was flown to a hospital in Tel Aviv, and I watered her house plants while she was up there with him.

Or, this may make it even clearer. In one of Benny's classes was a girl named Tamar, a funny-cute kid whose English was poor but audacious and whose class personality—the comic, but the genial, affectionate Carol Burnett kind, not the hostile anti-teacher variety—had probably been determined by the fact that her teeth were parted in the middle: she was small and skinny and she couldn't help grinning a lot, so the tall, sultry (closed-mouth) dignity path was closed to her. I liked Tami (pronounced like "Tommy") and invited her and a couple of others into my house one afternoon when I came across them walking home. And that's how I happened to find out—not then but the next time or the one after that: confiding in teachers doesn't come easily to Israeli youngsters—that Tami's brother was one of the soldiers thought to be in the hands of the Syrians.

Which was about the darkest of dark fates, and if it was a near-obsession with the Israelis, you could hardly blame them. For the Syrians, while blandly informing the Red Cross that they held no Israeli POWs, had exhibited several on their TV. (A gimmick thought to be aimed at making friends in the foreign press corps, but its blatant cruelty backfired even though the correspondents had been carefully chosen, so to speak: some things the Syrians are quite used to proved too much even for reporters considered duly qualified as "progressives.") Besides, there were lots of stories available—some in sickeningly graphic detail, others in the left-to-the-imagination style that may be even worse—about what the Syrians were "known" to do to prisoners. I put them firmly out of my writer-consciousness (getting them out of my personal one was understandably harder) for the same reason I've put "known" in quotes here: however sympathetic I feel, I remain suspicious of atrocity stories. But the people around me had no such fancy journalistic scruples, so they could just go ahead and suffer.

And after a while, so could I. For the Syrians in their first surprise attack had dropped helicopter-borne troops onto the Israeli outpost on 7000-foot Mt. Hermon—Israel's sole ski slope in peacetime, but always a defense essential because of the command of the surrounding territory it gave. Most of the Israeli soldiers inside on Yom Kippur, caught off guard (and being sloppy, too, from some

326

reports: an Israeli officer is said to have growled that somebody should be court-martialed), were killed; but some made their way out and got down the mountain to report that a small group had locked itself into the summit strongpoint and was still holding out. Since they were short of food and water, several attempts were made to relieve them; all failed—understandably, the Syrians were not about to let that mountain go again—one of them with the loss of thirty men, about five times the number to be rescued.

Not all of that was known to the public at the time, but Tami's parents had joined with other kin of similarly missing soldiers and they'd all gone to Jerusalem to demand that something be done; nothing much could be, but they were at least given all the news. Though much of it was bad—and the very worst was statements by captured Syrians that five Israelis had been shot as, weakened by lack of food and water, they finally came out with their hands up. Well, it might not be true: you can't trust Syrian statements (and the Syrian POWs, their captivity being supervised by the Red Cross, had no need to try to please their Israeli captors). The Israeli rescue attempts persisted, and finally, on the very last day of the war before the superpower-imposed ceasefire took hold, they made it—perhaps because by then they, too, could bring in troops by helicopter. And by then half the world's press was running loose all over the battle-fronts. So just about anybody with a press card got to see the corpses of Israeli soldiers, shot while blindfolded and with their hands manacled. And the bodies were mutilated in exactly the fashion described in the "atrocity stories." Among those reporting the find, unequivocally, was the *London Times*, a newspaper I consider at least as anti-Israel as the BBC. (My opinion isn't altered by the fact that the BBC frequently calls, for "outside" analyses, on people from the *Times*.) So scrupulous objectivity, you see, brought me out at precisely the same place occupied all along by Tami and her anguished parents.

(The story of the ceasefire, boiled down, is this: Kissinger flew to Moscow, found Kosygin persuaded that Egypt and Syria were no longer worth risking détente for, and the two K's worked out a ceasefire agreement that was then promptly passed by the UN Security Council—what else, with both the U.S. and the U.S.S.R. behind it? About eight hours before it was supposed to take effect, Kissinger flew into Tel Aviv and told Golda Meir about it. This exercise—it can hardly be called only "pressure"—appeared to effectively snatch victory, and in the crudest possible fashion too, from Israel, then virtually standing with one foot on Egypt's neck and the other on Syria's. However, Israel, though in need of U.S.

arms and thus unable to defy its "friend," knew its enemies: neither Arab nation had ever been known to respect an agreement, the ceasefire contained no arrangements for supervision, and the already cut-off Egyptian 3rd Army in the Canal area would undoubtedly grab at this last chance to try to break out. So the Israelis, going for broke, gathered everything in the country for a major push, and waited. And, at the very first violation of the ceasefire—which came in the Sinai, it appears, but nobody was timing the shots for comparison—the Israelis moved on both fronts, completing the surrounding of the captive Egyptian army in the south and retaking Mt. Hermon up north. Another ceasefire, for October 22, was promptly declared, this one with a supervisory force. And of course the air was filled with demands for a return to the October 21 positions. But the Israelis, with the legality on their side, managed to stand firm against even U.S. pressure.)*

Well, it was that kind of special suffering, arising from the feeling that all the rules of decency were being suspended whenever it came to Israel, that deepened and unquestionably legitimized the darkness of late October and November. When, at the end of the first week of war, American transports carrying much-needed supplies were seen over Tel Aviv, people had wept in the streets and blessed the Americans. (I didn't see that myself. But I did see the great lumbering things plodding across the sky toward Ashdod. That was later, when it was no longer a matter of survival, and I *still* felt like singing "God Bless America.") The public wasn't privy to what Mrs. Meir and Moshe Dayan knew—that Israel, attacked on two fronts, had been down to about ten days' worth of tank ammunition—and maybe to the Israeli public, accustomed to unbelievable bureaucracy, it sounded credible that the Americans couldn't get here sooner because of delays caused by paper shuffling at the Pentagon, as Kissinger was reported to have explained. (The Pentagon promptly said it wasn't true, it was State that was holding up the works. But *that* routine would hardly startle an Israeli citizen into incredulousness either.) Here and there, a few sophisticates wondered why the hell it should take so long. True, Israel is right far away; but it isn't that much farther than Europe—so the long delay, if truly unavoidable, would indicate NATO had something to worry about . . .

But no man-in-the-rechov suspected that it might be because Kissinger was trying to prove to Sadat the sincerity of his friendship.

*Is the old saying, *Fool me once, shame on you; fool me twice, shame on me,* really American in origin? If it is, maybe neither Golda nor Henry had grown up with it. But she sure had the idea; and if he didn't, he learned.

However, Mrs. Meir (who apparently could suspect that) flew to Washington to talk to President Nixon directly—then an unparalleled move for the leader of a nation in the middle of a war—and both House and Senate passed help-Israel measures by such overwhelming majorities that they could hardly be the result of either just the Jewish vote or a sudden rash of Congressional profiles in courage but must actually be reflecting public opinion. And Nixon ordered the stuff sent out at once. God bless America.

However, from the moment it began to look as though Israel really wouldn't get massacred—at least, I tell myself it was only after people abroad felt assured of that—the oil weapon came into play and a kick-Israel epidemic began. Out of all the new African nations that Israel had once gone to help—with practical advice about how to grow food in former wasteland and the loan of advisers who'd had firsthand experience with the hazards of new-nationhood, the Israelis had come with the zeal of good neighbors and agrarian socialists—only one of those who'd accepted with gratitude now refrained from obeying the Arab order to break diplomatic relations with Israel. (Since then, quite a few have in effect reversed themselves, after having discovered that the Arabs wrecked their frail economies just as cruelly anyway.) In Europe, nation after nation followed Britain's lead in denying cooperation to U.S. efforts, and refusals to let the U.S. use territory or fly through somebody's airspace on the way to help Israel were almost unanimous. The guilty-rich* Germans mollified their consciences by tactfully turning their backs, and only when the job was about finished "discovered" what was going on and sternly forbade the U.S. to use their territory for such an outrageous purpose. But the single European exception was Holland, whose government announced that no outsider was going to dictate *their* foreign policy: The Netherlands not only did not break relations with Israel, the Dutch promptly restricted recreational use of gasoline and took to riding their bikes instead of driving. The stiff-necked people who'd once tried to save Anne Frank from the Nazis hadn't changed, God bless 'em.

But by ceasefire time, the situation had gone beyond mere heartbreak to a bewildering sense that we'd somehow all landed

*I know—the Germans (the West Germans, that is) have paid lots of reparations money to Jews who suffered at the hands of the Nazis. But ask yourself how much money, and what could have been done with the money, Thereza's father's thriving factory might well have made in the missing thirty years. And how much similar wealth accrued to Germany in the end at what amounts to very bargain rates indeed—and to the East Germans, for nothing. (To the credit of the West Germans, many of them readily acknowledge the profits that could never be returned in reparations.)

inside *Alice in Wonderland*. Because what Kissinger was trying to get the Israelis to do, at that point, was provide food and water (they'd already sent blood plasma for the wounded) to the surrounded Egyptian 3rd Army. Nobody doubted the men's need, but prisoners taken by Israel are given food, water, and medical care—and the Red Cross had long since been invited in to see that that was true this time, too—so all they had to do was surrender.* Which Sadat couldn't afford to let them do, for domestic reasons: the 3rd Army's plight was still a secret from the Egyptian public, presumably because of fear of their reaction (they'd been led into defeat, in 1967, by Nasser—and they wouldn't take another Nasser). But the press of the world knew it and sooner or later the news would probably seep into Egypt, so Sadat couldn't keep the situation under wraps forever. Thus he was moved to offer a bargain, via Kissinger: in return for having his army turned loose, he would give Israel the names of Israeli POWS held by Egypt.

That this was only what he was supposed to do under the Geneva convention of 1949 (and by long-honored international custom) escaped nobody, yet Kissinger was pressuring the Israeli leaders to accept the deal.† If you wonder how he could have, well, Kissinger's response to the news of Syrian murder and mutilation of prisoners had been that Syria was "using the North Vietnam model." A right cool view, but true enough—and in Israel the public anguish was, as it had not been in the U.S. about POWs in Vietnam, a substantial political force. Thus, with the Israeli leaders facing a public demand to do anything, anything at all, for news of its sons, you could—if you were Kissinger—see that if leaned on enough by the U.S. too, the Israelis would have to surrender. And then Sadat would save face and would owe the U.S. for it, and another blow would have been struck for world peace. See?

The last thing the Israel government needed, right then, was more talk at home about those prisoners. But it's a free country (which is a great handicap when playing chess with Kissinger) so the government couldn't stop something happening that set out, for me at least, the cruel absurdities in maximum poignancy. It turned up one day on the half-hour English news broadcast, where a reporter, as had often been done with controversial issues, was buttonholing English-speaking Israelis to ask them what they

*One Israeli offer was to open the road back to Cairo: the 3rd Army could then, by simply leaving their arms behind, go home for food and water. It sounded fair enough to me, considering who was on top. But of course it didn't even get debated.
†Actually, some sources say the prisoner list wasn't even part of the deal originally and had to be demanded by the Israelis. Kissinger must have seen, though, that Sadat would have to give that much, whether it was part of the first offer or not.

thought of the proposed deal. One of the interviewees, in a minute or less, put everything in starkly simple human terms: But how can this be, asked a woman—a lady-like voice, speaking in the precise English of educated Israelis. For her son, now presumed to be in the hands of the Egyptians (though of course nobody knew for sure) had been a baby in Jerusalem in 1948, when the city was under seige by the Arab Legion. There was no milk for her baby then, she said—the voice trembling a little, but still clear and only sad—and not even enough water for the starving civilians huddled in the Jewish Quarter. But nobody, not the Red Cross or the UN or anybody except, eventually, Israel itself, did anything to feed her son then: and nobody could tell her who, if anybody, was feeding him now. And yet here was the whole world worrying about professional soldiers—no babies, no old people, just young men who only needed food and water in order to be able to fight some more. She didn't want the Egyptian army to suffer: they were somebody's sons too, so let them go home and live in peace, please God . . . But she just couldn't understand, the woman said humbly—she sounded apologetic, as if she thought she should have paid more attention (I've heard that tone at PTA meetings, from women nervous about talking up in public and afraid everybody's going to say *Now you show up with your complaints! Why didn't you come to the last meeting?*). Why were there always different rules for Israel? . . . Her time running out and the tears apparently close, she said desperately that things never seemed to change. Would anybody out there ever begin to care about her son too?

Her question* hung on the air for a fraction of a second, and then another citizen was being asked for his reaction to the U.S. proposal. Nobody tried to answer the woman. But her voice—frightened, controlled, wondering, free of hatred and not even willing to be angry—so haunted me that maybe it always will.

And it spoiled, by the way, the choice bit of fun that emerged from the Through the Looking Glass goings-on, a chance to contemplate the plight of the BBC. Which had been faithfully reporting things the Egyptian way: there was no surrounded army, see. (Anybody in Egypt who had a mind to get around Sadat's controlled press wouldn't get help from the BBC, would they.) But there was a fatal difference between the two now: Sadat didn't have to tell the folks back home he was now negotiating for that army's release, whereas the BBC could hardly ignore the travels of the U.S. Secretary of State, not to mention the Red Cross, the UN, and the whole

*I mean no irreverence by this, but doesn't it make you think of another—*How long, O Lord?*

megillah. So all of a sudden there they were, in what even they might be willing to describe as a difficult position, and I could just imagine the hair-tearing in London: What in the world do we do now, chaps? Well, what they did was bet on blandness again—with incredible *chutzpah,* the BBC proceeded to report the negotiations for, and afterward the whole business of UN convoys, etc., feeding and watering that non-existent captured Egyptian army! Delicious. And, laughing last, I could've laughed best—if only I hadn't kept hearing that agonized lady-like voice in my head.

And if only, winding in and out of every day, there weren't always sudden glimpses. Like Tami, still being the comic but developing a too-determined, almost professional edge that made her less good at it. Her father was in Paris as part of a delegation whose fare was being paid by one of those unofficial groups stirred to life by the Syrian cruelties—e.g., actors in England, writers in France—to make in-person appeals to Something-or-other meeting there (sorry, but I'd forgotten to be a reporter and recorded it like an Israeli: it didn't matter which marble palace, because whoever lived in it wasn't going to do a damn thing anyway). Her mother had broken down, not all the way yet but she was zombie-ing around in a fuddle of sedatives; and Tami, who at first had been sent to school, over her own objections, in a proud family insistence on life-as-usual, was now skipping classes to take care of the little kids at home . . .

And then there were my own three pet students: as seniors, Estie and Elie and Amir had been allowed to skip school for special group duties in certain crunch situations. At one point, those included picking carnations for a moshav that had a contract to sell them abroad (The moshavim and kibbutzim are predicated, of course, on the labor of every member, man and woman. So, especially in the case of the smaller ones around Beer-Sheva, the departure of the men when crops were to be harvested was as devastating as a plague of locusts or a flood to farmers elsewhere.) It was hard work, Estie said, but enjoyable—she'd come then to my house, late in the evening, to tell me they'd be down in the desert every day for a while and so couldn't make our English-conversation date. That was okay, I assured her: what they were doing was of importance for their country (which is putting it mildly, all right: the carnations were even more important than food, because you can cut the food rations but not the need for foreign currency) and the least I could do was give them extra time whenever they could get back to their English lessons.

But, a couple of days later, all three of them turned up in the afternoon anyway, and Estie presented me with a great bunch of carnations. I hesitated, embarrassed, but then did my duty: it was very sweet of them, I said, and I was happy to have the flowers; but it was wrong to have taken, even from the kindest motives, any part of what represented a major factor in Israel's economy . . . The three youngsters were looking at each other sadly while I was talking, but they're well-mannered—so they let me finish my lecture before they told me to enjoy, enjoy. Because the carnations would have gone to waste anyway: when they arrived at the fields that morning, the flowers they'd collected the day before were still lying around because the trucks that were supposed to take the whole now-withering mass to the airport never showed up. So the high-school seniors had been sent back to Beer-Sheva . . . What could I say? Well, listen, I told their closed faces, things like that simply happen in wars, when choices have to be made and always cost *something*. When a silly-sounding order to a single squad may make enormously good sense to some larger strategy. So it's necessary to imagine reasons you can't see . . . Yes, they said politely, willing to let teachers teach.*

Or sometimes the whole story, what all the defeats and victories and then negotiations and agreements were all about—and the answer to the recurring question of just who *were* the good guys, if any—could get handed to you in a single everyday event. Like Martha and Avi coming by to say hello when Avi had a weekend leave. He looked handsome in his uniform,† particularly as he'd grown a neat spade-shaped Machiavelli-type beard (which didn't last too long after the war, come to think of it. Maybe Martha didn't share my opinion). Avi's unit was about to be transferred, but he didn't know where yet: they were hoping for the Jordan border but they might get Africa anyhow, he told me, sipping appreciatively at my best whiskey. (Nothing too good for our boys—I'd even gone directly into the pantry to get it, since I didn't want to waste his precious leave-time on my lizard-warning ritual.)

The preference puzzled me: things were quite quiet by then on the Egyptian front, but if Jordan should be successfully pressured to relieve her allies' plight by a sudden stab across the Jordan, wouldn't that be a less safe place to be? Well maybe, Avi said. But he

---

*This one, though faking it at the time, may have been right: figuring back, it's possible that was the day everything on wheels was being scooped up to make the final push in "Africa." So it could be that the drivers were right then trundling the flower-delivery trucks across pontoon bridges over to the west side of the Canal.

†When I was pregnant and my uniformed husband came home on leave, a bit of dialogue from a then-popular Broadway comedy—"Him in his uniform and me in my condition," the girl says wryly—set us laughing. I thought of it again when Martha and Avi came in that day, but they wouldn't have recognized the line. Middle age can be lonely sometimes.

333

figured he'd be better off taking a chance of getting shot than catching bilharzia.

You see what I mean by glimpses? Because now that I've got all this hindsight information about all the fabulous weaponry, the Soviet missiles that had never before been seen in combat (95 percent of Israel planes lost in the war succumbed to what is now said, by the *London Times* among others, to have been the most complete missile system in history, a combination never likely to be massed again on such a small, single front)—all that technical data that I'm very damn glad I didn't know at the time—I see that probably the clearest difference between the Israelis and their enemies lay in what was behind Avi's half-humorous remark in my salon. For when the Israeli troops first crossed over to the lush country (said to be the "Land of Goshen" of the Bible) on the other side of the Canal, the contrast with their own forbidding desert land awed everybody. But the next thing they noticed was the miserable condition of the *fellahin* there ("I never imagined people could live like that," a young Israeli soldier wrote to his mother). Then the realities began surfacing: word came home to Israel that Zahal was in more danger from Egypt than from Egypt's armies, for the local hygienic conditions were incredible—and though the boys might be persuaded not to drink the water, making sure they wouldn't bathe in it was, considering the dirt and heat and weariness, next to impossible. Yet that would be all it would take to pick up any of a large number of thriving parasites (including, apparently, the one that causes bilharzia: Avi's unit, scheduled for "Africa," must have been given preparatory lectures).

Well, lights burned late in labs in Israel. And then, zippety-zip, a team from Hebrew University was down in the Sinai injecting everybody with a new disobedient-soldier-proof serum against the hazards of life in Egypt. That's what seems to me so significant. For it's only in TV dramas that the scientist comes up with Eureka-juice while the clock ticks away suspensefully, so this coming through so fast in the clinch means somebody in Israel must have been studying these things all along. And, true, wartime emergencies tend to zippety-zip things up a lot—but the fact is that Egypt, which does have the problem (while bilharzia is hardly a household word in Israel) and also has educated people,* had done nothing effective about it, zippety-zip or otherwise, for its own *fellahin*.

*If you own stock in one of the lusher oil corps., you get handsome booklets describing, with beautifully colored photos, how much love and money has been expended in providing worthy Arabs with higher ed. And of course, we have the Arab exchange-student shtick, which now gets such fraudulent use in the U.S. that a university backlash seems to be forming against it, at last.

A similar example (though this one also exemplifies the international screw-the-Jews game) was the Gaza strip, which Egypt made the mistake of using for a jumping-off point in the war in 1967. The Israelis moved in, at first giving medical care only for humanitarian reasons, to Egyptian soldiers found wandering half-dead of thirst in the desert. (One of the now-generals, a hero in the Egyptian army, is celebrated because he *didn't* run off and desert his men in that war, by the way. Admirable. But it'd never make him a special case in Israel.) Then the thing snowballed, and pretty soon the Israelis—in their own self-interest as well as for humanitarian motives, since epidemics don't recognize boundary lines—were coping with the results of the squalor the Arabs there lived in. Israel did, by any objective public-health standard, a marvelous job; but it also conscientiously reported on the status of Gaza to the World Health Organization, which members of the UN are supposed to do. That turned out to be a mistake: the Egyptians had reported no tuberculosis in the area to the WHO, so the published figures went abruptly from zero to whatever total the honest Israeli medicos considered still unarrested cases. And the result was Arab propaganda charges that the Israeli aggressors, doubtless bent on genocide, had introduced TB into the Gaza strip: see, here are the WHO statistics to prove it. (I haven't trusted a WHO figure since.)

Well, what both of those add up to is pretty clear: the *"Machar"* of the Israeli song, that peaceful tomorrow when all the peoples of the region will live together and help each other, is not just talk; it has solid work behind it, in hopeful preparation, and genuine gifts to offer. That alone, whatever exasperations the Israelis also have to offer—and they *can* be maddening—makes the persistent Arab war-making impossible to see as anything understandable by the exercise of reason.* Some kind of abstract evil, of dementia, or whatever is your pet way of explaining the irrational destructive impulse. For when the two societies are thus glimpsed side by side, no Israeli sin seems grave enough to outweigh the difference between the long-time reverence for life visible on one side of the Canal and the contempt for it that has prevailed on the other.†

However, as 1973 darkened toward its end, I wasn't thinking

---

*Anyone who believes the cry of "Palestinian homeland" lies within the province of reason should try explaining why Egypt and Jordan—who could have set up homelands any time before June 1967 in Gaza and the West Bank, respectively, but didn't—should six years later find it worth starting a war for.

†Unlike Nasser, Egypt's Sadat does seem to have some comprehension (now, anyway) that maybe Egyptians don't really have to serve as troops in other Arab nations' hate-wars. If his populace backs him up, it's possible that the old Arab game of fighting Israel till the last Egyptian isn't going to be played again.

long thoughts like that, and I doubt that many people in Beer-Sheva were either. If I had to pick a single example of the way we *were* thinking and feeling in that death-haunted, tear-laden time, I'd choose the night of the concert postponed from October but then firmly rescheduled for a night in November—when the buses in town still stopped running after the evening rush hour and most people's lives were still so hard you'd swear they wouldn't give a damn about woodwind quintets. It was also the coldest night we'd yet had. Hilda and her two sons picked me up (no, not in a car: you called for people just to walk with them through the black night), the boys frankly shapeless with wrappings but Hilda glittering with earrings and brooches and scarves and anything else that could be fancy without costing warmth. I was even wearing my elegant evening sweater—only it was the bottom layer under two more utilitarian numbers. And pajama pants under my slacks, and two pairs of socks inside my lined boots. This regalia was topped with my shin-length winter coat, a New Look in Massachusetts in about 1971, and a woolen cap from a ski "shoppe" in Colorado; I thought the latter's blue-green color festive, but I didn't care to risk the mittens that went with it so I took my Israeli flannel-lined leather gloves instead.

Practically everybody in town was there, it seemed—all the women glittering from the neck up and bulkily bundled below. There were more men than I'd expected, because the newer groups of immigrants, American and Argentinian and Russian, all had men who weren't in the army. And there was a heavy sprinkling of doctors from the hospital—always well represented among the town's music-lovers anyway—plus an assortment of uniformed men who happened to be off duty that night.

Lord, was that place cold! The great barn of a hall, the one built by the original settlers, is rather like an enlarged version of the "spring house" in which butter used to be kept during a rural Maine summer: you could probably keep an elephant carcass nicely in the Beer-Sheva model. (The new Conservatory, my own chief civic pride, was of course not finished—and who knew, now, whether it would ever be?) I'd had some foolish notion that I might take my coat off during the concert, but that got junked during the first Divertimento; then I also discovered it wasn't a great idea to take my gloves off; and finally I ended up alternating my gloved hands, keeping one over my nose and the other warming up in my coat pocket. The musicians were a little better off, for two kerosene heaters had been provided on stage. The first violinist warmed his hands at one of them, but it didn't sound as if that had quite done the job; and the woodwinds seemed to me to be showing audible

336

effects of the cold . . . Not that there were any complaints, though: the packed audience—you could count the house handily via the visible puff of exhaled breath hovering above each seat—listened the way musicians must dream of in the long hours of practice. In November in Beer-Sheva, nearly everybody has a cold; but there was hardly a sniffle or cough to be heard. If the players had had any reluctance to schlep down to the Negev in midwinter, they soon knew better. For surely, it was a memory for them to cherish, that funny flat, slapping sound of hundreds of pairs of gloved hands applauding as if they'd never stop. The bowing musicians, obviously moved—a French horn looked as though he might cry—gave us encore after encore, playing as if Mozart (a man who knew plenty about living in the dark and the cold, come to think of it) had just handed them the finished score.

Even by intermission time, the lifting of spirits, the slash of light in the darkness, had already begun to appear. It was all greetings, some pretty emotional: people who hadn't seen each other since the war started asked low-voiced questions, sighed with relief, and began to smile. One of the acquaintances I met was Ruth, the house mother from the mercaz klita; her husband was in the army but okay, and she'd brought along a visitor who was staying with her, a woman from Holland. As Ruth introduced us, speaking in English of course, the key word was apparently overheard (much of that audience was English-speaking, either natively or, like the doctors, because they'd had to learn it for professional reasons). For, while I was still shaking hands with the lady from Holland—and saying foolishly, "Welcome to Israel," perhaps as a way of telling her the *Thank you, thank you* I felt like saying—I could hear "Holland" going around the lobby. Because of my Washington experience, plus the recent months of being Mrs. America in my neighborhood, probably nobody there knew better than I did how embarrassing it is to be forced into being a national symbol; and for all I knew, this particular woman might even have opposed her government's support of Israel (not to mention the most memorable boon: they sent us trucks, *with* drivers!). So I quite understood the pink flush rising along her cheekbones. And I certainly knew *I* was in no way a legitimate spokesman for Israel. But I still wanted to say *Tell them back home, we're so grateful* . . .

Everybody had the same impulse: people were pressing in from all sides, wanting to meet or even just to see the woman said to have come from Holland. Some of them ventured remarks in English—"Vun from your great country is velcome alvays in Israel," said a voice from over her shoulder, in a heavy accent and absurd pomp. The Dutch lady said "Thank you" but began to look alarmed: the Israeli concept of personal space takes a little getting used to anyway,* and these people were really crowding in. It was pathetic, embarrassing... "Everyone is so grateful to The Netherlands, you see," I told her, ridiculously slipping into the proper diplomatic usage. ("Holland" is what I usually say, and so do English-speaking Israelis—except Abba Eban, I guess.) There I was, appointing myself ambassador again, I thought wretchedly. Or maybe, worse, a social worker explaining the natives so she wouldn't think them just pushy...

Ruth had also seen the problem. She proceeded to extricate her friend from the crowd, with the help of Hilda—who also is a native Dutch speaker, and I heard her say something to the visitor. So, on the way home, I asked Hilda what she'd told the lady from Holland.

"I said 'Thank you,' of course. And that she should tell the people at home, Israel is most grateful to them all. What else should I say?" She gave me one of her boy-are-you-dumb-sometimes looks. Which are pretty wilting, and Hilda knows it, so she patted my bundled shoulder with her thickly gloved hand to take some of the curse off. Then she wrapped her muffler around her mouth and we shuffled off into the night for the long walk home. During which there was almost no conversation, but I kept thinking wistfully how nice it would be to be as sure of everything, including myself, as Hilda.

So yes, I think that evening does show dejected, rejected, and suffering Beer-Sheva in the dark and the cold. And don't let anybody tell you love really warms anything, for even though the world couldn't love us on account of loving Arab oil more there was plenty of love around, all kinds, at the concert—but it was cold as hell anyway. Still, love does do *something*: if my nose got just as frozen as it would have anywhere else, something as basic to my health as the circulation of my blood was nevertheless benefited that night.

I am most grateful to them all. What else should I say?

*People waiting behind you to enter a bus stand so close that you get the impression they're pushing. They aren't, usually—they're just used to taking up less room in the world than Americans, I guess.

From the diary: 19
Three wartime vignettes (Oct.–Nov.)

Three scenes you could maybe use to show them back home what it's like in a war when there's nothing to do but hang on, together or separately, and try to keep your head straight.

I. Rob was here. We ate dinner and washed the dishes, and then played anagrams (a real concession by him, because I always win and he hates that). He'd brought his portable radio, which can be plugged in so I could save my batteries—it's getting harder and harder to buy batteries now—and by the time we'd listened to the "Voice of America," it was late for him to be starting the long hike home. Besides, he was probably as uptight as I was: the distance between the tear-laden air around us and the cheery m.c.-type voices from Washington can get a little hard to take. So he decided to stay over. I made up the sofa-cot in the salon and we both went to bed.

And then it started, the sound that's been tightening my nerves every night—the helicopters bringing wounded up from Sinai to the hospital. I was sitting up in bed, trying to read, and with the trissim blackout-closed it was too warm to close my bedroom door, so I saw Rob go by on the way to the bathroom. But when he didn't say anything about the sound overhead, neither did I, in case he didn't know what it was: his apartment is at the other side of the hospital grounds, and maybe over there they don't hear the flights.

He went back to bed—apparently ready for sleep, because he turned off the big lamp in there. I kept mine on: it couldn't possibly disturb him, and I couldn't possibly sleep. But neither could I get up and roam around, not without waking Rob. So I had to stay where I was, propped in bed and trying not to listen for the next copter-load of hurt boys. Trying not to think of the lines from somebody's forgotten poem—"Somewhere out there/A man died for me today"— that kept creeping into my head. And trying to swallow the great load of grief filling my throat.

I don't know how long it took me to realize that those odd soft sounds from inside were Rob, tiptoeing around in the kitchen: since he had the advantage of occupying the salon, he didn't have to pretend, only to be quiet. Gratefully, I got up and went to join him.

He knew about the helicopters, all right. We got a drink and then turned out the lights and pulled up the trissim. The night air was soothing—until the next copter came beating by. Not particularly noisy, and invisible in our own patch of black sky, but there like a heartbeat in the dark. Rob and I talked, but it wasn't exactly talking: what we were really doing, sitting there in our helpless dark, was to talk as the dry heaves are to vomiting. We were not-crying together, that's what.

II. It's getting chilly enough so people now welcome a chance to be in the sun. And you can't let little children play outside the courtyard alone, as the street is too trafficky, so there was a small group of mothers out there with them this morning when I went to buy cigarettes at the kiosk. I said "Shalom" and so did they, but none of them speaks English so I just went on across the street. When I started back, an army jeep was pulling into the curb over there, two soldiers already climbing out. For a minute it looked rather like the aftermath of a near-accident, with the mothers gathered into a knot and several of them holding on to their toddlers or reining them in by overall straps. But it couldn't be that one of the children had run into the street: there'd been no squeal of tires, no outcries—and when I crossed over to that side, one of the soldiers was talking to one of the women and neither of them was angry. In fact, she was giving him directions, it sounded like.

Then some more clues began to add up. Like, the soldiers carried neither packs nor weapons, and if they had to ask directions, they couldn't be coming home on leave. And like that the group was becoming larger, the newcomers people like me, without children: women going with shopping bags to the macaulet were pausing on their way, as if to watch—but nothing was visibly going on except the soldiers walking through the courtyard to the next house and then halting before the third entry to look up at the number. And finally, there was a decisive absence of laughter or joshing: the soldiers had dodged a tricycle without saying something teasing to its rider, the woman giving directions had not smiled at the soldier or he at her—and in fact, they had almost not been looking at each other at all . . .

So I knew, I guess, before a new arrival, looking scared, asked "Le mi?" (To whom?) Somebody said Geveret This and then somebody else said no, her husband was b'beit so it must be Geveret That. We all stood there in the warming sun, our eyes on the empty entry where the soldiers had gone in. The mothers called children to them in soft, anxious voices and then held them there, wiping noses and smoothing hair and tugging shirts down—anything, it was clear, to be touching the child for a moment . . . Suddenly I envied them terribly.

340

I took my cigarettes on home. But when I got there, all I did was stare at my framed photograph of Debbie, smiling broadly around the toothless frontal gap of the six-year-old, and Maggie, smaller and less certain, her hand twiddling with the end of a pale pigtail. Both of them perfectly safe with Mommy and Daddy in the U.S.A.—where I couldn't touch them but messengers like those I'd just seen couldn't either.

III. First full session of our English-conversation class since the enemy attack, though I had a few words with Estie and Elie and Amir, singly or in various combinations, in hurried moments in the interval. I've mentioned here how they always seem to sort of elect a spokesman for important pronouncements, and I'm pretty sure it was as spokesman that Elie told me, during one of those brief encounters, "In only one year, we could have been already soldiers. But we were born one year too late, and that is our misfortune." Even if he hadn't concluded with "It is useless to be angry," I'd have recognized it as a consensus: back then, when everybody was aching for an active part in the war, the kids had talked over their sad lot and come up with this hard fact to be faced. I remembered that it had been Elie—but speaking then for himself—who'd once (see Chapter 9) complained of military service as a useless interruption in your life. I didn't say anything about that, only that when there was time we'd talk about the war . . .

But I rather had it in mind today when, seating myself in my rocking chair (my "command post" for these seminars), I invited discussion on the changes we'd seen, in ourselves and the people around us, since we last met. It was an obvious opening but no less satisfactory therefor, loose and general and leaving them free to go in any direction. The one I assumed they'd go in was political: the elections, postponed from October, are scheduled for December 31, and there's been a lot of talk. What it amounts to, summarized crudely, is strong feeling against Ma'arach, the Labour coalition headed by Golda Meir, because of charges of mismanagement during the war—and possibly because of a general desire for change, since they've been in power for as long as there's been a state—but also a marked reluctance to get instead Menachem Begin, who heads the opposing Likud coalition. So voters have, in effect, no place to go. Which predictably has caused a lot of third-party-type activity.*

*Well, I had the right idea, but it took until still another election and a third party that hadn't yet got started in 1973. Nobody questions, though, that the loss of Labour votes to that third party had a large part in electing Begin's Likud coalition eventually.

341

Politics was the direction a group of American teenagers would have taken the discussion in, I think. And, these youngsters did too, for a few minutes: Shulamit Aloni, one of the more experienced women politicians, is attracting some attention here with her Civil Rights Party (a woman I know is even working for her campaign. And what with the straightforward women's-bloc vote, I'd guess Aloni will get a couple of seats) and the kids seemed interested in some of the American touches in her campaigning. Like passing out leaflets outside places of employment. Was it true, Amir asked, that American Presidents stood outside factories, the way people said they'd seen on TV?

I said it was, and explained about the difference under the U.S. system, where, though you may vote a party line if you choose to, you elect a regional representative rather than a party representative to Congress and the President is chosen by popular (except for a complication called the Electoral College, which I forbore explaining) rather than party vote. Then I told them about an intensive New Hampshire primary I'd once covered, with freezing 6 A.M. handshakes and personal appeals by the candidate... While I was talking, I noticed with some amusement a kind of shift in my audience. For it was Amir who'd asked the question, but it was Elie who was apparently seeing himself in the picture I was describing: he stood over by the front window, idly playing with the cord of the trissim, and the look on his face reminded me of when Phil was seven years old and played left field for the Boys' Club—and I would see that he was dreaming, out there, of being Joe Di-Maggio... Well, I certainly don't know enough about Israeli elections to be making pronouncements, but I don't think Elie would be unrealistic if he did entertain fantasies: he's a charmer with wit and a loving heart, and that's apt to prove a winning combination on anybody's hustings.

That's the way I was thinking, anyway, when it all began to blow up in my face. Because Estie (did she see the same thing I did, over there at the window?) said things here were very different from America, and not just in the way elections were conducted. She spoke sadly, and Amir followed her bitterly: Israelis, he said, would do better not to compare themselves with other countries, since they could never have what people in other countries had.

That was something of a shocker. First, because of course what Israel was all about was the desire to be a nation among nations: that was what the sunbrowned, energetic, pragmatic idealists who founded their country had dreamed of. But secondly—well, I don't know how to say this, it's too appalling. What emerged,

342

in that opening and the conversation flowing from it, was a picture too frightening for me to have been able to see it at first. For what I was dealing with was in fact a group of kids who, at seventeen, had been looking at the possibility of their own death. And you couldn't blame them: the view of the future, from that afternoon in Beer-Sheva—a dusty little frontier town in a poor little country that much of the world was busy cold-shouldering if not actually kicking in the teeth—held no guarantees and not even really great odds that these kids would make it to thirty. Or maybe even twenty-five, since the Soviet Union was already rearming the Arab nations (and the U.S. was apparently willing to, too), who seem to have international permission to make war at will and without blame.

I couldn't stand it. So, when I could manage it, I said lightly that prophets of doom always sounded convincing because if you predict disaster long enough and steadily enough, sooner or later one will happen and then you can say See, I told you so . . .

"He tsodecket," Elie said, looking across the room at the others. It means "She's right." And it meant both that I had made a small dent, and also that I couldn't win. For I understood those Hebrew words only because, by lucky chance, I'd happened to have had them translated for me just the night before. But there was no reason to think I would know them, and they don't say anything my students can't say in English: Elie, normally the one for whom English comes most easily, had deliberately spoken in Hebrew in order to make an argument without publicly breaching the group's united front. Something had been decided, a conclusion reached, I saw. And I had no direct entrée to it.

Not even, it turned out promptly, an indirect one. For Estie shook her head at Elie—not No to the argument, but Don't—and then looked anxiously at Amir. He did what she apparently feared he would: his head lowered bullishly, Amir burst out with a harsh objection that "for we in Israel," none of this mattered. The truth was, he went on (the voice thick and heavy, his English gnarly again for lack of recent practice) that they were Jews and the whole world wanted to kill Jews. As it always had wanted to, and always would . . . Nothing about the way he spoke indicated discovery; he didn't even look to see the others' reaction. Because clearly he already knew it, and was only reminding them of the "truth" they might be forgetting.

So he didn't see their half-ashamed, acknowledging faces. But I did. What should I say to them? I could offer evidences that it wasn't true, for Israel has not been without its comforters—not only organizations and ad hoc groups but aching, ardent letters from individuals in a dozen countries, sitting in their homes and painstakingly

343

writing (to the Jerusalem Post, *usually: as the only newspaper in English, it's where foreigners write*)* You are brave, good people and We are with you—*sometimes with passionate shame, too, for the actions of their governments . . . Still, the fact is, they cannot stand between Amir and the latest billion-dollar missiles that may come seeking him next year, or in two or three years. So, while it's indecent that decency should be only a tidbit, that's what it is. (But tidbits are for children, and are these children, even if they are only seventeen years old?)*

I could tell them what I think myself is the truth, that some people do hate Jews but what most people want is not to kill anyone, just to be warm and comfortable and let alone—and that that in itself kills a lot of people, but not especially Jews. However, what chance has the voice of reason, particularly when it has something so un- shiny to say? And what chance do you ever have to convince any adolescent, even one not afraid of being killed in tomorrow's war, that he isn't the center of the universe?

Well, I don't know whether I did the right thing. But I looked at a red-haired boy with pimples who'd added up the score and come out with total doom, and I thought of a way to say (to begin with, so maybe I could get to say those other things) It's too soon to add everything up, you're still just a boy. *So what I did was, I corrected his grammar.* "'For us in Israel,' Amir," *I said in a voice that turned his outburst into just one of the arguments brought up in discussion.* "The pronoun is the object of the preposition, you see."

I won that little bit, anyhow: he lifted his head, eyed me blankly, and repeated "For us in Israel" *obediently. And then I said the other things I had to say, and maybe they listened; maybe Elie did, anyway, and he can be pretty persuasive. So victory is possible, for I have nature going for me too, I guess—surely even adolescents don't want to believe in their own doom? Not when it's real, anyway, without romance and with blood . . .*

But, since they've gone, I am sick at heart. For why aren't those three, the heirs of hard times and pioneer struggles, just as entitled as Americans to believe in change and progress and can-do because they've seen that it can happen? It didn't take Americans two hundred years to start feeling that way—all it took was the first generation that hadn't been exiled or transported from English jails or pushed around somewhere by kings. And twenty-odd years was all it had taken to do the same for these Israeli children. Until Yom Kippur

---

*A notable exception was a letter from a Danish lawyer, wry and full of swift grown-up truths—it may well have been one of the war's best pieces of writing—to the Israeli columnist Ephraim Kishon, who writes in Hebrew but is widely translated abroad.

came, and they saw what they saw. And now they're snatched back into the synagogue lamentations, the rhythm of wail and appeal and dark convictions about forever—among the old men with a fondness for ghettos, because they wall out as well as in, who are always waiting to say See, we told you, you can't trust anybody except Jews.

Dammit, these youngsters don't belong to ancient history and lost temples and old hurts and the stink of doom, they belong to their own sundrenched and justice-loving Now land. They're entitled to the membership their fathers won for them, among us. I don't care about God's covenants. But we had one, we men of good will who care about each other, for God reasons or no reasons—and it's supposed to include anybody alive who's willing to take a fair share in the working and the caring. Have we now let graceful Elie, tender Estie, thoughtful Amir be stolen away from us? If so, we have connived—in the name of oil or sloppy thinking or maybe just plain willingness to be seduced by the ignorant and selfish and rich—at the cruelest theft in mankind's whole cruel history.

This, what I saw this afternoon, is the most terrible thing I've seen happening in the war.

16 ɐ Ring Out the New

If you keep in mind that the Jewish year usually starts in September (on Rosh HaShana) and Yom Kippur is only about ten days into it, you'll see why I didn't feel much like ringing that particular new year *in*. For in Beer-Sheva it began grim and got grimmer: as the end of my own year* approached, so did a conviction of being at the bottom of a deep, smooth-sided hole. I kept remembering a marvelous cartoon from about 1960: it featured two guys chained hand and foot in just such a spot, with long beards and clothing reduced to rags making it clear that they'd been down there for a very long time; they were obviously unable to move a muscle—yet one of them was saying earnestly, "Now here's my plan . . ." That drawing used to delight me (so, at around the same time, did Sinatra singing "High Hopes," a then-popular song with a lighthearted never-say-die message) because I guess I *stamm* dig examples of human indefatigability. Only, by mid-December of 1973, I was short of delight and the cartoon was beginning to seem exclusively a satire on the human proclivity for self-delusion. Possibly that was because I couldn't even kid myself that I had a plan. For wherever I looked, no prospect pleased—and if man is only confused and not really vile, that doesn't make things better but just sadder.

*Back in the Washington days when I was a housewife, my own family's and the Congress's rhythms stirred me to the (quite independent) conclusion that September is when the new year "really" starts. But when I found myself living in a society that had things so arranged, I *dahfke* couldn't get used to it. Like, I forgot to buy a new calendar in September. And I got sad at Christmas and positively morose on New Year's Eve, just as if I were still in the U.S.

Well, there *was* one light instant, in late November when the long hassle about prisoners of war half-concluded with the return from Egypt of 241 Israeli POWs. The Red Cross plane bringing them home touched down to bouquets of flowers and hugs and the band playing in the bright air—a teeny-tiny moment of national gala. (No matching one in Egypt, though: their 8301 returned POWs were slipped quietly into military airfields where the homecoming would be kept secret from the citizenry at large. And though Mrs. Meir had barely managed not to compromise the dignity of a head of state by weeping openly when she greeted the boys, Sadat had no such control problem—he was reportedly somewhere else when his troops arrived. A student in need of a capsule example of the differences between Israeli and Egyptian societies probably couldn't go wrong with that single contrast.) But many of the returning chyellim went directly to hospital, and the marks of captivity were noticeable on even the unwounded.* So, since we all knew Egypt was a "moderate" Arab state—certainly as compared with Syria, where the fate of captured Israelis was still unknown—the joy was there, but not unconfined.

Heigh-ho, though, that was the *happy* day . . . What filled the rest were things like the "voluntary" war loan clipped from paychecks, which affected all workers (including foreigners employed by an Israeli university or hospital, and thus most of my "Anglo-Saxon" friends); in addition, the truly voluntary contributions made or pledged in October were now beginning to bite. And the mobilization was of course still on, which meant that personal finances continued to suffer among those accustomed to a paycheck fatter than the Zahal allowance: e.g., Avi was still in uniform, with the effect on the family finances that I described in Chapter 15. So everybody was getting mighty poor. Savings became daily-bread money, large purchases were postponed indefinitely, and the more frilly budget categories— Recreation, Entertainment, etc.—tended to vanish altogether. And that was *before* the cost of electricity jumped 30 percent, right in the season of short, cold, electricity-consuming days! That blow swatted just about everybody, even those like me whose income was out of the paycheck-notchers' reach or people like Fran and Rob, who got clipped but had leeway (as singles living on faculty salaries that could support at least two). The government's explanation was a

*A few Israelis reported incidents of Egyptian officers trying to stop their men from beating the POWs—and one boy said an officer who failed made a point of coming around later and apologizing to him. (These accounts appeared in the newspapers: the Israel government has never been interested in encouraging anybody to hate the enemy.) However, most of the chyellim weren't so lucky, and some had been very unlucky indeed.

desperate need to save energy*—which meant that even if the new rate per kilowatt hour was financially bearable, you were stuck with a moral obligation. And that's *really* tough. Because so long as you can tell yourself wotthehell-Mehitabel, it's only money (and I'll economize on something else, I will, I will), you can switch on your heater. But for a moral obligation, you keep on shivering.

And let us not leave out of this category of gloom an ongoing no-joy proposition, the frenzied public squabbling that has been aptly tagged "the wars of the Jews." Those can take off from nearly any topic and happen at just about any time in Israel, but right then there was spectacular Yom Kippur ammunition—the kind of charges and countercharges that the columnist Kishon summed up as *Yossi dropped the keys in the Canal.* (Kishon is generally dismissed as a lightweight by Israeli intellectuals, so I don't suppose any lecturer on Modern Poetry noted that that line encloses all aspects in a single visual image and thus is a veritable feat of poetry.) Naturally, the hullabaloo was associated with pre-election fighting, which was fierce and dirty anyhow.† But even so, Kishon's triumphant line reflects a basic benignity that's absolutely accurate but awfully hard to describe. Maybe because it's so un-American? Like, despite a no-holds-barred ambience, nobody even *tried* to toss around any "disloyalty" charges, conspiracy theories, etc. So yes, it was recognizable as part of political campaigning in a democracy—except conducted according to the rules of the wars of the Jews, under which you apparently go for the jugular and squeeze like hell, but the one thing you don't do is cut it. This cultural phenomenon (if that's what to call it) adds an extra price to what Israel always pays, by contrast with the Arab countries, for being a democracy. Because all that in-fighting produces an incessant babble the basic terms of which escape foreigners (old-hand correspondents usually understand, but it's the quick-visit capital-J Journalists who write the syndicated stuff) and so make their "leaks" and "sources" seem shifty and unreliable. And that tends to anger reporters, especially the network men who have to present a less-than-a-minute wrapup that appears to know everything. It's much, much easier to interview Sadat . . .

And now for the final item in the list of new-year discoveries I

---

*For us Americans, that was then a brand-new idea, so I was slow to believe at first. But what administration seeking re-election would pull a quantum price rise in a basic commodity only weeks before an election? You can always postpone a mere need for revenue, so it *had* to be that this was something unpostponable.

†When I commented on that to Mrs. Ben-Ari, she asked me what politics was like in America when the country was only twenty-five years old. Fierce and dirty, of course. *Touché.*

could cheerfully have done without. I guess it was those years and years of "year-end reviews" stirring in my memory cells that inspired me to a mid-December look at the Israeli economy, and that was a *big* mistake. For what I saw was a landscape in which it didn't really matter where you came in because there was no exit anyway. Because each of the elements of the economy was in its own little box, with the lid nailed on tight. Like this:

(a) Trade. A country can get solvent the easy way by being born with oil or uranium within its borders, or it can do it the hard way, like Japan, by being whiz-bang productive and trading like mad. Israel, as usual, can forget the easy way. But the hard way looks distinctly dim too, what with large hunks of the work force pulled off for military service* (to city only one reason for non-productivity); and trading like mad is just a jot difficult when what you have to offer isn't oil or uranium and none of the trading can be with anybody nearby because they're all hostile, underdeveloped, or both.

(b) Wages. Israel has a suicidal little gimmick that for all I know is unique: it's called "linking" and means that if you raise teachers' salaries you automatically must raise, say, engineers'—even though you may be sorely in need of schoolteachers and up to your neck in surplus engineers. (That's just a simple example: actually, it's more complex than one-tweaks-one, for a twitch anywhere can yank half a dozen elsewheres. And I hope your eye didn't slide over the word "automatic" above—this isn't something for union meetings to argue about, it's written into the system.) I suppose it was the sacred we-are-all-workers idea that produced "linking," which would make it an ideological chicken come home to roost. But it sure roosts: in Israel, founded on a socialist-worker ideology, everybody belongs to a union; and the union of unions, the Histadrut, is—like the Jewish Agency—a pseudo-governmental phenomenon that has no American equivalent.+ It's not just that the Histadrut owns valuable real estate, whole industries, the health service with the most members, and I don't know what-all else. Nor is it only like George Meany's voice

---

*Avi, who has no special military talents, spent at least five months in the army. A man I know, a mechanic whose peacetime work would clearly get added into the gross national product, was so good at converting captured Syrian (i.e., Soviet) tanks that he remained on virtually permanent miluim. And Yoshua of the coffee bar, a reserve tank battalion man, was home only long enough for me to discover he'd survived the war; then he was off again, for retraining—the army having learned a few lessons during the war.

+It does have something close to a British equivalent, in the TUC (Trades Union Council), whose displeasure is said (by some: others say it was because Prime Minister Heath was chicken) to have brought down the last Conservative government. Under a Labour government, the TUC's weight is like the Histadrut's—anything either of them doesn't want to happen, won't.

getting listened to in the White House—it's more as if he were the landlord of the White House, actually . . . But what it all means is that Israel, a small enough society so it should be adaptable (and one that sure as hell needs to be) is locked into an all-or-nothing wage setup that, given the ever-rising cost of living, must go to "all." And then, there we go—if the government resists wage demands, the resulting strikes hold export industries hostage; if Israel can't compete abroad because strikes at home keep it from delivering the goods at the contracted time, there goes trade. But if the government does yield on wages, there goes any hope of even edging toward solvency. Anybody want to waltz around again?

(c) Revenue. One unhappy result of linking has been the development of a complex structure of "perks" (perquisites) that amount to disguised salary increases (e.g., if you need a top man but can't offer him any more pay without also raising the wages of all the janitors too, what you do is throw in a "book allowance"—which may or may not be for books—and a car, trips abroad, university tuitions for all his children, and anything else he'd like). None of this fringe stuff is taxable as income,* so an Israeli who does manage to live soft can continue that way. And the straightforward paycheck earner is already drained virtually white (except for what perks *his* union has been able to acquire: some people who really don't read books much have book allowances), so there isn't much revenue to be had from income taxes anymore. Other sources of revenue are trade, which has—see (a)—its hazards, and gifts, which tend to have certain expensive stings in their tail. Like, American aid money is not, as most Americans seem to believe, all a great big present: the interest on the debts can be very, very hairy—and the same is true for the Israel bonds bought abroad . . . I could go on about sources of national income, but it's a really irrelevant consideration when a country is under attack. However much a Phantom costs, Israel probably can't afford it, in theory. But with Egypt and Syria already replacing their Yom Kippur War losses (the oil revenues from Saudi Arabia and Libya—to cite only two—are always available to buy what the U.S., U.S.S.R., and France—to cite only the busiest businessmen—are always willing to sell), Israel *stamm* has to afford not only Phantoms but whatever else it takes . . .

All right, enough. Though there are more boxes: the way I know that is, when I looked at the picture I'd painted, I figured I

---

*A tax-law revision that would make these perks taxable as income was later launched. But the Knesset watered it down before passing the bill, and then administrative difficulties caused more dilutions; when I last looked, the exceptions seemed likely to be numerous enough to bring everything back to Square One.

must've got some color in the wrong number because this didn't make sense. So I summoned Rob to come give me the benefit of his professional expertise. He came, and said I'd left a few things out (e.g., import prices also rise, because there's inflation in countries abroad too—ah there, Maggie, did you forget about One World?—and since Israel can't make everything it needs, the need to import drives the cost of living up no matter what. Etc. etc.) But Rob's addenda just closed the boxes more tightly. I'll spare you his statistics because they only gave me a worse headache—and anyway, if you're that fond of statistics you probably know where to look these up. But what they showed was that no, I hadn't caught the Israeli habit of dark foreboding (that had been my last, wistful hope). As for what could be done, well, Rob mentioned a few moves that I instantly recognized as total political impossibilities in a democracy. And then he blew even those away by adding that he wasn't sure of their abstract efficacy to begin with, and anyway things could well be past the point where any corrective measures would do much good anyhow . . . For once, I think Rob would rather have spent the evening playing anagrams.

So much, then, for the news of the day at the beginning/end of the year. Many people sank entirely under the load: practically every time I went to the macaulet I seemed to hear about another American family "going back" (that delicate usage is preferred because it avoids offending the Zionist belief that Israel is "home" for every Jew). It's socially unacceptable to say a word against such folk,* but I could let down my hair with Rob, so I said bitterly (and unfairly, I admit) that it was rotten to walk out on the Israelis just when they needed friends most. He looked at me oddly and then murmured that by that kind of reasoning, probably nobody could ever leave Israel. Buoyant is not the word for Rob . . . Ah, but Thereza is an Israeli, which somehow seems to include a sure sense of when to grab somebody going down for the third time. So she produced, at the critical moment, her Shabbat Theory. I'd got sprung from my high-school-English stint, but what had I done, Thereza demanded. Turned immediately to working all day every day on my novel, that's what, Thereza replied. So look at how thin and gray-faced I was (perfectly true, but I'm always thin and gray-faced in the winter, and it's working on novels that tends to put the roses back in my cheeks), and I hadn't even been out of Beer-Sheva since before the war. In short, anybody who never takes a Shabbat—any kind of shabbat—is

*Even the hyper-Zionist Yehuda Artzi reproached me when I mocked the "deserters," and he's certainly against neither partisanship nor mockery. But the feeling seems to be that at least these people tried—it's no disgrace to fail, and maybe they'll try again and succeed next time.

351

bound to become sunk in gloom, lose perspective, and doubtless develop pimples. Well, maybe Thereza didn't say that last. But she did say I needed to go down to Eilat and lie in the sun.

What that indicates most clearly is probably that Thereza, who loves to travel (how is it I get so fond of people so utterly unlike me?) would love to go down to Eilat. But she did have a point. The fact was, I had indeed been having nothing but work days—metaphorical certainly, and literal, too. Whereas before Yaakov and Sara left for their year in the U.S., going to Jerusalem had more or less forced an occasional "shabbat" on me whether I realized it or not . . . So in the end I adopted Thereza's theory and started on a series of deliberate "sabbaths," in which I stirred myself out of my usual ways (sometimes even actually going somewhere!) at least once a week. The name of this game was to stop worrying and even thinking, and stamm breathe in and out, looking around but never-never-never drawing conclusions. (Yeah. You can probably imagine how perfectly I managed that last.) The remainder of this chapter comprises the results of that Rest and Recreation shtick—a kind of ragbag of notebook jottings, letters home, snatches of conversation, and other bits-and-pieces. I think they may provide a better picture of a jumbled time than smoothing them all out would. And if they don't, well, at least they'll have whatever it is that's so engaging about poking into your friend's sewing basket or inspecting strangers' grocery carts in the supermarket checkout line. Here they are, in no particular order:

Item 1—Dec. 9, Ben-Gurion died. A national occasion but the old boy had just turned eighty-seven and he'd been out of office a long time, so no public trauma. Large-scale media reviews of his life, which covered the entire history of the state—interesting, and it quieted the wars of the Jews. But not for long, because by reviewing the years of the *yishuv* (yi-SHOOV, the community of pre-state Palestinian Jews) the obits disinterred some *old* wars of the Jews. Which then meant screams of "revisionism," etc., followed by equal-time panel shows— relicts of various yishuv factions shouting at each other in Hebrew. Oy va voy. As long as they don't pre-empt the Saturday-night "Ironside," the public will simmer but not explode . . . I'm getting quite fond of the photo of the young B-G in his fez.* And since I'm free of old fervors and past battles, maybe I mourn more purely than the official mourners. Because Ben-Gurion had admirable horse-sense and guts,

*Yep, I said "fez"—it's interesting how hard it is to remember that the Turks owned Palestine right up until 1917, when the British took it. It was the Turks who granted "administrative rights" to Egypt in Gaza—which now provides a basis for those casual assumptions that Gaza really "belongs" to Egypt.

and he and his Paula (she died some time ago—I saw her grave at Sde Boker) seem more like what I think marriages ought to be about than most I've seen or known . . . I wish I could be sure there was a young B-G growing up somewhere, and I don't mean just in Israel.

Item 2—Visit to Elizabeth, a British woman married to an Israeli for oh, twenty years or more: I met her and Natan (Nah-TAHN), an ex-American of at least as long Israeli citizenship, last spring at Yaakov and Sara's. Elizabeth and Natan play in an amateur chamber-music group on the old established moshav (it's practically just Exurbia now, about halfway between Tel Aviv and Haifa) where they both live—Elizabeth and her family luxuriously; Natan and his, somewhat closer to original moshav style. Elizabeth's house is in fact rather like Janice's in Massachusetts (perhaps because of the grand piano in its music-room alcove), but of course there are those special Israeli touches like the kerosene heater in the salon that moves around on a little wheeled platform to follow us from the preprandial sherry to the dining table. And like another difference: at Janice's, I slept in their eighteen-year-old son's room, which was empty because he was away at college; but Elizabeth's son's room was available for guests because, having recently turned eighteen, he'd just gone off to begin his army training.

Ah, but Saturday morning was *all* Israel (though the sea outside isn't something that's usual in my own Israel). Elizabeth is beautiful-people-ish, but Natan is, like his house, still close to the youth who came from America full of Zionist dreams. And what became of him is surely a tribute to that movement, for a sweetness shines out of this smallish, slight, shyly smiling man who loves music, his country, and apparently everybody in the world who'll let him. He still works in the moshav industry, and hard physical labor has seamed his face and shows in his hands; but at fifty-something he's straight and sturdy and moves springily, and he seems willing and able to take all kinds of trouble to make things happen (which may in fact be *the* youthful quality).

Saturday morning in Natan's house: all the furniture in the small salon—except the old upright piano—is scrunched into a corner to make room for music-stands. The flute player, who's in the navy, has made it home on leave in time. The viola couldn't, so one of Natan's sons, collared on his way out to basketball practice, was pressed into service on the violin to free Natan to take the viola part. The youngster (maybe sixteen? Who can tell about boys at that lanky-gawky age?) seemed good-natured about being drafted and waited patiently—his basketball in its yellow net carrier on the floor between his huge sneakers—while the sheets of music were reshuffled. Elizabeth was at the piano under the window, softly trying out different bits: beyond her bent head I could see the blue Mediterranean lying calm as a lake in sunlight; but up close there must have been a breeze, because a branch of brilliant bougainvillea tapped lightly at the window. Oh, it was a lovely day. And lovely, lovely too the stops and starts and murmurs of reproof ("B *flat*, please") and apology ("Oh. *Slicha*"), and then an outburst of congratulation at the end of the effort to play not only all the notes but even the music. "Oh, wasn't that something!"—Natan, his face bright with happiness. ("Let's play that last part again," said his son, too young to know you never can and you'd better not try.)

Then all the heads bent once more to the business at hand, which this time meant catching every intent of Johann Christian Bach, who lived in Europe I don't know how many centuries ago and doubtless couldn't have begun to imagine any of this: a room with the unlikely combination of gorgeous jungle-colored flowering outside and bare cold floor within; the thicket of dilapidated musicstands like a field of strange steely grasses sprinkled with worn sandals and sneakers (and one great yellow-net orb!); and, most weird of all, the motley men and women, soldiers and civilians, old and young—all of them, incredibly, nobody's subjects, neither grand duke nor church their patron. Oh God, I would have prayed (and maybe did), give them Time. At least those intervals that music and maybe everything else depends on, God help us all . . . I sat in the corner collating the scrawled pages of a quartet they wanted to try next—though, because of the war and other interruptions to life, the flute would have to sight-read. When I finished, I ate the cookies Natan's wife and his daughter (who, like Natan, was home on leave from the army) had set out for the musicians' coffee break. There cannot have been, ever, a lovelier sabbath.

Item 3—Rob had a problem: come rather recently from American campuses and with all his "progressive" connections still intact, he'd been discovering that some of his friends' letters were busily pushing the left-wing anti-Israel party line. When things were rather dicier, they'd mostly been silent. And it was still a little early to start calling Israel an aggressor again, but not to start burying the fact of who attacked whom on Yom Kippur. (In fact, "neutral" terminology had begun in the media almost at once—war "broke out" in the Middle East, they kept saying, as if nobody had actually lifted a finger to make it.) Well, Rob didn't need any help with the substance of what his correspondents said: that sort of twaddle never survives

354

a brush with reality very well. But he wanted to counter them, and the Israelis were getting in his way by looking so bad—what was he supposed to fight back with, the unedifying spectacle of the wars of the Jews? So that's how I happened to deliver a lecture (was it really Rob I was lecturing? Ah well, it's against the rules to speculate here) on popular perception of heroism: "You can be a hero for ten years and fifteen days, and if on the sixteenth day you stop being a hero, you're instantly a bum—and everybody says you've been one for over ten years, too." I also reminded him that people most in need of sympathy often make themselves least attractive to it. Like, the deep schizophrenic, who's so sick he wouldn't even know you were there if he hadn't been shot full of miracle drugs, is one of the most charming guys in the hospital—whereas the patient in the next corridor only ails with something human attention could make better, but he picks his nose or is incontinent . . .

Hmm. I could've put it better: the Israelis, even the wrangliest of them, are neither bums nor booby-hatch inhabitants (and Maggie should control the loose habit of hyperbole). Like, why not have simply told Rob, "Love always has to mean dahfke, too?" But dammit, I get upset—these people are all so tired, so awfully, awfully tired, and still they don't get a vacation from everybody else's great expectations. There's been all the genuine heroism, big and little (and sometimes going on for years and years), the expenditures of love and kindness and self-sacrifice—hearts full of noble emotions, bloodstreams full of adrenaline. So now their emotional bank accounts are all overdrawn, Rob, don't you see? The whole scene shrieks "aftermath," like coming downstairs to a weak dawn light revealing overflowing ashtrays and spilled booze, somebody's tie hanging from a lamp and a sequinned slipper lying on its side under the coffee table.

Oh wow, where do you get that party image (and what the hell is Rob supposed to make of it: who wears ties anymore, or sequinned slippers?). I suppose it's because of those bright-and-shining moments, even now, and the God-how-beautiful-everyone-is insights that can come of one kind of intoxication or another. But no, it wasn't like a party; it was more like a flood. And the aftermath is some houses swept away and others still in place but damaged, the skies gray and threatening still, and a foot of stinking mud all over everything—with the fact of your own survival becoming, for now anyway, only an obligation to go help pick up the pieces. Except, Israel can't count on any Red Cross showing up with blankets; and even when the victims can be got to the firehouse and the high-school gym, they may find not shelter but the doors shut in their faces.

Item 4—These people are at once the most politically naïve I've ever seen and the most sophisticated. E.g., a wounded chyal interviewed in hospital urged, "We should let them [the Egyptians] think they won. We should even keep telling them they're great fighters. Then maybe that will make them happy and we can have peace." That's more contemptuous than most people seem to feel (but he's nineteen, so what do you expect?); the sophistication, however, is quite typical. Kissinger's maneuvers are less than popular with lots of Israelis, chiefly because they don't believe he realizes the risks of some of his coups. But a large and surprisingly broad sample of the population recognizes that if Sadat should get swept out of office, his replacement would be far less likely to be willing to talk peace . . . Aha, but on the other hand—an election ad in the newspapers: it's for Ma'arach, the Labour coalition currently in power, and it's signed by a whole string of Big Names (many of them important academics) of influence and repute. So would you believe the ad says, in virtually so many words, Ma'arach stinks but please vote for it anyhow?!? These ish-chacham types, all dignity and tradition, make American frank-and-open fans look positively skulking. It's not their sentiment that makes the mind reel, because practically the same situation can be found in England (and doubtless for the same reason, ideological party grouping plus the mechanisms of a parliamentary system). But who else would collect money—and not at a rock festival, either: these are the Establishment's babies—to announce the fact in an ad?

Item 5—Christmas. A great big occasion in Jerusalem and of course in Bethlehem, but in Beer-Sheva it's just another day. An American Christian I know, one of the very few in town (he's also one of the few who offer you Scotch the way nearly everybody else offers you coffee or tea, but I don't know that the two facts are connected), drove up to Jerusalem for Christmas Eve and I could have gone along. I didn't, and when I watched the church services in Bethlehem on the TV (which stayed on late for the occasion), I knew it was because all that official ceremonying isn't what Christmas means to me anyhow. That's not what I miss, any more than I miss the annual sense of panic and the shopping and the exhausting party chores. What I miss is the pretty tree and the giggles over those Tab A/Slot B toys and my daughter objecting once because in "The Night Before Christmas" it says Mother's in her kerchief and I wasn't. The bathrobed children in fuzzy slippers (who probably stand for Myself When Young), that's what I miss . . . Ah well, one of the things I always liked best about Christmas was having a glass of brandy while Dylan Thomas told about Christmas in Wales (marvelous Miss Protheroe, who knew just the right thing to say to the firemen!)—and I can still have that, if not with the same company, because I brought the record along. And my favorites, "Joy to the World" and "Good King Wenceslas" and "Little Town of Bethlehem" weren't yowling out of every department store but I did hear them (plus "Bring a Torch, Jeannette, Isabella," which isn't easy to run into in the U.S.!) So okay, if I couldn't have everything I like about Christmas, at least I didn't have to have the things I *don't* like. Happy Christmas, Dylan Thomas.

Item 6—Watching TV in an R&R frame of mind can be a real ball. For the standard obeisance to the kibbutz ideal turns up at least once an evening—usually on the news, when some MK (member of the Knesset) or Cabinet Minister shows up tieless and with open shirt collar—thus delivering, along with his comments, the important message that after all he's still one of the agrarian socialist chaverim just like thee and me. (Abba Eban thus *en déshabillé* is especially giggle-provoking.) It's a little like American campaigning (the *Ahm jus' a li'l ol' country boy* routine—in either its Lyndon Johnson version or later ones—and the Indian war bonnet and the eating of soul-food-and-knish sandwiches); but this is funnier because, unlike American pols, these guys are often conning *themselves.* For the we're-all-simple-workers-here shtick is genuinely important to their sense of themselves, though they haven't worked in a kibbutz field for thirty years and they're not even as *au courant,* common-folk-wise, as they could get by riding buses in Tel Aviv.* But put 'em before a TV camera and out pops the standard naked Adam's apple. (One of the few who doesn't seem to con himself is Moshe Dayan, who wears not only a dress-up shirt and tie but even matching coat and pants: he was actually a farmer once, and then a soldier, and dressed accordingly; and he apparently figures that now he's a politician he ought to wear *that* raiment . . . Dayan is an odd man,† with some ideas I don't approve of, but he is in the best sense a genuinely simple person, I suspect. Which may be why the West Bank Arabs seem to prefer him to other Israeli officials.)

Anyway, I call this phenomenon "chaverim-ism" and have so

---

*I've not come upon any Israeli equivalent of the late Sen. Theodore Green, Democrat of Rhode Island and a longtime chairman of the Senate Foreign Relations Committee, who used to ride around Washington on the public transport—and at the age of ninety or so, too.
†There's a little of Coriolanus in him, I sometimes think. (Live long enough, and you'll run into *all* Shakespeare's characters!)

described it to Thereza and Jan, who are also amused by the egalitarian posing. Thereza likes having a name for it, but Jan is torn: he sides with my sentiment, but he doesn't want to encourage the sort of liberties I constantly take with the Hebrew language.

Item 7—rosemary and rue. Went Shabbat-visiting, proper Israeli style, with coffee and cakes and conversation—in English for my benefit, though occasionally somebody got excited and forgot (but it was okay, Thereza was there). This was a liberal crowd, so its version of the public squabbling was a where-did-we-go-wrong discussion; and one suggestion was that it was back at the decision to accept German reparations money. The debate at the time on that very controversial issue came down to two propositions, it seems: one asserted that taking reparations amounted to saying suffering could be wiped out by mere money, and thus the offer should be scorned; the other view was probably best represented by Ben-Gurion's observation that it was stupid to allow your murderers to be also your heirs.* The latter prevailed. And now here was an Israeli arguing that the reparations money, injected into a there-tofore hand-to-mouth society, had created disproportionate con-sumer demand and an inflationary effect never entirely reversible since. Not to mention (said somebody mentioning it) a kind of psychic deflowering: when you can once satisfy your materialistic urges without working, there's a permanent effect on productivity . . .

Very fancy, and maybe true. Some folks might stifle their materialistic urges—after, maybe, one or two big whoopee pur-chases—and just put the money in the bank, but I guess it counts as inflationary pressure there too. And maybe money in the bank is enough all by itself to lose agrarian socialists their virginity. (That's the kind of group this was, anyway: if people are greedy it's because society done 'em wrong, the child-of-a-broken-home is the preferred rationale for anything uncomfy, and so on. Some of these Israeli liberals even manage to tuck terrorists under their rubrics.†)

Item 8—chicken again. Chicken is just about the only meat people can afford, so I wasn't surprised when that's what was for dinner at

*Both contentions seem to me absolutely valid. I wouldn't have known how to vote.
†Sometimes I can sympathize. For, hundreds of adolescent-rebellion-type Arab kids, often drug-dimmed too, are put over the border in the course of a year—after having been given a couple of months' "training" in a (UN-supported) refugee camp, plus a load of explosives. Israeli border patrols pick them up with ease, often before they blow themselves up; and most people here find them terribly pathetic. But *ma la'assot?* Their mission instructions are frankly genocidal, so they will kill you—or anyone else they come across—if they aren't stopped.

358

Martha and Avi's—especially since Avi's still in the army and thus runs into even more people to invite to dinner whenever he has leave, while the money coming in is not increasing likewise. I'd probably clobber him, but Martha brings her large array of cookbooks and her U.S. kitchen technology to bear on the problem and rings resourceful changes on the chicken theme. I wish I'd kept track from the start, but I estimate this was her two-dozenth chicken recipe . . . Anyway, Avi drove me home and I took occasion to tell him about the rue session I'd sat in on (Item 7) and ask him what he thought. He didn't say their conclusion wasn't so, but he suggested that where the society veered was just after the 1967 war. At that point the Israelis had beat the pants off the Arabs, who were thus good and sore; therefore it was essential to build defenses along the new perimeters in a hurry. And money to do it with was available, because the victory in the Six-Day War had brought an influx of contributions from Jews all over the world who'd had a bad scare (and maybe even guilty Christians, too? Lots of people had found it comfy to assume Nasser was just talking "Arab rhetoric"). So for a change a need and funds to fill it matched. And thus it suddenly became possible for an Israeli to make a pile of money by driving a truck in the Sinai—which up to then he'd done because it was a national duty. So the notion of demanding individual loot for helping out in social squeezes entered the Israeli psyche . . .

Avi is much tougher and more pragmatic than the people I'd listened to earlier, and I find his argument more persuasive. (If it *is* his: sometimes he'll advance a substantially held view that I might otherwise miss, even though he himself isn't in total agreement with it.) Nevertheless he too seems to start from some conviction of original purity, and a similar tenderness for the maiden Israel. Lord, how her people love her! I suppose it goes with being a beginner-state. But it's hard for me to keep that status up front, for I'm used to thinking of governments as old.*

Item 9—Went to visit Dick and Peg Hook, an American diplomatic couple who live in a suburb of Tel Aviv. (That's where the U.S. Embassy is, which irks the Israelis, who say Jerusalem's their capital: they feel it's the sort of thing a country ought to have the say

*Thus it was a real surprise to discover that Sara's mother had known a man for whom a street in Beer-Sheva was named. I mean, I know a couple of descendants of a couple of Presidents—but one's a great-grandchild and the other's even longer ago than that. In Israel, though, practically anybody over fifty may have been on coffee-and-cake terms with a Founding Father. For all I know, Sara's mother knew Ben-Gurion, too: I never thought to ask her, and she wouldn't have thought the information remarkable enough to volunteer it..

about, itself.) I knew the Hooks when we all had little children in the nursery school and strong views about burning issues in the local Civic Association back in Suburbia, U.S.A. So it was nice to see them, but from the moment they opened the door—Peg barefoot, that's how warm their house was!—I was primarily dazzled by the rediscovery of America the beautiful. I hadn't been in an American home for nearly a year. But that's what the State Department supplies its professional diplomats, as nearly as possible (e.g., it couldn't give them a house with central heating, but there was a heater/air conditioner in every room, and a separate dood for every bathroom!); and they get to shop Americanly at a special commissary. So, oh wow, talk about luxury: I spent the first hour of my visit peeling off sweaters in between bites of real bacon and eggs. Real hamburgers!* Not only perked coffee but my favorite brand thereof! Bourbon!! The guest room I used had its own bath and was twice the size of my salon. Oh soft warm easy-talking plenty-of-room America, where people work hard+ but they get something for it . . .

Then I came home to my apartment, icy because it had been closed up, to huddle by the heater, making my small room even smaller so I could get one spot warm to start with. And here's where my shabbat restrictions end and it's back-to-work time. Because sitting there wrapped in my afghan, I figured out the name of what had been ailing me. It was powerlessness, the one thing Americans really know nothing about. I know they think they do, every time Congress or the state legislature does something they dislike. But it's not at all the same, believe me: remember when I moved into my humble little apartment, I compared it with a lower-middle-class neighborhood I'd lived in, in a Massachusetts town? I've lived before among people who didn't have money or fame, I said, so I knew I could get along without glamor . . . Well, what I was too dumb to see was that though there isn't glamor in those American backwaters, there *is* power: what the donnybrooks at the Shamrock Bar and Grill or the imbroglios at the Napoli (Ladies Invited) in such a town are all about is power. And in fact if you ever need an inside story on local politics, the best place to go is the Shamrock or the Napoli. (In case you think that's hyperbole, listen: I've heard a man bellying up to a

*It's impossible to make hamburgers in Israel. Martha thought it was because the koshering process did something to the meat, so I bought some non-kosher beef—a bargain at about $3 a pound, and you should've seen the guy's face when I told him to grind it. But it still came out more like flattened meatballs.
+Dick had even been to Beer-Sheva (shortly before I arrived in Israel), and he knew a great deal more about it than, say, Yaakov. Hooray for our brave boys in the Foreign Service, who actually go and *look* at provincial towns important Israelis don't bother with! It warms the cockles of this taxpayer's heart . . .

bar in Somerville, Mass. start discussing the chances that the state legislature would prorogue soon. To prorogue is to break off meetings without ending the session, and I used to think it was a right technical term—but both the customer, a milkman by trade, and the bartender were using it quite casually.)

Power doesn't mean that you have to care about politics, only that if you do want to know you have to be told. But what powerlessness means is that nobody has to tell you in advance and nobody has to explain later: things *stamm* happen to you the way rain does. Or a sandstorm—a better example because it can do you great injury or even kill you, but all you can do about it is to get out of the way if you can and cower if you can't. Even if you're part of a majority, you can't make anything happen because not only are the decisions made by people who don't know how it is where you are, but in Israel they themselves are also finally powerless. So you roll with the punches for as long as you can, as long as they keep coming. But nobody knows how long that will be: the bell will ring whenever somebody somewhere, who doesn't know about you and doesn't want to, needs to have this round come to an end.

I'm glad I lived in it, I guess, for certainly nobody who hasn't ought to try to tell people what life in Israel is like. Besides, most of the world lives that way, just taking whatever blows are handed out. (And worse off than in Israel, with its *shelanu* spirit within and its well-wishers outside. What must it be like to be a citizen of Uganda?) Maybe someday Americans will have to live that way, too. Right now, a bell rung in Washington still is heard around the world; but for how long, considering that the Warms are always at a disadvantage against the Cools?

At any rate, I know now what it's like, and perhaps it was time I found out. But it's an awful, awful way to live.

From the diary: 20

"Election Central" (December)

On election day I decided to go watch the evening TV news at Thereza and Jan's so I could get some interpretative aid. My Hebrew's probably up to coping with the vote totals, but it's hardly enough to be told how a certain district voted if you don't also know whether that represents a "safe" seat or a breakaway, how likely it is to be part of a trend, etc. Thereza and Jan, both pretty immune to the joys of politics-watching, probably couldn't care less; however I'm an aficionado of politics at home and abroad, and they're willing to pay the price of friendship.

I was just about to leave for their place when Rob turned up on my doorstep. So I took him along. Which was socially a perfectly acceptable thing to do but was probably a mistake: alone, I might have managed to compose myself during the broadcast, but Rob's presence lowered the giggle threshold. And even when we managed to avoid each other's gaze, not-laughing was hard. Because what we were seeing on the TV screen was something like a made-in-Japan American flag: at a curved desk sat a Hebrew-speaking pair of young men, under a plaque that clearly said the equivalent of "Election Central." The rest of their regalia was mostly Early Huntley-Brinkley, with some of the newer rituals added; a few of those looked slightly misunderstood, but they were faithfully carried out anyhow. So we got the whole bit—tote boards, computer predictions, turning us over to Zvi or Tal (who might or might not actually be there) at various party headquarters—all rather like a color photo with the colors not quite right, streaked a little by being in Hebrew to begin with and then further shaded by distinctive touches of chaverim-ism . . . Thereza clucked impatiently and Jan's face pinched into the look of fine-boned disdain it acquires in moments of social distress, for intelligent and perceptive people know when they're in the presence of the inauthentic even when they've never seen the original. But Rob and I had seen it, and we lacked reverence to begin with; so the respectful copy was just out-and-out funny, and a poker face has never come easily to me.

What this was all about, you see, was a handful of votes in a country even I could ride across on a bicycle. And the choicest absurdity of the whole shtick was that behind the comic Huntley-Brinkleying lay a set of propositions that couldn't possibly fit what that machinery was devised for anyhow. (On second thought, forget that made-in-Japan American flag: what it was, actually, was chopsticks marked "Made in U.S.A." in Japanese) For in a U.S. election, once the numbers get added up, that's your story—except in rare instances, the only delay is a result of the multiple time zones. So speed makes some sense (if not exactly real good sense). But in Israel, all this whizzing is like having a guy come galloping into town on his foam-flecked horse, in order to start reading aloud to the gathered citizenry something like—well, let's say the tiny-print prose on the back of an insurance policy. I mean, immediate it ain't.

Nor is it decisive. For, leaving aside the question of a snappy computer vs. fumbling human fingers counting little pieces of paper, the Election Central bit has to go with a winner-take-all (or, as the British call it, "first past the post") voting system. And Israel has a form of Proportional Representation (hereinafter called just PR) laid on top of the parliamentary system copied from England. Which cumbrous combo is, whatever else you want to say about it notwithstanding, unlikely to lend itself to contest-type reporting.

It works like this: each party draws up a list of candidates (for the Knesset: in parliamentary government, all you get to elect is members of the parliament—they then choose the Prime Minister from among their number) in descending order of importance, e.g., Ma'arach's list would begin with Golda Meir. There are 120 Knesset seats, so the magic number is 61. Which no party is likely to get, because there are too many parties for that; but for a major party the first third of its list is a sure thing and thus contains all the current biggies. If the party wins, these will be running the government; if it loses, they'll still be chaverim haKnesset.* (A brand-new party, on the other hand, is likely to get actual seats for only two or three of its list—and sometimes only one, the founder.) None of this has anything to do with where the candidates come from, of course: as in Britain, they're simply assigned by the party. However, Israel's tradition is not horse-racing and "first past the post" would be considered a dirty gyp, an infringement of freedom, etc. So though in Israel, too, what you vote for is a party—like, you may be voting Ma'arach because you're for Golda or Abba Eban or Dayan or some other "star" on the list, but that just means they attract votes for Ma'arach—it's the total number of votes for the party rather than

*An American who read this had trouble grasping the setup around this point, so I'd better hammer it home: whereas in the U.S. a Hubert Humphrey returning to the Senate after he'd been Vice President was newsworthy, in a parliamentary system that's routine. Because the Prime Minister is a member of parliament anyway, see? This makes an important difference in political life because a Name like Dayan, say, remains before the public even when he's not a minister of something or other. And in the U.S., a Menachem Begin would have disappeared into the wilderness long before, but after half a lifetime as an Opposition MK, he finally became Prime Minister.

the number of constituencies won (i.e., in Britain if the Labour candidate gets a majority of a district's votes, that district is then Labour's) which determines how many Knesset seats the party will get.

That's because in PR, a predetermined number* of votes elects one MK; when the first man gets more votes than that—and for, say, Golda or Dayan there's always likely to be a sizable surplus—the "extra" votes are then applied to the next name on the list. When that candidate's quota is filled, the surplus goes to Number 3, and so on . . . One of the virtues of PR, you see, is that it does give "purity" a chance: if, say, you have an ish chacham who'd make a crackerjack finance minister but is short on charisma, you can tuck him into a handy spot on your list. And a similar sense of virtue-protected goes for little minorities, who can get represented in the Knesset if they have enough voters to make the quota just once, whereas in a winner-take-all setup they'd be simply washed away by the flood. Thus PR is perceived as the friend of the underdog—which may be why it persists in Israel, where being pro-underdog is part of chaverim-ism—and is everywhere especially beloved by voters who suspect they're in the clutch of some machine.

It was that kind of conviction, cherished in the town-vs.-gown context of Cambridge, Mass., that gave me my own most recent (pre-Israel) experience of the joys of PR. For in Cambridge the "town" folks were always sure the "gown" guys were up to something slick (which belief of course excuses the town guys getting up to something slick themselves). So "town" was not only unwilling to have winner take all but also brought about a final absurdity. Because if any operation is computer-meat, it's PR, and computer experts are thicker in Cambridge than grass skirts in a Hawaii tourist spa. But, said "town," shaking its head wisely, we ain't gonna have MIT (which is in Cambridge, and is "gown" in the eyes of "town" though snubbed as mere "Tech" by Harvard: these things are very complicated) making with fancy technological maneuvers an honest pol can't expect to follow. So, at least when I lived there,† the ballots were solemnly counted by hand—in a creaking neutral-turf municipal building and in the presence of eagle-eyed watchers . . . Which means that, in the audience of Israel Broadcasting's "election central" show that night was Maggie, who had once had the

*It's a formula based on the total number of votes cast in the last election. And let's not get any more nitty-gritty than that: this is complicated enough.
†Maybe by now "town" has acquired some computer types of its own, and therefore learned to trust. (But, judging from a recent letter from a friend familiar with the Byzantine local politics, it doesn't sound like it.)

doubtless unique experience of standing outside an MIT building within which people were computering away at umpty-thousand operations per second and buying the current week's Cambridge Chronicle to get the final, authentic totals for the School Board— which had not yet been all figured out when last week's Chronicle went to press. Groovy. I wouldn't have missed the experience for the world. But if I'd turned on the TV in Cambridge and found somebody sitting around Election Centraling there . . . Well, I think my persistent impulse to bestow a loud and unseemly horselaugh on the proceedings in Israel on that election night is excusable, I really do.

But when I have done I have not done, for I have more. (I must be hysterical: I'd never abuse John Donne like that if I were feeling myself.) Because I've not yet even begun to tap the absurdity of news-ticker goings-on for what won't be decided until long after Election Central's banner has been recycled and its set returned to the educational TV for tomorrow's English-lesson broadcast. For, even when it's finally certain (barring appeals, demands for recounts, etc.) how many Knesset seats each party has, that's still only the start of finding out who won what. (On second thought, make that "probably won.") Because whoever got the most votes won't have got 61, and you'd need more than that—a majority of one vote really isn't enough of an edge—to get effective control of the Knesset and thus get to run the government. So the name of the game is to collect enough coalition partners from among the smaller parties to make up a bloc that will choose you for Prime Minister (and then vote with you often enough to keep you there); and the name of that game is deciding what chunks of your platform you can give away in return for support from whatever party can give away a chunk of its platform to become part of your coalition.

But—lest that sound too simple—leave us not forget that your winning ticket was itself a coalition, of factions pasted together before the election out of a common desire to get elected. (That part is substantially the same as U.S. parties, which are in effect coalitions: the factions joined in Ma'arach and in the opposing Likud are no farther apart than, say, Ted Kennedy and George Wallace or Barry Goldwater and Nelson Rockefeller in their respective parties. But the small difference is a vital one, for the Israeli factions got under their representative umbrellas by going the other way—they don't have to debate whether to form a "third" party because they are "third" parties, all of them, which can decide to get out just as easily as they decided to go in.) So if a would-be Prime Minister compromises enough to pick up some Knesset coalition partners, *he may thereby lose a party coalition partner or two.* The potential Israeli Prime Minister is perhaps best seen as a man trying to get six kittens into a small basket, and keep them there long enough to put the lid on.*

The most interesting kitten is the National Religious Party, because it generally has a minimum of twelve Knesset seats to trade. (If a potential PM needs too much more than the NRP bloc of seats, he's probably not close enough to a majority to be making the run.) And since the religious stuff the NRP insists on, like Shabbat observance and rabbinate-approved marriages, are not the hardest concessions to make, it's likely to be the address applied to first. Which explains why, though Labour alignments have been governing since the start of the state, its voters—who are probably the closest ideological descendants of the non- and even anti-religious socialist pioneers—end up empowering religious laws . . . That situation no doubt explains the kind of feeling that inspired what's now my favorite item in my graffiti collection. (The previous Top Gem was "E=mc²" painted on a wall in Cambridge. Near MIT, where else?) I found this one when I walked into a Ladies at the university in Beer-Sheva and noticed some unfamiliar Hebrew words scrawled on the wall. I copied them on an envelope, but then I had considerable trouble getting them translated for me. Until Rob came through: what was on my envelope was "Fuck the National Religious Party."

I'd better make it clear, though, that the NRP doesn't include all "the religious" by any means: both of the major coalitions have religious parties as members, and there are some others so pure they don't go into anybody's coalition. Or if they do, they come out again at the first dispute. Because in the Israeli political scene, everything Matters and there's a party formed to prove it. The

---

*Moshe Dayan, a star frequently said to be waning but unmistakably still a star, probably provides a prime example. For Dayan, originally Ben-Gurion's baby, went with B-G when he broke away from Mapai (which is the core of Ma'arach) to form the Rafi party—which is small but replete with dazzling names and, since Dayan always means votes, gets wooed by everyone. In 1973 Ma'arach had wooed successfully, so Dayan was Defence Minister in Mrs. Meir's cabinet. He stayed won despite numerous "Phfft" rumors (Will Dayan Take a Walk? is to Israel journalism as C.I.A.-scandal items are to American—a headline you might as well always keep set in type) until, though Ma'arach was re-elected in 1973, Mrs. Meir resigned. For a while then, Dayan was just one of the chaverim haKnesset. But when Begin's Likud came in at the last election, the game began again—only this time the question was Will Dayan Walk *In?* At this point, he's Foreign Minister in Begin's government . . . None of this implies lack of principle, as it might in the U.S.: Dayan still has his own platform and tries to advance whatever plank of it he can. What it most closely resembles in U.S. terms, in fact, is the behavior of Independent voters who switch parties as it suits them.

Israeli voter, who doesn't have his very own Congressman and has to vote for a whole list or nothing, has much less individual representation in the legislature than we do; but he does have—thanks to the PR voting system—much more detailed representation of his opinion. Thus he can have the luxury of belonging to a virtually custom-tailored party. Like, red-haired religious kibbutzniks for water purification: if that's what he wants he can have it, and he doesn't have to go in with some brunette bunch just because they're also religious kibbutzniks, or make any of those other hard U.S.-type decisions ("How much can I forgive the Republicans/Democrats this year?"). But—and it's a big-big but—he's also likely to wake up in a coalition bed with anti-freckle atheists who want to tax the hell out of the kibbutzim, and discover that his vote has in the end empowered those who award water purification a priority somewhere below choosing the national flower. And his bellows when he finds it out can't fly upward or even be heard by anybody but his next-door neighbor.* For the leaders who took him into the coalition have no particular reason to listen for his voice: their future, if they went to be re-elected, lies in the hands of the party list-maker—who can put them where they can pick up a dozen anti-freckle votes for any pro-freckle voter they've lost. A couple of the new parties are now experimenting with a certain amount of small, still somewhat tentative, grass-roots wooing: that's the sort of activity my high-school students asked me about (since that's "American") right after the war. But that kind of messing around with the actual voter is what makes those new parties, see?

Well, what with all the above considerations (and those are simplified, habibi!) that wouldn't be exactly represented in the votes reported from Petach Tikva to Election Central, things could only get funnier as the joy-boys of the TV chatted in Hebrew about the weather at various polling spots or cut away to show us a cabinet minister (no tie, shirt button open) and his wife casting their votes. But I did pretty well at self-control, honest I did. Until, anyway, a small kibbutz somewhere did its bit for Election Central by rushing in its teeny total—à la that New Hampshire town that always gets its eleven votes in first . . . As "Huntley" and "Brinkley" began to dis-

---

*Americans complain of similar "double crosses," particularly in recent years. But quite often that's a product of the Silly Sixties fashionable notion that there's no difference between Republicans and Democrats. People who swallowed that twaddle then were outraged to discover that if you elect a Republican he'll govern Republicanly, and vice versa, because there are in fact real philosophical differences . . . But, instances of folly aside, American politicians do have a vested interest in finding out what you think, and the only Congressman without a reason to want to oblige you is one who's planning to retire anyway.

367

cuss these early returns solemnly, Rob announced (just in time, too!) that Maggie was tired and we ought to shove off. That allowed me to retreat to the bathroom and gain control over my face, so I could say goodnight nicely.

We took a cab home, thus offering a golden opportunity to complete the election ritual by interviewing the cabbie. But fortunately, it was too short a ride: I got dropped off at my house before I could gather myself enough to frame the first traditional question.

From the diary: 21

Happy New Year (Jan.—Feb.)

January brought a son for Miriam and Ze'ev—hooray and mazal tov. *He's our first not of two but of four: Yael and Selma are also pregnant, so even after Martha comes through, there'll be new babies well into the summer . . . This one is, as it happens, a quite remarkably beautiful infant. But after my October midwife-musings, I'd have welcomed a homely one with the same special pleasure.*

Miriam and Ze'ev also have a telephone now, which may be nearly as big a hooray. It happened because our local Beduin sheikh (pronounced "shaych") got elected to the Knesset, and it turns out there's a law that all MKs have to be on the telephone. He lives just outside Beer-Sheva;* but since the Communications ministry had sturdily refused to string more lines here, it was compelled to bring a line across the desert from Arad, which is over near the Dead Sea. And Omer, where M. and Z. live, is apparently on the way, so . . . The sheikh's compulsory phone is said to have cost the government IL267,000. Talk about the price of democracy!

I was visiting Miriam in the maternity ward at the hospital when I ran into the woman from my apartment block whose son-in-law was killed in the war. It was her flat the soldiers were looking for, that day in November. Her daughter, who's been staying with her since Yom Kippur, had the baby yesterday. A girl, said the grandmother wanly (she's not old, but she's had a rough time and the Fathers' Room waiting ordeal is meant for strong young men). I said I was so happy to hear it, and her face twisted: yes, it's better to have girls, she agreed as though I'd intended my congratulations to suggest that. At least girls don't grow up to get killed in a war . . . She speaks some English because her other child, also married (her English doesn't extend to the "—in-law" construct, so I can't make out whether she's talking about a daughter and son-in-law or the other way round), lives in the States and she's been there to visit previous grandbabies. It must be a strange feeling, having one part of your posterity far away but safe and the other jammed into a little apartment with you, and suffering.

Well, but once past those women's-page items, January isn't that good-newsy. The labor strife gets worse and worse, with devastating effect on the productivity so sorely needed. Israel has to buck

---

*Five kilometers off the Arad-Beer-Sheva road: he was born there, in a tent, and has built himself a villa on the same spot. Which says something about whither-the-Beduin, I think. (As does, to begin with, the fact that the sheikh belongs to the Labour alignment.)

poor resources, too much drain on manpower, the expenses of its geography, and an Arab boycott enforced by oil blackmail—all that just to get a chance to sell something abroad. So when you see an export contract (with all it means in terms of foreign currency earned and hopes of future solvency) demolished by a strike, it's like watching a starving family pour milk down a drain. I'm not the only one who perceives this, of course, so the worker-solidarity spirit is definitely fraying now; impatient things are being said even in the presence of foreigners and even by the chauvinistic. Though not yet, it seems, by the ebullient patriot I met at a neighbor's son's Bar Mitzvah party. (It's a very conservative, non-English-speaking family I barely know: I wouldn't have expected a hands-across-the-sea gesture from them, and I think Thereza was surprised, too). One of the out-of-town relatives, a thirtyish man who was tipsy and obviously unaccustomed to it, insisted that he had something to tell the American soferet and eventually they let him. This was his pronouncement: "In The Land some things are not so good and some are very good.* But there is nothing in Israel that is not good." His relatives seemed embarrassed, but I couldn't tell whether because of his flag-waving or his being in wine.

One Israeli phenomenon that's not-so-good was to be expected, I suppose: some of the effects of the war are now showing up in the children. Lately I hear stories from everyone I know who comes in contact with school-age children, and even music and dance teachers—whose pupils come by choice and are thus a select, motivated sample—tell me it's impossible to get the kids' attention, they don't carry out projects, have to be constantly yelled at to exact even minor obedience, etc.† I myself observe that the children in my neighborhood are even more groupy than before (Israeli children are very chevra-minded, but the chevra is not restrictive and individuals dart out at will, usually) and are silent rather than giggly; nobody has tried out his school English on me lately . . . And the effect can't all be ascribed to wartime absence of fathers, for Thereza and Jan's daughter is exhibiting what looks like some kind of war shock too. Suddenly, she refuses to stay alone at home, though she's quite old enough and the circumstances are such that

---

*I'm a timid translator, so I've stuck to literal meaning. But the expression, in general use, really is closer to the British "Super!" or the American "Great!"
†Much of the picture drawn by the complaints resembles the profiles of children in U.S. inner cities, particularly among families recently come from rural areas to the bewildering urban scene. I suppose that figures: in both cases the parents are seen as no longer quite in charge. And to the harsh logic of childhood, the fact that somebody else started the war is irrelevant.

fear is ridiculous: their house has no attic or basement for ghosties to be imagined lurking in, none of its few rooms is far enough from wherever you're standing to become at all mysterious, and it's right smack in the middle of a row of houses with people she's known all her life only a few feet away and doors always open onto the communal mews. But none of that tempers the girl's fear, which appeared out of nowhere. Thereza and Jan circle the problem but can't find a way in: questions get shrugs, and coaxing to tell Mama or Papa what she's afraid of—and they won't laugh, however silly it is—produces nothing but, if pushed, tears and/or a mad dash out of the room. The evidence is, though, that she isn't afraid of any thing; for her brother doesn't sit beside her and hold her hand when he's at home, but his presence somewhere in the house is enough. She's just afraid to be alone, I think. And she doesn't know why, and if you suggest reasons you may be putting ideas into her head. So once again, education and ratiocination bring you out right where common sense did: the only thing to do is not leave her alone until she gets over it.*

My three teenagers still come for English conversation but are less assiduous, I note—and Elie, who was always somewhat restless, now hardly sits still at all. But I can't assign that to the war because much of their behavior resembles American high-school seniors I remember: nobody anywhere seems to be able to devise a curriculum that will keep that last year in high school, and especially the last part of it, at all enchanting. The Beer-Sheva youngsters, headed for army service next, are spared the tortures of the college applications routine (and so are their lucky parents!); but the bagrut looms, and it's at least as nerve-wracking as the college entrance exams back home. So Estie and Elie and Amir are nervous and jumpy, and alternately too glib and too silent; but I can't unscramble that from the general facts of their age and station.

FEBRUARY—Nature doesn't have to consider whose calendar to accept. So the desert has its own New Year when one day, usually sometime in February, it suddenly bursts into bloom. That day isn't random, for it can be seen coming by the knowledgeable: someone like that came by one evening to say tomorrow was going to be The Day, and if I cared to see it, I must be ready at 5 A.M.—dress warmly,

---

*For the information of the concerned, yes, she did get over it. After a while, things got to a stage where she could be kidded about it: she'd grin shamefacedly but still found the kidding preferable to being left alone. Then finally, it *stamm* got forgotten about. Now she's a much-in-demand neighborhood babysitter and probably doesn't even remember how she felt back then.

and don't forget your canteen. And yes, it most certainly would be worth the trouble, Geveret . . .

Oh my, was it ever: I should've been struck by lightning for even asking. For, drunk on fatigue and shivering though wrapped in a blanket, I stood in gray light and tan-gray sand—everything had such a milky, pearly look—and, simply by getting up in the middle of the night and jolting in the back of a truck for a while, I got to see the Garden of Eden before Adam appeared. It's the suddenness that does it, I guess. During the winter, the caramel-color desert takes on a faint green fuzz; you can see it when you ride by in a car, but it's not really spring-like. I mean, it's not a reminder or a portent the way a crocus emerging through snow is—the chief effect is to make the landscape look a little more "normal" (i.e., like an empty piece of winter countryside back home on a non-snowy day). But then nothing else happens, so you forget about it.

Unless you happen to be acquainted with someone who works in the desert and knows its signs and will make you climb out of bed at 4 A.M. to get down to the right spot at the right moment. Then you can stand and look while, abruptly and as far as you can see in any direction, the flowers appear. There must be light-year numbers, 10-to-the-somethingth of them, little tiny blue and pink and purple and white flowers, all very close to the ground. The scene still has that absence of verticals peculiar to the Negev—where sometimes you yourself, your own five feet five inches sticking up, are the only connection between underfoot and overhead—but it's as though somebody had whisked the beige carpet away and instantly replaced it with one close-patterned as paisley. (Come to think of it, that may explain the teeny-tiny, crowded, over-and-over flowers characteristic of the indigenous art: that's what they see, when they see anything except a vastness too indifferent for imitation.)

The flowers remind me of lily of the valley, but they wouldn't remind a botanist, because I don't mean bell-shaped blossoms, scent, etc. Maybe it's only that I once tried to keep lily of the valley from taking over my backyard, and these have the same way of kind of appearing suddenly, by the dozens, while you pause to breathe. But also reminiscent is the way the flower is sort of tucked into a leaf that's itself just a broadened stem—as though the whole works had to be got into one fast shot: here we go, stem-leaf-flower-seed, all together now, one try is all we get, one two three SPROUT . . . Indeed, one try may actually be all they get, I gather. For, though there'll still be some wild flowers here and there, most of this will be shoved out by grasses—if where they came up was a good spot, it'll be good for the tough pasture grasses, too—or dead because it wasn't a good spot.

I see I haven't really described the flowers. But how can I? It's as impossible as describing an orgasm. Besides, I'd need a whole different vocabulary: does the word "flower" really fit something so incredibly numerous and sudden? How can I write that word and expect people to see something they'd never think of picking and that it seems quite natural to walk on? All I can describe is what it feels like to experience this sudden brief delicate flowering of the vast brooding Indifference: I know You don't care, but thank you, thank you anyway . . .

We couldn't cut through the wadi because it's still February and so long as there's still any possibility of rain, the wadis can be deadly. Because you don't get any warning at all before all of a sudden there's a wall of water racing toward you, squeezed into a torrent by the narrow, steep-sided gash it travels through. There's nothing to grab, and you can't get ahead of the water or survive the force of it; so if you can't get out of its way in one minute or less, you're dead . . . The Israelis, who are easily as smart alecky as Americans, lose a hiker or two—usually a student, or somebody aged seventeen to twenty-one—in a flooded wadi every year; the newspapers report it with the usual warnings, but the next year another bunch figures this once it'll be okay, and wham . . . The desert can be beautiful but it is never genial.

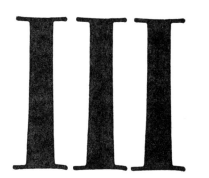

17 ⬀ Phil's Israel

By the time my son Phil came to visit, I was living on the other side of Beer-Sheva in a much classier neighborhood. By which I mean principally that there, I wasn't the only resident who put the cover back on the communal dustbin. (It's heavy, so I'd usually enlist the help of passing youngsters. That had the happy side effect of tagging closed-up garbage as American chic, with thus some chance of improving matters in the future.) Originally, I was motivated by concern for the public health, aided by my past discovery—in Washington's Georgetown—that rats do not happen only in slums. But then I learned a purely Beer-Sheva reason: if you don't cover the damn bins, cats jump in. And then, when you're passing by on the street at night, your footsteps frighten them—and something incredibly fast and frantic and sometimes yowling erupts from the bin, in a great leap that just misses you and does at least as much for your heart action as electric shock. (It's not true, by the way, that all cats are gray at night. Some of them are whizzing black streaks.)

Shikun Hay* is also a much better neighborhood for getting rides to and from concerts: before, only the yekke lady next door and I were regular concert-goers, but in my new neighborhood lots of people were. And a great many more people spoke English, either natively—"Anglo-Saxons" in Beer-Sheva tend to congregate in the classier quarters—or because they had been to university (both of these also explain better jobs, and thus more people with cars, too). The language of the macaulet still wasn't English, but the people

---

*The French *quartier* is probably a better translation of *shikun* than any one English word. And *hay* is simply the fifth letter of the alphabet: socialist city planners don't have to call a new area "Happy Knolls" or something imaginative like that.

who ran it were from Argentina; hearing me ask *"Quanto es?"* in there one day, Thereza remarked acidly on how much faster I seemed to learn Spanish than Hebrew. (Actually, I *can* ask "How much?" in Hebrew, too. But it's fun to see her simmer.)

Thereza and Jan were the friends who lived closest now, which was great for me—among the women I'd got to know in my year and a half in Israel, Thereza was as much a "natural" friend for me as Anita, but without any hampering language problems. And it was good for Thereza's kids to hear English spoken at home as well as in school lessons. It wasn't a bad idea for her husband, either: Jan had hidden his quite adequate but accented English behind Thereza's interpreting up to then, but once I moved nearby he was on his own. Because, since he's an expert on desert agriculture, I appointed him consultant for my balcony "garden." Where I'd insisted on planting blue American morning glories, which were beautiful and unique in the neighborhood; when they got badly assailed by Negev bugs, I'd summon Jan—who then had to reproduce, in quantities suitable for my four feet of garden, the remedies used to protect several thousand dunams of experimental agriculture down in the desert. That exercise cost poor Jan a terrible lot of intensive arithmetic, with fractions, but he was probably repaid in delight by the discovery that the word "dirt" also meant what was always "soil" in the English agricultural journals he read. (He couldn't believe it at first: I think he figured it was some kind of personal aberration. But then I found a reference to "dirt farmers" in a book and showed it to him. He went away marveling at American English.)

It was Thereza who went shopping with me again, this time for amenities like one of those aluminum-frame lawn furniture lounges made of woven plastic strips. It cost the equivalent of twenty-five dollars*—plus several days' wait while one was brought down from Tel Aviv, and then of course we had to carry it home on the bus—but I needed it because now I had a real *mirpesset* (mere-PESS-et, balcony) to sit out on. I was up on the fourth floor, so the view was gorgeous; and I had neat brick-edged planters along two of the walls and even hooks and strings for vines to grow up the walls and across the ceiling on. La de da, back to bourgeois splendor. Practically all the way, too, for, inside the apartment, I had kitchen cabinets. And a whole wall of closet in the front bedroom, which obviously had been the master bedroom. But it overlooked

*More than three times the price I just saw advertised in the U.S., three years and a lot of rising U.S. prices later. I hate to think what it must cost in Beer-Sheva now.

378

the street, so I preferred to sleep in the other one, which had been the children's room: what was out back was a courtyard and gardens and rows of one-family houses, and I can sleep past human starting-the-day noises but not the clatter of soda bottles being delivered and the empties taken away (with cheery 6 A.M. Shaloms) at the macaulet below.

My perversion of the bedrooms, I learned, puzzled and rather offended my landlords, who'd spent a great deal of do-it-yourselfing time and money making their boudoir as elegant as they could possibly imagine—and now saw it inhabited by bookshelves and utilitarian desks and a typewriter, the walls hung with notes reminding me when lilacs bloomed in Massachusetts and where the murderer really was at 2:15 P.M. on a mythical October 23, and not a ruffled lampshade anywhere in sight. I could understand their dismay. In fact I was rather more sympathetic than the neighbors' daughter, who was interpreting when my landlords came for their first look around. I'd caught their puzzlement, but I had to ask her what the Hebrew exchange had been about. "Oh, nothing," Judith said with casual contempt. "Rivka said it was a shame you didn't seem to know how much a closet like that costs. So I told her it was a shame *she* didn't know closets are no big deal to an American."

This tactless young interpreter was obviously a great factor in making my life convenient: Thereza was nearby but it still meant running down four flights of stairs to fetch her, whereas Judith was a lot handier. But meeting Judith before Phil came was also a stroke of luck, for—though I didn't realize the need at the time—it brought me into contact with the local university-student society and gave me a close-up view of some relations between grown-up but not yet married children and their parents. So that Phil found me rather more like he'd known me in Cambridge than he would have if he'd come six months earlier; and I was at least somewhat in tune with the mother-and-son picture into which he and I got inevitably cast.

A little later, I got to know a great many Israeli young couples, so I could place Judith among her age group. (She was not entirely typical: at about twenty-five, she was old to be still unmarried, which bespoke a certain independence of mind and successful bucking of parental urgings; and she was more moody and quick-trigger emotional than was entirely acceptable among the sabras I came to know.) But at the time, what I mostly knew to compare her with was American college kids, and there were quite a few similarities. Judith and her friends spoke a special iconoclastic language, for one thing: the university-student slang word *zabosh* (zah-BOSH) is an acronym made out of the three Hebrew words *Zeh*

379

byah shelchah (or *shelach*, if it's a female you're talking to), which mean "That's your problem"; if you understand the solemn social-responsibility-think of Israeli society, you can see the naughty tweaking of Mama and Papa's values in that saucy I'm-for-me announcement. Another expression, a mocking contraction of the Hebrew words for "When I came to The Land," is probably special to the children of immigrants (in America, what the children of immigrants kept hearing was, "In the Old Country . . ."); but it's not really too different from a repeated speech of my father's which my sister and I, rolling our eyes heavenward, thought of as the "I walked ten miles to school" number . . .

Since Judith was the only child of parents who'd come from Russia more than a decade before, she was in fact an immigrant. And indeed she gave me what I think is the most memorable picture yet of what changing countries is like for a child: "We walked out into the desert, my parents holding my hands, and my mother said, 'This is our land now.' I knew I was supposed to get to like it, but it was so empty! And then my father told me there wouldn't be snow out there, not ever . . ." But she was very much a child of the new land—pretty in the leggy sunbrowned unself-consciously sexy way of the local young women, with the characteristic rapid speech and quick motions, and an emphatic air of having decided everything really important. She'd recently finished being an English major at the university, and her mile-a-minute and virtually accentless English ranged from colloquialisms like "big deal" to A-student explications of *Hamlet*. Which latter she went in for rather heavily, perhaps out of a notion that one ought to Talk Literary to a writer.*

But of course as summer drew near, what most of my conversations were about was the coming of Phil, whom I hadn't seen for about a year and a half. And, since I'm never exactly close-mouthed about my own affairs—and certainly not when I'm joyous—everybody I knew was enlisted in the preparations. Phil had last seen me in a state of great disorder, about to set off for Israel and surrounded by packed trunks and lists of things with exclamation points after them. So I was determined that he should find me in everything-under-control calm now—which, since I'd just moved house, meant hurrying; and hurrying in Beer-Sheva can only be

---

*That Israeli respect for the arts can have maddening results sometimes: e.g., Estie (one of my three ex-high-school students) came home on leave from the army, managed to find out where I'd moved to, and came over—and then, because she heard the typewriter going, left a note in the door instead of knocking and interfering with my sacred art! I'd have given a lot to lay my eyes on her, and I was furious when I found the note, hours later.

done with lots of help, if at all. Thus everyone rallied, in a bustle rather like London preparing for a coronation. In fact, more like a coronation than I realized, I guess: I saw it as only the chevra coming to my aid, which we all did when something happened that was important to one of us. And with people like Fran, it probably was just that. But the Israelis probably made a distinction I didn't see: who was coming was a *son*. The young prince. So no wonder Maggie was all in a tizzy . . .

But Phil's own feeling fit even less than mine did the Israelis' notion. For he was then still young enough to be consciously wary of Mama's-boy booby traps, so he wasn't going to Israel to see his mother but to work as a volunteer in a kibbutz, which was something more "respectable" in his milieu. (He outgrew that nonsense, thank heaven: last time he came to Israel, it was frankly and bravely to visit his mother. By that time, it had become a perfectly manly thing to do.) Thus he dropped in to Beer-Sheva for a weekend and then vanished up north. Whence he would return after he'd finished his volunteer stint: part of the deal on that was a two-week period when the volunteers were free to roam the country at will, seeing the sights and staying at kibbutzim and hostels. At that point Phil would feel it acceptable, I gathered, to acknowledge me as an Israeli sight worth seeing—and everybody in Israel stays with relatives, so that would be socially acceptable.*

It was this arrangement, with Phil on the kibbutz up north and me typing away in Beer-Sheva, that first brought the Israelis' raised eyebrows to my attention. For it's almost impossible to call anyone on a kibbutz. The best chance is to try at mealtimes, since the phone is in the dining hall and whoever answers will yell, "Anybody here named Phil?" and he just might be within earshot. (But everyone in the country knows that, so kibbutz phones are always busy during mealtimes.) It's possible to call *from* a kibbutz, as there are pay phones—and the sophisticated, long-established one Phil was on had not only other, experienced volunteers who could wise him up on Israeli telephone techniques but also a kibbutz member whose summer assignment was to supervise the foreign volunteers.† So if Phil only had a phone to phone to——.

---

*If all this sounds a bit extreme and I remarkably patient, all I can say is, nineteen-year-olds aren't much for moderation—and I could remember easily my own taste for elaborate independence and symbolic gestures at that age.

†Inevitably, he was known as "Big Daddy"—another example of the way American culture appears to take over, for the volunteers came from many countries and Americans were in a minority. But they were all young, and among the young, "American" practically *meant* "chic," it seemed.

381

That's where Judith's parents, who had a phone and were generous, came in. Neither of them spoke English, but Phil learned to shout "Maggie, *bevakasha?*" If Judith wasn't at home, whoever was would tell him "*Rock rega*" and then run over and fetch me. I'd come into their house and stand there talking incomprehensibly, in their way as they were getting dinner or interrupting them while they were eating it. I felt awkward and guilty about these obvious impositions, even though Judith kept assuring me her parents didn't mind and they themselves did their best, via smiles and gestures, to make the point too. They meant it, and at last I understood why: up to then, Israeli feelings about the centrality of the family had been items for my notebook, but now I was seeing it up close and personally—the pain in Judith's mother's face as she reported that "*ha ben shel* Maggie" had called when I wasn't at home was unmistakable. This was more than neighborly kindness; a son trying to reach his mother meant a special, almost sanctified obligation to lend a hand.

Maybe it was these exposures to Israeli-style parenthood, which has established rights and is never meek, that emboldened me. Or maybe it was because I'd come to a good stopping place in my book. But one day I decided to hell with this so-near-and-yet-so-far shtick, and I boldly proposed that I come visit Phil on the kibbutz. He checked and found it could be done: sure, come on, he said, he'd arranged with Big Daddy for a place to put me up. Thus clapped on the back, so to speak, by the whole Israeli culture, I managed to overcome qualms, travel hang-up, etc. (Back in Beer-Sheva, they were probably saying, "*Now* she's acting like a mother . . .")

But when I got up there, after a long trip on several buses, those differences in notions about mothers promptly popped up again. For it turned out that Phil, in obtaining permission to have a guest, hadn't mentioned that the guest was his mother. So the quarters arranged for me were in one of the "barracks" inhabited by the volunteers, which had not quite all the luxuries of the mountain cabins available to hikers in the U.S.; and, since this was definitely the domain of the young, it also offered no more privacy or freedom from radio rock than a college dormitory. Still, I wouldn't have boggled. But Tova and Reuben, the middle-aged kibbutznik couple Phil was dining with when I arrived, were horrified: whatever had Pheel been thinking of? One simply didn't put one's mother up in a place like that! They wouldn't hear of it, I must come and stay with them.

I did: I was much too tired to argue, anyway. (And when I

later saw where I would have been, I was damn glad. For I don't mind roughing it, but the volunteers' dorms were a hell of a distance from the dining hall and everything else: the kibbutz, no more interested in losing their hearing than I was, had put all the rock-age young—their own as well as the foreign volunteers—well out of everybody's earshot.) Tova and Reuben's house was much more substantial than the one-room numbers provided the chaverim in a Negev kibbutz I'd visited, for this not only had a bedroom and a salon—the latter handsomely furnished and with an open-out sofa, on which I slept—and a quite modern bathroom, they also had a tiny kitchen and a dining table, so they could eat at home if they chose. What's more, they even had a beautiful garden complete with garden furniture: in short, it was all quite suburban except for the number of rooms. Which was more than sufficient, though, because their children (now grown and gone except for weekly visits) had been, in orthodox* kibbutz fashion, housed in the children's house.

It all really figured, though. When Tova and Reuben had first come, the land had literally been the malarial swamp that's since become an Israeli cliché (and that Arabs who couldn't be paid to work on it then have taken to calling their "homeland" since it got so much prettier). "We had one toilet for fifty people," Tova told me. She kept saying that sort of thing: people on the old kibbutzim have made it, and the fact is frequently embarrassing to them. I recognized that after a while and managed to stop being articulate about the comparative luxuries around me, but at first I was frankly dazzled. The kibbutz is huge, and beautiful—one feature, a long aisle of trees between which you walk in delicious cool and cathedral quiet, quite overwhelmed me after a year and a half of desert . . . All right, it *was* a malarial swamp once. But what I was looking at was very like a smoothly run country club: plenty of land perfectly tended, all sorts of luxuries; strolling through the grounds, or lying on my back beside the aquamarine waters of the gleaming swimming pool and looking up into the tops of great old trees, it was a little hard to think of stern, self-sacrificing pioneers. True, I was loafing and the kibbutzniks weren't. But they *were* swimming in the pool or bicycling about the paths or picking up what they needed in the kibbutz store or at the kibbutz's own Post Office (having spent hours and hours standing on sweaty lines in the one in Beer-Sheva, I'd surely notice that!), or even stopping by the ice machine in the porch of the dining hall on their way back from a leisurely game of

*I mean orthodox in terms of kibbutz philosophy: some of them have broken away from or modified the children's-house concept. I do *not* mean capital-O Orthodox, as in religion: at that kibbutz we had pork chops for Friday night dinner.

something. Because everybody worked, either in the kibbutz's fields or its produce plant—both far enough away to be quite out of my sight—or at some aspect of the communal housekeeping; but by early afternoon, what you saw was leisure, freshly showered people who wore clean clothes somebody else had laundered for them and ate meals planned and served and washed-up after by somebody else. Even if I'd been a worker rather than a guest, I'd still have lived more comfortably there than I did in Beer-Sheva.

But I learned quickly to keep judgments like that to myself. For this kibbutz was founded by people who mostly came from Russia and Poland and were the kind of Marxist-oriented Zionists the Soviet Union could be proud of. (The U.S.S.R. was the second country to recognize the new State of Israel in 1948, President Truman having just got the U.S. in first by pulling rank on the State Department.) The kibbutz still belongs to the Mapam party, which is not to be confused with Mapai: the latter is Golda Meir's faction of the Labour Alignment and is roughly equivalent to the Social Democrats of European parliaments, whereas Mapam is about as far left as you can go in the Knesset without bumping into the Communist seats. If the Soviets hadn't concluded that Marxist brotherhood rated rather lower than bases in the Middle East (which are even remunerative, too: arms sold to Egypt and Syria are really *sold*, with the money coming from Saudi Arabia—which isn't going to run out of it or use the funds for enlightened welfare programs instead, and where nobody has to get an appropriations bill through Congress), this Mapam kibbutz would still be flying the International Workers flag every May Day. They stopped that after the 1967 war, when the Mapamniks had to acknowledge that those really-truly had been Russian tanks shooting at them* . . . It's not kind to mention that, since one can imagine the hurt of those lifelong True Believers sold out by the Marxist Motherland. People used to laugh at them anyhow, but by now, enough other Israelis have been sold out by enough other ideologies and guilds and erstwhile old buddies so that the behind-the-hand giggles in Israel are dying down. Mapamniks are still very sensitive about it, though.

Well, you can see that this stern commune spirit (which is in fact quaintly reminiscent of the progressives of my own college

---

*Back in about 1968, I read a really touching "open letter" to world radicals from an Israeli writer (damn good one, too), asking, in effect, *Why did you turn me out?* The Israeli radicals had been just as radical as anyone else, labored just as loyally in the pro-Castro vineyards, etc., yet all of a sudden they were declared Other. It rather resembled a more emotional and personal *Just for a handful of silver he left us,/Just for a ribband to stick in his coat* . . . Except that Establishments, and sellouts, have grown more complicated since Robert Browning's time.

years) with its doctrinaire opposition to capitalist materialism can't endure very much of being complimented on its lovely home. But I could talk freely to Phil, so as he was showing me around the place one evening, I told him it reminded me of George Washington's plantation at Mount Vernon. (Which Phil has surely seen a lot of: a boy brought up in Washington, D.C. gets taken to Mount Vernon by his school, by his parents, and then for however long he's too young to be left at home when visitors have to be shown around. With Phil's memory, he can probably still map the wash houses, slave quarters, etc.)

Perhaps because he'd just finished work on the kibbutz kitchen crew, my son was moved to point to the obvious flaw in the analogy. But I brushed that aside: "Well okay, they're their own slaves here. But once the work day ends, everybody gets to be George and Martha." Which remark, now that I think of it, isn't quite accurate: George and Martha Washington didn't have to attend the endless meetings that go with kibbutz decision-making. (But on the other hand, Phil washed the dishes in a machine. So maybe it balances out, so to speak.)

Phil distrusts flights of fancy, and he apparently didn't feel that being your own slave was quite such a minor difference. But he did allow that as a "self-contained agricultural community," which Mount Vernon also was, there were certain resemblances. You see what happens when you send your boy to a good college?

So okay, the kibbutz is a self-contained etc. etc. And it's also chock-a-block with noble ideals and its children shudder at the very idea of materialism and nobody talks about money. But the clubhouse is still comfortable to the point of luxury and supplied with updated drawing-room graces, and there was even a discothèque (though that was for the volunteers, I was told: the implication that decadence seeps in from outside The Land is as commonly heard in Israel as is Hebrew being spoken in discothèques). And there's nothing hand-hewn about the consumer goods in Tova and Reuben's or in other salons I visited there, all of which featured furniture items that would drive lots of people in Beer-Sheva mad with envy . . . But it wouldn't occur to them to be furious, though the kibbutzim (which constitute a bloc with real clout in the Knesset) get all sorts of tax advantages, special rates for water, etc.—not to mention the priceless psychic feeding of being known as a noble few, purer than the grubbing average Israeli. Who will almost always tell you, the moment you even hint that what started out as *Ur*-egalitarianism seems to have picked up quite a few touches of elitism, that young kibbutzniks represent a disproportionate percentage of the casualties when there's a war.

385

Sure. Because they're officers (and in Israel's army, officers tend to go first), just like the young-subaltern sons of the British upper classes in World War I. And the aristocratic Washingtons didn't exactly get to escape the dangers of war either. So I say it's George and Martha, a lot more of the way than it seems: if an aristocracy exhibits *noblesse oblige*, that doesn't prove it isn't an aristocracy (though it's a real departure from the current one in the U.S., which has never heard of *noblesse oblige* and patronizes no Mozarts). Don't get me wrong— I admire a lot of kibbutzniks I know, sometimes for the same charms possessed by some of the rich Americans I know: people who never have to pay bills are, like those who never have to worry about money, often rather nicer than the harassed common man. But I admire more the right-naming of things. So I can quite understand that, in the vocabulary of Ivy League universities of the early 1970s, subsidies that don't go to arms manufacturers aren't subsidies; but me, I didn't see "self-contained." And I did see elitism, and anything that ignores that is hypocritical spinach.*

However, you should keep in mind (I didn't, as you'll learn) that Phil and I strolling the ordered grounds together and arguing about what we were seeing were ourselves being seen as Mother and Son, our conversations therefore personal and deeply important. (What was I supposed to be telling him, I wonder. Not to get his feet wet? To look out for bad girls who might give him VD?) So, the next day, the cultural-anthropology gap opened again. It was a Saturday and I was to leave on Monday, and I wanted to see Nazareth, where I'd never been, and buy some presents to take to the folks back in Beer-Sheva. I knew Nazareth wasn't very far away, but I wasn't sure whether there'd be a bus on Shabbat (though, inside the town, Saturday seemed as likely a shopping day as Sunday). Phil had the day off and was sleeping late and I didn't propose to wait around till he woke up, so when I was ready to go, I asked Reuben, who was lying out on a lounge taking the morning sun, for travel instructions.

He didn't seem to understand at first that I meant Today and right Now. But when he did, the culture-clash fat was immediately in the fire: "What?" he roared. "You go to Nazareth *alone*?" He came

*I may not be alone in these perceptions, as, despite the verbal defensive reflexes, virtually every Israeli you meet *used to* live on a kibbutz; and membership never climbs above about 3 percent of the population, even using the kibbutz movement's own figures. But all except a few rugged individualists believe that's because few people are noble and self-sacrificing enough: percentages don't affect the kibbutz-as-virtue image.

bounding off the lounge as though catapulted, demanding to know the whereabouts of Philip (not the familiar Pheel but the formal name obviously meaning "that blackguard"). He was asleep in the volunteers' house, I surmised. Reuben ordered, "You wait here," and was off while—the penny having finally dropped—I was trying to tell him I hadn't even mentioned to Phil that I wanted to go to Nazareth. Reuben heard me, I'm pretty sure. But he simply shook it off: naturally, the mother would try to defend her feckless son.

A few minutes later, Reuben was back. Phil was getting some breakfast, and I should go meet him; he'd been provided with all the necessary instructions. I paused long enough to get it on the record that Phil wasn't really a cad; it just wasn't our way, I said, to wake a sleeping son only because you wanted to go somewhere—and anyway, if I could travel to Israel by myself, surely I didn't need an escort to go a few kilometers? . . . Apparently I did succeed in saving Phil's reputation at least in part (though I think there was some feeling that if the boy had any character, he'd have risen above his culture), for when I left Reuben, what he was shaking his head about was less Pheckless Phil than the way some people live. In America, a strong young boy stays in the sack when his mother wants to go somewhere? Unbelievable.

I found Phil in the dining hall, munching a roll. He'd got the same message, but he said Reuben hadn't seemed angry—more sorrowful, like a probation officer disappointed in his charge but still patient and hopeful. But yes, he'd made it clear to Phil that day-off idling could never extend to ignoring your permanent built-in obligations to your dear old mom. I said I was sorry, and Phil shrugged and said he'd like to see Nazareth too, and now that he was up anyway . . . Then, smiled upon by the society, we took off.

It turned out to be a memorably pleasant day. But it was also the first time I was aware of myself as a kind of proprietor of Israel. I guess I'd been doing it before that—certainly I had often been the proprietor of Beer-Sheva—but it took Nazareth to really bring it out. For when Phil had visited me at home, what mostly went on in the brief time was Old Home Week, with him discovering household landmarks in their new setting ("Hey, you still have that old . . .") and getting to attach some faces to the names he'd grown familiar with in my letters. After that, at the kibbutz, we were on his turf, so to speak: "See, Mom, they've got this new irrigation technique . . ."

But now, in Nazareth, hilly and historic and colorful, and equally new to both of us, he was nevertheless the tourist and I the native. I recognized that when we passed a group of Russian immigrants (probably Georgians) who'd spread out blankets on the sidewalk and set out for sale a jumble of brummagem. Some of it had been brought from the Soviet Union but wasn't intrinsically valuable for that—rather as if you were to offer for sale your everyday, mass-produced hairbrush on the grounds that it's imported and thus valuable—and some of it, like cheap transistor radios, was simply the regular coin of illegal trade. You had to walk around this shoddy display to go up to the church (which, to be truthful, is a not much less shoddy display, only a lot older). Ladies with wisps of chiffon over their heads, presumably Christian pilgrims, were picking their way around the Russians. I winced with an Israeli kind of shame and caught myself thinking irritably, *Where the hell are the police?*

That's typical Israeli citizen-chutzpah, by the way. For the police could have been almost anywhere and wherever it was, it was pretty certain to be more important, since the jobs left to their small number are staggering in both quantity and complexity. But the recognition of the Russian-immigrant problem is also typically Israeli. I began explaining carefully to Phil that these characters didn't really need to be out selling their bric-à-brac, because machinery existed to supply all their needs (and in case it didn't touch individual circumstances, there was always a Vered to write a special social-worker chit for extra funds). But the problem was, the Georgians were the kind of people they were, trusting in no governments or official plans, always ready to try for the illicit buck. You could spend millions of lirot in tax money*—and in fact you had to, because there was no other way—on these immigrants and you'd still be, to these people, not much different (except less efficient, and thus perhaps less admirable) from all those, whether Tsarist or Bolshevik, whose function it had been to shove them around. For their culture is anarch and petty-crook: they are the street corner boys of anybody's society, the underworld smallchange, and nothing will make citizens of them—emotionally, anyway —except time, and maybe a whole generation's worth of that. So, *It just takes time,* the Israelis tell themselves, and go on trying . . . The only thing un-Israeli about all that was that I was saying it to Phil. If I'd been with Thereza, we might have simply looked at each other and shrugged, aware of what the tourists would think—and doubtless the Arab propagandists will make the most of it—but *ma la'asot?)*

In one specialized way, though, Phil turned out to be more "native" to the tiny winding bazaar streets than I: once we started

*I was getting a little hyperbolic there, implying that it was my money though I didn't pay Israeli income taxes and nobody had asked me to. But getting carried away like that is also part of the Israeli scene.

being shoppers, his haggling skills proved awesome. And surprising, for I'd never seen them before (where would I, come to think of it? At Sears, or the supermarket? And it wasn't with me that he'd traded baseball cards). I myself was useless except for minimal translating, which was usually unnecessary: numbers can be communicated easily, and most stallkeepers can manage enough English or French to do business. When we came upon a long embroidered dress (in the U.S., the style is called a caftan, and it's now fashionable, I believe) that I really wanted, I was so very unhelpful that Phil sent me into a back room to try it on—which was obviously unnecessary, since you don't have to try those on. I even tried to tell Phil that (you see what I mean about my helpfulness?) but he banished me sternly anyway—thus simultaneously removing me and my expressive face from the scene and establishing that he was not a man to be moved by the pleas of his mother. Which latter point he made again after I'd emerged with the news that the dress fit: the man had meanwhile come down to IL80, which was 20 lirot more than I'd meant to pay. But that was then only about three bucks' difference and I really wanted that dress, so I looked at Phil hopefully. Nope, he said. I lingered, fondling the embroidery (oh, Maggie!), and my son told me—in slow, careful English—to put the dress back and come on; then he took my arm and hustled me toward the door, talking over my protests that honest, I didn't care about a few lirot . . .

We got the dress for IL60, and I couldn't stop marveling at my son the haggler. (While he grumbled: he could have done better, he thought, if I'd only shut up.) Where had he been hiding this amazing talent, I kept asking him as we went on to buy baskets—with me, this time, shutting up . . . Now that I've had time to think it over, the answer is obvious. For Phil has always been good at games, and Arab buying is a game, a match in which each side uses information about the other as the principal weapon: Phil knew the Arab storekeepers doubled their prices (at least) for tourists, the Arab knew these American college boys all have fat books of traveler's checks in the pockets of their ragged jeans. And this one had an importunate Mama burdening him, too, so he'd be a pushover . . . (I hate to say this, but if their women are like me, maybe the Arabs know what they're doing when they keep bargaining the exclusive business of men.)

But then, when we decided to take a bus ride to see the non-tourist parts of town, gamesmanship was less important than acquaintance with realities, so it was suddenly my turf again. Though not entirely, or I'd have been willing to admit that I didn't understand what the driver was trying to tell me (with my quite justified feelings of inferiority about my Hebrew, I always assume the other guy is speaking it understandably—which this guy probably wasn't) and thus we wouldn't have got on that bus. In the downtown swirl of mixed populations where we embarked, it wasn't so noticeable that we were the only non-Arabs on the bus. But we were, and it went to exclusively Arab districts, and we were becoming more and more noticed and commented upon (apparently). So I finally realized why the driver had been trying to tell us we didn't want—*Atem lo rohtsim*—something. But, this bus? Or wherever it was he was going? The real answer was "Trouble," and suddenly I could see why he couldn't have been too specific. For he rather thought we'd made a mistake, but maybe our jaunt was deliberate—maybe the American college boy rather than the sensible-age Israeli-dressed woman was in charge? In that case, it would be useless to argue . . .

I found that last out for myself, when I did get the idea and told Phil we should get off and go back. We were sitting directly behind the driver and I think he understood some English: I could sense him pulling for me* as I argued with Phil. Who, to my surprise (but not, I think, the driver's), declared it all nervy nonsense. We clearly meant no harm, we were visibly foreigners walking around with our bundles of purchases, and it was broad daylight in a town that wanted tourists, so why would anyone treat us ill? (Oh my, logic yet, in the Middle East!) The bus stopped to let a passenger off and the driver turned; he caught my eye and we exchanged a look of dismay. For neither of us really thought anybody would start anything, but there's always the odd hothead around. We were united in simply not wanting trouble, the driver and I. But what in the world were we to do with this naïve American who had never seen a bombed market—Arabs and Jews equally bleeding and carted off to hospital—and couldn't understand whom the terrorists were really against?†

In the end, Phil and I compromised: we rode out to the end of the line, but we didn't get off there. It was just a sight-seeing jaunt, right? And then back on the same bus . . . I'm not sure the driver

*He may have had more specific reasons than I knew, for he could understand the passengers' conversations in Arabic. All I could tell was, they weren't humorous.
†This is taking Phil strictly in terms of his "uniform," and he wasn't as limited as that. But he *was* fed his news largely by the U.S. media, and now that I've seen what that's like, I can understand why Americans believe it's Jews-vs.-"Palestinians." (You'd think they'd begin to wonder, though, why it is that so few terrorist attempts are successful in Israel. The cops aren't that good, not without help from what you might call a Leave-Us-Alone coalition that has lots of Arab members.)

understood our negotiations; maybe I only imagined the man's shoulders looked less tense when the English voices behind him reached agreement. But he was clearly happy when we got off, safely returned to the center of town among tourists and policemen and people who don't want trouble either.

Once we were back at the kibbutz, though, there was no doubt whose turf we'd been on. For Tova and Reuben were disgusted with us: what, we'd not gone to the new town, Upper Nazareth? (*Ohhh*, a great light dawned then—that's probably where the driver was trying to direct us.) Such beautiful new buildings of many, most modern flats. A most innovative sewage system. (Or something like that: I didn't really listen to the glories of Upper Nazareth, because I know better—Israelis applauding social triumphs have a way of lumping present and future randomly. Thus, without meaning to mislead, they may well throw in all together actualities, measures currently in a Knesset committee, and a gift promised by a French sculptor.)

But we were forgiven: Israelis, great believers in education, generally find it possible to believe you'll learn better. So by Monday, when I was to leave, Phil and I were the kibbutz's babies again—and next time, everybody was sure, we'd know what to look at in Nazareth. Tova and Reuben earnestly declared all their kindness nothing whatever, and everybody assured me Pheel would be exquisitely cared for and I must come back again. Naturally, he was excused from work—it was simply taken for granted—to walk me out to the main road, where I'd catch my bus.

We stood by the roadside, sharing the patch of shade with a young girl and an older man who were waiting for a ride rather than the bus, and we talked companionably. Phil said he'd be coming down next weekend and I said I'd have another go at trying to cook hamburgers, and then the bus chugged up. My son dutifully got on with me so he could stow my original plastic bag, plus the dress and baskets I'd bought and gifts from the kibbutzniks, all in the overhead shelf. Meanwhile, I paid for one fare. So the driver knew that only I was going, but he made no attempt to hurry Phil-the-perfect-gent settling me in a seat near the window and making sure I had my glasses. Nobody at all seemed impatient, and the benign looks on nearby faces said it was only right and proper that a boy should take his time taking good care of Mama.

But, then Phil was finished, and the audience was not. When he said "Well, I'll see ya" and turned to go, there was an all but audible reaction from the passengers and the pink glow of approval darkened noticeably. I got the message promptly this time, but what to do with it was a problem. For Phil, raised in a Momism-fearing culture and mindful of the classic dangers of being the youngest son of a widow, was not really big on kissing Mama. (In fact, he never has been: when he was eight, I remember, he decreed that he could be kissed only on Mother's Day.) Yet precisely that was what everybody was waiting for—the *Nu?* murmurs in Hebrew were making that clear.

Well, Phil didn't understand the Hebrew commentaries. But he may have caught at least part of an observation, from a lady across the aisle, deploring the ways of "American hippies" (a term bearded American boys with unkempt hair hear a lot in Israel). Or perhaps he saw, coming over the driver's face, a look that must have been rather like Reuben's when he rousted the boy out of bed because a lad must learn . . . So Phil got the message, too. Bowing to public pressure, he bussed me soundly and then, to an audible accompaniment of satisfied sighs, swung down the steps. He's a nice kid, a bit stubborn but never niggardly. So he did it up handsomely: he was still standing there waving, as visibly devoted a son as any woman could ask, when I and my busload of defenders of motherhood set off for Beer-Sheva.

From the diary: 22

Of language and other barriers (August)

Having Phil around the house casts everything in a different light, with altered emphases jumping out at you. Like, he's the most unmaterialistic of kids—I remember the battles we used to get into whenever he had to be bought any clothes, and he went off to college with something like two pairs of pants—but his very presence in Israel instantly made it no longer so charming not to have a phone, and now that he's in Beer-Sheva, I'm constantly (silently) thankful for the greater bourgeois-ness of my current apartment. Maybe actively parenting just sort of pushes you in that direction?

Part of it is simply his American-ness, of course. For example, I found him rinsing out a glass he'd used and setting it on the drainboard—right, just the way he was taught as a boy. And he was also taught not to wipe his hands on the dish towel, so he took a paper towel (from the roll standing on top of the refrigerator: to mount the roller means getting Avi or Yehuda to come over with an electric drill, and I keep forgetting). But as I came into the kitchen, Phil was tossing the paper towel into the trash, though it was used only once and hardly even damp! I all but cried out in pain—if he'd been raised in Israel, he'd know how much paper towels cost! (Yeah. But if he'd been raised in Israel, we probably wouldn't even have had paper towels—only an American household in Beer-Sheva is likely to be that extravagant.)

In a way, he manages better here than I do, as temperatures in Centigrade don't confuse him and he's quite comfortable with kilos and grams. But he can't seem to get the hang of the non-customer-obliging culture: when he went up to Jerusalem, he had to stay over because he never imagined you couldn't get a bus back after about 9 P.M. (and I forgot to tell him because I took it so for granted). And he just doesn't seem able to grasp that stores don't stay open all day—we missed the supermarket the other morning because he loitered, though I kept warning him it was getting close to closing-time. That's easy enough to fix, of course: while he's here, I'll just have to alter my habits (e.g., working until the very last minute and then tearing down the stairs to get in under the wire). But it's funny, the things that are just too alien for him . . .

One not so funny: on the way back from that fruitless foray to the supermarket, a group of airplanes roared by overhead and Phil paused and looked up, shading his eyes. Which is what I used to do when I first came, I remember. Now I simply plod on, like the

Israelis. Knowing that if it wasn't some kind of practice exercise, I'd have heard, all right, so they're nothing to do with me.

(No, that's not quite all there is to that item. Because Phil looks up not because he thinks the Phantoms have anything to do with him but out of simple curiosity. And I don't look up because I'm always aware of the possibility of their relevance: I can probably never again hear planes overhead and react with Phil's American curiosity, so innocent that it doesn't even have to make the assumptions of irrelevance I—and Israelis—do.)

I'd forgotten about the little boy on the first floor (he's about three, with a cap of glossy black curls, rather like what Phil probably can't remember ever looking like) until he called out "Shalom, Sveedi" as we went by. I stopped and introduced ha ben sheli, of course. But as we climbed the stairs, Phil wanted to know what sveedi was: he knows geveret, but this one was new to him . . . Well, what it means is mostly that I couldn't cope with the little boy's name (which is Eres—two syllables, and I'm still not sure which is accented) when I first moved here, but I saw him every day as I went downstairs to buy my newspaper, and he was such a cute, friendly child. So I took to saying "Shalom, sweetie": it was easier than any of the Hebrew words I knew, all of which involve that irritating necessity to know the gender you're addressing* (which info isn't easy to come by when you're looking at a unisex-haired tot wearing only baby-clothes shorts, which have no fly anyway; gender is a mystery until you hear which form of "you" his mother uses to speak to him). Anyway, his mother speaks a little English and I guess she told him "sweetie" was just a nice name to call people, because the next day he surprised both of us by attempting it with me. Naturally we laughed, which pleased him, so he practiced. And by now it's—well, just part of my day. The last time I paid any attention to the matter was when his brother, aged about five, got jealous and told me "Gahm ani" (me, too). So I called him Sweetie Godol (Big Sweetie); that made him giggle and then, satisfied, he forgot about it. But the little one, more of a traditionalist, goes on singing out his "Shalom, Sveedi" every time we meet . . .

Luckily, my Hebrew still isn't great enough to interfere with playing outsider-games with the language: I may know more words than Phil, but I still hear them "objectively," too. So we invented a melodrama starring Rock Rega as the stalwart hero who falls in love with the Portuguese dancing girl Annie Lo Rosa (ani lo rotsa is the feminine form of "I don't want," thus offering handy plot possibilities). Also, Phil encountered on the kibbutz the startling fact that

*There is a comfily genderless word, I've since learned with relief: MO-tek is the same for both sexes and means "sweetie" too.

394

when you call "Boy!" a girl will show up; apparently it had the volunteer dining-hall crew in stitches (Bo-ee *is the feminine of the imperative of the verb "to come": to call a boy you say "Bo!"), as did the revelation that the Hebrew word for "she" is* he. *But I'm tickled that he spotted the same significance for the society I'd seen in the fact that functionaries in government offices "receive" the public. That's what the verb means, and their attitude reflects it beautifully. . .*

The volunteers at the kibbutz are taught some Hebrew, and Phil's picked up some more outside, too. So he uses "B'seder" easily* and drops the odd "Ken" or "Tov" with an almost convincing air; but he can still easily understand why I chose the name I did for my turtle. Sweetie Godol gave it to me and I was just establishing turtle quarters out on the mirpesset when Hilda came by and told me it was a female.† So I named the turtle Klita, which sounded appropriately dainty for a small girl creature. Of course I know it's the word for "absorption"—I lived in a mercaz klita, after all. But my Israeli friends can't think of it as anything but that, so they always giggle as they ask after Klita. (I can understand, I guess: suppose a foreigner in Mass. decided to name her kitten Jealousy, because it's a pretty word?) Phil, though, has enough of an outsider ear to think of it as a nice name for a turtle.

However, he's acquiring enough Hebrew to bring him to a certain loss of his faith in my linguistic abilities.‡ For, on a bus the other day, I had some difficulty making myself understood to the driver. And when I'd finished and staggered back to join Phil, he eyed me suspiciously and asked (a tad disingenuously, I thought) whether it could be that my Hebrew had been wanting? Stung into unusual cool, I said, "A lot of new immigrants are hired as bus drivers. They can learn Hebrew on the job, you see." Phil just nodded: he either believed me or was conceding that for thinking that quickly I deserved to see my run on the scoreboard, and I don't propose to find out which.

But the language fun-and-games stopped today, when another kind of language gap opened up—one so hard to close that

---

*And ingeniously, too: when he was leaving at the end of the summer, I asked him to cable me reporting his safe arrival. The subsequent wire from New York said, simply (and economically): "B'seder. Love, Phil."

†No, Ogden Nash fans, I don't know how she knew: my turtle does live "twixt plated decks," etc. But if you've met Hilda in these pages (see, e.g., "Geveret Maggie's Frigidaire"), you'll understand that I'd simply take her word for it. (And not only I: when Martha asked me how I knew the turtle's sex, I said "Hilda told me" and she just said "Oh," though neither of us knows whether Hilda even took Zoology I.)

‡Well, that was due to vanish anyway, as it was infirmly based on my once-remarkable ability to translate *"Achtung!"* and *"Alles im ordnung, Feldwebel"* back when they were barked out by Germans in the "Combat" series on TV. I was thought quite an asset, and a hard-up parent needs every bit of respect she can pick up . . .

I'm feeling rather gloomy about doing it for readers someday. For after all, you might say Phil constitutes my best shot, communications-wise . . . Still, maybe it was because I wasn't sitting at my typewriter but caught off guard, with no time to think. That's what I'm trying to tell myself, anyway.

What happened was, we'd been over to the university so I could show Phil the library, and we were headed back home for lunch and siesta (in August, you just don't stay outdoors in the middle of the day). Waiting for the bus, I realized we needed milk and our own macaulet would be closed by the time we got there. But there was one not far from the bus stop—a couple of streets this way, I told Phil. He trailed me doubtfully, by now convinced of the shop-closing game but still inhabited by a historic skepticism about my sense of direction. I know that's justified, so I was telling him nervously that I used to go into this macaulet sometimes when I lived over this way—when, glory be, there it was, a literal hole in the ground down some half-dozen rickety steps.

We came plunging into the cool dimness and the woman behind the counter looked up from waiting on a customer and said "Shalom, Geveret. Ma shlomech?" in obviously pleased welcome. Even before she went on to say she hadn't seen me in a long time, I knew I must know her. But she had the advantage of me, and I don't mean figuratively—coming in from the midday glare, I could hardly see in the shop. I said Shalom too, agreed that it had been a long time, and told her I lived in Shikun Hay now. Then suddenly my eyes adjusted and I saw her. And I remembered her and her shop and a day I'd come in, also just before closing time, and stood there holding my shopping bag, waiting in what was too ragged to be a queue but was an understood order . . .

It was like a film dissolve, I swear it: all at once, it just was that other day, with the bell tinkling over the door and another woman coming in, a dark figure not very visible because a rambunctious toddler had got loose up ahead and was darted after by its mother, thus causing a general shuffling of women and children and shopping bags in that narrow dimness. Airless too, for it was a cold day and the window at the back, behind the refrigerator case of cheeses, was closed tightly. Only the opening of the front door did anything to dilute the pungent smells: that macaulet catered mostly to Moroccans, who bought a lot of the kind of things I didn't eat but had learned to recognize the smells of. I always felt especially alien and "Anglo-Saxon" in there.

Once the mother with the naughty child had got safely finished and squeezed past me, I saw the woman who'd come in last.

She was very thin, in fact utterly haggard, and dressed altogether in dead black, including even her stockings; the pallor of her drawn face was pitilessly framed by a jet-black head scarf. Everybody seemed to know her, or at least about her. The customer whose turn it was motioned her forward instead, and when the woman in mourning hung back, her colorless lips saying something protesting, the whole group began coaxing her—Please, let us give you this was the obvious message. The proprietress, who looked like the plump and pleasant-faced aftermath of a pretty peasant girl, said " 'Vakesha, Geveret" softly, but with a kind of captain-of-the-ship authority that seemed to do the trick. The black-clad woman came forward and I could hear her answering questions in a dull voice: yes thank you, she was feeling better now.

Then she began to give her order, and I began to eavesdrop, as well as I could, on two women behind me who were discussing her. It wasn't easy—they were muttering, trying to be unnoticed, and besides they used the shorthand speech and half-sentences that suffice between people who know each other well. But I got enough to learn that the mourning woman had lost her elder son, a reservist, early in the war; he must have been one of those caught in the Bar Lev line by the Egyptian surprise attack. When the casualty lists came out and it was established that he was "fallen,"* there'd been an attempt to send her younger son home (it's against policy to take a family's only surviving son for active duty, and she was apparently a widow besides). But though the younger boy came home briefly, he suddenly slipped out again, after only a few days of the mourning period, and sneaked back to his unit. The army tried to find him, but his buddies lied for him; and then the war got so bad and everyone was just too busy... It was said he was still all right, though: he'd sent word via his married sister, who had a phone—

The gossipers broke off abruptly, like schoolgirls when a teacher enters, because the bereaved woman had finished and was turning to go. Somebody else asked her then how she was feeling, and she said it was easier now because all the family from up north had gone back home. So at least she no longer had to cook for a crowd. Heads nodded sympathetically at that, agreeing that it would be a relief. The woman's voice, thin to begin with, wound down to a wisp and then vanished altogether. She stood there in

---

*Most Israelis seem to use the frank "dead," rather than euphemistic equivalents of "passed away," etc. But to die in a war has a special verb, respectful but less fact-dodging than simply information-giving: someone who "fell" didn't die of natural causes or after his allotted fourscore-and-ten...

397

silence, looking at the busy comforters praising the convenience of solitude—and reading, I guess, the unacknowledged truth all the faces knew: it wasn't really better, in the lonely silence now with nobody at all to cook for. Her thin face crumpled and she began to cry quietly, great tears rolling down and splashing on her dead-black bodice.

I looked away, and then I saw the two women behind me. They were both weeping too, openly and without pretense, wiping their faces with a sleeve and the corner of a head scarf. It all seemed so blatant, almost as if they were enjoying themselves; they looked like an audience having a good cry at Stella Dallas or some other tearjerker. I felt disgusted, and then ashamed of that: they were a very emotional people, these Moroccans, I reminded myself. It was simply their way. And it was not only unkind but downright stupid to be judging them by the standards of an entirely other culture.

The woman in mourning didn't bother to wipe her tears—she just let them keep happening while she walked out slowly, carrying her shopping bag of yellow nylon net; it bloomed, unexpected and riotously gay, against the total blackness of her figure. The woman behind the counter said "Chaval" (alas, too bad) as the door closed after her. The two sniffling women behind me moved up to take their turn, and then began to talk and order. I stood there in the space they'd left, not paying attention anymore but thinking about that frail black figure going home to sudden empty leisure, to wait for word of the other son—the angry one who wouldn't let them make him somehow what his brother had died for... All of a sudden something splashed on my hand and I looked down at it, and that's when I knew I was crying. I couldn't feel it happening, I could hardly believe it: I didn't even know the living son or the dead one, the bereaved mother, any of these emotional people. All of whom were alien to me, the product of hundreds of years of northern culture, daughter of blue-eyed, light-skinned folk who don't ever grow fat or indulge in public displays of emotion. Or anyway, that's who I'd thought I was until—

The proprietress came out from behind the counter to get something from the shelf behind me. Which meant she walked right up to me, and I didn't know what to do about it: there was no room to turn aside, and to get out a handkerchief would involve setting my purse down somewhere and other utterly conspicuous maneuvers. None of the things I'd ever learned about how to behave fit any of the circumstances. So, panicky and helpless, I just stood there, utterly revealed to the plump woman who still resembled the pink-cheeked, wide-skirted girl twirling in a picture of folk dancers.

Turning now with a can of something in her hand to go back to her post behind the counter, she looked right into my eyes from a few inches away. And then she passed me, patting my tear-splashed hand as she went. But she did it almost furtively, and she didn't say anything about me to the other women, who didn't see. Somehow she knew saving my face was important to me . . .

The film dissolved again, and we were back in Now and I was presenting my son to the macaulet woman, who said he was a fine young man and I had luck. Phil understood the word mazal *and, recognizing the general content of what was being said, put on an appropriately modest look. I bought the milk and some cookies, and we left. After urgings that I should come back again, hear? And my not really casual promise that I'd try to.*

Outside, Phil looked at me curiously and wanted to know what that was all about. Nothing, I said—"The woman knows me, I told you I used to shop there. And she thought I was lucky to have such a nice son, that's all."

He didn't buy it. "I got the impression she was a real good friend of yours," he said. But he let it go at that—he's a man now, which means puzzling manifestations of Mom's secret life are no longer all that worth pursuing. Yet he's also my child, and he was always one who observed with swift, almost unbelievable accuracy. So I can recognize the kind of look he used to get when the data he collected seemed to him to add up to more than the adults were willing to explain.

A suspicion that parents are not telling him something doesn't really matter to Phil anymore, I guess. But it matters to me, so I tried: I told him about that day during the war, and the worn-out woman with a dead son and an angry son. And about the macaulet woman who saw me crying and somehow knew that I was bewildered and made ashamed by it. So, no, she wasn't a real good friend of mine; but she remembered me and would for quite a while yet, maybe. As I'd remember her.

"It's just—well, it's like that in a war," I fumbled. "Things, glimpses, little sort-of-intimacies happen between people. And afterward, there's just—something there. I don't know the name of it, but it's real. And different from anything else."

Well, he understood what I was saying, at least. And I know he tried to understand what I couldn't get said: he turned the best of his imagination to the task of trying to see how it must be between people in a war. But he doesn't know, not really. And I don't know whether, even with lots of time and quiet and my best typing, I can ever really tell him or anybody else.

399

From the diary: 23

Q, and A. (August)

Phil has spent a couple of weeks standing in the middle of my life in Beer-Sheva and looking around. He's met Martha and Avi, Thereza and Jan, and all the other American, Israeli, and "mixed" couples; he's been to their homes and seen the way we all interacted, watched me with their children, and listened later to my explanations of how and why (sometimes reporting, sometimes guessing) all these people happened to come and be where they were. He heard the jokes, was presented like a trophy—here he is, the boy in the photograph (except he's grown a beard)—to Anita and Rafaelo, and met the young "singles" who only a few years before had themselves been college sophomores. He went with me and a few other crazy people (because nobody in his right mind goes voluntarily tramping around in the desert in August) to Avdat and climbed to the ruins of the Nabbateans' well-planned town and stood among the broken columns to look out over the baked and baleful land that was once all comings and goings; and he did truly seem to understand how much it mattered to me. He even spent an evening with the redoubtable Hilda, beating her at games*; Hilda managed to contain her rage, but I took Phil away quickly because I knew how hard that was for her.

But all the time, of course, he's been asking questions—the kind that nobody in Beer-Sheva could have asked because none of them knows from where I'd started, so to speak. I myself hadn't begun to add things up yet, because it wasn't time: I was still writing a notebook, not yet a book. So it's been a little jolting—but doubtless good for my character—to have this checking-out of some of my advance pronouncements going on. Like, I'm supposed to have once labeled Israel a nation of Thoreaus governed by a Disraeli (I'd swear I said something less punchy and thus less absolute. But that's what you get for making pronouncements). And now that I'd had a close-up look, Phil wanted to know in the course of our Q, and A. session, had I changed my view?

Well of course I have: political-science-think always under-goes fuzzing up (if, that is, the thinker is really thinking) when actual people move into the statements. Like, for one thing, "Thoreau" was too glib. For if it meant the Walden Pond simple life

---

*He beat me at anagrams, too, to the great delight of Isaac, who was still trying though nearly everyone else had given up. It was no surprise to me, of course: I always knew I'd be chief honcho only until Phil moseyed into town.

in the minimal house, etc., then I was taking the kibbutz (and the idealized one, at that) for Israel. But if "Thoreau" meant a stubborn refusal to alter your values no matter how many people tell you you're crazy, why then it stands. In fact I thought of the legendary dialogue between Emerson and the jailed Thoreau (a kindly-concern question, Why are you in here? *from E. answered by T. with a tart* Why aren't you? *or words to those effects) as recently as last October. During the great silence from American progressives, who'd up to then been proclaiming loudly that war was never an acceptable policy. But after Egypt and Syria attacked Israel—it was a matter of policy, planned and prepared for, Sadat just told Barbara Walters or somebody, for at least two years—there was this posi-tively Yom Kippur-like silence on the American left. Israelis at the time lacked the physical safety Thoreau enjoyed in jail, so they mostly couldn't ask pointed questions* like his; but in logic and justice they were sure as hell entitled . . . As for Disraeli, I guess all that meant was the Victorian Parliament as a model for the Knesset. Which is a sloppy comparison to begin with, and then fails to take into account all the fancy wrinkles the Israeli system adds.*

But what's most seriously wrong with my advance estimate (even if it was more conservative than stated) is its Europe-and-America limitation of the imagination: it fits Israel as ill as my proposed Canterbury Tales *framework did the mercaz klita. Be-cause Israel is much more Middle East than I realized: something like half the current population has roots, its own or its ancestors', in Arab countries or an Arab culture (which includes North Africa, of course). In my own region, the percentage is probably even higher—so if I were to attempt the same kind of swingy one-punch statement about Beer-Sheva, I'd say it was largely populated by Jewish Arabs. The town does contain also a sizable group that was originally European and retains that cultural outlook to some extent. But even in extreme cases of hanging on to the past—like my yekke ex-neighbor, who remains so German though she's spent twice as many of her adult years in Palestine/Israel—the* Herr Doktor *briefcase is a rarer artifact than the sponja. Mrs. Yekke is not the*

---

*I did, confronting (by mail) some formerly ardent anti-war types who'd this time not found the weather right for demonstrations. Why? Well, naturally he'd felt just as bad for bleeding Israelis as he had for Vietnamese, one friend wrote, but when it wasn't his own country making war, what could he do? He couldn't tell another country what to do . . . A line that might have been impressive if he'd ever said a word before (a) against the UN declaration of human rights or (b) for apartheid, an internal policy of another country . . . I wondered whether his tenderness for national sovereignty has sent him out demonstrating against President Carter's human-rights stance now. (Somehow, I doubt it.)

401

only one in town, either, whose superego recites in her ear Morgen, morgen, nur nicht Heute/sagen alle faule Leute *(the equivalent of "Don't put off for tomorrow what you can do today," except it rhymes in German*). But none of them can keep the* morgen *of an energetic, ambitious culture wholly unaltered—first by Israel's* machar, *a tomorrow always more magical than specific, and then by the* mañana-*like tempo of Beer-Sheva.*

For inevitably, the warmer, more playful Mediterranean spirit dilutes the stream that came from cold northern seas: you simply can't live in the Negev the way you once could in brisk Berlin. (Or Russia either. Remember the little Judith being introduced to her new country, all desert and no snow?) But neither, having known a European kind of life, do you live in the Negev the way you might have otherwise: think of Jan, as at-home in the desert as the Beduin but with a Mozart sonata dancing in his head.† Thus what develops is the pattern of paradox my diary keeps despairing about. However, the permanent tension created when the mañana *shrug is perpetually being yanked up short by a git-up-and-go conscience may not be a bad thing: it could be that the pulling and tugging of the society, first one way and then the opposite, is essential to its health.*

Ah but—. Enter here clever Phil, asking about one hassle that visibly tugs the society but doesn't seem to be really good for it. Do I think, he wants to know, that the conflict between the religious minority and the rest of the country can ever be reconciled?

I don't see how. For, although the non-religious are prepared to live and let live, the religious minority tends to moral imperialism. It never gets quite as vicious as a crusade, but the same idea operates: e.g., since Shabbat is holy, everybody ought to keep it and it's your holy duty to make 'em. With Jews, that's not built-in in the religion; but it seems built into some religious Jews. (The beautiful triple question—"If I am not for myself, who will be for me? If for myself alone, what am I? And if not now, when?"—is a marvel of ethical insight. But the trouble with all great insights, whether religious

---

*Literally, " 'Tomorrow, tomorrow, only not today,' all lazy people say." I picked it up in my youth and got an amazing amount of mileage out of it in Israel, for every German-speaking person seemed tickled when I produced it. The revelation that that (plus one short poem by Goethe) is virtually all the German I know would subsequently emerge, of course—but by that time the ice had usually been broken.

†In a sense, Jan is a very model of the pre-World War II European intellectual (Jules Romains wrote him, you might say): unlike Thereza, who on certain subjects will go off like a rocket, Jan will consider soberly any view a turn of logic leads to. So it's significant that he's got annoyed with me only twice—once when I referred to the desert as "empty" (that was before I saw the February flowering: I'd never write that now) and once when he thought I was putting down the Beduin (I wasn't; he'd misunderstood).

or intellectual, is that somebody can grab them and start applying them narrowly or in part, and then where are you?) Of course if you could simply put the religious question in a referendum, it would at once be clear where the Israeli majority is. But that means what the majority thinks, not what it wants done: some issues simply don't lend themselves to a yes-no question, or to determination by majority rule.

We had an example of that in the U.S. when for years and years there was a Congressional majority in favor of civil rights legislation. Which would get passed by the House, but the Senate—where there was also a majority in favor—couldn't get it to a vote because it'd be stopped by a filibuster. It soon became apparent to us proponents of the laws that the only way to get them to a Senate vote was a cloture motion, which would set a limit to the debate and thus end the filibuster. Only, such a motion required a two-thirds vote—and we not only couldn't get that but some of the pro-civil rights Senators also refused to vote for cloture. Their reason was not lack of ardor for civil rights but a belief that the Senate's right of unlimited debate, which is necessary to its Constitutional role as the deliberative body able to put the brakes on majorities, was simply too important to chip away at, however urgent the reason. (I thought them wrong, of course. But we weren't given to simplistic political thinking back then, so everybody regarded their position as perfectly honorable.)

I have a feeling that any attempt at a referendum facedown in Israel would run into something like the cloture problem, for a good many people who have no patience with "the religious" would nevertheless balk at voting them into powerlessness. That may be partly because Hitler got voted into office in Germany, a fact that gets forgotten in the U.S.; but Israeli survivors of the Nazis have reason to suspect (as did the authors of the U.S. Constitution) that a majority can be wrong as hell. And in addition there's a general non-rational (though not necessarily superstitious) recognition that the Hittites and the Phoenicians have vanished but the Jews haven't—and who can say for sure that those impossibly stubborn old men who clung always and no-matter-what to their ridiculous rules and rituals aren't why?*

---

*I'm willing to try, for it seems to me that herding the congregation into the synagogue often only saved the SS the trouble of rounding them up. It's my hunch that lots more Holocaust survival came via the brawny, agnostic or atheistic Palestinian Jews who, with money and help from people all over the world, sneaked into Europe and wrestled or bribed the victims out. But if anyone wants to argue that that was the result of somebody else's fasting and prayer, well, how can that be disproved?

403

So I told Phil that the "religious-vs.-non" hassle seemed to me to resemble the continual struggle between Greek and Turkish Cypriots. Which is a non-starter as an answer, because it leads to having to decide which are the Greeks and which the Turks—and no thanks, I'll pass. But I don't think much of the often-heard notion that if it weren't for Arab hostility, Israel would split over this controversy. Because though that may sound inviting as poli-sci-think, one thing easily observed on the ground is that both the religious and the non often get along well with the Arabs: the right-wing Israelis and the older Arabs have rather similar ideas of what's an acceptable social contract, and the leftish Israelis and younger Arabs likewise. When they're all let alone, that is—once gathered into victor-and-vanquished groups, both natural alliances get suspended. (Another resemblance to Cyprus, for the most recent civil war there came when it wasn't let alone—when the left-wing Greek Cypriots tried a pro-communist coup. Turkey, which could have gone into Cyprus any time but hadn't, promptly intervened. And then the blood began to flow again.)

So the short answer to that question is, the religious-vs.-the-rest hassle in Israel doesn't look awfully reconcilable but I don't think that matters. Because if they're not left alone, they're still each other's shelanu in the crunch. (That goes for me, too, by the way: I'm not sure what men of good will all over the world were doing for me last October, but I am sure that among the young men who kept the hostiles off my Beer-Sheva doorstep were some who'd been fasting and praying when they were interrupted.) And if the machar of the Israeli song ever actually comes, wider shelanu feelings will have a chance to take over: there have already been some instances of people shaking hands across fences—a pursuit that seems to cut down the time available for stone-throwing at home.

So much for the "easy" Q. and A. The one that threw me came after my son finished looking around at Israel and Beer-Sheva and began to look at me. He saw me as thriving: I'd made a satisfying life for myself here, he said, in what seemed a comfortable role among a group of people loosely but warmly connected, and obviously it was good for me. But then he asked the natural question—did it have to be here, so far away? Couldn't the same thing be found at home?

Well, the simple answer was "I don't know"—I was here, not there. And I didn't propose to find out, not then anyway: less than a year after the war, with much of the price still being paid and new and wrenching anxieties still turning up every week, I wasn't about to say, "Well folks, it was interesting but now I must run." So how could I answer questions like that? . . . Well, he was just asking, Phil said peaceably; if it couldn't be answered, it couldn't. He opened his book, selected an apple from the bowl he remembered from home— only, now that it lived in Beer-Sheva, it had become Israeli and thus always held fruit—and proceeded to enjoy his vacation.

Denied the chance to blow off steam by slamming a door (in a Beer-Sheva winter you always close doors: but in summer, you might lose a stir of cool), I went into my workroom and proceeded to mourn. Because he had sure as hell put a worm in my apple: I had a notebookfull of Fascinating Characters sketches, not to mention a collection of those Beer-Sheva paradoxes—all stuff that's marvel- ously handy for light, mocking little essays on human absurdity. Or if I wanted to throw in the odd poli-sci seminar, I could get serious about the Ur-Absurdity, Israel itself. For what else is a bumptious upstart of a nation that wants to have everything at once—freedom and safety, a technologically advanced society and a tender and humane one, collectivism and individual rights, enshrined tradi- tions and innovative solutions to old problems? Pretty great expec- tations, my boy. Especially (since you insist on these comparisons) considering that the U.S., with all the advantages of size and wealth, hasn't managed that much in two hundred years. And here we've got an outfit that hasn't even been in business for thirty years and is so small that the distance from the Dead Sea to the shining Mediter- ranean* would make a nice training hike for Marine Corps recruits. Not to mention that every six to eight years, Israelis have to stop whatever else they're doing and start peering through the rockets' red glare and the bombs bursting in air. Their flag is still there, but let me remind you, junior: the citizen army it takes to keep it there can't also be at home boosting the Gross National Product... (I stopped as soon as I felt better: both humor and indignation are so easy to write, and so satisfying...)

I needed a drink of water, I decided, and trailed out to the kitchen to get it—pausing on my way back to observe loudly that everything didn't always have to be compared with America, and in fact in some cases that was downright unfair. My son looked up with an air of mild surprise (perhaps because the edge in my voice didn't seem to go with a scene where there'd been no sound except the hum of the electric fan?) and then, after a moment's consideration, asked politely whether I was planning to write a book about Israel without comparing it with America... I stopped off in the bath- room and dampened a towel to hang around my neck. It was incredibly hot, and it would be another hour before time to open up

---

*An especially hyperbolic trill, of course: the Mediterranean is lined with too many nations to be very shining (unless you count oil slicks?).

the trissim and maybe catch an apprentice night-breeze from the desert.

Later.

Dammit, it was never a question of Whether but of What. Because Phil's question really was What did you find out here that would be useful to me?—which is certainly legitimate for a nineteen-year-old collecting data, as they all must be, on the world Out There After College. And they're hardly the only ones: whose way of life is so safe and comfortable nowadays that he can read about a foreign country without in any way "shopping" for new slants and perceptions? Of course people would want to know what could be translated—so to speak—and of course that was always what I'd set out to tell them: I came and looked with my American eyes, didn't I? There isn't a single Olympian observation in my notebook, and I probably couldn't write one if I tried.

But I didn't answer Phil's question, I blew my obligation, because it was just too hard to find a way to say convincingly what I had to say. Which is Yes and No but not the yes-and-no of the-truth-is-somewhere-in-the-middle maturity—I mean Yes/No/Yes/No, a succession of practically simultaneous flashes about as easy to describe as a strobe light. And even if I could show him all of them at once, he'd be jerking his head back and forth fast enough to end up with a whiplash pain in the neck.

No, because you can't go home again and Beer-Sheva is a piece of the American past. The time varies: Avi setting off downtown with his little daughter riding on his shoulders belongs (except that we didn't carry toddlers around that way) to the 1950s in Bethesda, Md., with little Phil and his daddy off to do the Saturday chores. In a scene where people and automobiles, both moving more slowly then, actually shared the same streets and you were waited on by a real live sales clerk who sometimes even knew all about the paint he sold and in any case could be seen—the way the storekeeper Avi greets looks to his daughter—as a nice man and probably somebody else's Daddy. So much in Beer-Sheva now is like those days—e.g., a professional man young enough to be a two-year-old's father is also likely to be a war veteran; to have a baby is a good thing, pleasing to everybody; do-it-yourselfing is In and a new power-tool gismo is what your husband wants for his birthday . . . Or else it's a different time, longer ago: Thereza and Jan and their children, each of them doing his own thing but all gathered in the salon of a winter evening because that's where the heater and the good light are, are a vignette from back when my mother was a girl.

406

And sometimes the shape imparted to social life by the lack of telephones is not only long-ago but rural-America nostalgic: in Massachusetts I'd have phoned to ask after the pregnant Yael, but in Beer-Sheva I must go instead—so we have not ten minutes' contact but two hours', and I read Yehuda's poems too, and the little girls kiss me goodnight.*

Yes, I can see why you'd want to take this back home, my son: there is a gritty authenticity about a way of life in which you're cold when it's cold out and hot when it's hot out, and to every fruit there is a season and that's what's for dinner . . . I can understand why the wistful commune movements tried to get "purity" by imitating it. But that didn't work and never will, because in America it would have to be an enclave, caught and set aside—whereas this, here, is mainstream and moving: people in Beer-Sheva are just living along like everybody else in Israel. And their innocence (and maybe their warmth, too?) is in-process, and fragile: Time itself will probably take the shine off it, even if nothing else does. So, No. Because the trouble with authenticity is, it's like a bird's nest—the minute you handle it, it's no good anymore.

But Yes, it would be useful in an American scene hardening and darkening, full of public breakdowns and private frustrations. For these people know how to live in a world of good intentions gone wrong and no issue ever standing out in the light where you can see it clearly. The caring society, always handicapped by its virtues, must keep on stumbling under its own weight—and yet its weight must keep growing, for more and more rights must be more and more intricately guaranteed, and that takes ever more elaborated machinery. So you inheritors of an America no longer rich (it's somebody else who has the oil, and calls the tune) and now only one of the free minority at bay among the world's powerful tyrannies, Yes, you-all could use the Israeli know-how. They've got all this experience with being a minority unpopular with the rich and selfish; and, thanks to the socialist ideology with which they started out and the insistence on individual freedoms since, they contend regularly with a cumbrous, overgrown social machinery that would make New York's political and financial structures look simple and streamlined. Civic Man in Beer-Sheva is the final product of the doctrine of societal responsibility—an end-run individualist who carries out the society's consensual aims by outflanking the*

---

*Deciding what era of the past is "playing" at any given moment can be rather fun. But it has its painful moments, too: "Hey look out, you're walking right into the pollution booby trap!" I want to yell. Sometimes I do, too. But the Israelis are so American . . .

machinery set up to make them happen. (You see what I mean by a whiplash effect?) It's as if the whole country is in the counter-culture, because that is the culture: when a water pipe broke in my apartment house, I would have called City Hall or the Fire Department first; but my Israeli neighbors went to look for a wrench first instead. When Thereza met an immigrant who complained that it's hard to meet people in Beer-Sheva, she didn't write a letter to the Ministry of Absorption or even to the editor: having seen that the machinery wasn't working properly, she took a personal poke at it by marching over to the mercaz klita herself to implement the immigrant-absorption policy . . .

You see it sometimes in the U.S. in a crunch—in a blizzard, for instance, when most people are grimly struggling to keep on going where they were going, there is always one guy who'll jump out of his car and start directing traffic. But in Beer-Sheva that's done all the time, routinely: the obligation to whip out your screw-driver and tinker with the society, or bring your own needle and thread and take a tuck in the fabric that's supposed to fit but doesn't, is part of the Israeli notion of citizenship. But it's Yes/No because that, although frequently admirable (and I myself have lots of reason for gratitude to it), can also be feckless and high-handed. It's individual arrogation of power, that's what it is. And so, societally dangerous. (Isn't it?)

"I don't know" really was the right answer to Phil's hard question, I guess. Because how should I make the un-heroic Israeli-style hero sound heroic to him? (And should I, anyway?) Chaim, who can get you out of Catch 22 situations by locating some obscure Regulation 40266-aleph that will provide a loophole, is in fact the rescuer of the weak and confused who go to pieces in the clutches of bureaucracy—but won't he sound like just another wheeler-dealer to Phil? The trouble is, they're all so used to being (societally) rich, back home! They aren't, anymore; and it looks to me as if they're going to be poorer still. But they don't seem to know it, so they go on talking rich-talk and playing rich-games—"idealism" is no more demanding than striking a pose of moral purity that's convincing in the mirror, and "activism" is being nasty to a cop . . .

Well, Phil isn't like that. But he doesn't know. And I couldn't find a way to tell him. So I blew it. Yes/No/Yes, blink-blink, and on the other hand . . . Bah.

18 ↙ Oskar Schindler— and Gertruda and Elena and a Very Special Few

I've had some experience with the phenomenon known as "staircase wit"—where you think of the perfect answer after the party is over and everybody's gone home—but this is ridiculous: it was more than two months after Phil left that this turned up. By which I mean the answer to my own wrestle about how to explain the new heroism to the New World—and, more important, a way to confront, for myself and on behalf of other reluctant Americans, the question of the Holocaust. I'd put that off as long as I could, because you have to write about it—how can you talk about Israel and leave it out?— and yet every attempt, using every approach known to the mind and emotions, to explain it or somehow absorb it safely into the past seems to me to have failed. The insiders are too scarred, and the outsiders are left with hands full of facts and the name of it all still not named . . .

But then one day, too late for my try at instructing Phil, I opened my morning newspaper and this story appeared. What it does for me is give me a chance to enter the frightening territory by the path least scary for me, as a novelist looking out of the eyes of a particular person—a guy with a wife and a job and dandruff— instead of a symbol or a group. Only, I could probably never have invented a character who so well satisfies both needs, to shape the past in some form an outsider can expect to imagine and also to show my son and his contemporaries that while you're eating your wheat germ and meditating, things you never meant to happen will happen—and then will come biting back at you. Until finally, one day, you have to risk everything to stop them . . .

I had never heard of my "character" until this notice appeared in the *Jerusalem Post*:

"The coffin of the righteous gentile, OSKAR SCHINDLER, who saved one thousand two hundred Jews, has been brought to Israel in accordance with his wish to be buried in the country in which live so many of those he saved.

"There will be a requiem mass on Monday, October 28 . . .

"Transport will leave Tel Aviv at . . ."

Looking it up, I found there'd been word of Oskar Schindler shortly before that, in a small news item about his death in Germany at the age of sixty-six. The *Post* normally runs to a slim eight or ten pages, so, while you do find out what's happening in the rest of the world (often rather better, I find, than in a Denver newspaper), it's bound to be via very sparse mention. Schindler mattered to people in Israel, but the details given were still few. He'd been a factory owner during World War II, a friend of the State of Israel all through its short life, and he'd been designated a "righteous gentile." (That was all. Apparently the *Post* didn't know, then, about his wish to be buried in Israel.)

I'm still not quite used to the way they use that word "righteous," and maybe it startles other Americans as much as it did me. When I was young in the 1940s, what "righteous" meant was unattractive conviction of one's own rectitude—as in thin-lipped virtue, or Robert Burns's "unco guid." For me, it meant the lady downstairs who was always snooping, keeping track of just how late any visiting males left the apartment I shared with another girl. But by the late 1960s, when I no longer cared whether my Massachusetts neighbors thought me respectable, "righteous" had acquired a meaning quite opposite to thin-lipped virtue but no more attractive. The dubious characters, neither quite hippies nor quite students, who hung around Harvard Square and ripped off the doughnut shops in the name of anti-capitalism used "righteous" to mean people who made them feel good. Since that could be done by spouting the correct rhetoric, or merely by posing as poor but with Dad's credit cards in your pocket, it made the definition rather loose. (Which didn't matter: definitions weren't considered righteous in that set anyway.)

So, with this double-jointed history of Ugh, you can see that I was rather put off in advance by the name of the Avenue of Righteous Gentiles at Yad Vashem* in Jerusalem. But when I went there and looked, it turned out to be just a dusty, ill-tended path (maybe they spruce it up for official visitors?) lined with little

*The memorial to Holocaust victims at which are gathered documents, pictures, and artifacts. The impact is all but unbearable, but nobody ought to miss it: sometimes it can almost make you understand it was real.

plaques naming unknown people from places often equally unknown. The legends told briefly, in English, how Maria Unpronounceable had hidden Jewish kindergarten children from Nazi searchers. (Quite a picture implied there, isn't it: *Your mission, Hans, is to bring in every five-year-old Jew in the city . . . ?* Is it too much to hope that Hans, or at least one guy in his squad, proved willing to be flimflammed by Maria?) Or the neighbors of the Something-or-other family in a Dutch town wished to honor them for their courage in sheltering a family of fleeing Jews at the risk of their own lives. (All of a sudden you remember then that Anne Frank's diary was not a work of fiction.)

And so on—all so wrenchingly human-size that, in self-defense, you almost have to try to pretend they're not real. But they were, and are: a commission investigates the cases, often by taking testimony from the beneficiaries of those acts. I didn't count them, but it seemed to me there were a lot of teachers—and some nuns, who may also have been teachers—and that there were more Poles than I would have expected, given that land's history of anti-Semitism, and fewer French than I, as a (now ex-)Francophile, would have thought. My impression was that if you were a fleeing Jew in Europe in those days, your chances of survival improved if you happened to know a Dutch teacher (female).

But after that visit, I came to accept (though I still twitch a little at the sound of the word) a new—or, more precisely, old, thundering-Biblical old—use of "righteous." In Israel, a righteous gentile (usually capitalized) is a Christian who in the crunch behaved in what I'd been taught to call a Christian manner. Such Christians were apparently so sadly few that the Righteous Gentiles are, you could say, the Savior's saviors.

Oskar Schindler, the Righteous Gentile whose obituary appeared in the *Jerusalem Post* that October, was born into a middle-class Catholic family in the Sudetenland. He was still a Catholic when he died: on the night of his funeral we all saw on the TV news the presiding mitred figure with the big cross, and we heard part of the mass before the cameras tactfully switched away—to show us the middle-aged Jews who would have been dead for a generation except for Schindler. The men's faces revealed discomfort, possibly at being in a Catholic church, or perhaps at simply being in a place of worship with their heads uncovered; one or two also evinced disgust and anger at the presence of the TV camera.* Afterward, outside the church, there were too many pallbearers—several hundred

---

*A not-untypical hostility to TV presence. In small, stubborn Israel, coldheartednesses in the name of "the right to know" don't slide by as easily as they do in the U.S.

411

of what the *Post* called Schindler's "protégés" came to the funeral—
and some of them grimaced under the weight of the coffin; one,
clearly finding it too much for him, gestured hastily and a younger
man (his son?) came forward and took his place. We didn't get
to see the ceremony at the graveside: as in the U.S., the TV news
can't afford to linger long on any single event. And I didn't hear the
speech delivered by District Court Judge Moshe Bejski, but I did
learn that as a young man he'd forged German documents for use in
the Jew-saving factory Oskar Schindler ran while he was officially
running a kitchenware factory in occupied Poland. Judge Bejski
must surely be a notable example of the rehabilitation of a forger.

If that last remark strikes you as gagging it up over serious
matters, that's probably the way it once would have sounded to me,
too. But wry observations pretty well typify the attitudes (overtly,
anyway) of many Israelis toward what is always called the Holocaust. (I object to that word: it's fair enough in terms of the effects
and magnitude of the gas-oven murdering, but holocausts are not
man-made. So why use a name that implies natural forces, when
what came upon European Jews was as out-of-left-field and
destructive as an earthquake or an avalanche but *wasn't* a natural
disaster?) Although "typical" would have to mean somehow
averaging the Holocaust survivors and the sabra or child-immigrant
Israelis. The latter feel themselves connected to the ancient stones
of archaelogy rather than to the ashes of Dachau, and when they say
"I am an Israeli," they think of it as a complete sentence. Whereas
the survivor group remembers the Jews of Germany, who believed
themselves to be simply Germans, and the Jews of France who had
been officially declared just plain Frenchmen as long ago as
Napoleon. And yet, when the Nazis shoved, or sometimes just
tapped them lightly, both Germans and Frenchmen—the former
with a *Heil,* the latter with a shrug—generally saw their Jewish
neighbors deported and neither questioned nor protested. (Unlike
the Danes, who lined up behind their king in an organized effort to
save the Jews, and the Dutch, who seem to have done it even in the
absence of formal leadership or organization.) So the survivors say
"I am an Israeli" just as proudly, but not as matter-of-factly.

The Yom Kippur war altered that division between Israelis, I
think. I was very upset* at the post-war change in my seventeen-

So Israelis (so far, anyway) won't put up with stuff like turning a camera on an accident victim's wife as she hears the news. They believe that if you're lucky you'll never
know what it feels like, and in the meantime you're not entitled to prey on the unlucky.
*A considerable understatement, since I felt fiercer than I could ever have imagined:
right then, I'd have been willing to shoot any Egyptian or Syrian soldier without a
twinge of liberal-humanist thought for his helplessness in the clutch of the oily
warlords.

year-old students, who only months before had been just young Israelis—grumbling and confident and merry, much like any other free nation's young—and then suddenly were struggling to make themselves believe the world yearned to kill them because they were Jews. But later I couldn't decide whether the change had been permanent. When I ran into Amir about six months after, he was just starting his army service and the main thing on his mind seemed to be his recently cropped thatch of bright-red hair: if you don't get it done yourself, the army will do it, he told me—and then God help you. But otherwise he seemed much the same; if his old ducked-head, shy grin now covered a terrible consciousness of some "Jewish burden," it didn't show . . . And Estie came to visit me not long ago: she's soon to finish her army service and will be starting at the university. What she mostly talked about was Esperanto, which she'd been studying in her spare time. (She found it fascinating and wanted to recommend it to me.) So *that* didn't sound as though she'd really given up on the rest of the world, but how can you know?

Well, maybe some of the Righteous Gentiles honored at Yad Vashem were shaken by the kind of anger that filled me during that bitter discussion with the children of freedom and democracy suddenly demon-ridden in my Beer-Sheva salon. That's the kind of Righteous Gentile I myself can empathize with, as opposed to the doubtless-many who acted out of religious conviction. So I can imagine myself as, for example, Elena Chlopinaite, who was working for the Wolpert family as nursemaid to their little Rita in 1941. In what was then Latvia but is now part of the Soviet Union. (When the U.S.S.R. takes a land by conquest, you see, American professors don't chip in for ads in *The New York Times*, nobody suggests internationalization of the territory, and the Latvians' national rights don't get demanded in the UN.) When the child's parents were scooped into the Riga ghetto—which amounted to a sentence of death, for that was the authorities' plan—the nursemaid simply took the little girl home with her. As I would, wouldn't you?

Elena kept the child until the end of the war—what else could any woman of sanity and heart *do*, for heaven's sake?—and then, after it was established that Rita's parents had not survived, Elena went on raising the girl as her own. And ultimately came to Israel with her, for reasons not clear unless it's that the Palestinian Jews collecting Jewish orphans in Europe came for Rita, and Elena came along because women don't like to be separated from children they've raised. Or there could be an equally simple but less personal explanation: Rita now had a place to go, and the desire of residents of the Soviet Union to go someplace else can be assumed from the grim care with which the government there keeps them locked in. So maybe for Elena, who'd cast her bread upon the waters in 1941, it came back the honey cake of Israel.

It's harder, though, to see myself as Stanislaw and Maria W. (their family name still can't be published), who hid their Jewish neighbors Mr. and Mrs. S. Gorzyczanski in a bunker built under the floor of their barn. To understand how that situation could have continued for a whole year is easier, because even if Stanislaw and Maria rued what they've done and yearned to be rid of their illegal guests, how could they without getting themselves shot for having hidden Jews? But it's the initial step that I can't imagine: I'm afraid I would have, at the most, kept my mouth shut and packed sandwiches for the Gorzyczanskis to take along. Maybe Stanislaw and Maria, simply impulsive, lacked the imagination to see what they were getting into? And besides, their generous or defiant or just muddled impulse didn't have to fight its way through the American law-abiding tradition I was born into.*

Ah well, I don't feel guilty about not having been a hero back then (actually, I was too young as well as in the wrong place. Though that didn't stop me, and a lot of other people, from feeling guilty anyway right after the war, when it all came out), and the admission that I can't identify with some of the Righteous Gentiles doesn't upset me anymore. It used to: the establishment of the State of Israel in 1948 assuredly had something to do with a world-full of decent people's having just discovered what the Nazis and their allies—who, everybody now seems to have forgotten, included the Grand Mufti of Jerusalem, Anwar Sadat, and other Arab leaders swept by either enthusiasm for killing Jews or belief in the fascist wave of the future—had done and corrupted the whole civilized world into suborning, one way or another. But time passes, and there's a limit to people's ability to entertain feelings of shame and guilt. So I don't know exactly when I got tired of those six million victims; but I remember that in 1964 or 1965, when I was a book reviewer for the New York Herald Tribune, I wasn't enthusiastic about being assigned Hans Habe's The Mission, a half-documentary account of a failed attempt to buy Jews from the Nazis who offered them at a ransom of so much per head . . . I did read the book (I'm not only law-abiding, I also do what I get paid for), and then I found myself stuck with the problem of how to overcome my readers'

*Which, come to think of it, isn't the same as Americans of Phil's age live in. So, question: would it be easier for him to be Stanislaw and Maria, since breaking laws is done more lightly nowadays, or harder because nowadays what you do at nineteen goes on your résumé so you learn to think ahead?

probable resistance to the subject. Because I wanted everybody to read it, but I was almost certain that whatever I said in my review, people would feel much the way I had when the *Herald Trib* handed me the book.

Maybe some others read the public mood the way I did then, for in 1964—says the *Jerusalem Post*—Metro-Goldwyn-Mayer planned to make a film based on Oskar Schindler's story, starring Anthony Quinn. The project fell through, for reasons not specified— but I wouldn't be surprised if it was that somebody decided the public would never go for another Holocaust story.* If so, I'd guess they were right. There comes a point when you have to turn off generalized tragedy in the interests of your own sense of reality. And at that point in my life, these tales became irrelevant in terms of either awe or guilt: I can't in all honesty find myself in Gertruda Babilinska, a heroic Polish Christian schoolteacher who not only saved her neighbor's son, Michael Stolovitzki, but also brought him to Israel in 1948, after a previous attempt on one of the illegal immigration ships that were turned back by the British. And I certainly cannot see myself—nor can I be induced to by portentous thundering that deep-down we are all Hitlers—in the men Gertruda hid the boy from.

One thing Yad Vashem provides, though, is a clear image of those men: among the collected news photos is one showing a boy of perhaps seven or eight with a pointed chin and wide scared eyes under a peaked cap like the ones worn by Horatio Alger newsboys or the child actor Jackie Coogan in *The Kid*. The boy is being herded out of a building by several helmeted and uniformed men pointing automatic weapons. His hands are raised, somewhat tentatively, in the traditional surrender gesture, and the men, alert and wary, also fit perfectly into this perfectly standard news shot of the capture of a public enemy; the only thing that even may make it the tiniest bit different from a thousand other photographs is the startled look (maybe he was only blinking at the sunlight, though) on the small, pinched face. Even if you manage to subtract the future-knowledge you bring to the picture—like, that the little Jewish boy probably never got to grow up, and that the sturdy soldiers who flushed him out of hiding may well have gone on to the Russian front and ended up in the hands-up role themselves in another, later photograph—no matter what you do, it's still visually appalling. And unforgettable

---

*Not then, but the public has since: the fact just won't go away, and keeps coming back in waves. As is apparently understood by Israel's enemies—for a silly attempt to deny that it all happened is the latest move in the oil/terrorist complex's propaganda effort.

in its implications, because who took the picture? And for whom to see in his morning newspaper? It's a clear, sharp professional shot, of a quality you might expect from a good sports-page photographer with one of those big old Speed Graphics they used to use. So even if you try to imagine a fleeing Jew or anti-Nazi pausing to snap a candid-camera shot from hiding, the quality of the picture denies that: it looks like the work of a newspaper photographer, who had time to figure the correct aperture and had a place to stand—ahead and slightly to one side of the oncoming boy—to record the event for the public while the two lanes of uniformed men waited deferentially . . . Once I saw that photo, I knew with immovable certainty that there were not after all, there could not have been, any innocent Germans.

Sorry. I particularly wanted to avoid straying into pity. Or useless mourning for an unknown boy (he was wearing knickers and those high socks) who looks like Albert, a boy in my class who once lent me *The Boy Allies at Jutland*, which I didn't have because my mother would buy me only girls' books. Look, in a real, if harsh, sense, the boy in the photo is irrelevant: history crunched him up and went on by—and so, in all common sense, must we. Whatever there was to be learned from the startled eyes under the peaked cap was useful only then and perhaps only to those who fled or fought, or both. And to the likes of the Righteous Gentiles.

So let's get on to Oskar Schindler, who also shows how history can bite you—but from whom it's maybe possible to learn what you need to keep from being chewed up. For Schindler is translatable, and relevant: he was not only personally unthreatened when the Nazis came, he was welcoming. Because he thought he was being liberated. When the Germans took over his native Sudetenland, Oskar had finished his military service (in the Czech army: Czechoslovakia owned that hunk of the former Austro-Hungarian empire inhabited by the ethnic Germans that Hitler's *Putsch* was supposed to be liberating) and had entered his family business, a factory making agricultural machinery. After the annexation of the Sudetenland, Schindler was an insider of the New Order, presumably convinced, certainly well-connected, a young man on the way up. As a functionary in the German anti-espionage service run by the famous Admiral Canaris, Schindler did all right—or so one gathers from the *Jerusalem Post* story, which doesn't choose to dwell on his career with the victorious Germans. However, even its brisk summary includes the fact that he became friendly with senior Wehrmacht officers. And he seems to have been still doing fine after the Germans marched into Poland (the move, on September 1, 1939, that formally set off World War II).

Schindler left the service then and started up in business—an enamel and kitchenware factory in Cracow—in the newly conquered land. Which was not, one may imagine, a move permitted to people lacking spotless dossiers and good connections.

Yet something had started to go sour, it seems. Oskar Schindler afterward rejected offers to write a book about his experiences (though he apparently consented to the abortive movie idea in 1964), but he did contribute to a book published in Berlin.* There, he explained it thus: "The motive for my actions was the daily sight of the unspeakable suffering inflicted on Jewish persons and the brutal conduct of the Prussian supermen. This group of lying hypocrites and sadistic murderers promised to liberate my homeland, the Sudetenland, only to turn it into a colony, to be plundered at will."

Well, if you read that with the kind of suspension of both belief and disbelief that I used to urge on my students, some clues emerge to the insiderhood-gone-sour. For Jews suffered plenty before the annexation of the Sudetenland too, and it would be fair to assume that the government of Czechoslovakia had no reason to keep that news from its populace; so Sudeten Germans would seem to have had lots of time to note the hypocrisy and sadism before the colony-plundering even got started. Thus a probably more reliable clue to Schindler's alienation appears in his remark about Prussian—not "German," please note—supermen: maybe the arrogant German officer corps wasn't sufficiently aware of or attentive to the need to butter up the provincials, and some of the provincials developed grudges? A certain note of infighting is detectable, too, in a previous quote, which jabs at latecomers jumping on the anti-Nazi bandwagon: "I do not belong to that group of Germans who discovered their 'inner resistance' to Nazism on July 20, 1944 and later fashioned for themselves a halo of empty phrases." What that date means is the (failed) German officers' plot to assassinate Hitler; the reference shows, I think, whose decisions Schindler thought *really* mattered to the course of the war.

And finally, there's the all-but-obligatory pious tribute to the Jews: "The memory of a happy childhood, spent with many Jewish friends and schoolmates," Schindler concludes, "was for me a moral obligation that drove me on." *Jawohl*. Except that that happy childhood was Czechoslovakian and he talks and thinks of himself as a German—which, at the least, doesn't imply much intaking of loyalties from the boyhood landscape, right? As for those Jewish

Die Unbesungenen Helden (The Unsung Heroes) by Kurt R. Grossman, Arani Publishers.

friends and schoolmates, well, *their* happy childhood ended considerably before their old buddy Oskar seems to have developed a sense of moral obligation to them. "Yeah, but *when?*" is, quite amazingly often, the question Truth asks, raising its gritty voice in the chorus of acclaim for a hero.

Nevertheless, he was a hero, this non-Galahad Schindler; make no mistake about that. But the new kind, with an essential illogic to his heroism—the two-steps-forward, one-step-back human pace of it, the acts intending less than they came to mean, the specific becoming general while the man who started it all perhaps watched helplessly . . . Look: in 1940, Oskar Schindler employed 150 Jewish workers in his factory. Presumably he had about the same number when, in 1942, the Germans changed their policy—which had been to squeeze all Jews into ghettos where overcrowding, hunger, and disease would winnow them out—in favor of the more straightforward and efficient extermination camps. It was at that point that Oskar Schindler decided to have his workers declared prisoners assigned to work at his factory. Why? Well, what he said was, "I could not disappoint the absolute confidence they placed in me . . ." and maybe it's true. However, it could also be true, either additionally or instead, that he was interested in making sure of his labor supply.* But then comes this, tilting the presumptions a little farther apart: "Since the managers of three neighboring factories were about to hand over their 450 workers to the nearby Plaszow concentration camp, I volunteered to take in their men too." All sorts of people made all sorts of postwar boasts about what good guys they'd been, but the folks at Yad Vashem have heard them all and Schindler's claims have been verified by the world's least likely marks for a con. So it would seem he did what he said he did—and if it was only insurance for a future labor supply, it would've been incredibly overdone.

Not to say, also, perilous and expensive. "The factory kitchen alone cost me 50,000 zlotys a month," partly because he had to get most of his food supplies on the black market or through barter. I don't know how much a zloty was worth then, but 50,000 of them a month—when you got nothing for them that you couldn't have got anyway—had to matter. (Maybe it was only 25,000 zlotys a month? But even if it's been inflated by memory, it had to be *something*.) Besides, the thing began snowballing: men on Schindler's payroll

*Consider *all* the possibilities, I used to lecture—but I never said to give them all equal weight. And it seems doubtful that a man with connections would find it so hard to get slave labor as to make it worth while to set up a camp for the workers and their families on the factory premises.

418

brought in aged parents and other kin* for whom there was no work; but if they couldn't be stowed in the factory, they'd be sent to the camps. So they were added to the work list—and "for every name on my work list I had to pay the SS five zlotys a day." That was in addition to a constant need for bribes to "party functionaries, SS leaders, camp commanders, and other such parasites." Any one of whom could, of course, have turned Schindler in for attempting to bribe an official.

This is a harsh and insensitive way to put it, but I'm afraid Oskar and his wife, Emilia—who "shared my views on the importance of saving Jewish lives"—begin to sound like a couple of kids who didn't know what they were getting into when they decided to keep pet rabbits. The project was not only proving unprofitable (for no matter how many pieces of kitchenware the—clearly well-motivated—Jewish factory workers produced, how could they possibly offset the costs of *that* overhead?), it was also increasingly risky. One day a group of high SS officers, come to inspect the factory, became irritated by a "prisoner" named Lamus, who was pushing his wheelbarrow across the yard too slowly. They ordered him shot. (I've tried and tried, but I can't think of any way to write that so it will be really credible to people who have shop stewards, civil rights, and Congressmen. You'll just have to help me: put your mind back to the tales of kings and courtiers you read as children— the ones in which a king's off-with-his-head order was so taken for granted that it was only the starting point of the story.) Fortunately, the visiting biggies delegated the chore to a sergeant and then departed to inspect somewhere else. So, minutes before the scheduled execution, Schindler was able to buy Lamus's life from the SS man in charge of the firing squad. The price was a bottle of vodka.

Booze did the trick on another occasion too, by the way. This time a man named Wohlfeiler had bought forged Polish identity papers, and was found out. Two Gestapo men appeared at Schindler's office and demanded that the five members of the Wohlfeiler family be handed over for execution. Oskar sent out an

---

*I thought of this in 1976 when Israel army doctors stationed near the Lebanese border started treating Lebanese victims of the civil war there: first it was a pregnant woman who was brought to the wire, then a wounded child was slipped over (by grown-ups on both sides, some of whom were there specifically to *prevent* anything coming over), then the child's mother had to be let in to visit him in hospital, etc. etc. Eventually the government formally opened a section of the security fence and let aged parents, etc. be carried through to a special field hospital staffed with extra doctors. (Which led to sour jokes among patients waiting at the health clinics in Beer-Sheva: if you want to see a doctor quickly, go on up to the Lebanese border and . . .)

order to "search" for them and meanwhile got out the bottle, and the Gestapo proved to have no head for liquor: three hours later, they "reeled out of my office without their prisoners and without the incriminating documents they had demanded . . ."

It must have been nerve-wracking, all right. And I can easily imagine Emilia (who shared his views and all that, but there are limits) screaming *Why in God's name couldn't you just mind your own business, like everybody else?* Or Oskar seriously weighing the risk of simply going to one of his old big-shot friends, confessing the whole caper, and counting on astute handling and the size of the haul of Jews to keep the ax off his neck. But he didn't, and by the end of 1942, he had been enlisted in a more or less organized cause: the Jews had not been standing around hoping some good fairy would give them three wishes, so there was considerable activity—generally based on money from America and muscles from Palestine—aimed at stealing victims from the Nazis. A representative of such a group came to visit Schindler and told him the Jews in Palestine knew about his work; later, the man brought him money on behalf of "certain Jewish groups and mail from the Holy Land." All of which was helpful and inspiring—and also would have made it too late for Schindler to turn back, even if one assumes he wanted to. He went forward instead: "Dr. Kastner sent me lists with the names of certain prominent Jews in various ghettos, whom he asked me to take under my protection. I succeeded in doing this in 16 or 18 cases." So, more—and presumably bigger—risks, more mouths to feed, more faces to hide when the inspection teams came around, and finally, more and more people who knew and could betray what was no longer an individual dissent but part of a team. In short, Oskar was back to being an organization man—but, this time, not the kind of organization that offered pension plans or exposed you to the danger of boredom . . .

There were 1200 people, genuine workers and ringers combined, under Oskar Schindler's protection when he did get a chance to pull out—safely for himself, and who would have blamed him? For even if any of the 1200 were left alive afterward (assuming there was an Allied victory), all they could have said of Schindler was that he had tried and tried and was finally forced to give up . . . This crunch came a year before the war ended in Europe, at a time when the approach of the Russians was compelling the Germans to move all factories back from the Cracow area. Schindler could have moved with his machinery then to any point in Germany—but he would've had to leave the 1200 Jews behind.

He didn't do it. Those who resist heroism as an explanation (always a good idea, I think) may consider the possibility that he knew the Germans were going to lose the war, so why give up a winning ticket? I don't think too much of that notion, because the continued risks don't seem worth Schindler's while even if you argue him as a pure cynic. He already *had* a winning ticket, if that's what it turned out to be: the Jewish organizations knew what he'd been up to and could so testify, if everybody lived that long.* Also, you'd have to show that, from where Schindler sat, it was really so clear the Germans were going to lose the war. The folks in Berlin may have suspected it, and the officers who tried to get Adolf Hitler in July 1944 surely thought so. But, out there in Poland, I dunno . . . The most persuasive explanation of Schindler's behavior at that point, even if you eliminate the dimension of heroism, seems to me to be simple human protectiveness of one's own labors and personal history. City planners in America see that phenomenon often: after years of consultants and hard-won legislation, whole projects can teeter because some small householder, however tempted by money and other goodies, stubbornly refuses to sell out and leave the rosebush he planted with his own hands. So whatever Schindler's reasons, I suspect they start with the fact that he had too much invested in those 1200 Jews to give them up—and if he was also behaving like a hero and a Catholic, driven by either glory or morality, he was first of all behaving simply like other men.

He pulled strings with the highest authorities in Berlin and succeeded in getting permission to move with all his workers to Bruennlitz in the Sudetenland, where he set up in business all over again. Starting from scratch, and this time surrounded by antagonistic neighbors who objected to the "Jewification" of the area. (*They* certainly don't sound as though they were getting ready for an Allied victory, do they?) By spending practically his last penny, Schindler managed to feed his "wards"—it would be tempted to build a psychoanalysis on that word, but remember it's a translation—and pay for the SS guards until the factory began to become a going concern again.

It's at this point that I think even the most careful skepticism, and even Monday-morning quarterbacking, must give up and acknowledge Oskar as an authentic honest-to-God hero. The story's "turn" is as sharply dramatized as any novelist could contrive: one day, a friend who worked for the German railway told Schindler

*And Oskar didn't have anything to fear from them: the Joint Distribution Committee doesn't shoot people's kneecaps for letting down the Cause.

that a transport train with about 100 prisoners had been standing in the station at Zwittau (Oskar's hometown—how's that for dramatic irony?) for several days. The train, come from the quarries in Auschwitz-Golleschau, had already been shunted from factory to factory; nobody it seemed, wanted the unsatisfactory labor-force consignment represented by its cargo of half-dead freezing and starving men. "Sixteen of the men were frozen corpses when we opened the wagon doors," Schindler recalled. "All the others needed months of hospital care, which my wife worked hard to provide for them. One day she traveled 300 km. in subzero weather to trade two suitcases full of vodka for medicines and vitamin pills." (You know, I get the feeling that if the Nazis had been teetotallers they could've got every Jew in Europe instead of a mere six million. For drinking certainly seems to have impaired their efficiency.)

"The dead of the transport," Schindler reports, matter-of-factly as any head of a well-run little duchy, "received a Jewish funeral conducted by our camp rabbi, Lewetov." Something about the tone of that makes you sort of wonder whether Schindler's 1200 might not also have had calisthenics every morning and a movie in the mess hall on Tuesday nights. It sounds like an early-Israeli kibbutz—a bunch of Jews surrounded by dangers but settled-in and organized and intending to stay. But it wasn't that, of course: that would be old-hero stuff (probably played by Humphrey Bogart). In the new hero's camp, the inhabitants had not so much joined as simply landed there, doubtless thinking themselves lucky at first; and then, I'm pretty sure, becoming increasingly discontented and suspicious. Because they just weren't in shape for idealism—how many of those people, yanked abruptly out of their lives and even out of their identities and then hunted like vermin, could have been even quite sane by then? Or in any way trusting: people who had so recently learned that their nationality and all its connotations—of taxpayer, citizen, patriot—could be whisked away in a day, even in an hour, were unlikely to become wholehearted song-on-the-lips followers of little-king Schindler. No way. True, he was known to have taken in So-and-so's old parents, who were clearly too feeble to be of any use to anybody and thus had to represent an act of pure charity. And it was said that he (read: The Man, Mr. Charley, the Irish "himself") had saved Lamus's skin, and that could hardly be because Lamus was such a great wheelbarrow-pusher. But he must be getting *some* kind of payoff, or be counting on one later. And meanwhile, the food was miserable. It was supposed to be the best he could manage, but only a fool would believe Schindler wasn't holding out something . . .

I don't know, but I think it must have felt like that if you were one of the 1200. For Oskar Schindler was in a spot any executive knows enough to avoid: his responsibility was total, but his authority was uncertain. True, his 1200 "subjects" could hardly afford to overthrow their monarch; but he was an outsider and no part of their own everybody-must-be-heard, endlessly debating culture (even to contemplate the co-existence of Talmudic hairsplitting and the police-the-barracks personality that shows up in Schindler's prose boggles the mind!). They had neither elected nor inherited him, so they could not be relied on to obey or trust him.* Not as a group, anyway—there would be some who, like the future Israeli judge Bejski, assisted Schindler in the daily crookeries needed to keep them all alive. But it had to have been a small, special corps; otherwise, it couldn't work.

However, if Schindler didn't take a vote, he certainly took responsibility. Listen to the benevolent-despot sound of this: "With the approaching collapse of the German army in the spring of 1945 I feared that the SS troops at Bruennlitz would kill all my Jews as an act of desperation. Against that danger I created an illegal self-defense group among my workers from men who had served in the Polish army." Ah yes—add the word "veteran" to those Jews' lost connotations of nationality I listed above. Not that it's a surprise to anyone who's seen Yad Vashem: the souvenirs gathered there include identity cards of men who were, one day, German enough to have won the Iron Cross for valor in World War I; the next day, they were no longer Germans and even their names were changed. With characteristic thoroughness and swiftness, machinery and manpower were provided to correct the identity papers of all Jews by inserting "Israel" or "Sarah" in the sudden ex-German's name. Yad Vashem has some more good clear photos of this—Jews lined up, waiting patiently for a man at a desk to make the change in their papers.†

Well, back to Schindler's account of the end of all that: "Under the pretext that I needed weapons for the protection of my factory, I wangled rifles, machineguns and ammunition from the SS

---

*Wohlfeiler's individualistic efforts to deal in the false-documents market on his own (with the narrow-escape result reported earlier in this chapter) was presumably an example of this—and the effect, endangering others, was probably also typical. This bunch was definitely *not* kibbutzniks.

†This sort of thing is now used to support the myth that Jews went sheep-like to slaughter—a notion properly answered only by a trite, scatological word. For if Washington suddenly sent me a registered letter telling me I was henceforth not Maggie but Beulah, I might start learning how to make Molotov cocktails; but I'd sure as hell stand on line in the meantime.

423

chief of Moravia." (Israel's national anthem, *"Hatikva,"* is based on a Moravian folk air picked up by the Czech composer Anton Dvorak. So what, you say? Well, I put it in parenthesis because I'm not sure. Except that I don't know where the SS chief of Moravia is now, but Moshe Bejski was singing *"Hatikva"* at Schindler's funeral. So I guess what I'm afraid or ashamed to say right out in the open is that maybe, sometimes, hope—which is what *tikva* means—and ardor do win out over the efficient death-men. And that Israel made a more loving home for the Moravian folk tune than Moravia did.) "The transaction," Schindler's report says of the arming of the 1200 via the SS chief, "was also smoothed by the gift of a diamond ring for his wife." Not vodka this time. But it would seem that those who may have muttered in the corners of the camp that The Man was holding out could have been right. If Schindler had been running a democracy—or a kibbutz—the diamond ring would maybe have been cashed in and shared around as an extra ration of bread.

On May 9, 1945, it was all over: the SS had left Bruennlitz, running. So it was safe for Oskar Schindler to leave "his" 1200 charges and make his way to the American lines—which, considering that the other choice was perhaps to be taken by the Russians, was the more sensible direction for a capitalist factory owner, not to say also a guy with friends in the Wehrmacht. Back at the camp, the Jews were armed but they didn't need to be, not any more: those Germans whose careers were too much to expect even the easily conned Americans to overlook were running; the others were working up résumés showing their busy-busy anti-Nazi activities all those years. Schindler later said proudly—and he was surely entitled to pride—that he'd kept his word to his people "to remain with them until five minutes after midnight. None of those who had come under my protection had died a violent death." There weren't many Christians in Europe in 1945 who could make that statement, a righteous boast any way you want to use "righteous."

Is he the new hero, this influence peddler, corrupter of public officials, anything-goes protector of his accidental earldom? Well, look at it: swindled in the name of liberation, he turned around and wielded the power his own victimhood had given him. (For surely his ability to pull strings with those high authorities in Berlin had something to do with his erstwhile stint in Admiral Canaris's outfit—a good place to have learned where bodies were buried, and other tidbits wieldable later when strings had to be pulled?) And 1200 survivors could attest that Schindler knew how to work the machinery. For a heartful nursemaid had sheltered little Rita Wolpert, and an idealistic schoolteacher not only snatched

Michael Stolovitzki from death but also defied the world and the British navy to make him a citizen of the baby state of Israel. But Oskar Schindler's "protection" included trouble he went looking for in a boxcar-full of men dying of callousness in the station of a tidy town. His own hometown, remember: among those probably peeking from behind their starched curtains were, maybe, his old teacher and his first girlfriend. Everybody in town knew who that was out there in the cold, messing about with all those trouble-making Jews . . .

And man, did it cost him! In 1945, Oskar Schindler was thirty-seven years old. He'd begun by inheriting a thriving business, and he obviously knew how to run one well: whatever his subsequent factories manufactured, he always managed to make a living (*and* lay in a stock of vodka, presumably) for himself and his Jewish dependents—even when he had to start over again and again, and without good will among his assets. All of which sounds like executive ability at least in the running for the Chamber of Commerce's young-men-of-the-year banquet. Also, he'd successfully played the black-market game in a time when fortunes were made that way in Germany (and in France, and occasionally in the U.S. Army, too); but when the war ended, Schindler had neither money nor medals. He'd lost his property and possessions in the Russian Zone, where he was not likely to get a sympathetic hearing to any request for repayment, and he had frittered away—in 1200 directions—the pretty penny civilians in his position were assumed to have made on the war. He did, of course, have what he had once wanted so badly, the right to be a German. But by then he couldn't have felt it exactly a thrill: "Schindler," the *Jerusalem Post* obit notes chastely, "did not feel at ease in West Germany." You betcha.

However, he had one earned asset: as Golda Meir once pointed out in her flat and tactless way, the Jews don't forget their friends. So Oskar Schindler emigrated to Argentina, where he bought a farm with money supplied by a private Jewish charitable organization. How he fared in Argentina is left to the imagination, but it clearly wasn't too well. And it's not difficult, I guess, to see why: in the expatriate colony there, he could hear the sound of his native language, all right, but it's hard to imagine this Sudeten upstart with no money to throw around finding a very warm welcome. What with the snobbishness of expatriate societies in general and the title-nuttiness of the German besides, that bunch wasn't likely to roll out the Welcome Wagon for a title-less provincial who had been a—so to speak—premature anti-Nazi.

The *Jerusalem Post* passes over all that with remarkable

economy and/or tact: in one sentence, we read that Schindler is in Argentina and in the next, "In 1956 he returned to Frankfurt and started a cement factory, which, however, did not succeed." No explanation. Maybe the business whiz kid, now aged forty-eight, had lost his touch. Certainly he seemed to have lost some official phone numbers, because it was not until 1968(!) that the West German government awarded him the *Verdienstkreutz Ersten Ranges* (Service Cross, first class) and a monthly pension of 200 Deutschmarks. When he died, that was worth around $80 a month. And at no time was it ever close to what a fellow who at thirty-two had had capital, business acumen, and influence might have expected to own at the age of sixty.

But if Schindler was poor, he wasn't friendless. "Over the years," the obit says, he'd stayed in touch with former "protégés," who apparently didn't forget "the debt they owed him." I remember reading that he'd made seventeen trips to Israel, and I doubt that he paid the fare on his 200-DM pension. So he had fringe benefits, shall we say. He died in Hildesheim, as a German in Germany—the identity he had once so devoutly sought. But it was to Israel that, by his last wish, he came home.

Well, that's the way the costs add up, based on the *Post* story. But there must have been some not included in that account, because what's strangely missing (oh, so you noticed too, did you?) is Emilia, who once worked fourteen- and sixteen-hour days at her husband's side while they tried to lick the problems of running that unorthodox factory in Poland. Emilia gets mentioned in the newspaper only by implication: Schindler was childless, it notes, thus indicating the sometime existence of a wife. The remarks I've quoted about Emilia are in the newspaper's obituary, but it's only quoting Schindler's contribution to that single postwar German book. Something looks funny here: if Emilia had also been honored as a Righteous Gentile, why wouldn't the *Jerusalem Post* say so? And if she'd perished at the hands of the Nazis—if that had been part of the price of Schindler's helping the Jews—surely it would also be part of the obit? Where *is* Emilia, then? She's not buried in that Catholic cemetery in Jerusalem. And if she's buried back in Hildesheim, why did Oskar ask to be laid to rest in Jerusalem?

What seems likely is that Emilia isn't buried anywhere—Schindler was sixty-six, so she could be in her early sixties, or even younger. And maybe she's somebody else's wife now: Oskar's lost magic touch at building businesses could have been at least in part a result of personal depression over a domestic crisis. Perhaps, either

426

by Oskar's choice or Emilia's, the marriage ended with the war (and those postwar references to her comradely sharing of labors and perils were, for all their stiff language, elegaic). If so, it wouldn't be the first marriage to survive *Sturm and Drang* and then collapse when the storm's blown over and the sun is coming out. So if Emilia was still alive in 1974, when Oskar died, she was either remarried (and thus presumably controversial, since she was presumably also Catholic) or just separated, but in any case she was no longer Oskar's next of kin.

What makes these speculations especially interesting, aside from the gossip-curiosity, is the number of special hazards Emilia must have encountered as the wife of a new hero—and, whatever actually happened, they're part of the costs. Like, I'd find it entirely believable that sometime back in the dark days, there was just one freezing 300-km journey too many, and Emilia simply ran out of steam. Or say she *stamm* got fed up with being in the hero trade— though not, obviously, to the point of defecting, or Schindler's 1200 would've been goners: Emilia knew where those bodies were not buried. But suppose she'd come to want, for all her virtuous "sharing" of Oskar's Jew-saving passion, what she'd after all been promised when she married the handsome (from his photo, Schindler probably *was* a handsome young man, in a blond and big-toothed German way), dashing, well-fixed Oskar. I can see her realizing, desperately and maybe shamefacedly, that the years of her youth were passing—who knew, in say 1943, how long the drudgery and horror would go on?—and longing to have a baby and settle down in a respectable house with a nice garden. Which was what plenty of people in Germany were doing, and right outside of Dachau, as a matter of ugly fact . . .

I think it's a fair guess that Emilia was a daughter of the bourgeoisie: she married Schindler, and there wasn't that much marrying between classes in that milieu. So how prepared could she have been, what with having been taught the management of maids and how to play the piano gracefully, for life in a fog of fatigue and danger, day after day going by in grim service as chief healer of wretched people? Some with psychic wounds she couldn't hope to heal, either: "Those to whom evil is done/ Do evil in return," said W. H. Auden*. So there was doubtless no lack of ugliness, nastiness, and meanness of spirit in the crowded and fear-ridden camp on the factory grounds. Emilia's life must have been not unlike those for

*In his poem "September 1, 1939"—which title makes it clear what evil he was taking off from.

which the Roman Catholic church gives canonization candidates brownie points . . .

So maybe one day Emilia said the hell with her reward in heaven and her share of the guilt for the *verdammte* suffering Jews, and she just took off. Or it happened later, when, pushing forty and perhaps condemned by then to childlessness, she found herself living alone with a husband shunned by the best people, in psychic and then in actual exile, always grubbing for money—and she couldn't help taking out her rage on him, chopping him down every day in deadly little remarks and killing silences. Or maybe it was Oskar who turned onto the one person he thought couldn't leave him, a Catholic wife, the bitterness of his regrets and dismays. Perhaps that farm in Argentina was just too much for Emilia. Or it could be that she *liked* Argentina and refused to go back and try again with a cement factory in Frankfurt.

I can think of more variations, some of them pretty lurid. But it doesn't matter what details you write into the scenario: they're all part of the cost of the new heroism that saved those 1200 Jews. The *Jerusalem Post* writer, either *nihil-nisi*-ing for Schindler's funeral or preferring as a matter of policy not to belabor the costs—beyond failed factories, anyway—of being a Righteous Gentile, gave Emilia credit for what she did (it was the reporter, after all, who chose those quotes from Schindler that mentioned her) but tactfully omitted the end of the story. And now that I consider it carefully, I think he was right. For the lesson for our times is clearer without the narrowing details: Emilia had only one life to be affected, but heroism has more possible outcomes than any one life can demonstrate. Oskar is specific: the portrait of a man seduced by ideology into (at least tacitly) accepting cruelty, and then so far revolted by particular cruelties as to bet his life, repeatedly and for years and years, on snatching its victims away—well, that already stands out clear and humanly complicated enough. We can recognize the line of descent, from the erring Lancelot rather than the pure Galahad,* to the hero who cannot be hero-worshipped, which is the only useful kind for the current climate of moralism and simplistic judgments. We can leave Emilia to represent later possibilities, some guessed at and some still unguessable, and zero in on

---

*Like many other readers, I never did warm to him. But when I got tipped to the heroes of the Old Testament, the whole King Arthur shtick seemed comic-book stuff anyway besides Moses (peeking even when the Lord of Hosts himself said not to!) or the flawed King David. The Jews, most of whose greats have to be apologized for as well as admired, may have had the inside track on the right kind of heroes all along.

Schindler the daily deliverer, coping over and over again in weariness and danger and dismay, coaxing and scheming and maybe
dragging the fainter-hearted one more step, one more day. Not a
pure-soul hero. And not a big-moment hero.

That last is the kind we used to have. But I've been a big-
moment type hero myself, so I know why it's not good enough
anymore. I once ran out into a street and snatched a toddler from
the path of a truck: the driver was freewheeling down a steep grade
and couldn't possibly have seen the baby. Afterward, I was embarrassed by the praise because what I'd done was not brave but
impulsive, almost mindless, and with none of the intent to sacrifice
myself that the hallelujahs were implying. I was young and athletic,
and I'd seen that I could launch myself in a kind of flying tackle and
grab the baby and then roll away, and that's what I did. Maybe I
expected to scratch my knees and elbows, but I didn't really expect
to get hurt: when I saw the tire marks of the truck on my white skirt
(fortunately, wide skirts were in style then), I nearly fainted with
surprise and retroactive fear—in the midst of a group of people
acclaiming my heroism . . .

Well, they didn't know any better. And neither did I, back
then: the straightforward act based on a person-to-person impulse
and a shot of adrenaline into the bloodstream seemed, to all of us,
enough. But it isn't. In an age of big-number death, when babies are
saved it isn't by youth-with-muscles but by somebody with a stack of
file cards and an ability to keep on working when he's very, very
tired. Oskar Schindler was a transitional figure, I think, in the sense
that he probably began, as old-fashioned heroes did, with only
rudimentary planning and no intention of really getting hurt; from
there on, though, it was on-the-job training, with lives hanging on
his every trial-and-error move, his every attempt to bully the bullies
and con the con men. The world had no model, thirty-odd years ago,
for a state's conning millions of innocents into gas ovens; and
Schindler didn't have any handbook on how to cheat the state. But
his experiences provide a model now.

Learn from it, I would have said to Phil if only I'd been luckier
in the timing, by imagining how things felt—which nobody can tell
you with facts—and selecting what's usable in a different time and
place. If the silhouette, recognizable though not wearing the same
uniform, looms again. And in case Righteous Gentiles—or their
equivalent, involving some other noun next time—are what helpless
people come to depend on again.

The Israelis already have learned, some at first hand and

others at memorial services. But they aren't the only people who are going to need the new hero. And if enough others learn, maybe it won't cost so much to be a hero next time.

From the diary: 24
Phil's last day (September)

Phil stayed on a little longer than he'd meant to, as a result of a complicated airline maneuver he'd put together. It was far less expensive than my own whizzes via El Al, but part of his return ticket was on the Greek airline—and it suddenly went on strike. Oooh-ah, said Beer-Sheva, shaking its head. (This indicates overt sympathy plus either the covert or just unrealized satisfaction that occurs whenever something outside Israel turns out not to work efficiently either.) Finally some sort of lend-lease arrangement among airlines was evolved, so Phil would get back to school in time to do whatever he'd planned before the new term began, and after that the extra days were pure velvet. He even had time to borrow a saw and make me a shelf (out of some more of my leftover crate wood) on my kitchen balcony. There I was, having my cake and eating it too—in Israel and still with a son around—and I loved it.

What was especially nice was that so did everybody else, on my behalf. I noticed that when Phil carried a table over from Thereza and Jan's for me. (It was light enough for one person, so long as I wasn't the person; thus it was at their house, waiting for Jan to carry it over to my place for me on Saturday. Except that now, I had Phil around and didn't have to wait.) He picked it up and put it upside down on his head, Israeli-style, and carried it easily down the length of the mishol. With me scurrying proudly beside him: everybody see my big strong helpful son? Everybody did, coming to their doors to smile benignly—it's nice that the American woman turns out to have a son, like other people. A dutiful son is the culture's necessary resource for help-needing middle age, and Thereza's neighbors were pleased to learn that I am duly equipped. If it had been Jan carrying the table for me, the neighbor-faces would have shown pleasure, too: Thereza and Jan's kindness to a lone immigrant is regarded as not only individual goodness but a patriotic act in this community where nobody can ever quite feel free to stop being a symbol. But this was even better, for now I was visibly getting the hang of being Israeli, looking openly proud, and so was my American son, who had somehow already learned the right way of doing things . . .

Well, today was the last-last day, though. A Saturday, so when I wanted Phil to see that anti-war monument (see Chapter 12), Avi was home from work and could take us. Of course he could: it was hot as hell and it meant missing the sacred 2-to-4 P.M. nap time, and

God only knew how many lirot-worth of incredibly expensive gasoline it would cost (and you can't pay Avi back for it)—but of course Martha and Avi would come get us and take us over to the Dead Sea. Once I expressed the wish, that was that—it's just everybody's job to see that a visitor sees Israel, and if you can help, you stamm do. So they packed up the baby and the water bottles and plastic bags of fruit and diapers and off we went, in the hottest part of Avi's only day off from work . . .

The baby is about four months old. I took care to remind Phil in advance that she's a girl, because a non-Hebrew speaker couldn't tell from her name and Martha's a bit sensitive about the fact that you sure can't tell from her hairdo. Her hair is there all right, a pale yellow fuzz; but the general look is still that Winston Churchill one . . . She was in fine fettle, though even with the car in motion it was still unbelievably hot. (What good is a breeze when it itself is like furnace breath?) She wasn't too hot though, at least not at first, for all she was wearing was a diaper and plastic pants, and her sweet plump pink-and-white body—the skin so perfect and blooming that she looks positively unreal!—had been freshly sponged. What's more, she was enjoying the outing, so much livelier than some dull old nap. So she crawled up Martha's front to peer into the back seat. Where I was of course immediately willing to forswear attention to everything else but, equally of course, it was Phil she fixed her round china-blue eyes on with delight. Phil doesn't dislike babies, but they're not the most important part of any scenery for him—and yet, as always happens, it was he whom the baby set out to enchant. She laughed, she cooed, she tried to grab his hair (which she apparently believes is a real winner in her charm-the-biggies routine) and Phil smiled politely and said what a cute baby she was and went on looking out at the scenery.

She finally got him, though: annoyed, she began to berate him, in a series of non-word but nevertheless clear sentences. The cadence was unmistakable, and eventually Phil could no longer resist answering her. "Burrabzzbzz bz," said the baby reproachfully; and "Burraburrabzzbzz burra," protested Phil in self-defense. It was a veritable dialogue, lines out of some domestic bicker ("you could've taken a minute just to call"—"I did try to call you, but you're never at home"), and it was ridiculous and fascinating. We should have been caught like that as some kind of cosmic metaphor, in our carful of innocent inanity—Martha and Avi and I laughing as we supplied possible dialogue in two languages, the pleased baby flirting with Phil while still busily lecturing him, and Phil beguiled by his interesting experiment demonstrating how close you can get to language without actually speaking words*— rolling along under the burning sun through the still, empty afternoon. On our way to the bottom of the world, the Dead Sea, and guided by Avi's sure hand down that perilous road: accidents are frequent there, especially at night but also in the early morning and at any other time when visibility is less than absolutely perfect, for you could drive right off it in a minute, any time you got inattentive or failed to see one of its hair-raising turns. You have to drive that road with the exact, unwavering attention of a proofreader.

And if you miss a typo, wow. Because your car would plunge into the abysses that change only with changes in their own shadows, and you'd be instantly lost from sight. You might well land softly, since there's nothing but the caramel-colored sandy dirt to hit, but surviving wouldn't do you much good; trying to climb out, you'd be like a bug in a washbasin. Only, far less conspicuous—and the traffic that normally goes by is sparse and also the kind least likely to contain anybody scanning the endless hills and valleys of dead sand. Terrorists wouldn't find them any more life-supporting than anyone else, so a police patrol doesn't usually have any reason for turning its binoculars on that scenery. (Or any such paternalistic routine, either: the police in Israel are as undermanned as in the U.S. and have much more constant perilous business besides, so there's not much automatic watching-out for citizen follies. Israelis are expected to be mostly self-sufficient—which they generally are— and to call the cops themselves, which usually happens only when the problem is beyond the capacities of the men of the neighborhood.)

Thus if we'd gone off that road almost anywhere along the way, the odds were that the sun would get us, and if it didn't thirst would, long before anybody started looking for us. It's a landscape in which you simply don't matter, so empty that it makes the Nabbatean ruins of Avdat, down in the Negev, look bustling. These deader-than-dead hills and folds of sandy stuff, in which nothing lives, it seems—I doubt that there's even the odd lizard: they must have learned by now that there's nothing to live on there, and gone elsewhere—would swallow outcries as easily as they'd swallow attempts to slog out of there or set something on fire or anything else you might think of to do to try and get noticed. Nothing happens

---

*What it most resembled, I guess, was those photography tricks where the dots that make up a newspaper picture are selectively removed—the idea being to see how many dots you can take away and still have the photo recognizably Lincoln. Phil, who once had a summer job teaching a computer to speak, may well have become especially fascinated by the small, highly evolved computer in the front seat.

433

among those hills of Time: "If I should die there," I wrote in a poem about them, "nothing, nothing, would come of my bones."

Avi is not a daredevil or a fool; he's checked the gas and water and done what he could to ensure that a tire won't blow out. But if it does, he'll be ready; he looks relaxed, laughing at the baby with the rest of us, but his eyes are alert and wary behind the tinted glasses. And I can see in his posture the small but important differences between his relaxation and the American Sunday driver's, idling along with an elbow propped on the window ledge and the other hand tapping out a tune on the steering wheel. (Seeing those differences, I am suddenly full of love for Avi, who would be so good at being that Sunday driver: what good care he would take of the comfortable American suburban house I wish I could give him! He's such a happy man—how he would flourish, what a good neighbor he'd be, among the eases and safeties of some Wildwood Manor or Crestview Homes!)

Avi thinks it's safe enough, or we wouldn't have come here: he doesn't need to make daring gestures. But Israeli-safe is always in peril, from either nature or man, and Avi knows he's bringing his wife and child within probable range of Jordanian artillery or rockets or missiles or whatever. He relies on skill and preparation, and finally on luck, betting that the Jordanians won't fire, not this Saturday anyway. And that some idiot shelanu won't do anything fatally stupid either—not even if he belongs to the government (which, in any normal Israeli's calculations, always represents odds against you*). Because what else can you do? You have to live, and in Israel that never means alone. You're hooked up to not only your own family and friends and neighbors but also to the despised "religious," assorted Israeli nuts, and all the Jews in the world—a pain-in-the-ass folk who keep sending money and artwork and ambulances. And then, if they can afford the trip, turn up in person to add a kibbutz duncecap to their tribal costume of Bermuda shorts and loud shirts and the slung cameras they pay so ridiculously little for. They can be seen prancing around Tel Aviv or peering at the Wall in Jerusalem or, in the Negev, emerging from their air-conditioned buses to climb puffing up the ramparts of Masada. Then they go home, and—from the safety of places like New York and London—start poking their busybody noses into whatever Israeli cabinet decision is currently being chewed over.

Though how safe are New York and London now? It's hard to

*For a couple of days after some feat like the raid on the Entebbe airport, Israelis will concede that the government occasionally uses its head. But it's recognized that that feeling is only a passing exhilaration, and people will soon come to their senses.

see a friend as a hero, but now that I've written out the definition, how can I deny that Avi has the earmarks of the new hero who'll be needed there too? He knows how to work the bureaucratic machinery and does work it, and he takes risks if he has to because he's decided enough-is-enough. His scorn is easy and widely inclusive, but so also is his sense of obligation: it reaches back into the past as well as into the trying daily business of doing favors for friends in the little bit of time off you have after you earn a living and defend your country. People like Avi don't think of themselves as heroes, of course. They think of themselves as more like perpetually in trouble and just hoping it won't prove too much—or, in short, as Israeli. Which means being neither a hero nor an ideologue but a dahfke man, stamm beating the odds as long as you can. Hoping it won't take all the time you have, and trying to have a little fun in the interstices meanwhile . . .

Well, we weren't in New York or London but on our way to the Dead Sea. The baby, who would have gone on with her game if she could (have you ever noticed how long an infant's attention span really is, no matter what the books say? Incredible!), was being overtaken by that missed nap. She was still trying to bat those saucer eyes, but the delicate blue-traced lids kept closing over them and she was now doing her gurgling from inside the crook of Martha's arm. Clearly, the baby hasn't finished exploring the possibilities of Phil—but she just can't stay on her toes to peer into the back seat anymore. Not right now, but for a few minutes . . . Don't go 'way, Phil . . .

But Phil did: there was a good place to pull off the road, so he and Avi and I climbed out of the car and went over to look down at an abyss beginning to purple a little in the late-afternoon light. What makes this one special is, it's non-empty at the bottom, though you can't really tell what that sand-colored crumble way down in there once was. A customs post, Avi says: a lost nation had soldiers stationed there, to collect tribute from whatever commerce was going on across the Dead Sea. It would have been hard duty, that's for sure—maybe the soldiers got incentive pay? I asked whose soldiers they were and Avi told me, but I forgot the next minute; they all sound alike to me, those long-gone peoples with their strange names.

We stood there looking long enough for the baby, still fighting, to be conquered. Martha came to join us, carrying the sleeping baby wrapped in a shawl that goes around both of them, like a Beduin woman's black cape. I want to remember us always as we stood there, all of us, looking down at the silted-over eons but *being our now and separate selves too . . . Martha is not a Beduin woman—born in the American heartland, she left it for love of a stranger, but she brought her people's ways with her. And added her new people's ways too, so American Martha wants to see what there is to see and take part in the talk; but Israeli Martha doesn't look for a babysitter or take turns with her husband, she just naturally totes the baby along. And Avi isn't an Arab, so he makes room for her. And he also puts himself between her and the edge he's already warned Phil and me away from because it's more crumbly than it looks. Avi is responsible, he takes care: Martha and the baby are under his protection, but so am I—no longer as much the stranger within the gates as I was on Yom Kippur, when Ze'ev (who is younger and was not yet anybody's father but nevertheless is an Israeli) also took care of me. And Phil is the youth Avi never was, safe and fathered. And therefore perhaps inclined to be heedless; so Avi, who is not afraid of responsibility, takes care of Phil too.*

When Martha came over, I was just asking how long ago those soldiers camped down there at the hostile, shadowed bottom of the world. Avi tells me and I turn to my-son-the-mathematician: how many generations have there been, then, between the four-month-old baby and the crew who manned that outpost? Phil reckons for a minute, decides it's probably eighty. We all stand there trying to imagine eighty generations, the "greats" having to be represented by a little exponent number, as in math. Meanwhile Martha, in a gesture light-years old, pulls up the shawl to cover the baby's peach-fuzz head against the hot wind that blows and blows.

It will never stop, God help the brave, tired people who live in its forever path. Quintessential Warms in an increasingly Cold world, they want more than just to survive. That was maybe good enough for the gone soldiers in that outpost down there, but these caretakers of past and future want to live, with not only their loves but even their hobbies, with glories and homelinesses firmly joined (which is the only way to make glory safe to keep around the house). And maybe also to be able to go about on holiday, with the baby and the picnic basket and the general sun shining, somewhere where there are no walls.

Tomorrow. Or if not tomorrow, then the day after.

Glossary

A: pronounced "ah" unless otherwise indicated.

aba—*father*
achbar—*mouse*
adoni (a-doe-NEE)—*mister, sir,* form of address (literally, *my lord*)
agora—unit of currency, a coin worth 1/100th of a lira; pl., "agorot"
alenu (a-LAY-noo)—*to us, among us, in our midst*
aleph—first letter of the alphabet (hence, "aleph-bet" for *alphabet*)
almana (al-ma-NA)—*widow*
anachnu (a-NACH-noo)—*we*
anashim (a-nash-EEM)—*people.* ("Nashim" is *women,* which sounds as
    though it must have some connection)
anglit (ahn-GLEET)—*English* (not capitalized in Hebrew)
ani (a-NEE)—*I*
arba-im (EEM)—*forty. (Four* is "arba." But I never thought to ask how
    you'd say four-plural without ending up at forty)
Artzoat Habrit (ha-BREET)—*United States*
asimon (a-see-MOAN)—telephone token; pl., "asimonim"
at—*you* fem. sing.; masc. is a-TAH. (The masc. pl. a-TEM is used when
    addressing mixed genders)
avoda—*work* (noun); b'a-voh-DA, *at work*
ayin (EYE-in)—sixteenth letter of the alphabet
az—*then* in the sense of *well, then* or *okay, so . . .*—but not meaning
    "ago." (Probably best translated by French *alors*)

B: in Hebrew, this is only minimally different from V; so whether it's B or V
in English is often up for grabs (e.g., Beer-Sheva vs. Beersheba)

b'—*in* ("b'anglit") or *at* ("b'avoda"); occasionally, *on* (see "regel")
bagrut (bog-ROOT)—exam at end of secondary school

437

Beer-Sheva (Bear-SHEV-uh)—literally, *well of the oath*
beit (bite)—*house*; "b'beit" is *at home*
ben—*son*; in names like the suffix —*son* in English names
bevakasha (beh-vok-a-SHA)—*please* (interjection); also used like *You're welcome* after being thanked
binyan (bean-YON)—*building* (noun)
blee—*without* (prep.)
bo—imperative of *come*, masc. sing; fem. is "bo-ee," which comes out "boy" and leads to inevitable jokes in English
boker—*morning*
Brit Hamo-azoat—U.S.S.R.
b'seder—*okay*; b'seder gah-MOR, A—*okay*

C: "k" sound only
[The listing for *ch* follows *H*]

ca-ah-SHARE—*when*, but as in "When the war is over . . ."; for the specific "What time?" meaning, there's another word
cadur (cah-DOOHR)—*ball*
cadur-regel (REH-gull)—*football*
cah-SHARE and cosh-ROOT—*kosher* and *kosherness*. These belong here according to the Hebrew (kosher is Yiddish). But see "K"
col (cole)—*all, everything*

D:

dahfke—*despite*?? (This is one of the two untranslatables—see Chapter 2)
daled—fourth letter of the alphabet
dood (oo as in *goon*)—hot-water tank and/or heater

E: as in *leg* unless doubled

ech—*how*; "ech omrim," which is (roughly) *How do you say?*, is a vital tool for foreigners
echod—the number *one*, masc.(fem., "achat"); the expression "echod-shtym"—literally *one-two*—means *at once, pronto*
eem—*if*
efshar (ef-SHAR)—*it is possible*; as in English, this is mild whereas its opposite, "EE-efshar," is weighty and forceful
Egged (EGG-ed)—intercity bus line
esh—*fire* (noun)

F: Hebrew has an "f" (or "ph") sound, but no entries occur in the book

G: all hard, as in *gun*

gadol (ga-DOLE)—*big, large*, masc. (fen., ga-dol-AH)
gahm—*too, also*

438

gan—*garden;* "gan yeledim," a *children-garden* (kindergarten)

ganenet (gan-EN-et)—*kindergarten or nursery-school teacher,* fem.

gar—*live* (verb), masc. sing.; fem. is ga-RAH

geshem (GEH-shem)—*rain;* "yored geshem," *rain is coming down* (N.B.:
   not to be confused with "gesher," which means a *bridge.* I once got
   lots of attention by announcing "Yored gesher!")

geveret (3 syll., accent on 2nd)—*Ms.,* I guess, since it means both *Miss*
   and *Mrs.* When used without a name, it's like *Madam* or *(Hey) Lady,*
   depending on how formal the scene

goomi (GOOH-me)—*foam rubber* or various objects made therefrom

H: hay, the fifth letter of the Hebrew alphabet, is pronounced just like our *H;*
   so I don't know why Israeli students ave such a ell of a time in English

ha—*the*

"habibi"—(Arabic) slang for *buddy, pal, old chap,* or—also in the slang
   and mocking sense— *"baby"*

hafsaka (3 syll., accent on last)—*intermission, interval* (In combining
   form, a final *"t"* is added: as, "hafsakat—ma-im," a break in the water
   supply)

Hatikva (ha-TIC-vah)—Israel's national anthem ("The Hope")

he—*she**

holech (ho-LECH)—*go, go out,* masc. sing. (Hard to define because of
   numerous uses, but it may be helpful to note that the imperative
   "Lech!" means *Beat it! Scram!*)

hoo (pronounced *who*)*—*he*

CH: This is the gargle pronounced like the *ch* in *och*

chacham (chah-CHAHM)—*intelligent, shrewd* (I brightened life in
   Israel by consistently confusing this with the word for *fever.* And
   when I applied it to an ambitious politician . . .)

cha-DAHSH, cha-da-SHA—*new,* masc. and fem.

chalav (cha-LAHV)—*milk*

chalutz (chah-LOOTS)—*pioneer* (This is often seen transliterated
   "halutzim," as virtually all towns have a Street of the Pioneers; such
   aids to the English-speaking keep them mispronouncing the name)

chamsin (cham-SEEN)—Arabic word for desert weather phenomenon:
   see "sharav," which is the Hebrew name for it

chash-MAHL—*electricity* ("hafsakat-chashmal," an electricity cutoff,
   is handy for comparing *h* and *ch* sounds)

chaval (chah-VAHL)—*alas, too bad, pity*

chaver (chah-VAIR)—*comrade, friend*—originally, only a member of a
   collective (in chalutz days, what else would your comrade be?) and so

*These work out nicely when sung to the tune of *Tea for Two:* "Who is *he* and he is
she; this tongue will be the death of me . . ."

439

used still in, e.g., "chaver haKnesset"; but now, it can even mean your boyfriend. Fem. is cha-ver-AH.

"chaverim-ism"—my own term for the self-consciously egalitarian dress and mannerisms of public figures, whether they're being cynically folksy (in Israel folksy is chalutz-y) or just nostalgic

cheder (CHAY-dare)—*room;* in the mercaz klita, your flat or part of one

chevra (chev-RAH)—*group, circle, intimates,* etc. Derivation from "chaver" is obvious, but one's associates no longer stem only from institutional memberships

choseret (cho-ZE-ret)—*return* (verb, intrans.), *come back* or *come home,* fem. sing.

chyal, chyelet (chigh-AL, chigh-ELL-et)—*soldier,* masc. and fem.

I: pronounced *ee*

ish—*man*

J: there isn't any—for a foreign word, a special squiggle is added to the letter gimmel *(G)* to indicate *J* sound. The *J* place names are usually more accurately rendered with a *Y:* e.g., the Hebrew name of Jerusalem is Yerushalayim

K

ken—*yes*

kibbutz—Well, isn't this practically English? Noun from the Hebrew verb *to collect:* a community where all ownership is collective, and so are labor and decisions—the historic form of Jewish settlement in Palestine

kibbutznik (accent 2nd syll.)—a member of any kibbutz (A member of a specific kibbutz is a "chaver" or "chavera" of it)

kipah (kee-PAH)—the *skullcap* worn by religious men; (called *yarmulka* —that's Yiddish—in the U.S.)

klita (klee-TAH)—*absorption* is the English word chosen (unhappily, I think, but it's hard to find a better) by the Israelis for the process, more profound than mere orientation and less legalistic than naturalization, by which immigrants take root in Israel

Knesset (KNES-set, and the K is not silent)—Israel's parliament, unicameral, 120 seats

"kosher"—Yiddish word applied (in America, anyway) loosely to all the ritual complications of "cashrut," which is rules about diet and a resulting religious bureaucracy. The best-known rules are the prohibition against eating the flesh of some animals altogether, the slaughter ritual required for others, and the strictures against mixing meat and milk

Kupat Cholim—literally, *patients* (or *the sick) fund*— not unlike an American health-insurance plan; this one is the largest of several. Thus, to newcomers, its name tends to mean simply *a clinic*

la'assot (la-ah-SSOAT)—infinitive of the verb *do* (also sometimes *make:* its usages are reminiscent of the Latin verb *facio*). "Ma la'assot?" —literally, *What to do?*—is a general expression of helplessness

le (pronounced like the French article)—*to*

lekabel (3 syll.)—infinitive of verb *receive*

liat (lee-OTT)—*slow* (adj.); the adverb is "liat-liat," which is what everybody tells you is the way you'll learn Hebrew

lira—100 agorot, the Israeli pound (a coin)—not to be confused with pound sterling, Italian *lire,* and certainly not American dollar

lo—*no* by itself; *not* in, e.g., "lo na-im" *not nice* (q.v.)

lomed (low-MED)—*learn* or *study,* masc. sing.; fem., "lomedet"

m or m'—*from* (combining form)

ma—*what* (as in "ma la'assot," etc.)

macaulet—*small neighborhood grocery store,* Mom-and-Pop type

machar (ma-CHAR)—*tomorrow*

machberrot—*notebooks*

machrotym (ma-chro-TIME)—*day after tomorrow.* (The "tym" suffix doubles—which led me to some ingenious and/or desperate uses of it)

ma-im (MAH-eem, so it actually sounds like *mime*)—*water* (And if you want to talk about hot or cold water, remember it's plural)

malka (MOLL-kuh)—*queen*

ma-od(mah-OAD)—*very;* "na-im ma-od," *very nice,* you say when you're introduced to someone. (But if logic then leads you to try "b'seder ma-od," you'll inspire giggles)

mashbir (mosh-BEER)—part of the name of what is neither quite a chain store nor quite a co-op, and I couldn't explain further without writing a treatise on Israel's weird mix of capitalism and socialism. But in Beer-Sheva, "the mashbir" is the *department store.*

mazal (ma-ZAHL)—*luck.* "Mazal tov" is the original of the Yiddish "mozzle tuff" Americans are familiar with. (Mazal is also a girl's name)

medabrim—*speak,* masc. pl.

"megillah"—I meant this English-Yiddishly, as a whole-long-story; the Hebrew meh-gill-AH is the service read at Passover (which is in fact a whole long story), but it's not used in extended sense

melach—*salt* (N.B.: do not confuse with "melech," which means *king.* I was never able to remember which was which, and thus had to mutter a lot at dinner parties)

melamedet—*teach,* fem. sing.

mem—thirteenth letter of the alphabet

mercaz (mair-KAHZ)—*center;* "mercaz klita," *absorption center*

mi—*who;* "le mi?" is *To whom?*

mi-eyn—*from where, whence;* "Mi-eyn at?" is *Where are you (fem.) from?*

miklat—*shelter* (noun)

miluim (3 syll.)—*military reserve duty*

minyan—minimum number of congregants needed for prayers

mirpesset (meer-PESS-et)—*balcony*

mishpacha (mish-pah-CHAH)—*family;* if followed by name, "mishpachat"

mishtara (mish-ta-RAH)—*police* (noun)

misrad (2 syll.)—*office*

mitz (meets)—any fruit juice or drink (i.e., orange *juice* or orange*ade*) so long as it's not carbonated. Then it becomes so-DAH.

mitzva (mitz-VAH)—one of the acts of generosity (i.e., a good deed not paying off for the doer) the pious Jew must perform; pl., "mitzvot"

"moderni" (moe-DARE-nee)—*chic, up-to-date, dernier-cri:* probably not a proper Hebrew word, for you can hear the quotes when people say it

morah (mo-RAH)—*teacher,* fem.; masc.,mo-REH

moshav (moe-SHAHV)—a cooperative (usually farming) community, like a kibbutz but with more individual self-determination: the life in a particular household may be very like American suburbia

motek (MO-teck)—*"sweetie,"* and (oh, mazal!), the same for masc. and fem.

N:

nachal—a form of army service in an agricultural-cum-military settlement, usually in some awful place where nobody would choose to live

na-im (nah-EEM)—*nice* (see "ma-od") and as mild as that in the positive; but "lo na-im" is stronger than just *not nice,* more like *unacceptable*

nekadot (neck-a-DOAT)—*points* (noun), as in a game; the singular, neck-a-DAH, is used for the *decimal point*

Negev (NE-gev)—either the Negev Desert or the region of which Beer-Sheva is the principal city; on the weather report, the latter extends from just north of Beer-Sheva down to the Sinai

"ness"—any instant non-Turkish coffee (prob. orig. "Nescafé")

nissooi (3 syll.)—*married* (adj.)

nu (noooo)—usually inquiry, and meaning virtually anything: e.g., *Well?/ Aren't you ready?/Speak up!/What's going on?/Isn't it time you . . .?* (I once got a postcard with "Nu?" the only message—eloquent and economical.) The word may not be Hebrew but Yiddish; it's used, though, by people who speak neither

nuhn—fourteenth letter of the alphabet

O: the basic "o" sound is as in the English word *forth*

ohev (oh-HEV)—*love* (verb), masc. sing.; fem., "ohevet"

oleh, olah (oh-LEH, oh-LAH)—*immigrant,* masc. and fem.; pl., "olim" and "olot"

omeret (3 syll.)—*say* (verb), fem. sing., as in "zot omeret" (q.v.); "omrim" (see "ech omrim") is the plural of the same verb

oolye (ooh-LIE)—*maybe, perhaps*

oy va voy—literally, "oy *and* voy"—which I think is the Israelis' imitation of the Yiddish *oy-oy-oy* (However, their own equivalent is an "ooh-AH" rather like the chorus of an American baseball crowd when a foul rolls down the overhead screen)

P: like our *p,* but can be altered to the equivalent of *ph* (or *f*)*

parparim (3 syll.)—*butterflies*

platta (PLATT-tuh)—a sort of gas hot plate, with several burners

Q: no equivalent in Hebrew, but one school of thought favors using Q for that gargled *h.* Thus you see road signs for, say, "Petaq Tikva" (It's a theoretically sensible idea, but a Q without a U is just too puzzling, I think)

R: rolled, but up front, not like the back-of-the-throat French *r*

raba (rah-BAH)—in "toda raba," thanks *very much* (never heard it else)

rah-boh-TIE—*ladies and gentlemen* (apparently exclusively in address)

rechov (ruh-CHOHV)—*street* (though not *gutter* or *road*). Usually anglicized as "rehov," which leads to mispronunciation. Interesting special use: a "rechov word" means an everyday one (but no connotations of naughtiness) as opposed to a fancy "Shabbat word"

rega (REH-guh)—*second* (noun), but most commonly heard in some such extended form as "Rega, rega!"—*Hold it!, Wait!*

regel (REH-gull)—*foot; on foot* is "b'regel"

rock—*only*—as, typically, "rock rega," literally *only a second* but in effect *wait a minute* (Untypically, Rock Rega was the muscular hero of a fractured-Hebrew epic composed by my son and me. Rock is loved by the exotic beauty Liat-Liat, but . . .)

rotsim (roh-TSEEM)—*want* (verb), masc. pl. (The fem. sing. is "rotsa"—as in Ani Lo Rotsa, another lady in Rock Rega's life)

S: Hebrew has one letter that's pure *S* and another that may mean *S* or *Sh.* Thus there's lots of room for choice/error in transliteration.

savlenut (sahv-luh-NOOHT)—*patience* (nearly always heard with "liat-liat")

seder (SEH-dare)—*order* (noun): "b'seder" *(okay)* is, literally, *in order*

---

*I got a bank order once from a friend named Preston, which later resulted in incomprehensible Hebrew on my bank statement. Appealed to Hebrew-learned American pal, who read it as "Firestone" and told me I must've ordered something and forgotten it. I accepted that meekly, and I'd still be wondering what I bought if Avi hadn't dropped in and figured out what it must be if it wasn't "Firestone."

Shabbat (shah-BOTT)—*sabbath, Saturday.* Comes from "sheva," *seven* (which is not the same as in "Beer-Sheva": that one comes from the verb to *swear*)

shaliach (shah-LEE-ach)—*emissary* to would-be immigrants (not a diplomat)

shalom—*peace*—also, both *hello* and *good-bye*

shameyim (shuh-MIME)—*sky* (plural, so watch those adjectives!)

sharav (shah-RAHV)—a hot wind accompanied by ionic disturbance: it turns up periodically and makes everybody feel bloody-awful for a couple of days (Arabic word, *chamsin*, is better known)

shel—*of.* Followed by noun, makes simple possessive: "shel Maggie" is *Maggie's.* Inflected for possessive pronouns: "sheli"—"shel" plus "ani"—is *my* or *mine.* And you already know "shelanu," right?

shem—*name* (noun)

sherut (sheh-ROOT)—*service*—commonly, an intercity taxi service in which you buy a seat as for a bus. But, N.B.: the plural, "sherutim," is not several taxis but the *toilet** (like "the *facilities*," I guess)

shesh—*six*

shikun (she-KUHN)—*neighborhood* or *quarter* (though neither quite, exactly—a real-estate development in the U.S. may be closer)

"shmatta" (SHMAH-tuh)—*rag,* and probably Yiddish—though the plural, "shmattot," is the Hebrew plural for feminine nouns

shuk (rhymes with *kook*)—a *market* usually described as open-air though it's often roofed-over; the kind of farmers' market commerce seen in some form in lots of countries (The word is taken from the Arabic *souk,* which is pronounced to rhyme with *cook*)

slicha (slee-CHAH)—*pardon, excuse me*

Sochnut—*agency* in general, but here the Jewish Agency

soferet (so-FERR-et)—*novelist,* fem. (Though, since "sefer" is *book,* it seems to be literally a *book-writer* and so may mean non-fiction too)

sponja (*sponge* + uh)—a sort of cross between mop and squeegee (described in Chapter 6) used for washing floors: "sponja" (a rechov word) is both noun and verb

stamm—*just because??*—one of the two real untranslatables. Better see Chapter 4, where it's explained if not defined

T: Hebrew has two letters with our *T* sound (which makes correct spelling difficult)

talmidim (tal-mee-DEEM)—*pupils,* masc. (or a co-ed classful)

tarbut (tar-BOOT)—*culture* (in anthropological sense)

tikva (tic-VAH)—*hope* (noun); "Petach Tikva," *gate of hope*

toda (toe-DAH)—*thanks, thank you;* "toda raba," *thanks very much*

tor—*line* or *queue* (noun)

tov (tohv)—*good.* As interjection, can be no more than *Uh huh* or (if "tov ma-od" and suitable tone of voice) as enthusiastic as *"Super!"* As adjective, has variety of benevolent intents—e.g., "Shana Tova," a

*For the benefit of travelers, the question is "AY-fo sherutim?" Or just look for any door numbered 00.

good year, the New Year's greeting—but it doesn't seem to mean
  virtuous (except maybe in Tova, a girl's name)
tremping—*hitchhiking*, and strictly a rechov word. As is "trempiada," a
  somewhat-sheltered spot where hitchhiking soldiers wait for rides
trissim—slatted window blinds, like jalousies but with extra slits that
  you can leave open or close so it isn't so all-or-nothing (but you can't
  tilt the slats, as in Venetian blinds). They can keep out not only light
  but also air—a factor desirable in desert sumers
tsava (tsav-AH)—*army*
tseva (TSEV-ah)—*color* (Avoid confusing this with the one above!)
tsipor (tsee-PORE)—*bird*

U:

ulpan (ool-PON)—here, an intensive course in Hebrew for adult
  newcomers. But it seems to be any kind of adult school: people I knew
  went to an Arabic ulpan, for instance

V: see note on B

va—*and*
vad (va-odd, one syllable but with a kind of hesitation) . . . *committee*
" 'vak' "sha—*please* as "bevakasha" is usually pronounced
vav—sixth letter of the alphabet, sometimes a V sound but more often a
  vowel, equivalent of *oh* or *oo* (A note on results of this handy
  arrangement appears in diary extract "Prometheus in the P.O.")

W: no such critter in modern Hebrew—gets turned into V

X: don't know of any words (*X ray* doesn't happen because the Hebrew is
  "roentgen"); but the algebraic symbol is pronounced "icks" as in *six*

Y: see note on J

yachad (YAH-chad)—*together*
yafeh, yafa (both accent on 2nd syll.)—*beautiful*, masc. and fem. (Yaffa is
  also a girl's name, which is as risky as naming your daughter Mazal)
  The slang form "yofi" is used like the American *Beautiful!* (with as
  tiresome frequency, too) and recently I heard that American
  volunteers on some kibbutz had coined "yofey-tofey"—which ought to
  make the Israelis rethink their summer-volunteer program . . .
yeheeye (ye-HEE-yeh)—*will be*, sing.: "yeheeye tov," literally *it will be
  good,* is what you tell people who're feeling "lo-tov"
yeledim (yell-e-DEEM)—*children* (plural of *boy*, YELL-ed; *girl* is
  yal-DAH). This term applies longer than in U.S.: my seventeen-year-
  old students, who I thought would use a word for *teenager,* described
  themselves as "yeledim"
yesh—*there exist(s),* a substitute for some of the missing present-tense

forms of *be*. You ask the greengrocer "Yesh bananot?"—*Are there bananas?*—or you proclaim "Yesh tor!"—*A line exists* (so wait your turn)—to somebody shoving; but *I am a novelist* is just "Ani soferet," no verb

yored (yo-RED)—*come down, descend*, masc. sing.—e.g., "yored geshem" means it's raining (rain is coming down), and I say "Ani yoredet" when I'm getting off a bus

Z: Hebrew has two—one like ours and the other like *ts*. I put the *ts* words under *T*, so these are all the buzzing-Z

"Za-BOSH"—a slang coinage created by compressing three words meaning *That's your problem* (accent on *your*). Thus it's the equivalent of *Get off my back, Don't bother me, Don't tell me your troubles*, etc. I don't know whether it's university-student or army slang, as I've heard it credited to both; but in Israel many people *are* both. In any case, it's not used by nice middle-aged ladies (except me: people are used to being startled by my Hebrew anyway, so . . .)

zeh—*this*, masc. sing.

zot (zoat)—*this* (fem.), as in "zot omeret," which means *that is, which is to say* (I don't understand why that's feminine. But I couldn't answer the cheerful "Why not?" I got when I asked)